HANDBOOK TO LIFE IN ANCIENT ROME

LESLEY ADKINS AND
ROY A. ADKINS

Oxford University Press
New York   Oxford

Oxford University Press

Oxford   New York
Athens   Auckland   Bangkok   Bogotá   Bombay
Buenos Aires   Calcutta   Cape Town   Dar es Salaam   Delhi
Florence   Hong Kong   Istanbul   Karachi
Kuala Lumpur   Madras   Madrid   Melbourne
Mexico City   Nairobi   Paris   Singapore
Taipei   Tokyo   Toronto   Warsaw

and associated companies in

Berlin   Ibadan

Copyright © 1994 by Lesley Adkins and Roy A. Adkins

First published by Facts on File, Inc.,
460 Park Avenue South, New York, New York 10016

First issued as an Oxford University Press paperback, 1998

Oxford is a registered trademark of Oxford University Press

Library of Congress Cataloging-in-Publication Data
Adkins, Lesley.
    Handbook to Life in Ancient Rome / Lesley Adkins and Roy A. Adkins.
        p.   cm.
    Includes bibliographical references and index.
    ISBN 0-19-512332-8 (pbk.)
    1. Rome—Civilization—Handbooks, manuals, etc. 2. Rome—History—
Chronology—Handbooks, manuals, etc. 3. Rome—Pictorial works.
    4. Heads of state—Rome—History—Chronology—Handbooks, manuals, etc.
    I. Adkins, Roy (Roy A.) II. Title.
DG75.A35 1998
937—dc21   97-49394

10 11 12 13 14 15 16 17 18 19 20
Printed in the United States of America

CONTENTS

ILLUSTRATIONS

TABLES

This book is dedicated to Mike Lang Hall

ACKNOWLEDGMENTS

We are particularly grateful to Ernest Black for his immeasurable help in reading and commenting on the entire manuscript. Also, for reading and commenting on specific chapters, we are most grateful to Miranda Aldhouse-Green, Valerie Maxfield and Stephen Minnitt. All errors are, of course, our own. For help in obtaining or supplying photographs, we would like to thank Stephen Minnitt (Somerset County Museums Service, Taunton, England) and Ralph Jackson. We would also like to express our thanks to the Joint Library of the Hellenic and Roman Societies for their assistance in obtaining books. We are of course indebted to all the authors of the published sources that we have consulted. Finally, we would like to thank our editor, Sheila Dallas, for all her work.

INTRODUCTION

From the 8th century BC, when Rome was a small settlement, to the fall of the western empire in the 5th century AD, the Roman period lasted more than 1,200 years. By then the empire was divided into eastern and western halves. The eastern half survived as the Byzantine Empire, ruled from Constantinople (originally called Byzantium) rather than from Rome. In this *Handbook*, we have tried to include as much useful factual information as possible relating to the entire Roman period up to the 5th century AD.

The chapters are organized thematically rather than chronologically, in order to give readers easier access to particular topics. All too often archaeological evidence and historical evidence are used in isolation from each other. We have therefore tried to select the most important aspects of both disciplines. No attempt has been made to separate historical from archaeological elements in the text, and so there are no specific chapters devoted solely to archaeological evidence or artifacts.

Because often a particular topic can be viewed in more than one way, it may be covered in more than one section. For example, wall paintings can be considered from the structural viewpoint (under building techniques) or as works of art. Where this occurs, repetition of information has been kept to a minimum. The reader should make full use of the index to find all references to a particular subject and also the meanings of Latin words and other terms. Inevitably, there is room to do no more than summarize the various topics, but we have tried to provide further references for readers wishing to know more about any subject. As well as technical, historical and archaeological terms, we have also tried to give the meaning of Latin words and phrases in common use.

Place names are usually in English, except where convention prefers the Latin or where no English equivalent exists. Where the names of modern countries are used, only the names of properly defined territories at the time of writing have been used. Measurements are given in metric with standard U.S. equivalent measurements in parentheses. Where only approximate measurements are known, U.S. and metric equivalents are given in round figures, for example, "approximately 60m (200 ft)." Roman measurements (such as Roman feet and Roman miles) are described as such to distinguish them from U.S. measurements. Precise dates are given wherever possible, but at times only approximate dates are known. One written as c. 60–c. 50 BC means approximately 60 BC to approximately 50 BC. Written as c. 60–50 BC, it means approximately 60 BC to precisely 50 BC; and 60–50 BC means precisely 60 BC to precisely 50 BC. The same applies to dates AD, although AD is not usually stated except for reasons of clarity.

REPUBLIC AND EMPIRE

DATES OF EVENTS

The history of ancient Rome can be divided into three periods: monarchy, republic and empire. The Principate describes the early empire from Augustus (27 BC–14) to Diocletian (284–305) when the emperor was *princeps* (first citizen). The Dominate is the late empire, when the emperor was *Dominus* (Lord). In 395 the empire was divided into east and west. The western empire is believed to have fallen in 476, as there were no more Roman emperors in the west, but the east continued as the Byzantine Empire for nearly 1,000 years, until 1453. The date of the beginning of the Byzantine Empire is disputed. The following list of dates relates largely to events and excludes dates associated with authors of literature (see chapter 6) and with emperors. For problems of dates, see chapter 9.

Monarchy

753 BC	(This is a traditional date accepted by ancient historians, but for which there is no certain evidence.) Rome was allegedly founded on 21 April by Romulus (in myth a descendant of the Trojan hero Aeneas), who later killed his twin brother, Remus, in a quarrel. Likely there were many more kings in early Rome.

THE SEVEN KINGS OF ROME

753–715 BC	Romulus. After Romulus, the position of king was held by men of Sabine, Latin and Etruscan extraction. The kingship was not hereditary.
715–673 BC	Numa Pompilius (Sabine).
673–641 BC	Tullus Hostilius (Latin).
641–616 BC	Ancus Marcius (Sabine).
616–579 BC	Tarquinius Priscus (Tarquin I) (Etruscan).
579–534 BC	Servius Tullius (Roman or Latin).
534–509 BC	Tarquinius Superbus (Tarquin the Proud or Tarquin II) (Etruscan).

509 BC	The king was expelled from Rome. Foundation of the republic.

Republic

508 BC	Treaty between Rome and Carthage. Horatius Cocles held back the Etruscan army at the Bridge of Sublicius at Rome.
496 BC	Romans defeated the Latins at the battle of Lake Regillus.
494 BC	Office of tribune of the plebs was established.
493 BC	The Latin League treaty was signed.
458 BC	Cincinnatus was summoned from his plowing to the dictatorship to save the Roman army.
451–450 BC	Laws of the Twelve Tables were published.
405–396 BC	Siege of Veii.
396 BC	Veii was captured and destroyed.
391 BC	A 30,000-strong force of Gauls crossed the Apennines.
390 BC	(July) The Roman army was defeated by the Gauls at the Allia River. Rome was sacked, but the Capitol resisted for seven months.
378 BC	The Servian wall was constructed around Rome.
366 BC	The first plebeian was elected to the consulship.
348 BC	Second treaty with Carthage.
343–341 BC	First Samnite War.
340–338 BC	Latin War.
338 BC	Rome dissolved the Latin League.
327–304 BC	Second Samnite War.
323 BC	Alexander the Great died.
321 BC	Roman disaster of the Caudine Forks, where the Roman army was forced to surrender to the Samnites.
312 BC	Construction began on the *via Appia* and the *aqua Appia* (Rome's first aqueduct).
298–290 BC	Third Samnite War.
293 BC	The cult of Aesculapius was introduced into Rome.
290 BC	Rome's victory over the Samnites forced them to become allies of Rome, completing Rome's domination of central Italy.

287 BC	The *lex Hortensia* abolished the Senate's right of veto on *plebiscita*.
280–275 BC	War with Pyrrhus, who had invaded Italy to help the Greek cities against Rome, but won only costly and inconclusive "Pyrrhic victories."
275 BC	Pyrrhus was defeated at Benevento and left Italy.
275–270 BC	Romans took control of southern Italy.
264–241 BC	First Punic War against the Carthaginians.
260 BC	Rome's first naval victory at Mylae.
241 BC	Naval victory against the Carthaginians at the Aegates Islands ended the First Punic War.
235 BC	The doors of the temple of Janus were closed in Rome, indicating that Rome was at peace with all nations for the first time on record.
229–228 BC	Rome attacked the pirates along the Illyrian coast (First Illyrian War).
226 BC	Ebro River treaty with Carthage.
225 BC	A huge army of Gauls crossed the Apennines but was defeated by the Romans at the battle of Telamon.
219 BC	Second Illyrian War against the pirates. Hannibal of Carthage attacked Sagunto and then marched out of Spain.
218–201 BC	Second Punic War.
218 BC	Hannibal crossed the Alps and invaded Italy. He defeated the Romans at the battle of Trebia. A law was passed limiting the size of cargo ships senators could own.
217 BC	Hannibal defeated the Roman army at the battle of Lake Trasimene. 15,000 Romans were killed.
216 BC	Hannibal defeated the Roman army at the battle of Cannae. 50,000 Romans were killed.
215 BC	*Lex Oppia* restricted the amount of jewelry and luxury clothing women could own and wear.
214–204 BC	First Macedonian War between Rome and Philip V of Macedon.
213 BC	Romans besieged Syracuse.
211 BC	Syracuse was captured.
204 BC	Philip V of Macedon was defeated.
203 BC	Hannibal was forced to leave Italy.
202 BC	Roman victory in Africa by Scipio over Hannibal at the battle of Zama.
201 BC	End of the Second Punic War.
200–197 BC	Second Macedonian War between Rome and Philip V of Macedon.
197 BC	The campaign to pacify Spain began.
195 BC	Repeal of *lex Oppia*.
194 BC	Rome withdrew from Greece.
192 BC	Antiochus III invaded Greece.
191 BC	Roman victory at Thermopylae. Outbreak of war against Antiochus III, who was driven out of Greece.
190 BC	Romans invaded Asia Minor and defeated Antiochus III at Magnesia.
187 BC	Antiochus III died.
186 BC	A senatorial edict suppressed Bacchic rites throughout Italy.
184 BC	Cato the Elder became censor.
179 BC	Philip V of Macedon died, succeeded by his son Perseus.
173 BC	Greek philosophers were expelled from Rome.
172–168 BC	Third Macedonian War.
168 BC	Perseus was defeated at the battle of Pydna on 22 June, ending the Macedonian War.
167 BC	Deportation to Rome of 1,000 Greek hostages, including Polybius. Delos was declared a free port.
161 BC	Greek philosophers were expelled from Rome.
149 BC	Outbreak of the Third Punic War. Rebellion in Macedonia.
149–146 BC	Third Punic War.
148 BC	Fourth Macedonian War and war against the Achaean Confederacy.
146 BC	Carthage was razed to the ground, ending the Third Punic War. Corinth was destroyed following the rebellion in Achaea. The Achaean Confederacy was dissolved.
135–132 BC	Slave revolt in Sicily, put down by the Roman army in 132 BC.
134–133 BC	Siege and destruction of Numantia.
133 BC	Tiberius Gracchus, a tribune, initiated land reforms. He was later assassinated.

The kingdom of Pergamum (later the province of Asia) was bequeathed to the Romans by Attalus III.

123–122 BC Gaius Gracchus, a tribune, attempted to pass agrarian reforms.

121 BC Gaius Gracchus was declared a public enemy and was put to death along with 3,000 supporters.

112–105 BC Wars in north Africa against Jugurtha, king of Numidia.

107 BC Marius was elected consul for the first of seven times. He was sent to Africa to fight Jugurtha.

105 BC The Roman army was annihilated at Orange by Germanic tribes advancing toward Italy.
Marius defeated the Numidians in north Africa.

104–101 BC Slave revolt in Sicily.

102 BC Marius defeated the Teutones at Aquae Sextiae.

101 BC Marius defeated the Cimbri at Vercellae.

90–88 BC Social War (after *socii*, allies), also known as the Marsian or Marsic War (after the Marsi tribe that began the revolt). This was a civil war against Rome by its Italian allies who demanded citizenship and other privileges.

89 BC Roman citizenship was granted to the Latins and Italian allies.
Mithridates, king of Pontus, invaded Roman territory in Asia Minor.

89–85 BC First Mithridatic War.

88 BC Sulla was consul. He marched on Rome with six legions.

88–82 BC Civil war at Rome between supporters of Sulla and Marius.

87 BC Sulla obtained command in the east and went to Greece, besieging Athens. Marius and Cinna seized Rome.

86 BC Marius died.
Sulla defeated Mithridates at Chaeronea and attacked and captured Athens.

85 BC Sulla imposed a heavy war indemnity on Asia, ending the First Mithridatic War.

83 BC Sulla returned to Italy and marched on Rome.

83–82 BC Second Mithridatic War.

82–80 BC Sulla was dictator.

79 BC Sulla retired.

74–63 BC Third Mithridatic War.

73–71 BC A slave revolt in Italy was led by Spartacus. Verres was governor of Sicily.

71 BC Pompey and Crassus put down the revolt of Spartacus.

70 BC Pompey and Crassus were consuls. Verres prosecuted by Cicero for extortion.

67 BC Pompey was granted power to rid the eastern Mediterranean of pirates, a task that took three months.

66–62 BC Pompey campaigned in the east. He advanced as far as Jerusalem and acquired much new territory for Rome.

63 BC Cicero was consul.
Conspiracy of Catiline.
Mithridates died.

62 BC Pompey returned to Rome from Jerusalem after his campaigns.

60 BC Pompey, Crassus and Julius Caesar formed an unofficial alliance (now called the First Triumvirate).

59 BC Julius Caesar became consul.
Pompey married Julia, Caesar's daughter.

58–51 BC Caesar campaigned to conquer all of Gaul.

58 BC Clodius was tribune. He promoted legislation for the free distribution of grain to citizens to gain popularity.

58–57 BC Cicero was exiled.

56 BC The First Triumvirate was renewed at Lucca.

55–54 BC Caesar's invasions of Britain.

54 BC Death of Pompey's wife Julia (Caesar's daughter) caused a split in the alliance. Crassus went to Syria.

53 BC The Parthians defeated the Roman army at the battle of Carrhae and Crassus was killed. The First Triumvirate ceased.

52 BC Siege of Alesia. Milo killed Clodius as civil unrest in Rome increased; Pompey was elected sole consul and restored order.

51–50 BC Cicero was governor of Cilicia.

49 BC	The Senate ordered Caesar to disband his army, but on 10 January he crossed the Rubicon River (a stream on the border of Italy and Cisalpine Gaul) and invaded Italy, beginning a civil war. Pompey and his supporters fled to Greece.
49–45 BC	Civil war at Rome.
48 BC	Caesar defeated Pompey at the battle of Pharsalus. Pompey escaped to Egypt but was murdered.
47–44 BC	Caesar was dictator.
47 BC	Battle of Zela.
47–45 BC	Caesar campaigned against Republicans in the east, Africa and Spain.
46 BC	Cato committed suicide at Utica. Battle of Thapsus.
45 BC	Caesar defeated the Republicans at the battle of Munda. Caesar returned from Spain. Julian calendar introduced on 1 January.
44 BC	Caesar was assassinated on the Ides (15th) of March. He had appointed his great-nephew, Octavian, as his heir. Civil war broke out between Caesar's assassins and his successors (Mark Antony and Octavian).
44–30 BC	Civil wars at Rome.
43 BC	Mark Antony, the official head of state with Lepidus, went to Cisalpine Gaul. The Senate declared him an enemy. Octavian was sent against Mark Antony and defeated him in two battles near Mutina, where both consuls Pansa and Hirtius were killed. The Senate refused Octavian the position of consul so he marched on Rome, taking it by force. Octavian was reconciled with Antony and Lepidus and formed the Second Triumvirate. Cicero and others were proscribed.
42 BC	Lepidus was consul. Octavian and Antony went to war in the east against the republicans Brutus and Cassius, and defeated them at the battle of Philippi.
41–40 BC	Perusine War (rebellion against Octavian). Perusia was besieged.
40 BC	Lepidus was given charge of Africa, Antony the eastern provinces and Octavian the western provinces. Treaty of Brundisium between Antony and Octavian. Antony married Octavia (Octavian's sister).
40–31 BC	Tension between Mark Antony and Octavian developed and increased while Antony was in the east.
37 BC	The Second Triumvirate was renewed.
36 BC	Lepidus made an unsuccessful bid for power and was forced to retire from politics. Antony suffered several disasters in Armenia and against the Parthians and their allies.
33 BC	End of the Second Triumvirate.
31 BC	The Senate deprived Antony of his powers. Octavian went to war against Cleopatra, and defeated Antony and Cleopatra on 2 September in the naval battle of Actium (a promontory off the west coast of Greece), giving Octavian control of the whole Roman world.
30 BC	Antony and Cleopatra fled to Egypt and committed suicide at Alexandria.
29 BC	Octavian celebrated a triumph for his successes in Illyricum, Actium and Egypt.

Fig. 1.1 Obverse of a denarius of Augustus. Courtesy of Somerset County Museums Service.

Imperial Period

27 BC	Octavian assumed the title Augustus (fig. 1.1) in January and claimed to have restored the republic, but was effectively in sole charge of the Roman world.
27 BC–AD 68	Julio-Claudian period.
27–24 BC	Augustus directed campaigns in northwest Spain.
27–19 BC	Agrippa completed the conquest of northwest Spain.
23 BC	Augustus received tribunician power for life.
19 BC	Augustus was probably granted consular power for life.
18 BC	*Lex Julia* was passed regulating marriage and adultery.
17 BC	Secular Games at Rome.
11 BC	Augustus forced his stepson Tiberius to divorce Vipsania Agrippina and marry Augustus' daughter Julia.
4 BC	Herod the Great died.

AD

6–9	Major rebellion in Pannonia.
9	Varus was ambushed in the Teutoberg forest and his entire force was massacred (three legions and auxiliaries).
14	Mutiny of legions in the Rhine and Danube areas.
c. 30	Crucifixion of Jesus.
31	Sejanus was executed.
43	Invasion of Britain.
59	Nero had his mother, Agrippina, put to death.
60	British rebellion began under Boudicca.
61	Paulinus suppressed the Boudiccan rebellion.
62	Nero had his divorced wife, Octavia, put to death.
64	Great Fire at Rome, for which the Christians were blamed.
65	The Pisonian Conspiracy to assassinate Nero was discovered, resulting in many suicides and executions, including Seneca the Younger, Petronius Arbiter, Lucan and Piso.
66–73	Jewish Revolt.
69	Year of the Four Emperors (Galba, Otho, Vitellius and Vespasian).
69–70	The German Batavian tribe under Julius Civilis and his allies on the Rhine rebelled and set up a Gallic empire, which was overthrown.
69–96	Flavian period.
70	Vespasian arrived in Rome, leaving Titus in Judaea. In May after a five-month siege, Titus captured and destroyed Jerusalem, including its temple.
71	Plague and fire at Rome.
78–85	Agricola was governor of Britain.
79	Eruption of Vesuvius (24 August).
80	The Colosseum was inaugurated.

Fig. 1.2 Lower bands of spiral relief on Trajan's Column, Rome. They depict various activities during the wars in Dacia and would have originally been painted.

	A fire at Rome destroyed Vespasian's new temple to Jupiter Capitolinus.
83	Domitian completed the conquest of the Agri Decumates.
85	Roman victory at the battle of Mons Graupius.
88–89	A revolt by the army commander Lucius Antonius Saturninus in Upper Germany was suppressed.
101–102	War against Dacia by Trajan (fig. 1. 2).
105–106	War against Dacia by Trajan.
109–111	Pliny the Younger was governor of Bithynia.
115	Trajan captured the Parthian capital Ctesiphon.
116	Jewish revolt throughout the eastern world.
	Revolt in southern Mesopotamia.
117	Hadrian abandoned the Parthian territories.
121 or 122	Hadrian visited Britain and authorized the construction of Hadrian's Wall.
130–134	Revolt of Jews led by Simon Bar-Cochba (Son of the Star) in Palestine. It was suppressed with great devastation and loss of life, and led to the final dispersal of the Jews.
135	Hadrian forbade the Jews to enter Jerusalem.
138–193	Antonine period.
c. 145–150	Revolt in Mauretania.
162–166	Wars under Lucius Verus against the Parthians.
166	The Marcomanni (a German tribe) surged across the Danube.
	Plague swept across the western empire, brought back by armies returning from the east.
167	Barbarian tribes invaded the northeastern and eastern frontiers.
168–175	German wars of Marcus Aurelius.
170	German tribes broke across the upper and middle Danube and penetrated deep into the empire.
193–197	Civil wars.
197	Septimius Severus defeated the last of his rivals, Clodius Albinus, at Lyon. The prohibition of marriage for soldiers was lifted.
197–198	Severus waged a war against the Parthians (fig. 2.12), whose capital Ctesiphon fell in the winter of 197–198.
208–211	Severus campaigned in Britain.
212	The constitutio Antoniniana granted citizenship to all free inhabitants of the empire.
213	In Germany, Caracalla campaigned against the Alamanni, who were threatening the Rhine/Danube border.
215	Caracalla moved to the Parthian frontier and extended the frontiers of Mesopotamia, but suffered a failure in Armenia.
235–285	50 years of anarchy.
247–270	Individual army garrisons proclaimed 30 generals emperors.
250	Persecution of the Christians under Decius.
251	The Goths and other barbarians began invasions across the Danube River.
260–274	Separate Gallic Empire of Britain, Gual and Spain.
266–273	Separate Palmyrene Empire Under Zenobia.
270	Aurelian built a wall around Rome for protection from invaders.
272	Aurelian captured Palmyra.
274	Aurelian defeated Tetricus near Châlons and recovered the Gallic Empire.
283	Carus captured the Persian capital Ctesiphon.
287	Carausius proclaimed his own empire in Britain (continuing to 296 under Allectus).
293	Diocletian made the empire into a Tetrarchy (four-man rule), led by two Augusti (co-emperors), himself in the East and Maximian in the West. Two Caesars were appointed below the rank of Augusti.
296	Britain was regained as a province (fig. 1.3).
301	Diocletian published an edict on wage and price controls.
303	Great persecution of Christians.

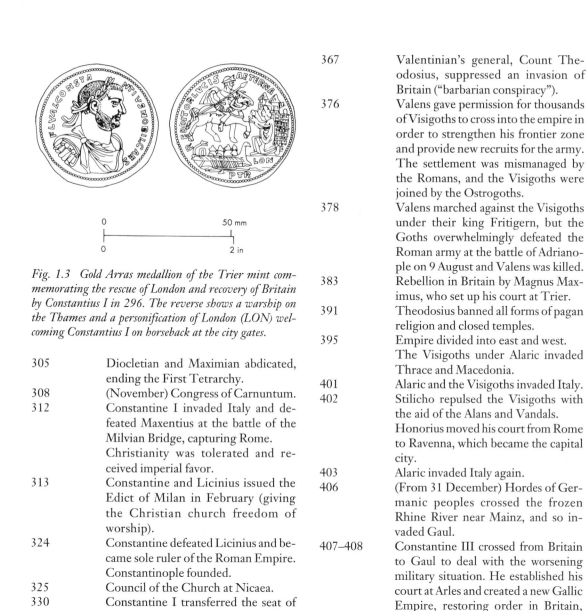

0   50 mm

0   2 in

Fig. 1.3 Gold Arras medallion of the Trier mint commemorating the rescue of London and recovery of Britain by Constantius I in 296. The reverse shows a warship on the Thames and a personification of London (LON) welcoming Constantius I on horseback at the city gates.

305	Diocletian and Maximian abdicated, ending the First Tetrarchy.
308	(November) Congress of Carnuntum.
312	Constantine I invaded Italy and defeated Maxentius at the battle of the Milvian Bridge, capturing Rome.
	Christianity was tolerated and received imperial favor.
313	Constantine and Licinius issued the Edict of Milan in February (giving the Christian church freedom of worship).
324	Constantine defeated Licinius and became sole ruler of the Roman Empire.
	Constantinople founded.
325	Council of the Church at Nicaea.
330	Constantine I transferred the seat of the Roman Empire to Constantinople.
351	Constantius II defeated Magnentius at the battle of Mursa (28 September).
357	Julian succeeded in forcing the Germanic tribes back across the Rhine. With a force of 13,000 men, he defeated 35,000 Alamanni at the battle of Argentorate.
359	Constantius II gave Constantinople a senate.
361–363	Julian the Apostate tried to revive pagan religion.
367	Valentinian's general, Count Theodosius, suppressed an invasion of Britain ("barbarian conspiracy").
376	Valens gave permission for thousands of Visigoths to cross into the empire in order to strengthen his frontier zone and provide new recruits for the army. The settlement was mismanaged by the Romans, and the Visigoths were joined by the Ostrogoths.
378	Valens marched against the Visigoths under their king Fritigern, but the Goths overwhelmingly defeated the Roman army at the battle of Adrianople on 9 August and Valens was killed.
383	Rebellion in Britain by Magnus Maximus, who set up his court at Trier.
391	Theodosius banned all forms of pagan religion and closed temples.
395	Empire divided into east and west.
	The Visigoths under Alaric invaded Thrace and Macedonia.
401	Alaric and the Visigoths invaded Italy.
402	Stilicho repulsed the Visigoths with the aid of the Alans and Vandals.
	Honorius moved his court from Rome to Ravenna, which became the capital city.
403	Alaric invaded Italy again.
406	(From 31 December) Hordes of Germanic peoples crossed the frozen Rhine River near Mainz, and so invaded Gaul.
407–408	Constantine III crossed from Britain to Gaul to deal with the worsening military situation. He established his court at Arles and created a new Gallic Empire, restoring order in Britain, Gaul, Germany and Spain.
408	Stilicho was executed on Honorius' orders for alleged complicity with Alaric.
409	(Winter) Vandals, Suebi and Alans invaded Spain, and Constantine III's Gallic Empire disintegrated.
410	Britain never recovered from the disintegration of the Gallic Empire. The year 410 is regarded as the end of Roman Britain. On 24 August the Visigoths under Alaric besieged, captured and sacked Rome for three days.

411	The imperial army from Ravenna defeated and executed Constantine III.
412	The Visigoths seized part of southwestern Gaul.
418	The Visigoths reached agreement with the Roman government to settle in Aquitaine.
429	The Vandals and Alans, led by Gaiseric, crossed the Straits of Gibraltar into Africa.
431	Council of Ephesus.
438	Law Code of Theodosius issued.
439	The Vandals conquered Roman Africa.
451	A combined force of Visigoths and Romans under Aëtius defeated the Huns under Attila on the Catalaunian Plains in Gaul. Council of Chalcedon.
452	Attila and his forces invaded Italy, but were persuaded by Pope Leo I to withdraw without entering Rome.
453	Attila the Hun died, and the Empire of the Huns disintegrated.
454	Aëtius was assassinated.
455	The Vandals under their king Gaiseric sacked Rome for two weeks.
468	Basiliscus led an unsuccessful campaign against the Vandals in Africa.
476	The last emperor of the west (Romulus Augustulus) was deposed. Italy was controlled by Germanic kings from their court at Ravenna. Fall of the western Roman Empire.
489	Theodoric, king of the Ostrogoths in the Balkans, was asked by Zeno to recover Italy for the eastern empire.
493	Theoderic defeated and killed Odoacer and had himself proclaimed king (until 526).
532	Serious riots occurred in Constantinople and large parts of the city were burned.
533	Justinian's Digest of Laws was published.
533–554	Justinian started to recover the western empire, securing Italy, Africa, Dalmatia and parts of Spain.
534	The last Vandal king, Gelimer, was defeated by Belisarius.
565	Justinian died, but the Byzantine Empire survived for another 900 years until conquered by the Ottoman Turks in 1453.

Emperors and Main Usurpers

The dates refer to the main period of rule, although some emperors ruled jointly with their predecessors for a time (such as Caracalla).

27BC–AD14	Augustus
14–37	Tiberius
37–41	Gaius (Caligula)
41–54	Claudius
54–68	Nero
68–69	Galba
69	Otho
69	Vitellius
69–79	Vespasian
79–81	Titus
81–96	Domitian
96–98	Nerva
98–117	Trajan
117–138	Hadrian
138–161	Antoninus Pius
161–180	Marcus Aurelius
161–169	Lucius Verus
180–193	Commodus
193	Pertinax
193	Didius Julianus
193–194	Pescennius Niger
193–197	Clodius Albinus
193–211	Septimius Severus
211–212	Geta
211–217	Caracalla
217–218	Macrinus
218	Diadumenian
218–222	Elagabalus
222–235	Severus Alexander
235–238	Maximinus I
238	Gordian I
238	Gordian II
238	Balbinus
238	Pupienus
238–244	Gordian III
244–249	Philip the Arab

247–249	Philip II	268–269	Marius
248–254	Uranius	268–270	Claudius II
248	Pacatian	269	Victorinus
248	Jotapian	270	Quintillus
249–251	Decius Trajan	270–275	Aurelian
251	Herennius Etruscus	271–272	Vaballathus
251–253	Trebonianus Gallus	271–272	Zenobia
251	Hostilian	275–276	Tacitus
251–253	Volusian	276	Florian
253	Aemilian	276–282	Probus
253–260	Valerian	280	Saturninus
253–268	Gallienus	282–283	Carus
260	Saloninus	283–285	Carinus
260–261	Macrianus	283/4–285	Julian
260–261	Quietus	283–284	Numerian
260	Regalianus	286/7–293	Carausius
260–268	Postumus	293–296	Allectus
268	Laelianus	284–305	Diocletian

Western Empire   Eastern Empire

Western Empire		Eastern Empire	
286–305	Maximian	286–305	Diocletian
293–305	Constantius Chlorus (Caesar)	293–305	Galerius (Caesar)
305–306	Constantius I (Chlorus)	305–311	Galerius
305–306	Severus (Caesar)	305–309	Maximinus Daia (Caesar)
306–307	Severus II	309–313	Maximinus II Daia
306–312	Maxentius		
306–308	Maximian	308–324	Licinius
306–324	Constantine I	314	Valens
310	Maximian		
317–337	Constantine II (Caesar)	317–324	Licinianus (Caesar)
317–326	Crispus (Caesar)	324	Martinian
324–337	Constantine I		
333–337	Constans (Caesar)	324–337	Constantius II (Caesar)
337–340	Constantine II		
337–350	Constans	337–361	Constantius II
350–353	Magnentius	335–337	Dalmatius (Caesar)
350	Vetranio		
350	Nepotian		
351–353	Magnus Decentius (Caesar)		
353–361	Constantius II		
355	Silvanus	351-354	Gallus (Caesar)
355–361	Julian (Caesar)		
361–363	Julian (the Apostate)		
363–364	Jovian		
364–375	Valentinian I	364–378	Valens
375–383	Gratian	365–366	Procopius
379–395	Theodosius I		
375–392	Valentinian II		

Western Empire		Eastern Empire	
383–388	Magnus Maximus		
387–388	Flavius Victor		
392–394	Eugenius		
395–423	Honorius	395–408	Arcadius
407–411	Constantine III	408–450	Theodosius II
409–411	Maximus		
409–410	Priscus Attalus		
411–413	Jovinus		
412–413	Sebastianus		
414–415	Priscus Attalus		
421	Constantius III		
423–425	Johannes		
425–455	Valentinian III	450–457	Marcian
455	Petronius Maximus		
455–456	Avitus		
457–461	Majorian	457–474	Leo I
461–465	Libius Severus		
467–472	Anthemius		
472	Olybrius		
473	Glycerius	473–474	Leo II
473—475	Julius Nepos	474–491	Zeno
475–476	Romulus Augustulus	475–476	Basiliscus
		476	Marcus
		491–518	Anastasius
		518–527	Justin
		527–565	Justinian

Barbarian Kings of Italy

476–493	Odo(v)acer
493–526	Theodoric
526–534	Athalaric
534–536	Theodahad

PROMINENT PEOPLE

Some of the prominent people of the Roman world are described. See also emperors (below) and literary authors (chapter 6). The following list is selective; through Rome's history there were over a thousand-million Romans.

AËTIUS: Flavius Aëtius. Born at Durostorum. Died 454. Pursued a military career, being master of the soldiers from 430 to 454. He was virtually in charge of the west during Valentinian III's reign. He particularly controlled barbarian invasions, and de- feated the Visigoths and Burgundians in Gaul. Later he called on the Visigoths to defeat his old allies, the Huns, under Attila in 451. The Huns invaded Italy in 452, and Aëtius was assassinated by order of Valentinian III on 21 September 454.

AGRICOLA: Gnaeus Julius Agricola. 40–93. Born at Fréjus. A biography about Agricola was written by his father-in-law, the historian Tacitus. Agricola followed a military career and was governor of Aquitania, consul for part of 77 and governor of Britain from late 77 or 78 to 85. He was victorious at the battle of Mons Graupius in Scotland in 85, after which he was recalled to Rome and received no other command.

AGRIPPA: Marcus Vipsanius Agrippa. 64–12 BC. Wives: Attica, Marcella, Julia (Augustus' daughter, married 21 BC). Children: Vipsania Agrippina (by Attica; married Tiberius), Gaius and Lucius Caesar (died AD 2 and 4 respectively), Agrippina the Elder, Julia and Marcus Vipsanius Agrippa Postumus (born after Agrippa's death, died AD 14) (all by Julia). Agrippa was a lifelong supporter of Augustus and was involved in many of his campaigns. He defeated Sextus Pompey in 36 BC and took part in the battle of Actium. He subsequently held numerous public offices and undertook an extensive building program in Rome.

AGRIPPINA THE ELDER: c. 14 BC–AD 33. Parents: Agrippa and Julia. Husband: Germanicus (died AD 19). Children: nine, including Agrippina the Younger, Caligula (emperor) and Drusilla. She was exiled to the island of Pandateria in 29, where she starved herself to death.

AGRIPPINA THE YOUNGER: Julia Agrippina. 15–59. Parents: Agrippina the Elder and Germanicus. Husbands: Domitius Ahenobarbus (married 28), Sallustius Passienus Crispus, Claudius (married 48, emperor). Son: Nero (by Domitius Ahenobarbus; emperor). Agrippina was exiled in 39 and was recalled in 49. She was very influential during the reigns of Claudius and Nero. She apparently poisoned Claudius, and was herself murdered at Baiae by order of Nero.

ANTINOUS: From Claudiopolis, Bithynia, Antinous died by drowning in the Nile in 130. He was a youth of great beauty and a favorite of Hadrian, who founded the city of Antinoopolis on the Nile and erected temples and statues in his memory.

ANTONIA: 36 BC–AD 37. Parents: Mark Antony and Octavia. Husband: Drusus (died 9 BC). Children: many, including Germanicus and Claudius (emperor). She became very influential during Tiberius' reign and inherited great wealth from her father.

ANTONY, MARK: Marcus Antonius. c. 83–30 BC. He followed a military career, served under Caesar in Gaul and assumed power at Rome with Lepidus after Caesar's assassination. His leadership was challenged by Octavian, who sided with the Senate in opposition to Antony. Civil war ensued and Antony was defeated at Mutina in 43 BC, but an alliance (Second Triumvirate) was formed among Lepidus, Octavian and Antony. In 42 BC the Republican opposition was defeated at Philippi, and Antony remained in the east. He entered into a political and personal alliance with Cleopatra. A split between him and Octavian developed, and he was defeated at Actium in 31 BC. He committed suicide at Alexandria.

ARBITIO: Flavius Arbitio, 4th-century soldier who rose to the rank of master of cavalry (c. 351–361). He was consul in 355.

ARBOGAST: Died September 394. Frankish born and master of the soldiers. He was a general at the court of Gratian, played a leading part in Theodosius' defeat of Maximus and was commander-in-chief (388) to Valentinian II, with whom he quarreled. After Valentinian's death, he declared Eugenius emperor, and with Nicomachus Flavianus he revived pagan cults. His army was defeated by Theodosius I and he committed suicide.

BALBUS: Lucius Cornelius Balbus. 1st century BC, from Cadiz. Balbus gained Roman citizenship in 72 BC through Pompey's influence and assumed a Roman name. He moved to Rome and became a man of considerable importance. In the civil war his allegiance was to Caesar and then to Octavian. In 40 BC he became Rome's first foreign-born consul.

BELISARIUS: Wife: Antonina (a former actress). Belisarius was an outstanding general of the emperor Justinian. His greatest victories were the recovery of Africa from the Vandals in 533 and of Italy from the Ostrogoths in 540. In 563 he was accused of a conspiracy and died in 565, possibly ending his life as a beggar in the streets of Constantinople.

BRUTUS: Marcus Junius Brutus. c. 85–42 BC. In the civil wars he fought with Pompey against Caesar, but was pardoned by Caesar and was appointed praetor in 44 BC. With Cassius he led the Republican resistance against Caesar and was his prime assassin. He was forced to leave Italy, was defeated at Philippi in 42 BC and committed suicide.

BURRUS: Afranius Burrus. Died 62. He was of an equestrian family from Vaison. In 51 he became praetorian prefect. He and Seneca acted as advisers to

Nero and helped weaken Agrippina the Younger's position. Burrus' death may have been due to poisoning.

CAESAR: Gaius Julius Caesar. Born 12 July 100 BC. Wife: Calpurnia. He was associated with the *populares*. A senator before 70 BC, he held various public offices and achieved a reputation as a military leader, initially in Spain. He made an informal alliance in 60 BC with Crassus and Pompey (First Triumvirate). As proconsul of Gaul and Illyricum, he undertook the conquest of the rest of Gaul. He was declared a public enemy by the Senate, and started a civil war by crossing the Rubicon with his army from his province to Italy. He defeated Pompey at Pharsalus in 48 BC and became dictator at Rome. He wrote the famous epigram *veni, vidi, vici* ("I came, I saw, I conquered") after the battle of Zela in Asia Minor against Pharnaces, son of Mithridates. Caesar was also a renowned orator and author. He was assassinated on 15 (Ides) March 44 BC.

CAMILLUS: Marcus Furius Camillus. 5th–4th centuries BC. He was a statesman and general whose deeds are obscured by legend. He captured Veii in 396 BC and in 391 BC was exiled. After the sack of Rome in 390 BC, he was recalled as dictator, and allegedly conquered the Gauls, Volsci and Aequi. He was five times dictator in the period from 390 to 367 BC.

CASSIUS: Gaius Cassius Longinus. He was quaestor of Crassus in Syria in 53 BC and saved some of the forces at Carrhae. Cassius supported Pompey in the civil war but was pardoned by Caesar. He was *praetor peregrinus* in 44 BC and a leading conspirator in Caesar's assassination. He left Italy and joined Brutus in Thrace. He was defeated at the battle of Philippi and committed suicide in 42 BC.

CATILINE: Lucius Sergius Catilina. He was from an obscure patrician family but rose to political prominence in the 60s BC. He was defeated by Cicero for the consulship of 63 BC and exploited the widespread unrest in Italy. He was involved in a conspiracy of rebellion against the state, against which Cicero took action. Catiline was defeated and killed in 62 BC.

CATO THE ELDER (or "the Censor"): Marcus Porcius Cato. 234–149 BC. Born at Tusculum of a peasant family. A military tribune in the Second Punic War, subsequently he held various public offices. He was a prominent orator. He was opposed to the Scipios and was censor in 184 BC, noted for his severity. Cato was known for his stern morality and resisted the introduction of Greek culture to Rome. His ideal was to return to the primitive simplicity of a mainly agricultural state. He also wrote literature. Obsessed with the threat from Carthage, at the end of every debate in the Senate he declared *Carthago delenda est* ("Carthage must be destroyed").

CATO "UTICENSIS": Marcus Porcius Cato "Uticensis" ("of Utica"). 95–46 BC. Great-grandson of Cato the Elder, Cato held Stoic principles, became leader of the *optimates* in 63 BC and supported the Senate and Republican cause. He dominated the Senate in the late 60s BC and opposed the triumvirs. In 58 BC he was sent to administer Cyprus. He continued his opposition on his return, but then retired from public life. After the battle of Pharsalus, he continued the Republican resistance in Africa, but committed suicide at Utica after Caesar's victory at Thapsus.

CICERO: Marcus Tullius Cicero. 3 January 106 BC–7 December 43 BC. Born at Arpinum. Wives: Terentia (married 77 BC, divorced 46 BC), Publilia (married 46 BC, divorced shortly after). Daughter: Tullia (c. 79–45 BC). Son: Marcus Tullius Cicero (by Terentia, 65 BC – after 30 BC). Cicero was from an equestrian family, a *novus homo* and orator who held numerous public offices. He became consul for 63 BC when he crushed Catiline's conspiracy. He was opposed to Caesar and was exiled through a bill of Clodius in 58 BC. In 57 BC he was recalled. From 51 BC he was governor of Cilicia and was a supporter of Pompey in the civil war. He was reconciled with Caesar but supported his assassination, and delivered a series of speeches (the Philippics) to the Senate against Antony in 44 and 43 BC. However, Octavian made an alliance with Antony, proscriptions followed and Cicero was executed.

CINCINNATUS: Lucius Quinctius Cincinnatus. He was a legendary hero who was recalled from his plow in 458 BC to save Rome when its army, under the consul Minucius, was being blockaded by the Italian Aequi tribe. He defeated the enemy, resigned his dictatorship after 16 days and returned to his farm.

CLAUDIUS: Appius Claudius Caecus. He was censor in 312 BC and consul in 307 and 296 BC. While censor, he constructed the *via Appia* and *aqua Appia* and extended membership of the Senate to rich citizens of lower classes and sons of freedmen. As consul he undertook various military campaigns in Italy. When old and blind (*caecus*), he successfully opposed peace with Pyrrhus in 280/79 BC.

CLODIUS: Publius Clodius Pulcher. c. 92–52 BC, of a patrician family of the Claudius *gens*. He was a political opportunist who used the plebeian form of his name (Clodius) and sought adoption (possibly aided by Caesar and Pompey) by a plebeian family, enabling him to hold the tribunate legitimately in 58 BC and so extend his popularity. He was unsuccessfully prosecuted by Cicero in 62 BC for religious sacrilege, and in 58 BC he secured Cicero's exile. To further his own career, he subsequently turned against the triumvirate and was notorious for his violence toward his opponents. He was himself killed violently by Milo's gangs.

CRASSUS: Marcus Licinius Crassus. 115–53 BC. He was one of Sulla's officers in 83 BC, praetor in 73 BC and suppressed Spartacus' slave revolt in 71 BC. Crassus acquired great wealth, particularly through buying property cheaply after fires and rebuilding using his many slaves. He formed an alliance with Pompey and Caesar (First Triumvirate) in 60 BC, and went to Syria to acquire wealth and glory by victory over the Parthians, but was defeated and killed at Carrhae.

FABIUS: Quintus Fabius Maximus Rullianus (or Rullus). 4th–3rd century BC. He was a Roman general who won victories against the Samnites, Etruscans and Gauls. He was five or six times consul (322, 310, 308, 297 and 295 BC), dictator in 315 BC and possibly 313 BC, and censor in 304 BC.

FABIUS (FABIUS CUNCTATOR — Fabius the Delayer): Quintus Fabius Maximus Verrucosus, c. 275–203 BC. He was a general in the Second Punic War and dictator in 217 BC after Hannibal destroyed the Roman army at the battle of Lake Trasimene. Fabius fought a defensive war against Hannibal, avoiding pitched battles. This was criticized until the Romans were defeated in 216 BC at Cannae, after which Fabius' evasive strategy was resumed. He was

consul for the fifth and last time in 209 BC and captured Tarento.

FAUSTINA I (Faustina the Elder) (fig. 1.4): Annia Galeria Faustina. Died in 140 or 141. Parents: Marcus Annius Verus and Rupilia Faustina. Husband: Antoninus Pius (emperor). Children: Faustina II (married Marcus Aurelius) and three who died before Antoninus Pius became emperor.

FAUSTINA II (Faustina the Younger): Annia Galeria Faustina, c. 135–75. Parents: Antoninus Pius and Faustina I. Husband: Marcus Aurelius (emperor; married 145). Children: 12 or 13, including Commodus (emperor). Faustina was with Marcus Aurelius in the east when she died at the foothills of the Taurus Mountains in a village that was renamed Faustinopolis.

FLAMININUS: Titus Quinctius Flamininus. 228–174 BC. He was consul in 198 BC and was given command against Philip V, defeating him at Cynoscephalae in 197 BC. He controlled Rome's eastern policy in the 190s BC and gave Greece independence. In 194 BC he withdrew his forces from Greece, but returned in 192 BC as unrest broke out and his Greek

Fig. 1.4 Obverse of a denarius of the deified Faustina (DIVA FAVSTINA). Courtesy of Somerset County Museums Service.

settlement failed. He was censor in 189 BC, but then his political influence at Rome declined.

FLAMINIUS: Gaius Flaminius. Died 217 BC. A popular leader in opposition to the Senate. He was consul first in 223 BC and defeated the Insubres north of the Po River. As censor in 220 BC he built the Via Flaminia and Circus Flaminius. He was killed at the battle of Lake Trasimene fighting Hannibal's army.

GERMANICUS: Nero Claudius Germanicus, later Germanicus Julius Caesar. 15 BC–AD 19. Parents: Drusus the Elder and Antonia. Wife: Agrippina the Elder. Children: nine including Caligula (emperor), Agrippina the Younger and Drusilla. Germanicus was adopted by Tiberius in AD 4 when the latter was adopted by Augustus. He undertook military campaigns against the Germans in 14–16 and in 17 was sent to the east. He died at Antioch in suspicious circumstances, possibly poisoned. His death caused widespread grief at Rome. Germanicus also wrote literature.

GRACCHUS, GAIUS: Gaius Sempronius Gracchus. Died 121 BC. Parents: Tiberius Sempronius Gracchus and Cornelia (daughter of Scipio Africanus). Brother: Tiberius Gracchus. Gaius Gracchus was in Spain when his brother was murdered. He returned to Rome as a member of the agrarian commission. In 126 BC he was quaestor in Sardinia and was elected tribune for 123 and 122 BC. He proposed a series of radical administrative and agrarian reforms, designed to alleviate poverty, curb the power of the senators and extend rights to non-Roman Italians. The rival tribune M. Livius Drusus (who had senatorial support) undermined his popularity, and Gaius failed to obtain reelection. Violence erupted, and the Senate passed a declaration of public emergency (the first recorded use of the *senatus consultum ultimum*). Gaius ordered a slave to kill him.

GRACCHUS, TIBERIUS: Tiberius Sempronius Gracchus. c. 164–133 BC. Parents: Tiberius Sempronius Gracchus and Cornelia (daughter of Scipio Africanus). Brother: Gaius Gracchus. Wife: daughter of Appius Claudius. He was quaestor in Spain and negotiated peace in 137 BC, which the Senate rejected. He was tribune in 133 BC and proposed an agrarian bill, which was hastily passed. It

involved redistribution of land and affected large landholders. He also undermined the Senate's authority by proposing to the popular assembly that the bequest of Attalus III should be accepted to finance the new smallholdings. He unconstitutionally sought reelection, and was attacked and killed by a mob led by Scipio Nasica.

HORATIUS COCLES: He was a legendary one-eyed ("Cocles") hero who held back the Etruscan army led by Lars Porsenna in 508 BC while the wooden Bridge of Sublicius over the Tiber was demolished. He drowned or, according to some sources, swam to safety.

JULIA: 39 BC–AD 14. Parents: Augustus (emperor) and Scribonia. Husbands: M. Marcellus (married 25 BC, died 23 BC), Agrippa (married 21 BC, died 12 BC), Tiberius (married 11 BC). Children: (by Agrippa) Gaius and Lucius Caesar, Julia, Agrippina the Elder and Agrippa Postumus. Julia quarreled with Tiberius and was exiled by Augustus in 2 BC for adultery.

LEPIDUS: Marcus Aemilius Lepidus. Died 13 or 12 BC. Wife: Junia. Lepidus was praetor in 49 BC, consul in 46 BC and cavalry commander in 46–44 BC. He was a supporter of Caesar, after whose death he formed a triumvirate with Antony and Octavian. He challenged Octavian, but his soldiers deserted to Octavian, and he was forced to retire.

MANLIUS CAPITOLINUS: Marcus Manlius Capitolinus. Died 395 or 394 BC. Consul in 392 BC. He allegedly held the Capitol at Rome when the Gauls sacked the city, having been woken by cackling geese. He became a supporter of the poor but was accused of tyranny and was thrown to his death from the Tarpeian rock.

MARCELLUS: Marcus Claudius Marcellus. Died 208 BC. Consul in 222, 215, 214, 210 and 208 BC. In 222 BC he won a triumph for victories in Cisalpine Gaul in which he killed a Gallic chieftain in single combat. He then won distinction in the Second Punic War against Hannibal, being more aggressive than Fabius Cunctator. He captured Syracuse in 211 BC but was later killed in a Carthaginian ambush.

MARIUS: Gaius Marius. 157–86 BC. Born near Arpinum of an equestrian family. He served at the siege of Numantia under Scipio Aemilianus in 134–133 BC and became plebeian tribune in 119 BC. In 109 BC he went with Metellus as legate to the war in Numidia, and was elected consul in 107 BC after intriguing against Metellus. He ended the war in Numidia, celebrating a triumph in 104 BC, and in both 102 and 101 BC defeated Germanic tribes that were invading Gaul and Italy. Marius also was responsible for a reorganization of the army. From 104 to 100 BC he was consul every year, apparently with the agreement of the Senate. Marius forged close ties with Saturninus (plebeian tribune), who used violent methods to promote legislation. The Senate passed an emergency decree (*senatus consultum ultimum*) to suppress Saturninus, which Marius undertook. Marius then withdrew to Asia Minor (99–97 BC) and his influence declined. He gained command of the war against Mithridates, contrary to the expectations of Sulla, who marched on Rome, causing Marius to flee to Africa. Marius returned to Italy in 87 BC, became consul in 86 BC, undertook a massacre of his enemies but died shortly after.

MILO: Titus Annius Milo. Died 48 BC. Wife: Fausta (Sulla's daughter, married 54 BC). Tribune at Rome in 57 BC. Milo was encouraged by Pompey to act against Clodius, which he undertook by violence and rival gangs for the next five years. He aimed to become consul in 52 BC and precipitated a crisis in which Pompey became sole consul to restore order. Milo was prosecuted, Cicero was apparently intimidated in his defense of Milo and withdrew, and Milo was exiled. In 48 BC Milo joined an abortive rebellion against Caesar and was killed in southern Italy.

NICOMACHUS: Virius Nicomachus Flavianus. 334–394. He was a prominent senator, pagan and friend of Symmacchus. He used violent means to oppose Christianity and further his career. Under Theodosius I, he became quaestor in 388 and praetorian prefect of Italy in 390. After Eugenius' usurpation, he collaborated with Arbogast. When his army was defeated by Theodosius I, he committed suicide.

PISO: Gaius Calpurnius Piso. Died 65. He was a wealthy senator and orator who was exiled under Caligula and was consul under Claudius. He was the major conspirator against Nero, but the conspiracy was betrayed, and Piso and his colleagues were condemned to death.

PISO: Lucius Calpurnius Piso Caesoninus. 1st century BC. Daughter: Calpurnia (married Julius Caesar). Piso was consul in 58 BC and refused to support Cicero against Clodius. He was given the governorship of Macedonia, and his administration was criticized by Cicero. He tried to prevent civil war after Caesar's assassination but died shortly after. He was an Epicurean and may have owned the Villa of the Papyri at Herculaneum.

POMPEY (THE GREAT): Gnaeus Pompeius Magnus, 106–48 BC. Father: Pompeius Strabo. Wives: Aemilia, Mucia (married 80 BC), Julia (Caesar's daughter, married 59 BC, died 54 BC), Cornelia. He was a successful military leader. In 83 BC he won victories for Sulla and then suppressed anti-Sullan forces in Africa and Sicily for which he was allowed a triumph in 81 or 80 BC, although ineligible as he had never held high office. In 77 BC he was sent to Spain with proconsular command against Sertorius, who was murdered in 72 BC. Pompey returned to Italy in 71 BC. With Crassus, he suppressed Spartacus' slave revolt. He was elected consul for 70 BC, despite never having held lower offices. In 67 BC he acted against the pirates in the Mediterranean, and in 66 BC he campaigned in the east against Mithridates. He returned to Rome in 62 BC, but the Senate refused to ratify his settlement of the eastern provinces and client states or provide land allotments for his veterans. He therefore formed the First Triumvirate with Caesar and Crassus to secure his aims. In 55 BC he was consul with Crassus, and in 53 BC he was sole consul to restore order following the violence led by Milo and Clodius. Pompey came into increasing conflict with Caesar, and his forces were defeated by Caesar at Pharsalus in 48 BC. He fled to Egypt, where he was murdered.

RICIMER: Flavius Ricimer. Died 472. German by birth and an Arian. Wife: daughter of Anthemius (married 467). He was master of the soldiers from 456 to 472 and was the real ruler of the west for 16 years through successive emperors. He arranged for concessions to be made to the Germanic tribes, which further weakened the empire. In 456 he deposed Avitus in favor of

Majorian, who was subsequently executed by Ricimer in 461. He then controlled Libius Severus. He reluctantly accepted Anthemius (a military officer from the eastern empire) as emperor but executed him in 472. Ricimer replaced him with Olybrius but died soon after.

SATURNINUS: Lucius Appuleius Saturninus, 2nd–1st century BC. He was quaestor in charge of the corn supply at Ostia in 104 BC when there were shortages at Rome, and he was replaced by the leader of the Senate. Saturninus became increasingly anti-senatorial. He was plebeian tribune in 103 and 100 BC and cooperated with Marius to obtain land for his veterans. He often used organized violence to pass legislation. He stood for the tribunate in 99 BC with the help of Glaucia, who stood for the consulship. Memmius, a rival of Glaucia, was assassinated, and Marius disassociated himself from Saturninus. The Senate took action, and Saturninus and Glaucia were imprisoned and killed.

SCIPIO (SCIPIO AFRICANUS): Publius Cornelius Scipio Africanus Maior, 236–183 BC. Father: P. Cornelius Scipio. Wife: Aemilia. Children: included Cornelia (mother of the Gracchi) and P. Scipio. He held various military commands in the Second Punic War. By 206 BC he had driven the Carthaginians from Spain. In 205 BC he was consul. Contrary to the policies of Fabius Cunctator, he crossed to Africa and defeated Hannibal at the battle of Zama in 202 BC. In 199 BC he was elected censor and became leader of the Senate. In 194 BC he was consul for the second time. He led the army into Asia in 190 BC and was unsuccessfully prosecuted for misconduct on his return to Rome. His influence waned, and he retired to his estate at Liternum, where he died.

SCIPIO: Publius Cornelius Scipio Aemilianus. c. 185–129 BC. Father: L. Aemilius Paullus. Wife: Sempronia (sister of the Gracchi). No children. He fought at the battle of Pydna in 168 BC and undertook military campaigns in Spain and Africa. He was consul in 147 BC (although ineligible) and was given command in the Third Punic War, destroying Carthage in 146 BC. He was censor in 142 BC. In 140 BC he led an embassy to the east, and in 133 BC he was consul for the second time, when he concluded the Numantine war in Spain by capturing and destroying Numantia. On his return to Rome, he opposed Tiberius Gracchus and condoned his murder. He himself may have been murdered.

SEJANUS: Lucius Aelius Sejanus. Died 31. Father: L. Seius Strabo. Sejanus was praetorian prefect from 14 to 31 and gained increasing influence with Tiberius. He was suspected of poisoning Tiberius' son Drusus in 23. When Tiberius withdrew to Capri in 26, Sejanus became very powerful, but was later accused of plotting to overthrow Tiberius and was executed.

SPARTACUS: Died 71 BC. A Thracian slave-gladiator. He escaped from a gladiator school at Capua and led a large slave revolt in 73 BC. His army defeated the Roman forces and plundered southern Italy. He was defeated and killed by Crassus and Pompey.

STILICHO: Flavius Stilicho (fig. 1.5). c. 365–408. He was half Vandal by birth. Wife: Serena (niece of Theodosius I, married c. 384). His daughter married Honorius. Stilicho was master of the soldiers from 394 to 408 and virtually ruled the west as Honorius' regent. He undertook successful campaigns against Alaric and the Visigoths in 401 and 403. He later cooperated with Alaric but was accused of treason and was executed by Honorius.

SULLA: Lucius Cornelius Sulla. c. 138–78 BC. He campaigned with Marius in the wars in Africa and against German tribes in Gaul. He was legate in the Social War. In 88 BC he was consul and was allotted the prized command of the war against Mithridates, who had invaded Asia. However, the command was transferred to Marius by the tribune P. Sulpicius Rufus, and Sulla was forced to flee Rome in the subsequent violence. Sulla assembled his army and marched on Rome, and Marius fled. In 87 BC Sulla campaigned against Mithridates, driving him out of Greece and then proceeding without authority to Asia. He amassed substantial booty and then prepared to invade Italy. Civil war broke out and Sulla finally seized Rome. In 82 BC he was elected dictator and had his enemies proscribed and their property confiscated. He adopted the cognomen Felix (fortunate). Sulla proceeded to reform the constitution and restored constitutional government. In 80 BC he was consul, and he retired in 79 BC.

EMPERORS

Augustus was a title held by all reigning emperors except Vitellius. *Caesar* was a title for the emperor's designated heir or second-in-command. In 293 Diocletian established a tetrarchy by dividing the empire among four rulers. He established two nominally joint emperors, who shared the title *Augustus*, to rule the eastern and western halves of the empire. Each had a subordinate ruler, designated a *Caesar*, who might expect to succeed to the higher rank. The system failed as a means of establishing the succession,

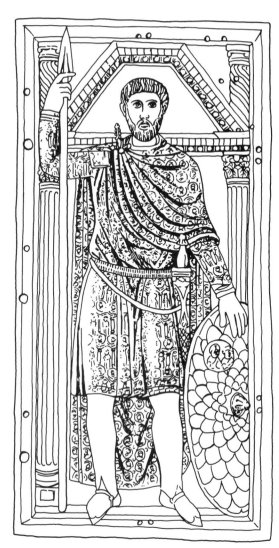

Fig. 1.5 *Stilicho (master of the soldiers, 394–408) represented on an ivory diptych of c. 396.*

Fig. 1.6 *Statue base of Caracalla showing the various titles held by emperors. ("For Marcus Aurelius Antoninus Caesar, son of the emperor Caesar Lucius Septimius Severus Pius Pertinax Augustus, conqueror of Arabia and of Adiabene, father of his country, chief priest, in his 4th year of tribunician power, hailed* imperator *8 times, consul twice, proconsul, the colony of Flavia Augusta Puteoli had this erected.")*

THEODOSIUS (COUNT THEODOSIUS): Flavius Theodosius. Died 375/6. Son: Theodosius I (emperor). From 367 to 369 he restored security in Britain as comes (count) following barbarian invasions. He became master of the soldiers and was sent to suppress an uprising in Africa. He was executed in Carthage shortly after Valentinian I's death, possibly because he was judged to be a threat to the new emperor.

but the titles and their general application survived. The title *Augusta* was bequeathed by the emperor Augustus to his wife Livia, and after Domitian it was held by the wife of reigning emperors.

In inscriptions, a Roman emperor is mentioned by *praenomen, nomen, cognomen* (or *cognomina*) and his official titles in a fixed order. Apart from *Augustus*, other titles held by emperors included *princeps*, short for *princeps civitatis* (first citizen), *pontifex maximus* (head of the priesthood), *pater patriae* (father of the country), *consul* and *imperator*. On accession emperors assumed *tribunicia potestas* (tribunician power equivalent to that of a plebeian tribune). Accompanied by a numeral, the *tribunicia potestas* indicates the number of years an emperor reigned (fig. 1.6).

The following biographies are in chronological order. Unless stated to the contrary, an emperor's death date marks the end of his reign.

Julio-Claudian Dynasty

AUGUSTUS (figs. 1.1, 1.7): Gaius Octavius, later Gaius Julius Caesar Octavianus. Born at Rome 23 September 63 BC. Great-nephew and adopted son of Julius Caesar. When Caesar was deified in 42 BC, Octavian became *divi filius* (son of a god). Wives: Scribonia (divorced 38 BC), Livia (married 38 BC, died AD 14). Daughter: Julia (by Scribonia, 39 BC–AD 14). Grandsons: Gaius Caesar (20 BC–AD 4), Lucius Caesar (17 BC–AD 2) and Agrippa Postumus (12 BC–AD 14). Octavian was head of the Roman world after Antony's defeat in 31 BC. In 27 BC he formally restored the republic, but in effect he had enormous powers, including the consulship and power over most of the army. On 16 January 27 BC he was proclaimed *Augustus* (reverend), by which title he was subsequently known. Emperor until 19 August AD 14, when he died of natural causes at Nola. He was then deified and accepted among the gods of the state.

Fig. 1.7 Bronze statue of Augustus as a young man. His breastplate has scenes of imperial propaganda. He carries a scepter and addresses victorious troops.

Fig. 1.8 Obverse of a denarius *of Tiberius.* Courtesy of Somerset County Museums Service.

Fig. 1.9 Obverse of an as *of Claudius.* Courtesy of Somerset County Museums Services.

Paetina, 27–66), Octavia (by Messallina, c. 40–62), Britannicus Caesar (by Messallina, c. 42–55). Father: Nero Claudius Drusus (38–9 BC). Until his accession Claudius led a retired life, hampered by some physical disability. He was the last surviving adult male of the Julio-Claudian line and was proclaimed emperor by the Praetorian Guard on 25 January 41. Emperor until 13 October 54, when he died, possibly poisoned by Agrippina.

NERO (fig. 1.10): Lucius Domitius Ahenobarbus, later Nero Claudius Caesar Drusus Germanicus. Born 15 December 37 at Antium. Stepfather: Claudius (emperor). Uncle: Caligula (emperor). Wives: Octavia (daughter of Claudius, married 53, divorced 62), Poppaea Sabina (married 62, died 65), Statilia Messallina (married 66). Daughter: Claudia (by Poppaea, born and died 63). Heir-apparent from 50 and emperor from 13 October 54 to 9 June 68, when he committed suicide.

TIBERIUS (fig. 1.8): Tiberius Claudius Nero Caesar. Born 42 BC. Stepson of Augustus (and son of Livia). Wives: Vipsania Agrippina (divorced 11 BC, died AD 20), Julia (Augustus' daughter: married 11 BC, died AD 14). Son: Drusus (by Vipsania, 13 BC–AD 23). Nephews: Germanicus Caesar (15 BC–AD 19), Claudius (emperor). Tiberius was heir-apparent from AD 4 and emperor from 19 August AD 14. He retired to Capri in 26 and died of natural causes on 16 March 37 at Misenum.

CALIGULA: Gaius Julius Caesar Germanicus. Caligula was a nickname meaning "little boot" given by his father's soldiers. Born 31 August AD 12 at Antium. Great-uncle: Tiberius (emperor). Wife: Caesonia. Father: Germanicus Caesar (15 BC–AD 19). Emperor from 16 March 37. Soon after his accession he became seriously ill, which may have affected his sanity. He was assassinated by a tribune of the guard at the Palatine games at Rome on 24 January 41.

CLAUDIUS (fig. 1.9): Tiberius Claudius Drusus. Born 1 August 10 BC at Lyon. Nephew: Caligula (emperor). Uncle: Tiberius (emperor). Wives: Plautia Urgulanilla, Aelia Paetina, Valeria Messallina (married c. 39, divorced and executed 48), Agrippina (married 48, died 59). Children: Claudia Antonia (by

Emperors of the Civil Wars

GALBA: Servius Sulpicius Galba. Born c. 5 BC, from a patrician family. After a distinguished military

Fig. 1.10 Obverse of an as *of Nero.* Courtesy of Somerset County Museums Service.

career, Galba became governor of eastern Spain from 60. The Praetorian Guard declared Galba emperor on 2 April 68, and he was encouraged by Gaius Julius Vindex, governor of Gallia Lugdunensis, who had rebelled against Nero in March 68. Galba marched to Rome with Otho, and was emperor from 9 June 68 to 15 January 69, when he was assassinated in the Forum at Rome.

OTHO: Marcus Salvius Otho. Born in 32. Wife: Poppaea (left Otho for Nero in 62, died 65). Otho was governor of Lusitania from 58 to 68 and had hoped to be Galba's heir. (Instead Galba adopted Piso.) He conspired with the Praetorian Guard and had Galba and Piso murdered. Emperor from 15 January 69. His forces were defeated by Vitellius' legions at the first battle of Bedriacum, and he committed suicide at Brixellum on 17 April 69.

VITELLIUS: Aulus Vitellius. Born in 15. Children: a son and a daughter. Father: Lucius Vitellius (three times consul and Claudius' colleague as censor, died 52). Vitellius was notorious for his gluttony. He was proclaimed emperor by his troops in Lower Germany on 2 January 69 in opposition to Galba, and again by soldiers and senators in Rome on 20 April 69. His forces were defeated by those of Vespasian in October 69 at the second battle of Bedriacum. Vespasian captured Rome and Vitellius was killed on 20 December 69.

Flavian Dynasty

VESPASIAN (fig. 1.11): Titus Flavius Sabinus Vespasianus. Born 9 at Reate. Wife: Flavia Domitilla (married 39, died before Vespasian's accession). Children: Titus (emperor), Domitilla (predeceased her father), Domitian (emperor). Vespasian was a successful soldier and was responsible for the pacification of southern Britain in the invasion of 43. In 67 he was placed in charge of subduing the Jewish Revolt. He was proclaimed emperor in opposition to Vitellius on 1 July 69 by the legions at Alexandria, Egypt, and was also supported by the Danubian legions. He was recognized as emperor by the Senate on 20 December 69. Emperor until 24 June 79, when he died of natural causes.

Fig. 1.11 Obverse of a denarius of Vespasian. Courtesy of Somerset County Museums Service.

TITUS (figs. 1.12, 8.4): Titus Flavius Vespasianus. Born 30 December 39 at Reate. Father: Vespasian (emperor). Daughter: Julia Sabina (c. 65–c. 91). Brother: Domitian (emperor). Titus is famous for the capture of Jerusalem in 70 after a long siege (commemorated by the Arch of Titus). He fell in love with Berenice, the daughter of the Jewish king Herod Agrippa I, causing much criticism. Titus was nevertheless universally popular. Caesar from 69 and emperor from 24 June 79 to 13 September 81, when he died at Reate, probably of natural causes but possibly by the action of Domitian.

DOMITIAN: Titus Flavius Domitianus. Born 24 October 51. Brother: Titus (emperor). Father: Vespasian (emperor). Wife: Domitia Longina (died 150). Caesar from 69 and emperor from 13 September 81 to 18 September 96, when he was assassinated as the result of a palace plot involving his wife.

NERVA (fig. 1.13): Marcus Cocceius Nerva. Born 8 November 30 at Narnia. He was chosen by the Senate as emperor after Domitian's assassination, having previously held public office. Emperor 18 September 96 to 25 January 98, when he died of natural causes.

Adoptive Emperors

TRAJAN (fig. 8.1): Marcus Ulpius Traianus. Born probably in 53 at Italica, Spain. Wife: Pompeia Plotina (died 129). Father: Marcus Ulpius Traianus (died 100). Trajan came from an Umbrian family that had settled in Spain. He had a highly successful military career and was adopted as Caesar by Nerva in 97 when governor of Upper Germany. Emperor from 25 January 98. On his accession, he did not proceed to Rome but organized the Rhine and Danube frontiers. He later conquered the Dacians (fig. 1.2), forming a new province, and much of the Parthian empire,

Fig. 1.13   *Bronze statue of Nerva.*

Fig. 1.12   *Marble statue of Titus wearing a breastplate and tunic.*

reaching the Persian Gulf. He died of natural causes at Cilicia on 8 August 117 as he returned from the Parthian campaign.

HADRIAN (fig. 1.14): Publius Aelius Hadrianus. Born 24 January 76 possibly at Rome, but his family was from Italica, Spain. Grandson of Trajan's aunt and married to Trajan's grand-niece Sabina (married 100, died c. 136). Adopted sons: Aelius (L. Ceionius Commodus, Caesar 136–138), Antoninus Pius (emperor). At his death Trajan adopted Hadrian. Emperor from 8 August 117. Hadrian abandoned

Fig. 1.14 Obverse of a denarius of Hadrian. Courtesy of Somerset County Museums Service.

Trajan's conquests in the east and spent many years (120–131) touring the provinces and consolidating Rome's territories. Hadrian also undertook reforms in administration. He died of natural causes on 10 July 138 at Baiae.

Antonine Emperors

ANTONINUS PIUS: Titus Aurelius Fulvus Boionius Antoninus. Born 19 September 86 at Lanuvium. Wife: Annia Galeria Faustina (died 140 or 141). Children: four, including M. Galerius Antoninus (died very young) and Annia Galeria Faustina (c. 135–175). Adopted sons: Marcus Aurelius (emperor), Lucius Verus (emperor). Antoninus Pius had been proconsul of Asia and had joined Hadrian's circle of advisers. He was adopted by Hadrian as son and successor on 25 February 138. The Senate conferred the title of Pius on him in recognition of his sense of duty toward Hadrian's memory. Emperor from 10 July 138 to 7 March 161, when he died of natural causes at Lorium. He was succeeded by Marcus Aurelius and Lucius Verus.

MARCUS AURELIUS: Marcus Annius Verus, later Marcus Aurelius Antoninus. Born 26 April 121. Nephew of Faustina (wife of Antoninus Pius). Father-in-law: Antoninus Pius (emperor). Wife: Annia Galeria Faustina (daughter of Antoninus Pius, married 145, died 175). Children: 12 or 13 including Commodus (emperor), Annius Verus (163–169), Annia Lucilla (149–183). Marcus Aurelius was adopted by Antoninus Pius in 138. Caesar from 139. Co-emperor with Lucius Verus from 7 March 161 until the latter's death in 169. His reign was dominated by warfare against invaders on all key frontiers. Emperor until 17 March 180, when he died of natural causes at Vienna.

LUCIUS VERUS: Lucius Ceionius Commodus, later Lucius Aurelius Verus. Born 15 December 130. Father: Lucius Aelius Caesar. Wife: Annia Lucilla (daughter of Marcus Aurelius, married c. 164). Caesar under Hadrian from 136 to 138. Co-emperor with Marcus Aurelius from 7 March 161 until early 169, when he died of natural causes near Altinum.

COMMODUS: Lucius Aelius Aurelius Commodus, later Marcus Aurelius Commodus Antoninus. Born 31 August 161 at Lanuvium. Father: Marcus Aurelius (emperor). Grandfather: Antoninus Pius (emperor). Wife: Bruttia Crispa (married 178, died c. 183). Caesar from 166. Co-emperor with Marcus Aurelius from 177. Sole emperor from 17 March 180. Later in his reign Commodus became insane, and renamed Rome *colonia Commodiana* (colony of Commodus). He was assassinated by his ministers on 31 December 193.

Emperors of the Civil Wars

PERTINAX: Publius Helvius Pertinax. Born 1 August 126 at Liguria. Wife: Flavia Titiana. Son: Pertinax Caesar (executed by Caracalla following Geta's assassination in 212). Pertinax was the city prefect and had held many previous posts, including governor of Britain from 185 to 187. He was proclaimed emperor by the Praetorian Guard following Commodus' murder on 1 January 193. Emperor until 28 March 193, when he was assassinated by mutinous guards.

DIDIUS JULIANUS: Marcus Didius Julianus, later Marcus Didius Severus Julianus. Born c. 135.

Wife: Manlia Scantilla. Daughter: Didia Clara. Didius Julianus was a wealthy senator and apparently gave the highest bid to the Praetorian Guard for the throne on the death of Pertinax. Emperor from 28 March 193. The armies refused to recognize him as emperor, and he was executed at Rome on 1 or 2 June 193 on the Senate's orders.

PESCENNIUS NIGER: Gaius Pescennius Niger. Probably born between 135 and 140. While governor in Syria, he was proclaimed emperor in 193 by his troops as a rival to Didius Julianus. Septimius Severus then set out for the east and defeated him at the battles of Cyzicus, Nicaea and Issus. He was captured in Antioch and put to death in autumn 194.

CLODIUS ALBINUS: Decimus Clodius Septimius Albinus. Born at Hadrumetum, probably 140 to 150. He was governor of Britain in 192. As his loyalty was dubious, Severus promoted him to Caesar in 193 to avoid trouble, but Albinus was proclaimed emperor by his own troops. He crossed to Gaul, which he held from 195, but committed suicide after defeat in a battle at Lyon on 19 February 197.

CARACALLA: Septimius Bassianus, later Marcus Aurelius Antoninus (figs. 1.6, 1.15). Caracalla was a nickname derived from the long hooded Celtic cloak, which was his favorite dress. Born 4 April 188 at Lyon. Father: Septimius Severus (emperor). Wife: Plautilla (married 202, banished 205, died 211). Brother: Geta (emperor). Caracalla was Caesar from 196 and co-emperor with Septimius Severus from 198 (probably the beginning of the year). He may have been mentally unstable and murdered Geta. He was obsessed with the desire to become an Oriental conqueror like Alexander the Great. His most significant act was to grant citizenship to all free inhabitants of the Roman Empire in 212. Caracalla was emperor until 8 April 217, when he was assassinated by an army officer between Edessa and Carrhae.

MACRINUS: (Not a member of the dynasty.) Marcus Opellius Macrinus, later Marcus Opellius Severus Macrinus. Born c. 164 at Caesarea in Mauretania. Son: Diadumenian (emperor). Macrinus was a praetorian prefect who had planned Caracalla's murder. Hailed emperor by the troops on 11 April 217, he was the first emperor not to have been a senator. Emperor until June 218, when he was executed following defeat in battle against the forces of Elagabalus at Chalcedon.

Severan Dynasty

SEPTIMIUS SEVERUS (fig. 1.6): Lucius Septimius Severus. Born 146 at Leptis Magna. Wives: Paccia Marciana (married c. 176, died a few years later), Julia Domna (married 187, died 217). Sons: Caracalla (emperor), Geta (emperor). Severus had held numerous public offices and was proclaimed emperor on 13 April 193 by his troops at Carnuntum, in opposition to Didius Julianus. Emperor until 4 February 211, when he died of natural causes at York. He was succeeded by Geta and Caracalla.

GETA: Lucius (later Publius) Septimius Geta. Born 27 May 189 at Milan. Father: Septimius Severus (emperor). Brother: Caracalla (emperor). Caesar from 198. Co-emperor with Septimius Severus and Caracalla from autumn 209. Co-emperor with Caracalla from 4 February 211 to early 212, when he was assassinated at Caracalla's instigation.

Fig. 1.15 Obverse of a denarius of Caracalla (called here ANTONINVS PIVS AVG). Courtesy of Somerset County Museums Service.

DIADUMENIAN: (Not a member of the dynasty.) Marcus Opellius Diadumenianus, later Marcus Opellius Antoninus Diadumenianus. Born c. 208. Father: Macrinus (emperor). Caesar from 217, co-emperor with Macrinus in 218 for a few months until June 218, when he was killed by troops following defeat in battle against the forces of Elagabalus at Chalcedon.

ELAGABALUS: Varius Avitus Bassianus Marcus Aurelius Antoninus. Elagabalus (incorrectly Heliogabalus) was named after the Syro-Phoenician sun-god El Gabal of Emesa of whom he was priest. A Syrian, he was born at Emesa. Second cousin of Caracalla and Geta (emperors). Great-uncle: Septimius Severus (emperor). Wives: Julia Cornelia Paula (married 219, divorced 220), Julia Aquilia Severa (married c. 220, divorced 221, married again late 221), Annia Faustina (married and divorced 221). Cousin and adopted son: Severus Alexander (emperor). Elagabalus was proclaimed emperor in opposition to Macrinus on 16 May 218 when age 15, because of a resemblance to Caracalla. He probably was Caracalla's illegitimate son. In Rome he was totally preoccupied by his religious duties. Emperor until 6 March 222, when he was assassinated by the Praetorian Guard at Rome.

SEVERUS ALEXANDER: Marcus Julius Gessius Bassianus Alexianus, later Marcus Aurelius Severus Alexander. Born 1 October 208 at Arca Caesarea in Phoenicia. Wife: Sallustia Barbia Orbiana (married 225, exiled 227). Adopted as Caesar by Elagabalus in 221. Emperor from 6 March 222. The affairs of the empire were conducted largely by his mother, Julia Mammaea, with her chief adviser Ulpian (the jurist, murdered in 228). Severus Alexander and his mother were assassinated by mutinous troops at Moguntiacum in mid-March 235.

Age of Military Anarchy

MAXIMINUS I (THRAX): Gaius Julius Verus Maximinus. Born c. 172/3, of Thracian peasant stock. Wife: Paulina (apparently died before her husband's accession). Son: Gaius Julius Verus Maximus (Caesar 235–238). Maximinus was over 2.4 m (8 ft) tall and a successful military commander. He was proclaimed emperor by his troops in mid-March 235. He spent his time successfully dealing with the Rhine and Danube problem, and was hated by the Senate because he never visited Rome. In 238 the Senate pronounced the two Gordians co-emperors, followed by Balbinus and Pupienus, also co-emperors. Maximinus therefore abandoned the northern frontier and invaded Italy, but was murdered at Aquileia on 24 June 238.

GORDIAN I AFRICANUS: Marcus Antonius Gordianus. Born c. 157. Son: Gordian II (emperor). Grandson: Gordian III (emperor). Governor of Africa. Proclaimed co-emperor on 22 March 238 in opposition to Maximinus, a move supported by the Senate. Emperor until 12 April 238, when he committed suicide on hearing of his son's death.

GORDIAN II AFRICANUS: Marcus Antonius Gordianus. Born c. 192. Father: Gordian I (emperor). Nephew: Gordian III (emperor). Co-emperor with Gordian I from 22 March 238 to 12 April 238, when he was killed in battle against Capellianus (governor of Numidia and supporter of Maximinus).

BALBINUS: Decimus Caelius Calvinus Balbinus. Born c. 178. Adopted heir: Gordian III (emperor). Balbinus was an elderly senator who was elected co-emperor with Pupienus by the Senate on 22 April 238 in succession to Gordian I and II. Emperor until 29 July 238, when he was assassinated by the Praetorian Guard.

PUPIENUS: Marcus Clodius Pupienus Maximus. Date of birth unknown. Adopted heir: Gordian III (emperor). Pupienus was an elderly senator who was elected co-emperor with Balbinus by the Senate on 22 April 238. Emperor until 29 July 238, when he was assassinated by the Praetorian Guard.

GORDIAN III: Marcus Antonius Gordianus. Born c. 225. Grandfather: Gordian I (emperor). Uncle: Gordian II (emperor). Wife: Furia Sabinia Tranquillina (married 241). Caesar from about May 238. Emperor from 29 July 238. From 241 the empire was ably controlled by Gordian's adviser and praetorian prefect Timesitheus, but he died in 243. Timesitheus' successor, Philip the Arab, persuaded the soldiers to assassinate Gordian III near Zaitha on 25 February 244 and proclaim him emperor.

PHILIP (I) THE ARAB: Marcus Julius Philippus. An Arab, born c. 199. Wife: Marcia Otacilia Severa. Son: Philip II (co-emperor 247–249). Philip I was praetorian prefect and had Gordian III assassinated, Emperor from 25 February 244 to September 249, when he was killed in battle against his city prefect Decius near Verona.

PHILIP II: Marcus Julius Severus Philippus. Born c. 237. Father: Philip the Arab (emperor). Caesar from 244. Co-emperor with his father from about May 247 until September 249 when he was murdered by troops after his father's defeat by Decius.

URANIUS: Lucius Julius Aurelius Sulpicius Uranius Antoninus. Date of birth unknown. A Syrian, proclaimed emperor by his troops in 248. He was possibly assassinated in 254 on the arrival of Valerian in Syria.

PACATIAN: Tiberius Claudius Marinus Pacatianus. Date of birth unknown. Proclaimed emperor by Pannonian and Moesian troops in early summer 248 but was assassinated by his soldiers a few weeks later.

JOTAPIAN: Marcus Fulvius Rufus Jotapianus. Date of birth unknown. Proclaimed emperor by troops in summer 248 in Cappadocia or Syria but was assassinated by troops a few weeks later.

DECIUS, TRAJAN: Gaius Messius Quintus Decius, later Gaius Messius Quintus Traianus Decius. Born c. 201 at Budalia in Lower Pannonia. Wife: Herennia Cupressenia Etruscilla. Sons: Herennius Etruscus (co-emperor), Hostilian (emperor). Decius was a city prefect in Rome and was given military command in Pannonia and Moesia by Philip I. He was declared emperor by his troops and defeated and killed Philip I in battle. The Senate honored him with the name Traianus (after the emperor Trajan). Emperor from September 249 to June 251, when he was killed in battle against the Goths at Abrittus.

HERENNIUS ETRUSCUS: Quintus Herennius Etruscus Messius Decius. Date of birth unknown. Father: Decius Trajan (emperor). Caesar from 250. Co-emperor with Decius from May to June 251, when he was killed in battle against the Goths at Abrittus.

TREBONIANUS GALLUS: Gaius Vibius Trebonianus Gallus. Date of birth unknown. Wife: Afinia Gemina Baebiana. Son: Volusian (co-emperor). Emperor from June 251 to summer 253, when he was killed in battle against Aemilian in northern Italy.

HOSTILIAN: Gaius Valens Hostilianus Messius Quintus. Date of birth unknown. Father: Decius Trajan (emperor). Caesar from December 250. Co-emperor with Trebonianus Gallus from about July 251 to about November 251, when he died of plague.

VOLUSIAN: Gaius Vibius Afinius Gallus Vendumnianus Volusianus. Date of birth unknown. Father: Trebonianus Gallus (emperor). Caesar from about July 251. Co-emperor with his father on the death of Hostilian from about November 251. Emperor until summer 253, when he was killed with his father in battle against Aemilian in northern Italy.

AEMILIAN: Marcus Aemilius Aemilianus. Date of birth unknown. Wife: Cornelia Supera. Proclaimed emperor by the soldiers of Moesia in summer 253 in opposition to Gallus and Volusian. Emperor until autumn 253, when he was assassinated by his soldiers while advancing against Valerian near Spoletium.

VALERIAN: Publius Licinius Valerianus. Born c. 193. Wife: Mariniana (died before her husband's accession). Son: Gallienus (emperor). Valerian was a senator and governor of Raetia. He was proclaimed emperor by his troops in Raetia about September 253 in opposition to Aemilian, and marched on Rome, making Gallienus co-emperor. He undertook campaigns in the east but was captured by the Shapur of Persia about June 260 and spent the remainder of his life in captivity. Date and cause of death unknown.

GALLIENUS: Publius Licinius Egnatius Gallienus. Born c. 218. Father: Valerian (emperor). Wife: Cornelia Salonina (married c. 240, died 268). Sons: Publius Cornelius Licinius Valerianus (Caesar c. 256–258), Publius Licinius Cornelius Saloninus Valerianus (co-emperor). Caesar, then co-emperor, from 253 and emperor from 260. He spent much of his reign campaigning against barbarian invasions. In 267 the commander of the cavalry, Aureolus, revolted and had himself proclaimed emperor at Mediolanum. Gallienus defeated and killed him, but was assassinated by other officers (including Claudius II) about August 268.

SALONINUS: Publius Licinius Cornelius Saloninus Valerianus. Born c. 242. Father: Gallienus (emperor). Caesar from 258. Co-emperor for a few weeks in 260 with Gallienus while being besieged by Postumus at Cologne. Executed in 260 by Postumus, who declared himself emperor.

MACRIANUS: Titus Fulvius Junius Macrianus. Date of birth unknown. Brother: Quietus. Proclaimed emperor with Quietus about September 260 on the capture of Valerian by the Persians. Emperor until spring 261, when he was killed in battle by Aureolus, general of Gallienus.

QUIETUS: Titus Fulvius Junius Quietus. Date of birth unknown. Brother: Macrianus (emperor). Proclaimed emperor with Macrianus about September 260. Emperor until about November 261, when he was besieged and killed at Emesa.

REGALIANUS: Cornelius Publius Regalianus. Date of birth unknown. Wife: Sulpicia Dryantilla. Proclaimed emperor by his troops in Upper Pannonia in autumn 260 and probably assassinated by his soldiers shortly afterward at the approach of Gallienus' army.

CLAUDIUS II GOTHICUS: Marcus Aurelius Valerius Claudius. Born May 214 in Dardania (Moesia Superior). Brother: Quintillus (emperor). Claudius II led a distinguished military career. When the Alamanni invaded Italy, he defeated them and won several additional battles against the Goths, earning himself the title Gothicus Maximus. Emperor from about August 268 to January 270, when he died of plague at Sirmium.

QUINTILLUS: Marcus Aurelius Claudius Quintillus. Date of birth unknown, but he was the younger brother of Claudius II. Emperor from January to about April 270, when he possibly committed suicide.

AURELIAN: Lucius Domitius Aurelianus. Born c. 215 at or near Sirmium. Wife: Ulpia Severina (in whose name the government was run during the six-month interregnum between Aurelian's death and the election of Tacitus). Aurelian was a man of humble origins and a brilliant soldier, the cavalry commander of Claudius II. He was declared emperor by his troops from about April 270 in opposition to Quintillus. He started his reign with victories against invading Germans in north Italy and then defeated Tetricus in the west and Zenobia in the east. Distrusting the future, he surrounded Rome by a massive fortified wall. Emperor until about April 275, when he was assassinated as the result of a conspiracy of his officers.

TACITUS: Marcus Claudius Tacitus. Born c. 200. Half brother: Florian (emperor). Elected emperor by the Senate in September 275, six months after Aurelian's assassination. Emperor until about April 276, when he died, possibly of natural causes, at Tyana in Cappadocia.

FLORIAN: Marcus Annius Florianus. Date of birth unknown. Half brother: Tacitus (emperor). Emperor from about April to end of June 276, when he was assassinated by his soldiers at Tarsus.

PROBUS: Marcus Aurelius Probus. Born August 232 at Sirmium. Proclaimed emperor by his troops in late April or early May 276 in opposition to Florian. He undertook successful campaigns against the Germans and Vandals. Emperor until autumn 282, when he was assassinated by mutinous soldiers at Sirmium.

SATURNINUS: Sextus Julius Saturninus. Date of birth unknown. He rebelled against Probus at Alexandria, Egypt, and shortly afterward was probably assassinated by his own soldiers.

CARUS: Marcus Aurelius Carus. Born c. 230, possibly at Narona in Illyricum. Sons: Carinus (emperor), Numerian (emperor). Proclaimed emperor by his troops in Raetia in autumn 282, shortly before Probus' assassination. Emperor until about August 283, when he died during a Persian campaign near Ctesiphon—officially struck by lightning, but possibly through the treachery of Arrius Aper, the praetorian prefect.

CARINUS: Marcus Aurelius Carinus. Born c. 249. Father: Carus (emperor). Wife: Magnia Urbica. Son: (?) Nigrinian (apparently died before his father's accession). Brother: Numerian (co-emperor). Caesar from autumn 282 and emperor from about August 283 to spring 285, when he was assassinated by his own men at the battle of Margus against Diocletian.

JULIAN (of Pannonia): Marcus Aurelius Julianus. Date of birth unknown. He rebelled against Carinus in Pannonia in 283 or 284, and was defeated and killed by him in battle near Verona in spring 285.

NUMERIAN: Marcus Aurelius Numerianus. Born c. 254. Father: Carus (emperor). Brother: Carinus (emperor). Caesar from late autumn 282. Co-emperor with Carinus from about September 283 to November 284, when he was assassinated while returning from the east, probably by Arrius Aper, the praetorian prefect.

Gallic Empire

POSTUMUS: Marcus Cassianius Latinius Postumus. Date of birth unknown. He rebelled against Gallienus in Gaul in 259 and became emperor there in 260, extending his territory to Britain and northern Spain. He was the first of the usurpers of the Gallic Empire. He was killed by troops in late 268.

LAELIANUS: Ulpius Cornelius Laelianus. Date of birth unknown. He rebelled against Postumus in summer 268 but was killed by him at Moguntiacum about four months later.

MARIUS: Marcus Aurelius Marius. Date of birth unknown. Proclaimed emperor in late 268 following Postumus' death but was probably assassinated by his soldiers in early 269.

VICTORINUS: Marcus Piavonius Victorinus. Date of birth unknown. He was proclaimed emperor following the death of Marius in early 269 and was assassinated at Cologne in 270 by one of his officers.

TETRICUS: Gaius Pius Esuvius Tetricus. Date of birth unknown. Son: Gaius Pius Tetricus (Caesar 270–273). Proclaimed emperor by the Gallic army in 270 following the death of Victorinus. Deposed and pardoned by Aurelian late in 273 (ending the Gallic Empire). He died several years later, probably of natural causes.

Palmyrene Empire

VABALLATHUS: Wahballat. Date of birth unknown, but very young at the time of Odenathus' assassination. Father: Odenathus. Mother: Zenobia. Vaballathus became king of Palmyra in 267 and was proclaimed Augustus in 271 in opposition to Aurelian, who deposed him in summer 272. His fate is unknown.

ZENOBIA: Septimia Zenobia. Date of birth unknown. She ruled Palmyra through her son Vaballathus as a nominal ally of Rome after the death of her husband, Odenathus, in 267. She declared herself Augusta in 271 and moved into Asia Minor and Syria in opposition to Aurelian. He defeated her forces and besieged Palmyra. After its surrender in 272, she was allowed to retire on a pension in Rome, and lived to an old age.

British Empire

CARAUSIUS: Marcus Aurelius Mausaeus Carausius. Date of birth unknown. Commander of the channel fleet. Proclaimed emperor of Britain and northern Gaul in late 286 or early 287 in opposition to Maximian. Assassinated by his colleague Allectus in 293.

ALLECTUS: Name and date of birth unknown. Emperor of Britain and northern Gaul after he assassinated Carausius in 293. Emperor until 296 when he was killed in a battle in southeast England by Constantius I, a victory commemorated by the gold Arras medallion (fig. 1.3).

The Tetrarchy

DIOCLETIAN (figs. 1.16, 1.17): Gaius Aurelius Valerius Diocletianus, originally named Diocles. Born c. 245 in Dalmatia. Daughter: Galeria Valeria (died c. 315). Diocletian was of humble birth and became commander of the imperial guard. Emperor from 20 November 284 following Numerian's death. He was extremely successful in administration, many of his measures lasting for centuries. He divided the rule of the empire into four (a tetrarchy) to make government more effective. Many provinces were divided into smaller units, and frontiers were strengthened. The size of the army was greatly increased, and he instituted a regular system of tax

Fig. 1.17 Reverse of a silver coin showing Diocletian, Maximian, Constantius I and Galerius sacrificing in front of a camp gateway with the enclosure shown in perspective behind. Courtesy of Somerset County Museums Service.

Fig. 1.16 Early 4th-century porphyry statue group of the tetrarchy, portraying Diocletian, Maximian, Constantius and Galerius. They are indistinguishable except for Diocletian, who is bearded. Height 1.3 m (4 ft 3 in). Probably once part of the imperial palace at Constantinople. Now in St. Mark's Square, Venice.

revisions, but was less successful in curbing inflation. Diocletian and Maximian abdicated on 1 May 305, the tetrarchic system collapsed and civil war ensued. Diocletian died of natural causes at Split, c. 316.

MAXIMIAN (figs. 1.16, 1.17, 8.5): Marcus Aurelius Valerius Maximianus. Born c. 250 near Sirmium. Son: Maxentius (emperor). Stepdaughter: Flavia Maximiana Theodora. Daughter: Flavia Maxima Fausta (died 326). Grandsons: Constantine II (emperor), Constantius II (emperor), Constans (emperor), Romulus (died 309). Co-emperor with Diocletian from April 286, with responsibility for the Rhine and from 293 the western Mediterranean (leaving the north to Constantius the Caesar). Maximian abdicated 1 May 305. His son Maxentius brought him out of retirement in November 306, but he was forced to abdicate again in November 308 at the Congress of Carnuntum. He took power again in spring 310 when he rebelled against Constantine at Arles, but died a few weeks later, possibly by suicide or more likely executed on Constantine's orders.

CONSTANTIUS I (CHLORUS—"the pale") (figs. 1.16, 1.17, 1.18): Flavius Valerius Constantius.

Fig. 1.18 Obverse of a denarius *of Constantius I.* Courtesy of Somerset County Museums Service.

Born c. 250 in Dardania. Father-in-law: Maximian (emperor). Wives: Flavia Julia Helena (born c. 248, divorced 293, died c. 328), Flavia Maximiana Theodora (Maximian's stepdaughter, married 293). Son: Constantine I (by Helena; emperor). Daughter: Constantia (by Theodora; died c. 330). Caesar from 1 March 293 under Diocletian's tetrarchy. He was given charge of all provinces north of the Alps with a base at Trier and overthrew Allectus (fig. 1.3). Western emperor from 1 May 305 to 25 July 306, when he died of natural causes at York.

GALERIUS (also known as Maximianus and Armentarius) (figs. 1.16, 1.17): Gaius Galerius Valerius Maximianus. Born near Serdica, date unknown. Father-in-law: Diocletian (emperor). Wives: one name unknown; Galeria Valeria (married 293, died c. 315). Caesar from 1 March 293 under Diocletian's tetrarchy. Eastern emperor from 1 May 305 to beginning of May 311, when he died of natural causes.

SEVERUS II (SEVERUS THE TETRARCH): Flavius Valerius Severus. Born in Pannonia, date unknown. Caesar from 1 May 305. Western emperor from 25 July 306 to spring 307, when he was deposed

and imprisoned by Maximian and Maxentius. He was executed in summer 307, probably on the orders of Maxentius.

MAXIMINUS II DAIA (MAXIMIN DAIA): Gaius Galerius Valerius Maximinus, originally called Daia. Date of birth unknown. Uncle: Galerius (emperor). Caesar from 1 May 305. He became eastern emperor early in 309 not long after the Congress of Carnuntum. Emperor until autumn 313, when he was defeated and killed by Licinius at Tarsus.

MAXENTIUS: Marcus Aurelius Valerius Maxentius. Date of birth unknown. Father: Maximian (emperor). Brothers-in-law: Constantius Chlorus, Constantine I (emperors). Son: Romulus (twice consul, died young in 309). Proclaimed western emperor at Rome on 28 October 306, in opposition to Severus II. He brought his father, Maximian, out of retirement as support. Emperor until 28 October 312, when he was drowned in the Tiber at the battle of the Milvian Bridge (just north of Rome) against Constantine I.

LICINIUS: Valerius Licinianus Licinius. Born c. 263. Wife: Constantia (half sister of Constantine I, married 313, died c. 330). Son: Flavius Valerius Licinianus Licinius (Caesar 317–324). At the Congress of Carnuntum in November 308, Licinius was proclaimed Augustus as colleague of Galerius, with responsibility for the Danube area. On Galerius' death, Licinius defeated Maximin Daia, and the empire was split between himself (east) and Constantine I (west). He was deposed by Constantine I in autumn 324 and was executed in 325 on charges of attempted rebellion.

VALENS: Aurelius Valerius Valens. Date of birth unknown. Proclaimed co-emperor by Licinius in autumn 314 during the wars against Constantine I. He was deposed in late 314 after a truce between Constantine I and Licinius and was then executed by Licinius.

MARTINIAN: Marcus Martinianus. Date of birth unknown. Proclaimed co-emperor by Licinius in late summer 324 during wars against Constantine I. He was deposed by Constantine I in autumn 324, retired to Cappadocia, but was executed by Constantine I in 325.

Dynasty of Constantine and Rivals

CONSTANTINE I (THE GREAT) (fig. 1.19): Flavius Valerius Constantinus Augustus. Born 17 February c. 285 at Naissus, Moesia. Father: Constantius I (emperor). Father-in-law: Maximian (emperor). Wives: Minervina, Flavia Maxima Fausta (married 307, died 326). Sons: Flavius Julius Crispus (by Minervina; Caesar 317–326; executed by Constantine in 326), Constantine II (by Fausta; emperor), Constantius II (by Fausta; emperor), Constans (by Fausta; emperor). Daughters (by Fausta): Constantina, Helena (died 360).

Constantine I was proclaimed western emperor by his troops at York on his father's death in 306, although Galerius, emperor in the east, granted him only the rank of Caesar. A complex power struggle ensued. Constantine sided with Maxentius at the latter's usurpation in October 306. Maximian (father of Maxentius) rebelled against Constantine in 310 and was possibly killed by him. Galerius died in 311, and Constantine made an alliance with Licinius. In 312 Constantine invaded Italy and defeated Maxentius. Licinius became emperor of the east, but in 313 and again in 323 war broke out between him and Constantine. In 324, after several battles, Constantine defeated Licinius and became

sole emperor. He moved his capital to Byzantium in 330, which he renamed Constantinople. He was baptized a Christian on his deathbed. He died of natural causes on 22 May 337 at Ancyrona, near Nicomedia. He had put to death his eldest son, Crispus, in 326 and was succeeded by his three remaining sons who each took the title Augustus and divided the empire among themselves.

CONSTANTINE II: Flavius Claudius Constantinus. Born 316 at Arles. Father: Constantine I (emperor). Brothers: Constantius II, Constans (emperors). Caesar from 1 March 317. Western emperor from 9 September 337. (Following Constantine I's death on 22 May 337, there was an interregnum of over three and a half months during which time the government was carried on in the dead emperor's name.) Emperor at Trier until spring 340, when he was killed in an ambush while advancing to attack Constans near Aquileia.

CONSTANS: Flavius Julius Constans. Born 320. Father: Constantine I (emperor). Brothers: Constantius II, Constantine II (emperors). Caesar from 333. Western emperor from 9 September 337. In 340 he defeated and killed his brother Constantine II and took over the whole of the west. He was assassinated by Gaiso, barbarian emissary of Magnentius, early in 350 at the fortress of Helene, at the foot of the Pyrenees.

CONSTANTIUS II: Flavius Julius Constantius. Born 7 August 317 at Sirmium. Father: Constantine I (emperor). Brothers: Constantine II, Constans (emperors). Wives: one name unknown, Eusebia, Faustina. Posthumous daughter: Constantia (by Faustina). Caesar from 8 November 324. Eastern emperor from 9 September 337 and sole emperor from 353 (on the death of Magnentius) to 3 November 361, when he died of fever at Mopsucrenae.

MAGNENTIUS: Flavius Magnus Magnentius. Born c. 303 at Amiens, of German descent. Brother: Magnus Decentius (Caesar 351–353). Proclaimed emperor at Autun 18 January 350 in opposition to Constans. He was defeated at the battle of Mursa on 28 September 351 by Constantius II and retreated to Italy and Gaul, but was encircled and committed suicide at Lyon on 11 August 353.

Fig. 1.19 Obverse of a bronze coin of Constantine I. Courtesy of Somerset County Museums Service.

VETRANIO: Name and date of birth unknown. Proclaimed western emperor by the troops in Illyricum on 1 March 350, possibly with the connivance of Constantius II to block Magnentius' eastward progress. He abdicated in late 350, retired to Bithynia and died c. 356.

NEPOTIAN: Flavius Julius Popilius Nepotianus Constantinus. Date of birth unknown. Uncle: Constantine I (emperor). Proclaimed emperor at Rome by opponents of Magnentius in early 350, but was killed one month later by Magnentius' troops.

SILVANUS: Claudius Silvanus. Date of birth unknown, of Frankish descent. An army officer, Silvanus deserted Magnentius for Constantius II before the battle of Mursa in 351. He was made master of the infantry and sent to Gaul to repel barbarian incursions. He was implicated in a political plot and so declared himself emperor at Cologne in 355 to save his own life, but was assassinated shortly afterward by his own soldiers.

JULIAN (II) THE APOSTATE: Flavius Claudius Julianus. Born April 332 at Constantinople. Father: Julius Constantius. Half brother: Flavius Claudius Julius Constantius Gallus (Caesar 351–354). Cousins: Constantine II, Constans, Constantius II, Nepotian (emperors). Uncle: Constantine I (emperor). Wife: Helena (Constantine I's daughter, married 335, died 360). Julian was proclaimed caesar by Constantius II on 6 November 355 and was put in charge of Gaul and Britain, where he was a very successful general. He was proclaimed emperor by his troops at Paris early in 360. Constantius died before Julian reached Constantinople, and he became sole emperor. He was named "the Apostate" by Christian writers because he reinstated pagan cults and temples, and was the last pagan emperor. In 361 he set out for Antioch to make preparations for the invasion of Persia. He was killed in battle against the Persians 26 June 363 at Maranga in Persia.

JOVIAN: Flavius Jovianus. Born c. 331 at Belgrade, son of a general. Sole emperor from 27 June 363 to 16 February 364, when he died at Dadastana en route to Constantinople — suffocated because a brazier of charcoal was accidentally left in his bedroom.

Fig. 1.20 Obverse of a miliarense *of Valentinian I.* Courtesy of Somerset County Museums Service.

Dynasty of Valentinian

VALENTINIAN I (fig. 1.20): Flavius Valentinianus. Born 321 in Pannonia. Wives: Valeria Severa (divorced 368), Justina (widow of Magnentius, married 368, died 387). Brother: Valens (emperor). Sons: Gratian (by Severa; emperor 367–383), Valentinian II (by Justina; emperor). Western emperor from 26 February 364. He was a great military leader and spent most of his reign on the northern frontiers. He died of natural causes at Brigetio on 17 November 375.

VALENS: Flavius Valens. Born 328 in Pannonia. Brother: Valentinian I (emperor). Nephews: Gratian, Valentinian II (emperors). Eastern emperor from 28 March 364. After Valentinian I's death, there were mass incursions on the northern frontiers, and Valens was killed in battle against the Visigoths near Hadrianopolis on 9 August 378.

PROCOPIUS: Born c. 326 in Cilicia and was related to Julian II. At Constantinople he was proclaimed emperor by troops in opposition to Valens on 28 September 365, but was defeated by Valens on 27 May 366.

GRATIAN: Flavius Gratianus. Born 18 April 359 at Sirmium. Father: Valentinian I (emperor). Uncle: Valens (emperor). Half brother: Valentinian II (emperor). Wife: Constantia (posthumous daughter of Constantius II, 362–383, married 374). Co-emperor with Valentinian I from 24 August 367. Western emperor from Valentinian I's death in 375 until 25 August 383, when he was killed while fleeing from Magnus Maximus at Lyon.

VALENTINIAN II: Flavius Valentinianus. Born 2 July 371 at Aquincum or perhaps at Trier. Father: Valentinian I (emperor). Uncle: Valens (emperor). Half brother: Gratian (emperor). Western emperor from 22 November 375. He was expelled by Magnus Maximus in 387 but was restored in 388 by Theodosius I. He died at Vienne on 15 May 392, possibly by suicide or perhaps assassinated by order of his general Arbogast.

MAGNUS MAXIMUS: Magnus Clemens Maximus. Date of birth unknown, of Spanish origin. Son: Flavius Victor (emperor). Proclaimed western emperor by his troops in Britain in July 383 in opposition to Gratian. He controlled Gaul and Spain and was recognized by Theodosius I until he invaded Italy. Emperor until 28 August 388, when he was executed following his defeat by Theodosius I's troops near Aquileia.

FLAVIUS VICTOR: Date of birth unknown. Father: Magnus Maximus (emperor). Proclaimed co-emperor by his father in mid-387. Executed in Gaul by the general Arbogast in August 388.

EUGENIUS: Full name and date of birth unknown. Proclaimed western emperor by Arbogast on 22 August 392 after a three-month interregnum following Valentinian II's death. Emperor until 6 September 394, when he was executed following his defeat by Theodosius I between Aemona and Aquileia.

Dynasty of Theodosius and Rivals

THEODOSIUS I (THE GREAT) (fig. 1.21): Flavius Theodosius. Born c. 346 at Cauca, Spain.

damage

Fig. 1.21 Theodosius I at a presentation ceremony of a charter to a kneeling official. Part of the scene on a late Roman silver dish of c. 388.

Father: Theodosius the Elder (Count Theodosius), the general who restored security in Britain between 368 and 370. Wives: Aelia Flaccilla (married c. 376, died c. 386), Galla (Valentinian II's daughter, married 388). Sons (by Flaccilla): Arcadius, Honorius (emperors). Daughter: Galla Placidia (by Galla, c. 388–450). Proclaimed eastern emperor by Gratian on 19 January 379. Theodosius spent the early years of his reign trying to drive out the invading Visigoths, finally assigning them lands in Thrace. He was a devout Christian and dealt harshly with heretics. In 391 he put an end to all forms of pagan religion in the empire and so founded the orthodox Christian state for which he acquired his title "the Great". He was sole emperor from the death of Valentinian II in 392. He died of natural causes on 17 January 395 at Milan. After Theodosius I the empire was permanently divided into eastern and western halves, with complete separation of administration and succession. The east was the forerunner of the Byzantine Empire.

ARCADIUS: Flavius Arcadius. Born 377. Father: Theodosius I (emperor). Wife: Aelia Eudoxia (daughter of Bauto the Frank, married 395, died 404). Son: Theodosius II (emperor). Daughter: Aelia Pulcheria (399–453). Brother: Honorius (emperor). Proclaimed co-emperor with Theodosius I from January 383. Sole eastern emperor from 17 January 395 until 1 May 408, when he died of natural causes at Constantinople.

HONORIUS: Flavius Honorius. Born 9 September 384 at Constantinople. Father: Theodosius I (emperor). Brother: Arcadius (emperor). Wife: daughter of Stilicho. Proclaimed co-emperor with Theodosius I from January 393. Sole western emperor from 17 January 395 but was dominated by Stilicho. Emperor until 25 August 423, when he died of natural causes at Ravenna.

CONSTANTINE III: Flavius Claudius Constantinus. No relation to his predecessors, he was a soldier who was proclaimed emperor by the army in Britain in 407. He invaded Gaul and established his court at Arles in 407. He gained brief control of Spain in 408, was recognized by Honorius in 409 but was later captured by Honorius' general Constantius and was executed in 411.

MAXIMUS: Name and date of birth unknown. Proclaimed emperor in 409 in Spain in opposition to Constantine III. He was deposed in 411 but was allowed to retire. He was executed by Honorius in 422 at Ravenna following an abortive rebellion.

ATTALUS: Priscus Attalus. Date of birth unknown. Attalus, a leading senator, was proclaimed emperor by the Goths at Rome in 409. He was deposed by Alaric in May or June 410. He was proclaimed emperor again by the Goths at Bordeaux in 414 but was deposed in 415 and was banished to the Lipari Islands. Date of death unknown.

JOVINUS: Name and date of birth unknown. Brother: Sebastianus (emperor). Proclaimed emperor by the Burgundian invaders of Gaul in 411. Executed in 413 at Narbonne.

SEBASTIANUS: Name and date of birth unknown. Brother: Jovinus (emperor). Proclaimed co-emperor by Jovinus in 412. Executed in 413.

CONSTANTIUS III: Flavius Constantius. Born at Naissus, Moesia (date unknown). Wife: Galla Placidia (daughter of Theodosius I, c. 388–450, married 417). Son: Valentinian III (emperor). Daughter: Justa Grata Honoria (417–454). Constantius was master of the soldiers by 411 and the most powerful political influence since Stilicho's fall. He was co-emperor of the west with Honorius from 8 February to 2 September 421, when he died of natural causes at Ravenna.

THEODOSIUS II: Flavius Theodosius. Born 10 April 401 at Constantinople. Father: Arcadius (emperor). Uncle: Honorius (emperor). Wife: Aelia Eudocia (originally named Athenais, 393–460, married 421). Daughter: Licinia Eudoxia (born 422). Proclaimed co-emperor by Arcadius on 10 January 402. Sole eastern emperor from 408. During his reign, he assisted the west in its defense, and his daughter was married to the western emperor Valentinian III. Theodosius undertook a compilation of legislation known as the Theodosian Code. He died of natural causes (after a fall from his horse) on 28 July 450 at Constantinople.

JOHANNES (JOHN): Name unknown. Born c. 380. Western emperor from 25 August 423 to October 425, when he was executed following his defeat by an army sent by Theodosius II to champion the cause of the young Placidius Valentinianus.

VALENTINIAN III: Placidius Valentinianus. Born 2 July 419 at Ravenna. Father: Constantius III (emperor). Uncle: Honorius (emperor). Cousin: Theodosius II (emperor). Wife: Licinia Eudoxia (daughter of Theodosius II, born 422, married 437). Daughter: Placidia. Western emperor from 23 October 425 (following the fall of the usurper Johannes) with his mother Galla Placidia as regent until 433, when Aëtius became influential. He was assassinated on 6 March 455 at Rome in revenge for the murder in 454 of Aëtius.

MARCIAN: Flavius Valerius Marcianus. Born c. 396 in Thrace. Wives: one name unknown, second was Aelia Pulcheria (sister of Theodosius II, 399–453, married 450). Marcian was previously a military tribune. Eastern emperor from 25 August 450 (having been selected for succession by Pulcheria) until January or February 457, when he died of natural causes.

Collapse of Western Empire

PETRONIUS MAXIMUS: Flavius Anicius Petronius Maximus. Born c. 396. Wife: Licinia Eudoxia (widow of Valentinian III). Petronius Maximus had held numerous public offices. Western emperor from 17 March to 31 May 455, when he was killed by a mob at Rome while fleeing from the approaching Vandal army.

AVITUS: Marcus Maecilius Flavius Eparchius Avitus. Born in southern Gaul, date unknown. Proclaimed western emperor at Toulouse by the Visigoths on 9 July 455. Emperor until 17 October 456, when he was deposed by Ricimer and Majorian and forcibly made bishop of Placentia. He died, possibly of natural causes, shortly afterward in 456.

MAJORIAN: Julius Maiorianus. Date of birth unknown. Proclaimed western emperor on 1 April 457 (more than five months after the fall of Avitus) with Ricimer's support. His fleet was captured by the Vandals in Spain. He was deposed by Ricimer, who executed him on 2 August 461 at Tortona.

LIBIUS SEVERUS (SEVERUS III): Libius Severus. Born in Lucania, date unknown. Western emperor from 19 November 461 (more than three months after the fall of Majorian) to 14 November 465, when he died at Rome, possibly of natural causes.

ANTHEMIUS: Procopius Anthemius. Born at Constantinople, date unknown. Father-in-law: Marcian (emperor). Descended from Procopius (emperor). Wife: Aelia Marcia Euphemia (daughter of Marcian). Daughter: Alypia (married Ricimer 467). Son: Marcian. Anthemius was a military officer from the eastern empire. Western emperor from 12 April 467 (almost 17 months after the death of Libius Severus) until 11 July 472, when he was executed by Ricimer at Rome.

OLYBRIUS: Anicius Olybrius. Date of birth unknown. Wife: Placidia (daughter of Valentinian III, married 462). Proclaimed western emperor by Ricimer in April 472 in opposition to Anthemius. Emperor until 2 November 472, when he died of natural causes.

GLYCERIUS: Flavius Glycerius. Date of birth unknown. Proclaimed western emperor at Ravenna on 5 March 473 (more than four months after the death of Olybrius). He was deposed by Julius Nepos on 24 June 473 and was consecrated bishop of Salonae. Date of death unknown.

NEPOS, JULIUS: Flavius Julius Nepos. Born in Dalmatia, date unknown. Western emperor from 24 June 473 (having deposed Glycerius) until 28 August 475, when he was deposed by Orestes, master of the soldiers. He fled from Italy to Dalmatia, where he remained in exile until his assassination near Salonae on 9 May 480.

ROMULUS AUGUSTULUS (AUGUSTUS): Romulus Augustus (nicknamed Augustulus). Date of birth unknown, but very young at the time of accession. Father: Orestes, master of soldiers under Julius Nepos (executed by Odovacer 28 August 476). Proclaimed western emperor by Orestes in late October 475, two months after the flight of Nepos, and remained emperor until late August 476. He was deposed by Odovacer, but was permitted to live in exile in a villa near Naples. Date and cause of death unknown. He was the last western emperor.

House of Leo

LEO I: Flavius Valerius Leo. Born c. 411 in Thrace. Wife: Aelia Verina (died 484). Daughters: Aelia Ariadne, Leontia. Grandson: Leo II (emperor). Eastern emperor from 7 February 457 (following the death of Marcian) until 3 February 474, when he died of natural causes.

LEO II: Name unknown. Born c. 467. Father: Zeno (emperor). Proclaimed co-emperor by Leo I on 18 November 473 and died of natural causes on 10 November 474.

ZENO: Originally named Tarasicodissa, but changed to Zeno on his marriage to Ariadne. Born c. 427 in Isauria. Father-in-law: Leo I. Wife: Aelia Ariadne (daughter of Leo I, married c. 467, died 515). Son: Leo II (emperor). Proclaimed co-emperor by Leo II on 9 February 474. Emperor until 9 April 491, when he died of natural causes. He was succeeded by Anastasius (491–518), who is generally recognized as the first Byzantine emperor.

BASILISCUS: Name unknown. Date of birth unknown. Brother-in-law: Leo I (emperor). Wife: Aelia Zenonis (died 477). Son: Marcus (co-emperor). Proclaimed eastern emperor in Constantinople in January 475 following the flight of Zeno to Isauria, but was deposed by Zeno in August 476. He was exiled to Cappadocia and starved to death in 477.

MARCUS: Name and date of birth unknown. Father: Basiliscus (emperor). Proclaimed co-emperor with Basiliscus in early 476 and was deposed in August 476. He was exiled to Cappadocia, where he was executed in 477.

ANASTASIUS: Born c. 430 at Dyrrachium. Wife: Aelia Ariadne (daughter of Leo I, married 491, died 515). Eastern emperor from 11 April 491, having been selected by Ariadne (widow of Zeno). Emperor until 1 July 518, when he died of natural causes.

House of Justin

JUSTIN I: Born in 450 or 452 at Bederiana near Skopje. Nephew: Justinian I (emperor). Eastern emperor from 10 July 518 until 1 August 527, when he died of natural causes.

JUSTINIAN I: Flavius Petrus Sabbatius Justinianus. Born c. 482 near the border of Thrace and Illyricum. Nephew and adopted son of Justin I (emperor). Wife: Theodora (married 523, died 548). Co-emperor with Justin I from 4 April 527. Sole eastern emperor from 1 August 527. Justinian tried to restore the Roman Empire by recovering the lost provinces of the west, by reforming the administrative system and by codifying and rationalizing the legal system. As part of this aim, he also suppressed heresy and paganism. Through his general Belisarius, he recovered Africa from the Vandals, occupied Rome, overthrew the Ostrogothic kingdom in Italy and freed Spain from the Visigoths. Emperor until 14 November 565, when he died of natural causes.

SOCIAL STRUCTURE

The *populus Romanus* (Roman people) was originally the body of citizens eligible to be soldiers but later came to mean the whole community. It was divided into two distinct classes or orders — patricians and plebeians. There was also an equestrian class. For slaves and freedmen, see chapter 9. In the later empire there were two classes — *honestiores* and *humiliores*.

Patricians

Patricians (*patricii*, probably from *patres*, members of the Senate, literally fathers) were a privileged group of families, many of whom were senators. Under the early republic they controlled politics by their influence over the Senate and the assemblies, by their positions of power and by controlling the state religion, in which they held the important priesthoods (augurs and pontiffs). They were in charge of all civil and criminal law, which they interpreted and administered. Patricians also dominated the army.

Patricians were large landowners. In 218 BC the *lex Claudia* prevented senators from engaging in commerce (which was left to nonsenatorial plebeians and foreigners, such as Greeks). Because there was a distinction between wealth from land and from commerce, though, patricians began to invest even more in land, in particular by leasing large tracts of *ager publicus*.

Until 445 BC, patricians were forbidden to marry plebeians. By the end of the republic the number of patrician families had declined significantly, and their political influence had diminished as well.

Plebeians

In the early and middle republic plebeians (from *plebs*, common people) were those Roman citizens who were not patricians. In the early republic they were excluded from the Senate and important priesthoods, did not have the right to hold public office and had no part in the administration of the law. Originally plebeians were also forbidden to marry patricians. They could, however, participate in commerce, and some became very wealthy, forming the "middle class" (*equites*) of Roman society. The "Conflict of the Orders" in the 5th and 4th centuries BC led to the plebeians achieving their political objectives.

In the late republic dispossessed farmers and unemployed laborers in particular drifted to the cities from the rural areas. The vastly increased urban population became the "urban mob." The *proletarii* at Rome were those citizens placed in the lowest property class who were exempt from military service and *tributum* and could serve the state only by contributing their children (*proles*) to it.

Equites

Equites (sing. *eques*; horsemen, knights or equestrians) originally formed the cavalry at Rome (see chapter 2), but the term came to mean the wealthy business or capitalist class (*ordo equester*). Particularly from 218 BC, when the *lex Claudia* prevented senators from engaging in commerce, there were numerous opportunities for the *equites* to make money in the provinces. These activities included tax collection, banking, money lending, operating mines and importing and exporting goods. The *equites* were also able to take on public contracts, such as road building and supplying equipment to the army. They could enter the Senate, but generally preferred a business life.

From the late 2nd century BC the *equites* were enrolled as such by the censors if they had property of a minimum value of 400,000 sesterces. The *equites* came to be of similar social standing to the senators and exerted much political influence, and could hold military positions in the army. Cicero tried to unite the *equites* with the senators in a *concordia ordinum* (concord between the orders). From the 1st century BC the equestrian order was increased by men of similar wealth and background from provincial cities.

In the empire the *equites* lost their influence as a political force but were able to fill military and administrative posts. *Vir ementissimus* was a title given to an equestrian praetorian prefect, *viri perfectissimi* to other prefects and procurators (fig. 2.3) and *viri egregii* to other equestrians in the imperial civil service. The latter title died out under Constantine, and *viri perfectissimi* was extended to minor officials. From the 3rd century nearly all higher posts were held by *equites*, but by the 4th century the equestrian order was no longer recognizable.

GOVERNMENT

Popular Assemblies

During the republic male citizens could vote on legislation and in the election of government officials. Voting was done in popular assemblies, of which every citizen was a member, and was oral and public until 139 BC, when secret ballots were introduced.

There were four assemblies in the republic, all held outdoors. Three were known by the plural noun *comitia* (meetings of all citizens—plebeians and patricians), a *comitium* being a place of assembly. These were the *comitia curiata*, *comitia centuriata* and *comitia tributa*. The *concilium plebis* was for plebeians only.

The assemblies met only to vote, not to discuss or initiate action. Legislation was initiated by a magistrate and discussed by the Senate, and was taken to one of the assemblies only for a vote. The senators therefore controlled the nature of the legislation that reached the assemblies. Laws or motions passed by the *comitia* were known as *leges* (sing. *lex*), and those by the *concilium plebis* were called *plebiscita* (sing. *plebiscitum*) (decrees of the plebeians). There was no opportunity for discussion during the assemblies, but very often informal public discussions were held — *contiones* (sing. *contio*) — before a vote was taken, which male citizens, women, slaves and foreigners could attend.

By the end of the republic many Roman citizens did not live at or near Rome and so would have had difficulty exercising their right to vote. The *comitia* continued in existence to the 3rd century but had lost their functions by the late 1st century.

COMITIA CURIATA

Originally the Roman people were divided into 30 *curiae* (wards), ten to each of the three original tribes. They were the basis of the political and military organization, and the people voted in their own *curiae*. Little is known of this *comitia*, from which the centuriate assembly developed, and it had no legislative powers. By the late republic the *comita curiata* met only for formal purposes, and conferred *imperium* on consuls and praetors.

COMITIA CENTURIATA

This centuriate assembly could be summoned only by a magistrate with *imperium*. It met in the Campus Martius (Field of Mars) at Rome, as it used to be a military assembly. Voters were divided into voting units called centuries (373 in all, of which 18 were for equestrians). The centuries were based on men's age and their property values, originally a means of organizing military forces. The poor had fewer votes; most of the power was with the rich. This assembly decided between war and peace and elected higher magistrates. It also acted as a court of appeal against the death sentence in criminal cases. In the early republic it was the main legislative and judicial body, but its functions declined.

COMITIA TRIBUTA

The assembly of the tribes (*comitia tributa*) met in the Forum at Rome, and the voters were divided into their 35 tribes. It could be summoned by consuls, praetors or tribunes. It elected lesser magistrates and acted as a court of appeal in cases not involving capital punishment. This assembly was also a legislative body and voted on bills put before it by the presiding magistrate.

CONCILIUM PLEBIS

The Forum at Rome was the meeting place for this assembly, which was restricted to plebeians, divided into their 35 tribes. It may have elected tribunes and plebeian aediles. After 287 BC its resolutions (*plebiscita*) were binding on all citizens.

Senate

SENATE IN REPUBLICAN ROME

The *senatus populusque Romanus* (SPQR) (fig. 1.22) was the Senate and the People of Rome. The Senate was a group of unelected men called senators, restricted to patricians in the early republic but later extended to plebeians. In the middle and late republic a man was automatically admitted to the Senate for life once he had been elected by the *comitia* or *concilium* to his first magistracy. He was expelled only if found guilty

Fig. 1.22 Reverse of an as of Nero showing Victory with a shield inscribed SPQR *and* SC *(senatus consulto, by decree of the Senate).* Courtesy of Somerset County Museums Service.

of misconduct. There were originally 100 members, which increased to 300, then to 600 in 80 BC, and to 900 under Julius Caesar.

The Senate was formally a body that advised magistrates, but from the 3rd century BC it increased its influence and power, particularly through the crisis of the Second Punic War. Among other work, it prepared legislation to put before the assemblies, administered finances, dealt with foreign relations and supervised state religion. In the 2nd and 1st centuries BC the Senate was the virtual government of Rome, having great influence and control over the assemblies and magistrates. It could not make laws but issued decrees (known as *decreta* or *senatus consulta*). The *senatus consultum ultimum* (final decree of the Senate) was a final resort for crushing political threats, last employed in 40 BC. It authorized magistrates to employ every means possible to restore order.

Senators had to have a private income as they received no payment. During the republic, the most important activity in adult life for the small group of families that constituted the senatorial class was the pursuit of political power for themselves, their family and friends. A boy's rhetorical education and a young man's activities in the law courts were preparations for a political career. Men would try to win election to their first magistracy in their early 30s. Friendships, marriages and even divorces were often a matter of political convenience. A politician was expected to greet everyone warmly and by name, and was assisted by a slave called a *nomenclator* whose duty it was to memorize names and identify people.

Only a small percentage of the population was deeply involved in politics. Rivalry was intense and political campaigns were bitter. Because elections were held every year, the process of campaigning was virtually unending. Political slogans were painted on walls of buildings at Pompeii (fig. 6.6) and presumably in other cities. Campaigns were also expensive, with bribery (*ambitus*) and corruption commonplace. Even if not running for office, a man was expected to campaign for family and friends.

Among the senators was an exclusive group of *nobiles* (well-known) whose ancestors (patrician or plebeian) had held a curule magistracy (later a consulship only). Up to the 1st century BC few men outside these families reached consular rank. Political alliances or factions (*factiones*) were common within these families, and various methods were used to undermine opposition factions. A *novus homo* (new man) was

the first man in a family (such as Cicero) to hold a curule magistracy, especially a consulship. These new men were nevertheless usually from wealthy families. In the empire the term *nobiles* was applied to the descendants of republican consuls.

OPTIMATES AND POPULARES

After the Gracchi, the politicians were divided into two opposing groups. The *populares* (on the side of the people) were reformers who worked through the people rather than the Senate. Their political opponents called themselves the *optimates* (best class) and were the larger and conservative part of the Senate.

MEETINGS

Meetings of the Senate were attended by senators, magistrates and the *flamen dialis* (see chapter 7) only, although the public could gather by the open doors in the vestibule. Meetings were held mainly in the *Curia Hostilia* in the northwest corner of the Forum, but they could also take place in any public consecrated place within 1.6 km (1 mile) of Rome. Senators sat on benches (*subselli*) down the long sides of the building in no fixed order.

THE SENATE UNDER THE EMPIRE

The Senate granted increasing powers to the emperor Augustus, and in turn its own power was greatly curtailed under successive emperors, although no emperor attempted to abolish it. By Augustus' reign there were over 1,000 senators. He reduced that number to about 600 and introduced a property qualification of 1 million sesterces for entry. A senatorial career was not necessarily safe under some emperors, and many members of the old senatorial families retired from politics, were executed or committed suicide. The Senate began to be filled by men from upper-class families from the provinces.

Under the empire the Senate retained some provinces, controlled the *aerarium* (state treasury), and became a legislative body, its *senatus consulta* having the force of law. Nevertheless, its power gradually diminished. In the later empire the number of senators increased, and Constantine also introduced a Senate in Constantinople, which in 359, was made equal to that of Rome. By c. 384 each Senate had about

2,000 members, and continued as legislative bodies. Senators at Rome tended to be wealthier and more conservative than those at Constantinople. The Roman Senate was last mentioned in 603.

Magistrates

MAGISTRATES IN THE REPUBLIC

In the republic magistrates were the elected government officials of Rome and had executive, judicial, legislative, diplomatic, military and even religious functions. The original magistrates were the two consuls (first called praetors). As Rome expanded, more magistrates were needed, and the consuls lost some of their original functions to other magistrates.

Each magistracy was filled by at least two officials to prevent power being held by one person. Magistrates holding the same office were *collegae* (colleagues). Not regarded as true magistracies were tribune of the people, censor, dictator and master of the horse. The term of office for magistrates was one year, and a senator would expect to be elected to at least two or three magistracies during his lifetime. A magistrate could hold other offices simultaneously, such as a priesthood.

CURSUS HONORUM

Before starting on a political career, young men were expected to have spent at least ten years in a military post (military tribune or legate—see chapter 2) or sometimes in a legal career in the courts. Magistracies were then sought, usually in a particular order—the *cursus honorum* (course of honors). This was fixed by law in 180 BC, although not everyone followed the normal career pattern—for example, Marius and Pompey. In the *cursus honorum*, the first political office was that of quaestor, then aedile (not obligatory), praetor, consul and finally censor. To gain a magistracy *suo anno* (in one's year) meant at the earliest possible age. The minimum interval between magistracies was normally two years. The republican senatorial career was based largely at Rome, interrupted by spells of provincial administration.

CURULE MAGISTRATES

Curule magistrates (praetors, consuls, censors and curule aediles) had the right to sit on a special chair (*sella curulis*) as a symbol of their office. The chair (of Etruscan origin) was an ivory folding stool.

MAGISTRATES UNDER THE EMPIRE

During the early empire the *cursus honorum* was extended. The magistracies of quaestor, aedile, praetor and consul were retained, but in between these offices there were numerous other posts. The political role of senators diminished, and their careers were largely administrative and outside Rome, with interruptions for holding magistracies at Rome. Senior posts were filled by senators and by *equites*, often from the provinces.

A senatorial career under the empire often started in the vigintivirate (a board of 20 minor magistrates) and could then proceed to the post of senior tribune (*tribunus laticlavius*) as a senator designate, then quaestor, praetor, commander of a legion (*legatus legionis*), governor of a praetorian (senatorial) province (*proconsul provinciae*), governor of an imperial province (*legatus Augusti pro praetore*) and finally governor of a consular (senatorial) province (*proconsul provinciae*).

IMPERIUM AND POTESTAS

The power held by a magistrate was either *imperium* or *potestas*. *Imperium* was supreme authority, involving command in war and interpretation and execution of the law, including the passing of the death sentence. *Imperium* was held by consuls, praetors, dictators (who had the *imperium* of two consuls) and the master of the horse. *Potestas* was a general form of power held by all magistrates to enforce the law of their office.

APPARITORES

Apparitores were public servants, in particular scribes and lictors, who attended magistrates. They received a salary from the state and were generally freedmen or sons of freedmen.

FASCES

The *fasces* was originally a double-headed ax enclosed in a bundle of rods to symbolize the king's right to scourge and execute. In the republic only dictators were allowed to carry axes in Rome, and so the *fasces* was normally a bundle of rods carried on the left shoulders of the lictors (*lictores*). Lictors attended magistrates with *imperium* and walked in front in a single file. Consuls were attended by 12 lictors each, praetors by 6 lictors each when outside Italy at the head of an army, and a dictator by 24 lictors. The *fasces* were a symbol of the magistrate's authority.

QUAESTORS

Quaestors were magistrates elected for one year by the *comitia tributa* at the minimum age of 27 (increased to 30 in the 1st century BC). Quaestors were financial and administrative officials who maintained public records, administered the treasury (*aerarium*), acted as paymasters accompanying generals on campaigns and were financial secretaries to governors. The number of quaestors increased as the empire grew, although their functions diminished. The office of quaestor remained the qualifying magistracy for entry to the Senate.

AEDILES

At Rome there were originally two plebeian magistrates, named from the *aedes* or temple of Ceres, which they administered. Their function soon was extended to public buildings and archives (of the *plebiscita* and *senatus consulta*). From 367 BC two curule aediles were elected from the patricians. The plebeian and curule aediles had similar functions at Rome; they were in charge of the maintenance and repair of public buildings (such as temples, roads and aqueducts), of markets (especially weights and measures), of the *annona* (to the time of Julius Caesar), and of public games and festivals (to the time of Augustus, when games were transferred to praetors). Aediles were elected for one year by the *comitia tributa*. The office was not an essential part of the *cursus honorum*, but for the wealthy there were plenty of opportunities for publicity and vote-catching, particularly in the staging of expensive games. Under the empire aediles formed part of the administration of local authorities.

PRAETORS

"Praetor" was the name originally given to the magistrates who replaced the king. In 366 BC the *praetor*

urbanus (city praetor) was introduced, who was almost exclusively concerned with the administration of law at Rome. The praetor, who had originally held military command, was the supreme civil judge. By the middle republic the praetors' powers were restricted to law and justice, and the consuls assumed the military role. By 241 BC a second praetor (*praetor peregrinus*—concerning foreigners) was established to deal with legal cases in which one or both parties were foreigners. As Rome acquired more territory overseas, the number of praetors increased, and there were eight by 80 BC.

Praetors issued annual edicts that were an important source of Roman law. They were elected for one year by the *comitia centuriata*, usually around the age of 40. Under the empire the functions of praetors increased, and included responsibility for games and festivals. Propraetors (literally, "in place of praetors") were chosen for military command as governors of some senatorial provinces.

CONSULS

When the monarchy was abolished in 509 BC, the king was replaced by two annually elected magistrates, originally called praetors and later consuls (*consules*). They assumed many of the duties of the king but could not themselves exercise supreme power, because they had to share power and served for only one year. The consuls were always patrician until 367 BC, when plebeians could stand for office. Their minimum age was 36 (increased to 42 in the 1st century BC).

Consuls were elected primarily as commanders of military forces. They presided over meetings of the Senate and implemented its decisions. They were elected by the *comitia centuriata* (although proposed by the Senate). In the republic consuls entered office on 15 March, and after 153 BC on 1 January. *Consules ordinarii* entered office at the beginning of the year and gave their name to the year, while *consules suffecti* were appointed later in the year, possibly to succeed a consul who was unable to complete his term of office.

In the empire consuls lost all responsibility for military campaigns, and the consulship became a largely honorary position. It was held for only two to four months, which increased the number of ex-consuls available for administrative posts. The emperors often proposed consuls or held the office themselves, and the age limit was disregarded. The consulship survived to 534 in the western empire.

PLEBEIAN TRIBUNES (TRIBUNES OF THE PEOPLE)

The tribunate had been established early in Rome's history to protect the plebeians from the patricians, when the patricians held all public offices. By 449 BC there were ten tribunes (*tribuni plebis*). They were responsible directly to the *concilium plebis* and could summon meetings of this assembly. Tribunes became indistinguishable from other magistrates but did not hold *imperium*. By the 2nd century BC the tribunate became an entry qualification to the Senate. Tribunes were elected from the plebeians for one year. Provided they did so in person, they had the unique power of veto (*intercessio*) against any action or plan of action within the city of Rome, including elections of magistrates, laws and decrees of the Senate, and actions of magistrates. Under the empire the tribunes lost all importance, and the emperor adopted tribunician power (*tribunicia potestas*), although the office remained to the 5th century.

CENSORS

Every five years two censors were elected by the *comitia centuriata* to hold office for 18 months. They were responsible for taking censuses of property, keeping a register of all citizens and assigning them to their centuries. They controlled public morals and could expel senators. They prepared lists of members of the Senate and had the right to take judicial proceedings against citizens suppressing information about their property. They also supervised the leasing of public land, decided on new construction and awarded government contracts. The censor was the highest position of magistrate in the middle and late republic, holding extensive powers, which were reduced by the legislation of Sulla. In the empire the role of censor tended to be adopted by the emperor.

DICTATOR

A dictator (also known as *magister populi*, master of the infantry — *populus* meaning those eligible to be soldiers) was appointed by the consul on the Senate's proposal for a maximum of six months (the length of the campaigning season) in emergencies, and had

supreme military and judicial authority, although other magistrates remained in office. The dictator appointed master of the horse (*magister equitum*) as his assistant. After Caesar's murder in 44 BC, the dictatorship was abolished.

PROMAGISTRATES

Prorogation — the extension of the *imperium* of a consul or praetor — was introduced in 326 BC to enable the consul to complete a military campaign as proconsul (literally, "in place of a consul"). Sometimes the promagistracy was extended to praetors who became propraetors. It became an important part of the administrative system, as there were otherwise not enough men to deal with the increased number of provinces.

MINOR OFFICES

There were minor magistracies, including the *vigintisexviri* (board of the 26 or vigintisexvirate). They had no special names but were named after the number of magistrates involved and their function — for example, *tresviri monetales* (board of three in charge of the mint). Under Augustus, the board was reduced to 20 — the vigintivirate — and it became common to undertake this magistracy before the quaestorship.

Civil Servants

In the republic the only civil servants were the treasury scribes (*scribae*) who assisted the quaestor. Some went to the provinces each year to assist the governor while the rest stayed at Rome.

Under the empire *scribae* remained the only civil servants of the Senate, while a huge civil service was established under the emperor. Many of the clerical positions were staffed by freedmen and slaves, especially Greeks, and often other posts were held by equestrians. Many of the civil service posts encroached on old magistracies. The *praefectus annonae* was an equestrian in charge of the grain supply from the reign of Augustus, taking over the role of aediles. Augustus also established boards (*curatores*) to take over the functions of many magistracies. They included *curatores viarum* (keepers of roads) who were in charge of maintenance of Italian roads, *curatores operum publicorum* (keepers of public works) who were in charge of public buildings and *curatores aquarum* (keepers of the water supply) who were in charge of Rome's aqueducts.

From the time of Hadrian, emperors also made use of *frumentarii* as spies throughout the provinces, but after Diocletian they were replaced by *agentes in rebus* (or *agentes in rerum*) who supervised the *cursus publicus*. After Julian their numbers reached several thousand, and by the mid-4th century they were attached to the *magister officiorum*. Senior ranks were often called *curiosi*.

In the late empire the emperor's court (*comitatus*) consisted of various officials and attendants. At the head of the court was the praetorian prefect, who had lost his military role and was now the emperor's deputy. He was responsible for finances and supplying the army and civil service. Second in importance was the *magister officiorum* (master of the offices), who was in charge of the administrative departments (*scrinia*) and of the *cursus publicus*, which was supervised by the *agentes in rebus*. Also part of the *comitatus* were finance officers: The *comes sacrarum largitionum* was responsible for gold and silver mines, mints and the collection of taxes levied in gold and silver, and the *comes rei privatae* was responsible for the administration of the emperor's extensive estates and property. There was also a quaestor who was responsible for secretarial departments and the drafting of imperial constitutions.

The vicars of the dioceses and the provincial governors each had a huge staff, including judicial, financial and clerical departments, and the total number of civil servants is estimated to have been at least 30,000. For civil servants, see also provincial government.

Provincial Government

GOVERNORS IN THE REPUBLIC

In the republic governors of provinces were appointed by the Senate and were originally changed annually. Governors were responsible for law and order, security, administration of justice and the collection of taxes. As Rome expanded its territory, a consul or praetor could expect to become a provincial governor (both called proconsul) at the end of his term of office, giving him money-making opportunities in the provinces. The *imperium* of a governor was restricted to his province. A consul (rather than proconsul) was put in charge of a conquered province only if there was a breakdown in law and order (such as the slave revolt in Sicily) or if the province was to be used as a springboard for a military campaign elsewhere.

Apart from a financial secretary (quaestor), each governor was accompanied by a small staff of *legati* (normally senators chosen by the Senate on advice from the governor) to act as advisers. A consular governor generally had three *legati*. Governors also took a body of friends (*amici*) and advisers to the provinces. If a governor left his province or died, the quaestor took responsibility as *quaestor pro praetore*.

GOVERNORS IN THE EMPIRE
(fig. 3.8)

Under the empire, governors were paid a salary, and their wives could accompany them to the provinces. The Senate retained nominal control of the peaceful (public) provinces and appointed governors, generally on an annual basis. The governors were proconsuls, usually recruited from ex-consuls for Africa and Asia (consular governors) and from ex-praetors for the rest (praetorian governors). The governors were still accompanied by a quaestor and *legati*. A law introduced by Pompey in 52 BC and later reintroduced by Augustus stipulated that five years had to elapse between holding a qualifying magistracy and being appointed governor. This was largely to curb bribery and corruption.

All other provinces were under a single proconsul, who was the emperor, and was not bound by a time limit in office. Governors of imperial provinces were appointed by the emperor and were his legates with propraetorian power (*legati Augusti pro praetore*). They were recruited from ex-consuls in provinces where there was more than one legion and from ex-praetors elsewhere, and were not bound by the five-year rule. Egypt was governed by a prefect (*praefectus Aegypti*) of equestrian rank, because no senator was allowed to enter Egypt without the emperor's permission, for fear that an ambitious senator would cut off the grain supply to Rome. Some unimportant imperial provinces also had equestrian prefects or procurators as governors. Increasingly, governors were equestrian with a military background. Imperial provinces did not use quaestors as financial secretaries but rather fiscal procurators of equestrian rank (as opposed to the procurators, who were governors).

PROVINCIAL GOVERNMENT IN THE LATE EMPIRE

From the time of Diocletian, the number of governors doubled because of the increase in the number of provinces, and most had a large staff. The main functions of the governor in the late empire were jurisdiction and taxation. Asia and Africa were under consular governors; Sicily, Achaea and Italy were governed by *correctores* of senatorial or equestrian rank, and other provinces by *praesides* (sing. *praeses*) who were equestrian. The latter undertook financial and judicial duties, having no financial secretaries.

Diocletian also created an intermediate system of administration between the court and the provinces—the dioceses. This three-tiered system of administration continued to the end of the Roman Empire in the west and to the 7th century in the east. The 12 dioceses were largely administered by equestrian vicars (*vicarii*), who were effectively deputies of the praetorian prefect. The civil and military administrations also were gradually separated, so that provincial governors had no military background.

Local Authorities

There were many differences in local government throughout the Roman world. Although each province had a governor, local authorities had wide-ranging control of their own affairs. Local magistrates and councils were responsible for areas such as the supervision of the water supply, public baths, construction of public and religious buildings and the food supply. Local authorities also were able to pass local laws. From the 1st century, problems of financial administration by local authorities led to *curatores* being appointed to individual cities to oversee their finances. The *curatores* were recruited from senators and equestrians and later from provincials.

Towns and cities often were administered by magistrates and by a council of ex-magistrates known as *curiales* or decurions (*decuriones*). The position of *curiales* and *decuriones* became hereditary, and they came to be responsible for tax collection. The magistrates included *duoviri iuredicundo* (board of two responsible for jurisdiction), aediles (responsible for public works) and sometimes quaestors (responsible for finance). In the Greek east the Romans retained the administrative systems of the former Hellenistic kingdoms—the local council was generally called a *boule* and the chief magistrates were archons. In Egypt the Ptolemaic system of administration was largely preserved, based on the village, not the city. Small towns and villages of east and west (such as the *canabae*) often had an administrative system despite their lack of official status.

From the time of Diocletian, local authorities lost much of their power.

TAXES AND FINANCE

In the early republic state income was obtained from rents for the *ager publicus*. The only direct tax paid by Romans was the *tributum*, a land and property tax levied in times of emergency. This was abolished on land in Italy in 167 BC as the treasury was enriched through overseas conquests. The *tributum* continued to be paid by citizens and non-citizens in conquered territory and was an important source of revenue. It consisted of *tributum soli* (land and property tax) and *tributum capitis* (poll tax).

The *aerarium* (treasury) (or *aerarium Saturni*, treasury of Saturn) was used for depositing cash and archives of the Roman state and was situated in the temple of Saturn below the Capitol. It was controlled by the quaestors under the general supervision of the Senate. The treasury was maintained into the empire, but many revenues were increasingly diverted into the *fiscus* (imperial treasury). The *aerarium* eventually became the treasury of the city of Rome. The *aerarium sanctius* was a special reserve fund drawn upon only in emergencies.

The *fiscus* was theoretically a fund containing the emperor's private wealth, but it came to mean the treasury for the imperial provinces.

New indirect taxes in the empire included *portoria* (customs). There were also taxes on the sale and manumission of slaves and inheritance taxes, levied at a rate of 5 percent. The inheritance tax was levied on the property of Roman citizens only, and the revenue went to the *aerarium militare* (military treasury), together with the revenues from the 1 percent tax on auction sales. In the imperial provinces taxes were collected by a procurator, and in senatorial provinces the quaestor was in charge, although *publicani* (tax collectors or publicans) were used. Tax collection was contracted out to the highest bidder, and many *publicani* were corrupt. In the late empire it was the responsibility of town councillors (*decuriones* or *curiales*) to collect taxes, and they were required to make up any deficits themselves.

From the late 3rd century the system of collection of money taxes was under severe strain. In 296 Diocletian introduced a new tax system. The collection of taxes in kind (such as corn, clothes and wine) became more common, particularly to supply the army and pay the civil servants. This tax included the *annona militaris*. The new system of collection of tax in kind was based on land (*iugatio*) and on the population (*capitatio*), and was based on the area of cultivable land (*iugum*) that could be worked by one man (*caput*), providing him with subsistence.

Censuses

Censuses were undertaken from the time of the monarchy for taxation and military purposes, normally every five years. In the late republic censuses were taken on a more irregular basis, but were revived by Augustus. The last known censuses in Italy were in the 1st century under Vespasian and Titus. Censuses became unnecessary because Italy was no longer subject to direct taxes.

In order to collect taxes from the provinces, it was essential to conduct regular censuses on which taxes were assessed. Censuses of land and population were undertaken by local authorities under the supervision of the governor, initially every 5, then 12 years.

LAWS

Legislation

Roman law was divided into public and civil law. Laws have been preserved in the works of ancient authors, in inscriptions and on papyri. The first Roman code of laws was the 12 Tables published around 451–450 BC. It was drawn up by a board of ten men (*decemviri legibus scribundis*, ten men for writing out the law). The 12 Tables survive only in references and quotations. Priests originally interpreted civil law, but this role was taken over by jurists (mainly of senatorial rank), and praetors administered the law and issued edicts.

The *comitia centuriata* was originally the main legislative body and passed laws (*leges*) named after the magistrates who proposed them. After 287 BC the people controlled legislation with their resolutions (*plebiscita*). The *comitia centuriata* rarely legislated after 218 BC. Senatorial decrees (*senatus consulta*, often written as one word) were strictly only advice to magistrates but were generally binding, and edicts of magistrates with *imperium* and interpretations of jurists also had the force of law.

Under Augustus, *plebiscita* and *leges* continued to be passed in the popular assemblies, but may have been proposed by the emperor. By the end of the 1st century these popular statutes were no longer being passed by assemblies. From the early empire *senatus consulta* appear to have acquired an undisputed legal status, though possibly influenced by the emperor. The Senate became practically the only legislative body, and *senatus consulta* continued to be important to the 3rd century. *Constitutiones* (constitutions) were legislative enactments by emperors that could take various forms, such as decrees (*decreta*), edicts (*edicta*) and rescripts (*rescripta*). Much of the work of emperors and their secretaries (probably often on the advice of jurists) was to issue rescripts, which were replies to questions of legislation and to petitions by litigants, and which seem to have carried the force of law. From the time of Constantine in the 4th century, rescripts were supplemented by the issue of *leges generales* (general enactments).

After the universal extension of Roman citizenship in 212, the distinctions between laws applying to Roman citizens (*ius civile*) and to noncitizens (*ius gen-*

tium) should have disappeared, but in practice this was difficult to achieve.

Theodosius II ordered the codification of all *constitutiones* of emperors from Constantine I, and this Law Code of Theodosius (*Codex Theodosianus*) was published in 438. Around 540 Justinian appointed a commission of jurists to publish a complete body of imperial legislation still in force. They published the *Digest* (or *Pandects*—a collection of legislation and commentaries by earlier jurists), the Justinian Code (a collection of the imperial constitutions), the *Institutes* (a legal textbook), and the *New Constitutions*. These publications are known collectively as *Corpus Iuris Civilis* (*Body of Civil Law*), which forms the code of Roman law inherited by modern Europe.

Jurists had particular learning and experience to interpret the law, and some of their commentaries survive. Jurists were held in high esteem, although their views sometimes conflicted. They often gave advice (*responsa*) to judges in legal matters.

cases at assize centers. Civil cases were referred to the courts run by local authorities, but they had no jurisdiction over Roman citizens. In the imperial provinces Roman citizens who were tried by governors could appeal to the emperor, and this privilege was extended to senatorial provinces.

Many crimes were capital offenses (such as treason), and lower-class defendants were more commonly executed than their upper-class counterparts. There were many nonstatute offenses, and provincial governors could fix penalties at their discretion, and so justice varied from province to province. In the 3rd century Roman citizens were divided into two classes for criminal jurisdiction—the *honestiores* (more honorable), which included senators, equestrians, local officials and soldiers, and the remaining citizens—the *humiliores* (more insignificant). Punishments for *honestiores* were far less severe.

Lawyers did not receive fees. Legal services were paid for not with money but with political help. It was therefore important for aspiring politicians to provide legal assistance to as many people as possible.

Courts

Cases could be tried by the kings (see p. 3) and later by magistrates, with rights of appeal to the assemblies. In certain cases special courts could be set up by the Senate, and permanent courts began to be set up from the mid-2nd century BC. Under Sulla the number of permanent standing criminal courts (*quaestiones*) was increased, largely for the trial of crimes such as treason and bribery committed by the upper classes. These *quaestiones* were presided over by praetors and continued into Augustus' reign, but ceased to exist by the 3rd century. Instead, the Senate became a supreme criminal court, and major political and criminal cases involving senators were tried before it. Other criminal cases were handled by the civil courts. The emperor also tried cases. In addition, courts were set up under the urban and praetorian prefects. The *centumviri* (hundred men) at Rome was a special civil court involving inheritance and property claims. It actually numbered 105 men in the republic (3 from each of the 35 tribes), and increased to 180 men in the empire, when they were usually divided into four courts.

In the provinces there were no standing courts, and so the governor toured the cities, hearing criminal

READING

Dates of Events
Bradley 1990: textbook largely on Rome's republican and early imperial history; Connolly 1981: illustrated account of military history from the early republic, including battles and an extensive account of Hannibal's campaigns; Grant 1974: an account of the military history in the empire; Hammond and Scullard (eds.) 1970 passim; Salway 1981: account of Rome's imperial history, with particular emphasis on Britain; Scullard 1980: 753–146 BC; Scullard 1982: 133 BC–AD 68.

Prominent People
Bowder (ed.) 1980: short biographies on many people of the republic and empire, with further reading; Bradley 1990: contains accounts of some of the major republican figures; Hammond and Scullard (eds.) 1970 passim.

Emperors

Bowder (ed.) 1980: short biographies of virtually every emperor with further reading; Grant 1974: information on many emperors in relation to military history; Hammond and Scullard (eds.) 1970 passim; Nicol 1991: Byzantine Empire; Salway 1981: contains much information on emperors; Sear 1981: chronological and genealogical tables of Roman and Byzantine emperors up to 1453.

Social Structure

Hammond and Scullard (eds.) 1970 passim; Shelton 1988, 6–11.

Government

Barnwell 1992: many aspects of provincial government and the imperial court in the late western empire; Braund (ed.) 1988: administration, including that of cities and client kingdoms; Burton 1987, 434–439: local authorities; Hammond and Scullard (eds.) 1970 passim; Liebeschuetz 1987: government and administration in the late empire; Lintott 1990: electoral bribery in the republic; Poulter 1987: administration of small settlements in east and west; Scullard 1981, 221–229: meetings of the Senate and the people, elections; Shelton 1988, 206–242, 270–289; Wiseman (ed.) 1985: politics of the late republic and early empire.

Taxes and finance

Burton 1987, 426–429: taxes in the empire; Hammond and Scullard (eds.) 1970, 437–440; Liebescheutz 1987: taxation in the late empire.

Laws

Burton 1987, 430–434: jurisdiction in the provinces; Green 1987; Hammond and Scullard (eds.) 1970, 583–590, 601–605: detailed account of law, listing individual laws by name; Howatson (ed.) 1989; Scullard 1981, 229–232: legislation and jurisdiction; Shelton 1988, 242–248.

2

MILITARY AFFAIRS

HISTORY OF THE LEGIONS

Legionary Development: Monarchy

Although there appears to have been an army from Rome's earliest days, little is known of it, except that it consisted of infantry and cavalry. At first it was probably a small patrician force led by the king, consisting of his bodyguard, retainers and some of the local population. Information about this early army derives from ancient historians, who thought that it was originally based on three ancient tribes (Ramnes, Tities and Luceres—Etruscan names). It was probably essentially Etruscan. Subdivisions within the tribes supplied 100 men (a century), and each tribe provided 1,000 men. These 3,000 men formed a legion (*legio*, literally "the levying"). An additional force of about 300 cavalrymen came from the *equites*, who could afford to equip themselves with horses and equipment.

Ancient historians state that in the late 6th century BC the king, Servius Tullius, conducted the first census of the Roman people, classifying them according to wealth for voting purposes and eligibility for military service, with a minimum property qualification established for the army. Despite these accounts, it seems unlikely that such a complex social and military organization was established as early as Servius Tullius, although it was certainly employed at a later date. Originally a single *classis* (call to arms) probably existed, composed of those able to afford to equip themselves, with the five classes developing later.

The population was grouped into centuries (100 men), and the 18 centuries of *equites* (the wealthiest people) continued to supply the cavalry. Below them, the remaining property-owning people were divided into five classes, from whom the infantry was drawn, with their specific arms and armor depending on their class. In each class men aged 47 to 60 (*seniores*, veterans) formed a home guard to defend Rome, while men aged 17 to 46 (*iuniores*) constituted the field army. Under Servius Tullius' system there was also a group called the *capite censi*—literally, "registered by headcount" because they owned virtually no property.

They were exempt from military service, but were formed into a single century for voting purposes.

During the monarchy, the total force (the "legion") was reckoned by ancient historians to be 60 centuries strong (4,000 men), with an additional cavalry force of six centuries (600 men). The number of men in a century may have varied considerably, since the division into centuries had more to do with the organization of voting than with army units.

Legionary Development: Early and Middle Republic (6th–2nd centuries BC)

The army of the early and middle republic was a citizen army led by elected magistrates. At the end of the campaign season, legions were disbanded, or if they were needed to secure conquered territory, only retiring soldiers were released. Over the winter, legions were raised to replace disbanded ones, and those not disbanded were formally reconstituted with new officers ready for a new campaign season, under the control of a new magistrate.

During the early republic small-scale warfare against neighboring communities was endemic, culminating in the ten-year war against Veii, which was captured in 396 BC. In the preceding years the army appears to have expanded from 4,000 to 6,000 men, probably with the creation of the second- and third-class infantry (previously attributed to Servius Tullius). The cavalry was also increased from 600 to 1,800 men, and their horses were provided at public expense. Financial assistance began to be given to the infantry and cavalry, probably reflecting the increasing amount of time soldiers were spending away from home.

In 390 BC the Romans were defeated by the Gauls, and Rome was sacked. Steps were taken, probably over many years, to remedy tactical weaknesses, including dividing the army into maniples (containing two centuries) and making changes in weapons and armor. By the mid-4th century BC the old class system was much changed—classes one, two and three were apparently grouped by age, not wealth, with *hastati* being the youngest, the *principes* being in the prime of life, and the *triarii* being the oldest. The *rorarii* were apparently the old fourth class. The century (*centuria*) was still the smallest unit of the legion, and the number of men in a century depended on the size of an army—nominally 100 men, but in practice fewer. Each legion comprised 60 centuries divided into 30 maniples (or later, into ten cohorts).

By 311 BC the army was split into four legions, recognizable as the forerunners of the more familiar legions of the civil war of the late republic. At this period, Roman armies were aided by *alae sociorum* (wings of allies). On campaign, two Roman legions were usually accompanied by two *alae sociorum* as well as a group of *extraordinarii* (elite troops drawn from the allies). This army of four legions plus allied forces probably was maintained to cope with any eventuality.

Over the next 150 years a series of wars (including the First and Second Punic Wars) necessitated an increase in the army and a continued refinement of its organization. During the 3rd century BC the number of legions increased, and several *legiones urbanae* (city legions) were formed from the old, unfit and underaged to protect the city of Rome itself.

Polybius provides an account of the army as it probably was during the Second Punic War (218–201 BC). According to him, the normal strength of a legion was 4,000 infantry and 200 cavalry, which could be expanded to 5,000 in an emergency. The legionaries were chosen from citizens aged 17 to 46 who had property valued at over 400 *denarii*. From these men, the youngest and poorest were selected as *velites* (cloak-wearers), who had weapons but no armor. Next in ascending age and wealth were the *hastati*, then the *principes*, and the final group formed the *triarii*. This legion of 4,200 men was divided into 30 maniples: the ten maniples of *hastati* and ten of *principes* each had 120 heavy infantry soldiers and 40 *velites*, and the ten maniples of *triarii* each had 60 heavy infantry soldiers and 40 *velites*. The composition of a legion appears to have been 1,200 *velites*, 1,200 *hastati*, 1,200 *principes* and 600 *triarii*.

Soldiers were originally needed for a short campaign season of a few weeks, and then returned to their farms. With the increasing number of new provinces, more men were needed for a longer time, and the campaign season stretched from March to October. Newly won provinces had to be held by a garrison, and inevitably the part-time character of the army changed to a full-time professional one. From c. 200 BC there developed a core of almost professional soldiers volunteering over several years up to the maximum of 16, probably largely in expectation of booty.

Legionary Development: Marius' Reforms (late 2nd century BC)

With longer and more distant campaigns, recruiting soldiers became increasingly difficult. The army's growing professionalism was put on a more formal basis by the reforms of Marius at the end of the 2nd century BC. The property qualification for enrollment in the army had become less stringent by this time, and in periods of crisis soldiers were conscripted from the poorest citizens, the *capite censi*. It is unclear whether Marius abolished the property qualification, but he certainly opened recruitment to the *capite censi*, equipping them from state funds. Otherwise, there seems to have been relatively little change in the recruitment and composition of the army. Marius' main reforms concerned its organization, tactics and equipment (in particular arming all legionaries with a modified *pilum*).

Marius seems to have been responsible for dropping the maniple in favor of the cohort as the tactical fighting unit, so that there were now ten cohorts in a legion rather than 30 maniples. The first cohort was always regarded as superior. It is also likely that Marius was responsible for abolishing the *velites*. The distinctions among the *hastati*, *principes* and *triarii* disappeared, and instead everyone was armed with sword and *pilum*. The strength of a legion at this time was probably about 4,800 men (80 men to a century), although some ancient historians believed that Marius increased the strength to 6,000 men (100 men to a century). There were nominally 600 men in a cohort, but the number varied between 300 and 600.

Legionary Development: Late Republic (2nd–1st centuries BC)

Further changes to the army occurred after the Social War. All soldiers recruited in Italy (south of the Po River) were now citizens and so served as legionaries.

The *alae sociorum* ceased to exist, and the Romans had to look elsewhere for support troops, especially cavalry. From this time a legion was a single force and not one matched in numbers by allied troops.

The cost of maintaining the army was now borne entirely by the state, and the number of legions was increased. Legions were now raised throughout Italy by officials called *conquisitores* working in conjunction with local magistrates. Armies ceased to be commanded by elected magistrates during their period of office, a further move from the earlier part-time citizen army toward a more professional organization.

The changes that led to the formation of the imperial army began under Julius Caesar. For his campaigns in Gaul, he widened recruitment, enlisting men from north of the Po River who were not full Roman citizens but had the status of Latins. He also recruited a militia of native Gauls that later became Legio V Alaudae. Soldiers' pay seems to have been doubled from the outset of the civil war.

In 49 BC, civil war was inevitable once Caesar crossed the Rubicon River, the boundary between Cisalpine Gaul and Italy; by leaving his province Caesar automatically lost his right to command troops and therefore was acting illegally. The Senate empowered Pompey to move against Caesar, and civil war followed. For the next 18 years, until the power struggle was resolved at the battle of Actium in 31 BC, various legions were formed, captured, reconstituted and destroyed.

The civil war increased the recruitment of legionary soldiers from non-Romans and noncitizens, moving the army even further from the original concept of a citizen army raised to defend its homeland. By this time most of the elements of the professional imperial army already existed. The civil war increased efficiency and the number of legions—to around 60 at the end of the civil war. It gave rise to more professional soldiers who served for an extended period.

Legionary Development: Early Empire (late 1st century BC–late 2nd century AD)

After the civil war, many of Augustus' and Caesar's troops were settled in colonies, and Augustus reorganized the remaining legions. He increased the period of army service to 16 and then 20 years. In AD 6 he established a military treasury (*aerarium militare*) for discharge payments. He established it with a large gift of money, but its revenues were subsequently drawn from taxes. Augustus also decreed that soldiers must not marry during their period of service, a ban lifted by Severus at the end of the 2nd century.

In the early empire the legions were still similar in structure to those of Caesar. Cohorts one to ten contained around 500 men each, organized into six centuries of about 80 men. In the later 1st century the first cohort was expanded to about 800 men and was reorganized into five instead of six centuries, with about 160 men per century. There were also about 120 horsemen attached to the legion who acted as scouts and dispatch riders, making a total force of about 5,500 men.

Toward the end of Augustus' reign, the post of legionary legate was introduced. Auxiliary forces of cavalry and other specialist soldiers began to be organized more systematically at this time as well, and Augustus also reorganized the navy. A further innovation was the garrison at Rome, in particular the Praetorian Guard.

Augustus left his successors an army that had been reorganized on a permanent professional basis, and further changes during the early empire were relatively minor. Legionaries were mainly recruited as volunteers, but increasingly from the provinces rather than from Italy. Because legionaries still were recruited from Roman citizens, there was an imbalance as there were many more citizens in the west than in the east. It became customary in the east for noncitizens to be granted citizenship on enrollment.

With frontier forces to be maintained, there was a constant need for recruitment to replace casualties and retirement of soldiers, and increasingly recruitment was from the areas where armies were stationed. Some armies acquired too many local ties, and from time to time attempts were made to break this trend, with fresh dispositions and postings in order to move troops from their home area.

By the end of the Flavian period, the imperial army was fully formed as a permanent professional army, and in many ways it had reached its peak. Once the frontiers of the empire had been pushed to their farthest extent, the role of the army was one of control, consolidation and defense, which did not provide the same stimulus for improvement and reform as the conquests of the late republic and early empire.

Legionary Development: Later Empire (late 2nd century–5th century)

The defensive role of the army led to stagnation and decline, and the weaknesses of the static defensive system became apparent in the late 2nd century when two new legions were hurriedly raised and armies improvised by Marcus Aurelius in 165 to defend northern Italy. At the end of the 2nd century Septimius Severus introduced reforms and increased the strength of the army one-tenth by raising three Parthica legions. He disbanded the Praetorian Guard, replacing it with ten new milliary (double-strength) cohorts. With one of the new legions (II Parthica), the milliary cohorts formed a mobile reserve for the frontier armies equivalent to three legions. Even so, this was barely enough to relieve the strain on the frontiers, particularly the pressure on the Rhine and Danube frontiers and in the east.

The 3rd century saw successive emperors fighting invaders outside the empire and usurpers within it. Gallienus appears to have been responsible for further military reforms, including recruiting extra cavalry forces and moving further from a static defensive army toward a mobile one. The infantry of the mobile army consisted of detachments (*vexillationes*) that were virtually independent of their parent legions. Gallienus also stopped the appointment of senatorial legionary legates, so that legions were commanded by prefects from the equestrian order. These reforms helped, but stability was not restored until Diocletian's reforms in the late 3rd century.

Diocletian strengthened the frontiers and the army. The army was doubled to around 66 legions (but possibly of lower strength), which were stationed in pairs at key points around the frontiers, accompanied by detachments of cavalry (called *vexillationes* rather than *alae*). Two new legions (Ioviani and Herculiani) raised by Diocletian were attached to the *comitatus* (literally, "emperor's traveling court") and became a mobile field force. Also attached to the *comitatus* were elite cavalry forces raised by Diocletian—the *scholae* (or *scholae palatinae*), the *equites promoti* and the *equites comites*. A 6th-century source estimated that Diocletian's army was around 389,704 strong; another 6th-century figure gave an estimate of 645,000 for the army of "the old empire."

Diocletian made hereditary military service obligatory, so sons had to follow their fathers into the army. The difficulty of recruitment led Valentinian (364–375) to reduce the height qualification. The army also recruited non-Romans, mostly Germans, some of whom were prisoners of war and others volunteers.

After Diocletian, imperial organization collapsed until Constantine I defeated his rivals to emerge as sole emperor in 324. Constantine abolished the garrison at Rome, including the Praetorian Guard, replacing it with the *scholae* cavalry units. He also increased the use of *auxilia*, which were old-style infantry legions, not auxiliary troops, and provided the shock troops of the late Roman army. They included the Cornuti (horned men), Bracchiati (armlet-wearers), Iovii and Victores. They were probably recruited from Germans in the Rhineland (as volunteers or prisoners-of-war) or from mercenaries from the *laeti* (Germanic settlements established mainly in Gaul from Diocletian's time to strengthen defenses against attack).

Constantine I also divided the army into mobile forces (*comitatenses*—from *comitatus*) and frontier troops (*limitanei*—from *limes*). Constantine withdrew troops from many frontier positions and instead concentrated mobile forces (*comitatenses*) at key points in the frontier zone in order to react to any local incursions, while the remaining army was posted in garrisons. The *comitatenses* did not have fixed garrisons, but were either on campaign or were stationed in towns. They were used for attacking opponents in the field. Mobile infantry units were 500 to 1,000 men strong and the cavalry (*vexillationes*) was below 500 men, except possibly for *scholae* units, which were probably 500 strong. Small mobile units were detached as required under the command of a *comes*. By the late 4th century the mobile army was divided into numerous detachments or small field armies.

The static frontier troops (*limitanei*) consisted of the old frontier troops and the *ripenses* (literally, troops stationed along riverbanks—*ripae*—and also on other frontiers). They had fixed bases in garrisons in *burgi* (towns or forts), which were all fortified for prolonged defense. These 4th-century *limitanei* were grouped into armies covering one or more provinces, except in Africa where the mobile army was used.

The trend toward larger numbers of more mobile forces continued, which gave better defense against invasion but fragmented the army, leading eventually to loss of overall control. After Julian's reign in 363, the empire was more or less permanently divided into eastern and western halves. Inevitably the weaker western half, with its vulnerable frontiers, gradually collapsed, while the eastern half, virtually free of invasion, survived.

After the battle of Adrianople in 378, a desperate shortage of trained soldiers forced the Roman government to enlist barbarian contingents (*foederati* or *federati*, from *foedus*, treaty) under their own chieftains. *Foederati* were tribes or groups that had entered into a treaty with Rome. They generally lived beyond the frontiers of the empire, but in the 4th and 5th centuries they were allowed to settle within the empire under their own laws. The Romans relied increasingly upon *foederati* into the 5th century, although *limitanei* are known on the upper Danube right up to when the last western emperor was deposed in 476.

NUMBERING AND STATIONS OF LEGIONS

Legions of the Republic

The division of the Roman army into units recognizable as legions seems to have occurred in the late 4th century BC. During the 3rd century BC the number of legions increased in response to various problems. By the end of the century there were around 20 legions in service, and several *legiones urbanae* were formed to protect the city of Rome. In 199 BC the number of legions was reduced to six; thereafter it appears to have fluctuated considerably according to the extent and gravity of threats to Rome's interests. After the Social War the number of legions was increased; on a few occasions there were less than 14, often there were many more.

Little is known of the numbering system of legions before the late republic, and that of the late republic is not fully understood. Legions were numbered according to the sequence of their formation in a particular year. Because they were raised and disbanded on an annual basis up to the end of the republic, it is possible that the legions sometimes, if not always, changed their number each year. Numbers I to IV were reserved for legions commanded by the consuls (if they needed to raise legions during their year of office), but it is not known on what basis other numbers were allocated. By the time Caesar began his campaigns in Gaul in 58 BC, there is evidence of legions numbered VII to X stationed in Gaul and of a legion numbered XVIII in Cilicia in 56–54 BC.

From 58 BC the trend was toward an ever-increasing number of legions, raised to cope with the needs of subduing and controlling new provinces, culminating in a dramatic increase during the civil war.

Legions Involved in the Civil War

Various legions were formed, captured, reconstituted and destroyed up to the battle of Actium in 31 BC. Since each commander that formed legions used his own numbering system (generally beginning with I), the situation is very confused, and duplicate numbers are common. Very often little is known about a legion other than that it had fought for a particular commander. There were about 60 legions by the end of the civil war.

CAESAR'S CONSULAR LEGIONS

These were legions that had been raised previously by Caesar under his consular power: I (possibly later became I Germanica, unless I Germanica was derived from legion I of Pansa's consular legions); II (present in Macedonia in 44 BC; later fought at the battles of Forum Gallorum and Mutina); III (later became III Gallica); and V Macedonica (served in Macedonia).

CAESAR'S GALLIC LEGIONS

These were legions that had been recruited previously for Caesar's campaigns in Gaul: V Alaudae (recruited from native Gauls); VI Ferrata; VII (later became VII Claudia); VIII (later became VIII Augusta); IX; X *Equestris* (later became X Gemina); XI; XII (possibly became XII Fulminata); XIII; and XIV.

LEGIONS RAISED BY CAESAR IN 49 BC

There were legions numbered XV to XXIII, of which the following is known: XV and XVI—both possibly destroyed in Africa in 49 BC; XXI in Spain in 49 BC; XXV in Africa in 46 BC; XXVI in Africa in 46 to 43 BC, moved to Italy in 43 BC and joined Octavian; XXVII at Pharsalus in 48 BC, at Alexandria in 47 BC, in Egypt from 47 BC possibly until 42 BC; XXVIII in Spain in 49 BC, at Thapsus in 46 BC, possibly at Munda in 45 BC, and in Italy and Philippi in 42 BC; XXIX at Thapsus in 46 BC, and remained in Africa until 43 BC when it moved to Rome and joined Octavian; XXX in Spain in 49 BC, at Thapsus in 46 BC and possibly at Munda in 45 BC; XXXI in Crete for an unknown period until 41 BC.

LEGIONS FORMED FROM POMPEY'S DEFEATED ARMY IN 48 BC

These were numbered: XXXIV; XXXV in Macedonia in 44 BC and in Italy at Forum Gallorum and Mutina in 43 BC; XXXVI at Alexandria in 47 BC and continued to serve in Egypt, possibly until 42 BC; XXXVII at Zela in 47 BC and in Egypt from 47 BC to possibly 42 BC.

LEGIONS RECRUITED 47 TO 44 BC

These were numbered: XXXVIII, XXXIX, XXXX and XXXXI. Likely several more legions were raised of which no evidence has survived.

LEGIO MARTIA

A Legio Martia (sacred to Mars, therefore warlike) appears in the writings of several ancient authors. From their evidence, this title belonged to one of the legions that were in Africa in 46 BC: XXVI, XXVIII, XXIX, XXX or possibly XXV, which may have been in Africa then.

PANSA'S CONSULAR LEGIONS

These were legions commanded by Gaius Vibius Pansa under his consular power: I (possibly later became I Germanica, unless I Germanica was derived from legion I of Caesar's consular legions); II Sabina (possibly became II Augusta); III (possibly later became III Augusta); IV Sorana; (indicating formation at the town of Sora, Italy); and V Urbana (urban; formed by Pansa to defend the city of Rome in 43 BC).

OCTAVIAN'S LEGIONS 41 TO 31 BC

Legions VII, VIII, and IV Macedonica were brought from Philippi. There were survivors from Pansa's consular legions including II Sabina, IV Sorana and V Urbana. There were also legions left in the west in 42–41 BC, including XXXXI.

Newly formed legions were numbered up to XIX. There may have been more legions (from XX), but no evidence for them has survived. The following legions newly formed by Octavian are known: V (possibly later became V Macedonica, unless it was V Urbana that became V Macedonica); VI (later became VI Hispaniensis and later still VI Victrix); IX (possibly later became IX Hispaniensis); X Fretensis; XI (possibly later became XI Claudia); XII Victrix (present at Perusia in 41 BC); XIII (possibly later became XIII Gemina); XIV (possibly later became XIV Gemina); XV (later became XV Apollinaris); XVI; XVII; XVIII; and XIX.

ANTONY'S LEGIONS 41 TO 30 BC

A series of coins issued by Antony to pay his army records the legions of that army. The coins indicate legions numbered from I to XXX, but coins attesting the legions numbered XXIV to XXX have been rejected as modern forgeries. The coin series is therefore accepted as evidence for legions I to XXIII. Of these, additional sources are able to provide extra identification and information: III Gallica (probably served in Gaul); VI Ferrata; X Equestris; V Alaudae (probably recruited from native Gauls); XII Antiqua; XVII Classica (probably served with the navy—*classis*); XVIII Libyca (probably served in Libya); VIII (with Pinarius Scarpus in Cyrenaica in 31–30 BC); and III Cyrenaica (possibly in Cyrenaica with Pinarius Scarpus). It is likely that the legion later known as IV Scythica was also formed by Antony.

Imperial Legions

After the civil war many of Augustus' and Caesar's troops were disbanded and settled in colonies. Augustus reorganized the remaining legions (25 or 26, increased to 28 in 25 BC) but kept the duplication within the numbering system that had arisen during the civil war. At one time, for example, five legions were numbered III. If a legion was lost, its number was never used again. The nicknames (*cognomina*) of the legions were largely retained and continued to be important in distinguishing legions with the same number. This situation appears to have continued throughout the empire.

KNOWN IMPERIAL LEGIONS

I ADIUTRIX (supportive): Formed by Nero from marines stationed at Misenum in 68 and taken over by Galba. It also had the title Pia Fidelis.

I GERMANICA: Formed during the civil war, possibly by Caesar in 48 BC or by Pansa in 43 BC. It appears to have been reconstituted by Octavian in 41 BC and was used against Pompey in 36 BC. It was disbanded in 69, apparently after collaborating with Civilis. Its title indicates service in Germany.

I ITALICA: Raised by Nero in Italy, probably in 66 or 67 for a projected Caspian expedition.

I MACRIANA: Its title indicates formation by Clodius Macer when he set himself up as emperor after Nero's death. The legion was disbanded after Macer's execution. It was reconstituted by Vitellius but was probably disbanded on his death.

I MINERVIA: Formed by Domitian in 83. Minerva was Domitian's favorite goddess. The legion also had other titles: Flavia Pia Fidelis Domitiana (indicating its loyalty to Domitian in the revolt of Saturninus; Flavia was Domitian's family name).

I PARTHICA: Formed by Severus in 197 for a campaign in the east.

II ADIUTRIX (supportive): Formed from sailors stationed at Ravenna during the Flavian advance on Italy in the civil war of 69. It was accepted as a legion by Vespasian. It also had the title Pia Fidelis.

II AUGUSTA (fig. 3.8): Possibly formed by Pansa in 43 BC, if it is the same legion as II Sabina. It served in Spain from 30 BC and on Germany's Rhine frontier until it was moved to Britain in AD 43. The move from Spain to Germany may have been in AD 9. Its title indicates reconstitution by Augustus, as does its use of the capricorn (Augustus' good luck symbol) as an emblem. The legion also had the titles Gallica and Sabina and had as its emblem the pegasus (the winged horse of Greek mythology), the reason for which is unclear.

II ITALICA: Raised by Marcus Aurelius in Italy in 168. It also had the title Pia.

II PARTHICA: Formed by Severus in 197 for a campaign in the east.

II TRAIANA: Formed by Trajan, possibly in 101, for the Dacian wars. It also had the title Fortis (Strong).

III AUGUSTA: Formed either by Pansa in 43 BC or by Octavian in 41–40 BC. It served in Africa from at least 30 BC, possibly earlier. Its title indicates reconstitution by Augustus. It also had the title Pia Fidelis. It may have had the pegasus as an emblem.

III CYRENAICA: Formed before 30 BC, possibly by Lepidus or Antony. This legion served in Egypt from 30 BC. It probably served in the province of Cyrenaica, possibly with Pinarius Scarpus in 31–30 BC.

III GALLICA: Probably formed by Caesar in 48 BC. It was at Munda in 45 BC, and at Philippi in 42 BC. It served with Antony from 40 to 31 BC and was involved in the Parthian War in 36 BC. From 30 BC it served in Syria. The title Gallica indicates that it served in Gaul, probably with Julius Caesar from 48 to 42 BC. It had a bull as an emblem, indicating that it was formed by Caesar.

III ITALICA: Raised by Marcus Aurelius in Italy in 168. It also had the title Concors (United).

III PARTHICA: Raised by Severus in 197 for a campaign in the east.

IV MACEDONICA: Formed by Caesar in 48 BC. This legion served in Macedonia from 47 to 44 BC and transferred to Italy in 44 BC. Originally on the side of Antony, it defected to Octavian at the battle of Forum Gallorum in 43 BC. It was at Mutina in 43 BC, at Philippi in 42 BC, at Perusia in 41 BC and possibly at Actium in 31 BC. It served in Spain from 30 BC to AD 43 and on the Rhine frontier from 43 to 69. The legion had a bull as an emblem, indicating that it was formed by Julius Caesar, and also a capricorn, indicating reconstitution by Augustus. It was disbanded and reconstituted in 70 as IV Flavia Felix.

IV FLAVIA FELIX: Formed in 70 as a reconstitution of IV Macedonica, which had been disbanded after collaborating with Civilis.

IV SCYTHICA: Formed before 30 BC, probably by Antony, although it may be the same as IV Sorana formed by Pansa in 43 BC. It served in Macedonia from 30 BC and at some time later served in Moesia. The title Scythica probably reflects victories over the Scythians, possibly under Crassus in 29–27 BC. It had a capricorn as an emblem, indicating reconstitution by Augustus.

V ALAUDAE: Formed from native Gauls by Julius Caesar in 52 BC and served with him in Gaul from 52 to 49 BC. In 49 BC it was in Spain and possibly at Pharsalus in 48 BC. It was at Thapsus in 46 BC and at Munda in 45 BC. In 44 BC it was in Italy and may then have been disbanded, since it was reconstituted by Antony in the same year. It was at Forum Gallorum and Mutina in 43 BC and at Philippi in 42 BC. It served with Antony from 41 to 31 BC and may have been at Actium in 31 BC. It was incorporated into Octavian's army in 30 BC and served in Spain until it was moved to the Rhine frontier, possibly in 19 BC, where it served until AD 69. It lost the eagle standard, a disaster for the legion, in Gaul in 17 BC. (See under "Military Standards," p. 90) The legion may have been disbanded in 70 for collaborating with Civilis, although it may have been transferred to the Balkans and was destroyed in 86. The legion was awarded an emblem of an elephant in 46 BC for success against charging elephants in the battle of Thapsus.

V MACEDONICA: Formed either by Pansa in 43 BC as V Urbana or by Octavian in 41 or 40 BC. It was at Actium in 31 BC and served in Macedonia from 30 BC to AD 6, and then in Moesia. It had a bull as an emblem, which usually indicates formation by Julius Caesar. When this legion was serving with Octavian, though, a legion with the same number that had been formed by Caesar is known to have been serving with Antony.

VI FERRATA (ironclad): Formed by Julius Caesar in 52 BC and served with him in Gaul from 52 to 49 BC. It served in Spain in 49 BC, was at Pharsalus in 48 BC, at Alexandria in 48–47 BC and at Zela in 47 BC. In the same year it was released and returned to Italy, but was at Munda in 45 BC. It was reconstituted by Lepidus in 44 BC and served under Antony in 43 BC. It was at Philippi in 42 BC and then with Antony in the east from 41 to 31 BC, where it was involved in the Parthian War in 36 BC. It was at Actium in 31 BC and from then on served in Syria. The legion also had the titles Fidelis Constans (Loyal and Steady), and had a wolf and twins as an emblem.

VI VICTRIX: Formed by Octavian, probably in 41–40 BC. It was at Perusia in 41 BC. From 30 BC to AD 69 it served in Spain. Its title *Victrix* indicates a notable victory, probably in Spain. It had an earlier title of Hispaniensis, reflecting its service in Spain. It may have had a bull as an emblem, which normally would indicate that it was formed by Julius Caesar, but the evidence for the legion using this emblem is inconclusive.

VII: Formed in 59 BC or possibly earlier. It served in Caesar's campaigns from 58 to 49 BC. In 49 BC it was in Spain and at Pharsalus in 48 BC. It was in Africa in 46 BC but was disbanded in the same year. It was reconstituted by Octavian in 45 BC and was at Forum Gallorum and Mutina in 43 BC. In 42 BC it was at Philippi, and in 41 BC it was at Perusia. From 41 to 31 BC it served with Octavian. From 30 BC to possibly 20 BC it was in Galatia, and from some point until AD 9 it served in the Balkans. From AD 9 it was in Dalmatia. It acquired the titles Claudia Pia Fidelis indicating loyalty to Claudius after the revolt of Camillus Scribonianus in Dalmatia in 42. It had two other titles: Paterna and Macedonica. It had a bull as an emblem, indicating that it was formed by Julius Caesar.

VII GEMINA: Formed by Galba in 70 from VII *Hispana*, which had suffered serious losses in the battle of Cremona.

VII HISPANA: Formed in Spain by Galba in 68 after he had been proclaimed emperor. It was reconstituted in 70 and then had the title Gemina instead. It also seems to have had the nickname Galbiana.

VIII AUGUSTA (fig. 2.6): Formed in 59 BC or earlier, and served with Caesar in Gaul from 58 to 49 BC. It served in Italy in 49–48 BC and was at Pharsalus in 48 BC. In 46 BC it was at Thapsus but was disbanded in 46 or 45 BC. It was reconstituted by Octavian in 44 BC, and was at Forum Gallorum and Mutina in 43 BC. In 42 BC it was at Philippi, and from 41 to 31 BC it served with Octavian. From 30 BC it served in the Balkans. Its title indicates reconstitution by Augustus, and may reflect a victory in the period from 27 BC to AD14. It had two other titles: Mutinensis (from Mutina) and Gallica. It had a bull as an emblem, which usually indicates that a legion was formed by Julius Caesar, but may derive from service with him in Gaul.

IX HISPANA: May have been formed as a new legion by Octavian in 41–40 BC, or from the legion IX formed before 58 BC and known to have been in Gaul then with Caesar; the latter legion IX was disbanded in 46 or 45 BC and was later reconstituted by Ventidius, but it is not known if it then became IX Hispana. The IX Hispana served with Octavian from 41–40 BC until the battle of Actium in 31 BC. It served in Spain from 30 BC, possibly until 19 BC. From AD 9 to 20 it served in Pannonia, from 20 to 24 it was in Africa and was again in Pannonia until 43. From 43 it served in Britain. Its title Hispana appears to have superseded its earlier title of Hispaniensis. It also had the title Macedonica, reflecting its service in the Balkans.

X FRETENSIS: Probably formed by Octavian in 41–40 BC. It may have been at Mylae and at Naulochus in 36 BC. It also may have been at Actium in 31 BC. From 30 BC it served in Macedonia, but by AD 14 (probably earlier) it was serving in Syria. The legion had four emblems: a bull, dolphin, galley and boar.

X GEMINA: Formed in 59 BC or earlier, and served with Julius Caesar in Gaul from 58 to 49 BC. It was in Spain in 49 BC and at Pharsalus in 48 BC. It was at Thapsus in 46 BC, was disbanded in 46 or 45 BC but was at Munda in 45 BC. It was reconstituted by Lepidus 44 BC, passed to Antony in 43 BC and served at Philippi in 42 BC. From 41 to 31 *BC* it served with Antony in the east and was at Actium in 31 BC. Possibly from 30 BC it served in Spain. Gemina indicates an amalgamation of legions, probably after the battle of Actium. It also had the title Equestris (mounted on horseback, knightly).

XI A legion numbered XI was formed by Julius Caesar in 58 BC but was disbanded in 46–45 BC. It is more likely that this was a new legion formed by Octavian in 41–40 BC. It served with him from 41 to 31 BC and was at Actium in 31 BC. It served in the Balkans from 30 BC to AD 9 and in Dalmatia from AD 9. It acquired the titles Claudia Pia Fidelis indicating loyalty to Claudius after the revolt of Camillus Scribonianus in Dalmatia in 42. It had Neptune as an emblem.

XII FULMINATA (equipped with the thunderbolt): Was probably the legion XII formed by Julius Caesar in 58 BC. It served with him in Gaul from 58 to 49 BC and was in Italy in 49 BC. It was at Pharsalus in 48 BC but was disbanded in 46–45 BC. It was reconstituted in 44–43 BC, possibly by Lepidus, and served with Antony in the east from 41 to 31 BC, possibly entirely in Greece. It was sent to Egypt under Augustus and served in Syria from the late Augustan period. It lost an eagle standard in Judaea in 66. (See under "Military Standards" p. 90.) The legion had two other titles: Paterna and Antiqua (ancient). Its emblem was a thunderbolt.

XIII GEMINA: May be the same as the legion XIII formed by Julius Caesar in 57 BC, but that legion was disbanded in 46–45 BC. Alternatively, XIII Gemina may have been formed by Octavian in 40–41 BC. The legion served with Octavian from 40 to 31 BC and was at Puteoli in 36 BC. It may have been at Actium in 31 BC. It served in the Balkans from 30 BC and is known to have been on the Rhine frontier after AD 9. The title Gemina probably refers to an amalgamation of legions, perhaps after the battle of Actium in 31 BC. The legion also had the title Pia Fidelis and had a lion as an emblem, which was the symbol of Jupiter.

XIV GEMINA: In 53 BC Julius Caesar formed a legion XIV after an earlier legion with this number had been destroyed, but Caesar's legion was disbanded in 46–45 BC. Alternatively, the legion XIV Gemina may have been formed by Octavian in 41–40 BC, since it served with him until the battle of Actium in 31 BC. It served in the Balkans from 30 BC to AD 9 and on the Rhine frontier from AD 9 to 43. From 43 to 66 it served in Britain. It was in transit in 67–68 and in Italy in 68, but returned to Britain in the same year, where it remained until 70. From 70 it served on the Rhine frontier. The title Gemina probably refers to an amalgamation of legions, perhaps after the battle of Actium in 31 BC. It also had the title Martia Victrix, apparently after victory over Boudiccan rebels in Britain in 60–61. It had a capricorn as an emblem, perhaps indicating formation or reconstitution under Augustus.

XV APOLLINARIS: Probably formed by Octavian in 41–40 BC, although it may have been formed earlier. It served with Octavian from 40 to 31 BC, and may have been at Actium in 31 BC. It was in the Balkans from 30 BC, and from AD 9 it was in Pannonia. From 58 to 66 it served in Syria and from 66 to 70 in Judaea. From 72 it was in Cappadocia. The title Apollinaris (sacred to Apollo) may be in commemoration of the battle of Actium, since Augustus was especially devoted to Apollo.

XV PRIMIGENIA: Probably formed by Caligula in 39, or possibly by Claudius in 42 in preparation for a planned invasion of Britain. Its number was chosen to fit the sequence of legions in Germany.

XVI FLAVIA FIRMA: Reconstituted from the disbanded XVI Gallica in 69. It was in Cappadocia by 72. It acquired the titles Flavia (indicating reconstitution by Vespasian) and Firma (Steadfast).

XVI GALLICA: Probably formed by Octavian in 41–40 BC. It served on the Rhine frontier from 30 BC or earlier. It was disbanded in 69 after collaborating with Civilis. By 72 it was reconstituted as XVI Flavia Firma and was transferred to Cappadocia. The title Gallica indicates service in Gaul, at an unknown date. It may have had a lion (a symbol of Jupiter) as an emblem.

XVII: Likely to have been formed by Octavian in 41–40 BC. It probably served on the Rhine frontier from 30 BC. It was also probably lost with legions XVIII and XIX in Varus' disaster of AD 9.

XVIII and XIX: Probably formed by Octavian in 41–40 BC. They served on the Rhine frontier from 30 BC to AD 9 and were destroyed in Varus' disaster of AD 9.

XX: Possibly formed by Octavian in 41–40 BC or after the battle of Actium in 31 BC. It served in Spain from 30 BC and in the Balkans until AD 9, possibly moving from Spain to the Balkans in 20 BC. It was on the Rhine frontier from AD 9 to 43, and in Britain from 43. It acquired he title Valeria Victrix (Valiant and Victorious) reflecting a victory over Boudiccan rebels in Britain in 60–61. The legion had a boar as an emblem.

XXI RAPAX: Possibly formed by Octavian in 41–40 BC or after the battle of Actium in 31 BC. It served in Vindelicia and on the Rhine frontier from 30 BC and was in Pannonia from 70. It appears to have been destroyed, probably on the Danube, around 92. It had a capricorn as an emblem, perhaps indicating formation or reconstitution under Augustus. *Rapax* is "greedy" or "grasping," like a bird of prey grasping its victim.

XXII DEIOTARIANA: Formed by transferring men from the forces of the kingdom of Galatia (whose king, Deiotarius, died in 40 BC), by 25 BC at the latest. It appears to have been stationed in Egypt, possibly from 25 BC.

XXII PRIMIGENIA: Probably formed by Caligula in 39, or possibly by Claudius in 42 in preparation for a planned invasion of Britain. Its number was chosen to fit the sequence of legions in Germany. It also had the title Pia Fidelis.

XXX ULPIA: The title indicates formation by Trajan (one of his names being Ulpius), possibly in 101 for the Dacian wars. It also had the title Victrix.

Late Roman Legions

Many legions were raised in the later Roman Empire, but in most cases very few details survive. Of the legions raised by Diocletian, Ioviani (sacred to Jupiter) and Herculiani (sacred to Hercules) were named after the patron gods of Diocletian and Maximian. The Solenses (sacred to Sol) were raised by Constantius I and the Martenses (sacred to Mars) by Galerius, and were named after their respective patron gods.

Titles of Legions

Legions began to use titles or nicknames (cognomina) during the civil war of the late republic. In the imperial army almost every legion had a title, and several legions had more than one. Some titles went out of use or were replaced by new ones. For example, the IX legion had the title Hispaniensis (stationed in Spain), but this was at some stage superseded by Hispana (Spanish). Some titles indicated distinguished service in battles or in particular provinces — Fretensis indicates participation in naval battles in the Fretum or Fretum Siculum, the channel between Italy and Sicily. Other titles appear to have described particular qualities of the legions, such as Pia Fidelis (loyal and faithful), Felix (lucky), or Sabina (Sabine) indicating recruitment in the Sabine area of Italy. Titles were given for various other reasons, and they provide useful evidence of the origins and careers of the legions. Alaudae, the Celtic word for crested larks and also great indicates recruitment from native Gauls. The title also may refer to a crest of feathers attached to the helmet, which was a Celtic custom. Flavia indicates formation by one of the Flavian family: Paterna indicates a connection with Julius Caesar as *pater patriae;* Gemella and Gemina (twin) indicate an amalgamation of depleted legions to form a single legion; while Primigenia (firstborn) indicates a new breed of legions.

DISPOSITIONS OF LEGIONS
IN THE EARLY EMPIRE

(after Balsdon 1970 and Cornell & Matthews 1982)

DISPOSITIONS IN AD 24

Province	Legions
Africa	III Augusta
Dalmatia	VII, XI
Egypt	III Cyrenaica, XXII Deiotariana
Germania Inferior	I Germinica, V Alaudae, XX, XXI Rapax
Germania Superior	II Augusta, XIII Gemina, XIV Gemina, XVI Gallica
Hispania Tarraconensis	IV Macedonica, VI Victrix, X Gemina
Moesia	IV Scythica, V Macedonica
Pannonia	VIII Augusta, IX Hispana, XV Apollinaris
Syria	III Gallica, VI Ferrata, X Fretensis, XII Fulminata

DISPOSITIONS IN AD 74

Province	Legions
Africa	III Augusta
Britain	II Augusta, II Adiutrix, IX Hispana, XX Valeria Victrix
Dalmatia	IV Flavia Felix
Egypt	III Cyrenaica, XXII Deiotariana
Germania Inferior	VI Victrix, X Gemina, XXI Rapax, XXII Primigenia
Germania Superior	I Adiutrix, VIII Augusta, XI Claudia Pia Fidelis, XIV Gemina Martia Victrix
Hispania Tarraconensis	VII Gemina
Judaea	X Fretensis
Moesia	I Italica, V Alaudae, V Macedonica, VII Claudia Pia Fidelis
Pannonia	XIII Gemina,

| | XV Apollinaris |
| Syria | III Gallica, IV Scythica |

DISPOSITIONS IN AD 150

Province	Legions
Africa	III Augusta
Arabia	III Cyrenaica
Britain	II Augusta, VI Victrix, XX Valeria Victrix
Cappadocia	XII Fulminata, XV Apollinaris
Dalmatia	XIII Gemina
Egypt	II Traiana Fortis
Germania Inferior	I Minervia, XXX Ulpia
Germania Superior	VIII Augusta, XXII Primigenia
Hispania Tarraconensis	VII Gemina
Judaea	VI Ferrata, X Fretensis
Moesia Inferior	I Italica, V Macedonica, XI Claudia Pia Fidelis
Moesia Superior	IV Flavia Felix, VII Claudia Pia Fidelis
Pannonia Inferior	II Adiutrix, XIV Gemina Martia Victrix
Pannonia Superior	I Adiutrix, X Gemina
Syria	III Gallica, IV Scythica, XVI Flavia Firma

DISPOSITIONS IN AD 215

Province	Legions
Africa	III Augusta
Arabia	III Cyrenaica
Britain	II Augusta, VI Victrix XX Valeria Victrix,
Dacia	V Macedonica, XIII Gemina
Egypt	II Traiana Fortis
Galatia–Cappadocia	XII Fulminata, XV Apollinaris
Germania Inferior	I Minervia, XXX Ulpia Victrix
Germania Superior	VIII Augusta, XXII Primigenia
Hispania Tarraconensis	VII Gemina
Italia	II Parthica
Mesopotamia	I Parthica, III Parthica

Moesia Inferior	I Italica, XI Claudia Pia Fidelis
Moesia Superior	IV Flavia Felix, VII Claudia Pia Fidelis
Noricum	II Italica
Pannonia Inferior	I Adiutrix, II Adiutrix
Pannonia Superior	X Gemina, XIV Gemina Martia Victrix
Raetia	III Italica
Syria Coele	IV Scythica, XVI Flavia Firma
Syria Palaestina	VI Ferrata, X Fretensis
Syria Phoenice	III Gallica

ORGANIZATION OF LEGIONS

Organization: Monarchy and Early Republic

The Roman army was at first under direct command of the king, but as the army increased in size, a hierarchy of officers was needed to control it. The 3,000 men of the three tribes who formed a legion in Rome's early monarchy were commanded by a tribune (*tribunus*, literally "tribal officer"), but otherwise virtually nothing is known about the chain of command before the 4th century BC.

At the end of the monarchy in 509 BC, the king was replaced as commander-in-chief by two consuls (originally known as praetors). They were elected each year (replacing the previous year's consuls) and held supreme civil and military power; it was not until Constantine I in the 4th century AD that full-time professional soldiers commanded the army. By 311 BC the army was divided into four legions, the command of which was usually divided equally between the consuls, although sometimes a single legion could act on its own under the command of a praetor (a lesser magistrate). Each legion also had six military tribunes (24 in total) elected by the *comitia centuriata*.

Organization: Middle Republic

The first detailed account of military hierarchy comes from Polybius. It is not clear if he was writing about the army of his day or as it was some 50 years earlier, but probably the latter. Two consuls were elected at the beginning of each year, and they normally had command of the army. Each controlled two legions — a total force of 16,000 to 20,000 infantry and 1,500 to 2,500 cavalry. Praetors also could command legions, and in times of crisis a dictator was appointed, usually for six months, who took command of the whole army instead of the consuls. A second-in-command to the dictator (*magister equitum*, master of the horse) was sometimes appointed by the dictator. In times of crisis, extensive forces could be called upon from Rome's allies.

From c. 190 BC, the army was still under the overall control of a consul or praetor, but parts of the army now could be commanded by legates (*legati*). When a governor (magistrate) took control of a province, he customarily took along one or more legates, to whom he delegated some civil duties and military forces. This was probably because one magistrate could no longer control the armed forces. Legates were senior senators appointed by the Senate on advice from the governor.

Below the consuls or praetors, the consuls elected 24 tribunes (six per legion). Ten senior tribunes were required to have served at least ten years with the army, and the remainder at least five years. Tribunes commanded any legions that had been raised extra to the four consular legions. The position of tribune was prestigious (even ex-consuls sometimes served as tribunes), and tribunes had to be of the equestrian order.

The tribunes selected ten centurions (prior centurions) from the troops, each of whom chose a partner (posterior centurions). The most senior centurion in a legion was the *centurio primi pili* (later called *primus pilus*, first spear), and he participated in the military council with the tribunes. Each maniple (composed of two centuries) had two centurions, and the *primus*

pilus commanded the extreme right-hand maniple of the *triarii*.

Each centurion appointed an *optio* (rearguard officer), and the centurions also appointed two of the best men as *signiferi* (standard-bearers). Each century was divided into ten units of eight men (*contubernia*) who shared a tent and a mule while on campaign and a pair of rooms when in barracks.

The legionary cavalry was divided into ten *turmae* (squadrons) of 30 cavalrymen. Each *turma* had three decurions (*decuriones*, leaders of ten men) and three deputies (*optiones*) appointed by the decurions. The decurion selected first commanded the whole squadron.

Organization: Later Republic

As Rome's territory continued to expand in the republic, the delegation of military power to legates became more common. They were normally senators who had held at least the post of quaestor. Toward the end of the republic, armies ceased to be commanded by elected magistrates (normally consuls) during their term of office, and in 52 BC a law was passed requiring a five-year gap between elected office at Rome and provincial military command. Since Rome was still a republic, there were several commanders-in-chief of the army, not a single one.

At this time, each legion was still commanded by six tribunes. Now, however, the post was held by young men, some hoping to enter the Senate, rather than by senior magistrates. Above them in command were the prefects who could command cavalry (*praefectus equitum*), naval fleets (*praefectus classis*) or be aides on the commander's personal staff (*praefectus fabrum*). These prefects were given individual commands (not in pairs like the tribunes) at the discretion of the commander, and their positions were often less permanent than that of tribune. Service as tribune and prefect led to the post of *legatus*.

As additional legions were raised to hold new territories, the need for more commanders grew. Extending the powers of senior magistrates beyond the usual one year of office was found expedient, so that propraetors and proconsuls retained military command of legions for extended periods of time (such as Caesar in Gaul).

Organization: Early Empire

Command of military forces was held by consuls, and later extended to proconsuls, praetors and propraetors, but under the empire the emperor technically commanded the army as proconsul. Augustus governed much of the empire through his *legati Augusti pro praetore* (legates with propraetorian power), a term covering both governors of provinces and commanders of legions within the provinces. The emperor, his close family or senatorial representatives usually led the army to war.

Toward the end of Augustus' reign the post of legionary legate (*legatus Augusti legionis* or *legatus legionis*) was introduced. These legates were appointed to command individual legions, often remaining with them for a number of years. At this time legates were young men who had held at least one magistracy at Rome, although later the post of legionary legate became more formally fixed within the senatorial career structure. The expansion of army and empire also increased opportunities for members of the equestrian order to become governors of newly won territory, commanders of naval fleets or prefects of auxiliary forces. There were also opportunities for centurions to rise into the equestrian order, becoming tribunes and prefects.

The internal command structure of a legion remained largely the same, however, with six tribunes under the legionary legate. The senior tribune, the *tribunus laticlavius* (tribune with a broad stripe), was a senator designate. He was entitled to the senatorial distinction of a broad purple stripe on his toga and would have had no previous military experience. The other five tribunes (*tribuni angusticlavii*, tribunes with narrow stripes) were mainly from the equestrian order and had some previous military experience, usually as prefect of an auxiliary unit. Tribunes were responsible for administration in a legion. The posts were far less prestigious than in the republic when tribunes were in command of legions.

Augustus established a new post equivalent to a quartermaster, the *praefectus castrorum* (camp prefect), whose functions had previously been carried out by the tribunes. In the hierarchy, he was usually between the *tribunus laticlavius* and the *tribuni angusticlavii*. During Augustus' reign, both ex-tribunes and ex-*primi pili* were appointed *praefectus castrorum*, but later it became the post to which a *primus pilus* was promoted before retirement. Originally there was one *praefectus castrorum* per camp rather than one per legion. He was the highest ranking officer to serve his entire career in the army.

There were 59 centurions in each legion, ranked below the tribunes. Centurions could rise from the ranks or be directly commissioned. They carried a cane as mark of rank, which they used to beat soldiers as punishment. The centurions were still named after the old maniples, except that *pilus* was preferred for *triarius*. The first cohort was divided into five double centuries commanded by five senior centurions known as *primi ordines* (first ranks). The most senior was the *primus pilus*, below which was the *princeps*, the centurion in charge of headquarters staff and of training. The other centurions were, in descending order of rank, the *hastatus*, *princeps posterior* and *hastatus posterior*. On retirement, a *primus pilus* was given a large gratuity (double that of *primi ordines*) and was known by the honorary title *primipilaris* (ex-*primus pilus*). He could then be promoted to posts such as camp prefect or tribune of the urban cohort.

In cohorts 2 to 10, the centurions did not have a hierarchy of rank but had equal status except for seniority due to length of service. These cohorts each had centurions known as *pilus prior*, *pilus posterior*, *princeps prior*, *princeps posterior*, *hastatus prior* and *hastatus posterior*.

Below the centurions were three main groups of soldiers — *principales*, *immunes* and *milites*. *Principales* were noncommissioned officers in each century who received double the pay of a legionary (a *duplicarius*) or pay and a half (a *sesquiplicarius*). *Principales* included the *signifer*, *optio* and *tesserarius*. The *signifer* (standard-bearer) was below the centurions in a century, and below him was the *optio* (deputy), who took control of the century if the centurion was absent or lost in battle. Below them was the *tesserarius*, who was in charge of the daily watchword and of the sentries. Each legion also had an *aquilifer*, who carried the eagle standard (fig. 2.11) and was responsible for the legionary pay chest and soldiers' savings, and an *imaginifer*, who carried the portrait (*imago*) of the emperor.

Under the officers were the *immunes*, who were skilled in particular crafts and were exempt from everyday tasks. Over 100 such posts are known, including *agrimensores* and *mensores* (surveyors); *acuarii* (bow makers); *adiutores corniculariorum* (assistants to the chief clerk); *aerarii* (bronze workers); *architectus* (master builder); *bucinator*, *cornicen* and *tubicen* (trumpeters playing different types of trumpet); *capsarii* (wound dressers); *carpentarii* (carpenters); *custodes armorum* (armorers); *fabri* (workshop craftsmen); *ferrarii* (blacksmiths); *librarii horreorum* (clerks of granary accounts); *lapidarii* (stonemasons); *librarii caducorum* (clerks of the accounts of the dead); *librarii depositorum* (clerks of deposit accounts); *medici* (medical orderlies or doctors); *optio fabricae* (*optio* in charge of a workshop); *optio valetudinarii* (*optio* controlling hospital orderlies); *plumbarii* (workers in lead); *sagittarii* (arrow makers); *stratores* (grooms); *tubarii* (trumpet makers); and *veterinarii* (veterinaries).

There were various clerical staff, also largely *immunes*. The rank of the *beneficarius* (clerk, literally "benefited one") and the *cornicularius* (adjutant) depended on the officer to whom they were attached. The headquarters staff (*tabularium legionis*) was headed by a *cornicularius*. The staff included *frumentarii*, who controlled the collection and distribution of food and the *quaestionarii*, who were legal staff responsible for investigation and policing, headed by a senior judicial clerk, the *commentariensis*. Lower in rank were accountants (*exacti*) and clerks (*librarii*). Some of these had special duties, such as the *librarii horreorum* (who kept the granary records), *librarii depositorum* (responsible for the compulsory savings of the men) and *librarii caducorum* (responsible for the property of deceased soldiers).

Below the *immunes* were the ordinary troops (*milites*). The career structure for a soldier was from basic pay to *immunis* (basic pay with exemption from everyday tasks), then to pay and a half (*sesquiplicarius*), double pay (*duplicarius*) and then to centurion and beyond.

Organization: Later Empire

The hierarchy of officers established in the early empire lasted for a long time, but just how long is unclear. From around the year 200 there was increasing emphasis on cavalry rather than infantry, and a move toward mobile field armies. Certain reforms occurred in the last half of the 3rd century. Gallienus stopped the appointment of senatorial legionary legates, so that all legions were subsequently commanded by prefects from the equestrian order. From the time of Diocletian, frontier armies were increasingly commanded by *duces* (who

were professional soldiers) rather than by provincial governors.

In the 4th century Constantine I made a complete division between military and civil careers, and from then all frontier armies were led by *duces*. So little evidence survives from the time of the later empire that it is not known if the hierarchy of officers was changed, or whether new types of commander such as the *duces* simply took control of the existing chains of command. Constantine created two commanders-in-chief of the *comitatenses*, the *magister equitum* (master of cavalry) and *magister peditum* (master of infantry), who took over many of the functions of the old-style praetorian prefect.

It was not possible to keep all the mobile forces under immediate command of the emperor, and regional field armies were formed, commanded in the emperor's absence by a *magister militum*. Smaller forces from mobile armies were detached as required, usually commanded by a *comes* (count).

ALAE SOCIORUM

By the early 4th century BC campaigning Roman armies were aided by contingents from towns in Latium, Latin colonies and allies elsewhere in Italy. These allies (*socii*) served as part of conditions of alliance with Rome. As these contingents became more common, they were put on a more organized footing. Contingents from individual towns probably consisted of about 500 infantry (later called a cohort) along with one or more squadrons (*turmae*) of cavalry. In particular, specialist troops were provided such as archers and cavalry. Where necessary, coastal towns were required to provide ships, sailors and marines.

On active service, lictors were not effective bodyguards for consuls, and so the *extraordinarii* were formed as bodyguards. They were selected from the best men of the allied cavalry and infantry, and were elite troops who also undertook scouting ahead and special assignments.

The allied contingents were formed into groups (usually ten, later known as cohorts) to form an *ala sociorum* of a size roughly equivalent to a Roman legion (about 4,000 to 5,000 strong plus about 900 cavalry). Later, under the empire, the term *ala* (wing) was used exclusively for groups of auxiliary cavalry. On campaign, two Roman legions were usually accompanied by two *alae sociorum*. The *alae sociorum* usually formed two flanking wings, one on either side of the legions.

It is likely that the Italian allied forces were commanded by Roman prefects (*praefecti sociorum*, prefects of the allies) appointed by the consul. Since the *ala* appears to correspond to a legion, it is likely that the six prefects in each *ala* matched the legion's six tribunes. Similarly, cavalry units were commanded by *praefecti equitum* (cavalry prefects), who were also Roman officers.

In the Punic Wars attempts were made to strengthen the specialist forces by increased use of allied troops and by hiring mercenaries, and in the 1st century BC the cavalry in particular was strengthened. After the Social War all soldiers recruited in Italy were citizens and so served as legionaries, and the *alae sociorum* ceased to exist. This forced the Romans to look elsewhere for support troops (especially cavalry) by recruiting auxiliaries.

GARRISON AT ROME

The garrison at Rome consisted of the Praetorian Guard, the urban cohorts and the *vigiles*. The most important was the Praetorian Guard. There were nine cohorts of Praetorian Guard, seven of *vigiles* and three urban cohorts, making a total force under Augustus of about 6,000 men. The organization of these troops was similar to that of the legions.

Praetorian Guard

During the siege of Numantia, Scipio Aemilianus formed a personal bodyguard that became known as the Praetorian Cohort (*cohors praetoria*, after *praetorium*, the area in which the general's tent was pitched in a camp). By the end of the republic it was customary for all generals to have a Praetorian Guard or Cohort, formed on an *ad hoc* basis on campaign. Under Augustus in 27 BC, this elite legionary force formed the permanent imperial bodyguard, and consisted of nine cohorts (total force of 4,500 men) with a small mounted contingent. In the 1st century AD under Tiberius the strength of the Praetorian Guard was increased from nine to 12 cohorts and to 16 under Vitellius. It appears to have been reduced to nine cohorts under Vespasian.

Soldiers of the Praetorian Guard were recruited mainly from Italy and a few neighboring provinces, in marked contrast to the legions, which were recruited from the entire Roman world. The Praetorian Guard usually went on campaign with the emperors. From the Flavian period a cavalry unit, the *equites singulares Augusti*, was formed from the *auxilia* to accompany the emperor on campaign.

The organization of the imperial Praetorian Guard was similar to that of the legions. Initially it had no overall command but was under the direct command of Augustus. In 2 BC Augustus put it under the joint control of two equestrian *praefecti praetorio* (praetorian prefects). There was no *primus pilus*, because the Praetorian Guard was not a legion in name or organization, although some officers may have ranked as *primi ordines*. Under Augustus three cohorts of the Praetorian Guard were kept in Rome and the rest in neighboring towns; under Tiberius all nine cohorts were based with the three urban cohorts in one camp (*castra praetoria*) on the northeast side of Rome (fig. 3.2).

The size of the Praetorian Guard varied in the early empire. It was always very powerful and often influenced the choice of emperors. At the end of the 2nd century, Septimius Severus disbanded the old Praetorian Guard and replaced it with ten new milliary cohorts from men of his Danubian legions. Henceforth the Praetorian Guard was recruited from the legions. Throughout the 2nd and 3rd centuries, the number of cohorts varied, but was generally ten, with 500, 1,000 or even 1,500 men in each cohort. Constantine abolished the garrison at Rome in 312, including the Praetorian Guard (which had supported Maxentius), and replaced it with the *scholae*, crack cavalry units 500 strong. At the end of the 4th century there were about a dozen units of *scholae*.

AUXILIARIES

German Bodyguard

Also stationed at Rome, but not part of the official garrison, was the *Germani corporis custodes* (German bodyguards), a force recruited by Augustus from tribes in the Rhineland as a personal bodyguard. It came to be an imperial bodyguard for later emperors, but was disbanded by Galba.

Urban Cohorts

Three *cohortes urbanae* (urban cohorts) formed a city police force at Rome stationed in the praetorian camp. They were recruited from Italians and could be promoted to the Praetorian Guard. Further units of the urban cohorts were sometimes sent to other towns and cities in Italy and beyond, such as Carthage (to guard grain shipments) and Lyon (to guard the mint). Originally there were 10 to 12, but the number of cohorts at any later period is uncertain. There were 500 men in a cohort under Augustus, but this rose to 1,000 under Vitellius and 1,500 under Severus. Each cohort was commanded by a tribune, all under the control of a senator appointed as city prefect (*praefectus urbi*).

Vigiles

After a fire in 6 a permanent fire brigade (*vigiles*) was established by Augustus at Rome to replace the previous ad hoc arrangements. The seven cohorts of *vigiles* were a semimilitary force each commanded by a tribune (*primipilaris*) under a prefect (*praefectus vigilum*) of equestrian rank. Each cohort had 500 (later 1,000) men. The *vigiles*, because of their fire-fighting role, had a greater variety of specialist troops such as *sifonarii* (men who worked the pumps) and *uncinarii* (men with grappling hooks). They were also used as a night watch. There was a detachment at Ostia as well.

History of Auxiliaries

From earliest times the Roman army relied on its infantry, which was the most effective part of the army. The Romans were not so adept at other types of fighting, and so during the early republic they began to use allied forces for specialist troops such as archers and cavalry. During the Punic Wars the need for an effective cavalry force in particular became apparent, and there were attempts to strengthen the specialist forces by increased use of allied troops and by hiring mercenaries. In the 1st century BC there was a noticeable move toward strengthening the cavalry.

From the 1st century BC it became common for the Roman army on campaign to be assisted by troops from local allied tribes within the region in which the campaign was being conducted. These foreign troops were called auxiliaries (*auxilia*). Julius Caesar made extensive use of such forces in his campaigns and during the civil war. After the civil war some of these auxiliary forces were disbanded, but others continued in service. Henceforth several auxiliary units were a permanent part of the standing army, while other units were recruited as the need arose.

Under the empire auxiliaries came to play a crucial role in the Roman army, providing a variety of fighting skills traditional to their home areas, including light infantry, archers, slingers and most of the cavalry. The role of the cavalry within the legionary army was correspondingly diminished, and the Romans came to rely on auxiliaries instead. As the empire expanded the Romans came into contact with different nations that used different methods of fighting, and were able to draw on a wide range of recruits for their auxiliary forces. For example, archers were drawn from Crete and the east, slingers from the Balearic Islands, and cavalry from Gaul, Germany and other parts of the empire (fig. 2.1).

By the end of the 1st century the recruitment catchment area of auxiliary troops became much more localized, as with the legions. During the 2nd century an increasing number of citizens enrolled in *auxilia*—often sons joining their father's regiment. Gradually many of the distinctions between legionary and auxiliary forces broke down, with noncitizens accepted into the legions and some citizens serving in the auxiliaries.

Organization of Auxiliaries

Auxiliary forces were organized into *cohortes* of infantry in parallel with the legions. Initially these units were called *quingenaria*, with a nominal strength of 500 men divided into six centuries, but from the Flavian period (late 1st century) *cohortes milliariae* with a nominal strength of 1,000 men were introduced, composed of ten centuries. There were also *cohortes equitatae* of combined infantry and cavalry. The cavalry units were called *alae*. Auxiliaries were often named after their area of origin, such as *alae* and *cohortes Britannorum* (units of British).

Where auxiliary units were raised from a particular tribe under treaty obligations, they were often commanded by chiefs or leaders from that tribe, who could be rewarded for their service by being granted Roman citizenship. Other units, including the ones that formed part of the permanent standing army, were usually commanded by ex-centurions or ex-legionary tribunes. By the Flavian period, the command of auxiliary forces had been rationalized. Prefects drawn from the equestrian order were now in command of auxiliary units, while the larger *cohortes milliariae* were commanded by tribunes. The tribune of a *cohors milliaria* had equal status to a legionary angusticlave tribune. Below these commanders were centurions, chosen from the ranks, who served all their time in the same unit. Below the centurions the chain of command was probably similar to that in the legions.

Cavalry

In early Rome a force of about 300 cavalrymen came from the nobility (*equites*). In the late 6th century BC the 18 centuries of *equites* (the richest section of the community) continued to supply the cavalry. Ancient authors believed the cavalry was 600 strong. In the early republic the cavalry was increased from 600 to 1,800 men, and their horses were provided at public expense. In the 2nd century BC the richest still served in the cavalry, for a period of ten years.

Fig. 2.1 Tombstone of an auxiliary cavalryman (4th cohort of Thracians), with spear raised to kill a native warrior. An attendant holds two extra spears. The cavalryman wears a helmet and has a long sword suspended from his belt. Photo: Ralph Jackson.

By the 1st century BC the legionary cavalry had largely disappeared, and foreign auxiliary horsemen were employed (fig. 2.1), led by their own chiefs or Roman commanders (*praefecti equitum*). Under the empire cavalry units were commanded exclusively by Roman equestrian prefects. The cavalry was divided into units called *alae* (unlike the *alae sociorum*, which were infantry with some cavalry) with a nominal strength of 500 men, although from the Flavian period there were *alae milliariae* of nominally 1,000 men. The *alae* were divided into 16 or 24 *turmae*, each commanded by a *decurio* (decurion). Below the decurion in each *turma* were two other officers, the *duplicarius* (double-pay man) corresponding to a legion's *optio* and the *sesquiplicarius* (1½ times pay man) corresponding to a legion's *tesserarius*. There was also a *curator*, who seems to have been responsible for the horses. Each *turma* had a standard carried by a *signifer*, and there was also an *imaginifer* and a senior standard-bearer (*vexillarius*) who carried the flag.

Cataphracti were heavily armored cavalry from the Sarmatian tribe and were employed by Rome from at least the time of Hadrian. They were armed with a heavy lance (*contus*). Rome also employed the Numidians, who were completely unarmored cavalry, and mounted archers.

Irregular Forces

During the 2nd century *numeri* (irregular units, literally "numbers of") and *cunei* (irregular cavalry units, literally "wedges") were raised from warlike tribes in some frontier provinces to match similar opponents outside the empire. Unlike the usual auxiliary forces, which by this time had become an established part of the army and were no longer considered to be irregulars, men from *numeri* and *cunei* kept their own weapons and identity and were probably commanded by their own native leaders. Also in contrast to auxiliaries, they do not appear to have received citizenship upon discharge from the army. They fought alongside legionaries and auxiliaries and undertook frontier policing work. In the 4th century *gentiles* (native or foreign troops) provided ethnic troops from within and outside the empire.

THE NAVY

Development and Decline

In the early republic the Romans did not have an effective navy and were not a maritime people. A small navy of triremes was built in 311 BC, but this was scrapped shortly afterward. A large fleet was then built in 260 BC in the First Punic War, consisting mainly of quinqueremes with a few triremes. By 256 BC there were 330 ships, built by naval architects and shipwrights from the Greek coastal cities of southern Italy and from Syracuse. This navy continued to be rebuilt after a series of disasters in the following years, and Polybius estimated that during the First Punic War,

Rome lost about 700 warships and the Carthaginians 500.

After 200 BC the navy was allowed to decline, and Rome relied on ships from the eastern Mediterranean, chiefly Rhodes and Pergamum, which it had bound by treaty to furnish naval forces. The events of the early 1st century BC, in particular the invasions of Mithridates and the increasingly aggressive attacks by the Cilician pirates, led to the formation of a large standing navy, initially by commandeering ships from allies. In the later 1st century BC, sea power was very important in Antony's campaigns in the east (a galley was a common symbol on his coins) and in the ensuing civil war between him and Octavian.

The events of the civil war, culminating in the sea battle of Actium between Octavian and Antony in 31 BC, had emphasized the importance of sea power to Rome and the need to maintain a naval force to protect transport ships. After the civil war Augustus reorganized the navy, and maintained a permanent standing navy with large fleets, originally based at Forum Iulii but later moved to Italy. By the early 1st century AD the Italian fleets based at Misenum and Ravenna were by far the most important naval forces in the empire, but other fleets were also established off Syria, Egypt, Mauretania, the Black Sea, English Channel, the Rhine and the Danube in order to meet specific local needs as the empire expanded. Each was assigned to a particular province, in which it had one or more bases, and generally took its name from that province, such as Classis Pannonica.

From the 2nd century the navy fell into decline. The republican method of hurriedly assembling a navy to meet each crisis was resumed. In the early 3rd century the fleets became smaller, and old units vanished or underwent change. Piracy and barbarian activity became prevalent. Of the ten fleets in existence in 230, only the two Italian fleets remained when Diocletian became emperor in 284. The provincial fleets of the Mediterranean had gone, and the carefully organized fleets on the northern frontiers gave way to new smaller flotillas, each based on a single port and patrolling a smaller area.

In the campaign of Constantine and Licinius in 324, sea power was very important, but there was virtually no navy. Constantine hastily amassed a large fleet, mainly from Greece, and Licinius levied a fleet in the east. This campaign marked the end of the recognizable Augustan navy, although the two Italian fleets officially lasted throughout the 4th century:

They appear in the *Notitia Dignitatum*, although they lost their title *praetoria* when the capital was moved from Rome. By the end of the 4th century there was virtually no navy, and in the 5th century the invading Vandals gained naval supremacy in the western Mediterranean, destroying the western fleet. The fleets at Ravenna and Misenum ceased to appear in formal entries on the army register.

Shortly after 500 in the eastern empire, the emperors began to build up a strong navy at Constantinople in order to maintain their control of the eastern seas and also aid their reconquest of the west. By the mid-6th century they gained control of much of the Mediterranean area and the Black Sea. This Byzantine navy remained a powerful force until the 11th century. A new type of warship was used, the *dromon*, although some of the traditions of the old western navy were retained.

Fleets and Their Bases

PORTUS IULIUS

This naval base was on the Bay of Naples at the Lucrine Lake. The lake was opened to the sea and linked by a channel to Lake Avernus farther inland, which offered a safe inner harbor. It was built by Agrippa in 37 BC and had extensive harborage and dockyards. It was soon abandoned, apparently because it was difficult to maintain, and silted up.

FORUM IULII

A naval base and harbor were also established at Forum Iulii around 37 BC as a base for operations against the fleet of Sextus Pompeius (son of Pompey), and this is probably where part of Octavian's fleet was built. A lagoon of the Argenteus River was made into a harbor by constructing moles and quays. The fleet here guarded the coast of Gaul and could proceed up the Rhône River. As Gaul became pacified, the importance of this remote harbor declined. Most of the crew and ships probably transferred to Misenum before 22 BC, although Forum Iulii continued as a detachment of the main fleet to AD 69, after which the harbor silted up.

MISENE FLEET (CLASSIS MISENENSIS)

The natural harbor at Misenum is at the northern end of the Bay of Naples. The main inner harbor (now a landlocked lagoon, the Mare Morto) was connected by a narrow channel to the outer harbor, which was improved by the construction of two parallel arched moles. It served as the headquarters of the naval fleet for four centuries, reserved solely for naval use. In 69 it probably had over 10,000 sailors and over 50 ships, mostly triremes, with some quadriremes and quinqueremes, and a "six" as flagship. Detachments from the Misene fleet were based in Ostia, Pozzuoli, Centumcellae (a harbor built by Trajan on the south Etrurian coast) and probably ports elsewhere such as Sardinia and Corsica. The largest detachment of men from the Misene fleet was at Rome, based in the praetorian camp.

RAVENNA FLEET (CLASSIS RAVENNAS)

The fleet based at Ravenna on Italy's Adriatic coast was smaller than at Misenum, probably with about 5,000 men in 69. It was established by 25 BC and consisted mainly of triremes. The harbor, designed for naval use only, consisted of an enlarged lagoon in the delta of the Po River, two miles south of Ravenna. It was equipped with moles, a lighthouse and a camp. A canal (Fossa Augusta) led from the harbor to the Po. There were only a few subsidiary detachments of the Ravenna fleet, such as at Salonae on the Dalmatian coast. A detachment at Brindisi may have been from Ravenna. The detachment at Rome was smaller than that from the Misene fleet. Other ports were probably used as well, but not on a permanent basis. The Ravenna fleet was active on occasions in the western Mediterranean. The harbor became silted up in the Middle Ages and is now inland.

CLASSIS ALEXANDRINA

The Alexandrian fleet or Egyptian squadron was based at Alexandria and was probably Augustan in origin. Under Vespasian it was rewarded with the title Classis Augusta Alexandrina for services to him in the civil war. In the 1st century it did not have regular duties on the Nile as the river was patrolled by ships of the *potamophylacia*, an independent service that exercised fiscal and police supervision over the waterways of Egypt and ferried detachments from the military forces. During the 2nd century the Alexandrian fleet took over this function. The fleet probably continued to 250.

CLASSIS SYRIACA

The Syrian fleet was based at Seleucia, the chief harbor on the Syrian coast, and was also responsible for patrolling the Aegean. It was possibly Augustan in origin, although it is first attested in the reign of Hadrian.

MAURETANIAN FLEET

A detachment of the Alexandrian and Syrian fleets was based far to the west along the African coast at Caesarea when Mauretania became a province in the 1st century.

CLASSIS MOESICA

The Danube divides into two at the Iron Gates in the Kazan Gorge, and it was probably difficult for ships to pass safely through this stretch in times of low

water. It was therefore necessary for two fleets to be based along the Danube. The Moesian fleet was based along the lower (eastern) Danube and also patrolled the northern coasts of the Black Sea. It was probably Augustan in origin.

CLASSIS PANNONICA

The Pannonian fleet was probably Augustan in origin, although its earliest record is in 50. It was based on the middle and upper (western) Danube and also patrolled the Save and Drave tributaries in Pannonia Superior. Its main base was at Taurunum, near the junction of the Save and Danube, and there may have been detachments at Brigetio, Aquincum and Carnuntum. The fleets on the Danube were useless in winter as the river freezes from December to the end of February. The Roman fleets on the middle Danube continued in some form to the end of Roman rule.

CLASSIS LAURIACENSIS

The first-known mention of this fleet is in the *Notitia Dignitatum* of the 4th century. It operated in the upper Danube and was probably based in a harbor at

Fig. 2.2 Neumagen wine ship tombstone (copy), early 3rd century. It represents a warship of the German fleet, with a ram, 22 oars and a steering oar, plus a cargo of wine barrels. The figures are shown too large in proportion to the warship.

the junction of the Enns River, near the legionary fortress of Lauriacum in Noricum.

CLASSIS PONTICA

The Pontus Euxinus (Black Sea) came partly under Roman control with the annexation of Thrace in 46, and there may have been a native Thracian fleet (Classis Perinthia). In 64 Pontus (previously a client kingdom) was annexed, bringing the whole of Asia Minor and the southern shores of the Black Sea as far as the Caucasus under Roman control. The Pontic fleet was established in 64 from the royal fleet of the former client kings and consisted mainly of liburnians (see p.73). Its base was at Trapezus, and it was responsible for the southern and eastern parts of the Black Sea. The fleet disappeared after 250 with the invasions of the Goths, and there were no Roman warships in the Hellespont until the 4th century.

CLASSIS GERMANICA

Apart from the Italian fleets, much more is known of the German fleet than any other (fig. 2.2). It was based on the Rhine River, with its headquarters at Alteburg, Cologne. There were also subsidiary stations, such as at Neuss, Xanten, Nijmegen, Velsen and Arentsburg. The fleet played a prominent part in campaigns against the German tribes, and several shipping disasters are known from literary sources. A canal (Fossa Drusiana) was constructed by Drusus the Elder in the late 1st century BC to shorten the distance from the Rhine to the North Sea. The fleet was Augustan in origin. It remained loyal to Domitian during Saturninus' rebellion and received the title Pia Fidelis Domitiana.

CLASSIS BRITANNICA

The British fleet was established in the reign of Claudius as massive naval operations were required to invade Britain in 43. Its main base was at Boulogne, and there were bases on the southern English coast, including Richborough, Lympne and Dover. It operated from the time of Claudius and is last attested in the mid-3rd century.

OTHER FLEETS

In Greece, Piraeus was used by naval forces but had no permanent detachment of any fleet, although sailors from the Misenum and Ravenna fleets are known to have served there. In southern France, despite the importance of the trade routes, the River Rhône did not have its own naval fleet until the 4th century.

TITLES

The honorific title of *praetoria* was given to both Italian fleets, probably during the first century, under Domitian. This placed them alongside the praetorian cohorts in the central system of defense. The provincial fleets were also honored by similar titles. The Alexandrian, German and possibly Syrian fleets received from Vespasian the title Augusta, and the Pannonian and Moesian fleets the title Flavia. In the 3rd century Gordian III gave the fleets the title Gordiana (fig. 2.3).

Warships

Roman warships were long war galleys based on designs from existing shipbuilding traditions, mainly Greek, with Latinized forms of Greek names, although no actual warships of Roman date have been found. The three main types of warship were the trireme (three-er), quadrireme (fourer) and quinquereme (fiver). The standard warship of the republican fleets was the quinquereme, but it lost its preeminence after the battle of Actium in 31 BC. The quadrireme then appeared, but the trireme remained the main warship in the Italian fleets. Occasionally "sixes" (probably outsize quinqueremes) were used as flagships, and Antony had galleys up to a "ten" in size. Augustus, though, kept nothing larger than a "six" for his flagship.

The fleets were apparently composed of a mixture of types of ship. The warships were narrow and long (generally 1 to 7 proportions). They were propelled by oars and so were superior to sailing ships as they did not rely on the Mediterranean winds. Contemporary representations show the ships with one, two or three banks of oars (fig. 2.2). They were probably built in the same way as merchant ships. Space was very restricted, and ships could not exceed a certain size in case they broke up in rough weather.

Warships are not known to have exceeded 60 m (200 ft) in length and were usually far less. They did not stand high above the water and were not very seaworthy or stable, although they were broader and sturdier than earlier Greek ships. There is little evidence for lead sheathing of warships, which were hauled ashore in harbor. They could not keep at sea for long periods and were normally laid up in winter.

From the base of the prow jutted a ram, made of a huge timber sheathed in bronze. However, the Romans adapted their warships to the tactics of land warfare by using a boarding rather than a ramming strategy. A movable boarding bridge or gangplank (nicknamed the *corvus*, crow or raven) was designed to fix itself into the deck of the enemy ship. It was a boarding plank 11 m (36 ft) long and 1.2 m (4 ft) wide with a heavy iron spike at one end. It was lowered and raised by a pulley system. When raised, it stood against a vertical mastlike pole in the bow of the ship. When lowered, it projected far over the bow, and the spike would embed in the deck of the enemy ship, allowing the sailors to board. The *corvus* was described by Polybius, but may have been used only for a few years around the First Punic War. It may have been scrapped as its design could have made ships unseaworthy.

Various types of grapnel (*manus ferrea*, *harpago* or *harpago-corvus*) were subsequently used, on a pole or chain, with soldiers probably boarding ships by light ladders. In the civil war Agrippa (who commanded Augustus' fleets) devised a new weapon, the catapult-grapnel (*harpax*), which fired a grapnel from a catapult.

Ships were given names, often of gods or rivers, but these were not inscribed on the hull as today. Above the ram, the prow was often surmounted by a carved figurehead (such as monster, animal or god) indicating the name of the ship (fig. 2.2), or else the prow terminated in a spiral decorated with a figure. On the sides above the ram and below the prow there were also carved figures or mystic eyes. In the center of the ship was a mast that could be raised or lowered at sea, and carried a big square sail; at the prow was a second smaller mast, inclined forward, for a smaller sail. On each side of the poop hung a steering oar.

The arrangement of oars is uncertain. In the earlier Greek triremes there were 25 groups of three rowers on each side, a total of 150 rowers, each of whom pulled an individual oar. There were three banks of oars, with the rowers in each group seated in a complicated staggered arrangement to save space. The arrangement of oars in a Roman quinquereme is unclear, and probably there were only additional rowers for larger craft, not additional banks of oars. The crews were larger than in a trireme, and five men seem to have pulled each great oar, with a total of 400 rowers. The quadriremes may have had two banks of oars with two men to each oar. The power of the rowers was limited and easily expendable, and so they probably worked in shifts on long voyages. When winds were favorable, sails could be used.

The *liburna* (pl. *liburnae*) or liburnian ship was not a system of oarage but a style of construction originally used by the pirate tribe, the Liburni, of the west coast of Illyria. It was a light, fast ship with one or two banks of oars and a very large lateen sail. By the 2nd century BC it had two banks of oars, with two men in each group in the style of a trireme. It began to be widely adopted from the 1st century BC, supplanting the quinqueremes. It occurs in limited numbers in the Italian fleets but became the standard vessel in the provincial fleets.

Vessels more suitable for river transport were also used in the naval fleets on the navigable rivers and canals (fig. 2.2).

The *dromon* (runner) appeared at the end of the 5th century and was the main Byzantine warship until the 11th century. It was similar in form to the earlier Roman warships and was a light, swift long galley with one or two tiers of oars. The dromons had a foredeck and poopdeck but were otherwise open, although the rowers were protected by the gangways and a light frame on which shields were hung. The name *dromon* referred to the largest type of war galley, with 100 to 120 oars, but it was also used loosely for smaller ships with fewer oars. The ships had two masts, a mainmast and a foremast, and in later centuries they had lateen sails. They relied on ramming and hand-to-hand combat, and from the 7th century carried incendiary artillery.

Ship's Crew

In the mid-2nd century BC the poorest citizens were sent to the navy, and, because of its foreign origins, the navy was organized as auxiliary units, not as legions. Throughout most of their existence, the two Italian fleets had a very considerable strength, with about 10,000 men at Misenum and 5,000 at Ravenna. The eight major provincial fleets in total may have been as strong.

The ship's crew consisted of various grades of officers and the rank-and-file sailors. The crew had both military and naval functions. Its military and administrative framework was borrowed from the army, but the Greek organization of the crew was adopted, with Greek titles for ships' officers. The relationship between the naval and military organization aboard ship is obscure. Military matters were left almost entirely to the centurion (not the trierarch). The crew of a trireme is estimated to be 200 (including 150 oarsmen); that of a quinquereme was 300, and the ship could also transport 100 men. The crew of a liburnian was smaller than that of a quinquereme.

OFFICERS

There were three senior officer ranks: ships' captains (*trierarchi*), squadron commanders (*navarchi*) and fleet commanders or prefects (*praefecti classis*), who were in charge of the administration of naval bases.

In the republic senators commanded individual fleets, but under the empire prefects were selected as commanders by the emperors. Under Augustus and Tiberius prefects were equestrian in rank and were drawn from the army. Under Claudius prefects became civilian in status, equivalent in rank to procurators; their title was *procurator Augusti et praefectus classis*.

Freedmen with no military experience were able to become naval prefects, since the use of freedmen as procurators had been common since Augustus' time. This situation proved unsatisfactory and was changed by Vespasian. The title *procurator Augusti* was dropped to prevent freedmen from holding the post, and the status of the praefecture was changed. This led to the praefecture of the Misene fleet (*praefectus classis praetoriae Misenensis*) becoming one of the most important offices in an equestrian career (fig. 2.3). The prefect of the Ravenna fleet (*praefectus classis praetoriae Ravennatis*) was of slightly lower rank. The length of tenure varied, but was normally four to five years in the 2nd century. In the 1st and 2nd centuries prefects were mainly Italian by birth. From the time of Nero there appears to have been a sub-

prefect, an insignificant post carrying the third-class honorific title of *vir egregius*.

The provincial fleets normally operated within the administrative system of their particular province in conjunction with the other troops. The provincial fleet commander or prefect was a junior equestrian under the control of the provincial legate, equivalent to an auxiliary command.

A navarch (from the Greek *navarchos*) was a squadron commander. In the late republic and Byzantine period the fleets were divided into squadrons, and this probably was true in the earlier empire as well. The number of ships constituting a squadron is unclear, but was possibly ten. A navarch was usually promoted

Fig. 2.3 An altar erected by the prefect of the Misenum fleet. The lower part of the inscription is in Greek.

from the position of trierarch, and under Augustus the post was usually held by experienced Greek sailors. The post was similar in rank to a centurion.

A trierarch (from the Greek *trierarchos*) was a ship's captain. He was probably promoted from the lower ranks, and under Augustus the position was usually held by experienced Greek sailors. The exact relationship between the trierarch and centurion is unclear.

The *beneficarius* headed the trierarch's staff and was equivalent to an equestrian tribune in a legion. He was head of a small administrative staff including a *secutor* and one or more other clerks. The *secutor* was the ship's clerk responsible for forwarding routine reports to the central administrative offices. An *auditor* was a higher clerk, a *librarius* was mainly concerned with financial records and the *exceptor* was a stenographer. Some of these clerks may have been carried only on larger ships.

Additional officers in charge of the oarsmen and of maintenance were promoted from the ranks of sailors. On the poop, the *gubernator* supervised the steersmen and controlled the sailors in the aft part of the ship. On the prow was the *proreta*, who was the chief assistant of the *gubernator* and relayed information on shoals and rocks to the steersman.

To obtain controlled motion, the rowers had to be supervised and a rhythmical beat established to achieve a synchronized rowing action. These duties fell chiefly to the *celeusta*, also known as the *pausarius*. No special titles distinguished the overseers of the rowers, but the numerous sailors known as *duplicarii* (double-pay men) may have fulfilled that role. To manage the sails each ship had a few *velarii* whose special skills entitled them to double pay.

Nothing is known of cooks on board ship, but each crew had its own *medicus duplicarius* (physician). The *nauphlax* was probably responsible for the care and physical upkeep of the ship. Under him were the *fabri*, trained workmen and carpenters who usually received double pay owing to their importance aboard ship. There were also officers with religious functions.

Besides the Greek naval organization of the crew into rowers, sailors and officers, both the Italian and provincial fleets had a Roman military framework. The crew of each warship, regardless of its size, formed one *centuria* (century). As each ship was a self-contained unit, the centuries were not organized into cohorts. A *centurio* (centurion) was in charge of a naval century and was responsible for the military training of the sailors.

The elaborate hierarchy seen in a legionary century was simplified in the navy. A small group of military officers assisted the centurion; the chief one was the *optio*, who would normally expect promotion to centurion. Among his duties was the supervision of the sick. Another aide, the *suboptio*, does not occur in the other armed forces. The *custos armorum* was the only purely military administrative officer aboard ship, and he looked after and repaired the weapons of the crew. There is no evidence for other officers, and military musicians on ship are recorded only rarely.

SAILORS

Sailors were ranked far below legionaries and somewhat below auxiliaries, as the navy was regarded as an inferior force. A sailor regarded himself as a *miles* or *manipularis* (soldier) rather than a *nauta* (sailor), because of the lack of status implied in the latter title. In the republic there was a distinction between rowers and marines, but this disappeared in the empire. The rowers and other crew members had to be soldiers as well, especially for boarding operations. After Actium there is no evidence that the legions provided marines on a regular basis, probably because there was no necessity for heavily armed troops to be present on board permanently.

The use of slaves or prisoners as rowers is not substantiated. From the time of Augustus sailors tended to be recruited from free men within the lower ranks of society, especially noncitizens. Freedmen were occasionally recruited, although they were generally too old by the time they had been freed. From about the time of Vespasian, there is evidence for the widespread adoption of Latin names by sailors, many of whom discarded their native names on enlistment. The sailors came from all over the empire, but in particular from the eastern Mediterranean.

Function of the Navy

The life of a sailor is not well documented, but in the sailing season the Italian fleets were probably often at sea practicing oarsmanship and carrying officials to their provincial posts. The navy was responsible for the transport of the emperor and his retinue, and the transport and supply of troops, often on a large scale, as in Trajan's campaigns in the east. About 60 warships were required to transport a legion of over 5,000 men on a long journey.

At Rome and elsewhere along the coasts, naval detachments were permanently stationed as guards, couriers and escorts. They probably acted as a police force in the thriving commercial ports as there was no other force to undertake this duty. A major task was to guard the grain supply to Rome: The Misene detachments guarded commerce along the Italian coast including the grain supply, and the primary function of the Alexandrian fleet was to protect the grain supply from Egypt. Occasionally the navy pursued pirates, although little piracy is known under the empire. Some sailors may even have been used for civil engineering projects. The duties of the detachments at Rome included organization of naval spectacles, assisting the watch and handling awnings in theaters and amphitheaters (where men skilled in rope and canvas were required).

In winter the warships were largely laid up, and the sailors must have had more spare time. They may have supplemented their income by private activities, and a large number seem to have had sufficient means to purchase a slave. When not at sea, they were based in camps, such as at Misenum and Ravenna.

The Roman navy fought no serious battle for the first two centuries of the empire, although on the northern frontiers the provincial fleets had a strategic military role.

CONDITIONS OF SERVICE

Length of Service

Soldiers were originally needed only for short campaigns and could return to their farms afterward. They were liable for intermittent service only between the ages of 17 and 46. With the increasing number of provinces, the campaign season extended from March to October, and permanent garrisons were required in newly won territory. From c. 200 BC

there developed a core of soldiers willing to volunteer over several years up to the maximum of 16, probably largely in expectation of booty, but at the end of each campaign season, it was still normal for legions to be disbanded.

Around the time of the Second Punic War (218–201 BC), the maximum period of service appears to have been 16 years for infantry and 10 for cavalrymen. Usually a legionary could expect up to about six years' continuous service and then be liable for recall as an *evocatus* up to the maximum. Under the reforms of Marius, the period of service appears unchanged.

Augustus increased army service to 16 years from the normal six, followed by four years as a veteran reserve *sub vexillo* (under the flag, rather than *sub aquila*, under the eagle), with this service rewarded by a fixed cash payment. These veterans were required to live near the camp for the five years. In AD 5 the period of service was raised to 20 years followed by an unspecified time (possibly five years) as a reserve, although often discharge was delayed. After Augustus' death service as a legionary became 25 or 26 years (as discharges were carried out every other year), with no separation of duties as a veteran after 20 years.

Praetorian Guards served for a shorter time than ordinary legionaries. In 13 BC the length of service was fixed at 12 years, but in AD 5 it was increased to 16. Consequently, Praetorian Guards were relatively young when they retired and could continue as *evocati*, often being considered for promotion to the rank of centurion in a legion or tribune in the *vigiles* or the Praetorian Guard itself. Urban cohorts served for 20 years and there was no *evocatio*. The *vigiles* served for six years.

Auxiliaries served for up to 30 years, but in the Flavian period service was reduced to 25. Sailors usually entered the navy between the ages of 18 and 23 and served for 26 years, one year longer than auxiliaries. Difficulty in recruiting increased in the 3rd century, and so the term was lengthened by two years, and sailors were also enlisted from the age of 15.

Soldiers' Pay

The earliest Roman soldiers were unpaid, as their main income was from their farms. Legionaries had to meet a property qualification before they were eligible for the army and had to pay for their own equipment, clothing and food. In the reforms following the war with Veii (captured in 396 BC), a daily cash payment (*stipendium*) was made to soldiers to help meet the cost of living expenses, and payments were also made toward the maintenance of cavalry horses while they were on campaign.

Polybius gives figures for payment in the early 2nd century BC in Greek currency. The figures are disputed, but a legionary possibly received half a *denarius* a day, a centurion one *denarius*, and a cavalryman one and a half *denarii*. They also received an allowance of corn, which was deducted from their pay.

By the mid-1st century BC, the *stipendium* was regarded as pay rather than an allowance. At this time legionary pay had been fixed for over 50 years at 112.5 *denarii* a year, with deductions being made for food and arms. Caesar doubled legionaries' pay to 225 *denarii* a year, probably to maintain their loyalty, although he also reintroduced a deduction for clothing. Caesar's opponents were presumably forced to take similar measures in increasing pay. Augustus continued legionary pay at this level, but greatly increased the pay of centurions, which ranged between 3,750 and 15,000 *denarii* a year according to their grade. Due to this massive increase, the lowest grade of centurion received nearly 17 times the pay of an ordinary legionary. Some specialist troops received more pay than the ordinary legionaries. Officers such as the *optio* and *signifer* received double pay and the *tesserarius* 1 ½ times.

In 83 or 84 Domitian increased legionary pay to 300 *denarii* a year, the Praetorian Guard to 1,000 *denarii* and centurions to about 5,000 to 20,000 *denarii*. Later, Septimius Severus increased legionary pay to 459 *denarii* and centurions' pay to a range of 8,333 to 33,333 *denarii*. Caracalla raised legionary pay to 675 *denarii*.

Generally in the early empire auxiliary infantry received one-third legionary pay and auxiliary cavalry two-thirds legionary pay or possibly slightly more.

The Praetorian Guard was paid substantially more than legionaries and received frequent donatives. At the beginning of Augustus' reign they were paid about 375 *denarii* a year, but by the end of his reign it had risen to 750 *denarii* and to 1,000 *denarii* under Domitian. The urban cohorts probably received about 375 *denarii* a year.

Under Diocletian the army was paid in rations, with some cash payments for salary and some donatives. Late Roman soldiers did not have to pay for arms, equipment and uniform. In the 4th century their regular salary was paid in vast quantities of bronze small change, and emperors gave donatives on accession and on five-year anniversaries. In 360 the accession donative was a pound of silver and five gold *solidi*. Emperors also gave gifts to officers, including inscribed silver plate and gold and silver belt fittings.

DONATIVES AND RETIREMENT GIFTS

As well as pay, soldiers expected a share of any plunder while on campaign, and from the late republic this was often the main source of remuneration for the army. From c. 200 BC soldiers volunteered for a period of several years, partly for the prospect of booty, which was probably a more realistic expectation than any gratuity during or on completion of military service. A general could grant booty in total or in part to his troops, and this system was widely used in the republic. Successful generals would sometimes pay a donative to the troops, often at a triumph, and soldiers were sometimes given land when discharged, but such prospects were less frequent than the opportunities for booty. *Spolia opima* were spoils taken from the enemy commander by the Roman commander.

Julius Caesar and successive emperors often found it expedient to issue bounties (donatives) to the army to ensure their loyalty during service, as well as gratuities and pensions to soldiers to ensure their loyalty after retirement from the army. In the late republic and early empire soldiers were sometimes given grants of land as well as or instead of gratuities on retirement, usually as part of a colony (*colonia*), a settlement either of soldiers or of soldiers and civilians. After Octavian emerged victorious from the civil war, many of his and Caesar's troops were rewarded with grants of land in colonies in Italy and the provinces, often after the ejection of the existing population. Land grants tended to disappear in the 2nd century, although in the 4th century veterans were encouraged on retirement to cultivate derelict land for which they received a small grant.

Initially there seems to have been no reward paid to auxiliary troops on completion of service, but from the time of Claudius auxiliaries serving 25 years were granted citizenship and *conubium* (the recognition of existing or future marriages so that children gained citizenship). There are indications that citizenship was granted to a few auxiliaries before Claudius' reign, probably as rewards for specific services. On retirement, auxiliaries were granted *honesta missio* (honorable discharge). Later in the 1st century honorable discharge and citizenship were both granted after 25 years' service. The grant of citizenship and *conubium* were confirmed on bronze diplomas. (See chapter 6.)

From the evidence of epitaphs, most sailors did not see the end of their full term of enlistment. Those who completed their 26 years were granted honorable dismissal (*honesta missio*) by the fleet prefect. Like auxiliaries, they were issued diplomas granting them citizenship and *conubium*.

Auxiliaries and sailors apparently did not receive a cash bounty or any other form of pecuniary reward on discharge. Very few naval veterans were ever settled in colonies, although Augustus settled some of his veterans at Forum Iulii and possibly at Nîmes. Vespasian also rewarded the veterans of the two Italian fleets who had aided his advance to the throne by settling them in colonies at Paestum and in Pannonia. Some veterans even stayed in service after their discharge date.

Marriage

Roman soldiers and sailors were forbidden to contract legal marriages during their terms of service. However, many had common-law wives and children and on retirement settled in the provinces where they had served. Septimius Severus lifted the ban on marriage in 197.

Food

Legionaries carried rations to last for 15 days in an emergency. The basic diet when on campaign was wheat baked in the form of wholemeal biscuits, supplemented by bacon, cheese and sour wine (all preserved foods). When in camp, there was a greater variety of food, with evidence for beef, mutton, pork and other meats and poultry, eggs, fish, shellfish, fruit, vegetables and salt, as well as the staple ration of wheat.

The requisitioning of foodstuffs for soldiers and their animals is uncertain, and may well have been undertaken locally, with farmers encouraged to overproduce to supply the needs of the military. The *annona militaris* was a regular tax in kind imposed upon Italy and the provinces to provide food for the soldiers. Originally it was imposed only in times of war, but gradually it became a permanent tax. It should not be confused with the *annona*. It may have been introduced by Septimius Severus, but was more likely gradually adopted and became more common through the 3rd century. It led to the organization of *horrea* (granaries and warehouses) and the development of the *cursus publicus* into a system for the collection and distribution of this tax.

TRAINING

Some kind of training of soldiers must have been carried out from earliest times. Polybius gives information about the retraining of experienced soldiers after Scipio captured New Carthage in 209 BC. It took the form of a seven-day schedule comprising running in full armor, cleaning of weapons and armor and weapons' drill (carried out with wooden swords and javelins with a button on the end to avoid accidents). The schedule was repeated until the soldiers were considered competent.

During the empire training of recruits seems to have been more wide-ranging. Recruits were taught to march and performed parade drill twice a day (whereas trained legionaries drilled once a day). They were taught how to build a camp, swim and ride. Weapons training concentrated on sword and javelin. For sword training, recruits used a wooden sword and wicker shield, both twice normal weight, and were taught to attack a wooden post using the sword to thrust rather than slash. More advanced training consisted of fighting in full armor, basic battle tactics and mock battles with the points of swords and javelins covered to avoid serious accidents. Practice camps have been identified, some of which were probably built for artillery practice. Much training took place in large parade grounds outside each fort. They were large flat enclosures, where ceremonial parades took place as well. Amphitheaters may also have been used as training grounds.

Battle Tactics

Little is known of the battle formations and tactics of the Roman army before the late 6th century BC, when the reform of the army by Servius Tullius is linked to the introduction of the Greek "hoplite" style of fighting. This method of warfare had been established in Greece around 675 BC. Hoplites were heavily armed infantrymen trained to fight in close formation, with their shields overlapping and their spears protruding forward. This formation (a *phalanx*, literally "roller") could be of any length, and eight, 12 or 16 rows deep. Casualties in the front row were replaced by men stepping forward from the row behind to maintain an unbroken front.

The phalanx seems to have remained the main battle formation for a considerable time, but when used against the Gauls in the early 4th century BC, it failed to be sufficiently maneuverable to counter their open-order tactics. Over the next 50 years, the phalanx was split into sections called maniples (*manipuli*, handfuls), so that instead of a single compact body of soldiers, there were several smaller units capable of limited independent action. This change in formation was combined with a change in emphasis from defensive weapons and armor to more offensive weapons, so allowing different tactics. Instead of fighting at short range in the close phalanx formation, legionaries used javelins to begin the battle at long range to disrupt enemy battle lines, before charging forward to engage the enemy at close range with swords and shields. The flexibility in battle allowed by this reorganization was a major factor in future Roman military successes.

Livy, writing nearly 400 years later, gives an indication of how the army was organized in 340 BC, although the degree of his accuracy is questionable: A further development in the 4th century BC appears to have been the complete abandonment of the phalanx and the division of the army into distinct battle lines. There were three lines of heavy infantry: the front line consisted of the youngest recruits (*hastati*, spearmen) and the second line of *principes* (chief men). Maniples of *triarii* (veterans, literally "third-rank men") formed the third line of battle but were rarely brought in except in an emergency. A screen of lightly armed infantry (*leves*) was in front, and two lightly armed groups, called *rorarii* and *accensi*, formed a reserve in the rear.

The *leves*, lightly armed skirmishers, began the battle by trying to break up the enemy ranks with light javelins. As the enemy advanced, the *leves* retreated through gaps in the Roman lines, and the *hastati* charged throwing heavy javelins. If this failed to break the enemy line, they also retreated, to be replaced by the *principes*, who also charged the enemy. If this failed, the *principes* retreated through gaps in the *triarii* line, the gaps were closed and the Roman army retreated.

Polybius, writing in the mid-2nd century BC, describes the army as it probably was around the beginning of that century. The battle tactics were similar to those of the 4th century BC, but now with *velites* rather than *leves*.

Until the time of Marius, maniples were the tactical fighting unit, although from the Second Punic War they seem to have been arranged in groups of three to form a cohort. Around the end of the 2nd century BC, the reforms of Marius appear to have included the grouping together of maniples to form cohorts. Certainly by the time of Julius Caesar, the maniple was dropped in favor of the cohort as the tactical fighting unit, and the legionary cavalry had been abolished. It is also likely that Marius was responsible for abolishing the lightly armed *velites* as a separate unit, sharing the men from this unit among the remaining centuries of the legions. The cohorts were composed of a maniple from each of the old *hastati*, *principes* and *triarii*, the differences between which now disappeared. The legion, made up of ten cohorts, had a battle formation of a front row of four cohorts and two rows of three cohorts behind, all armed with sword and *pilum*. The actual battle tactics appear to have remained largely unchanged, although the new units gave greater flexibility.

The use of cohorts enabled the army to be drawn up in a variety of formations, such as the wedge-shaped formation designed to break through the enemy line. Generally, though, the army of the late republic and early empire appears to have used simple formations and relied on established tactics rather than imaginative innovations. It continued to rely on well-trained, well-disciplined infantry as the main thrust of its attack.

In the 3rd and 4th centuries there was an increasing trend toward more mobile armies and a greater emphasis on cavalry rather than infantry. The cavalry had previously operated as lightly armed skirmishers to harass the enemy while keeping largely out of

Fig. 2.4 Testudo *formed by shields of the Ermine Street Guard, a group devoted to the research of Roman military equipment and re-enactment of maneuvers.*

range. Instead it changed to a light and heavy armored cavalry that played a significant role in battles. From the latter part of the 4th century, though, there was a decline in the training and discipline of the army. As the ability to finance a standing army was steadily reduced, the army's effectiveness dwindled until the frontiers were finally overrun.

SIEGES

Virtually nothing is known of Roman siege warfare until the 3rd century BC, but it was derived from Greek techniques. The city of Veii is said to have been besieged for ten years, and was finally captured in 396 BC when Romans dug a tunnel under the walls. At Agrigento, Sicily, at the beginning of the First Punic War in 262 BC, the technique of circumvallation was used, and it became the standard Roman system: Several camps or forts were positioned around the place being attacked, which were then joined by lines of trenches and ramparts (siege works), cutting off the place entirely. A second line of ramparts facing outward could be established, as well as booby traps such as pits with pointed stakes (known as lilies) covered with brushwood, to prevent reinforcements coming to the assistance of the besieged town. The town was stormed first, and if this failed it was starved out. Caesar used this technique at Alesia in Gaul in 52 BC, which was occupied by Vercingetorix' army of about 80,000 men. Alesia and Masada have particularly fine surviving remains of siege works.

Although the Greeks had used sophisticated and very large siege machinery, these machines were not extensively exploited by the Romans, who instead gained access to towns by building ramps and siege towers, undermining and using battering rams. Huge ramps of timber and soil were built up to town walls. Siege towers were built out of enemy range and were brought up on rollers. They were protected by screens made of wicker probably covered with hide, allowing the soldiers to launch attacks from cover. These siege towers and ramps required a vast amount of timber, and after the siege of Jerusalem, it was reported that no trees stood within an 18 km (11 mi) radius. Another means of gaining access to the walls was by the *musculus*, used by Caesar at Marseille. It was a long protective gallery on wheels with a sloping roof that shielded the soldiers. Soldiers could also be brought up close to the walls by the tortoise (*testudo*) formation. This could be formed of any number of men, who held their interlocking shields above and around them to act as a protective cover (fig. 2.4).

The battering ram (*aries*) was a heavy beam tipped with iron that was sometimes swung on ropes or, in more developed versions, was mounted on a wheeled frame. The Romans made use of some artillery in sieges.

After taking a town, the Romans could be very ruthless, committing atrocities, especially if the town had not surrendered. All inhabitants could be killed or some sent into slavery, pillaging undertaken in a systematic way, and the town itself destroyed, as occurred, for example, at Carthage in 146 BC, at Numantia in 133 BC and at Jerusalem in AD 70. After the 1st century BC most sieges were not against towns but against the hill forts of northern and central Europe. In the 4th century the only real sieges in the western provinces were during civil wars. Other sieges at this time occurred mainly in Mesopotamia, in warfare against the Persians. Techniques similar to those of previous centuries were employed, including use of battering rams, siege mounds, siege towers and undermining.

WEAPONS AND EQUIPMENT

As the army came into military contact with new people, various weapons and armor of those cultures were assimilated, including those of the Italians, Etruscans and Greeks, and adapted to suit the needs of the Roman army. Hoplite weapons and armor spread to Rome at the end of the 7th century BC. From the 4th century BC in particular, contact with the Celts influenced many aspects of army equipment, such as weapons, *vexilla*, armor, saddles and other cavalry equipment. The influence of the Celts (including the Gauls) probably had the greatest effect on the Roman army.

Ancient historians state that in the 6th century BC, the less wealthy property-owning people were divided into five classes who supplied the infantry. Men of the first class were hoplites (heavy infantry) armed with a helmet, cuirass, spear, sword, round shield and greaves; the second class were medium spearmen armed with spear, sword, shield (*scutum*) and greaves; the third class were lighter spearmen and had spear, sword and shield; the fourth class were skirmishers and had spear and shield; and the fifth class were slingers armed with slings and stones.

Livy says that in the mid-4th century BC, the *leves* were armed with spears and javelins and the *triarii* were armed with spears. The *principes* and *hastati* were probably armed with heavy javelins (*pila*) and swords.

In the time of which Polybius was writing, the *velites* were armed with swords, javelins and a small circular shield (*parma*); the *hastati* and *principes* were armed with the short Spanish sword (*gladius hispaniensis*), two long javelins (pila) and an oval shield (*scutum*); and the *triarii* were armed with the *gladius hispaniensis*, the *scutum* and a thrusting spear (*hasta*). The cavalry were armed with a circular shield and a long spear.

Marius was responsible for some modifications to the equipment of the army. It is likely that the short spear (*hasta*) had already been abandoned in favor of the javelin (*pilum*) by the *triarii*, and with the absorption of the *velites* into the other units, there was a move toward all legionaries being equipped in the same way. Marius is credited with a modification to the *pilum*. About this time, the differences between the *hastati*, *principes* and *triarii* disappeared, and all legionaries were equipped with sword and *pilum* and wore a mail shirt. In the empire the auxiliary infantry also carried a sword and a short spear, and the differences between auxiliary and legionary arms and armor may have been minimal. From the mid-2nd century the standardized arms and armor began to be abandoned, and archaeological evidence for military equipment from the 3rd century is very sparse.

Manufacture

Originally soldiers provided their own equipment. When Marius persuaded the state to take on the responsibility for arming new recruits (especially as they now all needed to be equipped as heavy infantry), the authorities responded by mass-producing armor. Early in the empire special workshops appear to have been set up in various parts of the empire to produce armor, and some of the surviving mass-produced helmets are very poor in quality. In the early empire workshops (*fabricae*) in forts produced most of the army's equipment on a fairly large scale. The *immunes* provided the labor, and much scrap material was recycled. In the eastern Mediterranean equipment does not appear to have been produced by the army.

Cavalry Equipment

Sculptural evidence of saddles appears in the early empire, but they were used by the Gauls by at least the mid-1st century BC. The saddles had a pommel or horn at each corner, which gave the rider stability, as stirrups were not used until about the 6th century. Bronze horn plates may have protected the pommels. The saddle may have consisted of a wooden frame with padding and leather covers. A saddle cloth was worn under the saddle. Spurs (of bronze or iron) were used throughout the empire.

There were two types of bridle bit in the Roman period, the snaffle and the curb, both of iron. The snaffle bit was of Celtic origin and was used with both draft and riding horses. It consisted of a solid (plain) or jointed bar that went into the horse's mouth. The most common type had a two-link bar. There were free-moving rings at each end to hold the reins and harness. The complex Italian curb bit was designed to produce a rapid response from horses, and so was used for riding horses, especially cavalry. It consisted of a plain or jointed bar that went in the horse's mouth and a straight bar that went under the chin. Metal hackamores were also used in conjunction with bits and consisted of a bar running across the nose and under the chin. They prevented the horse from opening its mouth.

Armor

LEGIONARIES

In early Rome (8th–7th centuries BC) only the wealthiest soldiers wore armor, and then only a helmet and breastplate of beaten bronze. The most common form of body armor was the Greek-style bronze cuirass consisting of a front and back plate held in position by leather straps passed through loops on the back of the plates. They date to the early 7th century BC and continued in use to at least the end of the 6th century BC. Several examples of Greek-style greaves are known dating from the 6th century BC to the 4th or 3rd century BC, of a type with no shaping for the knees.

In the mid-2nd century BC the *velites* wore no armor other than a plain helmet sometimes covered with a wolf's skin. At this time the armor of the *principes* and *hastati* consisted of a small square breastplate about 200 mm (8 in) square called a heart guard (*pectorale*). It was a descendant of the square breastplate of the 4th century BC. They also wore one greave (on the left leg), although by the mid-1st century BC greaves were no longer worn.

Officers in the late republic and early empire wore a Greek-style uniform consisting of a muscled cuirass under which was a tunic, probably of leather, with *pteryges* (strips of leather or fabric for the protection of thighs and shoulders). This was worn over the military tunic. In the empire a centurion's armor was silvered, and he wore greaves that had otherwise fallen from use. Animal skins were worn by standard-bearers—the *aquilifer* wore lion skins and the others bear skins. Some armor was decorative, worn only on parades.

Around 300 BC mail armor (*lorica hamata*) was invented by the Celts, but it was expensive to make and was restricted to the aristocracy. It was adopted by the legionaries and was made from rings of iron or bronze (fig. 2.7). In the 2nd century BC wealthier legionaries wore mail shirts, which were extremely heavy, weighing about 15 kg (33 lb). The use of mail armor by legionaries declined in the early empire.

From the mid-1st century, a new type of armor for legionaries was devised—articulated plate armor. Known now as *lorica segmentata* (not the Roman name), it weighed about 9 kg (20 lb). Metal

PRAETORIAN GUARD

The Praetorian Guard wore conventional body armor, but in peacetime they had a dress uniform which was similar to that of the republican era. The cohort on duty at the palace wore togas.

AUXILIARIES

Auxiliaries varied from lightly armed troops such as slingers who wore no armor and possibly no shoes, to fully armed troops whose armor was identical to that of legionaries. Archers wore mail shirts that were a longer variety of the cavalry type.

CAVALRY

In the mid-2nd century BC cavalrymen wore a cuirass or mail armor. In the early empire legionary cavalrymen wore mail or scale armor. The mail armor consisted of a shirt and a cape weighing about 16 kg (35 lb); the shirt was split at the hips so that the rider could sit on the horse. At this time horses wore no armor but were decorated with pendant disks (*phalerae*) of tinned bronze of Celtic origin.

In the late 1st century Rome came into contact with the Roxolani, a Sarmatian tribe that used *cataphracti*: heavily armored cavalry with both men and horses covered in armor. Rome began to employ this type of cavalry, and the first regular unit of *cataphracti* is known under Hadrian (117–138).

In the 3rd century the use of body armor was restricted to the heavy cavalry (*cataphracti*), who continued to wear mail and scale shirts. In the 5th century some are portrayed with knee-length hooded scale or mail shirts that must have weighed 25 to 30 kg (55 to 66 lb), similar in style to those later worn by Norman knights. In the 4th century *cataphracti* were lightly armored cavalry and the *clibanarii* were heavily armored cavalry. A *clibanarius* (oven man, describing what it felt like in the armor) was more heavily armed, covered from head to foot in a combination of plate and scale armor. *Clibanarii* were first used (unsuccessfully) against Constantine in 312. They were used mainly as parade troops. Similar armor must have covered the body, head and neck of the horses of *cataphracti* and *clibanarii*.

*Fig. 2.5 Legionary soldier from the Ermine Street Guard wearing a cloak (*sagum*), an imperial Gallic helmet and* lorica segmentata *armor. He wears a belt with an apron and a baldric for suspension of the sword.*

plates were held together by leather straps on the interior and on the exterior by straps and buckles or by hooks. With the shortening of the shield, articulated shoulder guards were developed (fig. 2.5).

Lorica squamata also came to be used mainly in the 1st and 2nd centuries. It consisted of rows of overlapping iron or bronze scales. The scales were 10 to 50 mm (½ to 2 in) long and were held in place by wire ties passed through holes at the top of the scales then sewn to a fabric backing.

The evidence for the use of body armor from the 3rd century is less common. *Lorica segmentata* may not have been used, but *lorica hamata* and *lorica squamata* are known, as well as heavily armored cavalry.

Helmets

From earliest times at Rome, many different types of helmet are known to have been used by contemporary tribes. Most of these early helmets and later Roman examples are considerably oversized and were probably all worn with a thick padded undercap or lining, mainly of felt. In the 8th and 7th centuries BC Villanovan-type helmets were most common, made of two pieces of bronze joined along the edge of the crest. Another common type was the "bell" helmet, most of which have cast bronze crest holders drilled through the center to take a crest pin. The Negau type of helmet was most common from the 6th to the 4th centuries BC, possibly even 3rd century BC. It had a flat ring of bronze inside the rim with stitching holes to hold the inner cap, and normally a crest, sometimes transverse. The significance of these crests is uncertain.

The Montefortino-type helmet spread across the Celtic world and was adopted by the Roman army from the 4th century BC. It became the most common form of helmet in Italy and remained virtually unchanged for four centuries until the 1st century AD. After this date, it continued to be worn by the Praetorian Guard with their traditional republican armor. It is estimated that some 3 to 4 million of these helmets must have been made. The bronze helmets had scalloped (some triple) cheekpieces. Some had a topknot to hold a long horsehair crest or plume. Beneath the peaked neckguard was a double ring attachment for attaching straps to hold it in position.

A second type of helmet was similar to the Montefortino type but lacked the topknot. It is known as the Coolus helmet or jockey cap. Although never as popular as the Montefortino helmet, its use became widespread in the 1st century BC. It was a round capped bronze helmet with a small neckguard, and appears to have been the forerunner of the early 1st-century legionary helmet. The bronze Coolus helmet disappeared in the 1st century; from then on all helmets were of iron.

In the 1st century the Port type of helmet (from Port bei Nidau, Switzerland) developed from the Coolus helmet. It was made of iron and had a topknot, now with a slit to hold the crest. The Port helmet developed into the type known as the Imperial-Gallic helmet.

The Imperial-Gallic helmet, usually of iron, was similar to the Port helmet but had an enlarged neckguard and cheekpieces. There was also a reinforcing strip across the front of the helmet to protect the face from sword slashes, and stylized "eyebrows" on the helmet bowl. By the mid-1st century ear guards had been added, so that the legionary helmet now had all the characteristics of the next two centuries. Reinforcing braces were added to the crown of the helmet. Most Imperial-Gallic helmets had a Y-shaped crest support, with a hook at the front and back to hold the crest in place. Imperial-Italic helmets were similar but lacked the eyebrows (fig. 2.5).

In the early empire the crest of a centurion's helmet was turned so that it ran transversely across the helmet (transverse crested helmet). The helmet continued to be tied on with two straps under the chin and tied to the cheekpieces. The latest known legionary helmets are late 2nd or early 3rd century in date and have a deepened neckguard. There is very little evidence for 3rd-century infantry helmets, which are not seen again until the 4th century.

The cavalry wore helmets that covered the whole head, leaving only the eyes, nose and mouth visible, the ears being completely enclosed. Toward the end of the 1st century a reinforcing strip was also applied to the forehead. Like legionary helmets, these helmets were reinforced with cross braces in the 2nd century.

The Intercisa helmets of the 4th century are not related to the early legionary helmets and may have been introduced by mercenaries in the Danube region. They were crudely made of iron, with the cap in two pieces joined along the crest. A separate neckguard was usually attached to the lining, as were the cheekpieces. Several elaborate Intercisa helmets are known, probably belonging to the cavalry (from which the infantry ones may have been derived). These include bronze examples where the neckguard is attached to the cap by straps and buckles. Both infantry and cavalry helmets usually have a slit along the crown of the cap to hold a crest. By the beginning of the 5th century the caps of the helmets were made in four segments riveted to a frame, forerunners of early Medieval examples.

Shields

In the 8th to 7th centuries BC shields varied from large body-covering types to smaller round shields — the *clipeus*. They all had a central handgrip. Some very thin bronze shields are known that could only have been used for ceremonial purposes. Functional shields were probably of wood covered with leather and decorated with metal studs.

In the early republic (before the siege and capture of Veii in 396 BC), the new groups of infantry seem to have adopted a long curved oval body shield (*scutum*) that gave more protection than a round shield, particularly if the soldier squatted behind it. It was about 75 cm (2 ft 6 in) wide and about 1.2 m (4 ft) long, and was made of sheets of wood glued together and covered with canvas and leather. It had a spindle-shaped boss with a long spine (*spina*). By 340 BC the *scutum* had

Fig. 2.6 *Tombstone of a soldier from the VIII legion Augusta who served 21 years and died at age 40. He is shown with a rectangular* scutum, *a pilum, a sword, helmet and apron. Late 1st century.* Photo: Ralph Jackson.

become the standard shield for the legionaries, most of whom were armed with a throwing rather than a thrusting spear. The *scutum* was now reinforced with an iron rim. By this time the smaller round shield (*clipeus*) had been abandoned, probably because the phalanx had been abandoned. In the 1st century BC all legionaries carried the *scutum* (fig. 2.11).

In the mid-2nd century BC the *velites* were armed with a round shield (*parma*) about 0.9 m (3 ft) in diameter. At the same time, cavalrymen carried a round shield (*parma equestris*). In the early empire the cavalry used a flat oval or sometimes a hexagonal shield of Celtic origin. When not in use, the shield was carried alongside the horse, sometimes hung from the saddle or saddle cloth.

Early in the 1st century, the oval *scutum* was replaced by a shorter rectangular shield that retained the name *scutum*. At first this was just the old oval *scutum* with the top and bottom cut off, but later the sides were also squared off (fig. 2.6). The shield was made in the same way, with thin strips of wood about 2 mm (⅛ in) thick glued together to form a curved piece of plywood that was covered in leather. The face of the shield was decorated with a painted design (fig. 2.4). The rim of the rectangular *scutum*, was reinforced with bronze or iron binding. Evidence from this binding shows that the shields were about 6 mm (¼ in) thick, probably thicker at the center where they were hollowed out for a horizontal handgrip. The handgrip was protected by an iron or bronze boss that was now hemispherical in shape. Shields had a separate leather cover with a drawstring and a round hole in the front for the boss. A carrying strap was probably attached to these covers.

The only difference between many legionaries and auxiliaries in the empire was that the latter used the flat shield rather than the curved *scutum* which could be oval, hexagonal or sometimes rectangular (fig. 2.7). In the early empire standard-bearers carried round shields. In the 2nd century the *scutum* began to be phased out, and by the mid-3rd century it had been abandoned, to be replaced by the oval auxiliary shield. Hexagonal shields may have been part of the equipment of the *cataphractus*.

Spears and Javelins

In the 8th to 7th centuries BC, spearheads were made of bronze and possibly sometimes of iron. The size of

Fig. 2.7 An auxiliary soldier of the Ermine Street Guard wearing a helmet, cloak (sagum), tunic, sandals and lorica hamata armor. He has a belt for his sword and an apron, and carries a pilum *and a flat oval shield.*

the spearheads varied greatly from about 0.01 to 0.5 m (4 to 20 in). Some spears found in graves had a total length of 1.5 to 1.8 m (5 to 6 ft). In the 4th century BC the spear (a thrusting weapon) was superseded by a heavy javelin (a throwing weapon), probably of Etruscan origin. It became the primary offensive weapon of the Roman legion and was known as the *pilum*, and in the 4th century BC it was probably used by the *hastati*.

In the mid-2nd century BC the *hastati* and *principes* carried two long javelins (*pila*). By now there were two methods of attaching the *pilum* head to the wooden shaft — a socket or a flat tang. The thin *pilum* had a long iron socketed head over 0.9 m (3 ft) long. The thick *pilum* had a broad flat tang secured by two rivets. There were various other types of spear and javelin.

By the mid-2nd century BC long spears (*hastae*) were carried by the *triarii*. At this time the *velites* were armed with javelins (*hastae velitares*), smaller versions of the thin *pilum*. They had a small head 0.25 to 0.3 m (10 to 12 in) long and a wooden shaft about 0.9 m (3 ft) long. In the mid-2nd century BC the cavalry carried a sturdy spear with a butt spike that could be used if the spear broke.

Marius is credited with a modification to the *pilum* whereby one of the two iron rivets that held the spearhead to the wooden shaft was replaced by a wooden peg. This shattered on impact, disabling the weapon so that it could not be thrown back by the enemy. Marius previously found that the long iron head did not always bend on impact and the *pilum* could be reused by the enemy. Caesar overcame the problem by tempering the point but not the shaft of the *pilum* head. The heavy version of the *pilum* was modified in this way; the lighter version continued to have a socketed iron head and shaft into which the wooden element of the shaft was fitted.

Both types of *pilum* remained in use throughout the 1st and 2nd centuries, with heads about 0.65 to 0.75 m (26 to 30 in) long (figs. 2.6, 2.7). In the early empire the flat-tanged *pilum* was made lighter, and a heavier *pilum* was introduced with a round lead weight inserted at the junction of the wood and iron. Barbed examples are found in the 3rd century.

A spear with a barbed head weighted with lead is found in the 3rd and 4th centuries and was probably known as the *plumbata*. The head had a split socket, although some also have been found with spiked tangs. Legionaries in the 4th century were armed with a weighted dart (*martiobarbulus*). In the late 4th century the infantry was still armed with throwing weapons — the *spiculum*, *verutum* and *plumbata*, all possibly derived from the *pilum*. The *spiculum* had an iron head with a triangular section and was 0.2 m (8 in) long, with a wooden shaft about 1.6 m (5 ft 6 in) long. It had an ovoid weight, probably lead, between the wooden shaft and the short iron head. The *verutum* was originally called a *vericulum* and had a head 120 mm (4¾ in) long and a wooden shaft just over 1 m (3 ft 3 in).

The *contus* was a heavy lance about 3.5 m (12 ft) long used two-handed without a shield by the cavalry. The lance could be used by the cavalry, either by charging or throwing. Lance heads were made of iron, and the lance was about 1.8 m (6 ft) long.

Daggers

Daggers (*pugiones*, sing. *pugio*) are known from the 8th century BC, when they can be divided into three types based on the shape of their blades (leaf-shaped, triangular, or straight-sided blades that narrow two-thirds down to form a stiletto-type point). The blades were of iron or bronze, 0.25 to 0.4 m (10 to 16 in) long. Handles were of wood, bone or even stone, capped by a T-shaped pommel. Little is known of daggers until the 1st century AD when they were very similar to their Spanish ancestors, with blades 0.2 to 0.25 m (8 to 10 in) long. They had a distinctive waisted blade and a central midrib. The dagger seems to have disappeared from legionary equipment by the 2nd century, to reappear in a much cruder form as part of the auxiliary equipment in the early 3rd century. In the early empire legionaries wore the dagger on the left, while centurions wore the dagger on the right.

SCABBARDS

In the 8th to 7th centuries BC sheaths or scabbards were usually made of beaten bronze with a cast bronze chape. Later there were two main types of scabbard—one of iron plates joined together at the sides, usually highly decorated on the front plate with silver inlay and with a lining of wood or leather. The second type was of organic material (wood and leather) with a decorated iron plate on the front face. Both types were probably contemporary in the 1st century.

Swords

In the 8th to 7th centuries BC swords varied from long slashing weapons to shorter stabbing ones. The longer ones are known as antennae swords, after their cast bronze handle with spiral horns. The blades were usually of bronze, sometimes iron, and were about 0.3 to 0.55 m (12 to 22 in) long. The short Spanish sword seems to have been adopted from Spanish auxiliaries serving with Hannibal in the late 3rd century BC. In the mid-2nd century BC, the *hastati* were armed with this short cut-and-thrust sword (*gladius hispaniensis*, Spanish sword). It had a two-edged blade about 0.5 m (20 in.) long tapering to a point.

In the 1st century AD swords still had the dagger shape and long tapering point of the earlier Spanish sword. The blades were 0.5 to 0.55 m (20 to 22 in.) long (fig. 2.6). Later on in the century a new sword was introduced with straight parallel sides and a shorter point. It owes little to the Spanish sword but was still called the *gladius hispaniensis*. The blade was 0.45 to 0.55 m (18 to 22 in.) long. In the late 2nd and early 3rd century the *gladius* was gradually replaced by the *spatha*, a sword about 0.7 m (2 ft 4 in) long. By the end of the 3rd century all legionaries carried it.

In the early empire much of the cavalry was Celtic and used the long *spatha* sword with a blade length of about 0.6 to 0.85 m (2 ft to 2 ft 9 in) derived from the long Celtic sword (fig. 2.1). At that time, legionaries and cavalrymen wore the sword on the right, the centurions wore it on the left and the *aquilifer* wore it on either side. From about 200 legionaries and cavalrymen began to wear the sword on the left side, possibly because of the abandonment of the *scutum* and adoption of the longer *spatha*.

Belts

During the early 1st century the sword and dagger were suspended from two individual belts that crossed over at the front and back. From these belts was suspended an "apron" of metal disks riveted to leather straps (figs. 2.6, 2.7, 2.11). Later a single military waist belt (*cingulum militare* or *balteus*) was substituted to which the dagger and apron were attached, but the sword was suspended from a baldric on the right (later the left) side (fig. 2.5). The belts were covered with rectangular plates usually made of bronze plated with tin, and many with enamel decoration from the 2nd century. The aprons continued to be worn with up to eight straps.

During the 3rd century the *cingulum* was replaced by a leather belt often worn on the hips rather than the waist. The sword was suspended from a wide decorated baldric. In the 4th century the influence of mercenaries led to the belt and baldric being abandoned in favor of the Germanic belt.

Clothing

Two types of cloak were worn by auxiliaries and legionaries—the *sagum* (draped around the shoulders and fastened with a brooch—figs. 2.5, 2.7) and the *paenula* (a large cape with an opening in the center). Footwear consisted of the *caliga*, a heavy hobnailed sandal (fig. 2.7), although in the later empire civilian footwear appears to have been worn instead.

Bows

Archers used the composite bow, which was much smaller than the English longbow. It was made of wood strengthened on the inside of the curve with horn and on the outside with sinew. A pair of horn nocks, to which the string was attached, reinforced each end. Arrows had wood or reed shafts, and arrowheads were of iron, sometimes bone. There were also fire arrows. When not in use, bows were unstrung to preserve the elastic qualities of the sinew and were kept for protection in a leather bow case or quiver. Arrows were also kept in the case, especially as the glue attaching the fletchings to the shaft could be affected by rain.

Caltrops

Caltrops were sets of usually four spikes joined at an angle at their blunt end. When dropped, one spike of the caltrop always projected upward. They were scattered on the ground against cavalry.

Artillery

Artillery was used in battles and in sieges. From the late republic the Romans used bolt-shooting machines and stone-throwers that had twisted ropes for torsion, and worked on the principles of a crossbow. The *ballistae* were two-armed stone-throwing machines that could hurl stones up to 0.5 km (a third of a mile) distance and could breach walls of brick and wood, although they were less effective against dressed stone. This type of machine may have continued in use to the early 3rd century but was obsolete by the 4th century.

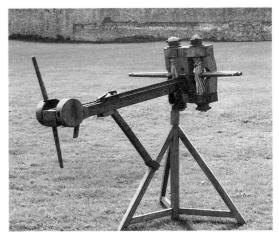

Fig. 2.8 Reconstruction (by the Ermine Street Guard) of a catapulta *bolt-firing machine.*

Catapultae (sing. *catapulta*) were two-armed machines that fired iron bolts or arrows (figs. 2.8, 2.9). Some were fairly portable, and the smaller ones were called *scorpiones*. They had a range of 300 m (990 ft) or more. The standard bolt-head had a square-sectioned tapering point, a neck of varying length and a socket, and was mostly 60 to 80 mm (2 to 3 in) long. In the 4th century the term *ballista* was used for bolt-

Fig. 2.9 Reconstruction (by the Ermine Street Guard) of an onager *stone-throwing machine. On its right is a* catapulta.

or arrow-shooting machines, and the stone-throwing *ballista* had gone out of use. The *carro-ballista* seems to have been mounted on a cart drawn by mules.

A new machine for hurling stones was used in the 4th century. This was the *onager* (pl. *onagri*), a fairly primitive one-armed torsion engine or sling that hurled large stone balls like a mortar (fig. 2.9). Due to vibration, it had to be fired on a solid platform. Ancient writers sometimes incorrectly called this machine a *scorpio*.

Musical Instruments

There were several different types of Roman military instrument, which were used for giving various signals and were all valveless (fig. 7.11). The *cornu* was a large curved instrument, played by a *cornicen*, similar to a French horn. The *tuba* was a long trumpet over 1 m (3 ft 3 in) long and was played by a *tubicen*. These two instruments were used for giving commands, whereas the *bucina* and *lituus* were probably for ceremonial occasions. The *bucina* (played by a *bucinator*) was possibly a trumpet or horn, while the *lituus* was possibly an elongated J-shaped instrument.

Chariots

Chariots were known from the 7th century BC but were never used by the Romans in battle, only in triumphal processions. However, peoples such as the Celts used chariots against Roman forces in battle.

Fig. 2.10 Scenes on Trajan's Column showing preparations for the Dacian wars. Bottom frieze: [left] *a harbor town and port with boats on the Danube*; [center] *river god Danuvius*; [right] *legionaries carry their equipment and march out of a fort or town gate over a pontoon bridge.* Upper frieze: [left] *Trajan addresses legionaries and auxiliaries*; [center and right] *legionaries build a fort of turves with timber walkways, while two auxiliaries remain on guard.*

Carriage of Weapons and Equipment

On the march, much equipment was carried by mules in long baggage trains. From the time of Marius, legionaries carried much more of the equipment on their backs, so reducing the size of baggage trains, which slowed down the army on the march. This earned the soldiers the nickname of "Marius' mules." Mules now carried tents and surplus baggage, while the legionaries carried their weapons and some other equipment. Their shields hung from their left shoulders and they carried javelins and palisade stakes for overnight camps. They marched bareheaded, with their helmets strapped to their right shoulders, but were otherwise fully armed. Over their left shoulder, each legionary carried a pole with a crossbar at the top to which his luggage was tied (fig. 2.10). Among the main luggage was a bronze mess tin (*patera*), cooking pot or bucket and a leather bag with a handle for clothes and personal belongings. A sack at the top probably held emergency rations for three days. In the 4th century the *comitatenses* had to carry rations for 20 days. Tools also had to be carried, including a saw, basket, pickax (*dolabra*), sickle, leather strap and chain, and sometimes an entrenching tool or turf cutter and double-ended wooden stakes (erroneously called *pila muralia*). It is likely that not every legionary carried every tool.

Normally soldiers would march about 30 km (18 mi) a day, but up to 50 km (30 mi) was common under forced marches. For crossing rivers, a bridge of boats (fig. 2.10) or timber piles could be used. (See chapter 5.)

MILITARY STANDARDS

The standards (fig. 7.11) were symbols identifying individual units. They also provided a rallying point during battle. It is therefore likely that the Roman army employed some kind of standard from earliest times. According to Pliny the Elder, when Marius reformed the legionary standards in 104 BC, a variety already were in use, with images of an eagle, wolf, minotaur, horse and boar. Marius kept the eagle as the legionary standard and abolished the others, although standards still identified subunits within legions. By the time of Julius Caesar, each legionary eagle standard (*aquila*) was made of silver and gold (fig. 2.11). It was the special responsibility of the *primus pilus* and never left camp unless the whole legion was on the move.

During the empire, the eagle was made entirely of gold, and each legion also had a portrait of the emperor (*imago*). There were also flags (*vexilla*) of Celtic origin, one of which belonged to the legion while others were used by detachments (*vexillationes*) serving away from the legion. The legion could also have a specific emblem, often a sign of the zodiac, which was usually connected with the origin of the legion or an incident in its history. Within the legion, each century had an individual standard called a *signum* (pl. *signa*). The standard of the Praetorian Guard carried images of the emperor and his family, crowns and victories.

Within the auxiliary cavalry, each *ala* had its own flag (*vexillum*), and each *turma* had a standard.

The standards were very important to the army. As cult symbols they were worshipped at various times during the year. In a fortress they were kept in a shrine in the *principia*, and if the standards were lost during a campaign, the unit suffering the loss might be disbanded.

MILITARY DECORATIONS

A system of rewards to the army gradually developed (parallel with a system of punishment). Initially rewards were a share of the spoils, a system that was widely used in the republic.

Military decorations (*dona militaria*) are recorded from the mid-5th century BC to the early 3rd century AD, although a few examples are known after this date. They could be awarded to soldiers who were citizens. A whole range of decorations existed depending, in the republic, on the deed performed. In the empire awards were standardized according to rank, except for the *corona civica*. By the 1st century BC there were several types of crown. The *corona obsidionalis* (siege crown) was the highest honor, given for raising a siege. It was made of grass or other vegetation from the area of the siege. The *corona civica* (civic crown) was next in importance, awarded for saving the life of a citizen. It was made of oak leaves and was sometimes known as the *corona querca* (oak crown). It was adopted as an imperial emblem, frequently appearing on coins.

The *corona muralis* (mural crown) was a gold crown ornamented with battlements, awarded for being the first to gain entry to a besieged town. The first to gain entry to an enemy camp was awarded the *corona vallaris* (rampart crown), made of gold ornamented with a rampart. The gold *corona navalis* (naval crown,

also called the *corona classica* or *rostrata*), was awarded in the empire to men of consular rank, and no longer had any connection with the sea. There was also a *corona aurea* (gold crown).

Other awards (fig. 2.11) included pairs of gold torques (neck rings), armlets (*armillae*) and *phalerae*, which were gold, silver or bronze disks decorated in high relief with mythological creatures. *Phalerae* were awarded in sets, usually nine, and were worn over the chest on a leather harness. The *vexillum* (flag) was also given as a decoration and was awarded to senior officers. It may have been an exact replica of the legionary and auxiliary *vexillum*, although some were silver copies. The *hasta pura* (ceremonial spear) was awarded for wounding an enemy in single combat. It appears to have resembled a spear with a small head, but its precise nature is uncertain.

It was rare for individual auxiliary troops to win military decorations, although whole units could be honored and even granted immediate citizenship as a reward.

Fig. 2.11 Legionary aquilifer, *first half of 1st century, with the eagle standard. In his left hand is an oval shield* (scutum). *He wears a tunic and mail shirt, a set of* phalerae, *two torques and two armlets. From his belt is suspended an apron.* Photo: Ralph Jackson.

TRIUMPHS

Triumphs were the celebratory procession of a victorious general and were the highest military honor of a general. They were Etruscan in origin and were guided by strict religious rules. The general had to hold a magistracy with *imperium* (not a prerequisite later on), to have won a decisive victory over a foreign enemy with over 5,000 of the enemy killed and to have brought home at least a token army. Although not common, 100 triumphs were held between 220 and 70 BC. The Senate had to allow the victorious general (*triumphator*) to retain his *imperium* inside Rome for one day, which he entered on a gilded chariot drawn by four horses, with a procession of magistrates, senators, soldiers, spoils, prisoners and sacrificial animals. The spectacular procession started in the Campus Martius, outside the city, to the Capitol, where a sacrifice was made at the temple of Jupiter Capitolinus, and one or more prisoners were executed.

Fig. 2.12 One of two triumphal arches erected by Septimius Severus in 203–204 after his wars against the Parthians and Arabs. The arch is in the Forum, Rome. Height 20.6 m (67 ft 6 in).

If a triumph was not allowed, an *ovatio* (ovation) was usually granted. This was less spectacular than a triumph, and the general entered Rome on foot or horseback (not chariot), wearing the *toga praetexta* and wreathed in myrtle. The use of the *ovatio* was sporadic, last recorded in 47.

Triumphs by generals outside the imperial family were forbidden by Augustus and by subsequent emperors because of the attention paid to one particular military person.

Triumphal arches were also erected to commemorate victories (fig. 2.12). (See chapter 4.)

CAMPS, FORTS AND FORTRESSES

During the republic military compaigns were conducted in the summer, at the end of which the legions were disbanded and the men returned home. There was therefore no need for more than overnight camps (marching camps), which were temporary fortifications to give protection against surprise attack. As Rome's territory expanded and the campaign season lengthened, there was an increasing need for legions to stay away from home for more than just the summer. Winter camps (*hiberna*) were therefore used as well as the temporary summer camps (*castra aestiva*). Winter camps were built in allied territory or in newly conquered regions, and had more substantial accommodation and stronger defenses. As Roman territory continued to expand in the late republic, some camps were used as semipermanent bases, but it was not until the early 1st century that frontiers were established and permanent camps (*castra stativa*) were built.

Camps (fig. 2.14)

The term camp usually refers to an overnight or temporary base (fig. 2.10). It was sited near water, on open ground (preferably raised ground) that did not offer cover to the enemy. The best viewpoint was selected for the general's tent (*praetorium*—from *praetor*, originally the chief magistrate), and the camp was

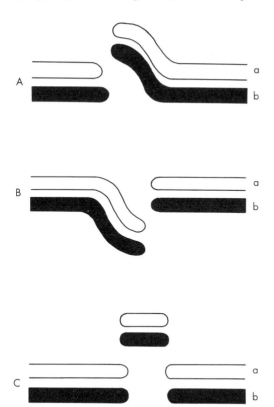

Fig. 2.13 Entrances of camps. a. external ditch; b. inner rampart. A. external clavicula. *B. internal* clavicula *C.* titulum

then laid out by a military surveyor using a *groma*. The three distinctive types of camp entrance known in Britain (fig. 2.13) are clavicular, Agricolan (or Stracathro) and titular (often erroneously called tutular). Tents, not buildings, were used for accommodation. Legionary tents (*papiliones*, literally "butterflies") covered an area 3 m (10 ft) square including guy ropes. Tents were made of leather and accommodated eight men and their equipment. Officers' tents were of various designs, some of which are shown on Trajan's Column (fig. 7.11). Tent pegs were of iron and wood.

POLYBIAN CAMPS (fig. 2.14)

The earliest surviving description of a marching camp is by Polybius in the mid-2nd century BC. He describes a camp designed to hold two legions and an equivalent number of allied troops, totaling around 16,800 infantry and 1,800 cavalry. The camp was square, with each side about 2,000 Roman feet (600 m; 1,950 ft) long defended by a ditch (*fossa*) outside a rampart (*agger*) that was surmounted by a palisade of wooden stakes. There were four entrances.

The site of the consul's tent (*praetorium*) was the point from which the rest of the fort was marked out by the surveyors. The *praetorium* faced the *via principalis* (main street) through a gap between the tents of the tribunes and was flanked on its left by the *forum* (an open marketplace). On its right, the *praetorium* was flanked by the *quaestorium*—the tent of the *quaestor* (a junior magistrate in charge of finance). The *forum* and *quaestorium* were in turn flanked by the tents of the cavalry (*extraordinarii equites*). Along the *via principalis* were tents of the tribunes.

Behind the area occupied by the *praetorium*, *quaestorium* and *forum* were the tents of the selected allied cavalry and infantry (*extraordinarii equites, extraordinarii pedites*) and local auxiliary troops. The tents of legionaries, flanked by tents of the allied troops, filled up the remaining space beyond the *via principalis*. The tents were divided into blocks by right-angle streets and by the *via quintana* (fifth street), which ran parallel to the *via principalis* at the fifth cohort.

Between the tents and the rampart was an open space about 200 Roman feet (61 m; 198 ft) wide called the *intervallum*, so that the tents were out of range of burning missiles, there was room to accommodate cattle and booty and there was good access between the tents and the rampart.

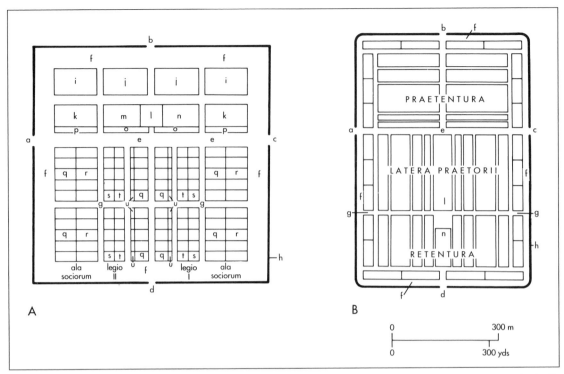

Fig. 2.14 A. *Polybian camp; B. Hyginian camp: a.* porta principalis sinistra, *b.* porta praetoria, *c.* porta principalis dextra, *d.* porta decumana, *e.* via principalis, *f.* intervallum, *g.* via quintana, *h.* rampart and ditch, *i.* auxilia, *j.* extraordinarii equites *and* pedites, *k.* extraordinarii, *l.* praetorium, *m.* forum, *n.* quaestorium, *o. tribunes, p. prefects, q.* equites, *r.* pedites, *s.* hastati, *t.* principes, *u.* triarii

HYGINIAN CAMPS (fig. 2.14)

The other full account of a marching camp comes from Hyginus writing in the empire. (See chapter 6.) The camp that he describes was designed to accommodate three legions and assorted auxiliary troops, with an approximate total of 40,000 men. The camp was rectangular with rounded corners. Its sides were about 490 by 705 m (1,620 by 2,320 ft), and so allowed much less space per man than the one described by Polybius. It was surrounded by a ditch outside a rampart of earth, turf or stone, with extra ditches protecting the gateways. The ditch was at least 1.5 m (5 ft) wide and 1 m (3 ft 3 in) deep while the rampart was about 2.4m (8 ft) wide by 1.8 m (6 ft) high.

The area within the camp was again divided into three portions by the *via principalis* and the *via quintana*, but the *praetorium* was situated in the middle of the central portion, which was called the *latera praetorii*. In this area was also the *auguratorium* (place for religious sacrifices), the *tribunal* (from which the commander addressed the troops), the tents of the commander's personal staff and the tents of the praetorian troops. These were flanked by the tents of troops of the first cohort and vexillations of troops from one of the legions.

The front portion of the camp, from the *via principalis* to the *porta praetoria* (front gate), was called the *praetentura*. Within this area were the tents of the legionary legates and tribunes, *valetudinarium* (hospital), *veterinarium* (where sick horses were treated), *fabrica* (workshop) and the quarters of specialist troops such as engineers and scouts. Also in this area were the *alae* of auxiliary cavalry and the *scholae* (meeting places) of the first cohorts.

The rear portion of the camp, the *retentura*, contained the *quaestorium* of the camp prefect where prisoners and booty were kept and the rest of the auxiliary troops. Around the perimeter of each part of the camp, nearest to the rampart, were the tents of the legionary cohorts, since these troops were thought more trustworthy than the auxiliaries. The *intervallum* was only about 18 m (60 ft) wide and there was also a perimeter road (*via sagularis*).

These two types of marching camp, although around 250 years apart in date, are recognizably similar, showing gradual development rather than radical change. This was probably due to the importance of having a standard plan for a marching camp so that a large group of men and animals could be accommodated rapidly. Marching camps with palisades were still used by *comitatenses* in the 4th century.

Forts and Fortresses

With the establishment of frontiers in the 1st century, permanent camps (forts and fortresses) were increasingly used to house troops in border areas. The "playing card" plan (rectangular with rounded corners) of the camps continued to be used. A distinction is usually made between fortresses, which were permanent camps designed to accommodate a legion (although some earlier fortresses appear to have accommodated a larger force), and forts, which were permanent camps for auxiliaries, smaller units of legionaries or a mixture of both. The internal area was determined by the size of the garrison. Fortresses were approximately 20 hectares (50 acres). Forts were 1 to 5.5 hectares (2.5 to 13.5 acres), according to the size and type of unit.

In the 1st and 2nd centuries forts and fortresses broadly conformed to the basic layout of the marching camp, with changes made to improve their suitability for a permanent garrison. These changes included strengthening the defenses with improved ramparts and ditches and the use of various traps and obstacles such as pits, sharpened stakes, thorn hedges and entanglements of thorn branches. The defenses of the permanent camps in the 1st and 2nd centuries were like those of towns, usually with a wall or rampart fronted by a narrow V-shaped ditch. The walls had gates defended by towers, normally rectangular, which did not protrude beyond the lines of the walls. There were sometimes corner and interval towers, also built within the lines of the wall.

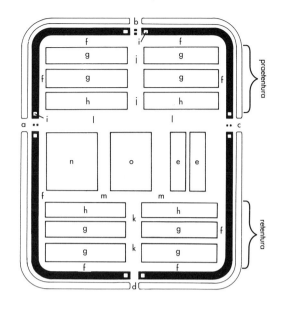

Fig. 2.15 Plan of a fort. a. porta principalis sinistra, *b.* porta praetoria, *c.* porta principalis dextra, *d.* porta decumana, *e.* horrea, *f.* intervallum, *g. barracks* (centuriae), *h. storebuildings/stables, i.* guard tower, *j.* via praetoria, *k.* via decumana, *l.* via principalis, *m.* via quintana, *n.* praetorium, *o.* principia. *The scale is arbitrary since fort sizes vary greatly.*

Forts and fortresses were divided down the center by the *via praetoria* and by the *via decumana* (because it was originally next to the tenth maniples). Laterally, forts and fortresses were divided by the *via principalis* (fig. 2.15). The buildings of permanent camps were originally of timber, but from the mid-1st century in Germany and at the end of the 1st century in Britain, they were being rebuilt in stone. Barrack blocks rather than tents were used to house troops, which were generally sited around the perimeter of the fort or fortress, about 30 m (100 ft) from the rampart, out of range of missiles. The centuries were housed in pairs (on the old maniple system), and each barrack block had ten or 11 sets of double rooms. Each double room consisted of a large bedroom about 4.5 m (15 ft) square for eight legionaries and a small room for their equipment. At the end of the barrack block were the centurion's living quarters and offices.

Bathhouses were introduced into legionary fortresses from the mid-1st century, and they also became common in or outside auxiliary forts. Amphitheaters (*ludi*) were provided outside fortress walls, but it is unclear if they were used for entertainment or for drill and exercise. There were also granaries and stores (*horrea*) for food. The increased administration needed for a permanent garrison led to the separation of the commander's office from his residence. The legionary headquarters (*principia*) now took the central position of the fortress, with the commander's residence (*praetorium*) being adjacent. The standards were kept in a shrine (*sacellum*) in the *principia*. The *principia*, *praetorium* and granaries were grouped together in the central range of buildings.

Under Diocletian many substantial rectangular forts were constructed in strategic frontier zones. They had stone walls at least 3 m (10 ft) thick, projecting towers and heavily defended gates. From the late 3rd century Roman fortifications were intended for prolonged static defense, and the defenses for towns and forts were similar. Late Roman walls required a wider berm for stability as they no longer had revetted embankments but were thick curtain walls of concrete rubble faced with masonry. There was a wide variety of building techniques, including brick facing, small ashlar with bonding courses of brick, and even irregular masonry and reused masonry were common. Towers or bastions projected above the walls for observation and also projected beyond the curtain wall for the deployment of artillery. Towers could be round, semicircular, D-shaped, fan-shaped, polygonal or rectangular. In front of the wide berm were wide flat-bottomed ditches.

In the late empire many existing forts and fortresses also had their fortifications updated, and numerous new forts built from the time of Diocletian were on elevated ground, which imposed an irregular shape on the defenses. Forts built or strengthened from the late 3rd century around the southeast coast of Britain are known as forts of the Saxon shore (a term used in the *Notitia Dignitatum*, probably signifying a shore threatened by attack from Saxons). The most characteristic element of the late Roman frontier defense is the *burgus*, a free-standing tower. These towers were small square structures, solidly built and more than one story high. Some were protected by an outer breastwork. They were first used from the 2nd century for frontier defense.

FRONTIERS

Limes means a trackway but came to mean a military road with a line of frontier forts and later a frontier zone. As Rome increased its territory, there was a continuous problem of holding frontiers, followed by

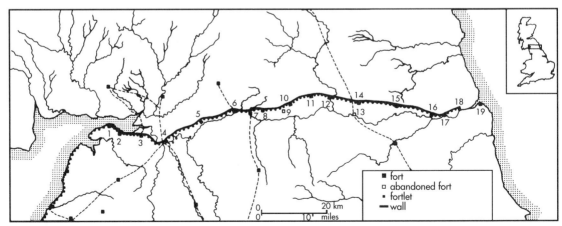

Fig. 2.16 Hadrian's Wall: 1. Bowness; 2. Drumburgh; 3. Burgh-by-Sands; 4. Stanwix; 5. Castlesteads; 6. Birdoswald; 7. Carvoran; 8. Great chesters; 9. Chesterholm; 10. Housesteads; 11. Carrawburgh; 12. Chesters; 13. Corbridge; 14. Halton Chesters; 15. Rudchester; 16. Benwell; 17. Newcastle; 18. Wallsend; 19. South Shields.

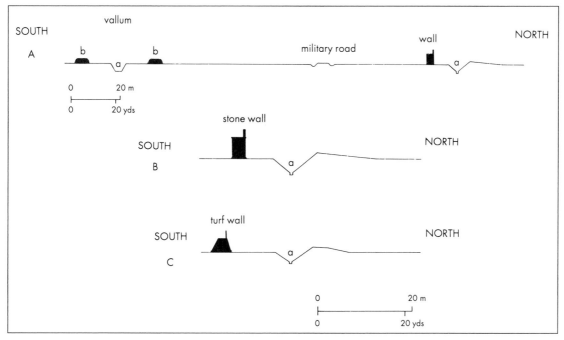

Fig. 2.17 Cross sections of: A. Hadrian's Wall zone; B. Hadrian's Wall; C. Antonine Wall (with reconstructed parapet): a. ditch, b. bank.

renewed expansion. When he came to power in the early 2nd century, Hadrian embarked on an entirely different policy from that of his predecessor, Trajan, consolidating the frontiers and abandoning provinces difficult to hold. The policy of subsequent emperors was subject to change, and from the 3rd century there were increasing pressures on the frontiers from invading tribes. Diocletian and his colleagues restored the old frontiers, except for the area beyond the Rhine and Danube rivers, southern Egypt and western Mauretania. From Diocletian (284–305) to Valentinian I (364–375), 6,400 km (4,000 mi) of frontier and lines of communication were fortified, with many bases for the new troops.

Hadrian's Wall (figs. 2.16, 2.17)

Hadrian established the building of a frontier wall (Hadrian's Wall) in northern Britain. Construction began in 122 from Newcastle to Bowness-on-Solway, later extended eastward to Wallsend. This frontier defense originally consisted of a wall with a pre-existing line of forts behind it. These forts were part of a previous frontier, known now as the Stanegate.

Hadrian's Wall was 117 km (73 mi) long, 3.1 m (10 ft) thick, and probably 4.65 to 6.2 m (15 to 20 ft) high, with a parapet and battlements. The wall was built in stone, in short lengths by centuries, and these lengths were marked by inscribed stones (centurial stones). The western section of the wall was constructed in turf (turf wall), possibly because limestone for mortar was not so readily available in this area.

Eighty fortlets (milecastles) were built, one every Roman mile (about 1,480 m or 4,856 ft), with two intermediate turrets or watchtowers about 490 m (1,618 ft) apart. The milecastles were built in turf along the turf wall and in stone elsewhere. They accommodated patrol troops and had internal buildings of stone or timber, and north and south gates. The turrets were all of stone, about 5 m (16 ft 6 in) square, with an upper story. In front of the

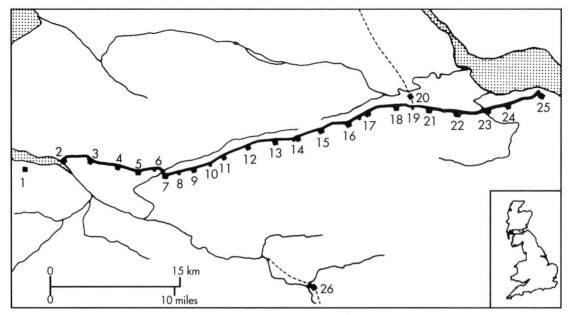

Fig. 2.18 Antonine Wall with forts and fortlets: 1. Bishopton; 2. Old Kilpatrick; 3. Duntocher (fort and fortlet); 4. Castlehill; 5. Bearsden; 6. Summerston (fortlet); 7. Balmuildy; 8. Wilderness Plantation (fortlet); 9. Cadder; 10. Glasgow Bridge (fortlet); 11. Kirkintilloch; 12. Auchendavy; 13. Bar Hill; 14. Croy Hill (fort and fortlet); 15. Westerwood; 16. Castlecary; 17. Seabegs fort and Seabegs Wood fortlet; 18. Rough Castle; 19. Watling Lodge (fortlet); 20. Camelon; 21. Falkirk; 22. Mumrills; 23. Inveravon; 24. Kinneil (fort and fortlet); 25. Carriden; 26. Bothwellhaugh.

wall was a broad berm and a V-shaped ditch about 8 m (26 ft) wide and about 3 m (10 ft) deep.

The first phase of the wall was altered before completion: The forts were transferred to the wall, and the broad wall was completed as a narrow wall 2.25 m (7 ft 6 in) wide. The forts were normally built astride the wall at about 10 km (6 mi) intervals. About 35 m (115 ft) to the south of the wall was a ditch (described by antiquarians as the *vallum* although the *vallum* should actually mean the wall) (fig. 2.17). The *vallum* was 3 m (10 ft) deep, 6 m (20 ft) wide at the top and had a mound 6 m (20 ft) wide on either side. It probably served as a boundary marker, keeping civilians away. A line of fortlets and turrets was built along the Cumbria coast, linked by a palisade and ditch. There were also outpost forts. The wall underwent a complex history of alteration, abandonment and reuse. It may have been completely abandoned only at the end of the 4th century.

Antonine Wall (figs. 2.17, 2.18)

In 138 Antoninus Pius succeeded Hadrian and extended the British frontier to Scotland, where the Antonine Wall was built. Construction began c. 140, initially to replace Hadrian's Wall as a frontier in a more northerly position across the Forth-Clyde isthmus. The wall was built of turf and clay on a stone base 4.5 m (15 ft) wide. The rampart was probably at least 3 m (10 ft) high with a wooden parapet and a ditch to the north (fig. 2.18). The wall was built in sections that were marked by distance slabs. The forts along the wall were smaller and more closely spaced than those along Hadrian's Wall — about 13 km (8 mi) apart. The fort ramparts were usually of turf, with main buildings in stone and others in timber. There were also fortlets, but no turrets, although beacon platforms made of turf have been found projecting from the south side of the wall, probably forming a system of long-distance signaling. Like Hadrian's

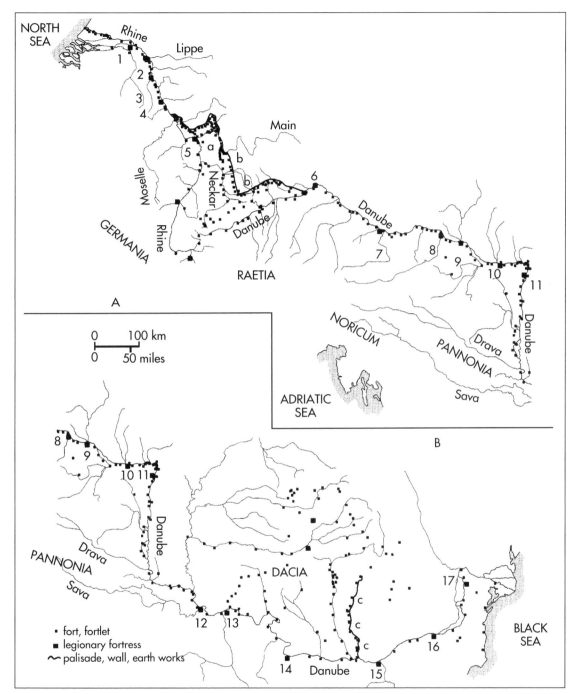

Fig. 2.19   Rhine-Danube frontier. A. German-Raetian limes *to the Middle Danube. B. Middle Danube, Lower Danube and Dacia. a. Odenwald* limes; *b. outer* limes; *c.* limes Transalutanus. *1. Nijmegen; 2. Xanten; 3. Neuss; 4. Bonn; 5. Mainz; 6. Regensburg; 7. Lorch; 8. Vienna; 9. Carnuntum; 10. Szöny; 11. Budapest; 12. Belgrade; 13. Kostolac; 14. Arar; 15. Stuklen; 16. Swisjtow; 17. Igliţa.*

Wall, the Antonine Wall underwent a series of changes. It may have been abandoned in the late 150s or in 163, the troops withdrawing to Hadrian's Wall.

Rhine-Danube Frontier (fig. 2.19)

During much of the empire the Rhine and Danube rivers formed the boundary of the European provinces, a distance of over 4,000 km (2,500 mi). From Claudius' reign (41–54), the west bank of the upper Rhine and south bank of the Danube were fortified with forts linked by roads. The Upper German *limes* was built c. 90, under Domitian, from the Rhine to the Danube and consisted of a road, watchtowers and fortlets. This line was later altered and made more permanent. Also under Domitian the Odenwald *limes* was constructed between the Main and Neckar rivers as a road with watchtowers, forts and fortlets. In the early 2nd century a similar fortification line was built along Raetia's northern boundary (Raetian *limes*).

Hadrian consolidated this German-Raetian *limes*, marking the frontier between the Rhine and Danube with a substantial wooden fence or palisade (except where the Rhine, Main and Neckar formed part of the boundary) and with forts, fortlets and timber watchtowers. This artificial frontier went from just south of Bonn to near Regensburg, a distance of about 450 km (280 mi). The watchtowers were gradually replaced by square stone towers.

By the early 2nd century there were lines of forts and watchtowers of timber or stone along the banks of the Danube. The frontier extended into Dacia and included the *limes Transalutanus*, a linear earthwork marking the eastern boundary of the province. It returned to the Danube when Dacia was abandoned. Various stretches of frontier earthworks are known in this area.

Antoninus Pius abandoned the Odenwald *limes*, moving to the outer *limes*, with a new palisade and stone watchtowers (none in timber), forts and fortlets. This was the last forward movement of the German-Raetian *limes* and remained for 100 years. A rampart and ditch (*Pfahlgraben*) was constructed behind the palisade of the outer *limes*, possibly in the late 2nd century. About the same time a stone wall (*Teufelsmauer*—Devil's Wall) 1.2 m (4 ft) wide replaced the palisade in Raetia.

Soon after 259–260, the Agri Decumates was abandoned and the frontier was again based on the Rhine and Danube, heavily reinforced by fortification on and behind the rivers. Chains of *burgi* (free-standing watchtowers) were built along stretches of the rivers between the forts. Towns behind the frontiers were also fortified with walls. By the early 5th century the frontier could no longer be held.

Eastern Frontier

The frontier in the east was a serious problem for centuries and was more of a military zone of forts than a physical barrier. It went from the Black Sea to the Red Sea, a distance of 1,400 km (870 mi), passing over varied and difficult terrain. The early imperial defenses relied on a buffer zone of client states and their armies, but these later disappeared. Particularly in the early empire, many military units were stationed in existing towns, but more forts and fortresses were built from the late 1st century. There was a major reorganization under Diocletian (284–305): the Strata Diocletiana was a military road from Sura on the Euphrates to the Via Nova Traiana in Arabia, and many forts and fortlets were built or rebuilt.

Africa

Like the eastern frontier, the frontier in Africa was more of a military zone than a physical barrier. This southernmost frontier of the empire was about 4000 km (2,500 mi) long. By Hadrian's time in Egypt there was a series of roads and forts in the Eastern Desert and along the southern Nile. The coastal zone of north Africa had numerous forts and fortlets. Hadrian may have been responsible for the *fossatum Africae* in Algeria and Tunisia, which consisted of stretches of ditch 2.5 m (8 ft 2 in) deep, with a mud brick wall not more than 2.5 m (8 ft 2 in) high and interval towers.

READING

History of the Legions
Anderson 1987: army of the early empire; Connolly 1981: development of the army; Grant 1974; Holder 1982: legions of 1st–4th centuries in Britain; Keppie 1984: army of the republic and early empire; Mann 1983: recruitment in various legions to Diocletian; Tomlin 1981 and 1987: late Roman army; Watson 1987: republican army; Webster 1985: army of the early empire; Welsby 1982: late Roman forces in Britain, including *laeti* and *foederati*.

Numbering and Stations of Legions
Balsdon 1970; Cornell and Matthews 1982; Holder 1982: legions of 1st–4th centuries in Britain; Keppie 1984: legions of the republic and early empire; Mann 1983, table 33: legionary movements and stations to 230; Webster 1985, 102–9: legions of the early empire.

Organization of Legions
Anderson 1987: army in the early empire; Connolly 1981: earlier republican army; Dobson 1981: army of the republic and empire; Grant 1974: the imperial army; Holder 1982: legions in Britain; Keppie 1984: army up to the early empire; Mann 1977: 4th-century army; Maxfield 1981, 21–32, 40–41: career structure and officers; Shelton 1988: army in the republic and empire; Tomlin 1981a and 1987: late Roman army; Watson 1987: republican army; Webster 1985: army in the early empire.

Alae Sociorum
Keppie 1984.

Garrison at Rome
Dobson 1981, 224–27; Keppie 1984; Maxfield 1984, 36–38; Webster 1985, 96–102.

Auxiliaries
Coulston 1985: auxiliary archers and their equipment; Dixon and Southern 1992: cavalry forces; Dobson 1981: organization of auxiliaries; Holder 1982: auxiliaries in Britain; Hyland 1990: study of the cavalry horse; Keppie 1984: auxiliaries of the late republic and early empire; Maxfield 1981: organization of auxilia-ries; Speidel 1984, 117–69: *numeri* and other irregular troops; Webster 1985: auxiliaries of the early empire.

Navy
Casson 1991, 143–56, 177–91, 213–16: detailed description of the history of the navy and the ships, mainly of the republic and early empire; Meijer 1986: includes a history of the navy in the republic and empire; Reddé 1986: detailed source on the navy; Starr 1960: navy from 31 BC to AD 324 (little changed from the 1941 edition); Thiel 1946: history of navy and events involving naval sea power in the republic to 167 BC, with a discussion of the *corvus* pp. 432–47; Webster 1985, 157–66: fleets in the 1st and 2nd centuries.

Conditions of Service
Davies 1985, 187–236: diet, medical service; Dobson 1981: auxiliary and legionary pay; Grant 1974: pay; Mann 1983: settlement of discharged legionary soldiers in the late republic; Maxfield 1981, 57–61: spoils, booty and donatives; Rickman 1971: organization of military food supply and *annona militaris*; Speidel 1984: includes the pay of auxiliaries; Watson 1969: many aspects of a soldier's life; Watson 1987: pay in the republic.

Training and Battle Tactics
Connolly 1981; includes an illustrated description of siege techniques of Greek and Roman armies; Davies 1985, 93–139: cavalry training grounds, practice camps; Holder 1982, 86–90: training in Britain; Keppie 1984: tactics in the republic and early empire; Marsden 1969: siege warfare and equipment; Oleson 1986: includes bibliography on siege equipment; Tomlin 1981c: siege warfare in the 4th century; Watson 1987: training of soldiers; Webster 1985: battle and siege tactics of the early empire.

Weapons and Equipment
Bishop 1985: production of weapons by the army; Bishop and Coulston 1989: weapons, armor and equipment from the middle republic to the late empire; Connolly 1981: detailed illustrated account of weapons and armor, including a discussion of early cultures; Connolly 1987: saddles; Coulston 1985: archery equipment; Dixon and Southern 1992: cavalry equipment; Hyland 1990: cavalry equipment; Manning 1985: various weapons, armor and cavalry equipment; Marsden 1969: artillery; Paddock 1985:

manufacture and supply of helmets; Scott 1985: illustrated account of daggers and scabbards with a gazetteer of finds; Tomlin 1981c: artillery of the 4th century; Webster 1985: equipment of various kinds of the early empire.

Military Standards
Connolly 1981, 218–19: illustrated description; Keppie 1984, 67, 139–40; Webster 1985, 133–39.

Military Decorations
Maxfield 1981.

Triumphs
Connolly 1981, 247–48: illustrated description; Maxfield 1981, 101–9; Scullard 1981, 213–18.

Camps, Forts and Fortresses
Bidwell et al. 1988: timber and stone fort gates across the empire; Connolly 1981: illustrated description of marching camps; Davison 1989: army barracks; Johnson 1983: late Roman fortifications; Lander 1984: detailed description of the design and defenses of stone forts and fortresses throughout the empire; Maxfield (ed.) 1989: Saxon Shore forts (including a gazetteer); Rickman 1971, 213–90: military granaries; Tomlin 1981b: late Roman fortifications; Webster 1985; early imperial fortifications; Welsby 1982: late Roman garrisons and forts in Britain.

Frontiers
Breeze 1982 and 1987: northern frontiers of Britain; Daniels 1987: African frontier; Isaac 1988: discusses meaning of *limes;* Isaac 1992: frontier in the east; Johnson 1983: frontiers of the Rhine, Danube and North Sea, with a gazetteer of *burgi;* Johnson 1989: Hadrian's Wall; Johnston (ed.) 1977: Saxon Shore forts; Kennedy 1987: eastern frontier; Kennedy 1992: frontier in Arabia (review article, with discussion and references); Kennedy and Riley 1990: the eastern frontier, illustrated by numerous aerial photographs and plans; Lander 1984: includes forts and fortresses relating to frontier defenses; Maxfield 1987: Rhine-Danube frontier; Maxfield and Dobson 1991: latest congress report on frontier studies covering many topics; Webster 1985: summary of the development of frontier policy throughout the empire in the 1st and 2nd centuries; Wilkes 1989: review article on the Danube frontier in Noricum.

3

GEOGRAPHY OF THE ROMAN WORLD

Expansion and Contraction of Rome's Territory

Founding of Rome (figs. 3.1, 3.2)

The origins of the city of Rome have always been obscure and controversial, even in the Roman period itself, when several myths and legends purported to explain its origin and development. There appears to have been some form of settlement in the area during the Bronze Age, as early as the late 2nd millennium BC. Traditionally, the first settlement was on the Palatine Hill, and there is evidence that settlement on this hill began to expand during the Iron Age, in the mid-8th century BC. Soon afterward there was another settlement, possibly of Sabines, on the Quirinal Hill.

At this time, Rome was surrounded by various communities, including Etruscans, Sabines, Faliscans and Latins. All these communities had an influence on the early development of Rome, although the majority of Rome's population probably came from the Latins. The early settlements were little more than villages, but those that grew up on neighboring hills gradually merged into a single large settlement, becoming recognizably urban by the 6th century BC. Rome was built on seven low hills: the Aventine, Caelian, Capitoline, Esquiline, Palatine, Quirinal and Viminal hills. As the city grew (fig. 3.1), the settlement expanded over these hills and the intervening valleys, and in the 4th century BC it was enclosed by the so-called Servian wall. The city in imperial times covered a much larger area around which the Aurelian wall was built (fig. 3.2).

Monarchy and Early and Middle Republic

During the monarchy Rome began an expansion of its influence and territory. This involved the conquest of neighboring settlements and the establishment of commercial links with cities much farther afield, such as Carthage and the Greek colony of Massilia. By the beginning of the republic in 509 BC, Rome had political and military dominance over many other cities in Latium. However, a struggle broke out between the Romans and the Latins that culminated in domination by Rome and in an alliance with the Latin League in 493 BC. This alliance allowed Rome to withstand attacks from neighboring communities during the first half of the 5th century BC and then to go on the offensive, capturing Veii after a long struggle in 396 BC. In 390 BC Rome survived a Gallic invasion from the north, recovering rapidly from this setback. It began to establish colonies at some of the major cities in Latium and to conduct campaigns against neighboring areas. After an unsuccessful fight for independence, the Latin League was dissolved in 338 BC, Rome's territory was greatly expanded and it took control of north Campania, finally defeating the Samnites in the early 3rd century BC.

During the 3rd century BC Rome expanded into southern Italy, coming into conflict with Magna Graecia (Greater Greece, the collective name for the Greek cities founded as colonies in southern Italy). It eventually subjugated southern Italy and, after successful wars in the north, came to dominate the entire Italian peninsula by the mid-3rd century BC. By then Rome ruled directly more than one-fifth of Italy, with strategic points secured by colonies of Romans or of Romans and Latins.

Before Italy was completely dominated, Rome and its Italian allies became involved in the First Punic War (264–241 BC). This was the first of a series of major wars over the next 100 years, in which Rome subdued Carthage and the major powers in the Greek east, becoming the dominant power in the Mediterranean by 167 BC. These rival powers were not completely destroyed, however, and further rebellions led to the destruction of Carthage and the annexation of Macedonia as a province of Rome in 146 BC.

Late Republic (figs. 3.3, 3.4)

BEGINNINGS OF THE EMPIRE (fig. 3.3)

A long series of Spanish campaigns ended in 133 BC when Numantia was captured and the provinces ex-

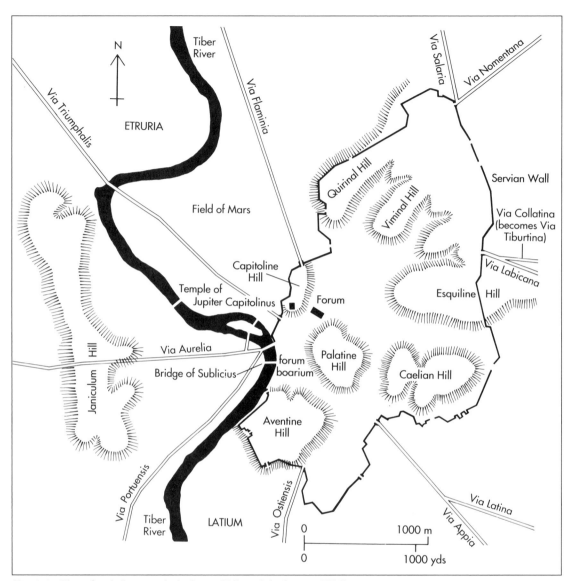

Fig. 3.1 Plan of early Rome with the Seven Hills and the Servian Wall.

tended over much of Spain. Also in 133 BC Attalus of Pergamum bequeathed his kingdom to Rome, which later became the province of Asia. By this time the Hellenistic kingdoms of Bithynia, Galatia and Rhodes had been subdued by various means. Rome had also interfered in the politics of Egypt and Syria and had become effective ruler of the Mediterranean. After campaigns against tribes in southern Gaul, the Romans established the prov-ince of Gallia Transalpina (later Narbonensis) in 121 BC.

During the 3rd and 2nd centuries BC Rome had established a largely overseas empire in the Mediter-ranean. From 133 BC to the end of the republic, though, attempts were made to secure this empire by dealing with threats to the borders from outside and revolts within as well as with establishing a system of control for the newly acquired territories.

RAPID EXPANSION OF THE EMPIRE (fig. 3.4)

The great expansion of the empire began in the last decades of the republic with the rise to power of Pompey and then of Julius Caesar. Pompey's campaigns in the east in 64 to 62 BC established Syria as a Roman province and enlarged Cilicia. Pontus was added to Bithynia, and the new territorial gains were protected by a series of adjacent client kingdoms. In the west Caesar embarked on the conquest of Gaul in 59 BC, advancing the frontiers of Roman control to the English Channel and the Rhine by 50 BC. In 46

BC, during the civil war, Caesar also enlarged the province of Africa by annexing part of the kingdom of King Juba II of Numidia during the struggle against Pompey's allies. However, there was little opportunity for expanding the empire during this civil war or during the civil war following Caesar's assassination in 44 BC.

Early Empire

At the end of the civil wars in 31 BC, Octavian (later Augustus) was in complete control of the empire. While Octavian's position was unassailable, his legal

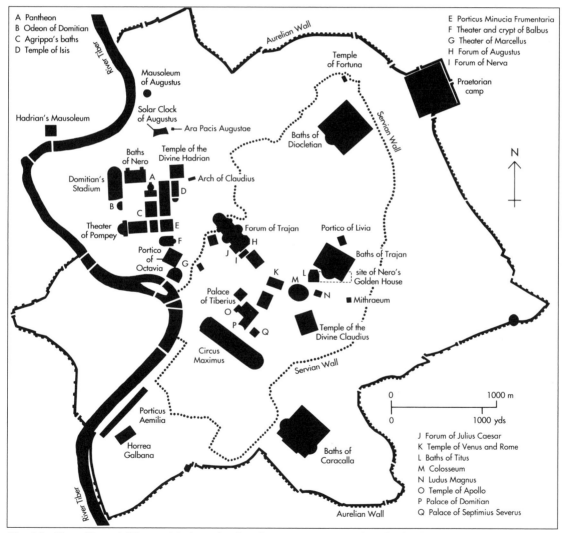

A Pantheon
B Odeon of Domitian
C Agrippa's baths
D Temple of Isis

E Porticus Minucia Frumentaria
F Theater and crypt of Balbus
G Theater of Marcellus
H Forum of Augustus
I Forum of Nerva

J Forum of Julius Caesar
K Temple of Venus and Rome
L Baths of Titus
M Colosseum
N Ludus Magnus
O Temple of Apollo
P Palace of Domitian
Q Palace of Septimius Severus

Fig. 3.2   Plan of imperial Rome with the major sites. Some monuments (such as the Ara Pacis) have since been moved.

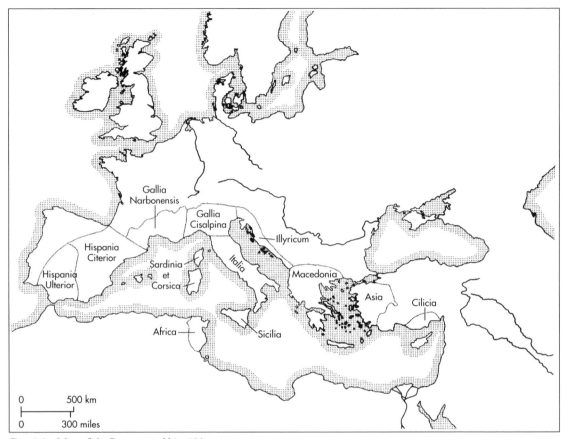

Fig. 3.3 Map of the Roman world in 100 BC.

position was difficult. In 27 BC he handed over the state to the Senate, but it was agreed that he should have a special command for ten years with a "province" including Spain, Gaul, Syria and Cilicia, which contained the bulk of the army.

The priority for Octavian (now Augustus) over the coming decades was the consolidation of existing provinces, which sometimes led to the extension of frontiers or the abandonment of territory. In the east plans for expansion were abandoned and an agreement was made with Parthia. Galatia was made a province in 25 BC and Judaea in AD 6. Spain was finally pacified, and both Spain and Gaul were reorganized. In the north the frontier was extended to the Danube, and the provinces of Raetia, Noricum, Pannonia and Moesia were established. To the west plans to advance to the Elbe were abandoned, and the Rhine-Danube became the northern frontier.

Tiberius largely followed Augustus' advice not to extend the empire, except that Cappadocia was made a province. The two Mauretanias, Britain, Lycia and Thrace were added during Claudius' reign. Nero's reign saw disorder and rebellion in the provinces, and at the end of his reign the civil wars of 69 caused disruption throughout the empire.

The Empire at Its Peak (fig. 3.5)

Vespasian emerged from the unrest to become emperor in 69 and established a policy of strengthening the existing frontiers. This policy was generally followed by succeeding emperors, with relatively

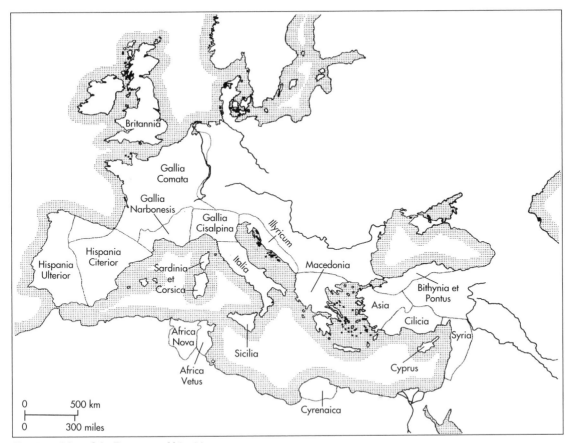

Fig. 3.4 Map of the Roman world in 44 BC.

little expansion of the empire. Under Domitian, Germany was divided into two provinces (Upper and Lower Germany). Trajan annexed Dacia and Arabia and took control of the new provinces of Armenia, Mesopotamia and Assyria from Parthia. Recurring problems had arisen on the northern frontiers in Britain and on the Rhine-Danube, and successive emperors attempted to strengthen these frontiers. During the early 2nd century, under Trajan, Pannonia was divided into two provinces (Upper and Lower Pannonia), and under Hadrian, Dacia was divided into two and then into three. The empire reached its maxiumum extent under Trajan, but his successor Hadrian was concerned with securing the frontiers and abandoned some of the territory won by Trajan. From the time of Hadrian, the empire ceased to expand and remained relatively stable.

End of the Empire (figs. 3.6, 3.7)

DISORDER AND INSTABILITY

The empire was relatively stable and peaceful until the death of Commodus in 192 resulted in civil war, from which Septimius Severus emerged the victor. Severus generally consolidated frontiers and improved administration of the provinces, dividing some of them in two (fig. 3.6). The empire was again relatively stable and peaceful during the reign of succeeding emperors until the death of Severus Alexander in 235, after which followed 50 years of military anarchy, with a rapid succession of emperors holding office for an average of less than three years each. The security of the empire was neglected and several frontiers were breached. Syria was overrun and Asia Minor was invaded, while in the west Postumus established the Gallic Empire (260–274), including Spain and Britain. Franks threatened the Lower Rhine, and the Alamanni crossed the Rhine and ravaged north Italy. Saxon pirates raided the English Channel coasts and Goths raided the Balkans and Aegean.

Claudius Gothicus and Aurelian managed to restore order. Relatively little of the empire was completely lost, mainly Dacia and the Agri Decumates. However, the rapid succession of short-lived emperors continued until Diocletian gained power in 284. In order to stabilize the succession, Diocletian divided the empire and the imperial power. He became joint Augustus with Maximian and established two junior Caesars (Galerius and Constantius Chlorus), who were destined to succeed as joint Augusti. The empire was

in effect split into west and east, with Maximian and Constantius Chlorus ruling the west and Diocletian and Galerius the east and was divided into smaller units, virtually doubling the number of provinces. These smaller provinces were grouped into 12 dioceses for administrative purposes (fig. 3.7).

Diocletian's plan for securing the imperial succession failed, and on his retirement civil war followed, from which Constantine I emerged in 324 as the sole emperor of both east and west. The division between east and west was maintained, however, and after his death in 337 the empire was again split between two Augusti. The dynasty established by Constantine I continued until the death of Julian in 363. By this time there was increasing pressure on the frontiers, with emperors continually having to respond to attacks and invasions. In the late 4th century this pressure contin-

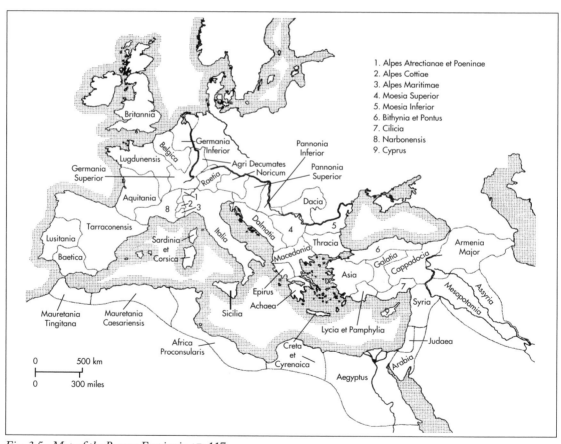

Fig. 3.5 Map of the Roman Empire in AD *117.*

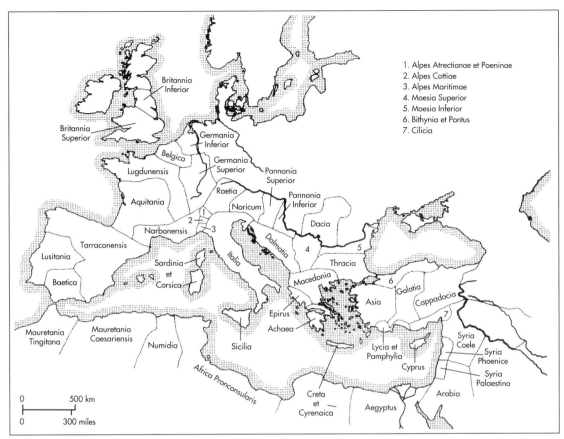

Fig. 3.6 Map of the Roman Empire in AD 211.

ued to grow, and large-scale movements of Germanic peoples such as Visigoths, Ostrogoths, Alans, Alamanni, Franks, Burgundians, Vandals and Suebi threatened the Rhine- Danube frontier.

COLLAPSE OF THE EMPIRE AND LOSS OF THE WEST

By the beginning of the 5th century the empire had begun to collapse. In 407 the Rhine frontier was overrun by various tribes; in 409 Vandals, Suebi and Alans crossed the Pyrenees into Spain; and in 410 Britain was abandoned. Also in 410 the Visigoths under Alaric invaded Greece and Italy, sacking Rome, but retreated northward when Alaric died. In 412 Visigoths took over part of southwestern Gaul but were forced into Spain and eventually agreed to settle in Aquitaine. In 429 Vandals and Alans crossed the

Straits of Gibraltar into Africa. Subsequently much of Africa fell to the Vandals, and by 439 they were as far east as Carthage. By 455, when Vandals sacked Rome and took over Sicily, the Visigoths had annexed most of Spain. By 476 little of the western empire remained.

In the east the empire was relatively untouched. Constantine I had moved his capital to Constantinople, from where the eastern or Byzantine Empire was ruled, and the city continued to grow. Several attempts were made to recapture parts of the western empire, but they met with little success before Justinian came to power. Parts of Spain were recaptured, Africa was recovered in 533 and after a long struggle Italy was recaptured in 553. Justinian died in 565, but the Byzantine Empire survived for another 900 years. However, most of Italy was lost to the Lombards in 568, and in the 7th and 8th centuries much of the

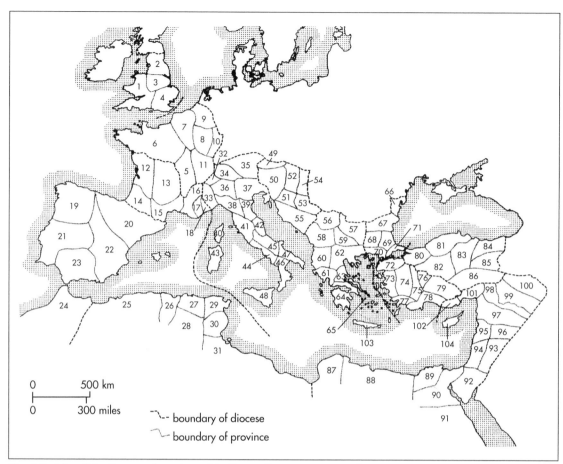

Fig. 3.7 Map of the dioceses and provinces of the Roman Empire in AD *314 after Diocletian's reorganization. The provinces are numbered 1 to 104, and the dioceses are in roman type:* Britanniae: *1. Britannia Prima (I), 2. Britannia Secunda (II), 3. Flavia Caesariensis, 4. Maxima Caesariensis;* Galliae: *5. Lugdunensis Prima (I), 6. Lugdunensis Secunda (II), 7. Belgica Secunda (II), 8. Belgica Prima (I), 9. Germania Secunda (II), 10. Germania Prima (I), 11. Sequania (Maxima Sequanorum);* Viennensis: *12. Aquitanica Secunda (II), 13. Aquitanica Prima (I), 14. Novem Populi, 15. Narbonensis Prima (I), 16. Viennensis, 17. Narbonensis Secunda (II), 18. Alpes Maritimae;* Hispaniae: *19. Gallaecia, 20. Tarraconensis, 21. Lusitania, 22. Carthaginiensis, 23. Baetica, 24. Mauretania Tingitana;* Africa: *25. Mauretania Caesariensis, 26. Mauretania Sitifensis, 27. Numidia Cirtensis, 28. Numidia Militana, 29. Proconsularis, 30. Byzacena, 31. Tripolitania;* Italia: *32. Alpes Graiae, 33. Alpes Cottiae, 34. Raetia Prima (I), 35. Raetia Secunda (II), 36. Aemilia, 37. Venetia et Histria, 38. Liguria, 39. Flaminia, 40. Corsica, 41. Tuscia et Umbria, 42. Picenum, 43. Sardinia, 44. Campania, 45. Samnium, 46. Lucania, 47. Apulia et Calabria, 48. Sicilia;* Pannoniae: *49. Noricum Ripense, 50. Noricum Mediterraneum, 51. Savia, 52. Pannonia Prima (I), 53. Pannonia Secunda (II), 54. Valeria, 55. Dalmatia;* Moesia: *56. Moesia Prima (I), 57. Dacia, 58. Praevalitana, 59. Dardania, 60. Epirus Nova (New Epirus), 61. Epirus Vetus (Old Epirus), 62. Macedonia, 63. Thessalia, 64. Achaea, 65. Insulae (islands);* Thracia: *66. Scythia, 67. Moesia Secunda (II), 68. Thracia, 69. Haemimontus, 70. Rhodope, 71. Europa;* Asiana: *72. Hellespontus, 73. Asia, 74. Lydia, 75. Phrygia Prima (I), 76. Phrygia Secunda (II), 77. Caria, 78. Lycia et Pamphylia, 79. Pisidia;* Pontica: *80. Bithynia, 81. Paphlagonia, 82. Galatia, 83. Diospontus, 84. Pontus Polemoniacus, 85. Armenia Minor, 86. Cappadocia;* Oriens: *87. Libya Superior (Upper Libya), 88. Libya Inferior (Lower Libya), 89. Aegyptus Iovia, 90. Aegyptus Herculia, 91. Thebais, 92. Arabia Secunda (II), 93. Arabia Prima (I), 94. Palaestina, 95. Phoenicia, 96. Augusta Libanensis, 97. Syria Coele, 98. Augusta Euphratensis, 99. Osrhoene, 100. Mesopotamia, 101. Cilicia, 102. Isauria, 103. Creta, 104. Cyprus.*

eastern empire and north Africa were also lost. The remains of the Byzantine Empire fell to the Ottoman Turks in 1453.

THE PROVINCES (figs. 3.3, 3.4, 3.5, 3.6, 3.7)

Once Rome began to acquire more territory, one of its prime concerns was to secure the frontiers of its empire. Often this was done by establishing buffer zones immediately outside the frontier, by controlling kingdoms within the empire through client kings, by alliances and in some cases by making a neighboring territory a protectorate of Rome. When political means of controlling a neighboring state failed and resulted in a threat to the frontier, such states often would be annexed, becoming provinces within the empire.

Most, if not all, boundaries and frontiers underwent some changes during the Roman period, and often the evidence from which a boundary line has been reconstructed is uncertain. For this reason provincial and diocesan boundaries shown on the maps should be taken as approximate indications only, rather than precise positions, of boundaries. In the following discussions of provinces, "Diocletian's reorganization" refers to the creation of dioceses and splitting up of provinces in the early 4th century.

Originally, "province" (*provincia*) meant the task a magistrate was given during his term of office, so that, for example, the *provincia* of a praetor at Rome was jurisdiction. Gradually "province" came to mean the territory that was governed, usually by proconsuls in the republic. Under the empire the provinces were divided into senatorial and imperial provinces. The senatorial (peaceful) provinces were administered by governors appointed by the Senate, while imperial provinces (ones needing a military presence) were controlled by the emperor who appointed provincial governors (fig. 3.8). Any new provinces automatically became imperial provinces.

Table 3.1 Chronological List of Acquisition of Main Provinces

241 BC	Sicilia
227 BC	Sardinia et Corsica
197 BC	Hispania Ulterior
197 BC	Hispania Citerior
146 BC	Africa, Macedonia
129–128 BC	Asia
121 BC	Gallia Narbonensis
74 BC	Bithynia, Cyrenaica
67 BC	Creta, to form Creta et Cyrene
65 BC	Western Pontus, to form Bithynia et Pontus
64 BC	Syria
58 BC	Cyprus
58–50 BC	Gallia Comata
30 BC	Aegyptus
25 BC	Galatia
15 BC	Raetia
c. 15 BC	Noricum

Dates AD

Before 6	Moesia
After 9	Dalmatia, Pannonia
17	Cappadocia
c. 42	Mauretania
43	Britannia, Lycia et Pamphylia
46	Thracia
106	Arabia
107	Dacia
197	Mesopotamia

Provinces

The provinces and dioceses created during Diocletian's reorganization are shown in Figure 3.7.

ACHAEA: Detached from Macedonia (of which it was part from 146 BC) to form a new senatorial province in 27 BC. The new province of Achaea incorporated Aetolia, Thessaly, part of Epirus and Arcarnania. Tiberius rejoined Achaea to Macedonia, but this was reversed by Claudius. After Diocletian's reorganization Achaea became a province in the diocese of Moesia.

AEGYPTUS (Egypt): Became an imperial province in 30 BC. Unlike any other province, it was governed almost like a huge imperial estate and retained much of the administrative structure that had existed under the Ptolemies. In Diocletian's reorganization, it was divided into several smaller provinces within the diocese of Oriens.

AFRICA: The original province was formed from part of conquered territory after the defeat of Carthage in 146 BC and corresponded roughly to northeast Tunisia. After the battle of Thapsus in 46 BC, Julius Caesar added a further area (Africa Nova, New Africa) to the original province, by then called Africa Vetus (Old Africa). Under Augustus further territorial gains were reorganized into a new province, Africa Proconsularis, which extended from Numidia in the west to Cyrenaica in the east. The coastal area of Numidia and Mauretania appears to have been incorporated into Africa Proconsularis soon afterward, forming a large senatorial province. Mauretania came under Roman control in 40 but was not fully subdued until several years later. Mauretania was split c. 42 into two imperial provinces: Mauretania Caesariensis and Mauretania Tingitana. Numidia was established as a separate imperial province under Severus. In Diocletian's reorganization Africa was divided into seven new provinces in the diocese of Africa, while Mauretania Tingitana became part of the diocese of Hispaniae.

ALPES ATRECTIANAE ET POENINAE: The third Alpine province to be created, established in the 2nd century. It remained a province, in the diocese of Italia after Diocletain's reorganization, but was renamed Alpes Graiae.

ALPES COTTIAE: Annexed and made into an imperial province during Nero's reign. It remained a province, in the diocese of Italia, after Diocletian's reorganization, but was restricted to the east of the Alps, although its territory was extended in other directions.

ALPES MARITIMAE: Became a province in 14 BC, later becoming an imperial province. It remained a province, in the diocese of Viennensis, after Diocletian's reorganization, but was limited to west of the Alps, although its territory was extended in other directions.

ARMENIA MAJOR: Armenia was the subject of a long power struggle between Rome and Parthia. After Pompey's campaigns Armenia became a Roman protectorate but continued to be the subject of dispute. Trajan annexed it in 114, creating the province of Armenia Major. In 117 Hadrian returned it to its earlier status of an independent kingdom, whose monarch was nominated by Rome.

ARMENIA MINOR: From the time of Pompey, this small kingdom was granted to a succession of neighboring kings. It may have been annexed by Tiberius, but in 38 Caligula granted it to king Cotys, and it was then held by a son of King Herod of Chalcis. Vespasian incorporated it into the province of Cappadocia. After Diocletian's reorganization the name Armenia Minor was reused for a province in the diocese of Pontica.

ASIA: This territory was bequeathed to Rome in 133 BC by King Attalus III of Pergamum, becoming a province in 129 BC. Under Augustus it became a senatorial province, and under Vespasian it was expanded to incorporate Rhodes. In Diocletian's reorganization the area was subdivided into smaller provinces within the diocese of Asiana, one of which continued to be called Asia.

ASSYRIA: This territory became a province under Trajan in 116 but was abandoned by Hadrian.

BITHYNIA ET PONTUS: Bithynia was bequeathed to Rome by King Nicomedes IV in 74 BC, and the western part of Pontus was added in 65 BC to form the province of Bithynia et Pontus. Under the empire it was initially a senatorial province, but eventually it became an imperial province under Marcus Aurelius. Under Diocletian's reorganization the territory was divided between several new provinces in the diocese of Pontica.

BRITANNIA: After Caesar's campaigns in 55 and 54 BC, Rome had a claim on Britain, but it was not until after the invasion of 43 that it became an imperial province. It was only toward the end of the 1st century that the main part of the province had been conquered. In the early 3rd century Britannia was divided into two provinces, Britannia Superior (Upper Britain) and Britannia Inferior (Lower Britain). Under

Diocletian's reorganization Britain became the diocese of Britanniae, divided into four provinces.

CAPPADOCIA: This province, previously a client kingdom, was annexed in 17. It was joined with Galatia under a single governor by Vespasian, but Trajan made Cappadocia a separate province with Pontus. In Diocletian's reorganization the territory was divided into several smaller provinces in the diocese of Pontica, one of which perpetuated the name of Cappadocia.

CILICIA: This territory formally became an imperial province in 72, although it was occupied by Rome as early as 102 BC in an effort to deal with pirates, who were finally suppressed by Pompey in 67 BC. For some time Cilicia included Phrygia and Pisidia, until these were returned to the province of Asia, and originally was part of the kingdom of Attalus III. Under Augustus Cilicia was reduced to the eastern part only, with part probably being attached to Galatia and part ruled by client kings. In 72 Vespasian reconstituted the province. In Diocletian's reorganization it was divided between the new provinces of Cilicia and Isauria in the diocese of Oriens.

CYPRUS: Annexed by Rome in 58 BC, this island became a senatorial province under Augustus. After Diocletian's reorganization it was a province in the diocese of Oriens.

CYRENAICA: Sometimes called Cyrene, after the province's capital city. The territory was bequeathed to Rome in 96 BC but was allowed to remain as a territory of free city-states. Following disorders, it was made a province in 74 BC. In 67 BC Creta (Crete) was incorporated into the province, and it was finally established as the senatorial province of Creta et Cyrenaica under Augustus. It may have been separated from Creta in the first half of the 3rd century. Under Diocletian's reorganization Cyrenaica became part of the diocese of Oriens.

DACIA: This area was made an imperial province in 107 after Trajan's campaigns in 101–102 and 105–106 (fig. 1.2). The province was divided into Dacia Superior (Upper Dacia) and Dacia Inferior (Lower Dacia) in c. 119, and probably in 124 part of Dacia Superior was detached to form Dacia Porolissensis. In the mid-2nd century a further reorganization of the

three provinces (the Tres Daciae, the Three Dacias) placed them under the control of a single governor. Dacia was abandoned under Aurelian, but after Diocletian's reorganization the name was later used for a province south of the Danube in the diocese of Moesia.

GALATIA: This province was formed in 25 BC, incorporating parts of Phrygia, Lycaonia and Pisidia as well as the area known as Galatia. During the empire it was an imperial province and underwent various changes, with territory being added under Vespasian and other territory being detached under Trajan and probably Hadrian. The general effect was a reduction in the size of the province. After Diocletian's reorganization the province of Galatia, in the diocese of Pontica, was approximately the same as the pre-Roman territory of Galatia.

GALLIA CISALPINA (Cisalpine Gaul): The area of north Italy that lies between the Alps and the Apennines. It was annexed by Rome in 224–222 BC and was lost and regained in subsequent campaigns. By 150 BC there were few un-Romanized Gauls left in the area, which was being settled by Romans and was sometimes known as Gallia Togata (Gaul of the Toga-wearers). It was constituted as a province by Sulla in 82 BC and incorporated into Italy in 42 BC. It finally became part of the province of Italia when Augustus conquered the tribes of the Alpine foothills.

GALLIA COMATA (Long-haired Gaul): This area was conquered by Julius Caesar in 58–51 BC and was divided into two areas, each governed by a legate. Augustus reorganized the area to form three imperial provinces called Aquitania, Lugdunensis (fig. 3.8) and Belgica (Gallia Belgica)—the Tres Galliae (Three Gauls). The area included what was later to become the provinces of Germania Inferior and Germania Superior, which was separated from the Gaulish provinces around 90. The area was completely reorganized by Diocletian, being divided into several smaller provinces and split between the dioceses of Galliae and Viennensis.

GALLIA TRANSALPINA (Transalpine Gaul): Sometimes used for the area normally called Gaul. The name was also used for the southern part of Gaul, which appears to have been a province from 121 BC. This area became known as Provincia (The Province) eral provinces—see GALLIA COMATA and GALLIA TRANSALPINA.

GERMANIA: This was for a long period an undefined area east of the Rhine and north of the Danube. After Caesar's campaigns the Rhine became a frontier of the empire, but Augustus' failure to advance the frontier from the Rhine to the Elbe and create his intended province of Germania led to the Rhineland being established as a military zone. Its civilian administration was under the governor of the adjacent province of Gallia Belgica. Under Vespasian and Domitian the military zone was increased to include the Taunus Mountains and the Agri Decumates. Around 90 the area was formally organized into the separate provinces of Germania Superior (Upper Germany) and Germania Inferior (Lower Germany). The Agri Decumates were lost by 260, and the frontier reverted to the Rhine-Danube line. In Diocletian's reorganization Germania Inferior became Germania Secunda and Germania Superior was divided into Germania Prima and Maxima Sequanorum (Sequania), all three in the diocese of Galliae.

HISPANIA CITERIOR: Two provinces, Hispania Citerior (Nearer Spain) and Hispania Ulterior (Farther Spain), were established in the Iberian peninsula in 197 BC. A long conflict ensued with the native tribes for nearly two centuries. During this time the two provinces expanded their territory, culminating in the conquest of the whole peninsula under Augustus in the 20s BC. The peninsula was then divided into three new provinces, Baetica, Lusitania and Tarraconensis. Baetica became a senatorial province in 27 BC, but the other two provinces remained under imperial control. It appears that the three provinces remained relatively stable until the 4th century, when the peninsula was reorganized by Diocletian into five new provinces, in the diocese of Hispaniae. The diocese also included a sixth province, in north Africa, Mauretania Tingitana.

ILLYRICUM: The Dalmatia coast and islands were originally a base for pirates threatening Roman shipping. The area therefore attracted intermittent action and increasing colonization, until it became a senatorial province under Augustus. Because of continued wars and rebellions, it was made an imperial province around 11 BC. After further warfare the province was divided into two imperial provinces after

Fig. 3.8 Statue base from Caerwent, Wales, erected by decree of the council, the commonwealth of the Silures [tribe] to [Tiberius Claudius] Paulinus, legate of the II Augusta legion. The inscription also records that he was previously senatorial governor of the province of Narbonensis and imperial governor of the province of Lugdunensis.

and later as Gallia Narbonensis or Narbonensis (fig. 3.8). The area was important for providing an overland route to Spain, and unrest and threats from the north provided the excuse for Caesar's campaigns in Gallia Comata. The area was constituted as a senatorial province in the reign of Augustus and subdivided into several smaller provinces during Diocletian's reorganization.

GALLIA TRANSPADANA (Transpadine Gaul): The part of the province of Gallia Cisalpina north of the Padus (Po) River.

GAUL: The area bounded by the Alps, the Pyrenees, the Rhine and the ocean, divided into sev-

AD 9, known by the Flavian period as Dalmatia and Pannonia. Under Trajan Pannonia was divided into Pannonia Superior (Upper Pannonia) and Pannonia Inferior (Lower Pannonia), also both imperial provinces. Under Caracalla the boundary between the two provinces was changed to enlarge Pannonia Inferior. In Diocletian's reorganization the main area of Dalmatia, Pannonia Superior and Pannonia Inferior, was replaced by five new provinces—Dalmatia (largely the same area as before), Savia, Valeria, Pannonia Prima and Pannonia Secunda, all part of the diocese of Pannoniae.

ITALIA: Modern-day Italy was originally a collection of city-states, often at war with each other. From the 5th century BC there was a number of Greek colonies in southern Italy, known collectively as Magna Graecia (Greater Greece). By 450 BC the name Italia referred to the southwest peninsula, and by the 3rd century BC it referred to the entire peninsula south of Liguria and Gallia Cisalpina. It was not fully unified until the reign of Augustus, when Gallia Cisalpina was formally incorporated into the province. Under the empire it had a special status, until the time of Diocletian when it lost its immunity from taxes. In Diocletian's reorganization Italia became a diocese, including the islands of Sardinia, Corsica and Sicily, and was divided into 16 new provinces.

MACEDONIA: This kingdom, divided into four autonomous republics in 167 BC, was made into a single province around 146 BC. In 27 BC Augustus divided the area into three provinces—Achaea, Epirus and Macedonia, the latter becoming a senatorial province. In 15 Tiberius joined the provinces of Macedonia, Achaea and Moesia under the command of a single legate, a move reversed by Claudius in 44, who restored Macedonia and Achaea as senatorial provinces. Nero proclaimed "freedom" for Greece in 67, which included exemption from taxes, but this proclamation was reversed by Vespasian. By the reign of Antoninus Pius at the very latest, Epirus was detached from Macedonia as a separate province. In Diocletian's reorganization the area was divided into five provinces within the diocese of Moesia.

MESOPOTAMIA: This territory between the Tigris and Euphrates rivers was made a province by Trajan but was abandoned by Hadrian. It was again the scene of campaigns by Lucius Verus in his wars against the Parthians from 162 to 166, and Septimius Severus formed a smaller province in the northwest part of the area in 197. This was lost to Persia in the 3rd century, but was then recovered and continued to act as a buffer zone on the edge of the empire, sometimes ruled by client kings. Part of Mesopotamia was divided into smaller provinces in the diocese of Oriens during Diocletian's reorganization, one of which retained the name Mesopotamia.

MOESIA: Originally occupied by the Thracian Moesi tribe, who were subdued by Crassus in 29 BC. The territory was initially attached to Macedonia or Illyricum, but appears to have become a province before AD 6 and was certainly organized as an imperial province under Tiberius. In the reign of Domitian it was split into two provinces—Moesia Superior (Upper Moesia) and Moesia Inferior (Lower Moesia). After Trajan's Dacian wars both these provinces were enlarged. During Diocletian's reorganization the area of Moesia was subdivided into several smaller provinces.

NORICUM: Originally an independent kingdom that supported Caesar in the civil war. It was peacefully absorbed into the empire about 15 BC, eventually becoming an imperial province. During Diocletian's reorganization it was divided into Noricum Ripense and Noricum Mediterraneum, in the diocese of Pannoniae.

PAMPHYLIA: This territory was ceded to Rome in 189 BC by King Antiochus III. Having successively been part of Cilicia, Asia and Galatia, it became part of the imperial province of Lycia et Pamphylia in 43. It became a senatorial province in Hadrian's reign, and after Diocletian's reorganization it was included in the diocese of Asiana.

RAETIA: Conquered in 15 BC. Later became an imperial province. In Diocletian's reorganization it was divided into two provinces, Raetia Prima (Raetia First) and Raetia Secunda (Raetia Second) in the diocese of Italia.

SARDINIA ET CORSICA: Became a province in 227 BC. During its history this province changed from a senatorial to an imperial province and back again several times. At some stage during the empire (date unknown), Sardinia and Corsica were made into sep-

Fig. 3.9   Map of Italy, Corsica, Sardinia and Sicily with major place names.

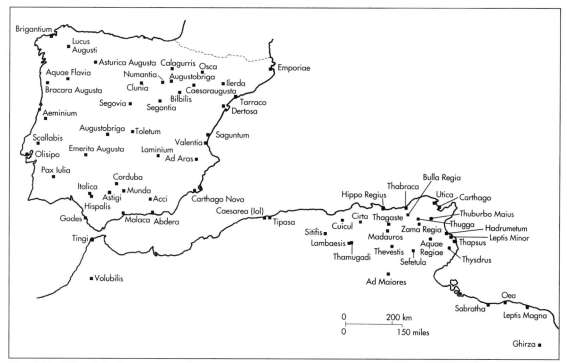

Fig. 3.10 Map of the Iberian peninsula and north Africa with major place names.

arate provinces. They were both in the diocese of Italia after Diocletian's reorganization.

SICILIA: In 241 BC Sicily was the first land outside Italy to become Roman territory. It became a province after the capture of Syracuse in 211 BC and was incorporated in the diocese of Italia in Diocletian's reorganization.

SYRIA: This territory became a province after Pompey forced its surrender in 64 BC. Under the empire it became a very important imperial province. After the Jewish Revolt in 70, Judaea was made a separate imperial province. Other territories were gradually added to the main province of Syria, but in 106 the southern end was detached to form the province of Arabia. Hadrian stationed an extra legion in Judaea, renaming it Syria Palaestina. Septimius Severus divided the remaining province into Syria Coele and Syria Phoenice. The reorganization by Diocletian divided the area into several provinces in the diocese of Oriens, four of which perpetuated the names Syria Coele, Arabia (I and II) and Palaestina.

THRACIA: Previously a client kingdom, this area was made an imperial province in 46. In Diocletian's reorganization it was divided into a number of smaller provinces in the diocese of Thracia, one of which retained the name Thracia.

GAZETTEER OF PLACE NAMES (figs. 3.9, 3.10, 3.11, 3.12 3.13)

This gazetteer gives the original Roman name of major places only (such as towns and fortresses), with English equivalents where available and the modern-day country. Numerous other place names are known from literary and epigraphic sources, some of which

1 Noviomagus
2 Anderita
3 Durovernum
4 Dubris
5 Rutupiae
6 Durobrivae
7 Durocortorum
8 Glanum
9 Tarasco
10 Avennio
11 Aquae Sextiae

Fig. 3.11 Map of Britain and Gaul with major place names.

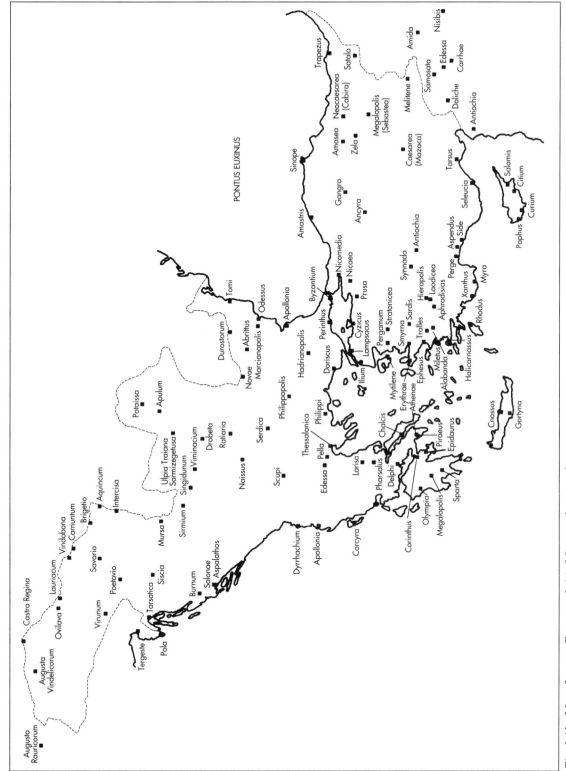

Fig. 3.12 Map of eastern Europe and Asia Minor with major place names.

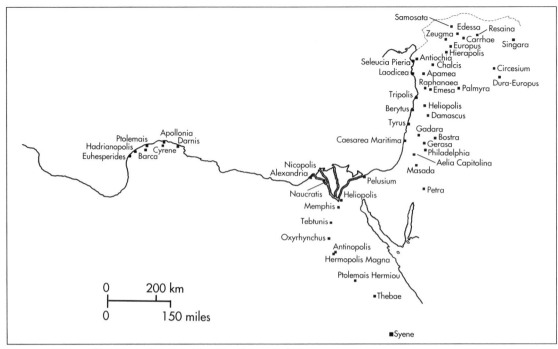

Fig. 3.13　Map of Cyrenaica, Egypt and Syria with major place names.

cannot now be precisely identified, while the Roman name of many other known Roman sites (in particular villas and farmsteads) are not known. Some places across the Roman world had the same name (such as Apollonia). Several places changed their name during their history — for example, Byzantium was changed to Constantinopolis. Alternative names are given in parentheses. Some place names have a suffix indicating the native pre-Roman tribe, such as Lutetia Parisiorum (Lutetia of the Parisi tribe). The suffix is often omitted in current use, and yet the modern word Paris obviously derived from the full name.

Place Names

Roman Name	Modern Name	Country
Abdera	Adra	Spain
Abrittus	Razgrad	Bulgaria
Acci	Guadix	Spain
Ad Maiores		Tunisia
Aelia Capitolina (Hierosolyma)	Jerusalem	Israel
Agathe	Agde	France
Agrigentum	Agrigento	Sicily
Alabanda	Araphisar	Turkey
Alba Fucens		Italy
Aleria	Alalia	Corsica
Alesia	Alise-St. Reine	France
Alexandria	Alexandria	Egypt
Altinum	Altino	Italy

Roman Name	Modern Name	Country
Amasea	Amasya	Turkey
Amastris		Turkey
Amida	Diyarbakir	Turkey
Amiternum	Amiternum	Italy
Ancona	Ancona	Italy
Ancyra	Ankara	Turkey
Anderita	Pevensey	Britain
Antiochia		Turkey
Antiochia (Antioch)	Antakya	Turkey
Antinoopolis		Egypt
Antipolis	Antibes	France
Antium	Anzio	Italy
Apamea		Syria
Aphrodisias	Geyre	Turkey
Apollonia	near Pojan	Albania
Apollonia	Marsa Susah	Libya

Roman Name	Modern Name	Country	Roman Name	Modern Name	Country
Apollonia	Sozopol	Bulgaria	Baiae	Baia	Italy
Apulum	Alba Iulia	Romania	Barca		Libya
Aquae	Baden Baden	Germany	Barium	Bari	Italy
Aquae Flaviae	Chaves	Portugal	Beneventum	Benevento	Italy
Aquae Regiae		Tunisia	Berenice		
Aquae Sextiae			(Euhespesides)	Benghazi	Libya
Salluviorum	Aix-en-Provence	France	Berytus	Beirut	Lebanon
Aquae Sulis	Bath	Britain	Bibracte	Mont Beuvray	France
Aquileia	Aquileia	Italy	Bilbilis	Calatayud	Spain
Aquincum	Budapest	Hungary	Bonna	Bonn	Germany
Aquinum	Aquino	Italy	Bononia	Bologna	Italy
Arae Flaviae	Rottweil	Germany	Bostra	Busra	Syria
Arausio	Orange	France	Bracara Augusta	Braga	Portugal
Arelate	Arles	France	Brigantio	Briançon	France
Argentomagus	Argenton-sur-Creuse	France	Brigantium	La Coruña	Spain
Argentorate	Strasbourg	France	Brigetio	Szöny	Hungary
Aricia	Ariccia	Italy	Brundisium	Brindisi	Italy
Ariminum	Rimini	Italy	Bulla Regia		Tunisia
Arpinum	Arpino	Italy	Burdigala Biturigum		
Arretium	Arezzo	Italy	Viviscorum	Bordeaux	France
Asisium	Assisi	Italy	Burnum		Croatia
Aspalathos	Split	Croatia	Byzantium		
Aspendus	Belkis	Turkey	(Constantinopolis)	Istanbul	Turkey
Astigi	Ecija	Spain	Cabira		
Asturica Augusta	Astorga	Spain	(Neocaesarea)	Niksar	Turkey
Atella		Italy	Caesaraugusta	Zaragoza	Spain
Aternum		Italy	Caesarea (Iol)	Cherchell	Algeria
Athenae	Athens	Greece	Caesarea Maritima	Kibbutz Sdot Yam	Israel
Atuatuca Tungrorum	Tongeren	Belgium	Caesarea (Mazaca)	Kayseri	Turkey
Augusta Praetoria	Aosta	Italy	Caesarodunum		
Augusta Rauricorum	Augst	Switzerland	Turonum	Tours	France
Augusta Taurinorum	Turin	Italy	Caesaromagus	Beauvais	France
Augusta Treverorum	Trier	Germany	Caesaromagus	Chelmsford	Britain
Augusta			Calagurris	Calahorra	Spain
Vindelicorum	Augsburg	Germany	Calleva Atrebatum	Silchester	Britain
Augustobriga		Spain	Cannae	Canne	Italy
Augustobriga	Talavera la Vieja	Spain	Capua	Santa Maria di Capua	
Augustodunum				Vetere	Italy
Aedorum	Autun	France	Carales	Cagliari	Sardinia
Augustomagus			Carcaso	Carcassonne	France
Silvanectum	Senlis	France	Carnuntum	Deutsch-Altenburg	Austria
Augustonemetum	Clermont-Ferrand	France	Carpentorate		
Augustonemetum			Meminorum	Carpentras	France
Aventicum	Avenches	Switzerland	Carrhae	Harran	Turkey
Augustoritum			Carthago	Carthage	Tunisia
Lemovicum	Limoges	France	Carthago Nova	Cartagena	Spain
Avaricum Biturigum	Bourges	France	Castra Regina	Regensburg	Germany
Avennio	Avignon	France	Catana	Catania	Sicily
Baeterrae	Béziers	France	Cavillonum	Châlon-sur-Saône	France

Roman Name	Modern Name	Country	Roman Name	Modern Name	Country
Cenabum	Orléans	France	Durnovaria		
Chalcis	Khalkis	Greece	Durotrigum	Dorchester	Britain
Chalcis	Qinnesrin	Syria	Durobrivae	Rochester	Britain
Circesium	Buseire	Syria	Durobrivae	Water Newton	Britain
Cirta	Constantine	Algeria	Durocortorum		
Citium	Larnaca	Cyprus	Remorum	Reims	France
Clausentum	Bitterne	Britain	Durostorum	Silistra	Bulgaria
Clunia	Coruña del Conde	Spain	Durovernum		
Cnossus	Knossos	Crete	Cantiacorum	Canterbury	Britain
Colonia Claudia Ara			Dyrrachium		
Agrippinensium	Cologne	Germany	(Epidamnus)	Durrës	Albania
Colonia Claudia Victrix			Eburacum	York	Britain
Camulodunum	Colchester	Britain	Edessa	Edhessa	Greece
Colonia Ulpia Traiana			Edessa	Urfa	Turkey
(Vetera)	Xanten	Germany	Emerita Augusta	Merida	Spain
Comum	Como	Italy	Emesa	Homs	Syria
Condate	Rennes	France	Emporiae	Ampurias	Spain
Constantinopolis			Ephesus	near Selçuk	Turkey
(Byzantium)	Istanbul	Turkey	Epidamnus		
Corcyra	Corfu	Greece	(Dyrrachium)	Durrës	Albania
Corduba	Cordoba	Spain	Epidaurus	Epidauros	Greece
Corfinium		Italy	Erythrae		Turkey
Coriallum	Cherbourg	France	Euhesperides		
Corinium			(Berenice)	Benghazi	Libya
Dubonnorum	Cirencester	Britain	Europus		Syria
Corinthus	Corinth	Greece	Fanum Fortunae	Fano	Italy
Cortona	Cortona	Italy	Florentia	Florence	Italy
Cosa	Cosa	Italy	Forum Iulii	Fréjus	France
Cremona	Cremona	Italy	Gadara	Um Qeis	Jordan
Cuicul	Djemila	Algeria	Gades	Cadiz	Spain
Cumae		Italy	Gangra		
Curium		Cyprus	(Germanicopolis)		Turkey
Cyrene	Shahhat	Libya	Genava	Geneva	Switzerland
Cyzicus		Turkey	Genua	Genoa	Italy
Damascus	Damascus	Syria	Gerasa	Jerash	Jordan
Darnis	Derna	Libya	Gesoriacum		
Delphi	Delphi	Greece	(Bononia)	Boulogne	France
Dertona	Tortona	Italy	Ghirza	Qirzah	Libya
Dertosa	Tortosa	Italy	Glanum	St. Rémy	France
Deva	Chester	Britain	Glevum	Gloucester	Britain
Divodurum			Gortyna	Gortyn	Crete
Mediomatricorium	Metz	France	Hadrianopolis	Driana	Libya
Doliche		Turkey	Hadrianopolis	Edirne	Turkey
Doriscus			Hadrumetum	Sousse	Tunisia
(Traianopolis)		Greece	Halicarnassus	Bodrum	Turkey
Drobeta	Turnu-Severin	Romania	Heliopolis		Egypt
Dubris	Dover	Britain	Heliopolis	Baalbek	Lebanon
Dura-Europus		Syria	Heraclea		
			(Perinthus)		Turkey

Roman Name	Modern Name	Country	Roman Name	Modern Name	Country
Hermopolis Magna	Al Ashmunein	Egypt	Mazaca (Caesarea)	Kayseri	Turkey
Hierapolis	Membij	Syria	Mediolanum	Milan	Italy
Hierapolis	Pamukkale	Turkey	Mediolanum	Évreux	France
Hierosolyma (Aelia			Mediolanum		
Capitolina)	Jerusalem	Israel	Santonum	Saintes	France
Hippo Regius	Annaba	Algeria	Megalopolis		Greece
Hispalis	Seville	Spain	Megalopolis		
Ilerda	Lerida	Spain	(Sebastea)	Sivas	Turkey
Ilium	Troy	Turkey	Melitene	Malatya	Turkey
Intercisa		Hungary	Memphis	Memphis	Egypt
Iol Caesarea	Cherchell	Algeria	Messana	Messina	Sicily
Isca Silurum	Caerleon	Britain	Miletus	Milet	Turkey
Isca Dumnoniorum	Exeter	Britain	Misenum	Capo di Miseno	Italy
Italica	Santiponce	Spain	Moguntiacum	Mainz	Germany
Iuliomagus	Angers	France	Munda		Spain
Iuliobona			Mutina	Modena	Italy
Caletorum	Lillebonne	France	Mursa	Osijek	Croatia
Lambaesis	Lambese	Algeria	Mylae		Sicily
Laminium		Spain	Myra	near Demre	Turkey
Lampsacus	Lapseki	Turkey	Mytilene		Turkey
Lanuvium	Lanuvio	Italy	Naissus	Nis	Serbia
Laodicea		Turkey	Narbo Martius	Narbonne	France
Laodicea	Latakia	Syria	Naucratis		Egypt
Larisa	Larisa	Greece	Nemausus	Nîmes	France
Lauriacum	Lorch	Austria	Neocaesarea (Cabira)	Niksar	Turkey
Leptis Magna		Libya	Nicaea	Iznik	Turkey
Leptis Minor		Tunisia	Nicaea	Nice	France
Lilybaeum	Marsala	Sicily	Nicomedia	Izmit	Turkey
Limonum Pictonum	Poitiers	France	Nicopolis		Greece
Lindinis	Ilchester	Britain	Nicopolis		Egypt
Lindum	Lincoln	Britain	Nisibis	Nusaybin	Turkey
Londinium	London	Britain	Nola	Nola	Italy
Luca	Lucca	Italy	Nora		Sardinia
Lucus Augusti	Lugo	Spain	Novae	Swisjtow	Bulgaria
Lugdunum			Novaesium	Neuss	Germany
(Condate)	Lyon	France	Noviomagus		
Lugdunum			Regnorum	Chichester	Britain
Convenarum	St. Bertrand de		Noviomagus	Neumagen	Germany
	Comminges	France	Noviomagus		
Luna	Luni	Italy	Batavorum	Nijmegen	Netherlands
Lutetia Parisiorum	Paris	France	Nuceria	Nocera	Italy
Madauros	M'Daourouch	Algeria	Numantia	Soria	Spain
Maia	Bowness	Britain	Odessus	Varna	Bulgaria
Malaca	Malaga	Spain	Oea	Tripoli	Libya
Mantua	Mantova	Italy	Olisipo	Lisbon	Portugal
Marcianopolis	Devnya	Bulgaria	Olympia	Olympia	Greece
Mariana		Corsica	Osca	Huesca	Spain
Masada	Mexada	Israel	Ostia	Ostia	Italy
Massilia	Marseille	France	Ovilava	Wels	Austria

Roman Name	Modern Name	Country	Roman Name	Modern Name	Country
Oxyrhynchus		Egypt	Scallabis	Santarem	Portugal
Paestum	Paestum	Italy	Scupi	Skopje	Macedonia
Palmyra		Syria	Sebastea		
Patavium	Padua	Italy	(Megalopolis)	Sivas	Turkey
Pax Iulia	Beja	Portugal	Segedunum	Wallsend	Britain
Pella		Greece	Segontia	Siguenza	Spain
Pelusium		Egypt	Segora	Bressuire	France
Pergamum	Bergama	Turkey	Segovia	Segovia	Spain
Perge	Aksu	Turkey	Segusio	Susa	Italy
Perinthus (Heraclea)		Turkey	Seleucia	Silifke	Turkey
Perusia	Perugia	Italy	Seleucia Pieria	Samandag	Turkey
Petra		Jordan	Serdica	Sofia	Bulgaria
Petuaria	Brough	Britain	Side	Selimiye	Turkey
Pharsalus	Pharsala	Greece	Singara		Iraq
Philadelphia	Amman	Jordan	Singidunum	Belgrade	Serbia
Philippi		Greece	Sinope	Sinop	Turkey
Philippopolis	Plovdiv	Bulgaria	Sirmium	Mitrovica	Serbia
Piraeus	Piraeus	Greece	Siscia	Sisak	Croatia
Pisae	Pisa	Italy	Sitifis	Setif	Algeria
Placentia	Piacenza	Italy	Smyrna	Izmir	Turkey
Poetovio	Ptuj	Slovenia	Sparta	Sparti	Greece
Pola	Pula	Croatia	Stratonicea		
Pompeii		Italy	(Hadrianopolis)	Eskihisar	Turkey
Potaissa	Turda	Romania	Sufetula	Sbeitla	Tunisia
Prusa	Bursa	Turkey	Syene	Aswan	Egypt
Ptolemais	Tulmaythah	Libya	Synnada		Turkey
Ptolemais Hermiou	El Manshah	Egypt	Syracusae	Syracuse	Sicily
Puteoli	Pozzuoli	Italy	Tarasco	Tarascon	France
Raphanaea		Syria	Tarentum	Tarento	Italy
Ratae Coritanorum	Leicester	Britain	Tarraco	Tarragona	Spain
Ratiaria	Arar	Bulgaria	Tarsatica		Croatia
Ravenna (Classis)	Ravenna	Italy	Tarsus	Tarsus	Turkey
Reate	Rieti	Italy	Tebtunis		Egypt
Resaina (Theodosiopolis)		Turkey	Tergeste	Trieste	Italy
Rhegium	Reggio	Italy	Thabraca	Tabarka	Tunisia
Rhodus	Rhodes	Greece	Thagaste	Souk Ahras	Algeria
Roma	Rome	Italy	Thamugadi	Timgad	Algeria
Rotomagus	Rheims	France	Thapsus	Rass Dimas	Tunisia
Rutupiae	Richborough	Britain	Thebae	Luxor	Egypt
Sabratha	Zouagha	Libya	Thessalonica	Thessaloniki	Greece
Saguntum	Sagunto	Spain	Thevestis	Tébessa	Algeria
Salamis		Cyprus	Thuburbo Maius		Tunisia
Salonae	Solin	Croatia	Thugga	Dougga	Tunisia
Samarobriva			Thysdrus	El Djem	Tunisia
Ambianorum	Amiens	France	Ticinum	Pavia	Italy
Samosata	Samsat	Turkey	Tingi	Tangiers	Morocco
Sardis		Turkey	Tipasa	Tefessad	Algeria
Satala	Kelkit	Turkey	Toletum	Toledo	Spain
Savaria	Szombathely	Hungary	Tolosa	Toulouse	France

Roman Name	Modern Name	Country
Tomi (Constantiana)	Constanta	Romania
Traianopolis (Doriscus)		Greece
Tralles	Aydin	Turkey
Trapezus	Trabzon	Turkey
Tridentum	Trento	Italy
Trimontium	Newstead	Britain
Tripolis	Tripoli	Lebanon
Turris Libisonis	Porto Torres	Sardinia
Tyrus	Tyre	Lebanon
Ulpia Traiana Sarmizegetusa		Romania
Uselis	Usellus	Sardinia
Utica	Utique	Tunisia
Valentia	Valence	France
Valentia	Valencia	Spain
Vasio Vocontiorum	Vaison-la-Romaine	France
Venta Silurum	Caerwent	Britain
Venta Icenorum	Caister	Britain
Venta Belgarum	Winchester	Britain
Venusia	Venosa	Italy
Vercellae	Vercelli	Italy
Verona	Verona	Italy
Verulamium	St. Albans	Britain
Vesontio Sequanorum	Besançon	France
Vesunna Petrucoriorum	Périgueux	France
Vetera (Colonia Ulpia Traiana)	Xanten	Germany
Vienna	Vienne	France
Viminacium	Kostolac	Serbia
Vindobona	Vienna	Austria
Vindonissa	Windisch	Switzerland
Viroconium Cornoviorum	Wroxeter	Britain
Virunum	Zollfeld	Austria
Volubilis		Morocco
Xanthus	Kinik	Turkey
Zama Regia	Zama	Tunisia
Zela	Zile	Turkey
Zeugma		Turkey

Rivers

Roman Name	Modern Name	Country
Addua	Adda	Italy
Anas	Guadiana	Portugal/Spain

Roman Name	Modern Name	Country
Arnus	Arno	Italy
Baetis	Guadalquivir	Spain
Bodotria	Forth	Britain
Danuvius	Danube	Central Europe
Dravus	Drava	Austria, Hungary, Croatia
Durius	Douro/Duero	Portugal/Spain
Duranius	Dordogne	France
Garumna	Garonne	France
Iberus	Ebro	Spain
Liger	Loire	France
Mosa	Meuse	France, Belgium, Netherlands
Mosella	Moselle	France, Germany Luxembourg
Nilus	Nile	Egypt, Sudan, Uganda
Padus	Po	Italy
Rhenus	Rhine	Switzerland, Germany, France, Netherlands
Rhodanus	Rhône	France
Sabrina	Severn	Britain
Savus	Sava	Croatia
Sequana	Seine	France
Tagus	Tajo	Portugal/Spain
Tamesis	Thames	Britain
Tiberis	Tiber, Tevere	Italy

Seas

Roman Name	Modern Name
Fretum Gallicum	Straits of Dover
Mare Adriaticum (Mare Adria)	Adriatic Sea
Mare Aegeum	Aegean Sea
Mare Caspium	Caspian Sea
Mare Erythraeum	Red Sea
Mare Ionium	Ionian Sea
Mare Mediterraneum	Mediterranean Sea
Mare Tyrrhenum	Tyrrhenian Sea
Oceanus Atlanticus	Atlantic Ocean
Oceanus Britannicus	English Channel
Oceanus Germanicus	North Sea
Oceanus Hibernicus	Irish Sea
Pontus Euxinus	Black Sea
Propontis	Sea of Marmara

READING

Expansion and Contraction of Rome's Territory

Cornell and Matthews 1982: illustrated with many maps; Hammond and Scullard (eds.) 1970; Talbert (ed.) 1985: illustrated by many maps; Wacher 1987.

The Provinces

Alföldy 1974: Noricum; Baatz and Herrmann (eds.) 1982: Germany (Hessen); Bowman 1986: Egypt; Buck and Mattingly (eds.) 1985: Tripolitania, with extensive bibliography; Cüppers (ed.) 1990: Rhineland; Cornell and Matthews 1982: descriptions of various provinces; Curchin 1991: Spain; De Alarcao 1988; Portugal; Drack and Fellmann 1988: Switzerland; Filtzinger et al. (eds.) 1986: southern Germany; Frere 1967: Britain; Hammond and Scullard (eds.) 1970: descriptions of several provinces; Heinen 1985: Germany (Trier region); Horn (ed.) 1987: Germany (north Rhineland, Westphalia); Jones and Mattingly 1990: Britain, with many maps; Keay 1988: Spain; King 1990: Gaul and Germany; Lengyel and Radan (eds.) 1980: Pannonia; Magie 1950: Asia Minor; Mócsy 1974: Pannonia and Upper Moesia; Potter 1987: Italy; Rivet 1988: Gallia Narbonensis and Alpes Maritimae; Salway 1981: Britannia; Sanders 1982: Crete; Talbert (ed.) 1985; Wacher 1987: description of various provinces, with bibliography related to individual provinces; Warmington 1954: north African provinces in the late empire; Wightman 1985: Gallia Belgica; Wilkes 1969: Dalmatia; Wilson 1990: Sicily.

Place Names

Cornell and Matthews 1982: color maps throughout, pp. 231–36 gazetteer of places with latitude and longitude; Rivet and Smith 1979: place names of Britain; Talbert (ed.) 1985: several maps of provinces with place names; Talbert 1992: detailed record of atlases and maps of the Greek and Roman world, with extensive references.

Many of the references under provinces have maps with place names.

4

TOWNS AND COUNTRYSIDE

TOWN PLANNING

In Italy the earliest Etruscan towns grew with little or no planning, and many of the Italian towns and cities, including Rome itself, were also unplanned and grew without restriction. Especially where the ground was uneven, their streets had no clear pattern and were often very narrow, lined by tall buildings, with *scalae* (flights of steps) on the slopes. Many Greek colonies in Italy from about the 6th century BC were deliberately planned. The Greek colony of Poseidonia (Paestum) in southern Italy was built in the 6th century BC and represents the standard Greek town plan that had developed by then. It had a central space for public buildings, such as temples and the *agora;* the rest of the town was divided by a regular grid of wide avenues intersected by narrower streets. This type of town plan influenced the development of Etruscan town planning, which used a similar grid pattern of streets but had two major streets intersecting at right angles to provide a crossroads as a focal point in the town center.

Greek and Etruscan town plans were influential in the evolution of Roman town plans. As Rome's territory expanded, new towns and cities were founded that were also deliberately planned. These were for military security, administration and the economic exploitation of newly acquired regions as well as for advancing the process of Romanization. In new towns the principles of classical town planning were introduced. The foundation ceremony of new Roman towns originated in Etruscan times. An augur marked out the axes of the town, the *cardo maximus* and the *decumanus maximus,* based on astronomical sightings. A ritual furrow (*sulcus primigenius,* original furrow) was plowed to mark the line of the wall or rampart. The strip of land immediately outside the town wall (*pomerium*) was the formal and religious boundary of the town and was not allowed to be inhabited or plowed.

In their developed form Roman towns consisted of a square or rectangular perimeter with two axes (usually the main streets, *decumanus maximus* and *cardo maximus*) intersecting at right angles in the town center. Streets parallel to these axes formed a grid pattern that divided the area into blocks of land (*insulae*) for building. The shape of the *insulae* (sing. *insula*) was largely determined by the shape of the town perimeter, but they were usually square or rectangular and of equal size. Often, however, the plan of a town had to be adapted to the topography so that the perimeter was irregular, the streets were not evenly spaced or always parallel, and the size and shape of *insulae* varied. Even so, a regular grid of streets and *insulae* was laid out as far as possible.

As well as a regular street pattern, planned towns usually had a unified complex of *forum* and *basilica,* and eventually acquired public buildings such as a theater, amphitheater, baths and various temples. Many of the public buildings and the *forum* were often sited in the town center, although amphitheaters and theaters were more usually situated toward the perimeter.

There are obvious similarities between the plans of towns and those of camps and forts, not surprisingly since many planned towns were established as colonies in conquered territory, often being designed primarily as defendable strongholds. Because military surveyors and engineers probably were responsible for the initial layout of many of these towns, the similarities between town and fort plans were maintained even where defense was not a crucial factor.

Unplanned Towns

Because they were the product of unrestricted development, towns that were not deliberately laid out to a pattern (such as those settlements that grew up around forts, religious sanctuaries and *mansiones*) have extremely varied plans, although broad groups can be distinguished. Some towns developed at the junctions of two or more main roads or at river crossings, being centered around the actual junction or adjacent to it along one or more of the roads. Some towns began as ribbon developments alongside main roads, giving rise to characteristically long, narrow town plans. These types of settlements could develop into larger towns with an irregular street pattern extending away from the main roads. For a variety of reasons, some towns were initially established away from main communication routes, such as those associated with mines and quarries; some were completely unplanned; while others show an element of planning with a partially regular street plan. Frequently these towns were native settlements developed under Roman control.

CENTURIATION

There was generally no sharp distinction between town and country because many people living in towns owned or farmed land in the surrounding countryside or were farmworkers who traveled from the town each day to work in the fields. This was particularly true of the colonies where the founding inhabitants were usually given grants of land near the settlement.

Centuriation took place on a small scale from the 4th century BC. It was a means of distributing land to settlers of colonies using a grid traced out on the ground. Such land was normally *ager publicus* — state-owned land that had usually been acquired by conquest. The surveying manuals stated that the *pertica* (the entire area of centuriation) should be divided initially into four equal areas starting from the center of the town, but this was done only occasionally. Usually two axes were marked out on the ground (*decumanus maximus* and *cardo maximus*) to form the main boundaries. Existing roads sometimes served as the *decumanus maximus* or were incorporated into the centuriation layout. The divisions between plots of land were called *limites* (sing. *limes*), which were primarily boundaries, but often became footpaths, tracks or roads. The land divisions were known as *centuriae* (originally one *centuria* for 100 men), and division of land in this way was known as *centuriatio* (centuriation) or *limitatio* (division of land by intersecting *limites*). The *centuriae* were further subdivided by roads or footpaths leading to the individual plots.

A *centuria* commonly measured 20 x 20 *actus*, with an area of 200 *iugera*. A *centuria* therefore consisted of 100 2-*iugera* units, which was an early size of smallholding. (See also chapter 8.) Surveyors were also responsible for the allocation of the plots of land to the settlers, which was usually done by lottery. Once the land was allocated, it was registered and mapped.

A *cadaster* was a detailed survey for taxation purposes, and parts of three cadastral registries survive for Orange in France. The boundaries of the *centuriae* were inscribed on stones, with information such as landscape details, the siting of the lots in relation to the axes, the areas of tributary or colonial land, the land tax and the name of the official adjudicator.

Traces of centuriation cover large parts of the Roman world and are particularly noticeable from aerial photography — in almost the whole of Italy, north Africa, the former Yugoslavia, the Danube Valley and Provence, with traces elsewhere in France, Greece, the Near East, Belgium, Germany and, more doubtfully, Britain.

Land outside but attributed to a town was called the *territorium*, which all *coloniae* and most *municipia* possessed. It was defined by natural features such as streams and rivers, or by man-made features such as walls. Alternatively, boundary stones (*termini*) were used, which were connected with the god Terminus and had a religious as well as legal significance.

On centuriated land, centuriation stones were supposed to mark all crossroads, but so few have survived that it is possible that wooden markers were normally used. Unlike boundary stones, centuriation stones had no religious significance.

TYPES OF TOWN

Various types of Roman settlement are now regarded as towns and cities, but not all would have been recognized as such at the time. This is particularly true of the many small settlements that were not administrative centers defined by Roman law. They are sometimes termed "small towns" to distinguish them from the main towns and cities in a region. The word city is usually applied to a planned urban settlement with its own municipal administration. However, some unplanned villages could acquire chartered status, and so the term town is preferred here, whatever the site's status in Roman times. Some settlements developed from villages to towns, became *municipia* and even *coloniae*, such as occurred in France at Vienne, in England at York and in Hungary at Budapest. The general Latin word for a city was *urbs* (pl. *urbes*), and *oppidum* (pl. *oppida*) for a town.

Coloniae

Coloniae (sing. *colonia*) were settlements or colonies established by the state to form a self-administering community, often with a strategic defensive function. Most colonies were founded on state-owned land, but sometimes they were established on land belonging to a *municipium* — an existing town incorporated into the Roman state, whose inhabitants might or might not be Roman citizens.

Colonies were founded from an early stage in Rome's history, with three Italian colonies apparently established during the monarchy and 11 more before 338 BC. These early colonies were settled by Romans to protect Rome from hostile Italian tribes. After the defeat of the Latin League in 338 BC, the Latin colonies (composed largely of Romans who did not have Roman citizenship) were independent states that were controlled by Rome only in matters of foreign affairs. They also had obligations to supply contingents to the Roman army. By the end of the 2nd century BC, colonies were established at key points throughout Italy.

As Rome's territory expanded in the late republic and early empire, increasing numbers of colonies were founded outside Italy as a means of establishing loyal communities in newly captured areas. Most settlers were usually retired legionaries, and in the 1st century BC, the main purpose of founding colonies was to provide land for legionary veterans. Within Italy, land was purchased or confiscated, and confiscation caused much discontent. Julius Caesar founded a large number of colonies, mainly outside Italy. Colonization appears to have reached a peak under Augustus, although subsequent emperors, such as Claudius, were eager to found colonies in the newest provinces.

The title *colonia* was also conferred on some existing provincial towns. After Hadrian's reign this became common, and the founding of colonies in unsettled areas became rare. Even small settlements (such as those attached to fortresses and forts) could be upgraded as they developed, eventually being given the status of *colonia*.

Municipia

During the republic the title *municipium* (pl. *municipia*) was given to Italian towns, the inhabitants of which had been granted Roman citizenship without voting rights. These towns had a certain amount of independence, but foreign affairs came under the control of Roman magistrates. Those that received this status were sometimes allied towns or were in conquered territory. After voting rights were conferred on all Italian communities in the early 1st century BC, citizens of *municipia* became full Roman citizens. As the empire expanded the status of *municipium* was conferred on towns outside Italy whose inhabitants were not Roman citizens. In these cases Roman citizenship was conferred only on the local magistrates, or sometimes on all the town councillors. During the early empire, therefore, a *municipium* could have a population of Roman citizens or of non-citizens governed by Roman citizens. A *municipium* was lower in status than a *colonia*.

Poleis

Throughout the hellenized eastern part of the Roman Empire, cities (Greek *poleis* — sing. *polis*) were already established before the area came under Roman control. These cities generally continued to act as administrative units within their regions, supplemented by *coloniae* and *municipia*.

Civitates

In the western empire there was no real tradition of towns and cities to compare with those in Italy and the east. Julius Caesar and other authors used the term *oppidum* very loosely, applying it to various fortified native sites in Gaul and Britain. During the empire native communities were originally administered on a tribal basis, and these were called *civitates* (sing. *civitas*). This term was used mainly for communities of noncitizens but came to refer loosely to the villages and towns that were designated the administrative capitals of these *civitates*, now often called *civitas* capitals.

Small Towns and Villages

In all parts of the empire, there were small towns and villages which had no official status or classification. In the west many were called *vici* (sing. *vicus*), a term meaning a district of a town, a native (noncitizen) town or village or a settlement attached to an auxiliary fort. In the eastern empire such settlements were called *comes* (sing. *come*). Some *vici* acted as administrative centers of rural districts (*pagi*). Outside the legionary fortresses, considerable settlements often grew up for the purpose of supplying goods and services to the legions. Such settlements were known as *canabae* or *cannabae* (sing. *canaba* or *cannaba*, literally "hut" or "hovel"). Many villages in the west were destroyed or abandoned from the 3rd century, whereas they continued to the 5th and 6th centuries in many parts of the east.

TOWN AMENITIES

Streets

All towns were based on a network of streets, which were in a regular grid pattern in planned towns and a loose irregular pattern in unplanned towns. The quality of the streets themselves varied. In more prosperous towns the streets were paved with stone, and the earliest recorded street paving dates back to 238 BC. Later on, raised stone walkways (*crepidines*) were also constructed to help protect pedestrians from litter and dirt in the streets. Stepping-stones enabled pedestrians to cross from one raised walkway to another without descending into the street. The gaps between these stepping-stones allowed passage to wheeled vehicles, attested by wheel ruts worn in the paved surfaces of many Roman streets (fig. 4.1).

In poorer towns and poorer districts of large towns and cities, the streets were of poorer quality, lacking raised walkways and stepping-stones, which forced pedestrians to walk in the streets. In small towns the streets might be little more than tracks with a rough surfacing of cobbles or gravel. The width of streets in towns also varied considerably. On the widest streets, wheeled vehicles could pass each other easily, while the narrowest were negotiable only on foot, being too narrow for litters and load-bearing animals. For roads and streets, see also chapter 5.

Fig. 4.1 Paved street at Pompeii with raised sidewalks, stepping-stones and wheel ruts.

Fora

The *forum* (pl. *fora*) was a large open space in a town but the term was used specifically for the main "square" — the meeting place, marketplace and political center, which functioned in a way similar to the *agora* in a Greek town. The *forum* was usually rectangular in shape, surrounded by public buildings, and often had a colonnaded portico with shops and offices, providing a covered walkway and shopping area. In most towns the *forum* was the central feature, but large towns could have additional *fora* devoted to specific purposes, such as a *forum olitorium* (vegetable market), *forum boarium* (cattle market), *forum piscarium* (fish market) or *forum cuppedinis* (dainties market). These types of *forum* were really more like *macella*, with which there is some overlap.

In early *fora* the layout of the surrounding buildings was usually haphazard, but from the mid-1st century unified planning of the *forum* complex became more common. In Gaul and parts of Germany and Dalmatia, the so-called Gallic *forum* developed, which was an open rectangle flanked on at least two sides by colonnades of shops and offices and at one end by the basilica.

CRYPTOPORTICOS

A *cryptoporticus* consisted of vaulted corridors that were separated by massive stone piers with arches. Some were underground (such as at Arles in France) and are found mainly in Gaul. They seem to have functioned originally as underground versions of the porticos normally found in a *forum*, and at Arles the *cryptoporticus* was below the *forum* porticos. In the late Roman period cryptoporticos seem to have been used for storage.

Water Supply and Drainage

WELLS AND CISTERNS

Although in some instances water was obtained from nearby springs and rivers, in most towns the supply came largely from wells. Towns such as London never had an aqueduct, but relied on wells, which were usually circular or square shafts dug to intercept the local water table. They were lined with stone or with wood, and in some instances wooden barrels with the ends removed were used for a lining. Stone-built cisterns, some extremely large, were also used in towns to store water, particularly in the eastern empire.

AQUEDUCTS

Some towns were supplied with water from a nearby source through an aqueduct. In most if not all cases, the initial reason for constructing an aqueduct was to supply a large quantity of water for use in the public baths. Once such a supply was established, it came to be used for drinking water and for private bathhouses as well.

Wherever possible, aqueducts ran at ground level or were buried just below it, in channels or in pipes. The water usually ran in a covered conduit built of stone and lined with waterproof cement. The conduit was normally only half full of water; the extra height was used to enable removal of calcium carbonate

Fig. 4.2 The arched bridge (Pont du Gard) in France carrying the covered channel of the aqueduct across the Gardon River to Nîmes. Height 49.38 m (162 ft).

deposits that formed inside the conduit and so narrowed the water channel. There were inspection chambers at ground level for access. In a few instances it was necessary to carry the channel of the aqueduct across a valley using a bridge, usually built on a series of arches (fig. 4.2). An aqueduct was built with a downhill gradient from the source to the town, so that water flowed to the town under gravity. In low-lying terrain, the aqueduct was carried on long masonry arcades in order to maintain the gradient. The ruins of these bridges across valleys and of arcades of arches across low-lying land are most easily recognized as the remains of aqueducts.

While pumps are known to have been used in Roman times, they were little used in the aqueduct system. Where it was not possible to build a bridge to carry an aqueduct channel across a valley, the water was diverted into a series of closed pipes (usually of lead or ceramic). The pipes passed down one slope of the valley and up to a lower point on the other side where the aqueduct became a channel once more. Using the inverted siphon principle, the water flowed through the pipes until it found its own level again. A bridge (*venter*) could be built across the bottom of the valley to take the pipes, and such bridges resemble ordinary aqueduct bridges or arcades. Pipes must have been difficult to clean and were probably more expensive to install than building aqueduct bridges with channels.

Because the water flowed under gravity, an aqueduct was routed to the highest part of a town. The water was passed through one or more settling tanks to a distribution tank (*castellum* or *castellum divisorum*), from where supplies were distributed to other districts using conduits or pipes. The one at Nîmes, France, distributed the water through 13 large lead pipes that supplied various parts of the town. For distribution at a local level, pipes of lead, ceramic, leather and wood are all known to have been used. Householders had to pay for a water supply based on pipe diameter, the standard measuring unit being the *calix* (pl. *calices*) or nozzle. Details of the aqueducts supplying Rome are given in the book *On the Water Supply of Rome*, written in the late 1st century by Frontinus, who was in charge of Rome's water supply at that time. It has been estimated that Rome was supplied with around half a million to 1 million cubic meters (17.5 million to 35 million cubic ft) daily.

Aqueducts delivered a continuous supply of water that could not be stopped, only diverted, so that

Fig. 4.3 Public drinking fountain and tank at the corner of two streets in Herculaneum.

provision of such a water supply also required provision of a drainage system. Underground sewers, usually built beneath the streets, carried overflow water and waste from latrines and bathhouses. Sewers were usually built of stone, sometimes of timber, and the main sewers of a town could be of a considerable size. They were equipped with manholes at regular intervals that provided access for cleaning and repair by the municipal slaves. Smaller drains consisted of covered stone or timber-lined channels, or were built of tiles mortared together to form a vault.

In some towns water was supplied to public drinking fountains in the streets, which fed stone tanks (fig. 4.3), the overflow from which drained into the sewers. Channels or gutters in the streets carried away surface water and may sometimes have acted as open sewers. The effluent from drains and sewers was discharged into cess pits and soakaways or into nearby rivers.

Public Buildings

BASILICAS (fig. 4.4)

The basilica was a large rectangular hall, usually with a central nave and lateral aisles, one or more apses and a timber or sometimes a vaulted roof. The nave was normally taller than the lateral aisles and had clerestory windows for lighting, and there was often a covered entrance porch (*narthex*). Basilicas were usually built on one side of the *forum*. In smaller towns the basilica could form the whole of one side of the *forum*, with colonnades on the other three sides.

Basilicas were used as public meeting halls, law courts and town administration. They performed a similar multipurpose function to stoas in Hellenistic towns but do not appear to be directly derived from them. The earliest known basilicas date back to the late 3rd century BC, and they rapidly became a standard feature of Roman towns. In the very late Roman period basilicas were a model for Christian churches, and several Roman basilicas were converted into churches.

CURIAE

Each *curia* (pl. *curiae*) had its own meeting place, and the word came to mean senate house. At Rome, the Curia Hostilia was thought to have been built by the king Tullus Hostilius in the mid-7th century BC. It was burned down by the mob in 52 BC and was rebuilt nearby by Julius Caesar in 44 BC. It was the meeting place of the Senate. Adjacent to the *curia* was the *comitium*, which was a consecrated open space for popular assemblies. The *curia* and *comitium* formed part of the forum complex in Rome, and this pattern was repeated in towns throughout the Roman world, where the *curia* was used as the meeting place of the town council (also called *curia*). The *curiae* tended to be rectangular in plan with benches along the side walls and the magistrates' dais along one short end facing the doors.

TEMPLES

The major temples in a town were usually situated in the *forum* complex or adjacent to it, but temples could

Fig. 4.4 The Basilica (Aula Palatina) at Trier was built c. 310 as an imperial reception hall (aula) by Constantine I as part of the palace when Trier was a capital. It was constructed entirely of bricks.

also be found elsewhere in towns. For temples, see chapter 7.

MACELLA

A *macellum* (pl. *macella*) was a meat market, but the term came to be used for a market hall housing shops and stalls selling provisions, and there was some overlap in function with *fora*. The most common design was similar to a *forum*, with an open square for market stalls surrounded by a portico of shops. *Macella* were often sited close to the *forum*. The most grandiose example of such a market is that known as Trajan's Market at Rome, which provided over 150 individual shop units. Virtually no *macella* are known in the northern provinces.

PUBLIC BATHS (figs. 4.5, 4.6)

Hot air or steam baths were known in the Greek world as early as the 5th century BC and seem to have become established in Italy by the 3rd century BC. Originally, public and private baths were called *bal(i)neae* (plural noun) or *bal(i)nea* (sing. *bal(i)neum*). They were small baths suites with individual baths that were filled and emptied by hand. The invention of hypocaust heating in the 1st century BC led to the development of bath suites with hot and cold rooms and plunge baths, and bathing became a communal activity. These large public and private bathhouses were known as *thermae*, a term first used for Agrippa's Baths (fig. 3.2), which were built at Rome in the late 1st century BC. They were the first of a long series of ever-grander bath buildings provided by emperors for the people of Rome (fig. 3.2). *Thermae* became a feature of Roman life that spread rapidly throughout the empire.

The design and layout of bath buildings varied, but typically comprised a suite of hot, warm and cold rooms. They included an *apodyterium* (changing room), *tepidarium* (warm room, usually without a bath), *caldarium* (hot room with hot plunge bath) (fig.

Fig. 4.5   The apse of the caldarium of the early 4th-century baths at Trier. The huge baths formed the southern boundary of the imperial palace, but were never finished because Constantine I moved the capital to Constantinople.

Fig. 4.6   Part of the system of huge service corridors with drains beneath the imperial baths at Trier.

4.5) and a *frigidarium* (cold room with cold plunge bath). Additional features could comprise a *laconicum* (hot dry room) or a *sudatorium* (hot room to induce sweating). Outside there could be a *natatio* (swimming pool) and a *palaestra* (porticoed enclosure for sport and exercise). *Gymnasia* (sing. *gymnasium*) were also sometimes part of a bathhouse complex. Originally the *gymnasium* and *palaestra*, terms that became virtually synonymous, were Greek institutions. The *gymnasium* was for athletics training and practice, with indoor and outdoor facilities, and was a meeting point for teachers and philosophers on the principles of training for mind and body, whereas the *palaestra* was technically a school for wrestlers and boxers.

LAVATORIES

Towns might have one or several public lavatories (*foricae*), often associated with the public baths. They consisted of a sewer over which a line of seats of wood or stone were set. The seating was communal, with no partitions. The sewer was flushed with waste water,

usually from the baths, and in front of the seats was a gutter with continuous running water for washing. The same system was used in latrines in forts and fortresses.

MANSIONES

Some inns and posting stations of the *cursus publicus* were sited in towns, though they were not always specifically built for the *cursus publicus*. (For the *cursus publicus*, see chapter 5.)

Monuments

Monuments in honor of prominent citizens were erected in towns throughout the Roman world, often in the *forum*. They included statues, equestrian statues, columns and inscriptions. Monumental honorific arches bearing statues and other sculpture were constructed from at least the early 2nd century BC. They were known as *fornices* (sing. *fornix*), a term replaced by *arcus* (pl. *arcus*) in the early empire. Triumphal arches (fig. 2.12) were also built to commemorate victories. (See chapter 2.) The term triumphal arch is often used for all types of honorific arch, whether or not they were associated with a triumph. The arches were free-standing, and imperial ones were usually dedicated to the emperor or members of his family, but they might also be dedicated to towns or gods. Arches were frequently positioned on bridges and on provincial or city boundaries. Early arches had one vaulted passageway, but later ones sometimes had two smaller passageways flanking the main one. The tetrapylon arch had two passageways intersecting at right angles. It was a type known at Rome (such as the Arch of Janus) but was particularly common in Africa. Above the arch was the attic, usually adorned with sculpture and a dedicatory inscription.

Buildings for Entertainment

THEATERS

From the late 3rd century BC plays were performed at Rome in temporary wooden buildings in the Forum or Circus Maximus. The first permanent theater at Rome was built by Pompey in 55 BC (fig. 3.2), but elsewhere permanent Roman theaters were built before this date, probably from early in the 1st century BC.

The design of Roman theaters was based on Greek examples. The latter were usually built into a hillside, with a circular orchestra and a low stage opposite the auditorium. Most Roman theaters, though, were built as free-standing structures with solid masonry or vaults supporting the curved and sloping auditorium (*cavea*), and there was a semicircular orchestra. The vaults gave easy access to the tiers of seating, and there was often a colonnaded gallery around the top row of seats. The masonry building behind the stage (*scaenae frons*) was as high as the auditorium. Unlike Greek theaters, the audience did not therefore have a view out of the theater directly over the stage. The *scaenae frons* had three or occasionally five doorways, which were usually flanked by projecting columns, and the entire front of the *scaenae frons* was decorated with columns and had niches with statues.

In front of the stage was a trough or trench for the curtain (*aulaeum*), which was lowered into the trough at the beginning of the performance and raised at the end. There were also smaller curtains (*siparia*) to screen off parts of the *scaenae frons* as required. The *orchestra*, the flat space between the stage and the auditorium, was used for seating for senators, priests and officials. Above the stage was a wooden roof that also acted as a sounding board. The audience was protected from sun and rain by an awning (*velum* or *velarium*) rigged on ropes from masts on the top of the auditorium. In some theaters, covered porticos were built as part of the auditorium or behind the *scaenae frons* to provide shelter for the audience between performances.

ODEA

A smaller, specialized type of theater was the *odeum* (pl. *odea*), which catered to musical performances and shows which were more refined than those performed in the theaters. *Odea* occurred mainly in the Hellenistic east and were of two types. The unroofed type was a smaller version of a theater, while the *theatrum tectum* (roofed theater) was enclosed in a square building with a roof. The unroofed type is sometimes classified as a theater, with the term *odeum* being reserved for roofed theaters.

AMPHITHEATERS

Unlike the theater, the amphitheater had a Roman, not a Greek, origin. Most amphitheaters are found in the west, with very few in the east where Greek influence was strongest. Gladiatorial and wild beast shows were first held at Rome in open areas such as the *forum* or circus. The earliest amphitheaters date back to c. 120 BC in Campania. The first permanent amphitheater at Rome is dated 29 BC.

Amphitheaters were elliptical or oval structures surrounding an elliptical or oval open space (*arena*) on which the shows took place. The sloping tiers of seats around the *arena* could be supported on solid banks of earth held by retaining walls with external staircases. Alternatively, the seating could be supported on vaulted masonry structures similar to that used in theaters. As with theaters, there was an awning (*velum* or *velarium*) to protect the spectators. In the larger amphitheaters, there were chambers and service corridors below the *arena* where

Fig. 4.7 The Flavian amphitheater (Colosseum) at Rome. The arched and vaulted structure would have supported tiers of seating around the elliptical arena. The arena's floor is no longer in situ revealing the service corridors and chambers beneath. Length 188 m (616 ft), width 156 m (511 ft).

animals for the shows were kept (fig. 4.7), with manually operated lifts to transport them to the *arena* through trapdoors.

It has been thought that *naumachiae* (mock sea battles) took place in specially flooded amphitheaters. However, there is little evidence that amphitheaters could have been flooded, and aquatic spectacles were probably staged elsewhere, such as in artificial lakes. In some towns the amphitheater provided the only entertainment. Because of their size, amphitheaters were usually sited on the edge of towns, sometimes even outside the circuit of the town walls. Military amphitheaters (*ludi*) were also built near forts and fortresses and were used for military training as well.

CIRCUSES AND STADIA

The circus was a building used primarily for chariot racing, with similarities to the Greek hip-

podrome, although it is unclear whether the Roman circus was a direct descendant of the hippodrome. A circus had tiers of seats for spectators, built around a U-shaped *arena*, within which the racing took place. Down the center of the U was a barrier (*spina*), with a *meta* (pl. *metae*, turning posts) at each end. At the open end of the U were the *carceres* (starting gates), from where up to 12 four-horse chariots (*quadrigae*) drove to the right of the *spina* and continued in a counterclockwise direction around the *spina* for seven laps. Toward each end of the *spina* were seven markers, one of which was removed as each lap was completed. The *spina* was lavishly ornamented with sculptures, obelisks, water basins and fountains. Circuses were also used for racing two-horse chariots (*bigae*), and in the republic and early empire various other events were staged, such as horse races, foot races, athletics and even gladiatorial shows and mock battles. The earliest circus at Rome was the *Circus Maximus* (fig. 3.2), reputedly constructed in the monarchy. In the east hippodromes were used for similar activities in the Roman period.

The *stadium* (pl. *stadia*) was a type of Greek building designed for athletics. *Stadia* were adopted by the Romans at a relatively late stage; the first permanent one at Rome was built late in the 1st century (fig. 3.2), although earlier temporary examples are known. *Stadia* were similar to circuses and are often confused with them, since they are long narrow structures with at least one semicircular end. However, a *stadium* was less than half the size of a circus, about 180 to 200 m (594 to 660 ft) in length, with a narrower arena about 30 m (96 ft) wide. Also, *stadia* had only two turning posts, instead of the ornate central barrier of the circus. There is some overlap between circuses and *stadia*, because circuses were used for athletic events in towns without a *stadium*. In general, circuses are found mainly in the west, whereas *stadia* are found mainly in the east where the tradition of Greek games persisted.

Town Houses (fig. 4.8)

The town house was usually a *domus*—a single-family house. As with modern houses, there were various styles of Roman town house, but probably the most common was the *atrium* house. The evidence for Etruscan houses comes largely from tombs (which were based on house plans). It is likely that the earliest Etruscan houses had a single main room with a smaller room opposite the entrance, or possibly a set of rooms around a small courtyard, from which the Roman *atrium* house developed. Early town houses, such as at Pompeii, were usually built around an *atrium*, an unroofed or partially roofed area. They were later roofed except for an opening (*compluvium*) in the roof to provide light and air. From the 2nd century BC the *atrium* often had a basin (*impluvium*) below the *compluvium* to collect

Fig. 4.8   Reconstruction of part of an atrium *town house (House of the Tragic Poet) at Pompeii, showing the* atrium *with its* impluvium. From W. Gell (1832) *Pompeiana.*

rainwater (fig. 4.8). From the late 2nd century BC this type of house had extra rooms, a peristyle courtyard and/or garden (a courtyard or garden surrounded by a portico), and sometimes baths. Such a house might have only one doorway and one or two windows opening onto the street, which presumably increased security and reduced noise and other nuisances.

The *atrium* was a reception hall and living room, leading off which was the *tablinum*—a small room or alcove containing the family records (*tabulae*) and portraits (*imagines*) of ancestors. There might also be *cubiculi* (bedrooms), *triclinia* (dining rooms), *oeci* (reception rooms), *diaetae* (outdoor rooms for relaxation), a kitchen and lavatory. The size of the house and number of rooms is a reflection of the owner's wealth. The more lavish houses might have luxuries such as bath suites and libraries.

Another common form of town house was linear in plan, often consisting of a strip of rooms. Particularly in the northwest provinces, such a house might be built with one of its long sides fronting the street, below which one or more wings of rooms extended. In towns where space was at a premium or street frontage was expensive, such a house might have been built with one of its narrow ends (usually a shop) fronting the street. This type of house is sometimes called a strip house.

Many other minor variations of town-house plan exist, and their methods of construction also varied, mainly reflecting local availability of materials and to some extent the wealth of the owner. Houses were commonly built of stone, but in the provinces timber frames with walls of wattle and daub infill were often used set on foundations or low walls of stone. In some areas houses were built of mud brick. Materials used for decoration are a more reliable indicator of wealth, as many were imported from a distance at great cost. Surviving evidence, such as at Pompeii, shows that the interior of most houses was decorated and that the street frontages of buildings were painted in red on the lower part of the walls and white above.

Because evidence so rarely survives, it is not known to what extent town houses had upper stories. Where upper stories have survived, some have been shown to be later additions. As with other features of town houses, the number of stories probably varied considerably. It is generally assumed that most town houses were single story, although there is increasing evidence for upper stories, particularly in strip houses. A few town houses also had cellars.

Apartments

By the end of the 1st century, there was growing pressure on land within some of the more overpopulated towns, and the single-family *domus* began to give way to the apartment block or tenement. The term *insulae* (rectangular areas of building plots within a town) was also used for rectangular apartment blocks. This did not imply that they were so large as to cover a whole *insula*: There might be six to eight apartment blocks within an *insula*. They were built around an open courtyard, usually with shops fronting the street at ground level. There were often three or more stories, making the courtyard more of a light well in the center of the building.

By the end of the republic the majority of the population at Rome was housed in rented rooms in apartment blocks owned by landlords. The apartment blocks acquired a bad reputation for being overcrowded and unsafe, although there appears to be some variation in their quality. They were constructed of timber and mud brick, which made them particularly vulnerable to fire and collapse. The upper stories lacked heating and running water, and apartments only occasionally had lavatories. Later *insulae*, such as ones at Ostia dating from the 1st century, were much more solidly built from concrete and fired bricks. They appear to have been very similar in design and function to the earlier apartment blocks, and so may not have been much of an improvement for the tenants. Augustus limited the height of *insulae* to 60 Roman feet (17.75 m, or 58 feet: a maximum of five stories), and Nero introduced fire regulations.

In the 4th century at Rome, *insulae* outnumbered the *domus* type of house by more than 25 to 1. *Insulae* continued to be the main type of housing for the majority of the population in some of the larger cities (such as Rome itself) until the end of the empire.

Palaces

Many imperial palaces came to be built at Rome (fig. 3.2), such as the huge *domus aurea* (Golden House) of Nero (demolished soon afterward). Some of the imperial palaces were built in the countryside, such as Hadrian's villa at Tivoli. In the late Roman Empire palaces were situated in cities such as Trier (figs. 4.4, 4.5) and Constantinople.

Shops

The single-unit shop was a common feature of towns, usually occupying part of the street frontage of a house or apartment block. Houses with a linear plan and narrow frontage often had shops (*tabernae*) or workshops fronting the street, the houses possibly deliberately designed to incorporate this feature. Shops and workshops are also found incorporated into apartment blocks and into every style of town house. In some cases the shops are obvious modifications to the original design of the house, while in others it is uncertain whether the shop was an original feature. Some shops had a single room only, while others had rooms behind for storage and production and a mezzanine floor for storage or living quarters (fig. 4.9).

Many shops had solid masonry counters for display and sale of goods. Some counters had large ceramic jars built into them (fig. 4.10), which were used for serving wine and foodstuffs. The mouths of the jars were flush with the surface of the counter, Some shops sold goods produced elsewhere, while others produced the goods for sale in an area behind the shop front. A bakery, for example, could have mills, ovens and storage for grain at the rear of the shop.

During the empire there was a tendency for some shops to be grouped into intentionally built markets (*macella*), which also acted as a focus for other shops to cluster in the surrounding area. The *forum* was another center attracting shops and market stalls. Inns and brothels were not uncommon in towns, but only the ones built specifically for that purpose are recognizable.

Fig. 4.9 A row of shops with upper stories at Herculaneum.

Fig. 4.10   A counter of a shop with large ceramic jars at Herculaneum.

Warehouses and Granaries

Towns throughout the Roman Empire had granaries and warehouses (*horrea*) that were used for storing goods—from building materials to foodstuffs, often grain. *Horrea* were built of stone or wood with tile or slate roofs, but their forms varied widely across the empire. Timber floors were raised to keep out vermin and to control the temperature and humidity of stored grain, allowing a good circulation of air beneath by means of ventilators set in the walls.

The need for large buildings for storage of food is a product of a large population concentrated in a small area. Rome itself had many *horrea* from the late republic, and as provincial towns expanded during the empire, the need for *horrea* correspondingly increased. At Rome and at its ports of Ostia and Portus, huge warehouses are known. The *Horrea Galbana* at Rome (fig 3.2) covered over 21,000 sq m (25,200 sq yd). Many warehouses consisted of rows of secure narrow rooms around a central courtyard. In time the courtyard was dispensed with owing to space pressure,

so that the warehouses became long narrow rows of rooms back to back. In Mediterranean areas *horrea* often consisted of walled yards, with *dolia defossa* (large storage jars set in the ground) for storing foodstuffs.

Town Fortifications

TOWN DEFENSES OF THE REPUBLIC AND EARLY EMPIRE

Most towns contemporary with early Rome were defended by fortifications, and the Romans adopted many ideas from other peoples, particularly the Greeks. The Romans believed the earliest defense of Rome to be the perimeter wall attributed to Servius Tullius, king of Rome in the late 6th century BC. However, excavations have shown that the earliest defense was an earth rampart from the first half of the 5th century BC, and that the "Servian" wall (fig. 3.1) was probably built in the 4th century BC. Other unplanned towns were also fortified relatively early in their history. In the east many *poleis* (cities) of the Greek world were built on sites specifically chosen for their defensive capacity—usually rugged hilltop sites or promontories.

The founding of colonies reached a peak in the reign of Augustus. Most newly founded colonies were provided with defenses, usually consisting of a wall with defendable gateways. One purpose of these colonies was to dominate their surrounding areas and implant the Roman way of life, but not all areas were hostile and so town walls may not always have been needed for defenses. However, impressive masonry walls provided the colony with enhanced status, representing the power of Rome.

Walls varied in plan and construction from town to town but were usually built as free-standing masonry walls with a carefully finished facing of small blockwork. Gateways were kept to a minimum (usu-

ally one per side if the town was planned as a rectangle), and were usually flanked by towers rising higher than the walls (fig. 4.11). There might also be interval towers on the perimeter wall itself. Gateways usually had single or double passageways for vehicles, flanked by narrower passageways for pedestrians. Beyond these general similarities, town gateways varied considerably throughout the empire. The flanking towers, for example, could be circular, rectangular, U-shaped or even octagonal in plan. Most gateways seem to have had architectural decoration, further enhancing the prestige of the town. In the late republic and early empire the portcullis, known at least as early as the Second Punic War, was introduced to strengthen some gateways (fig. 4.12).

After Augustus' death the establishment of new colonies and the building of town walls declined. By the early 2nd century many new towns had developed from smaller settlements and were not defended by walls, but during this century some of these towns

Fig. 4.11 The Porta Nigra *(Black Gate) was Trier's north gateway, probably built in the late 2nd century. It was constructed of blackish sandstone and decorated with pilasters. It had two passageways and two massive flanking towers. The apse (far right) was added in the Middle Ages. Height 30 m (98 ft 5 in).*

Fig. 4.12 One of the passageways through the Porta Nigra *gateway at Trier. It has a slot for the use of a portcullis in the nearest arch, which was raised and lowered by machinery above this level.*

were provided with defenses on a piecemeal basis (fig. 4.11). The most consistent approach was in Britain, where most major cities were defended by earth ramparts in the late 2nd and early 3rd centuries, and in many cases these were fronted by masonry walls soon afterward. There is no evidence that this was a centrally planned program of strengthening towns, and the reasons for it are unknown. Construction of defenses also occurred in the late 2nd century in some Thracian cities in response to threats from invading tribes from the north.

TOWN DEFENSES OF THE LATE EMPIRE

There was little further development in town defenses until the late Roman period. By the mid-3rd century the design of town walls was very similar to that of the Augustan period. Walls were 1 to 3 m (3 to 10 ft) thick, and any towers were usually circular or square in plan and set astride the wall, although the gateway towers could be larger and project farther beyond the wall. Generally there does not seem to have been any need to modify the design of town defenses in a drastic way in the 1st to 3rd centuries.

From the late 3rd century there were many innovations in the defenses of towns and forts, with similar methods being used for both types of fortification. Town gates still varied in design, the emphasis being much more on defense than prestige. The majority had only a single passageway between flanking towers. The plans of the flanking towers also varied, although the majority were U-shaped. However, there are so few remains of late Roman town gates that relatively little is known of their appearance. In some areas, particularly parts of Gaul, regional styles of construction can be recognized that may indicate contemporaneity of fortifications of those groups of towns sharing a similar style. It may also indicate imperial assistance with defenses implying that specific towns were chosen for strategic reasons.

By the late 3rd century in the west, towns in and immediately behind frontier zones were already fortified. Numerous towns of all sizes at strategic points deep in the heart of western provinces were also provided with defenses from this period in the face of increased invasions and the destruction of some Gallic towns. Many of these towns had circuits of walls considerably smaller than the town itself, even excluding major public buildings, although occupation continued outside the walls. Many walls were constructed of masonry from demolished buildings. Also in the late 3rd century, Rome received a new defensive wall (Aurelian wall) (fig. 3.2), the first since the Servian wall.

In the late Roman period many small settlements or road stations (*vici*) along major roads in Gaul were defended by a circuit of walls with bastions (such as Bitburg and Neumagen). They are often called *burgi* (sing. *burgus*), a term more usually applied to the smaller watchtowers of the frontiers. (See chapter 2.) These defended settlements may have housed military detachments.

VILLAS

Definition of Villas

During the middle and late Republic a *villa rustica* (house in the country) was a farmstead attached to an estate, with farm buildings and accommodation for the estate owner when he wished to visit. From the 2nd century BC the term *villa* was also used for large country houses that served as retreats from city life for wealthy Romans. The difference between these functions became blurred, and it is now virtually impossible to define precisely the function of Roman sites categorized as villas. The functions of such establishments probably varied with time, as they passed through the hands of different owners. These functions included farms run by an owner-occupier, by a bailiff for an absentee landlord or one who only visited occasionally, with the villa being a country retreat or even what might now be termed a stately home. The same villa might have performed all these functions over a period of time.

Villas had an element of wealth and luxury that distinguished them from other rural sites. The Romans were not consistent in their use of the term villa, and its definition is still disputed. In the widest sense, a villa was a farmhouse whose Romanized architecture distinguishes it from purely native farmsteads, and can range in size from a modest farmhouse to a mansion. Even this definition leaves a large number of borderline cases, particularly since the degree of Romanization recognizable from archaeological remains depends on the affluence and taste of the owner and occupier of the farm.

Villas developed and flourished during the empire, spreading to Africa, Spain, Provence, Gaul, Britain, Germany and the Danube provinces. A few villas are also known in the eastern provinces, but insufficient work has yet been done to establish their role and status.

In almost every case a villa was the product of a successful farm. Although villas may have been established from funds acquired from elsewhere, they were normally maintained from the profits of successful farming. Farming was dependent on a relatively local market, usually a town or city, and land was sometimes farmed by town residents. The distribution of villas tends to cluster around towns that provided profitable markets. A villa associated with farming together with its land (*ager*) formed an estate (*fundus*). However, not all farms were villas, and not all farms, particularly native ones in the provinces, developed into villas. A few villas appear to have been residences for Roman officials of various kinds, sometimes possibly attached to industrial enterprises or to imperial farming estates.

Types of Villa

The *villa suburbana* was common in Italy and was a farmstead built on the outskirts of towns in order to farm adjacent land. These villas were primarily residential and are often indistinguishable from town houses.

In Italy during the republic, the *villa rustica* developed from a simple building to a peristyle villa, which was a farmstead built around a courtyard or garden with a colonnaded portico on all sides. Some of the peristyle villas were large and complex. Luxury seaside villas (*villae maritimae*) became popular (fig. 5.17) and were retreats for the wealthy and for emperors. They included peristyle and porticus examples, the latter consisting of one or more rows of rooms with a colonnade.

The basic type of peristyle villa spread from Italy during the 1st century AD, but as the process of conquest and subsequent Romanization was not instantanous, the peristyle villa is more common in the first provinces to be conquered, such as Spain. In more outlying provinces, such as Britain, villas did not become common until the 2nd century. There was also a great deal of regional variation in the form and development of villas, reflecting the wealth and taste of the owners.

The most simple villa is sometimes termed the cottage type and consisted of a rectangular house, usually divided into a row of small rooms. These have much in common with native farmsteads and are not universally recognized as villas. This type of villa was often developed by the addition of a corridor or verandah (corridor villa) and then the addition of a wing at either end (winged corridor villa—fig. 4.13). In such villas the corridor may have been enclosed or an open verandah or portico; both types are known, and often the archaeological evidence is ambiguous.

Fig. 4.13   Reconstruction of a winged corridor villa at Mehring, Germany.

In outlying provinces the courtyard villa may have developed from forms such as the winged corridor villa rather than being a direct copy of the peristyle villa. The courtyard had buildings on between one and four sides, and is likely to have been a farmyard rather than a colonnaded garden as found in peristyle villas. In wealthier villas a second courtyard surrounded by farm buildings was built to separate the agricultural and residential functions of the villa. This separation of functions is a gradual process that often can be traced in the development of provincial villas, some of which became very grand country houses, where their residential function dwarfed their agricultural function.

A late development of villas, found in northern areas such as Britain, the Netherlands and northwest Germany, is the aisled building (sometimes called the aisled farmhouse, aisled house or basilica). The most simple form was a rectangular building with two rows of posts dividing the interior into a nave and two aisles. More developed forms also had internal divisions forming separate rooms, with mosaics, painted plaster, hypocausts and baths. Some aisled buildings, though, were outbuildings of larger, wealthier villas, and some had a specific agricultural or industrial, rather than domestic, use.

The main rooms in a villa broadly paralleled those in a town house. Depending on the wealth of the owner, there might be mosaics, painted plaster, hypocausts and baths. In large villas there were often many other rooms whose functions remain largely unknown, but probably included accommodation for guests, servants and slave quarters, and also storage rooms.

SURVEYORS AND SURVEYING

Much of Europe was explored in the 1st centuries BC and AD by military surveyors under Julius Caesar and the generals of Augustus. Surveyors are likely to have been used in centuriation; the construction of camps, forts and towns; and in road building. Although manuals on surveying are known, other literary evidence is sparse.

In late Latin a surveyor was called a *gromaticus* (groma man, from *groma*, a surveying instrument), but surveyors were more generally known as *agrimensores* (sing. *agrimensor*, land surveyors). A *mensor* (pl. *mensores*) was a surveyor or measurer who might be a land surveyor, military surveyor, architectural surveyor or even a corn measurer.

Surveying Instruments

Several authors, including Frontinus and Hyginus, wrote treatises on surveying that gave information on instruments such as the *groma* and *dioptra*. A *groma* (fig. 4.14) allowed surveyors to mark out lines at various angles to one another by taking sights from a central point. The metal parts of a *groma* have been found at Pompeii, and fragments are known from elsewhere, showing that it consisted of two bars of wood encased in iron sheeting, set at right angles to form a cross with four equal arms. This was reinforced near the center with bronze angle brackets. A plumb line was suspended from each arm to form the corners of a square. The center of the cross was attached by a bracket to a supporting staff so that the staff did not obscure the sight lines. The instrument was used by sighting through two plumb lines to distant markers that were moved until they were judged to be in line. Since the plumb lines provided sight lines at 45 degrees and 90 degrees to each other, lines at these angles could be marked out on the ground, enabling the surveying of straight lines, squares and rectangles.

The *dioptra* was a more sophisticated surveying instrument. It consisted of a sighting rod that could revolve freely about the center of a circular table that was marked with lines dividing the circle into quarters, eighths and so on. By revolving the sighting rod, lines at various angles could be surveyed. The circular table was set on a pillar, and plumb lines were used to set it up vertically. The circular table could be tilted from the horizontal for surveying sloping land. This tilting action was operated by a simple mechanism of cogs and screws. The *dioptra*, apparently made of bronze, is known only from a few ancient authors and appears to have been much less commonly used than

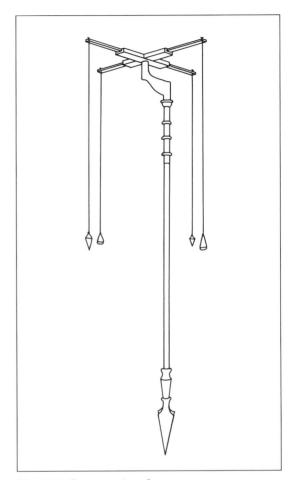

Fig. 4.14 Reconstruction of a groma.

the *groma*, probably because the latter was less expensive and more sturdy.

Accurate orientation during surveying was done by observation of the sun. For this a portable sundial was often used, several examples of which have been found. The most common method of orientation seems to have been the use of the sundial to calculate the position of the sun at midday (due south). This method, which is more accurate, was preferred to the observation of the rising and setting sun to establish due east and west.

Leveling, mainly of aqueducts, was done with a *chorobates*, which was a straight rule about 6 m (20 feet) long, supported at each end on legs of equal length. From the legs to the rule there were struts, alongside which were plumb lines. Lines perpendicular to the rule were marked on the struts, so that the rule was level when the plumb lines corresponded to these lines. An added refinement, used when strong winds made plumb lines inaccurate, was the use of a channel 1.5 m (5 feet) long in the top of the rule that could be filled with water. When the water touched the top of the channel at each end, the rule was level.

The *chorobates* was too unwieldy for field surveying, and the plumb line level (*libra* or *libella*) was used instead. This had a cross bar set on a post that was leveled by a plumb line in a similar way to the plumb lines on the *chorobates*. Sighting was then done along the upper surface of this cross bar toward a leveling staff marked with height graduations, in the same way that a modern optical level is used.

Measuring was done with measuring rods, ropes and cords for small distances, while elementary geometry was used for calculating longer distances, particularly over difficult terrain. Writing and drawing equipment was also commonly used. Although ancient authors refer to various other surveying instruments, it is unlikely that they were in common use.

ARCHITECTS AND ARCHITECTURE

The professions of architect and civil engineer were often closely linked. The main literary source on architecture and engineering was Vitruvius, himself an architect and engineer who had served with Julius Caesar and was later involved with the building of Augustus' new colonies in Italy. As is often the case today, many structures would have been constructed by building contractors without the aid of an architect or engineer. However, most of the large-scale projects, particularly the construction of public buildings, are likely to have been designed and supervised by an architect. Vitruvius stated that a large part of the job of an architect was supervision and organization of the building work itself.

It is unclear at what stage the profession of architect became recognized, but there is evidence of professional architects at least as early as the middle republic, with skills being handed down from father to son. They were employed by the army, the civil service or were in private practice. After the mid-2nd century BC the arrival in Rome of skilled Greeks seems to have had an impact, bringing new ideas and affecting the status of the profession, since many of the Greeks were slaves.

To draw plans, architects used dividers, calipers, folding rules and plumb bobs, all in forms recognizable today. A set of architect's tools has been found at Pompeii. Most architects would have had assistants and apprentices. For large projects an architect would have had an even greater work force under him, many of whom would have been responsible for elements of the work such as drawing the details of architectural mouldings.

Architectural Styles

ETRUSCAN AND GREEK INFLUENCE

The Etruscans were responsible for constructing Rome's earliest monumental buildings. Roman temples and houses were closely based on Etruscan models. Elements of Etruscan influence in Roman temples included the podium and the emphasis on the front at the expense of the remaining three sides. Large Etruscan houses were grouped around a central hall in much the same way as Roman town houses were later built around an *atrium*.

The influence of Etruscan architecture gradually declined during the republic in the face of influences (particularly Greek) from elsewhere. Etruscan architecture was itself influenced by the Greeks, so that when the Romans adopted Greek styles, it was not a totally alien culture. During the republic there was probably a steady absorption of architectural influences, mainly from the Hellenistic world, but after the fall of Syracuse in 211 BC, Greek works of art flooded into Rome. During the 2nd century BC, the flow of these works, and more important, Greek craftsmen, continued, thus decisively influencing the development of Roman architecture. By the end of the republic, when Vitruvius wrote his treatise on architecture, Greek architectural theory and example were dominant.

With the expansion of the empire, Roman architecture spread over a wide area, used for both public buildings and some larger private ones. In many areas elements of style were influenced by local tastes, particularly decoration, but the architecture remained recognizably Roman. Styles of vernacular architecture were influenced to varying degrees by Roman architecture, and in many regions Roman and native elements are found combined in the same building.

ARCHITECTURAL ORDERS

The Romans adopted the three orders of Greek architecture, the styles of which were defined mainly by the form of column, Doric, Ionic and Corinthian. The Doric order evolved in the 7th century BC and became the normal style in mainland Greece, Sicily and Magna Graecia. Greek Doric columns had no base, rising directly from the floor with a maximum diameter of about one-fifth or one-sixth the column height. The column had wide shallow flutings and tapered slightly from about one- quarter of its height from the floor. At the top of the column was a capital consisting of a basin-shaped circular molding and a plain square slab. Doric columns supported an entablature, the lowest portion of which was a rectangular stone beam called the architrave stretching from column to column. Above this was a frieze consisting of triglyphs (rectangular stones with surfaces divided into three by vertical grooves) interspersed with metopes (square sculptured stone panels set back from the triglyphs). Above the frieze was a projecting cornice, and at the end of a ridged roof were two sloping cornices, so that the three cornices enclosed a triangular panel (*tympanum*) to form the pediment.

The Greek Ionic order developed in the late 6th century BC. The Ionic column had a maximum diameter of one-eighth or one-ninth of the column height, giving it a more slender appearance than a Doric column. It also had deeper fluting, stood on a base and had a capital decorated with spiral scrolls. It supported an entablature in which the Doric triglyph frieze was replaced by a row of small projecting blocks (dentils) and sometimes also a continuous frieze of sculptured decoration.

The Corinthian order developed from the Ionic in the late 5th century BC, the main change being to the capitals of the columns, which became an inverted bell shape, decorated with acanthus leaves.

Besides copying these architectural styles, the Romans adapted them and developed new styles. Roman Doric columns, like all Roman columns, were set on a base, and were taller in proportion to their width, with slightly more complex moldings on the capitals. The Tuscan order of architecture seems to have been developed as a combination of the Doric and Ionic orders, with simple plain columns and entablatures. In the early empire the Corinthian order became the most popular style, and the Composite order was developed, combining the features of the Ionic and Corinthian orders.

BUILDING TECHNIQUES

At first the Romans built in stone, as did the Greeks, but concrete began to be used from the late 3rd century BC and increasingly replaced masonry. Concrete was cheaper and lighter and was more resistant to fire and damp. The main advantage of concrete construction was that, combined with arches and vaults, it allowed much larger areas to be roofed and stronger free-standing structures to be built. Various other building techniques, such as cob and mud bricks, were used, especially in the provinces.

Foundations

The first stage of a building was the preparation of the site, which might involve demolition of previous structures or leveling of the site. Foundations were also built by filling earlier buildings with rubble or incorporating earlier foundations into those of the new building. Sometimes the remains of earlier structures were encased in concrete or vaulted over. On a prepared site, foundation trenches were dug to bedrock or whatever was considered an adequate depth (as much as 5 to 6 m (16 to 20 ft) for a large temple). For large structures, the foundation trenches were usually filled with concrete, although stone was used

Walls

Walls were constructed on the completed foundations. At Rome the most common local building stone comprised relatively soft volcanic rocks, a factor that may have been instrumental in the use of mortared rubble construction and concrete walls with stone and brick facings, all of which were more sturdy than the soft volcanic rocks.

MORTARED RUBBLE AND CONCRETE WALLS

At least as early as the middle republic, walls were being constructed with a framework and facing of stone blocks and a rubble core set in clay. By the late 3rd century BC some walls were constructed at Rome with facings of mortared brickwork. They were filled with a core of small stones about 100 mm (4 in.) in diameter, over which mortar was poured to form a solid concrete wall (*opus caementicium*). The aggregate of small stones was known as *caementa*.

Concrete walls are more usually classified by their facings. The three main facings were *opus incertum*,

Fig. 4.15 Wall of opus quasi reticulatum.

where heavy loads were expected. Small buildings might have only a few courses of packed stone as a foundation.

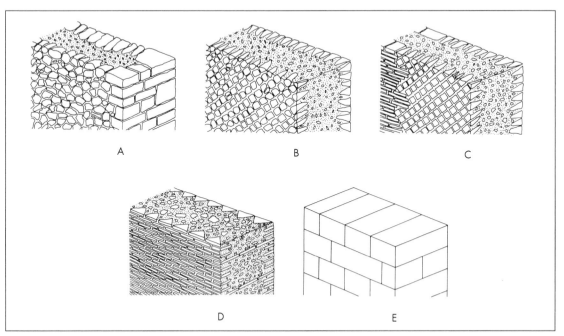

Fig. 4.16 Methods of constructing walls. A. opus incertum; *B.* opus quasi reticulatum; *C.* opus reticulatum; *D.* opus testaceum; *E.* opus quadratum.

opus reticulatum and *opus testaceum*. *Opus incertum* was mainly used in the 2nd and early 1st centuries BC and was a concrete core faced with small stone blocks in an irregular pattern. *Opus reticulatum* (figs. 4.16, 4.17) (from *reticulum*, net) was used mainly from the 1st century BC to 2nd century AD. The concrete core was faced with small square-ended stones set diagonally to form a regular netlike pattern. *Opus quasi reticulatum* (figs. 4.15, 4.16) is a term sometimes used where the diagonal netlike pattern was formed from irregularly shaped stones.

Opus testaceum (fig. 4.16) was used mainly from the mid-1st century and consisted of a concrete core faced with bricks or tiles. Bricks and tiles were occasionally used in buildings from the 2nd century BC, but *opus testaceum* was not predominant until the 1st century AD, during the time of Nero. The bricks and tiles were usually cut into triangles with one edge forming the facing of the wall. The wall construction normally began with the laying of a few courses of facing bricks, which were filled with a concrete core. At about every 25 brick courses, a bonding course of large bricks (*bipedales*) was laid, which extended across the width of the wall. The purpose of the bonding course is unclear since it separated the concrete core above and below it, creating a horizontal line of weakness. Bonding courses may have been connected with scaffolding, since scaffold (putlog) holes are usually found immediately above bonding courses. The exclusive use of brick as a facing material was rare outside Italy.

MASONRY WALLS

Even after concrete came to dominate Roman architecture, masonry was still widely used. Stone was expensive to transport, and so only particularly fine stones such as marbles were transported any distance, and then only for the most prestigious projects. Marble was not used in Roman buildings before the 1st century BC, but when it became popular, various colored marbles were imported (whereas the Greeks only used white marble), as well as other stones such as granites and basalts.

Generally any suitable local stone was used for building work, so that throughout the empire a great variety was used. The most popular at Rome was travertine, which was a form of limestone. Tufa, a volcanic rock similar to pumice, was also used at Rome, but there is some confusion since the term tufa is sometimes used for a type of travertine.

The Roman equivalent of Greek ashlar was *opus quadratum* (fig. 4.16), large square stones laid in horizontal courses. Walls were often built of massive stone blocks that were not mortared but stayed in position because of their great weight or were linked together by metal ties. The term *opus quadratum* is also sometimes used for a concrete wall faced with rectangular stone blocks.

Opus africanum was the use of massive horizontal and vertical dressed masonry blocks, containing panels of smaller masonry blocks, mud brick or faced concrete. It was particularly common in north Africa. *Opus vittatum* was the use of long and short masonry blocks.

Lewis holes enabled heavy stones to be gripped and lifted by the prongs of an iron lewis (lifting tackle). Cranes were also used to lift heavy materials such as masonry blocks, replacing the earlier method of lifting materials by ramps. The most common type was the shear-legs crane, consisting of two legs, pulleys and winches, and often with a treadwheel operated by slaves.

BRICK, EARTH AND TIMBER WALLS

Alongside these building methods, a wide variety of other methods of wall construction was used in the provinces, particularly for domestic and farm buildings. In some regions where there was a long-established tradition of building, such as the mud-brick architecture of the east or the stone architecture of the Greeks, the impact of Roman styles and methods was relatively small. In the Mediterranean area and the east, the use of unbaked mud brick was common, and examples of mud or earth-walled buildings have also been found in northern provinces.

Different types of earth walling were used to construct buildings of clay or cob. Various combinations of clay, earth, crushed baked earth or clay, stones and chalk were rammed between two boards held parallel by beams of wood. The resulting compacted clay or cob walls were plastered for protection from rain and to provide an even surface that often simulated stonework.

Bricks were used in walls throughout the Roman world, and there were two distinct types—baked and unbaked. Unbaked sun-dried bricks (mud bricks) were very common in the eastern provinces. They were made from loam or clay that was mixed with straw and chaff and then compacted, usually by treading with bare feet. The mixture was subsequently molded into bricks that were allowed to dry slowly— Vitruvius recommends at least two years, but this seems excessive, particularly as the bricks were only usually about 38 mm (1½ in) thick.

Baked bricks were also commonly used, and in some eastern areas they were preferred to unbaked bricks for use in large buildings. Baked bricks have a very long history, being used in Babylon in the 4th millennium BC, but do not appear to have been used in Rome before the time of Augustus. The preparation of baked bricks was more complicated than that of unbaked bricks. There were three main sizes of Roman brick: *bessales*, which were 197 mm (8 in) square; *sesquipedales*, which were 444 mm (1 ft 6 in) square; and *bipedales*, which were 592 mm (2 ft) square.

Opus mixtum was the use of leveling courses of baked bricks combined with *opus reticulatum*. A similar technique known as *petit appareil* was the use of small blocks of masonry laid in courses, with two or three courses of bricks at about 1 m (3 ft 4 in) intervals (fig. 4.5). Buildings were very rarely constructed entirely of brick; one such example was the basilica at Trier (fig. 4.4).

Also used for walling were various forms of timber frame, infilled with wattle and daub and then plastered or rendered. Buildings of timber are also known.

MORTAR

Simple lime mortar was commonly used throughout the Roman world, made from limestone and sand. The limestone was burned to form quicklime, which was then slaked by adding the correct amount of water to produce calcium hydroxide. This was mixed with sand (Vitruvius recommended one part slaked lime to three parts sand.) As it dried, calcium carbonate crystals formed from the slaked lime to produce the cohesion within the mortar. In some areas where it was obtainable, gypsum was used in plaster and mortar.

By the time of Augustus, a better cement using *pozzolana* had been developed. *Pozzolana* was a reddish volcanic earth found in large quantities around the harbor of Pozzuoli and from the Alban Hills. This cement, based on the reaction between lime and *pozzolana*, which is chemically much more complex than that of lime mortar, produced a fine hard mortar. It could set without first drying out and so could be used in damp conditions and even underwater. In other

Fig. 4.17 Window with an iron grille set in an opus reticulatum *wall at Herculaneum.*

Fig. 4.18 Reconstruction at Mehring villa of a window with an iron grille.

parts of the empire attempts were made to reproduce this hydraulic cement using local materials such as crushed volcanic stones. *Opus signinum* was a water-resistant cement used widely thoughout the Roman world. It was composed of a mixture of lime mortar and crushed tile, brick or pottery. The chemical composition of this mixture provided its water resistance. It was widely used in foundations, floors, bathhouses and as a sealant in other situations where water-resistant mortar or concrete was required.

DOORS AND WINDOWS

Doors were usually of wood, although they could be reinforced by ironwork, and bronze doors were used on some public buildings. Although doors themselves have rarely survived, their width and sometimes height can be determined from excavated buildings. Also, doors are portrayed in some wall paintings.

There is little direct evidence for windows, and many houses may have had no more than openings in the walls. Iron grilles are known (figs. 4.17, 4.18). The windows of

Fig. 4.19   A cast of a wooden window shutter at the Villa of the Mysteries, Pompeii.

most buildings were probably protected by wooden shutters (fig. 4.19), though evidence of this is rare.

Window glass dates from the 1st century and probably became cheaper and more commonly used with new manufacturing techniques. (See chapter 8.) The extent to which ordinary houses and other buildings had glazed windows is very difficult to estimate.

Roofs and Vaults

In many buildings a domed or vaulted roof was constructed. These constructions are based on the arch; a vault is an elongated arch and a dome is a series of arches meeting at their highest point. The Romans did not invent these techniques, but they developed them and used concrete for the first time. The combination of these elements made Roman architecture distinct from Greek. For example, it was the use of vaults and arches that allowed the Romans to build free-standing theaters, whereas Greek ones were usually built into a hillside for support.

The true arch built of voussoirs (wedge-shaped stones fitted together to form the shape of the arch and held in place by lateral pressure) was a relatively late development in western architecture. Arches were known in Egypt from the 6th century BC, but the Romans began to use them only in the 3rd century BC.

The width that can be spanned by an arch or barrel vault is unlimited, but the wider arches or vaults are, the higher they become. (See bridges in chapter 5.) To achieve greater spans with lower ceilings, barrel vaults were built side by side, supported on side walls pierced with arches. Groined vaults were used more often, consisting of two barrel vaults intersecting at right angles. These vaults could span a large rectangular area, with supporting pillars needed only at the four points of intersection. By increasing the number of intersecting vaults, a dome shape could be achieved, and by combining various vaults and arches, a new style of architecture developed. A striking example of this is the Colosseum (fig. 4.7), built at Rome in the late 1st century. Although its exterior was decorated with Doric, Ionic and Corinthian columns, the building is essentially a Roman structure of arches and vaults.

The use of concrete for arches and vaults necessitated precise carpentry during construction. To build a concrete arch, the centering (the wooden template, supported on wooden scaffolding, over which the arch was formed) had to function as shuttering for the poured concrete. Not only did the centering have to be of precisely the correct shape, but it also had to be strong enough to sustain the weight of the concrete until it had set. An added difficulty in building vaults and domes was the construction of centering with a complex shape using the same standards of precision and strength. The use of hollow terracotta vaulting tubes (*tubi fittili*) was very popular in the construction of barrel vaults from the 2nd century, particularly in north Africa.

ROOFING MATERIALS

Most commonly buildings were roofed with tiles over a timber framework. There were two types of roof tile, the *tegula* (pl. *tegulae*) and *imbrex* (pl. *imbrices*) (fig. 4.20) which were used in combination to form a weatherproof roof. *Tegulae* were flat, slightly tapering subrectangular tiles with a flange along both long sides. *Imbrices* resembled slightly tapering tubes that had been cut in half lengthways. The *tegulae* were fixed side by side and the *imbrices* were fixed over the gaps between the *tegulae* (fig.

8.9). Since the tiles were slightly tapering, each row of tiles could overlap the row below to eliminate gaps. (See also tiles in chapter 8.)

Throughout the empire there was a great deal of variation in roofing methods. Although roofs tiled with *tegulae* and *imbrices* must have been relatively common, roofing slates made of various stones were used in areas where such stone was available, and sometimes slates were chosen for decorative reasons. In many provincial areas a large proportion of buildings would have been thatched, and the use of wooden shingles is known. In drier areas in the eastern provinces many domestic houses had flat roofs of mud brick supported on timber or vaulting. Chimneys were not used in any area; smoke from hearths and ovens escaped through holes in the roof.

Floors

Apart from the suspended concrete floors of the hypocausts, there was a great variation in flooring methods. Beaten earth floors were found in the poorest

Fig. 4.20   Replicas of Roman tegulae *(left) and* imbrices *(right).*

Fig. 4.21 Stone-built flue of a hypocaust through which hot air passed from the furnace and under the floor. The floor is supported on piers of tiles (pilae).

houses, but they could also be of stone blocks, tiles (sometimes laid in a herringbone pattern—*opus spicatum*) or of wood. Another common method was concrete made with *opus signinum* for resistance to damp. Floors could be surfaced with small cubes of stone, tiles or other materials set in concrete to form a tessellated surface, or with very small cubes of various materials to form a mosaic (fig. 4.22).

for structural purposes, and poplar, lime and willow were regarded as particularly suitable for carving. Alder was regarded as good for piling and foundation work, and other species were chosen for particular tasks. Timber was also important during the construction of buildings since it was used for scaffolding, centering for arch construction, shuttering for concrete and many other purposes.

Timber

Timber was used extensively in building for a variety of purposes such as roofs, floors, wall frames and even cladding for walls. A great variety of trees provided timber for different purposes, and Vitruvius discusses the subject at length. Various species of oak were used

Metals

Metals were used mainly as fixings and fittings, rather than for structural purposes, although iron beams sometimes supported boilers over bathhouse furnaces. Lead, iron and bronze were all used to join blocks of masonry, and iron nails and dogs were used in woodworking. A variety of fittings such as locks, hinges and studs was made from iron and bronze, and decorations were often of bronze. Iron nails were driven into walls to help plaster adhere, and iron dogs and other fittings held in place various structural elements, such as flue tiles and drainage pipes. Lead was also used for water pipes.

Heating

One distinctive Roman feature was the underfloor heating system called the hypocaust, which was possibly invented in the 1st century BC. Heated rooms had floors supported on brick or stone piers (*pilae*), or occasionally had stone or brick-lined channels built into a solid foundation (channeled hypocaust), in order to allow the passage of hot air. The floor itself was of thick concrete, which warmed up slowly but retained heat. Hot air and gases from the furnace passed beneath the floor (fig. 4.21), providing the main heating, and then passed through tile-lined channels or flues in the walls, before escaping under the eaves of the roof. (See also box tiles in chapter 8.)

The hypocaust system was expensive in terms of labor and fuel, and the temperature was not easily controlled and could be very uneven, depending on the design of the particular hypocaust. Probably because of its cost, such a system usually heated only a few rooms within domestic houses, but it was used to great effect in public and private baths. In rooms without a hypocaust, charcoal-burning braziers provided the heating.

In baths, the hypocaust was designed for minimum heat loss, so that the hot air first passed to the hottest rooms (*laconicum*, *sudatorium* and *caldarium*), and then, as it cooled, to the next hottest and so on. A boiler over the furnace provided hot water.

Lighting

Candles, torches and lamps were the main forms of lighting. Torches were used largely outdoors, and candles of beeswax and tallow, and candlesticks, were used in provinces where olives were not cultivated. Lamps were commonly used for lighting from the 1st century BC, using olive oil as fuel. They were often placed on stands. Luxurious examples of bronze lamp stands and candelabra are known. Lamps were made of many materials, mainly pottery, but also bronze, lead, iron, gold, silver, glass and stone. (See chapter 8 for pottery lamps).

INTERIOR AND EXTERIOR DECORATION

Mosaics

A mosaic (*opus vermiculatum*) was a pattern or picture made by setting very small cubes (*tesserae*) of different colored materials in concrete, including stone, tile, pottery and glass (fig. 4.22). Some Greek mosaics are known dating to around the 4th century BC, but the Romans developed the technique from the 2nd century BC. Mosaics came to be used throughout the empire as a method of decorating floors in both private and public buildings and were used on walls and sometimes ceilings from the 1st century AD. In the Byzantine period mosaics became a popular form of church decoration on walls and ceilings, often using fragile and expensive materials such as glass and gold.

Opus Sectile

Opus sectile was also used as a surfacing for floors and walls. Different pieces of stone, such as various types of marble, were cut into shapes and formed into patterns.

Painted Plaster

Walls and ceilings of buildings were usually plastered, but in poorer houses the plaster might be left undecorated or simply whitewashed. In wealthier establishments walls and ceilings were painted with designs and pictures, as were the exterior walls. Roman wall paintings developed from Greek traditions, and figured paintings are known from Italy at least as early as the 1st century BC. Because painting on plaster survives relatively rarely, it is difficult to estimate the extent of the practice, but it is likely that the decoration of internal walls was very common. It is also possible that painting of external walls was more common than the surviving evidence suggests.

PAINT

Wall paintings were done either as a fresco technique (while the plaster was still wet), in tempera (on dry plaster) or a combination of the two. Fresco appears to have been the most common technique. In a fresco the lime-water from the drying plaster fixes the pigment, but for tempera something such as size is needed to bind the pigment to the surface.

The pigments were described by Vitruvius and Pliny, and most were derived from mineral, vegetable and animal sources. White could be obtained by grinding and slaking calcined marble, chalk or oyster shells, while black pigment was carbon obtained by burning materials such as resin, chips of pine wood or wine dregs. Red was obtained from the mineral cinnabar, which was heated and washed to remove impurities and then ground. Haematite (red ocher), composed mainly of iron oxides, was also used. Blue was made by heating a mixture of copper, silica and calcium, which formed a bright blue glassy substance (Egyptian blue, blue frit or Pompeian blue), which was then ground. Blue was also obtained by grinding the stone lapis lazuli, the mineral azurite or by using chalk colored with vegetable dye such as woad. Yellow was obtained from yellow ocher, a natural earth pigment consisting of a mixture of clay, silica and hydrated iron oxides such as limonite. Other colors could be obtained from other sources, or by mixing pigments.

Stucco and Sculpture

Three-dimensional decoration on walls and ceilings was provided by stucco and sculptured stone, which was generally painted in various colors.

Stucco was decorative plasterwork—usually patterns and pictures raised in low relief from a flat plaster background. There were many types of stucco, the finest being made of powdered marble, and the stucco designs were either formed in molds or done freehand.

Carved and sculptured stone was used as decoration both inside and outside, particularly on public buildings. Wealthier domestic buildings had carved stone ornaments such as columns and architraves, but public buildings were often decorated with panels and friezes of sculptured relief and even statues in niches. Some public buildings, such as monumental arches, might be almost completely covered in sculpture.

Furnishings

As far as is known, town houses and villas were furnished in a similar manner, and by modern standards rooms were sparsely furnished. The principal room was usually the dining room, equipped with tables and couches. In less Romanized areas chairs were used instead of couches. Bedrooms would have contained couches or chairs as well as a bed and cupboards or chests for storage of clothes.

The kitchen would contain an oven and probably a griddle over a raised open fire. Spits for roasting were also used, and in northern provinces cauldrons would have been suspended on chains over open fires. There would also be tables, a small mill for grinding grain, and cupboards, shelves, large jars and amphorae for storage.

Living rooms were furnished with chairs, tables and stools, and might also contain shelves and cupboards. Irrespective of the room, many shelves, cupboards and niches for storage and display were constructed as part of domestic buildings. Portable folding stools were used wherever they were required.

Under the empire new kinds of furniture were added to the basic range, such as sideboards for display of valuable items, and cupboards with drawers, sometimes for papyrus rolls. The quantity and quality of furniture varied according to the wealth of the owner, and the rich adorned their homes with many decorative items such as statues, vases and carpets from the east.

FARMING

Land Tenure

In the early republic most farming was done on a domestic scale by the landowner's family. Farms were self-sufficient, based mainly on the production of grain, and the ideal of the self-sufficient citizen farmer continued long after the establishment of large agricultural estates had engulfed many small farmers.

As Rome conquered Italy, land (usually one-third) was often confiscated from communities that put up strong resistance or later rebelled against Rome. This became *ager publicus* (public land) belonging to Rome. Some was assigned to individuals and much was allocated to colonies. The land became a source of dispute between the *plebs*, who were often tenants and workers on the land, and the patricians who made large profits from it.

In the early 2nd century BC some of the *ager publicus* in Italy was distributed by lease (largely to patricians), and much of it was formed into large agricultural estates called *latifundia*. Such estates, run for profit using a large staff of slaves, had the capital to produce new crops and breeds of animals. Peasant farmers, practicing mixed farming on smallholdings, could not compete and were compelled to sell their smallholdings, thereby increasing the size of large estates. Large estates were also established in the provinces, but apparently seldom on the same scale as the *latifundia* in Italy.

Eventually many of the land disputes were settled by an agrarian law of 111 BC that made most state-owned land (with several exceptions such as roads) the private property of those occupying the land. The question of *ager publicus* was subsequently raised several times, when generals such as Sulla and Julius Caesar wanted to grant land to discharged soldiers, and some lands in Italy and the provinces became *ager publicus*.

As Rome's territory increased, the pattern of land tenure became more complex. Under the empire the largest landowner was the emperor, who owned imperial estates in many parts of the empire, including industrial ones for mineral extraction and salt production. As well as the emperor, there were many other landowners and all sizes of agricultural estates. Such estates might be managed by the landowner, the tenant or a bailiff on behalf of an absentee landlord or tenant. Large estates could be split among a number of tenants. Other land was owned by municipalities, tribal communities or singly or communally by small freehold farmers. The tenure and ownership of land were constantly changing as land was bought and sold, leased, abandoned, recovered and occasionally confiscated by the state.

From the 3rd century there was a decline in agriculture, and some farms were deserted and land left uncultivated.

Farms

Farming was the major industry throughout the Roman period, and settlements of all sizes, from towns and villages down to individual farmsteads, were involved with agriculture. In many provinces a certain amount of farming was carried on by native communities, continuing their traditional methods, so that the countryside was often a pattern of Romanized towns and villas, interspersed with recognizably native villages, hamlets and farmsteads.

Many villas were farmhouses associated with agriculture, and there were also numerous small farmsteads that cannot be classified as villas. The native settlements include numerous small fortified structures and towers in north Africa. They are known as *gsur* (sing. *gasr*) and were probably late Roman fortified farms.

FARM OUTBUILDINGS

While the main residential buildings of villas and farmsteads are relatively easy to identify, outbuildings served a wide variety of purposes, few of which can be identified with precision. Storage buildings such as barns and granaries are known, as well as stables and byres, but the distinction between a cattle byre, stable, pigsty or sheep pen is very difficult to detect from archaeological evidence.

In Mediterranean areas mills and presses for the production of olive oil were used. In wine-producing areas buildings and equipment for wine making have been found. Large vats for the storage of both wine and olive oil are also known. In some of the northern and northwestern provinces, corn driers (sometimes called corn-drying ovens) were used to dry out cereals that had been harvested before they were fully ripe. These consisted of a T- or Y-shaped flue with a stokehole at one end, set within a building. The warm air from the stokehole passed along the flue to heat the grain, which was probably spread on a wooden floor above. Threshing floors are also commonly found on villa estates.

Land Use

In early Rome, grain production was most important, but as Rome's power expanded in Italy, sheep and cattle rearing became more profitable. In the 3rd and 2nd centuries BC Rome came into contact with the more scientific agriculture of Carthage and Greece. Few Greek writings on agriculture have survived, but many Greek ideas seem to have been incorporated into Latin agricultural works. Roman farming reached a peak of efficiency in Italy in the late republic and early empire, but with large agricultural estates and stock-rearing ranches, the small-scale family farm declined.

As Rome's territory expanded, newly conquered areas were forced to change from self-sufficient farming to the production of an agricultural surplus in order to pay tribute and taxes to Rome. The surplus produce supplied towns and cities and the army with food and encouraged the farming community to produce an even greater surplus to sell for profit. In some of the more distant provinces, producing a surplus was a relatively new concept that probably brought about far-reaching changes in land use.

In general, mixed farming was practiced, but the balance between animals and crops, and the types of animals and crops that were farmed, depended on local factors such as soil, topography and rainfall. In some areas irrigation or drainage was used to bring marginal land into production.

Crop Production

In Italy the Po valley and the coastal areas were used for pasture, cereals, fruit and vegetables during the republic, but cereal production declined during the empire. Olives and vines were grown on the lower slopes of the Apennines, while hilltop forests produced nuts both for human consumption and forage for pigs. Cleared upland areas were used as summer pasture for cattle.

The pattern of land use in provinces along the Mediterranean was broadly the same as that in Italy. Olives and to a lesser extent vines became extremely important in Spain, as did vines and some olives in southern Gaul, although before the time of Augustus the planting of vines was prohibited outside Italy. In Greece and the Asiatic provinces, vines, olives and figs were predominant. In Africa the area controlled by Carthage before the Romans took control had already been heavily cultivated, producing mainly cereals. The coastal areas of Tripolitania and Cyrenaica produced olives, and the production of olives in the African provinces was greatly expanded under Roman rule. Egypt became extremely important for the production of grain.

In the eastern provinces grain was grown in coastal areas, with vines and olives on the lower slopes of hills. Some areas were specifically irrigated for rice cultivation, and dates, figs, flax, hemp and cotton were also grown. Some areas produced specialist crops such as cedar trees in Lebanon, and marshy areas in the east grew rushes for papyrus.

In Gaul, Germany, Britain and the Danube provinces the emphasis was on cereals, with occasional vineyards but no olives.

Throughout the Roman world, a wide variety of vegetables was also grown. The most important were various types of legumes for human consumption and animal fodder as well as a large number of herbs for culinary and medicinal purposes. Grapes, peaches, pears, plums, apples and cherries were also cultivated, as were nuts including almonds, walnuts, hazelnuts and chestnuts. Vegetables and fruit were frequently grown on a domestic scale in the courtyards and gardens of villas and town houses, and there is some evidence for small-scale market gardens.

Hazel and willow were used for basketry, and other trees such as beech and chestnut were pollarded to provide a renewable crop for charcoal burning. Trees such as oak, elm and pine were grown for timber.

FIELDS

An important by-product of animal husbandry was manure for the fields, although this was in short supply in drier climates where transhumance was practiced. Residue from wine making and olive pressing was also used for manure. In some areas fields were both limed and marled to combat acid soils, and crop rotation and fallowing were also practiced. The size of fields varied considerably according to factors such as the type of soil and crops and the farming methods being used. Fields were bounded by ditches, fences, drystone walls and hedges, and upkeep of all boundaries was an important duty of tenants and owners, with some boundaries having a religious significance.

PLOWING

Plowing was usually done with an ard, which was a simple plow without a coulter or moldboard, drawn by one or two draft animals. Such plows scratched a furrow, rather than turned the soil over, and cross-plowing (plowing a second time at right angles) was needed to provide a good seed bed. Such plows are effective only on light soils, and so heavy clay soils were not efficiently used for arable cultivation until the heavy plow was developed during the empire. The heavy plow had a coulter to cut the ground and a moldboard that turned the soil over and buried weeds.

In many areas cultivation was carried out by hand using spades and hoes. These tools were similar to modern ones except that the spade has a wooden handle and blade, which was sometimes tipped with iron to give a cutting edge. Hoes were also used for weeding, and spades were essential for harvesting root crops as well as for general maintenance tasks such as digging ditches.

HARVESTING

Harvesting was done with a short reaping hook, and the introduction of the balanced sickle and scythe greatly improved harvesting efficiency. All these tools had iron blades, usually with wooden handles. In northern Europe a harvesting machine (the *vallus*) was used. It consisted of a bin or hopper, open on one side, which had broad, pointed blades projecting forward from the front edge of the base of the hopper. It was mounted on wheels with shafts pointing backward so that a donkey or mule could be harnessed to push it rather than pull it. As it was pushed through the crop, the blades stripped the ears of grain from the stalks and they fell into the hopper. A similar machine pushed by an ox was known as the *carpentum*.

Threshing was done by spreading the grain on specially prepared threshing floors and beating it with flails or having animals tread on it to separate the grain from the chaff. A Greek invention, the *tribulum*, may also have been used for threshing. This was a threshing sledge consisting of a weighted board, with flints embedded in the underside, which was dragged across the corn. An improved version of this machine (the Punic cart) used toothed rollers instead of flints.

After threshing, the process of separating grain from chaff was completed by winnowing—throwing the threshed grain into the air with a winnowing shovel or basket so that the chaff was blown away on the wind while the grain fell back down. The winnowing basket was shallow and open at one end, allowing the contents to be thrown up and caught again.

OTHER TOOLS

A great variety of tools, such as saws, knives and bill hooks, was used in agriculture, but, as today, the division between agricultural tools and general-purpose tools is often difficult to define.

Animal Husbandry

As with crops, the stock on mixed farms varied from area to area. Cattle were the most important and were farmed extensively on large ranches in parts of Italy, Sicily, Asia Minor, Gaul, Britain, the upper Danube region, north Africa, Egypt and Syria. Cattle were used to produce milk, butter, cheese, meat and hides. Bone and horn were used for the manufacture of artifacts, glue and size.

Sheep were also very important throughout the empire. They were bred mainly for wool, and in Mediterranean areas sheep rather than cows were used to produce milk and cheese. The finest wool reputedly came from sheep from Miletus in Asia Minor, and these were imported into Italy. Numidia was also renowned for its woolen goods. Goats were less widespread and less valuable than sheep, but were used to provide similar products. Sheep and goats also provided skins for parchment, and goat hair was used for products such as ropes and felt.

Fig. 4.22   Two hunters with spears carry home a doe hung on a pole. They are accompanied by a dog. Part of a mosaic from East Coker villa, Somerset. Courtesy of Somerset County Museums Service.

Pigs were widely reared, providing meat, lard, skin and bristle. Pork and ham were highly regarded, particularly in Gaul, Britain and Spain. Poultry, ducks, geese, pigeons, peacocks and doves were used for meat as well as for producing eggs, feathers, down and quills.

Other animals were bred for pulling and carrying, and in particular mule breeding was an enormous farming industry. Oxen were the main draft animals on farms. Donkeys were used to pull vehicles, occasionally to pull plows, and also to power machinery. Horses were little used on farms. In Africa and the eastern provinces camels were bred mainly for riding, as pack animals and for use by the army throughout much of Europe. They could also pull plows. Dogs were bred for herding, hunting (fig. 4.22) and as watchdogs but were also kept as pets, as were exotic animals such as monkeys.

HUNTING

Meat in the Roman diet was supplemented by hunting (fig. 4.22). Latin authors listed wild pig, geese, duck, hares, deer and various small birds as game, and it is possible that the pheasant was introduced into northwest Europe for hunting. Sea and freshwater fish and shellfish were eaten extensively. Oysters in particular were traded widely, and *garum* (a strong fish sauce) was very popular. Some varieties of fish were reared in fishponds as were oysters in artificial oyster beds (fig. 5.18). Honey was collected from wild beehives as well as domestic hives, and was very important as a sweetener.

READING

Town Planning
Chevallier 1976; Grimal 1983; Owens 1989 and 1991.

Centuriation
Chevallier 1976; Dilke 1971 and 1985.

Types of Town
Burnham and Wacher 1990: small towns in Britain; Dilke 1971: colonies; Drinkwater 1987: cities in western provinces; Hanley 1987: villages in Britain; Levick 1987: towns in eastern provinces; Owens 1989: town plans; Poulter 1987: townships and villages; Salmon 1969: colonies; Wacher 1974: town plans and types of towns, with particular reference to Britain.

Town Services and Buildings
Adam 1984: water supply, domestic architecture; Bateman 1985: warehouses, with particular reference to London; Bennett 1980: summary of towns in Britain; Blagg 1983: public buildings; Boethius 1970: early Roman public and private buildings; Brothers 1989: buildings for entertainment; Carter 1989: public buildings; Clarke 1991: town houses in Italy; Connolly 1981, 296–97: portcullises; DeLaine 1988: discusses the origins and development of baths as well as previous publications; de Ruyt 1983: discussion of *macella* throughout the Roman world, including goods sold, a gazetteer and detailed bibliography; Fabre et al. 1991: detailed analysis of the Nîmes aqueduct and Pont du Gard; Golvin 1988: amphitheaters; Grimal 1983: cities and their buildings; Heinz 1983: public baths; Hodge 1989 and 1992: aqueducts and water supply; Humphrey 1986: circuses and *stadia*; Johnson 1983: imperial town defenses; Kleiner 1989: review article on triumphal and honorary arches; McKay 1975: town houses, apartments and palaces; Oleson 1986: includes bibliography on hydraulic engineering; Rickman 1971: granaries and storage buildings; Sear 1982: types of buildings; Sear 1992: review article on architecture with numerous references; Thébert 1987: urban homes in various African cities, with numerous illustrations; Todd 1978: the walls of Rome; Tomlin 1981b: late Roman town fortifications; Ward-Perkins 1970: architecture of the empire.

Villas
Black 1987: villas in southeast England; McKay 1975; Percival 1976; Percival 1987: villas, especially of the western empire; Rossiter 1989: villas in the eastern empire; Todd (ed.) 1978: villas in Britain; Wacher 1987: types of villas; White 1978: translated extracts from ancient authors on villas and estates.

Surveyors and Surveying
Adam 1984, 9–24; Dilke 1971: detailed description of surveyors; Dilke 1985; White 1984.

Architects and Architecture
Andreae 1973: well-illustrated large-format book on art and architecture; Blagg 1983; Boethius 1970: early Roman architectural styles; Macdonald 1982 and 1986; Robertson 1945; Sear 1982; Sear 1992: review article on architecture with numerous references.

Building Techniques
Adam 1984: detailed well-illustrated account of numerous building techniques, materials, surveying and domestic architecture; Bailey 1991: major publications on metal and clay lamps since 1980; Blagg 1983; Boethius 1970: early Roman building methods; Brodribb 1987: brick and tile; Dodge 1990: influence of Roman building techniques and architecture in the eastern empire; Hill 1984: construction methods and materials; Landels 1978, 84–98: cranes; Macready and Thompson (eds.) 1987: architecture and building techniques in the eastern empire; MacDonald 1982: architectural styles, building methods and materials; Macdonald 1986: architectural styles; McWhirr (ed.) 1979: uses of brick and tile; Meiggs 1982: timber as a building material; Oleson 1986: includes bibliography on civil engineering and construction methods; Ramage and Ramage 1991: chronological account of architecture; Robertson 1945: architecture; Sear 1982: building techniques and materials; Ward-Perkins 1970: architecture of the empire; White 1984: building materials and methods; Wilson 1992: use of terracotta vaulting tubes, with a gazetteer of locations.

Interior Decoration
Adam 1984, 235–56; Clarke 1991: paintings and mosaics in town houses; Ling 1976: stucco; Liversidge 1983: wall and ceiling paintings and stucco; McKay 1975: furnishings; Pratt 1976: wall paintings and paint; Ramage and Ramage 1991; Sear 1976: wall and vault mosaics; Smith 1983: mosaics.

Farms and Farming
Anderson 1985: hunting; Applebaum 1987: animal husbandry; Greene 1986: agriculture, including a consideration of the sources of information and regional surveys, with bibliography; Manning 1985, 43–60: agricultural implements; Mattingly and Hayes 1992: fortified farms in north Africa;

Meiggs 1982: farming of trees; Morris 1979: agricultural buildings in Britain; Oleson 1986: includes bibliography on agriculture, tools and hunting; Rees 1979: agricultural implements; Rees 1981: summary of agricultural implements; Rees 1987: arable farming, horticulture and implements; Rickman 1980: corn-growing areas; Rossiter 1978: farm buildings in Italy; Thompson 1987: imperial estates; Wacher 1987: crops, animal husbandry and farming methods; White 1967: detailed description of agricultural implements; White 1970: all aspects of farming; White 1975: farm equipment other than implements of tillage and husbandry; White 1978: translated extracts from ancient authors on farming and hunting; White 1984: agricultural implements.

5

TRAVEL AND TRADE

—

One of the key elements in the expansion of the Roman world, and its subsequent consolidation and control, was efficient communications, which allowed effective policing of the provinces and encouraged trade throughout the empire. People who needed to travel included military personnel, emperors and their entourage, civil servants, couriers and envoys from the provinces and beyond. Travelers also included private citizens such as merchants, farmers, pilgrims, those seeking a cure for illness and even tourists. Travel was arduous and dangerous, particularly as piracy and brigandage were endemic, and wolves were a threat. It was not unusual for an altar to be erected or promised to a god for a safe journey, and wayside shrines existed for offerings en route. Most journeys were undertaken in favorable seasons, not in winter when conditions on the roads were treacherous and when sailings were suspended.

MAPS AND ITINERARIES

Cartography

There are very few records of maps dating to the republic, although they certainly existed, many probably associated with land surveys. In the empire maps and plans were fairly common. By the time of Augustus, geographical knowledge was extensive.

General maps, land surveyors' maps and town plans were drawn to scale. The Latin word for map is *forma* (map, plan or shape), and a world map is a *descriptio* (literally, "a drawing"). The term *itinerarium pictum* was also used, possibly referring to the Peutinger Table type of map or to an itinerary accompanied by paintings. A *mappa* is late Latin for a map, meaning literally "cloth."

Maps are mentioned by various authors, and many wrote about geography and cartography, including Strabo, Polybius, Pomponius Mela, Pliny the Elder and Ptolemy. Advances in cartography were significant from 50 to 150, particularly with the Greek scientists and mathematicians at Alexandria. One cartographer writing in Greek was Marinus, who worked around 100 or 110. He published the *Correction of the World Map*, but his work was criticized by Ptolemy for major errors. Ptolemy's *Geography* included six books of place names with coordinates, although not always accurate—for example, Ireland was placed about 6 degrees too far north. It is likely that Ptolemy also had maps drawn; maps were certainly drawn at some stage from his information, of which medieval copies exist covering an area from Thule (possibly Shetland) in the north to Africa south of the equator. Topographical information is shown, but Ptolemy excluded roads as his information was not designed for use by travelers. At the end of the Roman Empire, the standard of cartography appears to have declined.

Wall Maps

Wall maps of the world existed, but none survive. Julius Caesar commissioned one but did not live to see it. During Augustus' reign Agrippa undertook the creation of an official world map of the empire. Pliny the Elder mentioned it, but whether it was painted or engraved on the walls is unknown. After Agrippa's death, the map was completed by Augustus and publicly displayed on the Porticus Vipsania (named after Agrippa) so that the full extent of the empire could be seen. Although containing much detail, it is not known if it portrayed main roads. Pliny the Elder in his *Natural History* showed that some of Agrippa's distances were inaccurate. Agrippa's map was accompanied by notes or a commentary that travelers could consult. A world map was apparently compiled around 435 on the orders of Theodosius I; the only two previous official maps were those of Caesar and Agrippa. It was the last official map available in the west.

Wall maps of towns carved in stone also existed, of which fragmentary remains have survived, including a very large marble plan of Rome, which has been partly reconstructed. Known as the *Forma Urbis Romae*, it was completed sometime between 203 and 208. It was originally 18.3 m (60 ft) high by 13.03 m (43 ft) wide and was fixed to an outer wall of a library attached to Vespasian's temple of Peace. There may have been an earlier Flavian version. The average scale is about 1 to 300, although it does vary. Some features, such as aqueducts, are drawn in elevation and not as plans. Only a few fragments of other Roman town plans are known, such as one from Ostia. Three stone cadasters of Arausio show surveys of the territory of the colony. (See chapter 4.)

Mosaic Maps

Many floor mosaics have representations of landscapes that give geographical information in a maplike form. The most notable are from north Africa and show buildings in elevation. The mosaic map from a Byzantine church at Madeba (or Madaba) in Jordan dates to between 542 and 565 and probably originally measured 24 m by 6 m (79 ft by 20 ft). Its purpose was to portray the Bible lands, and place names are in Greek. Jerusalem is shown at a larger scale than the surrounding area.

Road Maps

The Peutinger Table (*tabula Peutingeriana*) is a 12th- or early 13th-century copy of a late Roman (possibly 4th or 5th century) road map of the Roman world. It was found at Worms at the end of the 15th century. It is so called after the scholar Konrad Peutinger who owned it from 1508. It is a narrow parchment 6.75 m (22 ft) long by 0.34 m (13½ in) wide and portrays the world from Britain to India. The most westerly parts of the parchment are damaged. The map is in five colors and shows the course of Roman roads. It is geographically extremely distorted because it was a schematic diagram for travelers and was not drawn to scale. Practical information is presented using various symbols, such as distances between towns, road stations, baths and the best way of traveling from one point to another. It shows the main highways of the empire and of the Persian lands to the east. There may have been a 1st-century predecessor, as it shows towns on the Bay of Naples that were destroyed by Vesuvius in 79. It is clearly a civilian and not a military map.

Another example of a road map is the fragmentary Dura-Europus shield, consisting of a papyrus fragment 0.48 m by 0.18 m (1 ft 7 in by 7 in) used for covering an infantryman's shield. It portrays a map of the Black Sea and part of the coast, with names of towns, mileages and principal rivers in Greek. It dates to before 260 when Dura-Europus was abandoned.

Itineraries

Itineraria (itineraries) were maps or lists of stations along roads, giving the distances between stations and other useful information. They covered the main routes of the empire, but not every existing road station was necessarily mentioned on an itinerary. Itineraries probably existed from an early date, but none survive from before the 1st century. They were common in the empire, probably on papyrus, parchment, stone or bronze, and copies could be kept in libraries. The most important surviving example is the *Itinerarium Antoninianum* or *Itinerarium Provinciarum Antonini Augusti* (*Antonine Itinerary*). This was a collection of journeys compiled over 75 years or more and probably edited in the late 3rd century. Some errors in later copying have occurred. It describes 225 routes or itineraries along major roads of the empire and gives the distances between places mentioned. The collection may have been used originally for journeys of emperors and troops, with many itineraries following routes of the *cursus publicus*, although few take the shortest route between two named places. The longest route (Rome to Egypt) may represent the plan for Caracalla's journey in 214 to 215. The itinerary also includes a short section on sea routes, entitled *Imperatoris Antonini Augusti itinerarium maritimum*.

The *Ravenna Cosmography* was a compilation by an 11th-century monk of documents dating back to the 5th century, which had been collated by an anonymous cleric at Ravenna c. 700. It gives lists of stations, river names and some topographical details, although there are numerous copying errors.

The *Notitia Dignitatum* is a late Roman collection of administrative information, including lists of civilian and military officeholders, military units and forts. The maps, of medieval date, were almost certainly derived from late Roman originals of c. 395 for the east and 395 to 408 for the west; the cartography is poor, but the originals may have been intended only as schematic.

Itineraries were in use from the late Roman to medieval period giving routes to the Holy Land for Christian pilgrims. They include the 4th-century *Jerusalem* (or *Bordeaux*) *Itinerary* (*Itinerarium Burdigalense sive Hierosolymitanum*), an itinerary from Bordeaux to Jerusalem that gives various routes on a pilgrimage to Jerusalem by way of Arles, Turin, Milan, Constantinople and Antioch, with an alternative return journey. The *Peregrinatio Aetheriae* (*Journey of Aetheria*) dating to c. 400 is an account of a pilgrimage to the holy places. Medieval itineraries and guidebooks can give valuable information on Roman roads and wayside buildings and monuments that were then extant.

PERIPLOI

A *periplus* (a sailing around) was the name given to the records of coastal voyages (*periploi*), which were probably fairly commonly used. Arrian wrote the *Periplus of the Euxine* (*Periplus of the Black Sea*) addressed to Hadrian in the form of a letter. Substantial fragments survive of the *Stadiasmus Maris Magni*, a Greek *periplus* of the Mediterranean of c. 250 to 300, the entries consisting mostly of distances with some description. The *Periplus Maris Erythraei* (*Periplus of the Erythraean Sea*) was compiled in Greek by an anonymous merchant in the 1st century and is the only such manual of the Roman Empire to survive. It describes two voyages that started down the Red Sea, the first to the Far East as far as India, and the second, which is less detailed, to east Africa as far south as Dar es Salaam. It concentrates on trade and was intended for ships' captains and as a guide to merchants.

The *Periplus of the Outer Sea* was written c. 400, in Greek, by Marcian of Heraclea Pontica. His work described the coasts beyond the Mediterranean including Britain to the west (book 2) and Sri Lanka to the east (book 1). No original Byzantine maps survive, but there are Byzantine *periploi*. There were also Greek *periegeses* (world guides), such as one by Dionysius Periegetes (The Guide), which describes the seas and continents of the world; it was translated into Latin by Avienius and Priscian. The 4th-century poet Avienus also wrote the *Maritime Shore*, giving a description of the coastline from Marseille to Cadiz and an account of maritime exploration from Cadiz.

Inscriptions

Itineraries and information on road systems can be derived from inscriptions on milestones, bridges, rock faces and various portable objects. The four Vicarello silver goblets, sometimes known as *vases Apollinaires*, were found at Aquae Apollinares (Vicarello) near Rome. They are cylindrical in shape and bear the names in vertical lists of *mansiones* and their distances apart. The lists are separated by pilasters. The itinerary, from Cadiz to Rome, is the same on each goblet, and appears to correspond to routes described by Strabo. The goblets vary from 95 mm to 153 mm (3½ in to 6 in) in height and probably date between 7 BC and AD 47. They may have been presented by someone from Cadiz to Apollo, the healing god, on a visit to Rome. The goblets may be copies of an elaborate milestone set up in Cadiz.

Several small bronze bowls or cups (*paterae*) of hemispherical form with colored enamel decoration are known from Britain and northern France, very occasionally with lettering. They may have been souvenirs and include the Rudge Cup, which was found near Froxfield. It is 102 mm (4 in) in diameter and 76 mm (3 in) high. It has a band of continuous lettering below the rim reading A. MAISABALLAVAVXELODVM-CAMBOGLANSBANNA, which is a list of place names at least partly on Hadrian's Wall. Similar forms of the names are in the *Ravenna Cosmography*, but no distances are given on the Rudge Cup. The body of the cup is covered with the schematic representation of a fortification with a crenellated wall, a design found on other bowls. It was probably one of a set like the Vicarello goblets. A similar bronze vessel from Amiens reads MAISABALLAVAVXELODVNVMCAMBOG . . . SBANNAAESICA. The place names are:

Ancient name	Modern name
Maia (Maium)	Bowness-on-Solway
Aballava	Burgh-by-Sands
Uxelodunum	Stanwix
Camboglanna	Castlesteads
Banna	Birdoswald
Aesica (not on Rudge Cup)	Great Chesters

ROADS

The earliest Roman roads were probably little more than tracks, mainly along river valleys in Italy, some following prehistoric lines of communication. The Etruscans had already constructed a network of well-built roads connecting their settlements, and some of their towns had paved streets. The Romans developed the road-building skills of their Etruscan and Greek predecessors, and from the late 4th century BC they began to undertake the construction of roads, with a further wave of construction from the late 2nd century BC. These roads were relatively straight, with good foundations and surfaces, and where necessary they had tunnels, embankments and bridges.

Roads were initially constructed for military, not economic, reasons. Their prime function was to facilitate the movement of troops and to link Rome with its colonies for good communication and administration. The main consideration was firm footing for infantry in all weathers, not vehicular traffic, and so steep gradients were not necessarily avoided. These strategically important military roads (*viae militares*) came to be used increasingly by the civilian population, and therefore led to an expansion of trade and the rapid spread of Roman ideas and way of life (Romanization).

Road Builders

In the republic construction of roads was the responsibility of magistrates—censors, consuls or provincial governors—who let out contracts, while resurfacing, paving and cleansing were the responsibility of aediles. The public main roads were known as *viae publicae*, *viae praetoriae* or *viae consulares*. In 20 BC a board of officials, the *curatores viarum*, was set up to manage state highways. No *curatores* of provincial roads are known, but governors acting through local authorities were responsible. Contractors were paid with money from the treasury, emperor, local authorities and landowners. Maintenance of main roads was always a problem, and for many roads a special curator was appointed for this purpose.

The actual builders of the strategic roads were army engineers (and later civil engineers), helped by an army and civilian workforce. Little is known of how the work was organized, but inscriptions sometimes give information. Roman roads came to be constructed throughout the empire, and under Diocletian 372 main roads (over 85,000 km; 53,000 mi) were recorded.

Road Construction

Roman roads are generally considered to be wide and straight, but this was the case only where terrain was suitable, such as in Britain. The first well-constructed road, the Via Appia, is attributed to Appius Claudius in 312 BC. Relatively little about road construction survives in contemporary literature, although roads were mentioned by several writers. Many Roman roads survive, and the ones that have been excavated show that there was no standard design.

Engineers were well aware of different terrains and constructed roads accordingly, often making use of local materials, even iron slag. The strip of land for the road was first marked out by furrows, and a road trench was dug to bedrock or to a firm foundation, often fairly deep (up to 1.4 m or 4 ft 7 in). The roads were built in sections, and the first stage was to reinforce the foundation by ramming, piles or brushwood. Successive layers of foundation materials were then added, all assisting drainage of the road. Across marshland, the foundations often consisted of a raised embankment made with a timber framework secured by vertical piles with a corduroy of tree trunks. Some main roads were built on a raised embankment (*agger*).

Over the foundations the surfacing material varied, from gravel to pebbles to cut stone slabs (fig. 4.1), held in place on each side of the road by a stone curb (*umbo*). Most roads were cambered and had side gutters or ditches to assist drainage. Some ditches were originally quarry ditches dug to obtain material for the road construction, while others acted as boundaries. Once constructed, roads required constant repair and maintenance.

The width of roads was commonly 4.57 m to 5.48 m (15 to 18 ft), but varied greatly, from about 1.14 m (3 ft 9 in.) to 9.14 m (30 ft). According to the Laws of the Twelve Tables, roads were supposed to be 4.8 m (15 ft 9 in) wide to allow two vehicles to pass. Decrees issued by Augustus stated that the *decumanus maximus* must be 12.2 m (40 ft) wide and the *cardo maximus* 6 m (20 ft), with other roads 2.43 m (8 ft), but in reality widths of roads varied according to their status. In towns, openings through surviving gateways indicate the width of their roads.

Minor roads were much less carefully constructed than major highways. They were mainly cross-country tracks used by traders and local roads and private ways leading from rural settlements to the main highways. Very few would have been constructed with firm surfaces, and they are difficult to locate and record. Caravan roads in the desert have left little evidence, as their courses were defined only by lines of stones cleared from the route. The other indications of such desert routes are posting stations, watchtowers and water supplies (wells and tanks).

Road Names

Few original names of Roman roads are known apart from those in Italy. In the republic roads were often named after the magistrate (usually the censor) who was responsible for their construction. For example, the Via Appia was named after the censor Appius Claudius Caecus; in northern Italy the Via Flaminia was named after the censor C. Flaminius; and the Via Domitia from the Rhône to Spain was named after Cn. Domitius. No original names for roads in Britain are known, if any existed, although some now bear apparently Latin names (such as Via Devana), which are of modern origin. Names such as Watling Street, Akeman Street and Stane Street in Britain were in use from Saxon times.

Roads tended to radiate from the center of towns toward neighboring towns and might be named according to the town to which they led (such as Via Ostiensis). Gateways in town walls often bear the same name as the roads passing through them (such as Porta Appia, Porta Ostiensis, Porta Aurelia).

Road Types

The Latin names for roads and streets were various and originally of rural origin but came to be applied to urban situations as well. Examples include:

actus local road or track for animals and vehicles, probably forming a large part of the communication network. Originally meaning a right to drive cattle (from *agere*, to drive cattle).

agger a causeway forming a road.

angiportus a narrow street or alley.

callis track, especially for seasonal transhumance.

clivus street on a slope.

crepido pavement.

iter route; right of way; path for travelers on foot, horsemen or litters.

limes path or track, often acting as a boundary; fortified frontier line.

pervium thoroughfare, passage.

platea street.

semita narrow path, lane.

strata embanked road. From the 3rd century, it replaced the word *via*.

trames cross-way, footpath, path.

via road for vehicles; street.

vicus the normal word for a city street, lane or district.

Roads in the Roman World

Roads developed with the conquest of territories and the setting up of colonies. Under the empire the road system expanded greatly, extending into Asia, to the Euphrates and the Red Sea. From about 200 the pace of road building declined, and by the 4th century the state was having increasing trouble maintaining roads.

Road networks within regions are still being recorded using a variety of techniques, including the study of topographical maps for alignments and place names, aerial photographs, ground survey and epigraphic evidence. More work is needed to elucidate the pattern of Roman roads, as it is still far from complete, but in many places there was a complex system of roads, from major highways to minor trackways.

ITALY (fig. 5.1)

Before the Romans, there were roads in Italy that had been constructed by the Greeks and Etruscans, some involving engineering work. There were also many existing transhumance routes between the coastal plain and the mountains. Under the Romans many roads were constructed radiating from Rome, several of which were based on preexisting tracks. The first well-constructed road (in 312 BC) was the Appian Way (Via Appia) from Rome as far south as Capua. Around 288 BC it was extended to Benevento and around 244 BC to Brindisi (the embarkation port for ships to Greece).

Roads probably built in the 3rd century BC include the Via Latina, which rejoined the Via Appia at Casilinum near Capua. The Via Amerina originally led from Rome to Nepi and later to Falerii Novi and beyond. The Via Valeria initially went from Rome to Alba Fucens. The initial stretch of road from Rome to Tivoli was also known as the Via Tiburtina. The

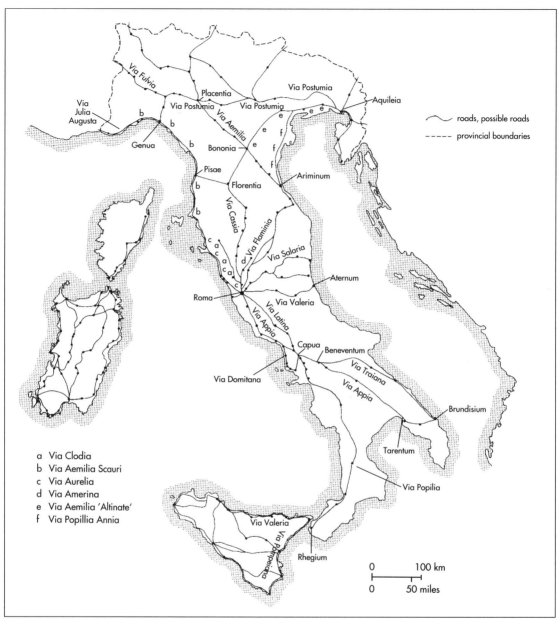

Fig. 5.1 Map of the road network in Italy, Sicily, Sardinia and Corsica. There was also a complex of minor roads in Italy.

a Via Clodia
b Via Aemilia Scauri
c Via Aurelia
d Via Amerina
e Via Aemilia 'Altinate'
f Via Popillia Annia

roads, possible roads
---- provincial boundaries

Via Valeria was extended to Aternum by Claudius and was also know as the Via Claudia Valeria. The Via Salaria (Salt Road) from Rome to Reate was on the line of an old trade route. After 16 BC it was extended to the Adriatic to Castrum Trueninum.

The Via Aurelia may have been constructed around 241 BC, and in 109 BC it was extended from Vada Volaterrana by the Via Aemilia Scauri as far as Genoa, and then by the Via Julia Augusta to the Via Domitia in Gaul.

The second main phase of road construction began with the Via Flaminia (Flaminian Way). It was built from Rome to Fanum Fortunae and to Rimini in 220 BC. It diverged into two roads at Narni, converging beyond Foligno. The Via Flaminia was restored several times, in particular by Augustus. In 187 BC it was extended from Rimini to Placentia by the Via Aemilia.

The Via Aemilia (or Via Aemilia "Altinate") was built from Bologna to Aquileia in 175 BC. The Via Cassia was built about 154 BC from Rome to Florence and Pisa. It was paved in the time of Augustus, having previously been a gravel surface. The Via Postumia was built in 148 BC from Genoa to Aquileia. The Via Popillia Annia or Via Popillia, built in 132 to 131 BC, ran from Rimini to Aquileia and carried the name of both its builders. The Via Fulvia (125 BC) ran from Dertona to Hasta and later Turin.

The Via Popilia extended the Via Appia from Capua to Rhegium. It is often incorrectly attributed to Popillius, who built the Via Popillia, and through this confusion it is sometimes called the Via Annia. The Via Clodia probably followed the same alignment as the Via Cassia to near Veii and then turned northwest to Saturnia.

The Via Domitiana led off the Via Appia at Sinuessa across marshy ground to Cumae, Puteoli and Naples. It was built in 95 by Domitian to avoid the longer route via Capua, and was 79 km (49 mi) in length. The Via Traiana was built from Benevento to Brindisi as an alternative shorter route to the Via Appia by Trajan from 112 to 117.

SICILY, SARDINIA AND CORSICA
(fig. 5.1)

In Sicily the Via Valeria was built in 210 BC. There were also secondary roads. Only one road is known in Corsica and a system of minor roads in Sardinia.

GAUL, GERMANY AND BRITAIN
(figs. 5.2, 5.3)

Prior to Caesar's invasions in Gaul, there was a well-established system of roads along major geographical routes. This was further extended by the Romans, with many roads crossing the Alps. The Via Domitia joined Italy with Spain and was built in 121 BC. Many

Fig. 5.2 *Roman road through the* burgus *of Bitburg, Germany, which led from Trier to Cologne on the Rhine. Its course is still in use today.*

of the main roads were the responsibility of Marcus Vipsanius Agrippa (64–12 BC), in particular the network radiating from Lyon. Along the German frontier, roads developed after the establishment of the *limes* frontier along the Rhine and Agri Decumates. There was a major road along the left bank of the Rhine.

In Britain numerous roads radiated from London and from tribal capitals. Watling Street ran from Dover to London and Wroxeter. The name Watling Street is also used for the road from Chester to Caerleon. The Fosse (or Foss) Way ran from the mouth of the Axe River in Devon to Lincoln. Ermine Street ran from London to York from where it continued as Dere Street to the Antonine Wall. Akeman Street ran from Verulamium to Cirencester, and Stane Street ran from London to Chichester. In all, there were over 9,654 km (6,000 mi) of road in Roman Britain.

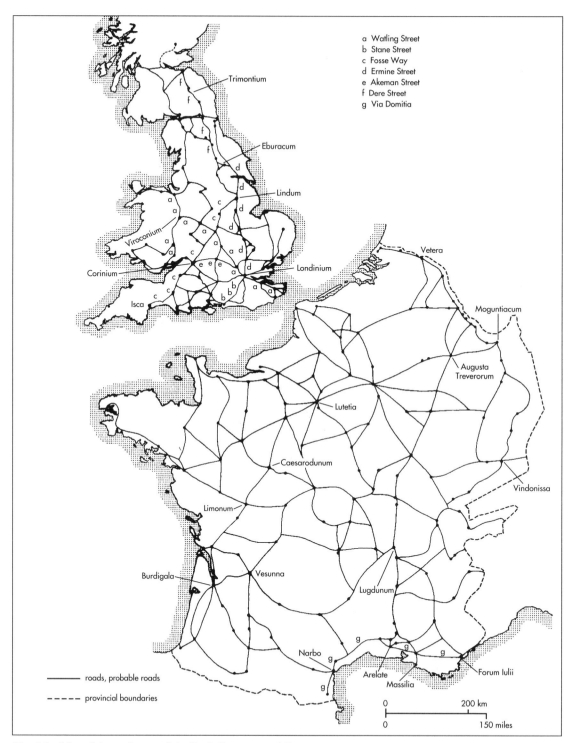

Fig. 5.3 Map of the road network in Gaul, Germany and Britain.

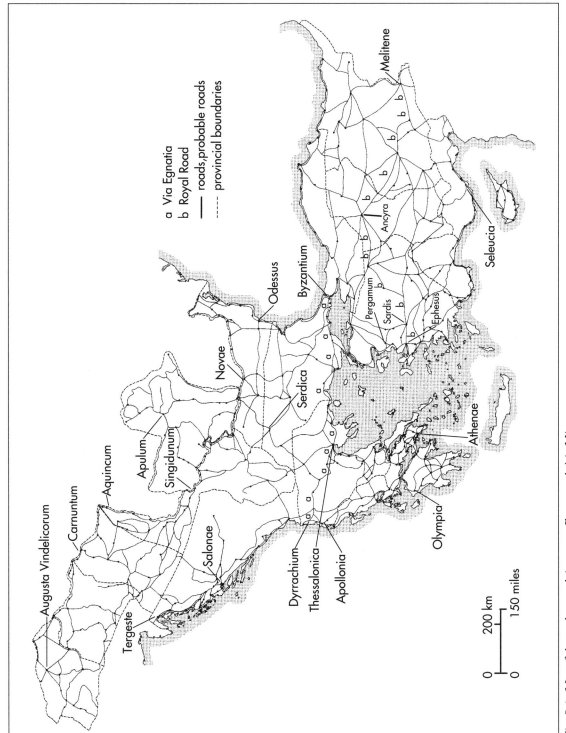

Fig. 5.4 Map of the road network in eastern Europe and Asia Minor.

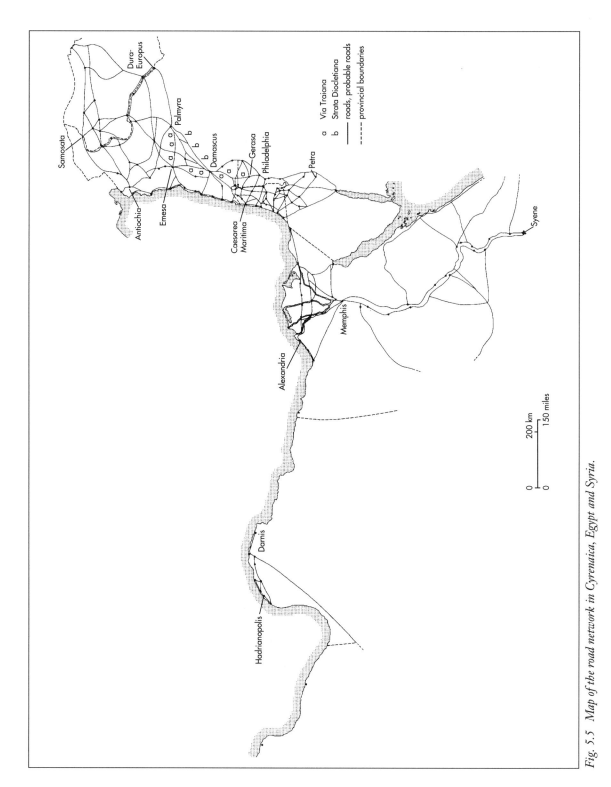

Fig. 5.5 Map of the road network in Cyrenaica, Egypt and Syria.

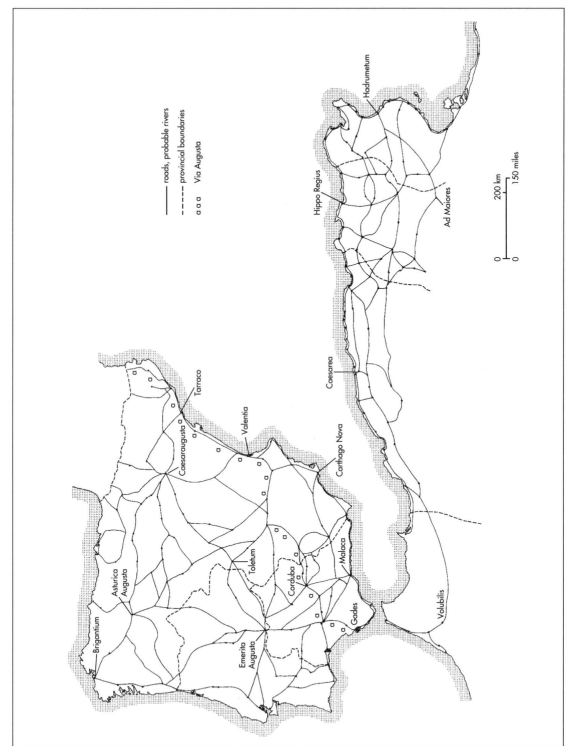

Fig. 5.6 Map of the road network in the Iberian peninsula and north Africa.

GREECE AND THE EAST (figs. 5.4, 5.5)

Due to the terrain, road construction in Greece was difficult. The Via Egnatia was a continuation of the Via Appia in Italy and became the main route from Rome to the east. It was built around 130 BC and was the first main road built outside Italy. It was of strategic importance in the civil wars of the late republic. The road started from two points (Dyrrhachium and Apollonia) on the eastern Adriatic, which converged shortly afterward, continuing eastward. The road crossed the Balkan Mountains along an ancient trade route and finally reached Byzantium. Other main towns in Greece were linked by roads, and numerous secondary roads existed, many of them sacred routes leading to sanctuaries.

Farther east there was a well-developed communications system long before the Romans, with many roads dating back to the Persian Empire. The Romans repaired these roads and built others. These routes included caravan trails and tracks. The Persian Royal Road (so called by Herodotus) led from Susa in the Tigris-Euphrates delta to Sardis and later Ephesus in western Turkey, a distance of 2,600 km (1,615 mi).

Antioch (Antiochia) was important as a center of communications between the Roman Empire and the Parthians, linking the *limes* of the Euphrates and of the Palmyran area. Roads also extended eastward to Ctesiphon and Lower Mesopotamia along the Tigris and the Euphrates rivers.

Under Trajan, there was road construction in 115 in connection with his campaigns against Parthia. The Via Traiana was built from Emesa to Philadelphia and from Emesa to Palmyra. Palmyra was later linked to Damascus through the desert by the Strata Diocletiana.

IBERIAN PENINSULA AND NORTH AFRICA (fig. 5.6)

In Spain and Portugal numerous roads were constructed, a total length of nearly 11,263 km (7,000 mi), many of which were connected with mining areas. The Via Augusta (originally called the Via Maxima) was the main route from Gaul to Cadiz, described on the Vicarello goblets.

A network of roads in north Africa was connected by a long coastal road, with few roads penetrating inland to the mountains.

BRIDGES AND TUNNELS

In difficult terrain it was not possible to construct long straight roads, and embankments, bridges and even tunnels were sometimes necessary to achieve a reasonably direct route.

Bridges (figs. 5.7, 5.8)

Bridges were constructed across rivers and depressions that were too deep for embankments. The earliest bridges were of wood. The oldest such bridge at Rome, and for several centuries the only bridge, may have been built by the Etruscans, although traditionally it has been attributed to King Ancus Marcius. This was the Pons Sublicius (Bridge on Wooden Piles, from *sublica*, pile or timber), which was defended by Horatius Cocles against the Etruscans in 508 BC, Afterward, it was rebuilt in wood in such a way that it could be dismantled easily in the face of attack. It was periodically swept away in floods and rebuilt.

Timber bridges were constructed by driving piles into the riverbed; the tips of the piles were sometimes protected by iron shoes. Transverse beams were fixed across the piles to form a trestle to support longitudinal timbers and the road decking. Although Roman timber bridges no longer survive intact, evidence for them has been found in excavations. They were frequently built in outlying provinces and for military use, but stone bridges became more common in the central provinces.

Pontoon bridges were constructed of boats placed side by side (fig. 2.10). They could be assembled quickly and were especially useful in military operations. On a swiftly flowing river, the boats were secured by anchors and cables. This type of bridge required constant maintenance, was liable to damage by floating debris and prevented traffic movement on the river.

By the mid-3rd century BC the weight-supporting arch was an important element of Roman construction techniques and was soon adopted for stone bridges supported on piers. In Mediterranean lands piers could be constructed directly on the dry riverbeds during the summer. In northern Europe, where rivers did not dry up, a cofferdam was first built. This could be a double-skinned box made of planks, with the space between the inner and outer planks being filled with clay. This box was floated into position and then weighted down until it sank. The water was pumped out by a device such as an Archimedean screw or tympanum.

To prevent the bridge from settling, the riverbed was excavated to a firm foundation and filled with hydraulic concrete for the pier foundations. Where there was no firm foundation, piles were driven into the riverbed, probably using a crane. The upper piles could be used as a superstructure for a trestle for a wooden roadway, or else they were cut short and capped with masonry and concrete foundations for piers.

Construction techniques for aqueducts and for bridges over rivers were similar. Masonry blocks were used originally, but from the 1st century concrete was more usual, with piers of concrete cores faced with masonry and brick. Piers tend to obstruct the flow of a river, but engineers tried to overcome this problem by constructing triangular cutwaters on the upstream end (fig. 5.7). This protected the pier foundations by diverting the water around the sides. Bridges over tidal rivers could have cutwaters on both the upstream and downstream ends of the pier foundations.

The bridge roadway was carried on arches that sprang from the piers and was either timber or masonry. Arches were almost all semicircular in shape, as Roman engineers could not build flattened (segmental) arches of great width. In order to minimize the number of piers, the height of the central arch was increased, so that its width could also be increased. The arches either side of the central arch were made progressively lower, which would give a humpback to the road surface. Many bridges had a single arch (fig. 5.8), while others had multiple spans. Bridges on navigable rivers had to have sufficient headroom for boats to pass underneath.

The use of headers and stretchers rather than plain voussoirs in arches was a structural improvement. Many surviving bridges have stormwater apertures in the masonry between the arches, so that the structure was not weakened when floodwater rose above the spring of the arches.

Towns such as Rome, London and Bordeaux were often sited at the lowest bridging point of rivers. At least 12 bridges existed at Rome, and hundreds more are known from the rest of the Roman world, including ones built in military operations. Bridges had to be designed to support the stresses from the structure itself. In particular, the piers and abutments had to withstand the vertical and horizontal thrusts from the arches. Because the bridges were so well built, they

Fig. 5.7 Roman bridge over the Moselle River at Trier. The pier foundations have triangular cutwaters. The superstructure is modern.

Fig. 5.8   The single-arched masonry bridge at Vaison-la-Romaine, Provence.

often can withstand modern traffic. Many are still in use, while others were replaced only in the 18th century when increased control of rivers led to a change in water flow.

In addition to bridges across rivers, there were also ferries, and river fords were used particularly for secondary roads.

Tunnels

There is evidence for tunnels, although they were used only rarely, when a major highway would otherwise have a long diversion. Examples include the Furlo tunnel, which was cut through a solid limestone outcrop at the Furlo Gorge on the Via Flaminia near Pesaro. Vespasian had it cut in 76 to 77. It was 5.48 m (18 ft) wide, 5.95 m (19 ft 6 in) high and 38.3 m (125 ft 7 in) long and is still in use today. It replaced another shorter older tunnel, which had been dug by the Umbrians. The road tunnel between Pozzuoli and

Naples (the Crypta Neapolitana) on the Via Domitiana was 705 m (2,313 ft) long, about 4 m (13 ft) wide and 5 m (16 ft 5 in) high and was lit with lamps. It was apparently always full of dust and remained in use until recently.

MILESTONES (fig. 5.9)

Milestones gave the distance in one direction only from a named place (usually Rome in Italy and the provincial capital in the provinces) to the unnamed point where the milestone was erected. Republican milestones were inscribed with the name of the consul or other officials concerned with the construction or repair, and the distance. In the principate the emperor's full names and titles often appear. Where successive repairs took place, several milestones could

Fig. 5.9 Upper part of an inscribed milestone recording 22 miles (M P XXII).

and some were quadrangular pillars. They vary in height from 2 to 4 m (6 ft 6 in to 13 ft), with a diameter from 0.5 to 0.8 m (1 ft 7 in to 2 ft 7 in). Some have their rear face shaped where they were set against a rock face or building. Over 4,000 milestones inscribed in Latin are known, and a similar number in Greek. About 600 milestones are known from Italy. Inscriptions were engraved directly onto the rounded surface of the column or within a flattened area. Some were not engraved but were probably painted, and some milestones are known to have been reworked or recarved. The earliest known milestone dates to 252 BC, but most date to the imperial period.

Some milestones are still in situ or recumbent nearby, and many more are in museums. Numerous milestones are mentioned in medieval documents as property boundary markers, a function some of them also performed in the Roman period. Some were converted to Christian use by adding a cross, while others were reused in buildings or broken up for road ballast. The recorded position of milestones can provide information on the course of a road and the frequency of repairs. If removed unrecorded from its original position, it is difficult to ascertain a milestone's original siting.

Boundary stones (*cippi* or *cippi terminales*) were used to mark boundaries between communities, and some inscribed slabs or pillars were erected by landowners to mark the construction of private roads. *Lapides tabularii* (stadia stones) were the equivalent of 100 m (330 ft) stones.

Apart from milestones, inscriptions painted on wooden signposts were probably sited close to towns or at crossroads, but none have survived. The "Golden Milestone" (*milliarum aureum*) was actually a marble column with gilt-bronze plates affixed to it. It was erected in the Forum at Rome by Augustus in 20 BC, and recorded the distances from Rome to all the main towns of the Empire. It had counterparts elsewhere, of which portions have survived.

be erected side by side, or more than one inscription could appear on a single milestone.

A milestone was generally positioned every Roman mile, with distances expressed in miles (MP). A Roman mile was 1,000 paces (*millia passuum*). The word for a milestone is *miliarum* or *milliarum* (pl. *miliaria*) which is derived from *mille* (thousand). PER M P on a milestone means *per millia passuum* (for a distance of . . .).

Distances on milestones could also be expressed in leagues (abbreviated to L). The league (*leuga* or *leuca*) was 1,500 *passus*, equivalent to 1.5 Roman miles (2,222 m or 7,285 ft). It was used in Gaul and Upper Germany from the time of Hadrian (117–138). Different local units of measurement also existed.

Milestones were usually cylindrical or oval-sectioned stone columns standing on a square base,

LAND TRANSPORT

Cursus Publicus

During the republic freedmen and slaves were employed by the state and by wealthy private citizens as couriers (*tabellarii*) to deliver and collect letters. Augustus created the *cursus publicus* (public transport or imperial post), a postal system used by authorized officials as a means of communicating messages along the military roads. It was used to send military and government dispatches and important information about laws. It also carried soldiers and official personnel on their journeys and state-owned baggage and military supplies. The requisitioning of supplies for the *annona militaris* became the responsibility of the *cursus publicus*. From the time of Constantine I, the *cursus publicus* was used extensively by the clergy.

A system of runners was used initially for the *cursus publicus* but was quickly replaced by stationing animals and vehicles along the roads to transport the same courier from start to finish of his journey. Road or posting stations (*mansiones*) were established along main roads at regular intervals, and some were based in towns. Couriers traveled an average of 75 km (46 mi) a day, but at high speeds they could cover up to 200 km (124 mi). Travelers on official business (mainly military personnel) carried an authorization document (*diploma*), and they could rest at the *mansiones* and obtain a change of animals. The words *mansiones*, *mutationes* and *stationes* originally had particular meanings. *Mansiones* (sing. *mansio*) were overnight stops and were on average 32 to 48 km (20 to 30 mi) apart; they offered fresh animals (horses, oxen and mules) and had overnight rooms and bathing establishments. *Mutationes* (sing. *mutatio*) were relays where horses and mules were changed, and *stationes* (sing. *statio*) signified a guard, with soldiers or road police to protect travelers against highwaymen; the word later came to mean a relay post.

In addition to the relays belonging to the *cursus*, there was a whole series of privately run hostelries offering civilians board and lodging.

On Foot

Civilians and soldiers often made long journeys on foot, carrying their own baggage. The legionary soldier was expected to carry a load on his back. (See chapter 2.) Loads were also carried by people using a neck yoke (*iugum*) with a basket suspended at each end. Human load carriers were cheap and were probably widely used. Travelers were also conveyed in litters (*lecticae, sellae*), borne by slaves or mules.

Horses

Horses were used primarily for riding, racing and warfare, and not as pack animals. Various breeds of horse are known from different parts of the empire, and there are references to Libyan horses. Some breeds were more suited to warfare and others to functions such as racing. Mules were also ridden, and in the eastern provinces camels were widely used. Evidence for horse equipment, such as saddles, comes largely from the cavalry. (See chapter 2.)

Pack Animals

Mules (a cross between a donkey and a horse) and donkeys were used as load carriers, being much hardier and more sure-footed than horses. A donkey was not as strong as a mule, and would probably carry loads of 100 kg (220 lb), while a mule could probably carry loads of 90 to 200 kg (198 to 441 lb). Three mules could carry the equivalent of one wagon load and were much less expensive than wheeled vehicle transport. Loads could be secured by ropes directly on an animal's back or carried in pack saddles consisting of a wooden frame covered in leather or cloth or in panniers, usually of soft basketry.

Trains of donkeys or mules may have been used far more than wheeled vehicles, and in eastern provinces camels were used to carry loads up to 200 kg (441 lb). Indigenous ponies would have been used as pack animals in more northern areas and draft horses for traction, as both types of animal can withstand a colder and wetter climate better than mules and donkeys.

Pack animals could go over the poorest of tracks that were unsuitable for wheeled transport. They could be used in towns for transporting building materials and goods from rivers and canals. They formed a major part of army transport for hauling and carrying equipment, and each legion may have needed as many as 1,000 mules or ponies.

Wheeled Vehicles (figs. 5.10, 5.11)

Not a great deal of information is known about wheeled vehicles from surviving remains or from literature. They are often represented in art form, particularly on tombstones, but are usually inaccurately or incompletely portrayed, especially the details of the harness.

Most equines seem to have been unshod, but precise information is difficult to obtain. Animals may have kept to the tracks alongside the roads in preference to the hard road surfaces. Most evidence for shoeing comes from the Celts and from Britain (where hooves can become very soft and break down quickly in the wet climate). There is archaeological evidence for pre-Roman Celtic horseshoes, and some horseshoes have been found in Roman contexts, but they did not become commonplace until the 5th century. Horseshoes had wavy or smooth edges with punched holes.

Equines could also wear light shoes: the *solea spartea* were made of tough sparta grass or other suitable materials, and the *solea ferrae* (hipposandals) had an iron (or occasionally leather) foot with an iron sole, and were attached to the foot by cords or leather straps. These shoes were a veterinary appliance used to protect an unshod sore foot or to hold a dressing in place, but were also used by animals such as oxen pulling vehicles over the hard road surfaces. They were clumsy and made movement very slow, and were most common in Gaul, Germany and Britain.

There are several methods of attaching a draft animal to a loaded vehicle, based on either a yoke or a collar. A neck yoke was more suited to oxen and a collar to equines (horses, mules, donkeys). Horses were little used because effective harness was not

Fig. 5.11 Relief on the Igel monument, Germany, showing mules pulling a four-wheeled cart laden with bales of cloth.

available, and they were more expensive to rear and maintain. They were also less adaptable to varying conditions than oxen and mules, although they had the advantage of speed. The lack of a suitable kind of collar for horses and mules prevented them from drawing wagons efficiently. Oxen were often used to pull wheeled vehicles, although they were very slow. Single pairs of oxen are shown drawing loaded goods wagons on a number of surviving monuments.

The design of wheeled vehicles was borrowed from the Celts, and nearly all the Latin names for vehicles were of Celtic (mainly Gaulish or British) origin. Latin writers did not necessarily use the terms correctly, and there are many problems with identification of vehicle types. Passenger vehicles (fig. 5.10) are more frequently portrayed in art form than commercial vehicles (fig. 5.11). The superstructure appears to have been light and flexible, at times made of wickerwork. No suspension was used, which must have made travel uncomfortable. For four-wheeled vehicles (fig. 5.11), it is uncertain if the Romans made use of a pivoting or a fixed axle, but the pivoting variety seems most likely. Horse-drawn wagons usually had an undercarriage or chassis, while ox wagons resembled boxes with wheels at each corner.

Various types of wheel were used. The primitive solid wheel continued to be used, especially on farms, but spoked wheels (figs. 5.10, 5.11) were more common, and a number of complete wheels have been found, with one-piece or multiple felloes (made from a single piece or several pieces of timber). The construction and fitting of one-piece felloes required more skill. These wheels usually had a single-piece

Fig. 5.10 Relief showing a mule pulling a two-wheeled passenger vehicle with spoked wheels.

iron tire, which was shrunk on, not nailed. Iron bands (nave hoops) protected the hub or nave, reducing the likelihood of the hub splitting, and an iron linchpin held the wheel in place. Heavier loads needed stronger wheels and substantial hubs or naves.

There is not much evidence for a braking system, but some means of keeping loaded vehicles under control on steep descents was necessary. A brake-pole dragging on the road may have been used.

Many roads were too narrow for two vehicles to pass, and it is possible that vehicles did not use the hard road surfaces except on bridges and in towns. Instead it has been suggested a dirt or grass verge alongside the paved road was used, which may have meant less wear and tear on the suspensionless vehicles. This may also explain why transport animals were not normally shod. The Theodosian Code and subsequent legislation imposed severe loading restrictions on various carriages, presumably to protect the imperial post animals and the road surfaces. Load limits included 90.8 kg (200 lb) for a two-wheeler carriage, 454 kg (1,000 lb) for a post carriage and 680 kg (1,500 lb) for heavy carts pulled by oxen. The size of the vehicles was also regulated.

The *lex Iulia municipalis* forbade the use of vehicles in town streets in the daytime, with the exception of certain vehicles such as rubbish carts and those intended for public works, although these concessions did not apply on holidays. These regulations remained in use in the 1st and 2nd centuries, and there were various subsequent bans on traffic.

MERCHANT SHIPS

While no tradition of Roman seafaring existed until the rapid expansion of Roman territory in the 4th and 3rd centuries BC, protracted wars against the Carthaginians led to a development of naval power. By the 1st century Rome was in control of the entire Mediterranean. More than 30 Greek and Latin ship types are mentioned in literary sources, but classifications of remains of ships from shipwrecks are difficult. Over 800 wrecks are known in the Mediterranean dating to before 1500 and mainly from Roman times. Of these, most have been identified as dating from the 2nd and 1st centuries BC, probably because of the discovery and recognition of their cargoes of amphorae. Keel timbers and anchors are the most common elements to survive. Wrecks from seas outside the Mediterranean are virtually unknown, although some river craft have been found in northern rivers. For warships, see chapter 2.

Ship Construction (fig. 5.12)

Mediterranean merchant ships were round-hulled or flat-bottomed, up-curving at the bow and stern (giving a symmetrical shape), keelless or keeled, with edge-fastened planking. The beam-to-length ratio was usually 1 to 4 or 1 to 3. Evidence for shipbuilding methods comes partly from representations in art but mainly from shipwrecks. Most shipbuilding techniques in the western world use a skeleton of keel and transverse frames to which the hull and deck planks are fastened. The Romans, though, used a hull-first (shell) sequence of construction, in which the watertight shell (stems, keel and planking) was built or partly built before the internal timbers were inserted for support. There are a few examples of Roman ships from the Mediterranean built with a mixture of shell and skeleton construction techniques.

In shell construction, the longitudinal planks (strakes) were fastened to each other edge to edge by mortise-and-tenon joints to form a complete hull or shell. The planking was often double. The mortises were cut into opposing edges of planks, which were held together by tenons, held firmly in place by wooden pegs (dowels or treenails). Long copper nails were also driven into the treenails for additional strength. Mortise-and-tenon joints were often close together. In later Roman ships the workmanship was not so precise: mortise-and-tenon joints were smaller, farther apart and lacked the pegs, and some showed signs of the skeleton-first method. Later Roman ships also tended to use only iron nails for fastening. In northern Europe shells tended to be constructed with overlapping, not edge-to-edge, planks, fastened by iron nails.

The frames (ribs) were then shaped and inserted in this hull. The use of half-ribs combined with one-piece ribs is common. The frames were commonly made of oak, and hulls mostly of pine, fir, cypress or cedar, and sometimes elm below the waterline. Oak

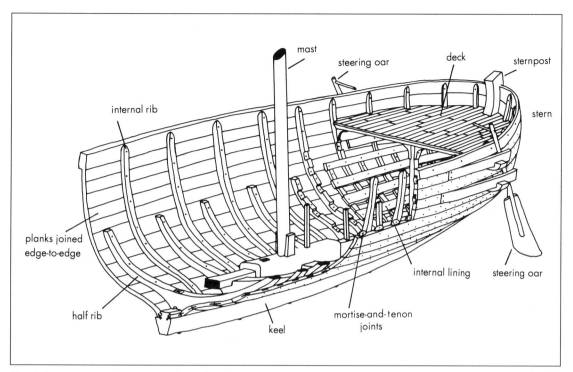

Fig. 5.12 Cutaway view of a merchant ship showing construction methods.

was also used for hulls in more northern areas. Tree-nails were often made of bog oak or a hardwood.

In order to strengthen the hull against heavy seas, large heavy timbers known as rubbing strakes or wales were attached to the exterior sides of the hull and were sometimes secured to the frames by long iron bolts. There were two heavy projecting structures on either side of the ship, which supported great steering oars or rudders. The ships had a pointed prow, like a ram, but this was only a means of completing the construction of the keel and was not for aggressive purposes. The stempost often carried a relief illustrating the ship's name, and figures on either side of the prow depicted the name of the ship. There is some evidence that ships were painted with encaustic paint (melted wax to which color had been added).

The final process was caulking—smearing the seams and sometimes the entire exterior and interior of the hull with pitch or a mixture of pitch and beeswax. Generally little caulking was necessary owing to the tightness of the mortise-and-tenon joints. The underwater surface of the hull was then often sheathed in lead as a protection against marine worms. Thin lead plates were nailed over a layer of tarred fabric using lead-dipped copper nails. As cargo ships were normally kept afloat, not hauled ashore, without the lead sheathing they would have been especially vulnerable to worm. The use of lead sheathing, though, appears to have ceased by the end of the 2nd century.

At the end of the Roman period, the eastern empire used merchant ships that were smaller in size than earlier ships. They were still rounded in shape and were similar in form to the earlier merchant vessels. The lateen sail may have begun to replace the square sail as the dominant rig.

Size

Most ships had a length of 15 to 37 m (50 to 120 ft) and a capacity of about 150 to 350 long tons, but much larger ships are known. Two imperial pleasure barges were uncovered by draining Lake Nemi in the 1930s. Although not intended as seagoing vessels, they were built to the same standards; one hull was 73 m (239 ft) long and 24 m (79 ft) wide, and the other was 71 m (233 ft) by 20 m (66 ft), tenoned, copper-fastened and lead-sheathed. Some exceptionally large ships were built in the early empire to convey special cargoes such as grain or obelisks from Egypt to Italy. The largest of the imperial grain carriers carried at least 1,200 tons of grain from Alexandria to Ostia. In the 2nd century one huge grain ship (the *Isis*) had to dock at Piraeus during bad weather. It was described by Lucian and was about 55 m (182 ft) long, 13 m (42 ft) deep, with a beam of more than 13.7 m (45 ft), and was able to carry up to about 1,300 long tons of grain.

Passengers and Crew

Besides cargoes, some ships also carried passengers. Between Dyrrachium and Brindisi a few ships carried only passengers, as the route was used so frequently. Most ships carried cargoes only and had little accommodation other than for the captain. Passengers (like most of the crew) generally lived on deck or under tentlike shelters. They brought their own food, which could be cooked in the ship's galley. Water was stored in a large wooden tank in the hold. Passenger ships as such did not exist in the ancient world—travelers used merchant vessels. The best service was on the grain ships, as they did a direct route from Alexandria to Rome with plenty of room for several hundred passengers.

Compared with warships, merchant ships had a relatively small crew. Unlike naval vessels, merchantmen often had crews entirely of slaves, including the captain, so that the owner of the ship might own the crew as well.

Sails (figs. 5.13, 5.14)

Merchant ships had sails; they rarely used oars, as far too many crew would be needed for rowing. There

Fig. 5.13   The ship Europa *was scratched in wall plaster in a house at Pompeii. It is a medium-size merchant ship and shows the rigging fairly accurately, as well as the shape of the keel and steering oar, not normally visible when the ship was afloat.*

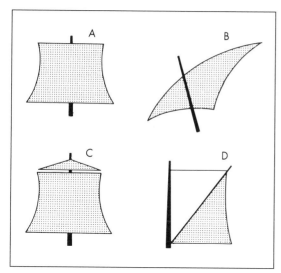

Fig. 5.14 Shapes of sails: A. square rig; B. lateen rig; C. square rig and topsail; D. sprit sail.

were two types of sail, square-rig and fore-and-aft rig. Square-rig was generally used; the mainsail was a broad square sail on a single mast, with occasionally a triangular topsail above. From the 1st century additional sails were used, including a large foresail called an *artemon* with its mast projecting over the bows.

There is also evidence for several versions of fore-and-aft rig—spritsail (or sprit-rig) and two varieties of the lateen sail. The spritsail was used from the 2nd century BC, the "Arab" lateen from the 2nd century AD and a triangular form from the 4th century. The lateen sail allowed a ship to sail more directly into the wind. The spritsail consisted of a sail more or less square in shape supported by a spar (sprit) that ran from a point near the base of the mast diagonally to the point of the sail. It was mainly used for small craft and fishing vessels. The sails were set in line with the hull and enabled the ship to tack and therefore sail into the wind. Fore-and-aft rig was not commonly used until the medieval period.

Sails were usually made of square and rectangular pieces of linen cloth sewn together, the edges protected by a boltrope and the corners reinforced by leather patches. Ropes were of flax, hemp, papyrus or esparto grass.

Merchant ships were not built for speed and could be rather slow, but were generally cheaper and quicker than land transport. They could not make reasonable progress without a following wind, and an adverse wind could make a journey take three or four times longer. If a contrary wind was met, a sailing ship would set its sails as close to the wind as possible and proceed by a zigzag course. Unlike oared warships, cargo ships needed to be towed in and out of harbor by smaller craft.

Navigation

Navigation was done by the stars at night and by landmarks and wind direction in the day. Although literary evidence for navigation has survived, no charts have survived. They probably existed along with *periploi*, which gave information such as rivers, ports, distances between ports and where fresh water was available. There were no compasses, and courses were probably plotted on charts. Depths could be tested with a lead line. Messages could be sent to other ships or to shore with signal flags. Sailings were largely suspended in winter: the *mare clausum* (closed sea) was from 12 November to 10 March, and there were also two uncertain periods, 10 March to 27 May and 14 September to 11 November. At these times there were storms and visibility was much reduced, making navigation hazardous.

Anchors (fig. 5.15)

The earliest anchors were anchor stones with a hole for a rope. These were replaced from the 7th century BC by the *agkura* (hook) anchor. Like some modern anchors, these had a stock, shank and two arms (flukes). The stock fell to the bottom causing one arm to dig in, holding the anchor cable at the correct angle. Large ships carried several anchors. Thousands of stocks and other parts made of lead have been found, and over 1,000 pieces of ancient wooden and iron anchors, most notably from the Sicily region. Many were made from a mixture of materials, such as lead, iron and wood.

Stocks were commonly of lead, sometimes of iron, and varied in size, with some weighing over a ton. Lead stocks were often cast directly onto a wooden core. By the Byzantine period fine-grade iron and movable stocks were in use. Stocks had a rectangular cross-section, but there is evidence of a circular section in the late Roman or early Byzantine period. They were often inscribed with names of gods, usually in Greek, but sometimes in Latin, reflecting the nationality of the sailors.

Over time the shape of the arms of the anchor and their angle to the stock changed. By the late Roman or early Byzantine period, the arms were set to form a right angle to the shank. Assembly pieces or collars were sometimes used to secure the arms to the shank, which probably added weight to this part. The collars were of lead and were cast in position, so giving the true shape of the arms and shank. Metal tips on the arms may have been of bronze or iron.

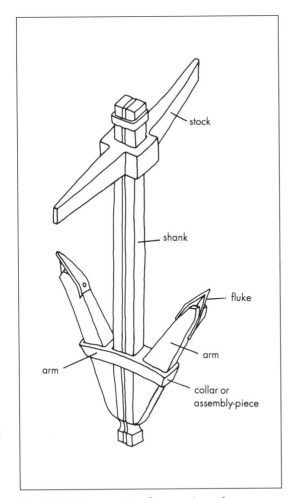

Fig. 5.15 Reconstruction of a composite anchor.

RIVERS AND CANALS

Many rivers were navigable, and some could be used by seagoing vessels. Rivers and canals were used by naval forces and by civilians. Canals were used either for interior transport or for drainage and flood control, and several are known to have been cut in the Roman period, although some were never completed. They needed a great deal of maintenance. The method of controlling the water level is not known, but could have included locks, barrages, sluice gates and weirs.

River Craft

There were several types of river craft, and cargoes were often transferred to these smaller vessels for journeys upriver. They could be propelled by rowing, although men and sometimes mules hauling the boats with ropes was the main means of propulsion upstream. The state of the banks of rivers and canals for towing boats is uncertain, but towpaths must have existed in some areas. The small boats that took goods up the Tiber River from Ostia to Rome were known as *naves codicariae*. These were barges with a rounded hull and a mast set forward to take a towline that could be kept well clear of the water and the riverbank.

Flat-bottomed barges were used on canals and rivers too shallow for seagoing vessels. Several boats of barge form have been found in northern Europe, mainly the Rhine region, dating to the 1st to 3rd centuries. They followed an indigenous western European or Celtic tradition of shipbuilding. Some were log boats, made from a simple dugout log, and others were made from large curved planks derived from logs. They were similar to barges, and the flat-bottomed floor planks were joined by several cross-members. They did not follow a true skeleton or shell technique of construction, and the strakes were not fastened by mortise-and-tenon joints. Instead, the seams were caulked with materials such as reeds and moss, and the timbers were fastened by nails. These barges were up to 34 m (11 ft 7 in) long. Some boats found in northern Europe were built in the Roman tradition.

Guilds

Guilds of watermen existed, the most powerful being the *nautae*, who were the river boatmen operating barges. They were usually associated with a particular river, such as the *nautae Druentici*, who were the boatmen of the Durance River. The most powerful guild was based at Lyon, working the Rhône and Saône. The guild of Codicarii operated the *naves codicariae* along the Tiber River. The *utricularii* (bladder-men) may have operated rafts with inflated skins or else transported liquids in skin containers.

under threat. In 67 BC Pompey took charge and commandeered ships from allies such as Rhodes, the Phoenician cities and Marseille. In a well-planned operation, he first cleaned up the western Mediterranean and then proceeded to the east, where many pirates surrendered. From then on, piracy was never a problem in the early empire.

By 230 piracy had erupted again, and between 253 and 267 mobs of Goths were using the waterways. The invasions of Germanic tribes in the late empire eventually made travel at sea more hazardous than in the days of the pirates of Cilicia.

PIRATES

Some states considered piracy a legitimate form of business. The ancient pirate chased and boarded merchantmen, but his main business was slave-running. Certain areas were particularly dangerous. The Illyrians on the Dalmatian coast were a notable threat until Rome took action after the First Punic War in the late 3rd century BC, but they were soon operating again, and at their height had a fleet of 220 ships.

The worst pirates were those of Cilicia on the southern coast of Asia Minor. They had enough crew and ships to organize themselves on naval lines and put their fleet at the disposal of Mithridates VI in his revolt against Rome in 89 BC. Attacks on shipping were a sideline, as their speciality was also slave-running. By the early 1st century BC the pirates of Cilicia controlled the seas and commanded over 1,000 ships. Rome had few ships, and wealthy Romans may have discouraged action against the pirates as they needed the slaves.

Shortly before 70 BC, though, the pirates began to raid the shores of Italy, carrying off high-ranking Romans for ransom, and the Via Appia along the coast was no longer safe for travelers. Pirates also destroyed a flotilla of Roman warships on the coast of Italy. In 69 BC a pirate fleet sacked Delos for a second time, ending the island's commercial life, and the seas became practically closed to shipping. This goaded Rome into action as its imported grain supply was

HARBORS (figs. 5.16, 5.17, 5.18)

There were many sheltered and unsheltered harbors in the Roman world as well as docks alongside navigable rivers for boats to berth and unload cargoes. The various types of harbor included open roadsteads operating offshore; natural harbors with a bay and headlands, which were often extended to enclose a larger expanse of water; and man-made harbors with great moles projecting on either side into the sea or else huge basins that were artificially excavated. Some harbors were solely for military naval use, but the majority came to be used for commercial purposes.

Evidence for Roman harbors has tended to be destroyed by changes in coastlines and in the course of rivers, or by the continued use of harbors. Subsidence of entire coastlines has also destroyed evidence for many Roman harbors, while some have become silted up beyond recognition. Roman harbor construction itself destroyed evidence for earlier harbors; between 100 BC and AD 100 the Romans refurbished and enlarged virtually every Mediterranean harbor and built new ones on previously inaccessible coasts. The coasts of Italy have few natural harbors, so artificial ones had to be constructed. Many were situated on the coastline north and south of Rome (fig. 5.16). In the Mediterranean and the Black Sea there were about 1,000 harbors in Roman times. There were

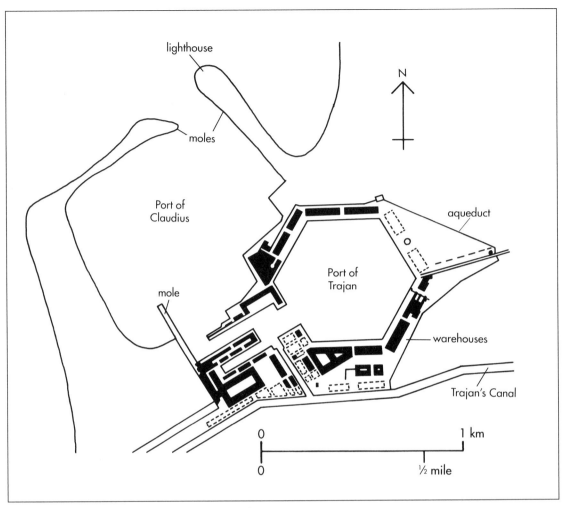

Fig. 5.16 Plan of the port of Rome at Portus near Ostia.

many other ports and harbors in the northern provinces and along rivers.

The Greeks had made considerable advances in the construction of harbors, and the Carthaginians probably built the first artifical harbor basins in the Mediterranean, dug back into the land rather than out to sea. It was not possible to pull the bigger warships and merchant ships up onshore for storage, loading and unloading, and so more sophisticated quays and harbors were constructed. Harbor construction was a very important element in the network of communications and played a vital role in the stability and success of the empire. Harbors

were prestigious structures and were fairly standardized throughout the Roman world.

The Romans developed earlier harbor construction techniques on a much larger scale, and they undertook some extensive engineering works, including the use of massive timbers and land reclamation in the construction of quays. There were also technical innovations, including the use of a hydraulic cement that set underwater. Two major problems affecting harbors were the deposition of silt at river mouths so that river ports became unusable (as at Ostia) and the deposition of sand caused primarily by the construction of moles and

Fig. 5.17 Wall painting from the House of the Little Fountain at Pompeii, portraying a harbor scene with an arched mole and a villa maritima. *From W. Gell (1832)* Pompeiana.

jetties projecting into the sea, leading to the silting up of the harbor (as at Leptis Magna). In order to overcome these problems, dredging was essential to maintain a sufficient depth in the approach channel from the open sea and at the quays. Man-made moles and jetties with arches were also constructed that allowed circulation of water and minimized silt buildup (figs. 5.17, 5.18). Some of the artificial breakwaters or moles built into the sea to construct an artificial harbor were extensive.

Fig. 5.18 Flattened illustration from a glass bottle. It shows a harbor scene at Baiae with a palace, oyster bed (ostriaria), *a lake, a mole with four arches and columns.*

Lighthouses

Lighthouses were built before Roman times, the first one being on the island of Pharos in front of the harbor at Alexandria. This acted as a model for lighthouses throughout the Greek and Roman world. It was apparently begun under Ptolemy I in the late 3rd century BC and was a three-tiered polygonal structure about 100 m (328 ft) in overall height. The light was provided by a huge fire in the base, which was said to be reflected by mirrors, probably of burnished bronze, at the top of the structure, which increased the intensity of the light. In the Roman period most harbors had a stone lighthouse, modeled on the one at Alexandria, but smaller. Known examples include the best-preserved one at Coruña in northwest Spain, and at Dover, Boulogne, Ostia (built by Claudius), possibly Delos, Ravenna, Puteoli, Leptis Magna and possibly Caesarea Maritima.

The method of using a fire to produce the light was probably universal, with mirrors used to reflect the sun's rays in daytime. A vast amount of wood or charcoal for fuel would have been required, a scarce commodity in some areas, such as Egypt. There a material such as dried animal dung may have been used instead. On coins, lighthouses are portrayed with flames coming out of the top of the structures. It has been suggested that this portrayal was stylized and that light was actually provided by several braziers at the top of the lighthouse, fuel being carried up by stairs or sometimes by external ramps.

TRANSPORT AND TRADE OF GOODS

Trade was carried on from early in Rome's history, with entrepreneurs buying goods in one location and selling them in another. In the late republic the term *negotiator* (pl. *negotiatores*) seems to have implied a financial dealer or banker, but it came to mean someone generally engaged in the trade of goods. *Negotiatores* handled the transport business and acted as middlemen, sometimes dealing in specific products. Some *negotiatores* were agents of large trading companies, which were owned by wealthy investors, and they were of many nationalities. *Mercatores* were merchants dealing with specific commodities and may even have been employed by *negotiatores*, along with sailors and river boatmen.

Most cities of the Mediterranean world were on the coast, and large quantities of materials could be traded fairly easily between them. Many goods from Spain, north Africa and Italy were transported along the rivers Rhône, Saône and Rhine, which provided a major link between the Mediterranean, the Rhineland and Britain. A great deal of early trade was to supply military needs, but as the empire expanded, goods were marketed to and from the farthest provinces and beyond. The trade routes stretched from China and Scandinavia to the Atlantic, and included the various routes of the Silk Road terminating at Loyang.

The two most conspicuous routes were those used for Rome's trade in the Indian Ocean and the Alexandria-to-Rome grain supply. The *Periplus Maris Erythraei* gave much information about trade to and from east Africa and India (as far as the Ganges), but the author was aware of lands farther east. Included is information about what could be bought and sold en route. Chinese records indicate that some Roman merchants reached Malaya, Java, Vietnam and the borders of China.

The Romans paid for the imported goods largely in gold and silver, and many Roman coins of gold and silver (not bronze) have been found in places such as east Africa, Afghanistan, India and Indochina. In the Indian area about 6,000 gold and silver coins have been found, mainly dating to the 1st and 2nd centuries but continuing to the 5th century and into the 6th from the eastern empire. The Romans exported finished goods such as jewelry, cut gems, glassware and clothing as well as amber, coral and purple dye. Some of the goods exported were made from raw materials originally imported from the east, including cameos and other cut gems. After gold, coral from the Mediterranean was Rome's most valuable export to India.

A vast and diverse amount of goods was imported to maintain a Roman way of life, including manufactured goods, foodstuffs, perishable goods, raw materials and building materials. Rome itself imported goods from the east, in particular raw materials and semimanufactured goods. The trade between India and Rome was on a large scale and included spices of all kinds, perfumes, silks, cottons, steel, certain drugs and precious stones. Some of the goods from India came from even farther afield, such as China, Afghanistan and Iran. The major imports were always silks and spices. In the 3rd century under Aurelian, silk was valued at its own weight in gold.

Trade between Britain, Spain, the Rhineland and Gaul apparently decreased considerably in the late 3rd century owing to the unstable political situation in those areas.

Some trade routes were by land, some by sea and land and some by river. Many goods were transported long distances by sea, and shipwrecks with their cargoes can reflect the date and type of trade. Ships sailed from the northwest shore of the Red Sea to India and back, with the desert being crossed by camel or donkey to the Nile. The bulk of seaborne cargoes consisted of grain, oil, wine, building stone and metals. During its journey, a cargo was often transferred to a smaller vessel and even to a river barge, which required much manpower.

Trade in Food and Drink

Food such as milk products, meat, poultry, fresh fruit and vegetables were probably produced locally, but less perishable commodities including olive oil, wine, grain, salt, preserved fish and fruit products were transported over long distances. They were carried in a variety of containers, such as amphorae, sacks, barrels, baskets and leather skins.

GRAIN

Already by the 2nd century BC, Rome was receiving large quantities of grain as taxes in kind from some of its provinces. Initially much came from Sicily and Sardinia, and then from Egypt and north Africa. To insure against starvation, political leaders started the practice of subsidizing grain, and later both *populares* and their opponents sought political support by distributing it free. During the first three centuries AD, about 200,000 inhabitants were receiving such handouts, after Julius Caesar had made drastic cuts to the number of recipients. The supply of grain for the city was called the *annona*, to which wine and pork were added in the 3rd century. A *praefectus annonae* was appointed as minister of supply under Claudius, and similar arrangements existed in other Italian towns.

The *annona militaris* was different from the *annona* and was not levied until the later 3rd century.

Although most commodities were free to Rome, as they were taxes in kind, they nevertheless posed a huge transport problem. Grain was carried by ship in bulk or in sacks, and in the 1st century, by the time of Nero, 20 million *modii* (about 135,000 long tons) of grain were shipped annually from Egypt. This served the requirements of about one-third of the population of Rome. The rest came from Egypt and north Africa, a total of over 300,000 long tons of grain, amounting to more than 10 million sacks. It was cheaper to transport grain by sea from Egypt and Africa than overland from southern Italy. During the summer months the prevailing winds are northwesterly, and so the ships were against the winds when fully laden on their return journey from Alexandria. The voyage took at least one month and was undertaken by huge grain carriers. The ships docked at Pozzuoli or Portus and had to shift their load to barges or small freighters. The grain was then unloaded to warehouses by porters and transported up the Tiber to Rome in the *naves codicariae*. On their return journey, these boats often carried refuse (such as rubble from the fire of Rome in 64).

The grain ships from Egypt sailed to Rome until 330, when Constantine I moved the capital to Byzantium, and the ships went there instead. Rome then was supplied by a shuttle service from north Africa. Navigating the Dardanelles was difficult, and in the early 6th century Justinian built a large granary on the island of Tenedos near the mouth of the strait. It was 85 m (280 ft) long and 27 m (90 ft) wide. When weather in the straits was bad, ships unloaded there.

WINE

The earliest wine trade began in the 6th century BC with the Etruscans, Greeks and Carthaginians. Wine was traded to Gaul from Italy from the 3rd century BC. The earliest wine amphorae with Latin inscriptions date from the first half of the 3rd century BC, but a great expansion of Roman wine exports began in the second half of the 2nd century BC from Etruria, Latium and Campania to all new areas of Roman territory. Wine was particularly in demand from the late 2nd century BC in southern Gaul, where viticulture had not yet been introduced. By 150 BC wine was being exported to southern France in Dressel 1 amphorae (see chapter 8), and also up the Rhône valley to areas then outside the empire, such as Britain and Britanny. The wine trade from Italy reached a peak in the mid-1st century BC, and Diodorus stated that when trading with the Gauls, a slave was exchanged for just one amphora of wine.

The Italian wine trade began to collapse from the end of the 1st century BC due to competition from new vineyards in Spain and Gaul and from traditional wine areas such as Rhodes and Cnidos. Rather than being a main market for Italian wine, southern France grew in importance as a wine-producing area from the 1st century, and by the reign of Augustus wine was exported in large quantities from Spain to Italy. However, wine production continued in Italy until at least the 4th century, as witnessed by the appearance of wine in Diocletian's price edict.

Defrutum—a sweet wine or grape syrup made from fruit juice boiled down to half its volume—was also traded.

OLIVE OIL

From the end of the 1st century BC, olive oil was a major export from Spain to Italy and elsewhere until the mid-3rd century, when that from north Africa became predominant. Much of the olive oil produced in Baetica was probably shipped to Rome. Dressel 20 olive oil amphorae constitute two-thirds of the sherds forming Monte Testaccio (see below), and show a peak in trade in the period from 140 to 165.

Containers

AMPHORAE

In the Mediterranean region, liquids such as wine, oil and fish sauce were usually transported in large clay jars known as amphorae. They were an important means of transporting liquid commodities, especially by sea, and were also occasionally used for solid food-stuffs such as olives, dates, oysters, figs and nuts.

Until the reign of Augustus, there was no safe land route to southern Gaul, and so much of the wine trade was by sea. Huge quantities of amphorae have been found stacked in the holds of wrecked ships, some packed with heather and rushes. The amphorae are known to have been stacked both upright and on their

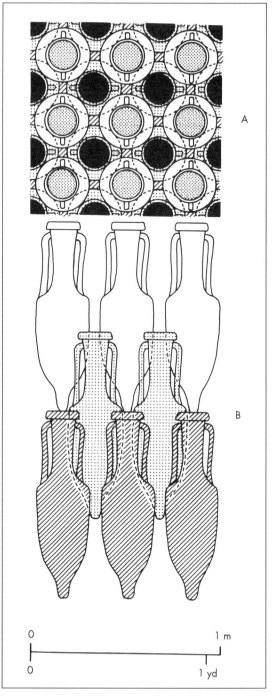

Fig. 5.19 Method of stacking amphorae as ship's cargo. A. Plan view of the amphorae; B. Three stacked layers of amphorae.

side, in up to five layers (fig. 5.19). It is estimated that the Madrague de Giens wreck (20 km [12 mi] southeast of Toulon) carried 4,500, possibly 7,800, amphorae, weighing 225 to 390 long tons, along with other cargo. The Albenga (Italy) wreck of the mid-1st century BC had five layers of amphorae, some 11,000 to 13,500 in number, a cargo of 500 to 600 long tons.

Many cargoes in Roman shipwrecks are partly or wholly of amphorae, some with a variety of amphorae types. On the outskirts of modern Rome near the point on the Tiber River where the ancient docks were situated is a substantial hill called the Monte Testaccio (Mount Potsherd) from *testae* (potsherds). This is composed entirely of amphora sherds, and represents containers for millions of gallons of olive oil from Spain and north Africa, mainly Dressel 20 amphorae. (See chapter 8.) This was presumably the point where the amphorae were offloaded from ships or riverboats and the contents transferred to smaller containers for distribution within the city.

BARRELS

In the Po valley and north of the Alps, wine was also transported in large wooden barrels, and some are occasionally found reused as the lining of wells. They are also commonly depicted in carvings (fig. 2.2). Barrels have been found in London with capacities of 400 to 1,000 liters (105 to 264 U.S. gallons). Barrels are likely to have been used to transport other products, such as fish sauce and salt, as well as wine. They were probably used more than amphorae in the later Roman period, when there is little evidence for amphorae manufacture in western Europe.

Spices

The word spice derives from the Latin *species*, a commodity of particular distinction or value. The opening up of the east introduced the Romans to many new spices for use in wine, food, medicines, perfumes and cosmetics. The Spice Quarter became a well-known part of Rome. Spices came from China and other areas of southeast Asia and included camphor, cassia, cloves, ginger, nutmeg, sandalwood and turmeric. From India spices included cardamom, cinnamon, sandalwood, sesame, turmeric and pepper, the latter being the major commodity of the Roman imperial trade with India. Other spices came from Persia, Arabia and east Africa, beyond the Roman Empire, in lands that were mainly desert or scrub with no rich rain forests. Their spices included balsam, frankincense, myrrh and ginger. Some spices were traded from within the Roman Empire, and many are mentioned in contemporary literature.

Pottery Vessels

Vessels such as amphorae were exported as containers, and other pottery vessels were used to transport salt. The pottery cooking vessels and tablewares themselves provided substantial trade. Many of the kitchen wares were made locally and transported over relatively short distances, but pottery with an intrinsic value was traded more widely, usually by sea. This pottery included mortaria from Italy as well as fine tablewares and drinking vessels from Italy, Spain and north Africa. Samian ware was exported in vast quantities, initially from Italy, then from southern Gaul and later central and eastern Gaul. This trade ceased from the mid-3rd century when the pottery industries of Gaul collapsed. For pottery, see also chapter 8.

Glass

Glass began to be mass-produced and exported from the 1st century. The centers of manufacture are not always easy to identify, but some was made in Spain, while much was made in Gaul and the Rhineland. It was transported mainly by sea. Some glass vessels were containers for their liquid or semiliquid contents, including square bottles and *unguentaria*. The original contents of these vessels is largely unknown. For glass, see also chapter 8.

Metals

No Roman wreck has been found with silver ingots, but lead ingots have been found. Ones from Spain date to the 1st centuries BC and AD and were marked with the names of Roman lessees of the mines. In the second half of the 1st century, export of Spanish lead seems to have slumped in competition with that from British and other mines. Lead ingots are of a standardized form.

Copper was exported from Iberia, and this was a flourishing industry in the early empire. Copper ingots are more varied in shape and bear more informative inscriptions. Gold came from Wales or Spain, and tin ingots, which vary greatly in shape, from Spain. Many were cast in decorated or inscribed molds, and all are marked by several stamps or inscriptions.

Stone

Most quarries seem to have served their local areas, although even nondecorative building stone does seem to have been transported some distance. For example, thousands of tons of stone were transported to London where no suitable local stone was available. Stone was usually carried by water and was a cargo liable to cause shipwrecks. Building stone and tiles may have been carried only on a return journey, with a more profitable cargo on the outward journey. Some cargoes of stone may even have been used as ballast.

There was an extensive trade in fine, exotic building stone, especially marble, which was an expensive and prestigious material for decoration. The use of white Carrara marble from Italy declined sharply in the late 2nd century and was largely supplanted by marble from the Aegean and Asia Minor. There was also a trade in colored marble and other colored stones, some from the eastern desert of Egypt. Marble was used extensively in Rome but is also found in provincial towns and villas. It was used for buildings, veneers, wall inlays and sarcophagi.

Huge marble blocks were quarried and shipped to Rome by the emperors, and marble and other stone were also shipped to Rome as semifinished objects such as columns, capitals, bases, sculptures and large blocks. Some needed only fine detail and polishing, some were half finished, while others were only rough outs. Nearly all the major quarries were by or near the sea or rivers. Old Egyptian obelisks were also shipped to Rome, and occasionally to provincial towns, to adorn circuses.

Off Sicily a wreck has been found (the "Church Wreck") containing prefabricated building parts for the interior architecture of a basilica. They date to the early 6th century, the early Byzantine period when Justinian I had embarked on an empire-wide program of church building. This basilica was probably destined for north Africa from Byzantium.

Textiles

The demand for finished textile goods must have been considerable. The textile trade included the import of luxury items such as silk and fine linen. For textiles, see chapter 8.

Animals

There was a considerable trade in animals for the amphitheater and also for pets and as draft animals in agriculture. There was even a trade in exotic animals from the east for food, including parrots, ostriches and buffaloes (also used as draft animals). Animals for the amphitheater and for pets included parrots, monkeys, lions, leopards, lynxes, tigers, elephants and the one-horned rhinoceros from Asia, and lions, leopards, giraffes and the two-horned rhinoceros from north Africa. Animals (such as horses, mules, camels and oxen) were also bred for military use, for the *cursus publicus* and for farm use. (See chapter 4.)

Slavery

In the late republic senators needed more and more slaves to run their huge estates. Rome's wars with Carthage and then with the east put thousands of prisoners on the slave market, and some slaves also came from the west. The supply eventually ran low, and pirates stepped in to replenish it. Slaves were obtained by raiding coastal settlements and seizing children and young adults. The pirates of Cilicia were particularly ruthless, preying mainly on the coasts of Thrace, Syria and Asia Minor. They supplied the bulk of the slaves who were sold at the great market at Delos, which could handle thousands daily, satisfying the ever-increasing demands of the Roman estate owners. The pirates eventually opened up a market of their own at Side, which became second only to Delos. This trade ceased only when Pompey cleared the seas of pirates in the late 1st century BC.

Customs

Portorium (pl. *portoria*) was a tax levied on the movement of imports and exports and was instituted by Augustus. It could be levied as customs (a tax paid at frontiers), as dues paid at the gates of some large towns and as tolls at important road junctions, passes, bridges and fords. It was usually levied at rates of 2 to 2.5 percent on the value of the goods but could be as high as 25 percent. The *portorium* was not a means of regulating trade but a source of public revenue, and was closely integrated with the transport network. The major source of revenue was on trade with the east. All goods, including personal effects, had to be declared, but some goods were exempt by law, such as animals and vehicles, property belonging to the treasury or emperor and soldiers' equipment.

In 167 BC Rome declared Delos a free port, open to trade without harbor or customs dues being levied, and gave it to Athens to administer. The island became a great center of exchange, dealing mainly in luxury goods and slaves, and eclipsed Rhodes, whose trade plummeted. The harbor was 3 to 4 m (10 to 13 ft) deep and was partially enclosed by two moles. Warehouses lined the quays but had no connection with the town itself because merchandise was moved in and out of the port of Delos so quickly. In 88 BC Delos was sacked during the war between Rome and Mithridates VI, and in 69 BC it was devastated by pirates and never recovered.

The method of collection of customs varied, and in the early empire customs offices (*stationes*) were leased out and were accompanied by military posts for security. Later on the collection was done by civil servants. Under Tiberius the empire was divided into five customs districts, and the revenue was paid into the *fiscus*, not the *aerarium*. The customs offices were generally sited in places determined by geographical factors, and sometimes gave rise to place names such as Ad Portum and Ad Publicanos. The collection of *portoria* by tax collectors or publicans was open to fraud. For other taxes, see chapter 1.

READING

Chevallier 1988: gives details on many aspects of travel and travelers including abundant literary sources and journeys of many civilian and military people as well as emperors.

Maps and Itineraries
Casson 1991: *Periplus Maris Erythraei*; Chevallier 1976, 28–39, 47–64; Dilke 1985: the most detailed source of information for mapmaking, maps and itineraries of all kinds, with many references; Miller 1969: discussion of the Periplus and early geographers; Oleson 1986: includes bibliography on maps.

Roads
Chevallier 1976: many details on roads, including their construction and specific routes in Italy and the provinces; Johnston 1979: roads in Britain; McWhirr 1987: summary of land and water transport; Oleson 1986: includes bibliography on roads; White 1984, 93–100, 209, 215–16.

Bridges and Tunnels
Chevallier 1976, 93–106, 200: includes details on many of the empire's bridges; Grant 1990, 126–28: bridge at Trier; Hill 1984, 61–75: construction of bridges, 127–54: water-raising machines; Milne 1985, 44–54: illustrated description of bridges, with particular reference to London; Oleson 1986: includes bibliography on bridges; White 1984, 86–87, 97–100.

Milestones
Chevallier 1976, 39–47, 71–72; Sandys 1927, 133–42.

Land Transport
Chevallier 1976, passim; Chevallier 1988: various aspects of carts, draft and pack animals, travelers and the *cursus publicus*, with many examples from Latin authors; Hyland 1990: contains much information on various aspects of horses and mules, in particular military uses; Manning 1985, 63–66: hipposandals, 70–75: vehicle fittings; Oleson 1986: includes bibliography on transport and vehicles; Piggott 1983, 229–35: literary evidence for wheeled vehicles in classical writing; Rickman 1971: the organization of granaries as part of the *cursus publicus*; White 1984, 127–40, 208–9.

Merchant Ships

Casson 1991, 191–212: various details of merchant ships and crews; Chevallier 1988, 83–122: includes details on various nautical matters, such as ships, harbors and literary sources; Käpitan 1973: discussion of anchors, largely of stocks; Marsden 1972, 114–23: boats in Britain; Meijer 1986, 220–31: merchant ships and shipping; Oleson 1986: includes bibliography on ships; Parker 1980: examples of wrecks and their cargoes; Rival 1991: construction materials and methods; Starr 1960: discussion of types of naval ships and crews as well as the various fleets, with much information relevant to merchant ships; Throckmorton 1972: ships, shipbuilding, shipwrecks and cargoes; Tusa 1973: includes an illustrated discussion of lead anchor stocks; van Doorninck 1972, 134–39: ships of the early Byzantine Empire; White 1984, 141–56, 210–13: most aspects of ships, shipbuilding, anchors, cargoes, navigation.

Rivers and Canals

Chevallier 1988, 123–32: interior waterways including canals; du Plat Taylor and Cleere (eds.) 1978: contains papers on river craft from the northern provinces; Johnstone 1988, 156–68: river craft.

Pirates

Casson 1991, 177–83: history of piracy in the republic.

Harbors

Clayton 1988: lighthouse at Alexandria; Flemming 1980: early harbors in the Mediterranean, including Roman ones, and sea level changes; Grant 1990, 100–4: Caesarea Maritima port, 182–84: port of Puteoli; Hague 1973: includes a discussion of some Roman lighthouses; Jones and Mattingly 1990, 198–200: harbors and canals in Britain; Miller et al. 1986: details of trade and an excavated quay at London, with numerous illustrations; Milne 1985: excavation of the harbor along the Thames River at London and the changing levels of the river; Oleson 1986: includes bibliography on harbors and lighthouses; Shaw 1972: Greek and Roman harbors and lighthouses; Starr 1960: discussions of naval ports throughout the empire; White 1984, 104–12, table 6.

Transport and Trade of Goods

Casson 1991: includes underwater finds, especially amphorae, transport of goods by ship, trade with the east and the grain supply from Egypt; Chevallier 1976, 195–97: customs; Chevallier 1988, 272–98: business travel, especially trade, including many literary sources; Dodge 1991: review article on marble industry; du Plat Taylor and Cleere (eds.) 1978: papers on trade between Britain and the Rhine provinces; Greene 1986; Grew et al. 1985: evidence for trade in London; King 1990: trade in Gaul and Germany, with bibliography; Miller 1969: spice trade, including countries of origin, trade routes and traders, the import and export of other goods beyond the Roman Empire and customs; Milne 1985, 98–102: handling cargoes in the port of London, especially amphorae; Parker 1980: cargoes of shipwrecks and seaborne trade; Peacock and Williams 1986: amphorae; Rickman 1980: corn supply.

6

WRITTEN EVIDENCE

LATIN LANGUAGE

Through much of Rome's early history, numerous languages were spoken in Italy, some of which were Indo-European, but little is known of these other than Latin. Etruscan was a non-Indo-European language, known from inscriptions, mainly short epitaphs and dedications. Etruscan literature is known to have existed, but none survives, and only a few words of Etruscan have been deciphered. The language had little influence on Latin, although it was spoken in early Rome, and Etruscan practices (particularly religious) were influential. Etruscan culture was dominant in the area of modern-day Tuscany from the 8th to 5th centuries BC.

Latin was the main language of the Indo-European Italic family of languages and was originally spoken by most of the people of Rome and the territory of Latium. It is known through inscriptions from the 6th century BC and through literature from the 3rd century BC.

With the expansion of the empire, Latin became widespread, particularly with the foundation of colonies, which created urban centers of Latin-speaking people. It eventually became the language of government of most of western Europe. Although there was no coercion to adopt Latin as a language, wealthy provincials especially were encouraged to adopt it as part of the process of Romanization. However, other native languages, such as Celtic, Punic and Syriac, continued to be used throughout the empire. In Greek-speaking areas Latin had little influence, and Greek remained the predominant language, although in the late 3rd century Diocletian encouraged the use of Latin in eastern provinces. Many books of the day were written in Greek, and educated Romans usually learned Greek from childhood.

"Early Latin" or "archaic Latin" describes the language up to 100 BC, "classical" or "Golden Age" Latin from 100 BC to about AD 14, and "Silver Latin" up to 150. The everyday speech, *sermo cotidianus*, of educated people occurs in letters such as those of Cicero. The everyday speech of uneducated people (vulgar Latin, from *vulgus*, mob) was less formal and is known mainly from inscriptions, especially graffiti. Even with the barbarian invasions of the 5th century, Latin continued to be the main medium of written communication in the west, but Greek remained dominant in the east. The last eastern emperor to use Latin as the language of government was Justinian in the 6th century. From c. 700 vulgar (spoken) Latin developed into the Romance languages, such as French and Italian. At the end of the medieval period, written Latin gradually gave way to the vernacular. Greek also underwent a comparable development.

Basic Rules of Latin

In English and other Romance languages the pronouns I, you, we and they are used with verbs, and the definite and indefinite articles (the, a/an) are used with nouns. In Latin no articles are used and pronouns are not essential: The sense depends on a combination of word endings and word order. For example, *amicum puer videt* and *puer amicum videt* both mean "the boy sees his friend," while *amicus puerum videt* and *puerum amicus videt* both mean "the friend sees the boy." *Ille amicum videt* and *amicum videt* both mean "he sees the friend" (*ille* being the pronoun he).

VERBS

English needs pronouns such as we or they to make the sense clear. In Latin the use of pronouns is unnecessary, as the verbs have personal endings to indicate their meanings. Verbs can be classified into four groups (called conjugations); their classification is determined by the final letter of the present stem: *a* in the first conjugation, *e* in the second conjugation, a consonant in the third conjugation, and *i* in the fourth conjugation.

1st conjugation: *amo* (I love), *amare* (to love). *Amo* is a contraction of *amao*.

2nd conjugation: *moneo* (I warn), *monere* (to warn).

3rd conjugation: *rego* (I rule), *regere* (to rule).

4th conjugation: *audio* (I hear), *audire* (to hear).

The most common endings for all conjugations are:

	SINGULAR	PLURAL
1st person	*-o* or *-m* (I)	*-mus* (we)
2nd person	*-s* (you)	*-tis* (you)
3rd person	*-t* (he/she/it)	*-nt* (they)

For example, these endings are used as follows:

1st-conjugation verb

amo	I love
amas	you love
amat	he/she/it loves

amamus	we love	
amatis	you love	
amant	they love	

2nd conjugation verb

moneo	I warn	
mones	you warn	
monet	he/she/it warns	
monemus	we warn	
monetis	you warn	
monent	they warn	

Different forms of the verb can indicate different tenses such as:

amabis	you will love
amabamus	we were loving
amaverant	they had loved

Different verb endings can also be used to indicate other states, such as the passive.

amantur	they are being loved
amabimur	we will be loved

There are also irregular verbs that do not fit the general pattern.

In dictionaries, it is usual for the first-person present tense and the infinitive of a verb to be given, to allow its conjugation to be recognized, such as: *scribo, scribere*—to write. The first-person singular of the perfect tense and the supine are also given, and these four principal parts (such as *scribo, scribere, scripsi,* and *scriptum*) allow the recognition of all the other parts of the verb.

NOUNS

Latin nouns also have various endings (called cases), which demonstrate their role in a sentence. Some endings have more than one function. The various cases are:

Nominative:	The subject of the verb.
Vocative:	Calling to or addressing a person or thing, such as "O, fortune!"
Accusative:	The direct object of the verb.
Genitive:	Denotes possession, such as "the altar of the god"—"of the god" is genitive. Used when one noun is dependent on another, or dependent on an adjective.
Dative:	Indirect object of the verb, translated as to or for. For example, "The priest gave the offering to the god"—"to the god" is dative.
Ablative:	This case has many functions, often in Latin (and always in English translations) used with prepositions such as by, with and from. For example "with money."

Nouns belong to one of five classes, called declensions. Nouns with an *-ae* ending in the genitive are first declension and are usually feminine, except for masculine-type words such as *agricola* (farmer).

Singular

Nominative:	*puella*	a/the girl
Vocative:	*puella*	o girl!
Accusative:	*puellam*	a/the girl
Genitive:	*puellae*	of a/the girl
Dative:	*puellae*	to/for a/the girl
Ablative:	*puell*	by/with/from a/the girl (used with a preposition)

Plural

Nominative:	*puellae*	(the) girls
Vocative:	*puellae*	O girls!
Accusative:	*puellas*	(the) girls
Genitive:	*puellarum*	of (the) girls
Dative:	*puellis*	to/for (the) girls
Ablative:	*puellis*	by/with/from (the) girls (used with a preposition)

Nouns with an *-i* ending in the genitive are second declension; ones ending in *-us, -er* or *-ir* in the nominative are masculine; and those ending in *-um* are neuter. More nouns belong to the third declension than to any other, and they can be masculine, feminine or neuter. There is a wide variation of spellings in the nominative singular, but the genitive case always ends in *-is*. For example, *pax, pacis* (peace) and *miles, militis* (soldier). Nouns that end in *-us* in the genitive singular are fourth declension and are largely masculine. Nouns that end in *-ei* in the genitive singular are fifth declension and are mostly feminine. In dictionaries, the nominative and genitive of a noun are usually given, with its gender, such as *stella, stellae,* f. (or *stella, -ae,* f.).

GENDER

In English the gender of a noun is determined by its meaning, so that "man" is masculine, "mother" is feminine and "house" is neuter. In Latin the gender of a noun does not necessarily reflect what it denotes. For example, *culpa* (fault or blame) is feminine, *iter* (journey) is neuter and *liber* (book) is masculine. Adjectives also carry different endings that relate to the number, gender and case of the noun.

WORD ORDER

In Latin there is much greater freedom of word order than in English, particularly for nouns, adjectives, pronouns and adverbs. The meaning of the sentence depends on the endings of words, not on word order as in English. The most emphatic positions are at the beginning and end of a sentence. As in English, the subject often comes at or near the beginning of a sentence, but the verb is usually at the end of a sentence or clause.

ALPHABET (fig. 6.1)

The earliest-known alphabet was the North Semitic, which developed around 1700 BC in Palestine and Syria and consisted of 22 consonant letters. The Hebrew, Arabic and Phoenician alphabets were based on this model. Around 1000 BC the Phoenician alphabet was used as a model by the Greeks, who added letters for vowels. From the 7th century BC Greek in turn became the model for Etruscan, from which developed the Latin alphabet, and ultimately all western alphabets.

Latin

The Latin alphabet was partly Etruscan and partly Greek in origin. In the early alphabet, *C* was used for both *C* and *G*. *C* was the curved form of the Greek gamma, but was also used to express the sound of kappa. For example, *virco* was pronounced *virgo*. To prevent confusion, *C* became slightly changed when used to represent the sound of gamma, which became the letter *G*. This occurred from the 3rd century BC, although names like Gaius and Gnaeus were still abbreviated in the archaic fashion as C. and Cn. *K* was originally used before the letter *A*, but this was replaced by *C*, and *K* became redundant.

Q was derived from koppa, found in some Greek alphabets after pi. It was originally written instead of *C* before *O* and *U*, and was later used only before *U*. *I* was used for *J*. *J* developed from handwriting and is occasionally seen from the 2nd century, although it

was adopted as an initial letter only in the 15th century. *V* was pronounced *W* up to the 3rd century, but was also used as a letter *U*. The Greek letter *X* represented the sound ks (not kh as in the Greek alphabet), and *H* differed from the Greek in representing the aspirate. Toward the end of the republic, *Y* and *Z* were borrowed for transliteration of Greek words, *Z* for 'ds' and *Y* for Greek words containing an upsilon. By this time, there were 23 letters in the Latin alphabet: A B C D E F G H I K L M N O P Q R S T V X Y Z

The alphabet was basically the same as modern English, but lacked the letters *J*, *U* and *W*.

Greek

Greek was also widely used in the Roman world. The standard Greek alphabet follows:

Lower case	Upper case	Greek name	English equivalent
α	A	alpha	a
β	B	beta	b
γ	Γ	gamma	g
δ	Δ	delta	d
ε	E	epsilon	ĕ
ζ	Z	zeta	z (pronounced ds)
η	H	eta	ē
θ	Θ	theta	th
ι	I	iota	i
κ	K	kappa	k
λ	Λ	lam(b)da	l
μ	M	mu	m
ν	N	nu	n
ξ	Ξ	xi	x (pronounced ks)
ο	O	omicron	ŏ
π	Π	pi	p
ρ	P	rho	r (or rh)
σ, s or c	Σ, C	sigma	s
τ	T	tau	t
υ	Y	upsilon	u (usually transliterated y)
φ	Φ	phi	ph
χ	X	chi	kh (sometimes transliterated ch)
ψ	Ψ	psi	ps
ω	Ω	omega	ō

WRITING (fig. 6.1)

Writing became widespread in Greece from 750 BC and subsequently spread to Rome via Etruria. In archaic Latin the letters closely resembled those of the Greek alphabet, but from around 300 BC they became much improved and more regular. The shape of letters depended on whether they were being used in a monumental context, for documentary use or as cursive lettering. Variations of the standard letters are often seen. Formal writing was done in the square capital (capital script), because angular capitals could be cut into materials such as stone and metal more easily. There were two types of handwriting, the ordinary cursive common to everyone and the carefully written bookhand used by trained scribes.

Cursive Writing

In cursive writing the characters are joined in a series of rounded, flowing strokes, to enable ease and speed of writing. It was in general use from the 4th century BC as everyday writing, both privately and by scribes for official letters and documents. It is known mainly from graffiti, writing tablets and

MONUMENTAL	ARCHAIC: PRE-3RD CENTURY BC	ARCHAIC: 3RD-2ND CENTURY BC	ORC	NRC	COMMENTS
A	AΛΛΛ	AΛ	ʎ	u	The height of the horizontal stroke in A varies in the monumental. Can also be written as Λ.
B	B	B	a	h	The size of the two lobes varies. An angular ꞵ is sometimes found. The upper lobe can be omitted and the stem curved upward.
C	⟨C⟨	C	ʹ	ʹ	The fully rounded C is the best monumental style, when C is sometimes larger than the next letter or even encloses it, such as ⓞ for CO.
D	DDD	D	∂	d	
E	EE‖ ⋀E	E‖	⨍	ⵜ	In the Augustan age, the three parallel lines are horizontal and of equal length, then the middle line becomes shorter. ‖ was also used in cursive.
F	ꞈ F ⌐ F	F ⌐	ꟻ	ⵏ	From the 2nd century, F is often taller than the other letters, especially at the beginning of a line.
G		G	ᴦ	ꓳ	
H	⊟H	H	ᴨ	ᴉ	H varies little, but does become narrower.
I	⏐	⏐	Ꮣ	ʔ	I is often plain in the republic and early empire, with no strokes. A tall I is often used for a long vowel, between two vowels or as the first letter of a word.

HANDBOOK TO LIFE IN ANCIENT ROME

206

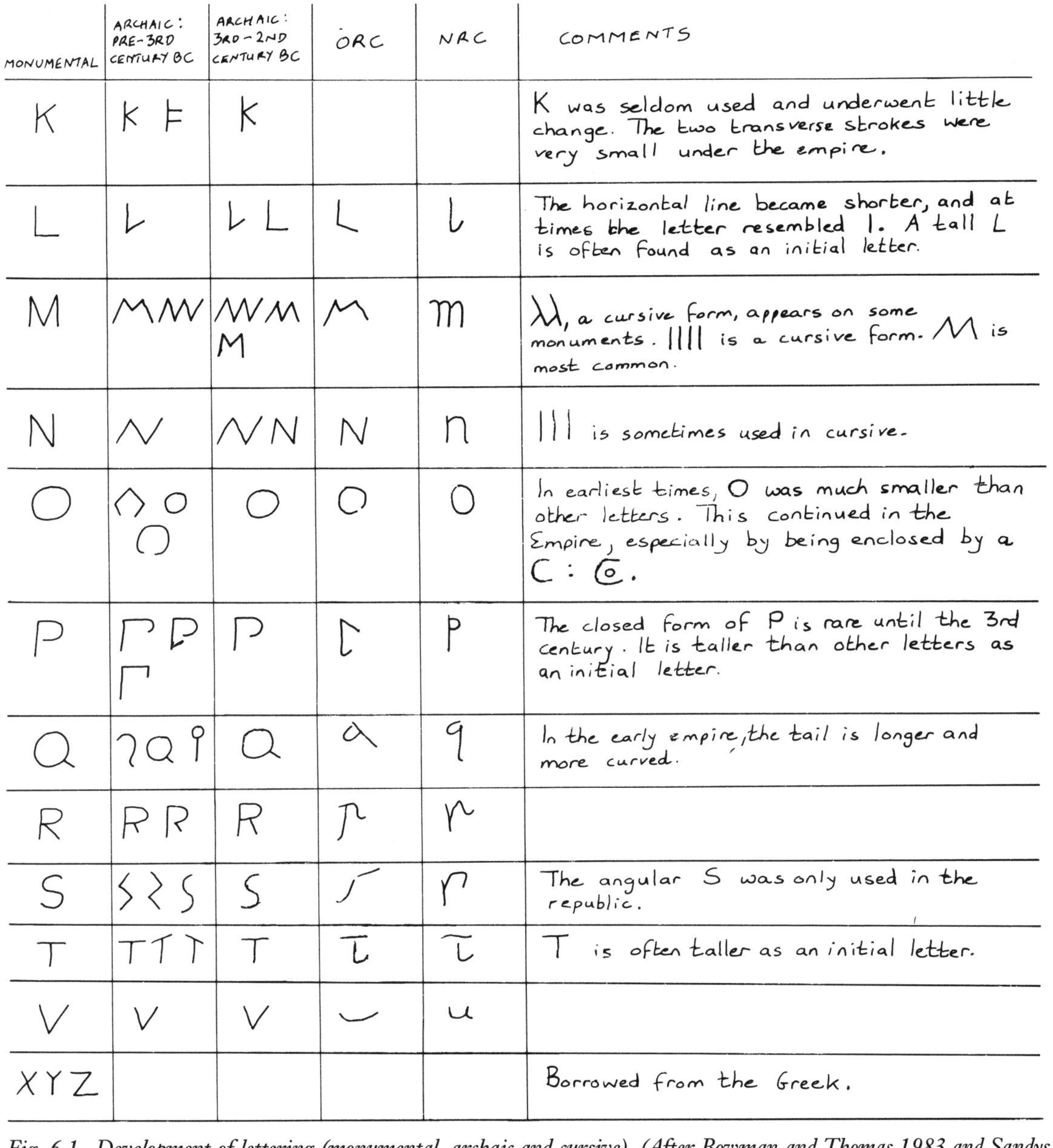

MONUMENTAL	ARCHAIC: PRE-3RD CENTURY BC	ARCHAIC: 3RD-2ND CENTURY BC	ORC	NRC	COMMENTS
K	K F	K			K was seldom used and underwent little change. The two transverse strokes were very small under the empire.
L	Ⴑ	Ⴑ L	L	Ⴑ	The horizontal line became shorter, and at times the letter resembled I. A tall L is often found as an initial letter.
M	ᨆ ᨇ	ᨆᨇ M	ᨆ	m	λλ, a cursive form, appears on some monuments. IIII is a cursive form. ᨆ is most common.
N	ᴧ	ᴧN	N	n	IIII is sometimes used in cursive.
O	◇ o ◯	O	◯	O	In earliest times, O was much smaller than other letters. This continued in the Empire, especially by being enclosed by a C: Ⓒ.
P	Γ Ɒ Γ	Γ	Ⲅ	P	The closed form of P is rare until the 3rd century. It is taller than other letters as an initial letter.
Q	ʔ Q ꝗ	Q	ɑ	ꝗ	In the early empire, the tail is longer and more curved.
R	R Ʀ	R	ᴦ	ᴦ	
S	ꙅ ⸝ ꙅ	S	⸝	ᴦ	The angular S was only used in the republic.
T	T Ⴕ T	T	ᴛ	ᴛ	T is often taller as an initial letter.
V	V	V	⌣	ᴜ	
XYZ					Borrowed from the Greek.

Fig. 6.1 Development of lettering (monumental, archaic and cursive). (After Bowman and Thomas 1983 and Sandys [ed.] 1921.)

papyri, and has many variants. The earlier form is known as Old Roman Cursive (ORC), which was gradually replaced from the late 3rd century by New Roman Cursive (NRC) or minuscule cursive, which developed into the handwriting of today and influenced the later bookhand known as minuscule. A capital script was sometimes used for headings and addresses on tablets and papyri, but otherwise cursive writing was a lowercase script. Abbreviations frequently occur in papyri and writing tablets. Handwriting seems to have been similar in style right across the empire.

The wall graffiti at Pompeii (pre-79) have been classified as baroque and were either a variant of ORC or were more likely undertaken by people familiar with the elegant contemporary bookhand writing, which used a capital script and carefully distinguished between thick and thin strokes (fig. 6.6).

Uncial Writing

Uncial writing was the careful bookhand used by scribes for literary purposes from at least the 3rd century and was especially used for manuscripts from the 4th to 8th centuries. The letters were in a majuscule (large letters), which were large, rounded letters, individually formed, resembling capitals and avoiding angles. The name may have derived from *uncia* (inch). Uncials were easier to write with reeds and other pens on soft materials such as papyrus, although they were still slow and took up much room. Uncial writing was replaced in the 9th century by minuscule (small letters), a new bookhand that could be written rapidly and in half the space.

Punctuation

Punctuation and spacing between words were rare, and enlarged initial letters were not used. The interpunct (stop) could be used to mark word division but is not seen after the 2nd century, and usually there is no spacing at all between words.

WRITING MATERIALS (figs. 6.2, 6.3)

Papyrus and Parchment

Papyrus was adopted from Egypt from the 3rd century BC, becoming the most common writing material throughout the ancient world. Papyrus was made from the pith of a water plant growing mainly in the Nile. The pith was sliced vertically into thin strips, and one layer of strips with fibers running vertically was superimposed on another layer with fibers running horizontally. The two layers were hammered together and adhered by means of the plant's natural gum. The sheet was dried and the surface was polished. Writing was usually done on the surface with horizontal fibers (recto), but sometimes the back (verso) was also used. The sheets were about 0.4 m (16 in) wide and 0.23 m (9 in) high and were pasted side by side to form a continuous roll. In good-quality papyrus rolls, the seams were barely visible. Papyrus was sold in rolls, about 10 m (33 ft) long, not by the sheet.

Writing was done by scribes in vertical columns 55 to 100 mm (2 to 4 in.) wide, with a margin between the columns and a broader margin at top and bottom. Scribes did not adhere to a regular number of lines per column or letters per line. Titles were written at the end of the papyrus roll (the part least likely to be damaged). When a papyrus roll (*volumen*) was being used, it was unrolled with the right hand and simultaneously rolled up with the left hand, and was rewound after use. Sometimes a wooden roller (*umbilicus*) with projecting knobs was attached to the end of the roll (fig. 6.2). In libraries, the rolls were placed in pigeonholes, identified by a suspended label (*titulus*).

Vellum (*vellus*, skin, hide) made from the skins of cattle, sheep and goats was an alternative writing material. The skins were scraped, rubbed with pumice and dressed with alum. Vellum was later known as parchment (from Pergamum, a city famous for its manufacture). Nowadays parchment is made from the

Fig. 6.2 Writing materials, including papyrus rolls, containers for papyrus rolls, writing tablets, an inkwell, pens and styli. From W. Gell (1832) Pompeiana.

skin of sheep and goats and vellum from that of calves, lambs and kids.

Sets of writing tablets led to the development from the 1st century of the modern book form, consisting of eight folded sheets of papyrus or parchment (giving 16 pages) stitched at the spine and bound with wooden boards. This type of book, known as a *codex*, was much easier to use than a papyrus roll. It was used by Christians from an early date and had superseded the papyrus roll by the 4th century, with parchment being preferred to papyrus. Nevertheless, the roll form was retained for public documents right through to modern times.

SURVIVING MANUSCRIPTS

Very few papyrus fragments of Latin works have survived because areas favorable to the preservation of papyrus, such as Egypt, tended to be Greek-speaking. Numerous Greek papyri have been found, some literary but the majority of a documentary nature (private letters and accounts and legal and administrative documents), which have yielded much information on Egypt under Roman rule. Most of the surviving Latin papyri date from the late 3rd century and are mainly legal and military documents, with occasional private letters. A few literary fragments have been found, mainly prose works and Christian texts. The earliest surviving manuscripts of classical authors date to the 4th century.

Ancient authors wrote on papyrus or waxed tablets, and the earliest extant copies made on parchment may postdate the author by 1,000 years. Authors' works were copied and recopied through the centuries, and have today been preserved mainly as copies produced during the medieval period. Letters have survived in various ways. For example, Cicero's secretary Tiro apparently kept copies of all the letters sent by Cicero, which were published after his death, whereas other letters were kept by the recipients. Translations and copying of texts were prone to error, especially by medieval scribes translating technical treatises. This has led to the corruption of texts, not all of which have been corrected today.

A palimpsest (from the Greek *palimpsestos*, scraped again) is a manuscript that was written over an earlier erased text. Monks in the Middle Ages frequently reused old parchment manuscripts, but the previous text could never be completely removed, so old texts were therefore preserved.

Libri Lintei

Libri lintei (books written on linen) were lists of magistrates at Rome from 509 BC, probably compiled around the mid-2nd century BC. They were stored in the temple of Juno Moneta and were consulted by historians such as Livy. No examples have survived.

Writing Tablets (figs. 6.2, 6.3)

The Latin word for book is *liber* (bark), which reflects the use of bark for writing in early Rome. Very thin sheets (leaves) of wood, known as leaf tablets, also were used. Recent finds (such as at Vindolanda) suggest that in northern provinces where papyrus was unavailable, leaf tablets may have been the most common form of writing material (rather than waxed tablets as previously thought). They were used for letters and ephemeral documents, and writing was done with pen and ink. While still supple, they could be folded over across the grain so that the writing was hidden. Some had tie holes through which individual sheets were joined together concertina-style. Notches show that several leaf tablets could be bound together by cord.

Waxed tablets or stylus tablets were used for more important documents, such as legal transactions, which needed to be stored. They were thick pieces of wood with recesses filled with beeswax; writing was scratched in the wax with a *stylus*. Sets of tablets were held together by a leather thong or ring passed through hinge holes in the outer edge. A *diptych* had two tablets. A *triptych* had three tablets (six pages): the first (outer) page was plain, the second and third pages were waxed, and the fourth page was waxed or plain and often had a groove down the middle. Signatures of witnesses were written in ink or wax on this page. Then the pages were bound together, and seal impressions of the witnesses were placed over the binding in the groove (fig. 6.3). The fifth page was waxed and contained a summary of the transaction on pages two and three, and the sixth (outer) page was plain. The fifth page could be read without breaking the seals. If the waxed tablets received repeated use, the stylus could penetrate the wood beneath the wax, leaving traces of one or more scripts. Some stylus tablets were not waxed but were written on with pen and ink.

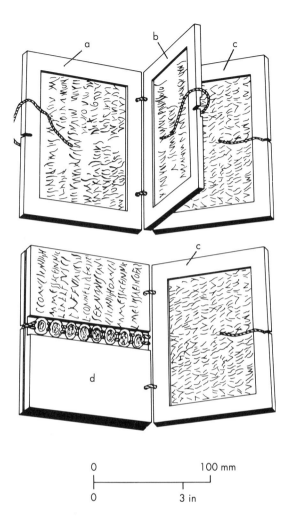

Seal Boxes

Seal boxes could be used to protect seals of documents, such as on papyrus rolls and waxed tablets. They had a variety of shapes and were usually made of bronze. They had a hinged lid that was often enameled. A cord was passed through perforations in the sides of the seal box, and wax was placed in the seal box and impressed by a seal (usually from a finger ring). The lid was closed to protect the seal.

LIBRARIES

The first libraries were established by the Greeks. The most famous was at Alexandria, possibly founded in the 4th century BC. It was the greatest library in antiquity and may have had from 100,000 to 700,000 volumes. Plutarch reported that the main library was burned down in 47 BC when Julius Caesar was in Alexandria. The Academy at Athens with its library was destroyed during the sack of the city by Sulla in 86 BC.

Libraries became commonplace in the Roman world. Private libraries were formed from Greek books looted during the wars in the east in the 1st century BC. After the Third Macedonian War, Lucius Aemilius Paullus kept many books that had belonged to Perseus, the Macedonian king, and formed the first private library at Rome, while Lucullus in the 1st century BC acquired the books of the Pontic kings as booty in the war, which became his private library. He was always ready to lend books from his library, which became a center for literary Greeks in Rome. In Herculaneum a small private library, excavated in the Villa of the Papyri, consisted of 1,803 carbonized papyrus rolls on wooden shelves.

The first public library at Rome was founded in the reign of Augustus by C. Asinius Pollio and contained Greek and Latin books. It was housed in the *Atrium Libertatis* (Hall of Liberty), the site of which is unknown. Augustus founded two more libraries, one in the Campus Martius (the Octavian) and another on the Palatine. The *Bibliotheca Ulpia* (Ulpian Library) was built at Rome by Trajan. Libraries were

Fig. 6.3   A triptych waxed tablet: a. page two; b. page three; c. page five; d. page four.

Pens and Ink

Ink was of dense carbon black, gum and water that could be made up when required. It was applied by a pen of reed or bronze that had a split nib. Inkpots were of bronze, samian (Ritterling 13) and other types of pottery. They had a small hole for inserting the pen and a concealed lip as an antispill device.

Writing on waxed tablets was done with *styli*. A *stylus* was made of iron, bronze or bone, sometimes decorated. The pointed end was for writing and the flattened end could be used to smooth the wax.

often given to provincial towns as gifts, such as at Ephesus and Athens.

Latin literature gives some information about books and the book trade. From the 1st century BC booksellers are known to have employed copyists. Cicero had his books published by Atticus, and Horace mentions the Sosii as booksellers at Rome. The demand for books increased, and it became fashionable for wealthy Romans to possess a library.

EDUCATION (fig. 6.4)

In early Republican times boys were taught by their fathers to read, write and use weapons, and they accompanied them to religious ceremonies and public occasions, including the Senate if their father was a member. At the age of 16, sons of the nobility were given a political apprenticeship by being attached to a prominent figure, and from the age of 17 they spent the campaigning season with the army. This method of education persisted into imperial times for some families.

From about the 3rd century BC a Roman system of education developed which was different from the Greek tradition, often with a Greek slave or freedman for teacher—the *litterator* or *ludi magister*. The education was based mainly on the study of Latin and Greek literature in order to produce effective speakers. The earliest education, from seven to 11 years, involved the teaching to both boys and girls of reading, writing and arithmetic, and Greek was sometimes taught by a *paidagogus*. Secondary education for boys from 12 to 15 years consisted of the teaching of literary subjects in Latin and Greek by a *grammaticus*, both for a general education and as preparation for rhetoric. From the 1st century BC contemporary poets, such as Virgil, were also studied.

From the 2nd century BC rhetoric was taught by Greek teachers in secondary education to pupils over 16, but a Latin style of rhetoric became increasingly predominant. The practice of political oratory with debates in the Senate declined under the empire, as political decisions were taken by the emperor and not through public debate. However, rhetoric was still the major element in education, preparing boys mainly

Fig. 6.4 Part of a relief sculpture (copy) from Neumagen, Germany, with a teacher sitting in a chair holding a papyrus roll.

for careers as advocates in the law courts, and rhetoric had a major influence on literature. Professorships of rhetoric were set up in the major cities of the empire. Famous teachers in the late Roman period included St. Augustine, St. Ambrose and Ausonius.

ANCIENT LITERATURE AND AUTHORS

The "classics" is a term derived from *classicus*, of the highest class, originally referring to the political divisions of Roman citizens. Cicero used the word *classis* to describe a class of philosophers, and in the 2nd century Aulus Gellius used the word *classicus* to describe a writer. Renaissance scholars adopted the adjective to describe Greek and Latin authors in general, from which the modern usage is derived. The term is also often used to describe the best cultural periods in Greek and Roman civilization (5th to 4th centuries BC for Greek and 1st century BC to the death of Augustus in AD 14 for Roman; the latter period is also called the Golden Age).

Types of Literature

Literary sources include history books, speeches, poems, plays, practical manuals, law books, biographies, treatises and personal letters. Authors were well educated, and many were very wealthy, so their opinions frequently reflect those of the upper class.

DRAMA

Drama was performed at Rome before the 3rd century BC in the form of mime, dance and farces. Atellan farces (*fabulae Atellanae*) were named after the town of Atella and were apparently popular at Rome from the 3rd century BC. Mime was introduced to Rome before the end of the 3rd century BC and was a dramatic performance acted by men and women, which ousted Atellan farce. The mimes were basically farces that developed into licentious farces and contributed to the decline of comedy. They were not like mime in the modern sense and were suppressed in 502.

Greek New Comedy was introduced to Rome in translation in 240 BC by Livius Andronicus and then by Naevius. Greek plays were subsequently adapted by Plautus, Caecilius Statius and Terence, and these comedies were known as *fabulae palliatae* (plays in Greek cloaks). By the mid-2nd century BC comedies tended to be about Italian life and characters, which were called *fabulae togatae* (plays in togas), although none survives. In the 1st century BC Roman comedy virtually ceased to be written but was replaced by mime, a more vulgar and popular form of entertainment with no literary merit.

A *fabula crepidata* was a Roman tragedy on a Greek theme. Like Greek New Comedy, this type of play was introduced to Rome by Livius Andronicus, and was followed by other adaptations, such as by Accius and Pacuvius. *Crepida* was the Latin name for the high

boot worn by Greek tragic actors. A *fabula praetexta* was a drama on a Roman historical or legendary theme, the invention of which is attributed to Naevius, but this type of play never became popular. In the late republic Roman tragedy declined, but it revived under Augustus, although no works survive. Seneca the Younger wrote highly rhetorical tragedies in Nero's reign, probably not intended for the stage. Roman tragedy was stifled by the repression of political life under the empire, which made it difficult to choose a "safe" subject.

POETRY

Meters in Latin poetry were borrowed from Greek, except possibly the saturnian meter, the oldest Latin verse form, named after the god Saturn by later poets to indicate great antiquity for this type of verse. Unlike English verse, which relies on stressed and unstressed syllables, Latin meter did not rely on accent but on quantity — the number of long and short syllables in a line. The various meters have different patterns of long and short syllables, indicated by the signs ¯ and ˘ (Rōme, sĕnate). The best known meter, the hexameter, was perfected by Virgil.

Fescennine verses were one of the earliest forms of Latin poetry, usually in the form of ribald songs or dialogues performed for amusement at festivals; they may have been the origin of Italian drama. *Naeniae* or *neniae* were funeral poems or songs performed at Rome by female relatives of the deceased or by hired singers. Later on this form of poetry gave way to funeral orations. Lyric poetry, to be sung, was not often written by Romans, although a song was composed for Juno by Livius Andronicus in 207 BC and Horace composed his *Carmen Saeculare* to be sung at the Secular Games of 17 BC. Only a few fragments of other lyric poetry survive, although some poets used the form but did not intend their poetry to be sung.

An elegy was any poem written in elegiacs (or elegiac couplets), which were alternate lines of hexameter and pentameter meter. It was a medium for expressing personal sentiments and was also commonly used in funerary inscriptions. Elegy developed at Rome under Greek influence in the 1st century BC and was used primarily for love poetry. The major poets were Gallus, Catullus, Tibullus, Propertius and Ovid. After Ovid, elegy was used mainly for short occasional poems and epigrams, notably by Martial.

An epigram (from the Greek *epigramma*, inscription) was a funerary inscription written in verse. From the late 2nd century BC literary epigrams were written in elegiacs on the theme of love, and Catullus wrote epigrams on love and hate. The literary epigram reached its peak with Martial, author of many epigrams with a witty and paradoxical ending. Apparently prominent men wrote many epigrams, but few have survived.

Bucolic poetry is pastoral poetry, and includes the *Eclogues* written by Virgil. Didactic poetry was intended to give instruction, and includes Lucretius' *De Rerum Natura* and Virgil's *Georgics*.

An epic is a narrative poem on a grand scale that relates the deeds and exploits of one or more heroes. It was introduced to Rome in the 3rd century BC by Livius Andronicus with a translation of Homer's *Odyssey*. It was further developed by Naevius in the 2nd century BC with an epic on the Punic wars and by Ennius with his *Annales*. The greatest Roman epic was the *Aeneid* by Virgil, but other epic poets whose work survives in part include Lucan, Silius Italicus, Valerius Flaccus, Statius and Claudian.

PROSE

Latin prose developed out of public speech and also partly in the *annales* (records) of the pontiffs. Unlike poetry and drama, it owed little to Greek influence, and reached its highest point in the writings and speeches of Cicero. *Controversiae* (judicial declamations) were Latin rhetorical exercises in the oratory of the law courts. *Declamationes* (declamations) were the exercises performed by students of oratory in rhetorical schools. *Suasoriae* (speeches of advice) were exercises in deliberative (political) oratory.

The earliest Roman historians wrote in Greek because Latin had not developed as a literary medium and because they wished to glorify and justify Rome's foundation and deeds to the Hellenistic world. The first historical work in Latin was by Cato (*Origines*). This inspired a study of the official records that were published after 130 BC as the *annales maximi* (the most important records) in 80 books covering the period from legendary times to about 130 BC, giving the history of Rome in chronological order. This method was followed by later historians such as Sallust, Tacitus and Ammianus Marcellinus.

The earliest form of biography was in the form of funeral orations and sepulchral inscriptions, subsequently followed by Republican generals and politicians writing their memoirs to justify their deeds. Under the empire emperors and members of their family wrote autobiographies, but none survives. Some biographies of famous men survive, such as one of Agricola by Tacitus and the 12 Caesars by Suetonius. Biographies are usually called *Lives* (*Vitae*). The *Confessions of St. Augustine* (written c. 397–400) is an autobiography revealing his own inner life and thoughts.

Other works of prose include letters, some of which were written for publication (such as those of Pliny the Younger), while others were written without publication in mind but have been preserved in a number of ways. The *Satyricon* of Petronius is the earliest novel to survive, and was partly a parody of other romantic novels. The *Metamorphoses* by Apuleius, dating to the mid-2nd century, is the only complete Latin novel to survive. Very little else is known about the Latin novel.

Dialogue was a literary genre that was Greek in origin and usually took the form of a conversation pursuing one main theme, with the interlocutor taking the leading role. It was a genre used mainly by Cicero in his political, rhetorical and philosophical treatises.

SATIRE

Satire developed as a separate literary genre in a variety of forms, such as dialogue, verse and a combination of verse and prose. It consisted of a personal commentary, ranging from good humor to invective on a variety of everyday topics. Ennius was apparently the first to write satires in verse, and Lucilius was the first to devote himself solely to this genre.

Chronology of Literature

3RD CENTURY BC

The beginning of Latin literature is traditionally dated to the performance of a play by Livius Andronicus at Rome in 240 BC, but the comedies by Plautus are the earliest works to survive. The main writers were Appius Claudius Caecus, Ennius, Caecilius

Statius, Livius Andronicus, Naevius, Pacuvius and Plautus.

2ND CENTURY BC

The main writers were Accius, Afranius, Cato, Ennius, Terence and Lucilius, as well as Polybius, who wrote in Greek.

1ST CENTURY BC

The Golden Age of Latin literature is a term used to describe the Ciceronian and Augustan ages of literature. The Ciceronian age is sometimes used to describe the period from c. 70 to 30 BC, the writers including Cicero, Lucretius, Catullus, Cinna, Nepos, Sallust and Varro. The Augustan age is a term applied to the period following the Ciceronian age, up to the death of Ovid in AD 17 (and largely covering the reign of Augustus). The main authors were Virgil, Horace, Tibullus, Propertius, Ovid and Livy. During this period support was given to poets and historians by Augustus and other patrons, such as Maecenas and Messalla, and this patronage was continued by later emperors. Such patronage tended to lead to a celebration of the emperor and his policies.

1ST CENTURY AD

This period is known as the Silver Age or post-Augustan phase of literature. The main writers were Arrian, Columella, Curtius Rufus, Frontinus, Lucan, Martial, Petronius, Pliny the Elder, Pliny the Younger, Quintilian, Phaedrus, Seneca the Elder, Seneca the Younger, Statius and Tacitus.

2ND CENTURY AD

The main writers included Appian, Aristides, Apuleius, Fronto, Florus, Galen, Gellius, Juvenal, Salvius and Suetonius.

3RD CENTURY AD

The main writers included Cyprian, Paulus, Papinian, Tertullian and Ulpian as well as Cassius Dio, who wrote in Greek.

4TH CENTURY AD

The main writers included Ausonius, Ambrose, Ammianus Marcellinus, Claudian, Donatus, Augustine, Hilary, Jerome, Lactantius, Nonius Marcellus and Symmachus.

5TH CENTURY AD

The main writers included Augustine, Paulinus of Nola, Orosius, Macrobius, Servius and Sidonius Apollinaris.

6TH CENTURY AD

The main writers included Benedict, Boethius, Cassiodorus, Procopius and Priscian.

Authors and Their Works

The following authors wrote in Latin, unless otherwise stated. Many other authors also wrote in Greek in the eastern empire: see Grant 1980, Hammond and Scullard (eds.) 1970 and Howatson (ed.) 1989. The authors are listed alphabetically under the name by which they are commonly known today.

ACCIUS or ATTIUS: Lucius Accius, 170–c. 86 BC. He came from Pisaurum and was a dramatist and poet. Only about 700 lines of his works survive, including fragments of 46 tragedies, mainly based on Greek tragedies, and two *fabulae praetextae* (*Aeneadae* or *Decius* and *Brutus*). His other works include the *Annales*, books of hexameter poetry on the calendar and festivals and the *Didascalica*, nine books on the history of the Greek and Roman theater and other literary matters from Homer to Accius himself. Accius lived mainly at Rome. He was influential in the development of Latin literature and was often quoted by Cicero and imitated by Virgil.

AELIAN: Claudius Aelianus, c. 170–c. 235. Born at Praeneste. He was a Greek rhetorician and Stoic who taught at Rome. His extant works (in Greek) include *De Natura Animalium* (*On the Characteristics of Animals*), 17 books of a moralizing nature, *Varia Historia*

(*Miscellaneous Stories*) and "Rustic Epistles" (brief stylistic exercises). His writings were much drawn on by later moralists.

AFRANIUS: Lucius Afranius was active c. 160 to c. 120 BC. He was possibly an orator and therefore a Roman citizen. He was a writer of *fabulae togatae*, but only fragments and 42 titles survive, even though they are known to have been popular in the empire. Nero staged a realistic performance of his play *The Fire* in which a house was actually set ablaze.

AMBROSE: Aurelius Ambrosius (St. Ambrose), c. 340–397. He was born at Trier, educated at Rome and entered a legal career. He became consul and governor of Aemilia province, and in 374 bishop of Milan, although he had not been baptized or ordained. He was very influential in eradicating heresy, paganism and Judaism, and Augustine was his most famous convert. He wrote copious treatises, sermons, letters, panegyrics and hymns, including *De Officiis Ministrorum* (*On Clergymen's Duties*), a practical manual for priests.

AMMIANUS MARCELLINUS: c. 325/330–395. He was a Greek, born at Antioch, and the last great Roman historian to write in Latin. In his early life he was an officer in the Praetorian Guard and participated in various campaigns. Around 378 he settled at Rome and wrote his history *Rerum Gestarum Libri* (*Books of Deeds*) in 31 books, a continuation of the histories of Tacitus, covering the years 96 to 378. The last 18 books are extant and start with the latter part of the reign of Constantius II (353), covering events in Ammianus' lifetime.

ANTHIMUS: An early 6th-century Greek doctor. He was author of *De Observatione Ciborum* (*On Dietetics*), which was written in the form of a letter to Theodoric the Great shortly after 511. It was a short Latin treatise, half medical and half cookery in content. It gives a picture of the eating and drinking habits of a Germanic people, who were the main source from which Anthimus learned his Latin.

APICIUS: Marcus Gavius Apicius. He was a proverbial gourmand who lived in Tiberius' reign and wrote about cookery. At least two other men called Apicius are known for their cooking, but the cookbook (*De Re Coquinaria*, *On Cooking*) under the name

of Caelius Apicius is thought to have been compiled at a later date, possibly in the late 4th century.

APPIAN: Appianos was born in Domitian's reign at Alexandria and lived to at least 160. From 116 he spent much of his life at Rome and held official positions in the imperial service. He was a historian and author (in Greek) of a 24-volume history (*Romaica*) of Roman conquests from earliest times to Vespasian. Nine books and portions of others survive, of which books 13 to 17 (*Bella Civilia*) describe the civil wars between 146 and 70 BC.

APULEIUS: Lucius Apuleius. Born c. 123/125 at Madauros, date of death uncertain. He was a renowned philosopher and rhetorician who studied at Carthage and Athens, traveled in the east and was influenced by the mystery religions. On his return to north Africa, he fell ill and was nursed by a rich widow, whom he subsequently married. His works include *Apologia*, his self-defense speech when he was charged around 155 with gaining his wife by the use of magic. He was acquitted and returned to Carthage, from where he traveled a great deal as an orator and philosopher. Many of his numerous writings are lost. His most famous work is the 11-book novel *Metamorphoses*, or *Golden Ass*, which was based on a Greek tale *The Ass*. It was written c. 180–190 and is the only complete Latin novel to survive.

ARISTIDES: Publius Aelius Aristides Theodorus, 27 January 118 to c. 180. Born at Mysia and educated at Pergamum and Athens. He was a Greek rhetorician who spent much of his life giving demonstrations of his oratory in the main cities of the Greek world. He also went to Rome, where at 26 years he developed a recurring illness, which ended his public appearances and caused him to spend much time at the temple of Asclepius in Pergamum and at Smyrna, where he spent the rest of his life. He subsequently wrote (in Greek) many speeches, of which 55 are extant, the best known being *Romes Encomium* (*In Praise of Rome*). He was also author of *Hieroi Logoi* (*The Dream Book* or *Sacred Tales*), an account in six books of the dreams and visions he experienced at the temple of Asclepius while seeking a cure from illness.

ARNOBIUS: Born c. 235 in north Africa. He taught rhetoric in Numidia and was converted to Christianity c. 295. A Christian Latin theologian, he was author of a seven-book polemic *Adversus Nationes* (*Against the Pagans*).

ARRIAN: Flavius Arrianus. Born c. 85–190/195. He was a Greek from Nicomedia and a successful officer in the Roman army. Under Hadrian he became consul, and c. 130–137 he was governor in Cappadocia. He retired to Athens and was archon in 145–146. He was author of various extant works (in Greek) including *Discourses* (*Diatribes*), which recount the lectures of the Stoic philosopher Epictetus, and a *Periplus* (a type of navigational guide for sailors) *of the Black Sea*. His most famous work *Anabasis of Alexander* (*Expedition Up-country of Alexander the Great*) was an account in seven books of Alexander's campaigns.

ATTICUS: Titus Pomponius Atticus, 110–32 BC. Born at Rome of an equestrian family. He was a close friend and correspondent of Cicero. He lived for many years in Athens (hence his cognomen "of Attica") and was very wealthy. He had strong literary tastes and kept many slaves trained in copying and binding manuscripts. He helped in the circulation of Cicero's writings. His own works have not survived, but included a *Liber Annalis* (Annals), a history of Rome in one book, and a genealogical treatise on certain Roman families and the magistracies they held. Nepos wrote a *Life of Atticus*.

AUFIDIUS BASSUS: Mid-1st century. He was apparently a major Roman historian, but little of his work survives. He was author of *De Bello Germanico* (*On the German War*) dealing with the campaigns of Tiberius from AD 4. He also wrote a Roman history, of which fragments survive.

AUGUSTINE: Aurelius Augustinus (St. Augustine of Hippo), 354–430. Born at Thagaste. He was a philosopher and rhetorician, educated at Carthage (never mastering Greek), where he subsequently taught rhetoric, as well as at Thagaste and Rome (in 383). He became professor of rhetoric at Milan in 384, where he met Bishop Ambrose and became a Christian convert. In 387 he was baptized and returned to Africa in 388. He became bishop of Hippo in 395, where he died in 430 while Vandals besieged the town. He was a prolific Christian writer, author of 93 books as well as a vast number of letters and sermons that influenced western theology into the Middle Ages. Many of his works are extant, including *Confes-*

sions (c. 397–400), 13 books in which he gives an account of his life and analyzes his feelings. *De Doctrina Christiana* (*On Christian Learning*) (397–426) was four books giving methods of education. *De Civitate Dei* (*City of God*), was 22 books written between 413 and 426 following the fall of Rome to Alaric in 410 and presented Augustine's philosophy of history in order to defend Christianity and attack paganism. *Restractiones* were two books written just before his death (426/7) and give a chronological catalog of his writings as well as the reasons for their composition.

AUGUSTUS: Emperor 27 BC–AD 14. He was author of *Index rerum a se gestarum* (*Record of His Enterprises*), usually known as *Res Gestae* (*Acts*). He also wrote literary works that have not survived, an autobiography, a poem on Sicily, epigrams and part of a tragedy (*Ajax*), which he destroyed. When Tiberius became emperor, copies of the *Res Gestae* were inscribed on stone tablets in many provinces, of which a large part survives as the *Monumentum Ancyranum*.

AURELIUS: Emperor 161–180. He adopted Stoic philosophy and was its last great proponent. He was educated in Latin and Greek by the best tutors, including Fronto, to whom he wrote a series of formal letters (mainly in Latin). He was also author, in Greek, of *Meditations* or *His Writing to Himself*, a work of a philosophical nature in 12 books written during the last ten years of his life while on campaign and posthumously published from his notebooks.

AUSONIUS: Decimus Magnus Ausonius, c. 310–393/395. He was a poet, educated at Toulouse and Bordeaux, who taught rhetoric at Bordeaux for nearly 30 years. He was then summoned to Trier in 364 and was appointed tutor to Gratian, son of Valentinian I. He accompanied Gratian on Valentinian's expeditions against the Germans in 368 to 369. He later held official appointments, but retired to Trier after Gratian's murder and then returned to Bordeaux for the rest of this life. He wrote a great deal of verse in a variety of meters on wide-ranging subjects. The *Ephemeris* is a description of his day from morning to night, and the *Mosella* is a long hexameter poem describing in detail the beauties of the Moselle River and life around it. He also wrote over 100 epigrams.

AVIENIUS or AVIENUS: Postumius Rufius Festus Avienus. 4th century. He was from Volsinii and was twice proconsul. He translated into Latin part of the poem *Phaenomena* (*Astronomy*) by the Greek poet Aratus. He was also author of "Description of the World" (a translation of the poem by the Greek poet Dionysius Periegetes) and *Ora Maritima* (*Maritime Shore*) about the Mediterranean and other coastal regions.

BALBUS: Lucius Cornelius Balbus, 1st century BC, from Cadiz. His published diary is not extant, but a few of his letters to Cicero survive.

BENEDICT, Saint: c. 408–543, from Nursia, the son of wealthy parents. He founded and ran a monastery at Monte Cassino, and his views on monastic life are contained in his *Regula Monachorum*, usually known as the *Rule of Saint Benedict*, which formed the foundations of the later Benedictine order.

BOETHIUS: Anicius Manlius Severinus Boethius, c. 480–524, a philosopher and Christian theological writer. He came from a family that held many high offices of state in the 4th and 5th centuries. He won the favor of Theodoric the Great and became consul in 510 and *magister officiorum* (head of the civil service) ten years later. In 523 he was suspected of treachery and was executed in 524. He was buried at Pavia and was regarded as a Catholic martyr, canonized as St. Severinus. His importance derives from his being the last Latin-speaking scholar of the ancient world to be well acquainted with Greek. After him, nobody in the West had firsthand knowledge of Greek philosophy until Aristotle's works were rediscovered in the 12th century. In his early life Beothius set out to translate into Latin and write commentaries on all the writings of Aristotle and Plato, a task that he never completed, although his translations of and commentaries on some of Aristotle's works survive. Some of his own writings also survive, including several Christian treatises and part of the *quadrivum*, handbooks on arithmetic, music, geometry and astronomy. These were much used in medieval schools, and the ones on arithmetic and music have survived intact. He is best known for *De Consolatione Philosophiae* (*Consolation of Philosophy*), a dialogue in five books between himself and a personified Philosophy that he wrote in prison. This work was very influential in the Middle Ages, and hundreds of manuscripts exist. It was translated

into more European languages than any other book except the Bible, its translators including Alfred the Great, Chaucer and Queen Elizabeth I.

CAECILIUS STATIUS: A Gaul from northern Italy, probably Milan, and taken prisoner of war in 223 or 222 BC. He was brought to Rome as a slave, and after manumission he became the leading comic dramatist of his day. He wrote in the period between the dramatists Plautus and Terence. He lived to at least 166 BC. No complete play survives, but 42 titles are known, 16 deriving from Menander, and some fragments survive in quotations.

CAESAR: Gaius Julius Caesar. 100–44 BC. His *Commentaries* were memoirs about the Gallic War and Civil War. The ones on the civil war (*De Bello Civili*) were an unfinished history in three books of the first two years of the war between him and Pompey, which was begun in 49 BC. His commentaries *De Bello Gallico* (*On the Gallic War*) cover 58 to 52 BC in seven books: books 1 to 7 were published in 51 or 50 BC, and an eighth book was later written by Hirtius on the events of 51 to 50 BC. These commentaries are Caesar's only writings that have survived. He was author of a number of other books, including a collection of jokes and sayings, a grammatical work (*De Analogia*) on declensions and conjugations dedicated to Cicero and a number of poems (a verse epigram to Terence survives). The extant *Bellum Africum* (*African War*), *Bellum Alexandrinum* (*Alexandrian War*) and *Bellum Hispaniense* (*Spanish War*) were probably written by soldiers in Caesar's army. See also chapter 1.

CALPURNIUS: Titus Calpurnius Siculus possibly wrote around 50-60 and was author of seven poems, largely pastoral in nature. Nothing else is known of him.

CALVUS: Gaius Licinius Calvus, 82–c. 47 BC. Son of Gaius Licinius Macer. He was a celebrated love poet in his day and a successful lawyer whose speeches against Vatinius were still used as models of oratory a century later. Only fragments of his poetry survive.

CASSIODORUS: Flavius Magnus Aurelius Cassiodorus, c. 490–583. Born in southern Italy, the son of a praetorian prefect of Theodoric. A senator, he held public offices including succeeding Boethius as *magister officiorum* (head of the civil service). He retired in the late 530s to devote himself to scholarship and a Christian life. In 540 he was taken prisoner by troops of the Byzantine Empire and was sent to Constantinople. He returned in the 550s and established two monastic foundations, including Vivarium in Bruttium. Around 537 he published *Variae Epistulae* (*Various Letters*), 12 books consisting of the most important letters and edicts he had written for the Gothic kings to important people of the day. He also wrote *History of the Goths* in 12 books, which has survived only as an abridged version, and *Chronica*, a brief world history to 519. In his retirement at Vivarium, he wrote *Institutiones* (*Institutions*), a guide to the religious and secular education of monks, including instruction about the copying of manuscripts.

CASSIUS DIO (DIO CASSIUS): Cassius Dio Cocceianus, 150–235, born at Nicaea, Bithynia. He was a Greek historian and Roman official. He went to Rome early in Commodus' reign, became a senator and followed a public career, returning to Nicaea c. 229. He wrote (in Greek) an 80–volume history of Rome (*Historiae Romanae*) from Aeneas' landing in Italy to AD 229. Books 36 to 54 (68–10 BC) are complete, books 55 to 60 (9 BC–AD 46) survive in an abbreviated form and books 17 and 79 to 80 (AD 217-220) survive in part. The rest of his history can be pieced together from the summaries by the Byzantine historians of the 11th and 12th centuries. Cassius Dio also wrote a biography of Arrian and an account of the dreams and portents of Septimius Severus, but these works are lost.

CATO: Marcus Porcius Cato (Cato "the Elder" or "the Censor"), 234–149 BC. He had a distinguished military and political career. He wrote several treatises for his son on various topics, including *Origines* (*Origins*) in seven books, which covered the foundation of Rome and the Italian cities and the history of recent wars. The first such history in Latin, as earlier works were in Greek, it was a model for later historians, but only fragments survive. Cato's only extant work is *De Agri Cultura* or *De Re Rustica* (*On Agriculture*), the oldest surviving complete piece of Latin prose. Cato was also a successful orator, and 150 of his speeches were known to Cicero, of which only fragments and about 80 titles survive.

CATULLUS: Gaius Valerius Catullus, c. 84–c. 54 BC. Born at Verona, the son of a wealthy man. He went to Rome in 62 BC and joined the fashionable literary circle. Extant are 113 of his poems (*Carmina*) of a varied nature, long and short, in various meters, including many love poems. Very little is known of his life except for information contained in his poetry, in particular a love affair with a married woman he calls Lesbia, to whom he addressed 25 poems.

CELSUS: Aulus (or Aurelius) Cornelius Celsus. Lived in Tiberius' reign (14–37). He was author of an encyclopedia covering many subjects, of which the first five books were on agriculture. Only the eight books on medicine survive, known as *Artes* (*Arts*).

CICERO: Marcus Tullius Cicero, 106–43 BC. He studied rhetoric and philosophy at Rome, Athens and Rhodes, and returned to Rome to pursue a public career from 75 BC. He was Rome's greatest orator, a statesman and successful pleader of court cases. He was a prolific writer and a master of the Latin language, considered to be the greatest Latin prose writer. His extant works include 58 speeches and fragments of others, numerous treatises on rhetoric and philosophy and over 800 private letters to various people (some with replies), which are an invaluable historical source. His letters date from 67 to 43 BC and were not originally intended for publication. Cicero also wrote poetry, a small amount of which has survived. His earliest speech was a plea, *Pro Quinctio* (*For Quinctius*) of 81 BC, the outcome of which is unknown. His four *In Catilinam* (*Against Catiline*) speeches are his most famous. They were delivered to the Senate in 63 BC and led to the execution of Catiline and his conspirators. *De Republica* (*On the State*) was written in 54 to 51 BC in six books and is incomplete. It was a fictitious dialogue between Scipio Africanus the Younger and some friends; *Somnium Scipionis* (*Dream of Scipio*) formed the epilogue and was a vision of the afterlife. *De Legibus* (*On Laws*) was a treatise written in 52 and 46 to 45 BC relating to political philosophy, of which three out of probably five books survive. It describes the legal enactments that would be introduced in Cicero's ideal state. Another famous speech was *Brutus* (or *De Claris Oratoribus*), a treatise on Roman oratory written around 46 BC in order to defend his own style of oratory. In it Cicero gave a critical history of Roman oratory from its beginnings to his own time. In the following months, he wrote numerous other philosophical and rhetorical works. His last work on moral philosophy was *De Officiis* (*On*

Moral Duties), which was finished in November 44 BC; it was in three books and was addressed to his son. Several months after Caesar's assassination in 44 BC, Cicero (who ardently wanted the return of the republic) delivered 14 violent orations against Antony. They were called the Philippics after Demosthenes' speeches against Philip II of Macedonia. The last one celebrated the defeat of Antony and is Cicero's last surviving speech.

CICERO: Quintus Tullius Cicero. Born at Arpino in 102 BC and executed in 43 BC. He was the younger brother of Marcus Tullius Cicero and had wide literary interests, but his works do not survive except for four letters to his brother. He was possibly the author of a treatise on campaigning for the consulship, *Commentariolum Petitionis* (*Some Thoughts about Political Campaigns*).

CINNA: Gaius Helvius Cinna, 1st-century BC poet. He was born at Brixellum and probably died in 44 BC. He was apparently leader of a literary movement known as New Poets or Neoterics. He was author of the short epic poem *Zmyrna*, which took nine years to write and of which only three lines survive, and of erotic poetry, of which only very small fragments survive. He was also author of *Propempticon*, a farewell poem for Asinius Pollio, who was about to journey to Greece, possibly in 56 BC. Cinna was apparently lynched by supporters of Julius Caesar in 44 BC in mistake for Lucius Cornelius Cinna who had approved the dictator's murder (or "for his bad verses," according to Shakespeare).

CLAUDIAN: Claudius Claudianus, c. 370–c. 404. He was born at Alexandria and went to Italy by 395. He was a native Greek speaker but wrote in Latin, and was the last great Latin poet writing in the classical tradition. Although a pagan, he became court poet of the western emperor Honorius (under whom the imperial house was Christian) and his regent Stilicho. He was author of numerous poems, many with political themes and savagely abused the emperor's political enemies, especially those of the eastern empire. His political poetry has provided much useful historical information about this period. One group of poems, the *Panegyrics*, was composed largely in honor of men appointed to consulships, including Stilicho. *De Raptu Proserpinae* (*Rape of Proserpina*) was in four books, of which 1,100 lines survive.

CLAUDIUS: Appius Claudius Caecus. 4th–3rd century BC. He was a noted orator, and some of his funeral orations were still read in Cicero's day. He also composed aphorisms in Saturnian verse, a few of which have survived.

CLAUDIUS: Emperor 41–54. Pliny the Elder described him as one of the foremost learned writers of his day. He was author of a number of works, including 41 books of Roman history, an eight-book autobiography (*Commentarii*) and many works in Greek. None of his work survives.

CLEMENT OF ALEXANDRIA: Born c. 150 at Athens, died between 211 and 216. He converted to Christianity and was head of the Catechetical School of Alexandria from 190 to 202, when he was forced to flee due to persecution. He was author (in Greek) of many works of a Christian nature.

COLUMELLA: Lucius Junius Moderatus Columella, 1st century, from Cadiz. He was author of a 12-book treatise on farming, *De Re Rustica* (*On Agriculture*), written c. 60 to 65, mainly in prose except for book 10, which is written in hexameters. He also wrote a shorter manual on agriculture, of which one book on trees, *De Arboribus*, survives.

CREMUTIUS CORDUS: Aulus Cremutius Cordus, 1st century. A senator and historian, he committed suicide when prosecuted by Tiberius for the contents of his history, possibly called the *Annales* (*Annals*). It was a history of the civil wars but has not survived.

CRINAGORAS: c. 70 BC–AD 15. He was a Greek elegiac poet of Mytilene who went to Rome. The *Palatine Anthology* preserves 51 of his epigrams.

CURTIUS RUFUS: Quintus Curtius Rufus, 1st-century historian and biographer. Virtually nothing is known of his life. He was author of a history of Alexander the Great in ten books, of which the first two are lost. It is the earliest surviving example of a Latin prose work not directly concerned with a Roman theme.

CYPRIAN, Saint: Thascius Caecilius Cyprianus, c. 200–258. Born in Carthage of a rich pagan family, he was educated in rhetoric and was converted to Christianity c. 246. A Christian churchman and a theological writer, he was made bishop of Carthage in 248. He was persecuted by the emperors Decius and Valerian and was executed in 258. He was a prolific author of mainly short religious treatises and letters that are a valuable source for ecclesiastical history. His *Life*, by his deacon Pontius, is the earliest surviving Christian biography.

DIODORUS SICULUS: 1st century BC (until at least 21 BC). He was a historian and native of Agyrium, Sicily. In c. 60 to 30 BC he wrote in Greek a general world history centered on Rome entitled *Bibliotheka Historike* (*Historical Library*), from mythical times to Caesar's Gallic War. Only 15 volumes are extant of the original 40. He lacked originality and copied his sources. In the 19th century Macaulay described him as "a stupid, credulous, prosing old ass."

DIONYSIUS: Died c. 8 BC. From Halicarnassus, he was a Greek rhetorician, literary critic and historian. He lived and taught in Rome from c. 30 BC to his death. He was author (in Greek) of treatises on rhetoric and literary criticism, including *On the Ancient Orators*. He also wrote a history of Rome from its legendary beginnings to the outbreak of the First Punic War in 20 books, *Antiquitates Romanae* (*Roman Antiquities*), of which the first half only is extant (to 441 BC). He learned Latin for this work and spent 22 years preparing it.

DIOSCURIDES: Dioskourides or Pedanius Dioscorides. He was a 1st-century Greek physician who served in the Roman army, presumably as a doctor. He was author (in Greek) of *Materia medica* in five books in which he described the medicinal properties of hundreds of plants and drugs. It became a standard textbook and was translated into Latin in 1526 and into several other languages in the following years.

DONATUS: Aelius Donatus. He was a mid–4th-century rhetorician and grammarian and teacher of Jerome. He lived in Rome around 353. He was author of two books of grammar, which were still used in the Middle Ages and formed the basis of subsequent grammars up to present times. He was also author of an extant commentary on Terence and one on Virgil, of which only the preface, a *Life* of the poet and an introduction to the *Eclogues*, survive.

DONATUS: Tiberius Claudius Donatus. He was a late–4th-century author of a rhetorical and stylistic commentary in 12 books on Virgil's *Aeneid* (*Interpretationes Vergilianae*).

ENNIUS: Quintus Ennius, 239–169 BC. Born at Rudiae. He was educated in Greek but wrote in Latin and served in the army during the Second Punic War. He lived much of his subsequent life at Rome as a teacher and poet. He was a versatile composer of tragedies, comedies, satires and a number of minor works. He was renowned particularly for his tragedies and for the *Annales*, an epic poem in 18 books on the history of Rome from Aeneas' flight from Troy to Ennius' own day. Very little of his work survives, including only 600 lines (out of 20,000 or more) of the *Annales*.

EPICTETUS: c. 55–135. He came from Hierapolis, was brought to Rome as a slave and was later manumitted. He taught Stoic philosophy, and after Domitian banished the philosophers around 89, he migrated to Epirus, where he spent the rest of his life. One of his students, the Greek historian Arrian, collected and published Epictetus' lectures in the eight-book *Diatribes*, four of which survive, as well as a summary of Epictetus' philosophy. These works greatly influenced Marcus Aurelius.

EUSEBIUS of Caesarea: c. 260–340. He was born in Palestine and was appointed bishop of Caesarea there c. 314. He was a Christian writer, author (in Greek) of 46 theological works, 15 of which have survived as well as fragments and translations of others. Among his extant works is *Historia Ecclesiastica*, an account of the rise of the Christian church from its beginnings to the early 4th century, which has earned him the title of Father of Church History. It was in ten books and is an important source for the rise of the church in the east from earliest times to 324. His other works include *Martyrs of Palestine*, an eyewitness account of the persecutions by Diocletian, and the two books of universal history — the *Chronikon* (*Chronicle*). The original Greek text of the latter survives only in fragments, but there is a Latin adaptation by Jerome and an Armenian translation. It is an extremely important source of dates and events in Greek and Roman history. After Constantine's death, Eusebius wrote a *Life* of him.

EUTROPIUS: 4th century, consul in 387, probably from Bordeaux. He was a historian who published in the reign of Valens a survey of Roman history in ten short books (*Breviarium ab Urbe Condita*) from the time of Romulus to the death of the emperor Jovian.

FABIUS PICTOR: Quintus Fabius Pictor (painter), late 3rd century BC. He took part in the Second Punic War, toward the end of which he published *History of Rome*, the first such history to have been written. His work (in Greek) survives only in quotations by other writers.

FAVORINUS: c. 81/82 to c. 150. He was born at Arles and learned Greek at Marseille, which he seems to have written and spoken in preference to Latin. He was a distinguished orator and teacher of Greek rhetoric in Greece and Rome, and enjoyed the favor of Hadrian. Around 130 he fell into disgrace and was exiled. Few examples of his works survive, but a fragment of his treatise *On Exile* survives. His other works included *Memoirs* (anecdotes about philosophers) and *Miscellaneous History* (an encylopedic work in 24 books).

FIRMICUS MATERNUS: Julius Firmicus Maternus, 4th century, from Syracuse. He was a writer on astrology and theology, including an eight-book treatise on astrology called *Mathesis* (*Learning*) of c. 334 to 337. Afterward he was converted to Christianity and wrote *De Errore Profanorum Religionum* (*On the Error of Profane Religions*) c. 343–350, which has survived incomplete.

FLORUS: Lucius Annaeus Florus, 2nd century. He was author of *Epitome Bellorum Omnium Annorum DCC* (*Epitome of all the Wars During Seven Hundred Years*), a history of Rome to the time of Augustus. He may be the poet Annius Florus who was friend of Hadrian, or the Publius Annius Florus who was author of a dialogue *Vergilius Orator an Poeta* (*Is Virgil an Orator or Poet?*).

FRONTINUS: Sextus Julius Frontinus, c. 30–104. He was consul in 73 or 74 and then became governor of Britain (preceding Agricola, Tacitus' father-in-law). He continued in public office, including a time as administrator of the water supply at Rome (*curator aquarum*) in 97. His extant works are *Strategemata*, a four-volume manual on military science published c.

84, and his famous *De aquae ductu* (*On the Conveyance of Water*), now more usually called *De Aquis Urbis Romae* (*On the Water Supply of Rome*), two books in which he describes the history of aqueducts and technical details and regulations in their construction. Fragments of a work *On Land-Surveying* also survive.

FRONTO: Marcus Cornelius Fronto, c. 100–166, born at Cirta. He was educated at Carthage and probably at Alexandria. He went to Rome, where he became the foremost orator and an influential figure in literature. At one stage he was tutor to Marcus Aurelius and Lucius Verus. He also held public office, becoming consul in 143. He was author of *M. Cornelius Fronto: Epistulae ad M. Aurelium* (*Fronto's Letters to Marcus Aurelius*). Very little of his writings was known until a collection of his letters (partly in Greek) was published in 1823, including letters from leading figures of the day. Very little of his speeches survives.

GAIUS: A distinguished 2nd-century jurist, about whom little is known, not even his full name. Between 130 and 180 he was author of treatises on law, including *Institutiones* (*Institutes*), a manual in four books for beginners. It was used as the basis of Justinian's *Institutiones* in 533, thereby greatly influencing later legal thought. It was known only in an abbreviated form until 1816 when a manuscript was discovered at Verona—the letters of Jerome had been written over it—and subsequently a 4th-century fragmentary papyrus has been found. It is therefore the only classical legal text to survive in its substantially original form.

GALEN: Galenos, 129–199. He was from Pergamum, where he became a doctor in 157, attending gladiators. He went to Rome c. 162, where he spent much of the rest of his life as physician to Marcus Aurelius, Commodus and Septimius Severus. He was a learned scientist and prodigious writer (in Greek) on medicine, philosophy, grammar, rhetoric and literature. Almost all his extant works are on medicine, which formed the basis of all later medical works into the Middle Ages. Over 150 medical works survive, including some in Latin and Arabic translations. He also wrote his own bibliography, *On the Order of His Works*, which mentioned 153 works contained in 504 books, but the list was not comprehensive.

GALLUS: Gaius Cornelius Gallus, c. 69–26 BC, born at Forum Iulii. He went to Rome at an early age. A soldier and poet, he fought in the civil war on Octavian's side and was made Egypt's first governor in 30 BC. After four years he was recalled in disgrace and committed suicide. His poetry was widely read and included four books of elegies entitled *Amores* (*Loves*), but only one line and tiny papyrus fragments survive. He also wrote *epyllia* (miniature epics), but virtually nothing survives.

GELLIUS: Aulus Gellius, c. 130–180 or possibly earlier. He studied at Rome and Athens. He was author of *Noctes Atticae* (*Attic Nights*), a 20-volume work, virtually all of which survives. A collection of anecdotes on people he had known, it includes various topics such as points of grammar, language, history, criticism, law and philosophy. For illustration he used passages from a large number of Greek and Roman writers, mentioning 275 by name, thus preserving extracts from many works that are no longer extant. The work is so called because he started collecting the material during winter nights in Attica.

GERMANICUS: Nero Claudius Germanicus, 15 BC–AD 19. He was adopted by Tiberius in AD 4 and died in mysterious circumstances at Antioch. He is said to have written comedies in Greek, all now lost. He also wrote epigrams in elegiac couplets, in Greek and Latin, a few of which have survived, as have fragments of his Latin translation of the Greek poem *Phaenomena* by Aratus.

GRATTIUS: (less correct: Gratius). He was an Augustan poet mentioned by Ovid and the author of a poem on hunting, *Cynegetica*, of which 536 hexameters survive.

HADRIAN: Emperor 117–138. He was devoted to literary activities and was author of several works, including a book on grammar and various poems, some of which are extant.

HERODES ATTICUS: Lucius Vibullius Hipparchus Tiberius Claudius Atticus Herodes, 101–177. He was a Greek, born at Marathon, consul at Rome in 143, and an orator, teacher and public benefactor. His villa at Cephissia in Attica was a literary center, but none of his writings (in Greek) survives except for one speech doubtfully attributed to him and a Latin translation of another by Aulus Gellius.

HERODIAN: Aelius Herodianus, 2nd century. He lived in Rome and wrote (in Greek) on a number of grammatical subjects. His main work was a treatise on Greek accents in 21 books, of which only excerpts survive.

HERODIAN: Flourished c. 230 and died after 238 (possibly c. 180–250). He was from Syria, probably Antioch, and held an administrative post. He was author (in Greek) of a history of the Roman emperors from the death of Marcus Aurelius to the accession of Gordian III.

HILARY, Saint: Hilarius, c. 315–367, from Poitiers. He was converted to Christianity and became bishop of Poitiers c. 353. He was opposed to Arianism and spent several years in exile in Asia Minor. He was author of numerous theological works, including *On the Trinity* in 12 books, a *Commentary* on Matthew, a *Commentary* on the Psalms and *De Synodis seu de Fide Orientalium* (*On Synods or on the Faith of the Peoples of the East*), which is a valuable source of information for ecclesiastical history. He is regarded as the greatest western theologian of his age.

HIRTIUS: Aulus Hirtius, 1st century BC. He was one of Julius Caesar's lieutenants in Gaul. Author of the eighth book of Caesar's *Gallic War*, he probably also wrote *Bellum Alexandrinum*.

HORACE: Quintus Horatius Flaccus, 65–8 BC, born at Venosa. He was Rome's great lyric poet and satirist. All of his published work survives. He was educated at Rome and then in Athens. He fought on the losing side in the civil war but was pardoned although stripped of his property. Poverty apparently led him to write poetry, and c. 33 BC his patron Maecenas gave him a farm in the Sabine Hills, which Horace celebrated in his poetry. His poems include the *Epodi* (*Epodes*), which were 17 short poems begun c. 40 BC and published c. 30 BC, and the *Sermones* (*Satires*—discourses) which consisted of two books of hexameters on a variety of topics, with the ones in the second book written in dialogue form; the first book was published c. 35 BC and the second c. 30 BC. The *Carmina* (*Odes*) were four books of 103 poems on a variety of subjects, composed in a variety of meters; the first three books were probably published in 23 BC, and book 4 was probably published in 13 BC. The *Epistulae* (*Epistles* or *Letters*) were two books of hexameter poems ostensibly written as poetic letters to friends. Book 1 contains 20 epistles and was published in 20 or 19 BC, and Book 2 contains only two epistles, which were published in 18 and 15 BC. A third epistle addressed to the Pisos, known as the *Ars Poetica* (*Art of Poetry*) since the time of Quintilian, was published c. 19 or 18 BC. It is in the form of a letter giving advice about the pursuit of literature and had a great influence on later European literature. It was translated into English in 1640 by Ben Jonson. The *Carmen Saeculare* (*Secular Hymn*) is a long ode written for the Secular Games of 17 BC and was commissioned by Augustus. It outlines the achievements of Augustus and welcomes the return of ancient virtues. Suetonius wrote Horace's biography.

HYGINUS: Gaius Julius Hyginus, c. 64 BC–c. AD 17, probably from Spain. A slave in Rome who was freed by Augustus, he was one of the greatest scholars of his day and a teacher. He was author of works on a wide range of subjects, including a commentary on Virgil, a treatise on agriculture, historical and archaeological works, and works on religion, but none survives. Under his name, but not actually by him, is a handbook of mythology, *Genealogiae* or *Fabulae*, probably compiled in the 2nd century. In Trajan's time there was a Hyginus Gromaticus (surveyor) who was author of treatises on boundaries, land tenure and land disputes. Wrongly attributed to him is an incomplete treatise, *De Munitionibus Castrorum*, on the laying out of camps, which has been variously dated to the 1st to 4th centuries. The latter author is often referred to as pseudo-Hyginus.

IAMBLICHUS: c. 250–330, born at Chalcis. He studied under Porphyry in Rome or Sicily. He was a Neoplatonist philosopher with an interest in magic, whose extant writings (in Greek) include *Exhortation to Philosophy* (*Protreptikos logos*), a work on Pythagoreanism and a defense of ritualistic magic, *De Mysteriis* (*On Mysteries*), a useful work for information on 4th-century superstition.

JEROME, Saint: Eusebius Hieronymus (Jerome is an English version of Hieronymus), c. 347–420. He was born at Stridon of a prosperous Christian family. He was educated at Rome where he was baptized c. 366 and then traveled a great deal. Around 374 he went to Antioch, where he began theological studies and learned Greek, although he remained devoted to Latin literature. From 375 to 378 he lived in the desert of Chalcis on Syria's frontier and learned Hebrew. He then returned to Antioch and subsequently went to Constantinople (c. 379) and Rome (382–385), where he was secretary to Pope Damasus. He aroused the pope's hostility and left Rome, finally settling in Bethlehem as head of a monastery, spending the rest of his life in scholarship and debate. Jerome was an unsurpassed scholar and wrote in classical Latin. His most important work, which took 20 years to complete, was the translation of most of the Bible from the original languages into Latin in order to correct the serious errors in the earlier Old Latin versions that were then current. The Vulgate (*editio vulgata* or *lectio vulgata*—common text) is the Latin version of the Bible most widely used in the west and consists mainly of St. Jerome's translations of the various texts. The oldest extant manuscript of the Vulgate is the Codex Amiatinus, written at Wearmouth or Jarrow between c. 690 and 700. His other main works included the *Chronicle*, a translation of Eusebius with a supplement covering the period 324 to 378. He also wrote *De Viris Illustribus* (*On Famous Men*), an account of 135 eminent Christian writers, and at least 63 biblical commentaries. In addition there is a collection of 154 letters (some forgeries) written between 370 and 419, including ten from St. Augustine.

JOSEPHUS: Flavius Josephus, 37 or 38 to after 94/95, born at Jerusalem, died at Rome. He was a Jewish historian of priestly descent and a Pharisee. He visited Rome c. 64 and returned to Jerusalem in 66 just before the Jewish Revolt. He was captured but predicted that Vespasian would become emperor and was spared. After the fall of Jerusalem in 70, he settled in Rome and received Roman citizenship, a house and a pension. His first work, *Bellum Iudaicum* (*History of the Jewish War*) in seven books, was originally written in Aramaic. His remaining works were written in Greek, including *Antiquitates Iudaicae* (*Jewish Antiquities*), a history of the Jews from the Creation to 66, published in 20 books c. 93/94. His third work was an autobiographical work *Vita* (*Life*), a reply to the allegations that he had instigated and organized the Jewish Revolt. His last work, in two books, was *Concerning the Antiquity of the Jews*, but is widely known under the title given to it by Jerome, *Contra* (or *In*) *Apionem* (*Against Apion*). This was a defense of Jews against anti-Semitism as personified in Apion, an Alexandrian Greek scholar.

JUVENAL: Decimus Junius Juvenalis, born between 50 and 70, died after 127. He was from Aquinum, but little is known of his life. The greatest of Roman satirical poets, he was author of 16 biting satires (*Saturae*) written in hexameters about the vices, follies and injustices of Roman society. They were probably published between 110 and 127 and were full of irony, pessimism and invective. The satires were in five books, but the last part of the final satire is missing. His poetry was well known from the 4th century and through the medieval and Renaissance periods, and influenced many satirists from the 17th century.

LABEO: Marcus Antistius Labeo, c. 50 BC–AD 10 or 11, from central Italy. He was an eminent jurist who spent six months each year teaching at Rome and the remaining time writing in the country. He was a man of great learning and reputedly author of about 400 works, now all lost but known from quotations by later jurists, from an epitome made by a 1st-century jurist Javolenus Priscus and from the *Digest* of Justinian.

LABERIUS: Decimus Laberius, c. 105–43 BC, a knight and distinguished writer of mimes.

LACTANTIUS: Lucius Caecilius (or Caelius) Firmianus Lactantius, c. 245–c. 325, from north Africa. He studied rhetoric, became a convert to Christianity and was an author and Christian apologist who achieved considerable fame. At Trier he became tutor to Crispus, the eldest son of Constantine I. Only his Christian works survive, most notably *De Opificio Dei* (*On God's Handiwork*) (303–334), *De Ira Dei* (*On the Wrath of God*) and *Institutiones Divinae* (*Divine Institutions*), written in seven books between 305 and 313.

LAEVIUS: Possibly Laevius Melissus. He flourished c. 100 BC, but little is known of his life. He was a poet and author of *Erotopaegnia* (*Diversions of Love*), which were love poems in a great variety of meters, of which only fragments survive. His work seems to have been ignored until the 2nd century.

LIVIUS ANDRONICUS: Lucius Livius Andronicus, c. 284–c. 204 BC, probably from Tarento. He was taken to Rome as a slave in 272 BC when the Romans captured Tarento. He was probably a tutor, later freed, and introduced Greek literature to a Roman audience. He translated Homer's *Odyssey* into Latin (*Odusia*), which remained a school book for over two centuries; only 46 lines survive. He also wrote plays, probably based on Greek versions: the first were a comedy and a tragedy, which were staged at the Roman Games of 240 BC. Very little is known of his further plays apart from 40 lines and eight titles of his tragedies. In 207 BC he was commissioned to write a hymn following a decree by the Sibylline Oracles.

LIVY: Titus Livius, c. 59 BC–AD 12 or 17, born at Padua. Very little is known about his life, but he seems to have spent much time in Rome. He was a historian and appears to have devoted his life to the study of literature and history. He was author of *Ab Urbe Condita* (*From the Foundation of the City*), a history of Rome in 142 books, from its foundation to 9 BC. It was published in installments and brought him immediate fame. Fragments and summaries made in later centuries exist for most of the volumes. (The summaries were made because the work was otherwise so large.) Only 35 original volumes are extant.

LONGINUS: Cassius Longinus, c. 213–273. He was an eminent Greek rhetorician and philosopher and adviser to Queen Zenobia. For supporting Zenobia, he was executed when Palmyra fell to Aurelian. Fragments of his writings survive.

LUCAN: Marcus Annaeus Lucanus, 39–65, born at Cordoba, grandson of Seneca the Elder. He lived at Rome from an early age, where he was educated in rhetoric and philosophy. He was a poet and author of several works, the only extant work being ten books of his uncompleted epic poem in hexameter verse on the civil war between Caesar and Pompey, *De Bello Civili* (*On the Civil War*), often miscalled *Pharsalia*. He was involved in the unsuccessful Pisonian Conspiracy to assassinate Nero and was forced by Nero to commit suicide.

LUCIAN: Lucianus, c. 115 to after 180, born at Samosata. His first language was probably Aramaic, but he received a Greek education and became an advocate and then a lecturer traveling across the empire. He was author (in Greek) of 80 extant prose works of various kinds, including dialogues, letters, essays, speeches and stories, mainly satirical in tone.

LUCILIUS: Gaius Lucilius, c. 180–102 BC, born at Suessa Aurunca. He came from a wealthy family of Roman citizens and was very well educated. He was a satirical poet and apparently developed poetical satire using hexameters as the standard meter. He wrote 30 books of verse on a variety of topics, including outspoken criticism of authors and men in public life. They served as a model for future satirists and were read until the end of the empire, but only 1,300 lines now survive.

LUCRETIUS: Titus Lucretius Carus, 98–c. 55 BC. He was a poet and philosopher about whose life virtually nothing is known. One work is extant, *De Rerum Natura* (*About the Nature of the Universe*), a philosophical didactic poem in six books of hexameters that explains the philosophy of Epicurus, but was unfinished at the time of his death. He was much admired by other poets but was almost completely forgotten in the Middle Ages, and only two primary manuscripts have survived. Fragments have been identified among papyri from Herculaneum.

LUCULLUS: Lucius Licinius Lucullus, c. 114–57 BC. He held military and public office, acquired great wealth in Asia and became an ardent philhellene, a lover of literature and the arts. He acquired a large library and was author (in Greek) of an account of the Marsian War (90–89 BC).

MACER: Gaius Licinius Macer, born in the late 2nd century BC, died 65 BC. He was a Roman politician and supporter of Marius. An orator and father of the poet Calvus, he wrote a history of Rome in at least 16 books (which Livy used) but only fragments survive. Macer was accused of extortion in 66 BC and died suddenly the following year, probably by suicide.

MACER: Aemilius Macer, from Verona, died 16 BC. He was author of the didactic poems *Ornithogonia* (*On Birds*) and *Theriaca* (*On Snakes*), which are no longer extant.

MACROBIUS: Ambrosius Theodosius Macrobius, lived c. 400, possibly from north Africa. Little is known of his life. He was a prose writer, philosopher and grammarian whose extant works include a seven-volume work *Saturnalia*, a miscellany of historical, philological, scientific and critical information, presented as a conversation at a banquet during the Saturnalia of 384 between a number of eminent Romans. The central topic is a criticism of Virgil. The work has survived virtually complete. He was also author of a commentary on the Dream of Scipio from Cicero's *De Republica* and of works of a grammatical nature that survive only as fragments.

MAEVIUS: Bavius and Maevius were two Latin poets sarcastically alluded to by Virgil in his *Third Eclogue*, but otherwise unknown. Maevius may be the Mevius who is attacked in Horace's tenth *Epode*.

MANILIUS: Marcus Manilius, lived at the beginning of the 1st century, but nothing of his life is known. He was author of a didactic poem *Astronomica* in hexameters in five books. It attempts to explain astrology and was possibly unfinished.

MARTIAL: Marcus Valerius Martialis, c.40–103/04, born at Bilbilis. He was educated in Spain, went to Rome in 64 where he spent the next 34 years and then returned to Spain. Martial was extremely poor, relying on the sale of his poetry for a living, and gradually his reputation increased. His first known work was *Liber Spectaculorum* (*Book of Spectacles*) to celebrate the opening of the Colosseum in 80, of which 33 poems survive. In 84–85 collections of elegiac couplets were published, later appearing as books 13 and 14 of the *Epigrams* (*Epigrammata.*) They consist mostly of light and ephemeral mottoes designed to accompany presents given or received in the Saturnalian festivals. From 86 to 101, books 1 to 12 of the *Epigrams* appeared, consisting of over 1,500 short poems similar to inscriptions on graves or works of art, mostly written in elegiac couplets. He used them to depict realistically detailed scenes of contemporary Rome, many of them satirical, usually very short, with a witty point or sting in the tail.

MARTIANUS CAPELLA: Martianus Minneus Felix Capella wrote c. 410-439. A lawyer at Madauros and a proconsul at Carthage, he was author of *De Nuptiis Mercurii et Philologiae* (*On the Marriage of Mercury and Philology*), an elaborate allegory in nine books, in prose with some verse.

MINUCIUS FELIX: Marcus Minucius Felix, wrote c. 200–240. He was possibly from Africa but lived much of his life at Rome. Very little of his life is known. He was an early Latin Christian author, and his extant work, *Octavius*, is an apology or defense of Christianity.

NAEVIUS: Gnaeus Naevius, c. 270–c. 190 BC, from Capua. He was a Roman citizen, a tragic and comic dramatist and epic poet. He was the first Roman to write on subjects drawn from Roman history, *fabulae praetextae*, but little is extant. Only 60 lines and seven titles of his tragedies, based on Greek plays, survive, and 30 titles of his *fabulae palliatae*. These were based on Greek New Comedy. He may also have written *fabulae togatae*, comedies with an Italian setting. His most important work was the *Bellum Punicum* (*Punic War*), an epic poem written in his old age in saturnian meter (the native Italian meter) and later divided into seven books; only about 60 lines survive.

NAMATIANUS: Rutilius Claudius Namatianus, 4th–5th century. He was born in southern Gaul, probably Toulouse, of a wealthy family. He held public office at Rome, but in 416 he returned to his estates in Gaul, which had been pillaged by German invaders. He was author of a poem about his journey home, which had to be made by sea as the overland route was too dangerous owing to the invasions. *De Reditu Suo sive Iter Gallicum* (*The Return Home*, or *The Gallic Journey*) consisted of one book of 644 lines and a few lines of a second book.

NEMESIANUS: Marcus Aurelius Olympius Nemesianus, late 3rd century, came from Carthage. He was author of four short *Eclogues*, or pastoral poems, totaling 319 lines and written in hexameters. They were once attributed to the pastoral poet Calpurnius Siculus. He was also author of *Cynegetica* (*On Hunting*), a hunting manual in verse, dating to 283 and of which only the initial 325 lines are extant.

NEPOS: Cornelius Nepos (praenomen unknown), c. 100–c. 25 BC, from a rich Cisalpine Gaul family. He was a biographer and historian and author of love poems. His prose works included a collection of anecdotes from Roman history (*Exempla*) in at least five books, all lost, and *De Viris Illustribus* (*On Famous Men*), a series of lives in at least 16 books. One book on foreign generals survives, as well as a short biography of Cato the Elder and one of Atticus.

NONIUS MARCELLUS: Probably Nonius Marcellus Herculius. He was from Numidia and lived in the first half of the 4th century. A Latin lexicographer and grammarian, he was author during Constantine's reign of *De Compendiosa Doctrina* (*Epitome of Learning*), an encyclopedia in 20 books, of which book 16 is lost. They were illustrated by quotations from many writers.

OROSIUS: Paulus Orosius, c. 380–c. 420. He was probably from Bracara Augusta. He was a Christian historian who took refuge c. 414 with St. Augustine in north Africa following the barbarian invasion of his homeland. In 417 he composed *Historiae adversum Paganos* (History Against the Pagans), a history from a Christian viewpoint of the world to his own day in seven books.

OVID: Publius Ovidius Naso, 43 BC–AD 17, born at Sulmo. He was educated in rhetoric at Rome but abandoned a legal career for poetry. He became a leading figure in literary and social circles at Rome, until he was banished by Augustus in AD 8 to Tomi on the Black Sea. A prolific and often irreverent poet, his extant works include *Amores* (*Loves*), 50 love poems dating to c. 20 BC, and *Ars Amatoria* (*Art of Love*, or *Treatise on Love*), a mock-didactic poem on the art of seduction published after 1 BC and possibly one of the reasons for his banishment. The *Heroides* (or *Heroidum Epistulae, Letters of Heroines*) are 20 amatory poems in elegiacs composed from c. AD 2, purporting to be letters from legendary heroines to their husbands or lovers. *Metamorphoses* (*Transformations*), an epic-style poem in 15 books (longer than the *Aeneid*), is a collection of stories from classical and Near Eastern legend, in particular the transformation of characters into another form. Ovid also wrote *Tristia* (*Sorrows*), elegiac poems in five books written AD 8 to 12 in the early years of his exile, and *Epistulae ex Ponto* (*Letters from Pontus*—his place of exile), written c. AD 12 to 16. He was also author of *Fasti*, a collection of elegiac poems in six books describing the Roman calendar and festivals; it was published posthumously, and only the first six books (January to June) survive. Most of his work was in elegiac couplets.

PACUVIUS: Marcus Pacuvius, 220–c. 130 BC, born at Brindisi. He followed his uncle Ennius to Rome as a young man and became a tragic poet and was well-known as a painter. Only 12 titles and fragments of his tragedies (based on Greek originals) and one *fabula praetexta* survive. He was considered to have been one of the foremost tragic poets of his time.

PALAEMON: Quintus Remmius Palaemon, 1st century. He was a former slave at Rome and became a famous grammarian and teacher. He was mentioned by Juvenal, and Martial referred to his poetry. He was also author of a book on Latin grammar, now lost, which was the basis of subsequent grammars.

PALLADIUS: Rutilius Taurus Aemilianus Palladius, 4th century. He was author of a treatise on agriculture, *De Re Rustica*, in 14 books, with an appendix on grafting trees. The last book, on veterinary medicine, was published for the first time in 1926.

PAPINIAN: Aemilius Papinianus, c. 140–212. He was possibly from Syria or Africa, although he moved to Rome where he became a famous jurist and praetorian prefect and accompanied Severus to Britain. He was executed by Caracalla. His main works were 37 books of *Quaestiones* (discussions of hypothetical or actual cases) completed before 198 and 19 books of *Responsa* (collections of opinions) completed after 204; many excerpts from these works are in Justinian's *Digest*. He also wrote a monograph *De Adulteriis* (*On Adultery*) and a collection of definitions (*Definitiones*).

PAULINUS OF NOLA, Saint: Meropius Pontius Anicius Paulinus, 353–431, born at Bordeaux of a wealthy Christian family. He held public office, and then became a priest and c. 409 bishop of Nola, where he remained until his death. He was a poet and letter writer. Of his work, 33 poems on Christian themes have survived. Also surviving are 51 letters written from 393, including correspondence with Augustine and Jerome.

PAULINUS OF PELLA: 5th century. He was probably born at Pella and was the grandson of Ausonius. He was converted to Christianity at age 46 and was author of the poem *Eucharisticus* (*Thanksgiving*), which gives a view of the collapse of the western empire and the ruling class.

PAULUS: Julius Paulus, active in the early 3rd century. He was one of the greatest jurists, a teacher and also a prolific writer (more than any other Roman lawyer). He published about 320 works on laws, constitutions and jurisprudence, including *Sententiae* (*Opinions*), part of which has survived; 26 books of cases (*Quaestiones*); and 23 books of rulings (*Responsa*). Extracts from his works constitute about one-sixth of Justinian's *Digest*.

PERSIUS: Aulus Persius Flaccus, 34–62, born at Volaterrae. He was educated at Rome and was greatly influenced by Stoic philosophy. He was a satirical poet, but only six satires (650 lines) and a brief prologue survive.

PETRONIUS: Possibly Titus Petronius Niger, known as Arbiter, He was governor of Bithynia in 61 and was later admitted to Nero's inner circle of intimate associates. In 66 he was accused of treason and committed suicide. He was the satirical author of a comic novel, the *Satyrica* (sometimes called the *Satyricon—Tales of Satyrs*), only fragments of which survive (parts of books 14, 15 and 16), It was written in prose interspersed with verse, and describes the disreputable adventures of two young men and a boy. The main episode in the surviving portion is known as *Cena Trimalchionis* (Trimalchio's Dinner Party). Trimalchio was a wealthy freedman, and the dinner party is a vulgar display of wealth. A few poems by Petronius also survive.

PHAEDRUS: Gaius Julius Phaedrus, c. 15 BC–c. AD 50. He was a Thracian slave who went to Rome and became a freedman in the household of Augustus. Apparently he offended Sejanus during Tiberius' reign and received some unknown punishment. He was author (in Latin) of a collection of works, mainly fables, in five books of poems and an appendix. They are based on the fables of Aesop and are mainly serious or satirical, but occasionally light and amusing. Many are well known today, having been handed down through medieval times to the present day.

PHILO: Philo Judaeus (Philo the Jew), c. 30 BC– c. AD 45, born at Alexandria. A prominent member of Alexandria's Jewish community, he traveled to Rome in 39 to 40 to persuade Caligula (Gaius) to exempt the Jews from worshipping the emperor. He was a prolific writer of philosophical works. His extant works (in Greek) include *Legatio ad Gaium* (*Embassy to Gaius*).

PLAUTUS: Titus Maccius (or Maccus) Plautus, c. 250 or 254 to c. 184 BC, born at Sarsina. He was apparently author of 130 comedies. His extant plays are 20 *fabulae palliatae* adapted from 3rd- to 4th-century BC works of Greek New Comedy. Like the Greek comedies, Plautus' plays are written in verse. They include *Aulularia* (*Pot of Gold*), *Amphitruo* (on the mythical subject of the cuckolding of Amphitryon), *Mercator* (*Merchant*), *Bacchides* (on two sisters called Bacchis who are prostitutes), *Rudens* (Rope) and *Asinaria* (*Comedy of Asses*). Fragments of another play also survive. His plays contained a quantity of song and so resembled musical comedy.

PLINY THE ELDER: Gaius Plinius Secundus, 23/4–79, born at Comum and probably educated at Rome. He held many public offices and spent much time on military service in Germany. In 79 he was appointed commander of the fleet at Misenum, from where he sailed on 24 August 79 on the eruption of Vesuvius, but was suffocated by the fumes. He wrote histories and biographies and treatises on oratory, grammar and military tactics, all of which are lost. Only his *Naturalis Historia* (*Natural History*) survives, a 37-volume encyclopedia of knowledge of the universe, published in 77.

PLINY THE YOUNGER: Gaius Plinius Caecilius Secundus, 61/2–111 or 113, nephew of Pliny the Elder. He was born at Comum and studied at Rome. A noted pleader and orator, none of his published orations is extant. He held various public offices. A surviving example of his oratory is *Panegyricus*, written for Trajan in 100. He is famous for ten books of letters (*Epistulae*). The last book was written while he was governor of Bithynia. It was published posthumously, and contained a selection of his correspondence with Trajan and the emperor's replies. He also wrote poetry, some of which is extant in the letters.

PLUTARCH: Lucius Mestrius Plutarchus, born at Chaeronea before 50, died after 120. He spent most of his life at Chaeronea. He was a Greek biographer, historian and philosopher, and was author (in Greek) of many philosophical works, most of them now lost, although the *Moralia* survives and consists of 78 miscellaneous works. He was also author (in Greek) of 50 biographies (*Vitae*) of famous historical figures. Most of these took the form of parallel lives, in which an eminent Greek was compared with an eminent republican Roman, a common exercise of the rhetorical schools.

POLLIO: Gaius Asinius Pollio, 76 BC–AD 4 or 5. He was a supporter of Caesar, then of Antony and then Augustus, but withdrew from public life c. 31 BC and became an advocate. He was also a historian, literary patron and sharp critic, and founded Rome's first public library. He was author of *Histories*, which dealt with the civil wars of 60 to 42 BC. This work was used by other authors, but only a fragment survives. He also wrote poetry, including erotic poems, and tragedies. He won a reputation as an orator and allegedly introduced the practice of authors reciting their own works to an audience.

POLYAENUS: 2nd century. Polyaenus came from Macedonia and was author (in Greek) of *Strategemata*, a collection of "ruses of war" in eight books dedicated to Marcus Aurelius and Lucius Verus to assist them in Verus' Parthian wars.

POLYBIUS: c. 200 to after 118 BC, born at Megalopolis. When the Romans defeated Perseus at Pydna in 168 BC, Polybius was among 1,000 Achaeans deported to Rome. He became tutor of the sons of Aemilius Paullus (commander of the Roman army at Pydna). Polybius returned to Achaea in 150 BC but joined the younger son Scipio Aemilianus at the siege of Carthage in 146 BC. He acted as an intermediary after the sacking of Corinth in 146 BC. Polybius was author (in Greek) of *Historiae*, a 40-volume history from 220 to 146 BC, which recorded the rapid rise of Rome to supremacy in the Mediterranean area. Only the first five volumes and fragments of the others are extant. Book 24 was devoted to geography but does not survive. Little is known of the last 20 years of his life, which must have been largely taken up with the writing of his *Histories*. Despite his admiration for Roman supremacy, Polybius attempted to be impartial.

POMPONIUS MELA: 1st century. He was born at Tingentera and was probably educated in rhetoric. He was author c. 43 of *De Chorographia* (or *De Situ Orbis*), *On Places*, a geographical survey in three books covering the world from Britain to the Persian Gulf, and recording more than 1,500 geographical names. It is the earliest surviving work in Latin on geography. There is no evidence that it contained maps.

PRISCIAN: Priscianus Caesariensis, 5th–6th century, from Caesarea, Mauretania. He was a teacher at Constantinople and author of *Institutiones Grammaticae* (*Grammatical Foundations*) in 18 books, the most extensive work written on Latin grammar. It contained many quotations from classical and earlier republican writers. He was also author of several minor works.

PROBUS: Marcus Valerius Probus, late 1st century, from Beirut. He was an outstanding Latin grammarian and scholar. He worked on the texts of many classical Latin authors, and some of his notes survive.

PROCOPIUS: c. 500 to after 562 (probably 565). He came from Caesarea in Palestine and was a Byzantine Greek historian and secretary to Belisarius, Justinian's general. He was made prefect of Constantinople in 562. Three of his works have survived. The *History of the Wars of Justinian* in eight books provides a general history of the first two-thirds of Justinian's reign and is the main source for much of his reign. He was also author of *On Buildings*, an account of buildings and works of art in Constantinople and the empire up to 560, a valuable source of information. His *Secret History* (*Historia Arcana*, also known as the *Anecdota*, The Unpublished) was a supplement to his *History* in which he makes a virulent attack on Justinian's entire policy. It could not have been published in his lifetime and was possibly not known until the 10th century.

PROPERTIUS: Sextus Propertius, c. 50 BC to after 16 BC, born at Assisi. He was trained in law at Rome but turned to poetry. He was author of four books of elegies, the first published in 25 or 28 BC and consisting almost entirely of elegant and witty love poems to his mistress Cynthia. (Her real name was Hostia, according to Apuleius.) Book 2 is long and may be a conflation of two books. It was published c. 25 BC and was similar in style to book 1. Book 3 was published soon after 23 BC and has a greater variety of topics. Book 4 did not appear before 16 BC and consisted mainly of poems on antiquarian and legendary subjects.

PRUDENTIUS CLEMENS: Aurelius Prudentius Clemens, 348 to after 405, from Zaragoza. He studied rhetoric, became a lawyer and held public office, but c. 392 he turned to writing poetry on Christian themes. His poetry included the *Cathemerinon* (*Hymns for the Day*), substantial lyric poems, extracts from which are still sung today. The

Peristephanon was a collection of poetry to celebrate the martyrs of Spain, Africa and Rome. The *Apotheosis*, concerned with the divinity of Christ and the nature of the Trinity, was over 1,000 lines long. His *Psychomachia* (*Battle for the Soul*) was an epic allegorical poem on the struggle between virtue and vice that became very popular in the Middle Ages. Another of his works was *Against Symmachus*, an argument in two books against the pagan senator Quintus Aurelius Symmachus.

PTOLEMY: Claudius Ptolemaeus, c. 90 or 100 to c. 168 or 178. He lived in Alexandria, where he made astronomical observations from 127 to 141. He was author (in Greek) of mathematical and astronomical works and of eight books of *Geographike Hyphegesis* (*Manual of Geography*, normally known as *Geography*), which includes a discussion of maps and mapmaking. Books 2 to 7 form a gazetteer of places throughout the Roman Empire and beyond, tabulated by latitude and longitude. Originally it may have been accompanied by the maps that now form book 8.

PUBLILIUS SYRUS: 1st century BC. He was brought to Rome from Syria as a slave, possibly from Antioch, and was manumitted c. 46 BC. He wrote Latin mimes, two titles of which are known: the *Pruners* (*Putatores*) and the *Myrmidon*. He was popular as an actor. He became well known for a selection of epigrams in alphabetical order that were supposedly taken from his plays to provide proverbial wisdom for schoolchildren.

QUINTILIAN: Marcus Fabius Quintilianus, c. 33/5 to before 100, born at Calahorra. He went to Rome at an early age and may have been educated there. He was an advocate and became a famous and wealthy teacher of rhetoric and oratory. The first rhetorician to receive a salary from public funds at Rome (under Vespasian), he retired c. 88 in order to write. Extant is a 12-volume work, *Institutio Oratoria* (*Education of an Orator*), probably published before 96. It describes the education and training of a pupil from infancy to early adulthood. A complete manuscript was discovered at St. Gall in Switzerland in 1416, and it became a standard textbook in the Renaissance. An earlier treatise, *The Decline of Oratory* (*De Causis Corruptae Eloquentiae*), is lost. He was also author of two volumes of rhetorical exercises (*Declamationes*) that may be transcripts of his lecture courses.

SALLUST: Gaius Sallustius Crispus, c. 86–c. 35 BC, born at Amiternum. He was a plebeian tribune in 52 BC when he acted against Cicero and Milo, and in 50 BC he was expelled from the Senate. In the civil war he sided with Julius Caesar. He became Numidia's first governor in 46 BC but subsequently withdrew from public life to write historical monographs after a threat of prosecution for extortion. He was author of *Bellum Catilinae* (*The Catiline War* or *Conspiracy*, usually known as the *Catiline*), which gave an account of the conspiracy against the government by Catiline in 63 BC. His *Bellum Iugurthinum* (*The Jugurthine War*) was written c. 41/40 BC and described Rome's war of 111 to 105 BC against Jugurtha, king of Numidia. His major work, *Historiae* (*The Histories*), was started c. 39 BC and was possibly unfinished at his death. It described late republican history from 78 to 67 BC, but survives only in fragments.

SALVIUS: Lucius Octavius Cornelius Publius Salvius Julianus Aemilianus, c. 100–169, born near Hadrumetum. He was a public official who held numerous posts and was also a jurist. He was author of *Digesta* (*Digest*) in 90 books, much of which is preserved in Justinian's *Digest* and by later authors. The views and rulings (*responsa*) of Salvius were collected by his pupil Sextus Caecilius Africanus.

SCAEVOLA: Quintus Mucius Scaevola, c. 140–82 BC. He was a noted orator who published the first systematic treatise on civil law at Rome.

SENECA: Lucius (or Marcus) Annaeus Seneca, Seneca "the Elder" or "the Rhetorician," c. 55 BC–c. AD 40. He was born at Cordoba of Italian parents and was educated at Rome. A wealthy rhetorician, in his later years he wrote on rhetoric and history. He assembled a collection of exercises in rhetoric, all extracts from Greek and Roman public speakers he had heard. This work was dedicated to his sons and consisted of *Controversiae* (debates) and *Suasoriae* (speeches of advice). The work was entitled *Oratorum Sententiae Divisiones Colores*. Like his history, it appears to have been published posthumously. Five of the original ten books of *Controversiae* and one book of *Suasoriae* are extant. He also wrote a history of Rome from the beginning of the civil wars almost to his own death, but virtually nothing survives.

SENECA: Lucius Annaeus Seneca, Seneca "the Younger" or "the Philosopher," c. 4 BC–AD 65. He was the son of Seneca the Elder and was born at Cordoba. He was educated in rhetoric and philosophy at Rome, and pursued a senatorial career as well as achieving a considerable reputation as an orator and writer. Appointed tutor to Nero, when the latter became emperor he exercised power along with the praetorian prefect Burrus. He withdrew from public life in 62 and committed suicide after being accused of conspiring to assassinate Nero. Seneca was devoted to Stoic philosophy and was a prodigious writer. Most of his extant writings have ethical and philosophical themes, including his longest work, a collection of 124 *Moral Letters*, *Epistulae Morales*, divided into 20 books. They were not real correspondence, but essays on various aspects of life and morality. Between 37 and 43 he wrote ten ethical treatises in 12 books with the name *Dialogi* (*Dialogues*). He was also author of *Naturales Quaestiones* (*Natural Questions*), a scientific work in seven books, which was written after 12/13. It is a collection of facts about nature from a Stoic and ethical rather than a scientific standpoint. He was also author of nine tragedies in verse that were adapted from the Greek.

SERVIUS: Probably Marius or Maurus Servius Honoratus. He was possibly born within the period c. 360 to 365, but his date of death is uncertain. He was a grammarian and commentator, best known for his commentary on Virgil's poetry *In Vergilii Carmina Commentarii*. Several other treatises have also survived.

SIDONIUS APOLLINARIS, Saint: Gaius Sollius Apollinaris Sidonius, 430/1 to the 480s. He was born at Lyon, the son of a prominent Christian family. A noted Gallo-Roman poet and letter writer, in 469 he became bishop of Clermont-Ferrand. He resisted the invading Visigoths but was imprisoned in 475. On his release in 476, he devoted himself to his diocese and literature until his death. He was one of the last major figures of classical culture. He was author of three panegyrics in verse to various monarchs. Also extant is a work of 21 other poems called *Carmina* and nine books of letters to friends and family that offer valuable information about life and conditions in Gaul in the 5th century.

SILIUS ITALICUS: Tiberius Catius Asconius Silius Italicus, c. 26–101, probably born at Padua. He won fame as an advocate and became consul in 68 and governor of Asia c. 77. He was a wealthy collector of books and works of art and a poet. He was author of the longest surviving Latin poem, *Punica*, an epic in 17 books of 12,200 hexameter lines on the Second Punic War, generally considered to be rather dull but pleasant.

SISENNA: Lucius Cornelius Sisenna, died 67 BC. He held public office and was author of a history of his own times in at least 12 books, which has not survived. He also translated into Latin the *Milesian Tales* of Aristides (c. 100 BC), gaining the stories popularity at Rome.

SOLINUS: Julius Solinus, 2nd–3rd century. He was author c. 200 of *Collectanea Rerum Memorabilium* (*Collection of Memorable Things*), an epitome of Pliny's *Natural History* and of Pomponius Mela's geography. He introduced the name Mediterranean Sea.

SORANUS: A Greek physician born in Ephesus who practiced and wrote about medicine in the first part of the 2nd century. Extant are several medical works (in Greek) including his four-volume work on gynecology, *Gynaecia*.

STATIUS: Publius Papinius Statius, c. 45–96, born and died at Naples, the son of a schoolteacher and poet. He moved to Rome and achieved a considerable reputation for his poetry. He was author of the *Thebaid*, an extant 12-book epic poem recounting the expedition of the Seven Against Thebes, published in 90 or 91. He also wrote *Silvae*, a five-volume collection of 32 short poems. The term *Silvae* was originally used for the raw material of a literary work, but was used by Statius as a title, and it came to mean collections of occasional poems. The first four books appeared between 91 and 95 and the fifth after his death in 96. The *Achilleid* (*Achilleis*) was his second epic poem on the story of Achilles, uncompleted at the time of Statius' death. He was also author of several lost works.

STRABO: 64 or 63 BC–AD 24. Born and died at Amasea. Strabo went to Rome in 44 BC to finish his education and thereafter visited the city several times. He became a Stoic and developed a profound admi-ration for the Romans. A Greek geographer and his-torian, he traveled extensively. Author (in Greek) of a 17-volume work, *Geographica* (*Geography*), in which he describes the physical geography of the chief coun-tries of the Roman world. He considered the world to be a sphere. The work, in an epitomized form, was used as a standard text for several centuries from the Byzantine period. His 47-volume history *Historical Sketches* is lost except for fragments. It was a continu-ation of the work of Polybius, from 146 BC to at least the death of Julius Caesar.

SUETONIUS: Gaius Suetonius Tranquillus, c. 70–c. 140. He practiced law at Rome and held posts in imperial service. He was author of the biographies of Julius Caesar and the first 11 emperors of Rome from Augustus to Domitian (*De Vita Caesarum*) (*Lives of the Caesars*), which are the earliest extant Latin biographies. Nothing is known of his life after 122, when he was apparently dismissed by Hadrian from his position as secretary of the imperial palace. He may have finished only the lives of Julius Caesar and Augustus when he was dismissed. He was also author of brief biographical sketches of famous literary men (*De Viris Illustribus*), including about 21 grammarians and 16 orators (*De Grammaticis et Rhetoribus*), 33 poets (*De Poetis*) and 6 historians. Fragments of this work survive. He was also author of works on Roman an-tiquities, natural sciences and grammar, much of which are lost.

SULPICIA: fl. c. late 1st century BC. A poet, the daughter of the jurist and orator Servius Sulpicius Rufus. She lived in the time of Augustus. Six short poems (40 lines in all) have survived in a collection of poems written by Tibullus.

SULPICIUS SEVERUS: 353–360 to c. 420. He came from Aquitaine and studied law at Bordeaux. He was converted to Christianity c. 389 together with Paulinus of Nola, to whom he wrote 13 extant letters. He was a historian and author of various works includ-ing *Vita Sancti Martini* (*Life of Saint Martin*) and a universal *Chronicle* (*Chronica*) in two books dealing with the period from the Creation to 400.

SYMMACHUS: Quintus Aurelius Symmachus, c. 340–402. He was a wealthy Roman noble, a distin-guished orator, an ardent supporter of the state pagan religion and a leading opponent of Christianity. Extant are ten books of over 900 of his letters, which he composed for publication; the first nine books are letters to friends and the tenth is official correspondence comprising 49 dispatches (*relationes*) including his unsuccessful appeal to Valentinian II for the restoration of the altar of Victory in the Senate.

TACITUS: Gaius (or Publius) Cornelius Tacitus, c. 56 or 57 to c. 117), possibly a native of Narbonese or Cisalpine Gaul. Tacitus studied rhetoric at Rome and followed a senatorial career, although not a great deal is known about his life. In his own lifetime he achieved popularity as a writer. He was a historian, and about half of his major works survive, including *Dialogus de Oratoribus* (*Dialogue on Orators*), a treatise set in the 70s in which four distinguished men of the day discuss oratory and the reasons for its decline. It used to be considered an early work but is now thought to have been published in 102 or soon after, and it is in a rather different style from his other works. *De Vita Julii Agricolae* or *Agricola* is a biography of Agricola, his father-in-law, dealing particularly with his accomplishments in Britain. It was published in 98. Tacitus was also author of *Historiae* (*Histories*) covering the period from Nero's death probably to Domitian's death. Only the first four books and part of the fifth are extant, although there were probably originally 14 books. The *Histories* were written in 106–107. The *Annales* (*Annals*) was a historical work consisting of at least 16 volumes covering the time from the death of Augustus to Nero's death: extant are books 1–4, a small piece of book 5, book 6, part of book 11, books 12–15 and part of book 16. They were published c. 116. Tacitus also wrote *Germania*, a monograph on the history, geography and tribes of the Germans to the north of the Rhine and Danube, published in 98.

TERENCE: Publius Terentius Afer, c. 195 or 185 to 159 BC, born at Carthage. He was brought to Rome as a slave and later manumitted. A writer of comedy, his plays are modeled on Greek New Comedy (*fabulae palliatae*) and were written in verse. Six of his plays survive: *Hecyra* (*Mother-in-law*), *Andria* (*Woman of Andros*), *Eunuchus* (*Eunuch*), *Adelphi* (*The Brothers*), *Heautontimorumenus* (*Self-Tormentor*) and *Phormio*. Suetonius wrote a biography of Terence c. 100.

TERTULLIAN: Quintus Septimius Florens Tertullianus, c. 160 or 170 to c. 230, born at Carthage of pagan parents. He received a literary and rhetorical education and was converted to Christianity before 197, possibly becoming a priest. He composed many works about the history and character of the church. His extant works include *Apologeticus* (*Apology*), written c. 197, in which he refutes charges made against Christians. He was the Father of Latin Theology and the first major Latin writer in defense of the church. He influenced the direction and thinking of the church in the Christian west.

TIBULLUS: Albius Tibullus, born between 55 and 48 BC, died 19 BC. Not a great deal is known about his life. He was author of two books of elegiac poems, his favorite themes being romantic love and the pleasures of rural life. The first book was published c. 26 BC, and the date of the second was possibly just before his death.

TIRO: Marcus Tullius Tiro, 1st century BC. He was a slave of Cicero, freed in 53 BC. Author of a biography of Cicero (now lost), editor of some of Cicero's speeches, he also wrote about grammar and developed a system of shorthand.

TITINIUS: 2nd century BC. He was a writer of comedies at Rome and the earliest known author of *fabulae togatae*. Only 15 titles and some fragments survive.

TROGUS: Pompeius Trogus. He was from Vaison-la-Romaine and was a historian in the time of Augustus. He wrote the first universal history in Latin. It was in 44 books, *Historiae Philippicae* (*Philippic Histories*), of which the central theme was the history of the Macedonian Empire. Only an abridgment survives, probably done by Justin in the 3rd century. Trogus also wrote a zoological work (*De Animalibus*) in at least ten books.

ULPIAN: Domitius Ulpianus, born at Tyre in the later 2nd century, murdered in 223 by mutinous soldiers of the Praetorian Guard. A famous jurist who held public office, he was also a prolific writer and published nearly 280 works on laws, legislation and constitutions, including an 81-book study on the praetorian edicts (*Ad Edictum Libri 81*) and *Regulae* (Rules), which summarized earlier legal writings. He became the main source for the legal scholars who compiled Justinian's *Digest*. One-third of the whole collection comprises quotations from Ulpian's work.

VALERIUS ANTIAS: 1st century BC, probably from Antium. He probably wrote c. 80 to 60 BC. He was author of a history of Rome from its beginnings to c. 60 BC in at least 75 books, fragments of which survive. Livy criticized him for his lack of veracity.

VALERIUS FLACCUS: Gaius Valerius Flaccus Setinus Balbus, 1st century, died in 92 or 93. Virtually nothing is known about his life. He was poet of the unfinished work, the *Argonautica*, an epic poem written in 5,593 hexameter lines divided into eight books, which described the mythical voyage of the Argo.

VALERIUS MAXIMUS: He lived during the reign of Tiberius, but little is known of his life. He was author of *Factorum et Dictorum Memorabilium Libri* (*Memorable Deeds and Sayings*), a compilation of historical anecdotes about Romans and foreigners (mainly Greek) in nine books intended for the use of orators.

VARIUS RUFUS: Lucius Varius Rufus, possibly born in the 70s BC, died c. 13 BC. He was a poet, friend of Virgil and Horace. He was author of tragedies, of which only one is known (on the story of Thyestes). He also wrote epic poems on death (with particular reference to Julius Caesar) and a panegyric of Augustus, but virtually none of his works survive.

VARRO: Marcus Terentius Varro, 116–27 BC, born at Reate. He was apparently also called Reatinus. Educated at Rome and Athens, he then entered a public career. He was proscribed by the Second Triumvirate in 43 BC but was reprieved, although his library and part of his property were taken. He spent the rest of his life studying and writing. One of the most learned Roman scholars, a poet, satirist, antiquarian, jurist, geographer, grammarian, and scientist, he also wrote on education and philosophy. Apart from Origen, he was the most prolific writer in antiquity, author of about 620 books on a wide range of subjects, although only two survive to any great extent. A three-book treatise about farming (*De Re Rustica*) has survived complete, and a 25-book treatise on Latin grammar and etymology (*De Lingua Latina*) is partly extant (books 5–10 with gaps). Also surviving from other works are 600 fragments of *Saturae Menippeae* (*Menippean Satires*), critical and humorous sketches of Roman life in prose and verse after the fashion of Menippus of Gadara, the 3rd-century BC

Cynic philosopher. The *Res Divinae* (*On Religion*) or *Antiquitates Rerum Humanarum et Divinarum* (*Human and Divine Antiquities*) was a huge 41-book compilation relating to Roman history and religion; large fragments survive because they were criticized by later Christian writers, including St. Augustine in his *City of God*.

VARRO: Publius Terentius Varro. He was also called "Atacinus", as he came from the valley of the Atax River in Narbonese Gaul. He was born in 82 BC, but nothing is known of his life. He was a poet who wrote verse of various kinds, preserved only in fragments. He was author of an epic poem on Julius Caesar's exploits in Gaul in 58 BC called *Bellum Sequanicum* (*Sequanian War*), a geographical poem called *Chorographia*, love poems, satires and a translation of *Argonautica* by the Greek poet Apollonius Rhodius.

VEGETIUS: Flavius Vegetius Renatus, lived in the last part of the 4th century. He was author of a treatise on the Roman military system, *De Re Militari* (or *Epitoma Rei Militaris*) in four books.

VELLEIUS PATERCULUS: Gaius Velleius Paterculus, c. 19 BC to after AD 30. He was born in Campania and served in the army. He was a historian, author of *Historiae Romanae*, a history of Rome in two books from legendary times to AD 30; the first book is incomplete. Included was a discussion on the evolution of Latin literature.

VERRIUS FLACCUS: Died AD 14. He was a freedman, learned scholar and tutor to Augustus' grandsons. Author of various works on antiquities, he was best known for *De Significatu Verborum* (*On the Meaning of Words*) in which he quoted from early republican authors. It is not extant but parts survive in a 2nd-century abridgement by Sextus Pompeius Festus and in an epitome of Festus by Paul the Deacon in the 8th century.

VIRGIL/VERGIL: Publius Vergilius Maro, 70–19 BC, born at Andes, near Mantua. He was educated at Cremona and Milan and later studied philosophy and rhetoric at Rome. He was a poet who abandoned public life and spent much of his time away from Rome. He was author of the *Eclogues* (or *Bucolics*), a collection of ten unconnected pastoral poems (*eclogae*

Fig. 6.5 Part of a figured mosaic from Low Ham, England, depicting the story of Dido and Aeneas as related in Virgil's Aeneid. *This central panel summarizes the story. It shows Venus between two Cupids, each holding a torch—one turned upright representing life and Aeneas, the other downward for death and Dido.* Courtesy of Somerset County Museums Service.

VITRUVIUS: Marcus Vitruvius Pollio (possibly Mamurra), 1st century BC. He probably wrote in the time of Augustus. An engineer and architect who saw military service c. 50 to 26 BC, he was author of a ten-volume treatise on architecture and engineering *De Architectura*, written toward the end of the 1st century BC and dedicated to an emperor, probably Augustus. *De Architectura* is a rare survivor of a Roman technical treatise. Book 1 is on general architecture and the principles of town planning and civic design, book 2 is on architectural history and building materials, books 3 and 4 on temples, book 5 on public and civic buildings, book 6 on domestic architecture, book 7 on interior decoration, book 8 on water supply, book 9 on sundials and other means of measuring time, and book 10 on mechanical engineering including machinery used in the building industry and by the military.

ZOSIMUS: Late 5th century. He was a Greek pagan historian and author (in Greek) of *Historia Nova* (*New History*), four books on the Roman Empire from Augustus to 410 (the sack of Rome). Book 1 is a summary of the first three centuries, and books 2 to 4 are of the 4th and some of the 5th centuries, with a particularly full account of the years 394 to 410, a most important source of information for this late period. As a pagan, he attributed the decline of the empire to the rejection of the pagan gods.

means selections). He apparently called the poems *Bucolica*, and they were written from 42 BC to c. 37 BC. Next he wrote the *Georgics* (*Georgica*—poems about the life and tasks of a farmer) from 36 to 29 BC. They were didactic poems totaling over 2,188 hexameter lines in four books, dedicated to his patron Maecenas. Virgil is best known for the epic poem the *Aeneid* (fig. 6.5), on which he spent the last years of his life. They were 12 books describing the search of the Trojan hero Aeneas for a new home for his people in Italy. Virgil linked this to the future foundation and greatness of Rome, and celebrates the achievements of the Roman Empire and of Augustus. In 19 BC he intended to travel to the east to visit some of the places he had described, but he fell ill in Greece and died at Brindisi on his return to Italy. The unfinished *Aeneid* was published on Augustus' orders. Virgil became famous in his lifetime but rarely appeared in Rome. After his death his fame increased to the point of superstitious reverence. The *Sortes Vergilianae* (*Virgilian Lots*) were attempts to prophesy the future by opening his books and picking a line at random, widely practiced from Hadrian's time.

INSCRIPTIONS

Epigraphy

Epigraphy is the study of the form and content of inscriptions and generally deals only with inscriptions cut, scratched or impressed on durable materials such as metal and stone, either in an official form or casually by an individual (a graffito). The Greek word *epigraphe* means an inscription, while the Latin for an inscription was *inscriptio* or *titulus*. Epigraphy does not usually cover coins, painted inscriptions and texts written in ink. Paleography is the study of handwriting on manuscripts such as papyri and writing tablets. Papyrology is the study of papyri and writing tablets.

Inscriptions date from the 6th century BC. (The one on a gold fibula from Praeneste dated to the 7th century BC is now classified as a forgery.) Early inscriptions are in archaic Latin. The *Forum Romanum Cippus*, commonly called the *Lapis Niger* (Black Stone), is Rome's oldest extant public document. It is a fragmentary stone inscription probably dating from the late 6th century BC, carved on four sides of a square pillar (*cippus*). The text is in very archaic Latin and is not fully understood. Most Latin inscriptions date to the early empire, but they continued beyond the collapse of Rome in the 5th century.

Unlike literature, which may have been copied many times, with the original version no longer extant, inscriptions provide an original record of writing. They have been found on various types of monument throughout the empire, although most are no longer in situ. Many inscriptions are fragmentary and mutilated, while a large number, reported from antiquity to the present day, is known to have been lost. New ones are being discovered constantly. It is estimated that well over 300,000 inscriptions are known (excluding coins), of which over 8,000 have been found in Rome and over 7,000 in Ostia. Inscriptions can be dated by their style of lettering, content (such as the subject matter and the mention of consuls) and spelling. Several thousand forgeries of Latin inscriptions are known, dating from the 16th century.

Writing (fig. 6.1)

Lettering on inscriptions was always in capitals, either monumental (deliberately formal) or cursive (as produced by the rapid use of a stylus or brush). The script of early inscriptions was similar to Greek, but by the 1st century the capital script had been formed, finely executed by stone cutters. In good-quality monumental work, the strokes of the letters were cut with a chisel to a V section (fig. 1.6). The guidelines used by the mason to keep the lettering straight are sometimes visible. Letters were usually highlighted by *minium* (cinnabar, vermilion). Traces of *minium* are rarely found, but in museums letters are sometimes restored with red paint.

Monumental lettering gradually became less formal and deteriorated in quality, and in poorer work a punch or mason's pick might have been used.

The normal material for monumental inscriptions was stone, but wood and bronze were also used. For large public monuments, the letters were sometimes made separately of bronze or lead and were fixed to stone or wood with rivets. Such inscriptions can sometimes be restored from the position of the rivet holes. Letters were usually cut in stone, or else cut, scratched, stamped or molded on metal, bricks, tile, earthenware and glass. Inscriptions could also be painted on walls, incised on writing tablets and written in ink on wood and papyri. Letters were even formed from tesserae in wall and floor mosaics. Cursive writing was usually used for curses, for graffiti on walls and objects, and for writing on wooden tablets (fig. 6.3).

A great deal of effort and skill was required to cut inscriptions, particularly those done from scaffolding. The Latin text of the *Res Gestae* at Ankara had 17,000 letters, and it was also carved in Greek. Errors are known to have been produced by the original carvers of inscriptions, which the carvers sometimes corrected.

Many inscriptions were in Latin, although in many parts of the Roman world they were in other languages, often Greek, and some inscriptions were in more than one language (fig. 2.3).

Types of Inscriptions

Inscriptions vary from very simple ones of two or three words to the *Res Gestae* of Augustus. Religious dedications (*tituli sacri*) are found on objects consecrated to the gods, usually on altars and votive goods, but sometimes on statues or temples. Religious dedications normally begin with the name of the god or gods (in the dative or genitive), followed by the name and status of the dedicator (in the nominative) and a verb or formula, usually abbreviated (such as VSLM). The reason for the dedication is sometimes stated. The verb of dedication is not always expressed but can be easily understood.

Honorific inscriptions (*tituli honorarii*) were usually on the base of a statue erected in a person's honor, with their name, rank and often their career (in the dative), followed by a statement of the dedicator (fig.

1.6). Commemorative plaques record subjects such as a victory or a vow of allegiance. *Tituli operum publicorum* were dedicatory inscriptions on public buildings and structures such as temples, theaters, walls, bridges, columns and aqueducts. These building inscriptions record construction or repair, from lengthy accounts to short statements. They usually record the name of the person responsible and the date. Many inscriptions record the building or repair of roads, and were sometimes on milestones (fig. 5.9).

Epitaphs on tombstones (*tituli sepulchrales*) are the most common type of inscription, and the form of words varies greatly both for men and women. From the Augustan age, they often begin with DM or DIS MANIBUS (to the divine shades), followed by the deceased's name (in the dative or nominative), or sometimes MEMORIAE ("to the memory of") with the name in the genitive. The name may be given in full, with that of the deceased's father, his voting tribe (if a Roman citizen) and his place of origin. The careers and ages of soldiers and prominent men are often recorded (fig. 2.6), with the addition of the name of the heir, relative or friend who erected the stone. Common last lines are HSE and STTL, sometimes written in full.

Military diplomas (*diplomata militaria*) were engraved on two linked bronze tablets. For more than two centuries from the time of Claudius to that of Diocletian, they were given to auxiliary soldiers on discharge and confirmed the grant of Roman citizenship. They were copies of edicts posted up in the Capitol at Rome (or, after Domitian, at the temple of Augustus on the Palatine). Each soldier was entitled to a copy of the enactment. The inscriptions included the name and titles of the emperor, the units to which the edict referred, the province in which they were serving and the name of its governor, followed by the date, the name and nationality of the individual soldier, and the names of seven witnesses to the accuracy of the copy. Each bronze tablet was the same size (c. 152 mm by 127 mm; 6in. by 5in.), and the text of the enactment was copied on the inner and outer surfaces. They were placed together, secured by wire through two or more perforations and sealed by the seals of seven witnesses to prevent forgery. Originally only the inner surfaces were used, but later the exterior surfaces were also used so that the contents were displayed without requiring the breaking of seals. Most diplomas refer to military cohorts, and hun-

dreds have been found in many parts of the Roman world, but all were originally made in Rome.

A huge number of tablets, mainly of bronze or wood, was also inscribed with state documents such as laws, treaties, decrees of the Senate and magistrates and religious documents. They were displayed in public places at Rome and in provincial towns. State documents included Diocletian's Edict on Prices and the text of many early laws and *senatus consulta*. Among the most important of Rome's historical inscriptions are the *fasti consulares* and the *fasti triumphales* (consular and triumphal *fasti*), inscribed on marble. They were placed on the outer walls of the *Regia*, not on inscribed slabs but on the actual marble of which the *Regia* was built. The *fasti* list under each year the names of the consuls and other details, and the *fasti triumphales* list triumphs. State documents written on wood may have been commonplace but none have survived, and very few bronze examples have been found as they were mostly melted down.

When Tiberius became emperor in 14, copies of the *Res Gestae* of Augustus were inscribed on stone tablets in many provinces. Much of the Latin text and a Greek translation are preserved on the walls of a mosque at Ankara, once the temple of Augustus and Rome and known as the *Monumentum Ancyranum*. The original inscription was incised on bronze tablets to be placed in front of Augustus' mausoleum at Rome (fig. 3.2). Fragmentary copies of Latin and Greek texts have been found elsewhere. This is considered to be the most important of all Roman inscriptions.

Public notices were also painted in black or red directly on walls or on wooden panels. Many on walls have been found at Pompeii, including a number that were professionally executed, while others were crudely done. These notices include advertisements, *fasti* and election pleas (fig. 6.6).

Fig. 6.6 An election notice for Lollius, professionally painted in red on a wall at Pompeii. Lollius ran for aedile in AD *78.*

Diptycha consularia were flat tablets of ivory, carved in the late Roman period as diptychs to commemorate consulates (fig. 1.5). They included the names and portraits of consuls. Ivory diptychs were also carved to commemorate important events and marriages.

Inscriptions are also found on portable objects known by the general term *instrumentum*, denoting articles used in public and private life, such as lead pipes, tiles, pottery vessels, weights and measures, stamps and seals. The term *instrumentum domesticum* refers more specifically to objects of everyday use such as amphorae. Seals (*signacula*) for stamping inscriptions in relief on softer substances, such as pottery and tile, were mainly of bronze. Stamped tiles were mainly flanged *tegulae*. Oculists' stamps of clay were for making impressions on cake ointment and gave the name of the oculist, the remedy and the malady. Stamps on metal ingots were made by casting the ingots in molds with raised letters. Lead water pipes bear inscriptions in relief from the age of Augustus to the end of the 3rd century. The earliest ones have only the name of the emperor; those from the 2nd century add that of the procurator.

Cursive writing was used in the curses written on tablets of lead or bronze (rarely stone) seeking the destruction of the writer's personal enemies. They were known as *exsecrationes*, *defixiones* or *devotiones*. Cursive writing is also found on *graffiti* scribbled on walls. Over 3,500 graffiti have been found on the walls of Pompeii, recording the trivialities of everyday life. Graffiti on walls are known as *inscriptiones parietariae*.

Words in Inscriptions

Words were usually divided by stops (interpuncts) known as *differentiae* (fig. 6.7), presumably to facilitate reading. *Differentiae* could be simple or decorative (such as ivy leaves) and were generally placed above the bottom line midway up the letters. Words were broken at any point to fit a line, and stops were sometimes introduced randomly midword. From the 3rd century stops were often put in the wrong place, a sign of illiteracy, and the use of stops gradually ceased. From c. 120 to 75 BC, a long *A*, *E* or *U* was denoted by a double vowel. Later an *apex* (pl. *apices*) was used, which was a stroke or accent above a vowel (for example, *á*) to denote a long vowel (fig. 6.7), although its use became merely ornamental. A tall *I* could also be employed to denote a long vowel, but its use was inconsistent and it also gave way to the apex.

ABBREVIATIONS

Words were commonly abbreviated by using the initial letter or letters of words, and most inscriptions have at least one abbreviation. Numerous abbreviations were used and some could have more than one meaning, depending on their context. (For example, *A* can be an abbreviation for many words, such as *ager*, *amicus*, *annus*, *Aurelius*, and *avus*.) Some words have more than one form of abbreviation, and there are also recurring formulas, such as HDSP. When a word was abbreviated, plurals could be expressed by doubling,

Fig. 6.7   An inscription on a tomb at Pompeii, with the words divided by differentiae and long vowels marked by the accents. There are several abbreviated numerals in the lower two lines.

trebling or quadrupling the last letter, such as AVGG (meaning two *Augusti*.) Some abbreviations, such as for personal names, were commonly used in litera- ture, while most were used only in inscriptions. The use of abbreviations in inscriptions seems to have been a fashionable trend as well as an attempt to save space.

EXAMPLES OF ABBREVIATIONS

See also abbreviations of personal names, tribes and numerals.

A	*amicus* (friend), *annus* (year), *aurum* (gold)
ADL, ADLEC, ADLECT	*adlectus*, (selected, chosen)
AED	*aedes* (building, usually a temple), *aedilis* (aedile)
AET	*aeternus* (*-a*) (eternal), *aeternitas* (eternity)
AN	*annus* (year)
ANN	*annus* (year), *annona* (corn supply)
AQ	*aqua* (water), *aquilifer* (eagle-bearer)
AS, ASO	*a solo* (from the ground)
A SOL REST	*a solo restituit* (he restored from ground level)
ASC	*ascia* (axe, trowel)
AVG	*Augustus* (Augustus), *augustalis* (priest of Augustus), *augur* (augur)
AVGG	*Augusti* (two *Augusti*)
AVGGG	*Augusti* (three *Augusti*)
AVG N	*Augustus noster* (our emperor)
B	*bene* (well), *beneficiarius* (beneficiarius), *bonus* (good)
BF	*beneficiarius* (beneficiarius), *bona fortuna* (good fortune)
B M	*bene merenti* (well deserving)
BR	*Britannia* (Britain), *Britannicus* (*-a*) (British)
⟩⊃	*centurio* (centurion), *centuria* (century) (⟩ and ⊃ are old Etruscan signs for K)
C	*Caesar* (Caesar, emperor), *civis* (citizen), *cohors* (cohort), *colonia* (colony), *coniunx* (wife, husband), *consul* (consul), *curia* (senate house), *custos* (guardian), *centuria* (century), *centurio* (centurion)
C A	*curam agens* (taking care, seeing to), *custos armorum* (keeper of arms)
CAES	*Caesar* (Caesar, emperor)
CC	*Caesares* (two Caesars)
CC VV	*clarissimi viri* (distinguished gentlemen — a courtesy title for senators)
C E	*coniunx eius* (his wife, her husband), *curam egit* (he took care, saw to)
C F	*Gai filius* (son of Gaius), *clarissima femina* (distinguished woman), *coniunx fecit* (his wife/her husband did this)
C F C	*coniunx faciundum curavit* (his wife/her husband took care to set this up)
CH, CHO, CHOR	*cohors* (cohort)
CL	*clarissimus* (distinguished — used for senators), *classis* (fleet)
COH	*cohors* (cohort)
COL	*collegium* (college), *colonia* (colony)
CON	*coniunx* (wife, husband)
CON KAR	*coniunx karissimus* (her most dear husband)
CONS	*consul* (consul)
COS	*consul* (consul), *consules* (consuls), *consularis* (consular)
COSS	*consules* (consuls)
CR	*civis Romanus* (Roman citizen)
CV	*clarissimus vir* (distinguished gentleman — a term used for senators), *cura* (care)
CVR	*curavit* (took care of)
CVR AG	*curam agens* (taking care, undertook)

D	*decretum* (decree), *decurio* (decurion), *dedit* (gave), *designatus* (designate), *deus* (god), *dies* (day), *divus* (deified), *dominus* (master), *donum* (gift)
DD	*decreto decurionum* (by decree of the town councillors), *dono donavit* (gave as a gift)
DEC	*decreto* (by decree of), *decurio* (decurion)
DED	*dedit* (he gave)
DES	*designatus* (designate(d))
DE S P	*de sua pecunia* (from his own money)
DIS M	*dis manibus* (to the spirits of the dead)
D M (S)	*dis manibus* (*sacrum*) ([sacred] to the spirits of the dead)
D N	*dominus noster* (our lord/emperor)
DO	*donum* (gift)
D P	*de pecunia* (from his own money), *donum posuit* (he presented a gift)
D P S (D)	*de pecunia sua* (*dedit*) ([he gave] from his own money)
D S D	*de suo dedit* (he gave from his own [money])
D S F	*de suo fecit* (he did this/set this up with his own [money])
D S P	*de sua pecunia* (from his own money), *de suo posuit* (he this up with his own [money])
DVPL	*duplicarius* (double-pay soldier)
EEQQ	*equites* (cavalrymen, members of the equestrian order)
E F C	*(h)eres faciendum curavit* (his heir had this made/set up)
EM V	*eminentissimus vir* (distinguished gentleman)
EQQ	*equites* (cavalrymen, members of the equestrian order)
EX AVC, EX AVCT	*ex auctoritate* (with the authority of)
EX OF, EX OFF	*ex officina* (from the workshop of)
EX T, EX TEST	*ex testamento* (according to his will)
F	*fecit* (built/did this), *faciendum* (to be built/done), *fidelis* (faithful), *filius* (son)
FAC CVR	*faciendum curavit* (had this set up)
F C	*faciendum curavit* (had this set up)
FEC	*fecit, fecerunt* (he/they did/made)
FID, FIDEL	*fidelis* (faithful)
FIL	*filius* (son)
F S ET S	*fecit sibi et suis* (he did this for himself and his own [kin])
GEN	*genius* (presiding spirit)
H	*heres* (heir), *hora* (hour), *hic* (here)
HAS P	*hastatus prior* (a centurion)
HAS PO	*hastatus posterior* (a centurion)
H D S P	*heres de suo posuit* (his heir set this up with his own [money])
HER	*heres* (heir)
H E T F, H EX T F	*heres ex testamento fecit* (his heir set this up according to his will)
H F C	*heres faciendum curavit* (his heir had this made/set up)
H L	*hic locus* (this place), *hoc loco* (in this place)
H M	*hoc monumentum* (this monument/tomb)
H M H N S	*hoc monumentum heredem non sequitur* (this tomb does not pass to his heir)
HON	*honoratus* (esteemed)
HS	*sestertius* (*-ii*) (sestertius)
H S E	*hic situs est* (he lies buried here), *hic sita est* (she lies buried here)
I	*invictus* (unconquered)
ID	*iure dicundo* (for administering the law)
IM, IMA	*imaginifer* (image-bearer)
IM, IMP	*imperator* (emperor)
IN H D D	*in honorem domus divinae* (in honor of the divine house)

I O M	*Jupiter Optimus Maximus, Iovi Optimo Maximo* ([To] Jupiter, Best and Greatest)
KAL	*kalendae* (the first day of the month)
L	*legio* (legion), *libens* (willingly), *libertus* (freedman), *locus* (place)
L A	*libens animo* (willingly)
L D D D	*loco dato decreto decurionum* (place given by decree of the town councillors)
LEG	*legatus* (legate), *legio* (legion)
LEG AVG	*legatus Augusti* (imperial legate)
LEG AVG PR PR	*legatus Augusti pro praetore* (imperial legate with powers of a praetor)
LEG LEG	*legatus legionis* (legionary legate)
LIB	*libertus* (freedman), *libens* (willingly)
L L	*legatus legionis* (legionary legate), *laetus libens* (gladly and willingly)
L L M	*laetus libens merito* (gladly, willingly and deservedly)
L M	*locus monumenti* (site of the tomb)
L M (D, F, P, S)	*libens merito* (willingly and deservedly) (*dedit, fecit, posuit, solvit* — gave, did, set up, fulfilled)
LOC	*locus* (place)
M	*manes* (spirits of the departed), *maximus* (greatest), *mensis* (month), *miles* (soldier), *mille* (thousand), *monumentum* (monument)
MAT	*mater* (mother)
MAX	*maximus* (greatest)
MED	*medicus* (doctor)
MIL	*miles* (soldier), *militavit* (served in the army), *millia* (thousands)
MON	*monumentum* (monument/tomb)
M P	*millia passuum* (thousand paces = one mile)
M V F	*monumentum vivus fecit* (he erected this monument while alive), *maritus uxori fecit* (her husband set this up for his wife)
N	*natalis* (native of), *natus* (born/age of), *nepos* (grandson/nephew), *noster* (our)
NA, NAT	*natio* (tribe), *natus* (born/age of)
NEP	*nepos* (grandson, nephew)
NN	*nostri* (our — plural)
NOB CAES	*nobilissimus Caesar* (most noble Caesar)
O	*officina* (workshop), *optio* (centurion's deputy)
OF	*officina* (workshop)
O H S S	*ossa hic sita sunt* (the bones lie here)
O M	*ob memoriam* (in his memory), *optimus maximus* (best and greatest)
OPT	*optimus* (best), *optio* (centurion's deputy)
P	*passus* (paces, feet), *pater* (father), *pecunia* (money), *pedes* (foot soldier), *pius* (dutiful, sacred), *populus* (people), *posuit* (he set up), *provincia* (province)
PA, PAR	*parentes* (parents)
PAT PAT	*pater patriae* (father of his country)
P F	*pia fidelis* (loyal and faithful)
P L L	*posuit laetus libens* (he set this up gladly and willingly)
P M	*pontifex maximus* (chief priest)
PONT MAX	*pontifex maximus* (chief priest)
POP	*populus* (people)
POS	*posuit* (he set this up)
P P	*pater patriae* (father of his country), *praeses provinciae* (governor of the province), *primus pilus* (chief centurion)
P R	*populus Romanus* (Roman people)
PR	*praefectus* (prefect), *praetor* (praetor), *primus* (first), *procurator* (procurator), *provincia* (province)

PRA, PRAEF	*praefectus* (prefect)
PRO	*proconsul* (proconsul), *procurator* (procurator)
PROC	*procurator* (procurator)
PROCOS	*proconsul* (proconsul)
PRON, PRONEP	*pronepos* (great grandson)
PRO PR	*pro praetore* (with powers of a praetor)
PROV	*provincia* (province)
PR POS, PR POST	*princeps posterior* (a centurion)
PR PR	*praefectus praetorio* (praetorian prefect), *pro praetore* (with powers of a praetor)
P S	*pecunia sua* (with his own money)
P S F	*pecunia sua fecit* (he set this up with his own money)
P S P	*pecunia sua posuit* (he set this up with his own money)
Q	*quaestor* (quaestor)
R	*restituit* (restored), *Romanus* (Roman)
R C	*reficiendum curavit* (he had this restored)
REF	*refecit* (he restored)
REG	*regio* (region)
RES, REST	*restituit* (he restored)
ROM	*Romanus* (Roman)
R P	*res publica* (the state)
S	*sacrum* (sacred to), *scripsit* (he wrote), *semis* (half), *servus* (slave)
SAC	*sacerdos* (priest), *sacer* (sacred)
S A D, S AS D	*sub ascia dedicavit* (consecrated, before the building — usually a tomb — was finished)
SACER, SACERD	*sacerdos* (priest)
SACR	*sacrum* (sacred)
S C	*senatus consulto* (by decree of the Senate)
SEN	*senatus* (Senate)
SIG, SIGN	*signifer* (standard-bearer)
S L L M	*solvit laetus libens merito* (he gladly, willingly and deservedly fulfilled his vow)
S P	*sua pecunia* (from his own money)
S P F	*sua pecunia fecit* (he did this/set this up from his own money)
S P Q R	*senatus populusque Romanus* (the Senate and the people of Rome)
ST, STIP	*stipendia* (years of military service)
S T T L	*sit tibi terra levis* (may the earth lie lightly upon you)
S V T L	*sit vobis terra levis* (may the earth lie lightly upon you — plural)
T	*terra* (earth), *testamentum* (will), *tribunus* (tribune), *turma* (unit)
TEST	*testamentum* (will)
T P	*tribunicia potestate* (with tribunician power)
T P I	*testamento poni iussit* (he ordered its erection in his will)
TR	*tribunus* (tribune)
TRIB	*tribus* (tribe), *tribunus* (tribune)
TRIB P, TRIB POT	*tribunicia potestate* (with tribunician power)
TR MIL	*tribunus militum* (military tribune)
TR PL	*tribunus plebis* (tribune of the people)
V	*victrix* (conqueror), *vir* (man), *vivus* (living)
V A	*vixit annos* (he lived. . . years)
V B	*vir bonus* (good man)
V C	*vir clarissimus* (distinguished gentleman — term used for senators)
V E	*vir egregius* (honorable gentleman — term used for equestrian ranks)

VET	*veteranus* (veteran soldier)
VEX	*vexillatio* (detachment), *vexillarius* (standard-bearer)
V F	*vivus fecit* (he did this/set this up while living)
V I	*vir inlustris* (distinguished man)
VIC	*vicit* (he conquered), *victoria* (victory)
VICT, VICTR	*victrix* (conqueror)
VIX	*vixit* (he lived)
V L	*veteranus legionis* (legionary veteran)
V L M S	*votum libens merito solvit* (he willingly and deservedly fulfilled his vow)
V L P	*votum libens posuit* (he willingly paid his vow)
V L S	*votum libens solvit* (he willingly fulfilled his vow)
VOT	*votum* (vow), *vota* (vows)
VRB	*urbana* (urban)
V S	*votum solvit* (he fulfilled his vow)
V S L L	*votum solvit libens laetus* (he willingly and gladly fulfilled his vow)
V S L L M	*votum solvit laetus libens merito* (he gladly, willingly and deservedly fulfilled his vow)
V S L M	*votum solvit libens merito* (he willingly and deservedly fulfilled his vow)
VV CC	*viri clarissimi* (most distinguished gentlemen)
VV EE	*viri egregii* (honorable gentlemen)

LIGATURES

Ligatures (combined letters) became increasingly common after the 1st century. Usually two, sometimes three, letters were joined (fig. 3.8). For example, VETVSTATE could become V⊢VSTA⊨ or TIB could become ⊤B. It can be difficult to know which letter comes first. Particularly from the later 3rd century, inscriptions show signs of decline in that they are less well cut and resort much to ligatured letters, economizing at the expense of clarity. Other examples of ligatures are:

	ABI
	ADI
	ENT
	ERI
	MAE
	NTI
	ATVR
	OHS (*ossa hic sita*—the bones lie here)
	OTSLT (*opto terra sit levis tibi*—may the earth lie lightly upon you)

ERASURE OF WORDS

Parts of inscriptions were sometimes deliberately erased as the result of a *damnatio memoriae* passed by the Senate on a deceased emperor. Over 30 emperors were condemned after death in this way.

Modern Conventions

In printing Latin inscriptions today, the following conventions are used to represent various aspects of the inscription, especially when it is being published for the first time.

[ ] Brackets represent restoration of *lacunae* and enclose letters that are thought to have been originally present but that have been lost through damage.

[[ ]] Double brackets indicate letters intentionally erased, such as through *damnatio memoriae*.

( ) Parentheses fill out abbreviations or, less commonly, words substituted to correct an error.

< > Angular brackets enclose letters that were accidentally omitted by the cutter.

| / A vertical bar or a stroke indicates the beginning of a fresh line on the stone.

$\overline{\text{PR}}$ $\widehat{\text{PR}}$ Ligatures are indicated by a straight or curved bar over the letters that are joined.

A̤ A dot placed beneath a letter indicates that it is not fully legible, due to decay or erasure.

[. . . .] Brackets with dots indicate the number of missing letters where restoration is not possible.

[- -] Brackets with dashes indicate that the number of missing letters is uncertain. Sometimes a number may be printed above the dashes to give an approximate number.

PERSONAL NAMES (fig. 6.8)

Knowledge of Roman names depends largely on inscriptions, where names are frequently mentioned. Inscriptions also play an important role in prosopography, the reconstruction of family trees, relationships and administrative hierarchies. Names underwent change throughout Roman history but started with simple forms, changed to multiple forms and then in the later empire reverted to simple or single names, especially under Christian and Jewish influence. As a rule, in the early republic, every man had two names—praenomen and nomen. Later three names (*tria nomina*) became common, in the order of praenomen, nomen and cognomen. The *lex Iulia municipalis* stated that the names of Roman citizens should be registered in the following order: nomen, praenomen, name of the father (or the former master in the case of a freedman), tribe, cognomen. This is the order used in imperial inscriptions, except that the praenomen was placed first.

The praenomen (today's forename) was the personal name used at home, although its popularity had declined by the late 2nd century. There were only a few personal names, which in writing were often abbreviated.

A.	Aulus
Ap(p).	Appius
C.	Gaius
Cn.	Gnaeus
D.	Decimus
L.	Lucius
M.	Marcus
M'.	Manius (originally M)
N.	Numerius
P.	Publius
Q.	Quintus
Ser.	Servius
Sex.	Sextus
S. or Sp.	Spurius
T.	Titus
Ti. or Tib.	Tiberius
V.	Vibius

The nomen (today's surname) was the more important name. It indicated the family or *gens* (clan) and is sometimes called the *nomen gentilicium*. For example, Titus Flavius Domitianus was a member of the Flavian *gens*. The nomen was abbreviated in inscriptions only rarely, for example, AEL for Aelius, VAL for Valerius.

Men often also had a cognomen, especially in the late republic and early empire when Roman male citizens commonly had three names (the *tria nomina*), such as Marcus Tullius Cicero. The cognomen consisted of one or more names and could refer to a personal characteristic, rather like a nickname, such as "Rufus" (redhaired) and "Brutus" (idiot). It was an extra personal name, and became a hereditary family name, thereby distinguishing the various branches of the same *gens*. Some cognomina were assumed later in life to commemorate a particular success in public life. The lack of a cognomen usually implies an early date or a person of humble origins, although this was not necessarily the case; Mark Antony, for example, had no cognomen. A *signum* was a nickname, found from the mid-2nd century.

An adopted son took his adoptive father's names but could add as cognomen the adjectival form of his own original name—for example, C. Octavius became C. Julius Caesar Octavianus (Octavian) when adopted by Julius Caesar.

In practice, men were usually known by their nomen and cognomen, sometimes reversed, or by the nomen alone, although the *tria nomina* remained the prerogative of the Roman citizen, distinguishing him from the noncitizen and the slave. At home family members addressed a man by his praenomen; by his friends he was addressed by his nomen or sometimes his cognomen; and in formal situations he was addressed by his praenomen and nomen, or by his cognomen as well.

From the mid-2nd century BC, the name of a man also included the *tribus* (tribe) to which he belonged, probably to indicate his Roman citizenship. The name of the tribe was usually abbreviated in writing, and the word *tribus* was omitted in writing and inscriptions. In very early Rome there were only three tribes, but by the end of the republic there were 35 voting divisions. Under the early empire every citizen was still assigned a voting tribe, quite often that of the reigning emperor for new citizens.

ABBREVIATIONS OF TRIBES

AEM	Aemilia
ANI	Aniensis
ARN	Arnensis
CAM	Camilia
CLA	Claudia
CLU	Clustumina
COL	Collina
COR	Cornelia
ESQ	Esquilina
FAB	Fabia
FAL	Falerna
GAL	Galeria
HOR	Horatia
LEM	Lemonia
MAEC	Maecia
MEN	Menenia
OVF	Oufentina
PAL	Palatina
PAP	Papiria
POL	Pollia
POM	Pomptina
PVB	Publilia
PVP	Pupinia
QVIR	Quirina
ROM	Romilia
SAB	Sabatina
SCAP	Scaptia
SER	Sergia
STE	Stellatina
SVC	Suburana
TER	Teretina
TRO	Tromentina
VEL	Velina
VOL	Voltinia
VOT	Voturia

Noncitizens who were granted citizenship regularly took the nomen of the reigning emperor, but from the time of the virtual extension of the citizenship to the whole empire under Caracalla in 212, the *tria nomina* came to have less importance as a mark of distinction. Some elaborate names continued to appear, but there was also a trend to simplification. It was increasingly common for men of foreign origin to have one foreign name coupled with a Roman one, such as Flavius Stilicho.

The use of inherited family names spread across the empire but gradually declined. By the end of the 3rd century the use of the praenomen had declined, and by the late 4th century many Christians had a cognomen (fig. 6.8), although upper classes tended to keep the three names. The use of inherited family names emerged once more to become the basis of most modern western nomenclature.

Women, slaves, freedmen and emperors had their own name systems. Whatever their origins, women were given only one name, their father's nomen in the feminine form, such as Cornelia. They did have two names in the early republic, the praenomen and nomen, but, especially in the upper classes, the praenomen came to be abandoned. All sisters were therefore called the same, and in order to distinguish them, terms such as the elder or the first were used. There is very little evidence for a praenomen being given to women, but from the end of the republic women had more names, most commonly a second name taken from her father's cognomen. For example, Fabia Honorata would be the daughter of Fabius Honoratus. On marriage a woman did not change her name, but could take her husband's name, in the genitive.

Slaves usually had only one name, but if granted their freedom, they often adopted their former master's praenomen and nomen and retained their slave name as cognomen.

Emperors' titles and names and those of their families became progressively longer and more complicated. Emperors were usually known by a short title in the form of one or two names or even a nickname. They adopted the name *Caesar* to prove their legitimacy even after the line of descent from Julius Caesar had died out with the end of the Julio-Claudians. This name eventually led to the titles kaiser and czar. There were very few praenomina in general use, but the title *Imperator* was adopted as a praenomen (not a title) by Augustus, Otho, Vespasian and all subsequent emperors, so that it came to mean emperor. It was originally a title given to a general after a victory, which he used until he had celebrated his triumph. Julius Caesar used the

Fig. 6.8 A late 4th-century Christian funerary inscription from Trier, set up to Maximianus by his sons Memoriosus and Prudens, all with single names.

title permanently. Inscriptions and other formal references to emperors therefore begin "Imperator Caesar. . . " before continuing with their other names, ancestry, titles, offices and honors. The formula *Imperator Caesar* was sometimes extended to members of the imperial family who shared the emperor's power. The title *Imperator* could also be used after an emperor's name if he had won a victory.

The term *Augustus* (reverend) was an honorary title decreed to Octavian by the Senate in 27 BC, and was used by all his successors as a cognomen. In inscriptions, an emperor is mentioned by praenomen, nomen and cognomen (or cognomina), followed by his official titles arranged in a fixed order (fig. 1.6). The three names or titles *Imperator Caesar Augustus* were used by nearly all the Roman emperors. The emperor Augustus and subsequent emperors also came to be called *princeps* (first citizen).

NUMERALS (figs. 6.7, 6.9)

The Roman system of numerals is clumsy. There is no symbol for 0 and no single symbols for 2, 3, 4, 6, 7, 8 and 9. The original Roman numerals are:

I	1	Apparently representing a single digit.
V	5	Apparently a rudimentary representation of the 5 fingers.
X	10	Apparently representing the two hands joined.
L	50	Originally ⊥ and ⊥ in the republic.
C	100	Possibly an abbreviation of *centum*.
IↃ or D	500	D usually had a middle bar but is now written as D.
CIↃ, M, ① or ∞	1,000	M was rarely used. It was an abbreviation of mille or milia, not used as an abbreviation until the 15th century.
Q	500,000	An abbreviation of *quingenta milia*.

Other numbers are made from the repetition, combination or both of these basic numerals. Repeated digits are usually added together, such as II = 2, CCC = 300. V and L are never repeated. A smaller digit is added to a larger preceding digit (on its left), such as LX = 60, DC = 600, but is subtracted from a larger number that follows (on its right), such as XL = 40. The latter procedure takes precedence within a number, such as CCXIV (214) = CCX+IV (not CCXI

Fig. 6.9 A tombstone to Tiberius Julius Pancuius, a soldier of the auxiliary cohort of Lusitani, who lived 55 years (AN, LV) and served 28 years (STIP XXVIII). He lies here. Photo: Ralph Jackson.

+ V). When a smaller numeral occurs between two larger ones, it is subtracted from the one on the right, such as MCM = 1900. Toward the end of the republic, a bar above a number multiplied it by 1,000, so that $\overline{VI}$ = 6000 and $\overline{D}$ = 500,000. It was also common for numerals to have a superposed bar in composite words such as IIvir (duumvir) to distinguish them from letters. Lateral lines were added to denote 100,000, so that $\boxed{X}$ = 1,000,000. Numerals are barred regularly

if used as, for example, an adverb; $\overline{XVI}$ "for the 16th time" (fig. 1.6). The numbers of a military unit (such as a legion) are always barred. The symbol IIS for *sesterdius* (II + *semis*, or two-and-a-half *asses*) often had a medial bar HS (or was written as HS). The *denarius* also had a medial bar ✕ (that is, ten [X] *asses*).

EXAMPLES OF NUMERALS (WITH ABBREVIATIONS)

1	I	*unus*
2	II	*duo*
3	III	*tres*
4	IIII or IV	*quattuor*. IIII is earlier and more frequent than IV
5	V	*quinque*
6	VI	*sex*
7	VII	*septem*
8	VIII or IIX	*octo*. VIII is more common.
9	VIIII or IX	*novem*. VIIII is more common in inscriptions.
10	X	*decem*
11	XI	*undecim*
12	XII	*duodecim*
13	XIII	*tredecim*
14	XIV	*quattuordecim*
15	XV	*quindecim*
16	XVI	*sedecim*
17	XVII	*septendecim*
18	XVIII or XIIX	*duodeviginti*. XVIII is more common
19	XIX or XVIIII	*undeviginti*
20	XX	*viginti*
30	XXX	*triginta*
40	XL or XXXX	*quadraginta*
50	L	*quinquaginta*
60	LX	*sexaginta*
70	LXX	*septuaginta*
80	LXXX or XXC	*octoginta*
90	XC or LXXXX	*nonaginta*
100	C	*centum*
200	CC	*ducenti*
300	CCC	*trecenti*
400	CCCC or CⅮ	*quadringenti*
500	IↃ or Ⅾ	*quingenti*
600	IↃ C	*sescenti*
700	IↃ CC	*septingenti*
800	IↃ CCC	*octingenti*
900	CIↃ CCCC	*nongenti*

| 1000 | CIↃ or M | *mille* |
| 10,000 | CCIↃↃ | *decem milia* |

NUMERALS IN INSCRIPTIONS

In inscriptions, many numbers are written as words, others appear as numerals, and many are abbreviated. Further examples of abbreviations are listed below. The basic shape of the abbreviations for 5,000, 10,000, 50,000 and 100,000 varies considerably.

VA XX VIII		Lived 20 years and 8 months
ꟗ	6	Possibly a ligature for VI
D	500	Half of CIↃ
CIↃ ∞	1000	The old form was sometimes changed to ∞
ꟗ ʜↄ ʜɪ ɪↄↄ	5000	Half of CIↃↃ
CIↃↃ ccↄↄ ɪⱮ	10,000	
ꟙ	50,000	Half of CCIↃↃↃ
CCIↃↃↃ ccↄↄↄ	100,000	
|X|	1,000,000	
|XI|	1,100,000	
|XVI|	1,600,000	
II. V(IR)	duumvir	
III. V(IR)	triumvir	
III. VIR	quattuorvir	
V. VIR	quinquevir	
VI. VIR	sevir	
VII. VIR	septemvir	
X. V(IR)	decemvir	
XV. VIR	quindecimvir	
XX. VIRI	vigint viri	
C. V	centumviri	

It was not until about 800 that Arab scholars at Baghdad adopted Hindu numbers, together with a sign for 0, so that there were ten numerals (0–9). During the Middle Ages in Europe the Roman system of numerals was widely replaced by this Arabic system, greatly simplifying mathematical calculations.

READING

Latin Language

Boardman et al. 1986: includes a discussion on the development of Latin in the early medieval period; Howatson (ed.) 1989.

Alphabet

Hammond and Scullard (eds.) 1970, 48; Sandys (ed.) 1921: includes archaic Latin and the alphabet.

Handwriting

Bowman and Thomas 1983: detailed analysis of cursive writing, with many references; Sandys (ed.) 1921: includes writing and changes in lettering.

Writing Materials

Bowman and Thomas 1983: discussion of writing tablets and papyri, with examples of writing tablets from Vindolanda; Chapman 1978: writing tablets; Crummy 1981, 103–4: seal boxes; Manning 1985, 85–87: *styli.*

Libraries

Grant 1990, 180–82: villa of the Papyri library; Hammond and Scullard (eds.) 1970, 607–8; Howatson (ed.) 1989.

Education

Balsdon 1969, 92–106; Bonner 1977; Hammond and Scullard (eds.) 1970, 371–73.

Ancient Authors and Literature

There are numerous books about individual Latin authors, both old and recent publications. For works of ancient authors in Latin and Greek, the Loeb Classical Library gives the original text, a translation and notes. The Penguin Classics series includes translations of Latin authors.

Boardman et al. 1986: includes discussions on many Latin authors; Bowder (ed.) 1980: profiles of major authors; Grant 1980: summary of authors' lives and their works as well as further reading and editions of their works in Greek and Latin and in translation; Gwinup and Dickinson 1982: provides a list of articles written about Greek and Roman authors; Hammond and Scullard (eds.) 1970 passim: discussion of literature of many authors with references; Howatson (ed.) 1989: handbook to the subjects, places and authors of Greek and Roman literature; Sandys (ed.) 1921: description of many aspects of Latin studies, including Latin authors; pp. 846–69 history of Latin scholarship from the Middle Ages to the 19th century; Shelton 1988: presents information on Roman social life by commenting on original sources in translation (texts, inscriptions, etc.); White 1984, 183–88: description of writers of technical works.

Inscriptions

The *Corpus Inscriptionum Latinarum* (*CIL*) is a corpus of inscriptions in many volumes, on which work began in 1862. Many other collections of inscriptions have also been published: see Gordon 1983, 8–12.

Collingwood and Wright 1965: gives illustrations, translations and notes on many inscriptions such as altars and tombstones; Frere et al. (eds.) 1990: illustrated description of inscriptions from Britain on military diplomas, metal ingots, tesserae, dies, labels and lead seals; Gordon 1983: photographs, text, translations and a commentary on 100 Latin inscriptions dating from the 6th century BC to AD 525, presented in chronological order; also contains an introduction to the subject, including past work, and a list of abbreviations used in inscriptions; Ireland 1983: methods of cutting inscriptions; Keppie 1991: illustrated guide to many aspects of inscriptions; London Association of Classical Teachers 1971: gives the text of original inscriptions, together with translations and notes; Sandys (ed.) 1921, 728–72: many aspects of Latin studies including inscriptions; Sandys 1927: explanation and description of all kinds of Latin inscriptions.

Personal Names

Allason-Jones 1989, 28–29: personal names of Roman and native women from the republic; Balsdon 1962, 17–18: personal names of women; Sandys 1927, 207–21, 231–33.

Numerals

Hammond and Scullard (eds.) 1970, 741–42; Sandys (ed.) 1921, 742–43.

7

RELIGION

STATE RELIGION

Development

Many different religions existed throughout the Roman world, but the citizens of Rome considered a collection of beliefs and rituals to be their particular religion. This was generally known as the state religion because it was thought to ensure the preservation and prosperity of the city-state. This state religion grew out of the rites performed by early farming families. As the agricultural community expanded, the gods who had been asked by individuals and families to provide such favors as beneficial weather, good harvests and protection from thieves were requested to provide these benefits for the community as a whole. To make these requests and perform rites and sacrifices for the gods, there grew up a hierarchy of priests and officials, led originally by the king. The basis of this religion was the belief that gods and spirits were everywhere, responsible for all natural phenomena, and that they all had to be propitiated by suitable offerings and rituals. Since gods and spirits were omnipresent, sacrifice and religious ritual became part of daily life. The state religion is therefore difficult to define precisely, and for many gods there is no surviving evidence of whether they were included in the state religion.

As the community grew into a state, religion became closely connected with politics and society. Religion governed all political activities because it was essential to ascertain the will of the gods before any state action. Eventually religion came to be manipulated for partisan purposes. Initially the king was a priest, but after the expulsion of the kings, the title was retained in *rex sacrorum* (king of sacred things) Priests were state officials, and temples and religious festivals were sometimes financed by the state.

The state religion was not static but developed alongside Roman society, largely by absorbing gods from other cultures, particularly from Etruria and the Greek colonies in Italy. Probably the greatest change was caused by the influence of the Greek gods, who were anthropomorphic and had a developed mythology, in contrast to the early Roman *numina* (sing. *numen* — spirits or divine powers, often representing natural or abstract forces). By the end of the republic, state religion was substantially different from that of early Rome because of the absorption of gods from other cultures.

While religion was flexible enough to absorb foreign cults, it was nevertheless also highly ritualized. There was a strong element of magic in rituals, and they were rigidly observed. The smallest mistake in performance would render a ritual invalid. Many rituals had been handed down unchanged, and gradually their meaning became forgotten, so that in later times they were barely understood. Rituals were occasionally performed to honor gods whose character and attributes had been forgotten, with only the name of the god surviving.

The Romans had no sacred writings other than the formulae of prayers, and so they were not bound by dogma. They were free to think and believe what they wanted about their gods, provided that rituals were performed correctly. The gods, though, were regarded as being in favor of many of the principles of Roman life, such as patriotism, family devotion and a sense of duty, and were closely associated with these virtues.

After Caesar crossed the Rubicon, resulting in civil war, the turmoil was attributed to neglect of the state religion. When order was restored, Augustus did much to revitalize the state religion by building temples, reviving rituals and cults (such as that of Apollo), and encouraging people to attend the public religious ceremonies. The state religion remained a powerful force for another three centuries, despite the increasing popularity of other religions adopted by many Romans, such as Mithraism, Christianity and the worship of Isis. Within the empire there was a contrast between the west, where the Roman pantheon was often adopted and merged with indigenous cults, and the east where Greek deities, already established and linked to local gods, continued in predominance.

Emperor Worship

With the expansion of the empire, Rome came to rule eastern nations that were accustomed to worshipping their kings as gods and that readily transferred their worship to Roman rulers. Augustus and his successor Tiberius, thought that this practice of worshipping living rulers as gods would be provocative if transferred to the west, but since the practice could not be

Fig. 7.1 "Maison Carrée" temple at Nîmes, a classical temple originally dedicated to the Imperial Cult of Roma and Augustus, but later to Gaius and Lucius Caesar.

eradicated in the east, they instead encouraged the worship of Roma, the divine spirit of Rome. Augustus tried to defuse future unrest by encouraging the worship of the *genius* or *numen* (spiritual power embodied in the emperor) and not the living emperor. In the west the cult of Augustus grew, often associated with Roma (fig 7.1). Evidence from inscriptions shows how various virtues were personified and worshipped, including Virtue, Victory, Discipline and Fortune (fig. 7.2). For example, several altars were dedicated to Fortuna Augusta (the fortune or luck of the emperor) the focus of this cult being at Lyon. Temples were also dedicated to Fortuna Augusta, as at Pompeii (fig. 7.2).

After his death in 44 BC Julius Caesar was regarded as having joined the ranks of the gods (that is, to have been *deified*), and after Augustus, who died in 14, it was common for an emperor to be deified after his death. In the west deified emperors were closely associated with the cult of Roma, but in the east worship of living emperors continued. The worship of the emperor became a test of loyalty to Rome—subjects were free to worship whatever gods they chose, provided they paid homage to the emperor. There is evidence from fragments of calendars from the Augustan period that festivals or celebrations devoted to the emperor or his family took place about twice a month.

Christianity

In the 4th century emperors began to support Christianity. After the Edict of Milan in 313, the practice

Fig. 7.2   Reconstruction of the temple of Fortuna Augusta, Pompeii, dedicated to the Imperial Cult. From W. Gell (1832) *Pompeiana.*

of Christianity was no longer an offense. In the late 4th century, Theodosius I, in a series of edicts banned all non-Christian rites and many Christian ones that were considered heretical, and Christianity became the official state religion.

Priesthoods

ORGANIZATION OF PRIESTS

There were no full–time professional priests of the state religion at Rome. Most priests were elected from the aristocracy, who had a duty to serve the state, and were trained in their duties as officers of the state religion. There was a hierarchy of priesthoods, organized in "colleges." The two major colleges were the *augures* and the *pontifices* (*collegium pontificum*);

the latter also included the *flamines*, the Vestal Virgins and the *rex sacrorum*. Two lesser colleges were the priests who looked after the Sibylline books and the *epulones*. Minor priesthoods included the *fetiales*, the Arval priests, the *salii* and the *luperci*.

The priests operated in parallel with the family *paterfamilias*: the latter performed rites to maintain good relations with the gods on behalf of his family, while priests performed rites to maintain good relations with the gods on behalf of the state.

Temples usually had a hierarchical staff headed by priests (*sacerdotes*, sing. *sacerdos*), who were either recruited as part-time priests from the magistrate class or were full-time paid officials. Priestesses also served in some cults, usually those of goddesses; the most well-known were the Vestal Virgins. Temples also had a range of servants such as gatekeepers for security, slaves and menials for general maintenance, clerks, acolytes for processions and ceremonies, and in some cases guides and interpreters to look after visitors.

PONTIFICES (PONTIFFS)

The *collegium pontificum* was the most important college of priests at Rome. The *pontifices* (sing. *pontifex*) had overall control of the state religion. In the monarchy they formed the religious council of the king, assisting him in the duties of the state cult. During the republic they were responsible for the organization of the state religion. It is thought that there were originally three pontiffs, but their number gradually increased to 16 by the time of Julius Caesar. Originally the pontiffs were all patricians, but after 300 BC half were plebeians. The *pontifex maximus* (head of the pontiffs) exercised control over the entire state religion and so was particularly powerful. This post was held by Julius Caesar and then by all the emperors until Gratian dropped the title after 381.

Pontiffs determined the dates of festivals, of *dies fasti* (days when it was permitted to conduct legal business) and of *dies nefasti* (days when it was not permitted to conduct legal business). They also kept a record of the main events that occurred each year. Pontiffs were allowed to participate in public affairs. They were not formally responsible for private worship, but were present at the solemn form of marriage known as *confarreatio*.

REX SACRORUM

After the expulsion of the kings in 510 BC, the office of *rex sacrorum* (king of sacred things) was established to carry out some of the king's religious functions. The *rex sacrorum* was a priest appointed for life from the patricians and was disqualified from holding any other office. He and his wife (*regina*, queen), who had some religious duties, performed various state sacrifices. The *rex sacrorum* was superior in rank and precedence to the *pontifex maximus* but inferior in religious authority.

AUGURES

The *augures* (augurs) were a college of priests who alone were officially authorized to take the auspices (read and interpret signs from the gods). This procedure, called augury or *auspicium*, was not to foretell the future but to find out if a proposed course of action had divine approval. Signs from the gods could be unsolicited but were usually sought in various ways, mostly by observing the flight patterns of wild birds or the feeding habits of captive birds such as chickens. The auspices were taken before any major event, such as a voyage or battle. For this purpose, sacred chickens were sometimes carried by armies in the field, so that auspices could be taken before battles. The methods of taking the auspices were governed by strict rules, and augurs were elected for life and trained for the role.

HARUSPICES

Haruspices (sing. *haruspex*, literally "gut-gazer") were originally Etruscan diviners at Rome. Believed to be interpreters of the will of the gods, they came to rival the *augures*, although they had no religious authority at Rome and were probably not organized into a college until the time of the empire. They interpreted the entrails from sacrificed animals, unusual births or growths ("prodigies") and lightning, all of which were regarded as indications of the will of the gods. (Prodigies and lightning were warnings.) Entrails were interpreted by the color, markings and shape of the liver and gallbladder, and there is evidence that models of livers were used in the training of *haruspices*. An interpreter of lightning was called a *fulgurator*. Lightning was interpreted by its frequency and the region of the sky in which it appeared. Confraternities of *haruspices* are known from many parts of the empire.

FLAMINES

Flamines (sing. *flamen*) were priests appointed to serve particular gods at Rome. There were 15 *flamines*, who served at least 12 gods: Ceres, Falacer, Flora, Furrina, Jupiter, Mars, Palatua, Pomona, Portunus, Quirinus, Volturnus and Vulcan. The *flamines* were part of the *collegium pontificum* under the authority of the *pontifex maximus*. The major *flamines* (the most ancient and most dignified) were patricians, and consisted of the *flamen dialis* of Jupiter, the *flamen martialis* of Mars and the *flamen quirinalis* of Quirinus. The minor *flamines* were plebeians. The characteristic dress of a *flamen* was a white conical leather hat (an *apex*). Municipal towns also had *flamines*. With the deification of Julius Caesar and subsequent emperors, *flamines* were also appointed in Rome and in the provinces to attend to their worship.

FETIALES

The *fetiales* were a college of priests selected for life from noble families. They were present in dealings with foreign nations and were particularly responsible for the rituals involved in declaring war and making treaties. To declare war, a priest would hurl a spear across the border into enemy territory, or alternatively hurl it into a special area in the temple of Bellona that represented the enemy territory. A treaty was solemnized by a priest pronouncing a curse on Rome if it was the first to break the treaty; the priest confirmed this ritual by killing a pig with a *lapis silex* or flint stone. This college of priests may have lapsed by the end of the republic, but it was revived during Augustus' reign.

ARVAL PRIESTS

Arval priests or brothers (*fratres arvales*) were the oldest college of priests in Rome. They offered public sacrifices for the fertility of the fields (*arvum* is a plowed field). The college consisted of 12 priests chosen for life from the highest senatorial families. Their most important ceremony, in honor of the goddess Dea Dia, took place in May in a grove on the Via Campania outside Rome. The song of these priests (*carmen arvale*) represents the oldest surviving example of Latin poetry. It is preserved in an inscription of 218 but probably dates to the 6th or 5th century BC.

AUGUSTALES

Augustales was the name given to several priesthoods or virtually honorary offices in Rome during the empire. Tiberius established the *sodales Augustales* (companions of Augustus) to preside over the worship of Augustus and his family. Similarly, priests were appointed to attend to the worship of other emperors after their death. In many Italian towns and some provincial ones, a board of six men (*seviri*) was set up to oversee the cult of Rome and Augustus. These were freedmen who were normally barred from other priesthoods and positions of authority.

EPULONES

A college of priests called *epulones* (feast organizers) was established in 196 BC, originally three in number and later increased to ten. They arranged the *epulum*

Iovis (the feast held for senators after the sacrifices at festivals of Jupiter Optimus Maximus) as well as the public banquets at other festivals and games.

SALII

The *salii* were a group of 24 priests of Mars, divided into two groups of 12. These were the "leaping" or "dancing" priests of Mars who danced in procession during his festivals. They were chosen from patricians and had to have both parents still living when chosen. For processions, they wore military dress and carried arms, halting at certain places to carry out ritual dances and to sing the *carmen saliare*, their ancient hymn.

LUPERCI

The *luperci* were a group of priests who officiated at the festival of Lupercalia. They were divided into two colleges, Luperci Quinctiales or Quintilii and the Luperci Fabiani or Fabii, believed to have been founded by Romulus and Remus respectively.

VESTAL VIRGINS

The Vestal Virgins had the duty of watching and tending the fire on the state hearth in the temple of Vesta at Rome. They also made a *mola salsa* (a sacred salt cake) and looked after a number of sacred objects, such as the Palladium—an image of the Greek goddess Pallas Athena, who was identified with Minerva. The Romans believed that it was a powerful talisman that protected Rome.

There were originally four Vestals (later six) chosen by the *pontifex maximus* from girls of patrician families aged between six and ten. They were required to serve for 30 years but usually continued to serve for the rest of their lives. They lived in the Hall of Vesta (Atrium Vestae) near the Forum at Rome. They were maintained at public expense and were controlled by the *pontifex maximus*. Their purity was all-important, and they were entombed alive if found guilty of unchastity. They were held in high esteem and could be very influential when intervening on behalf of someone in trouble.

Gods and Goddesses

Groups of Gods

The major Roman gods were often thought of in groups, the best known being the Olympians (Jupiter, Juno, Mars, Venus, Apollo, Diana, Ceres, Bacchus, Mercury, Neptune, Minerva and Vulcan), who paralleled the Greek Olympian gods. *Di consentes* were the 12 great gods (six gods and six goddesses). According to the poet Ennius, they were the same as the Olympians but with Vesta instead of Bacchus. As Roman religion developed, a triad of gods was formed who shared a temple on the Capitoline Hill at Rome and so became known as the Capitoline Triad. They were originally Jupiter, Mars and Quirinus. Under Etruscan influence, the triad later became Jupiter, Juno and Minerva, and it is the latter three who are usually referred to as the Capitoline Triad. *Di inferi* were gods of the underworld, such as Dis and Proserpina. A *dius fidius* was a god sworn by in oaths, usually Jupiter or the hero Hercules.

Evidence for Gods

Because the Romans had so many gods, often presiding over very specific areas of daily life, not all the gods had names. Of those who did, it is likely that only relatively few names have survived today. The amount of extant information about each god, such as function, attributes and rituals, also varies considerably. A distinction can be made between full-fledged gods and goddesses and more impersonal spiritual powers (*numina*). Most, if not all, of the gods developed from *numina*, which were much more numerous and covered specific functions. For example, Insitor was a deity of sowing. Because of a lack of information, it is often impossible to tell if a deity is a *numen* or a full-fledged god.

Assimilation of Foreign Gods

Unlike the Greeks, whose gods had anthropomorphic personalities and shapes and much wider spheres of influence, the Romans believed vague spirits presided over a place or activity. When gods from Greek and other traditions were absorbed into the Roman pantheon, they were also equated with Roman gods. For example, the Greek god Zeus was equated with the Roman god Jupiter, who had similar characteristics; the Celtic goddess Sulis in Britain became equated with Minerva; while in Cappadocia the war goddess Ma of Comana became equated with Bellona. Some of the original Roman gods acquired several names, and in prayers to gods a formula such as "hallowed be thy name, whatever name it is that you prefer" was often used, in case the supplicant had omitted a name and rendered the prayer ineffectual. Similarly, the Romans tried hard not to offend any god, to the extent that they invited over to their side to be worshipped the gods of cities they were besieging.

Descriptions of Gods

The following descriptions are of the main gods and goddesses and *numina* whose names are known. They are given in alphabetical order and are known to have been worshipped during the republic and empire. Many were adopted from other cultures or were local deities of pre-Roman origin (such as Celtic, Italian, Germanic and Syrian deities) and were often equated with traditional Roman deities. They were all tolerated within the Roman state.

ABNOBA: A Celtic goddess of hunting and possibly fertility, associated with Diana. She was worshipped in the Black Forest region.

ACCA LARENTIA: The origins of this goddess (also called Larentina) are obscure. There were various explanations of who she was, such as mistress of Hercules or wife of Faustulus (the herdsman who found Romulus and Remus with the wolf). Her festival, the Larentalia, was on 23 December.

AERICURA: A Celto-Germanic goddess, also called Herecura. She was sometimes depicted as a mother goddess but appears to have been regarded mainly as a goddess of the underworld. In southern Germany and the Balkans, she was worshipped in partnership with Dis Pater.

AESCULAPIUS: The Roman name for the Greek god Asklepios, who was the son of the healing god Apollo and the mortal Coronis (daughter of Phlegyas). Epidaurus was the most famous center of the cult of Asklepios, and from there lesser shrines were founded, such as at Athens (in 420 BC) and Rome (in 293 BC). The deliberate importation of this cult was the result of the Romans consulting the Sibylline books during a severe pestilence. The temple of Aesculapius at Rome stood on an island in the Tiber River. He was sometimes identified with the Phoenician god Eshmoun. There was a festival of Aesculapius on 1 January.

AIUS LOCUTIUS: An altar to this deity was erected at Rome after a voice was heard warning of the approach of Gauls who sacked Rome in 390 BC. Aius Locutius means "announcing speaker."

ALISONUS: Worshipped as the deity of Alesia.

AMON/AMMON/AMUN: One of the chief gods of the Egyptians and sometimes identified with Jupiter.

ANCAMNA: A Gaulish goddess, worshipped as the partner of Mars Lenus and of Mars Smertrius. She appears to have been a goddess of the Treveri.

ANDRASTE: According to ancient authors, Andraste was a Celtic goddess of victory, worshipped by the Iceni in Britain. Andraste may be the same as the deity Andarte, worshipped by the Vocontii in Gaul.

ANGERONA: Also called Diva Angerona. She was the goddess of secrecy, believed to give relief from pain and worry as well. She was usually depicted with a finger placed on her sealed mouth, warning silence. A festival in honor of this goddess, the Divalia Angeronae, took place on 21 December.

ANGITIA/ANGUITIA: An Italian goddess worshipped in the area of Lake Fucinus.

ANNA PERENNA: This goddess is usually considered to be a personification of the year because her festival was at the first full moon of the new year (15 March), but this explanation is uncertain.

ANTENOCITICUS: Sometimes called Anociticus. He was a Celtic god known from a shrine at Benwell, on Hadrian's Wall.

ANUBIS: The jackal-headed Egyptian god of the dead. The Romans usually portrayed him with a dog's head. His cult was introduced into Rome during the empire, along with other Egyptian deities, such as Isis.

APOLLO: This Greek god was never properly identified with a Roman deity. First introduced as a healing god, he became a god of oracles and prophecies as well as of hunting, music and poetry. The Sibyl at Cumae was a priestess of Apollo. To the Romans Apollo was the god of poetry, and "to drink the waters of Castalia" signified poetic inspiration. Castalia was a nymph in Greek mythology who, being pursued by Apollo, threw herself into the spring on Mount Parnassus near Delphi.

As Phoebus Apollo, he was worshipped as a sun god. Apollo Atepomarus, who was worshipped by the Celts, was sometimes associated with horses, and was probably a god of horses and riders. Apollo was also identified with the Celtic god Belenus: Apollo Belenus was a sun god and a healing god, popular in parts of Gaul, northern Italy and Noricum. Apollo Cunomaglus was a Celtic deity known from a shrine at Nettleton Shrub, Wiltshire: The shrine may have been a healing sanctuary, but Diana and Silvanus were also worshipped there, which may suggest that Cunomaglus (meaning hound lord) was a god of hunting. However, hunting and healing cults were often linked. Apollo Grannus was a Celtic god of healing known at Rome and over much of Europe; he was often associated with medicinal springs and was also worshipped as a sun god. Apollo Moritasgus was a Celtic god of healing known from a dedication at Alesia, which also mentions his consort Damona. Apollo Vindonnus was a Celtic sun god and god of healing who had a temple at Essarois near Châtillon-sur-Seine; Vindonnus means clear light, and many worshippers at the temple appear to have sought relief from eye afflictions. Apollo Virotutis was a Celtic god worshipped in Gaul; Virotutis means benefactor of humanity. At Rome games in honor of Apollo took place in July, and there was a festival on 23 September.

ARDUINNA: Celtic boar goddess of the Ardennes Forest. She was probably a goddess of hunting and the animals of the chase, particularly boars. See also DIANA.

ARNEMETIA: A Celtic goddess known from Aquae Arnemetiae (Buxton), where she was probably a goddess of the medicinal springs.

ARTIO: A Celtic goddess of forest animals, particularly associated with bears (*artio* means bear). She was probably also a goddess of plenty, hunting and fertility, and is known from evidence at Berne and from near Trier.

ATARGATIS: Also called Dea Syria (the Syrian Goddess). She was worshiped as a fertility goddess at her temple at Hierapolis (the greatest and holiest in Syria). Her consort was called Hadad. Her cult spread to a number of Greek cities in the 2nd century BC but appears to have gained little ground in the west. She was worshiped in Arabia, where she was known as Allat. See also BAALS.

AURORA: The goddess of the rosy dawn.

AVETA: A Celtic goddess worshiped at Trier. She appears to have been a goddess of fertility and prosperity, sometimes depicted with a basket of fruit, at other times with lapdogs or swaddled infants. She may also have been a goddess of healing, renewal or rebirth.

BAALS: Sun and sky gods (sing. Baal) worshiped in Syria and Arabia. At Baalbek, the center of worship of the great Syrian sun god, Baal was first identified with the Greek sun god Helios and later with Jupiter, so that he came to be invoked as Jupiter Optimus Maximus Heliopolitanus. Also at Baalbek Baal was associated with Atargatis. At Palmyra Baal Shamin was associated with local deities Aglibol and Malakbel and was sometimes represented in Roman armor, with thunderbolts and ears of corn, denoting that besides being a sky god, he was also a god of protection and fertility. In north Africa a god Baal was worshiped in a monotheistic cult and was identified with Saturn.

BACCHUS: The Roman name for the Greek god Dionysus. Because of reports that the Bacchic rites had become immoral and corrupt drunken orgies, the Bacchanalia was suppressed in 186 BC and the Bacchic

sanctuaries were destroyed. Bacchus was also worshipped during the festival of Ambarvalia (29 May).

BEL: A Syrian sky god, linked with Jupiter. At Palmyra he was associated with local deities Iarhibol and Aglibol.

BELATUCADRUS: A Celtic war god. He is known from inscriptions around Hadrian's Wall referring to Belatucadrus and Mars Belatucadrus. Belatucadrus means fair shining one.

BELENUS: An important Celtic sun god, sometimes identified with Apollo. He was associated with horses and may have been connected with the Celtic solar fire festival of Beltene on 1 May. See also APOLLO.

BELLONA: The goddess of war, also called Duellona (the old Roman form of the name). Bellona was equated with the Greek goddess Enyo and was sometimes regarded as the wife or sister of Mars. The war goddess Ma, from Comana in Cappadocia, was also identified with Bellona. Bellona's festival was on 3 June.

BENDIS: A mother goddess worshipped in Romania and Bulgaria.

BONA DEA: An earth and fertility goddess, sometimes identified with Fauna. She was worshipped exclusively by women. Her festival was on 3 December.

BONUS EVENTUS: The god of successful enterprises. Probably originally an agricultural god, he became very popular and had a temple on the Capitoline Hill.

BORMANA: A Celtic goddess of healing springs. Sometimes worshipped on her own, she was more usually associated with Bormo.

BORMO: Also known as Bormanus, Bormanicus and Borvo. A Celtic god associated with healing springs, he was worshiped in Spain and Gaul. He was sometimes associated with Apollo, and at Aix-les-Bains he may have been equated with Hercules. He was frequently associated with a female counterpart called Bormana, and at Bourbonne-les-Bains he was associated with Damona.

CAMENAE: Italian goddesses, probably originally associated with water. They were identified with the Greek Muses, and had a spring and grove outside the Porta Capena at Rome where the Vestal Virgins drew water for their rites. The festival of the Camenae was on 13 August. See also EGERIA.

CARDEA: The goddess of door hinges.

CARMENTIS: Also called Carmenta. She was a prophetic goddess of protection in childbirth and possibly a water goddess. In mythology she was mother of Evander, the first settler at Rome. A minor *flamen* was assigned to her, and her festival, the Carmentalia, was on 11 and 15 January. The Porta Carmentalis, the gate at the foot of the Capitoline Hill, was named after her.

CARNA: This goddess was the protector of people's health.

CASTOR: Castor and Pollux were worshipped at Rome from an early date. Castor was always more popular, and their temple at Rome is usually called the temple of Castor. They had festivals on 27 January and 13 August. They were popular gods, particularly with the *equites*, and the common Latin oaths *mecastor* and *edepol* were derived from their names. Castor and Pollux were identified with the Germanic twin gods, the Alci.

CERES: An Italian goddess representing the regenerative power of nature. She was identified with the Greek goddess Demeter and was associated with the earth goddess Tellus. During a famine in 496 BC, the Sibylline books recommended Demeter, Kore and Iacchus (Greek gods) to be identified with the Roman gods Ceres, Liber and Libera. At Rome there was a *flamen cerialis*. The Cerialia festival was 12–19 April, and Ceres was also worshipped during the Paganalia in January and the Ambarvalia in May. As an earth goddess, Ceres received a sacrifice to purify the house after a funeral. There was a fast in honor of Ceres on 4 October.

CERNUNNOS: A Celtic god of fertility, abundance, regeneration and wild animals. He is known from pre-Roman sites and was worshipped widely in Roman times. Cernunnos means the horned one, and at least one named image shows him with antlers.

Many other similar but unnamed images are identified as representing this god. Occasionally he is linked with a female partner, and representations of antlered goddesses, probably female equivalents of Cernunnos, are also known.

COCIDIUS: A Celtic god whose worship seems to have been confined to north and west Cumbria and Hadrian's Wall. He appears to have been a god of woodland and hunting. At Ebchester there was an inscription to Cocidius Vernostonus (meaning alder tree). He was sometimes equated with Silvanus and also Mars (when he was regarded as a god of war).

COLLATINA: A goddess of hills.

CONCORDIA: This goddess was the personification of concord, with a festival in July.

CONDATIS: A Celtic god of the confluence ("condate") of rivers in the Tyne-Tees region of Britain. Although a god of water and possibly of healing, he was sometimes equated with Mars.

CONDITOR: A deity associated with storing agricultural produce.

CONSUS: A god of the granary, probably connected with harvest and autumn sowing. He had an underground barn and altar in the Circus Maximus that was uncovered only during his festivals, the Consualia, on 21 August and 15 December. There was also a festival of Consus on 12 December. He was associated with horses and so was sometimes identified with the Greek god Poseidon. See also NEPTUNE.

CONVECTOR: A deity associated with binding the sheafs.

COTYS: Also known as Cotyto or Cotytto. She was a Thracian goddess associated with Cybele and had an orgiastic cult that eventually spread throughout Greece and Italy.

COVENTINA: The Celtic goddess of a spring at Carrawburgh, Hadrian's Wall. The spring fed a small pool or well that became a shrine. Although the spring had no medicinal properties. Coventina may have been regarded as a healer and also a water goddess. She is also known from Gaul and northwest Spain.

CUPID: The boy god of love, son of Venus and Vulcan. Cupid is an adaptation of the Greek god Eros; both are portrayed with wings and a quiver of arrows. Cupids are found as symbols of life after death on coffins (fig. 6.5), and this symbolism was continued in Christianity, where cupids became winged cherubs.

DAMONA: A Celtic goddess worshipped in Burgundy. She seems to have been goddess of fertility and healing, and was sometimes associated with Apollo Moritasgus, with Bormanicus and with other water gods at healing springs. At Arnay-le-Duc she was associated with Abilus. The name Damona means great (or divine) cow.

DANUBIAN RIDER GODS: In Pannonia, Moesia and Dacia, representations on small marble and lead plaques show two riders, accompanied by a goddess, trampling a defeated enemy. Little is known about these deities who have been named the Danubian Rider Gods.

DANUVIUS: A deity of the Danube River (fig. 2.10).

DEA NUTRIX: pl. *deae nutrices*, nursing goddesses. This term is used to describe a particular form of Celtic mother goddess, usually depicted sitting in a high-backed wicker chair suckling one or two children. Pipeclay statuettes in this form are found in Celtic areas of the empire and were manufactured in central Gaulish, Breton and Rhineland factories in the 1st and 2nd centuries. Finds of these statuettes in graves suggest that she was also a goddess of renewal and rebirth. Pipeclay figurines resembling the classical Venus (sometimes called pseudo-Venus figurines) are also probably connected with a Romano-Celtic domestic fertility cult rather than the worship of Venus. See also MATRES.

DIANA: A goddess of wild nature and woods whose cult spread widely from her native Italy. Identified with the Greek goddess Artemis, she came to be regarded primarily as a goddess of hunting and of the moon and as a protector of women. There was an early temple to Diana on the Aventine Hill. In a grove at Aricia she was worshipped as Diana Nemorensis in association with Egeria and Virbius. She was sometimes associated with Celtic gods, such as Apollo Cunomaglus at Nettleton Shrub, Wiltshire, and she was sometimes conflated with Celtic hunting goddesses such as Abnoba and Arduinna. There was a festival of Diana at Rome on 13 August. See also HECATE, JUPITER and LUCINA.

DIS: A contracted form of *dives*, "rich." Dis was also known as Dis Pater, Dives, Hades, Haides, Aides, Aidoneus, Orcus and Pluto. A god of the dead and the ruler of the underworld, equated with the Greek god Hades, he was also known as Plouton (Pluto in Latin) and associated with the Etruscan god Februus. In Greek myth Hades was one of the three sons of Cronus and Rhea. (The others were Zeus and Poseidon.) Hades ruled the underworld and the dead with his wife Persephone. When he was in the underworld, only oaths and curses of men could reach him, and men invoked him by striking the earth with their hands. Black sheep were sacrificed to him, and those who performed the sacrifice averted their faces. Hades had almost no cult, and there are few statues of this god. In 249 and 207 BC the Senate ordained special festivals to appease Dis and Proserpina. In southern Germany and the Balkans Dis Pater had a Celtic goddess, Aericura, as a consort. In literature Dis was regarded only as a symbol of death.

DOLICHENUS: A mountain god, worshipped at Doliche. He was regarded as a god of sky and weather (a Baal) and so became equated with Jupiter.

EGERIA: She was worshipped in association with Diana and Virbius in a grove at Aricia and with the Camenae at a grove outside the Porta Capena at Rome. Egeria was an Italian water nymph, said to be consort to the second king of Rome, Numa Pompilius. Pregnant women sacrificed to her for an easy delivery.

EL GABAL: A Syro-Phoenician sun god imported to Rome by Elagabalus, who had been a boy priest of this deity at Emesa.

ENDOVELLICUS: A god of the underworld worshipped in Spain.

EPONA: The Celtic horse goddess. Her name derives from the Celtic word for horse. Her worship was most popular in eastern Gaul and on the German frontier, but she was also worshipped in Britain, former Yugoslavia, north Africa and at Rome, where she had a festival (unique for a Gaulish deity) on 18 December. She was always portrayed on or with horses, and sometimes with *paterae* full of corn, ears of corn, baskets of fruit, a dog and a key, suggesting other aspects of the goddess, such as fertility, water, healing, and death and rebirth.

ESUS: A Celtic god known from the writings of Lucan and from two inscriptions from Paris and Trier. He had a strong connection with willow trees and was supposed to have demanded human sacrifices. He is depicted as a woodman cutting or pruning trees.

FAGUS: A Celtic god, personifying the beech tree, worshipped in the Pyrenees. *Fagus* means beech tree.

FALACER: A deity served by a *flamen*, but little else is known.

FAUNA: A goddess of fertility, the counterpart of Faunus. She was equated with Bona Dea.

FAUNUS: Also known as Pan. He was an Italian pastoral god, a hunter and a promoter of agriculture. Evidence for his cult has been found as far afield as Thetford, Britain. He also had the title "Fatuus" (speaker) because he was an oracular god, revealing the future in dreams and voices in sacred groves. He was worshipped at the Lupercalia, but also had festivals on 13 February and 5 December. The idea evolved of many Fauni (fauns) who were identified with Greek satyrs.

FEBRIS: The goddess who averted fever.

FEBRUUS: An Etruscan god of the underworld equated with Dis.

FELICITAS: Goddess of good luck. Unknown before the mid-2nd century BC, she played an important part in the state religion during the empire. Fausta Felicitas had a festival on 9 October.

FERONIA: An Italian goddess of spring flowers whose cult was quite widespread. She was associated with Flora and had a festival on 13 November.

FIDES: Goddess of good faith and verbal contracts, with a festival on 1 October.

FLANONA: A goddess worshipped at Istria in Dalmatia, and identified with Minerva.

FLORA: An Italian goddess of flowers and the spring. She had a temple at Rome near the Circus Maximus that was founded in 238 BC and was served by a *flamen floralis*. Her festival, the Floralia, was 27 April to 3 May. There was another festival of Flora on 13 August. *See also* FERONIA.

FONS: A god of springs whose festival, the Fontinalia, was on 13 October.

FORCULUS: A god of doors.

FORNAX: The goddess charged with preventing grain from burning in grain-drying ovens. She appears to have been invented to help explain the festival of Fornacalia in early February.

FORTUNA: Also known as Fors Fortuna. She was probably originally a fertility goddess, but came to be identified with the Greek goddess Tyche and so was regarded more generally as a goddess of fate, chance and luck. She had a temple in the Forum Boarium at Rome and a shrine and oracle at Palestrina. She had festivals on 25 May and 24 June. Fortuna Redux was Fortune the Home-Bringer. Fortuna Publica (Luck of the People) had a festival on 5 April, and Fortuna Virgo (Fortune the Virgin) had a festival on 11 June. There was a festival of Fortuna Huiusque (Fortune of the Day) on 30 July and a festival of Fortuna Equestris (Fortune of the Knights) on 13 August. The festival of Fortuna Primigenia (Fortune the Firstborn) was on 13 November.

FURRINA: Also called Furina. She was a goddess whose festival, the Furrinalia, was on 25 July. Little else is known about her.

GAIA: An earth goddess who appears to have been worshipped with Tiberinus at his festival on 8 December.

GENII CUCULLATI: (Hooded spirits; sing. *genius cucullatus*) The name given to a series of representations, usually relief carvings in stone, of hooded deities. On the continent they usually appear singly, as giants or dwarves, but in Britain three identical dwarves are usually portrayed, although a few single ones are known. They appear to be Celtic deities associated with fertility and prosperity, and possibly with renewal and rebirth.

GENIUS: A festival in honor of the Genius Publicus (public spirit) was on 9 October.

GLANIS: The patron deity of Glanum, where an altar was set up to Glanis and the Glanicae, a triad of mother goddesses associated with its healing springs.

HAMMER GOD: This Gaulish god was an important Celtic deity. He was represented either with a consort or alone, and a few representations are dedicated to Sucellus. Most representations depict the god bearded, with a short belted tunic, a heavy cloak, a long-handled hammer and a small pot or goblet. In different areas he appears to have been associated with wine production, healing springs and the sun. It is likely that he also had many other associations. His function is complex and not fully understood.

HECATE: The goddess presiding over magic and enchantments. She was the sister of Latona and was often identified with Diana.

HERCULES: The Roman equivalent of the Greek hero Heracles. He was worshipped as a god of victory and also as a god of commercial enterprise. He had an altar, the Ara Maxima, in the Forum Boarium at Rome. He was sometimes identified with the Phoenician god Melqart. Hercules was linked to a number of Celtic names, the most popular being Hercules Magusanus in northeastern Gaul; in Gallia Narbonensis he was called Ilunnus and at Silchester he was called Hercules Saegon, which may be a different form of the name Segomo meaning victorious. As Hercules the Great Custodian, he had a festival on 4 June, and there were festivals of Hercules Invictus (Unconquered Hercules) on 12 and 13 August.

HONOS: The personification of honor and also called Honor. There was a festival of Honos on 17 July.

IALONA: A Celtic goddess and female equivalent of Ialonus. She was worshipped at Nîmes.

IALONUS: A Celtic god who was a personification of a concept connected with the land. He appears to have been a god of clearings, glades and even cultivated fields. At Lancaster he was worshipped as Ialonus Contrebis (Ialonus who dwells among us).

IANUARIA: A Celtic goddess known from a shrine at Beire-le-Châtel. She was portrayed as a young girl in a heavy pleated coat holding a set of pan pipes. She was associated with Apollo and may have been a goddess of music and/or healing.

IARHIBOL: A Syrian deity, associated at Palmyra with Aglibol and Bel.

ICOVELLAUNA: A Celtic goddess worshipped at Metz and Trier. She appears to have been a goddess of healing springs.

IMPORCITOR: A deity associated with harrowing.

INSITOR: A deity of sowing.

INUUS: An ancient Italian god, probably a god of fertility or sexual intercourse, named by Livy as the god originally worshipped at the Lupercalia.

IOVANTUCARUS: A Celtic god equated with Lenus at Trier, where he appears to have been worshipped as a protector of youth. He is also known to have been equated with Mercury.

JANUS: The god of beginnings and also of gates and doorways. He was frequently represented as having two faces (Janus Bifrons) looking in opposite directions, just as a door has two faces. To denote his different functions, he was sometimes described as Janus Patulcius (the god that opened doors) and Janus Clusivus (the god that closed doors). As Janus Pater (Janus the Father) he was regarded as a god of creation. As god of beginnings, he was the first to be named in any list of gods in a prayer and the first to receive a portion of a sacrifice. The first month of the Roman calendar was named after him, and 1 January was dedicated to him. His temple in the Forum at Rome was a small shrine consisting of an east-west arched passageway, with doors at both ends that were closed only in time of peace (fig. 7.3). There was a festival of Janus on 17 August.

JUGATINUS: A god of mountain ridges or of marriage.

Fig. 7.3 Reverse of an as *of Nero, showing the temple of Janus with its doors closed, signifying peace.* Courtesy of Somerset County Museums Service.

JUNO: (or Iuno) An ancient and important Italian goddess. She was the Roman form of the Etruscan goddess Uni and wife of Jupiter. She was identified with the Greek goddess Hera, who was the daughter of Cronus and Rhea and the sister and wife of Zeus. The Kalends of every month was sacred to Juno, and she had festivals on 1 July and 13 September. There were temples to Juno in the Campus Martius and one on the Aventine Hill, which was dedicated in 392 BC.

Juno had many epithets: Juno Lucina was goddess of childbirth who was worshipped at the Matronalia festival on 1 March; the Romans identified Lucina with Eileithyia or Eileithyiae, a Greek goddess of childbirth. Juno Opigena was also a goddess of childbirth. Juno Regina (Juno the Queen) was one of the Capitoline Triad and had a festival on 1 September. Juno Caprotina seems to have been a goddess of fertility and was worshipped at the Feast of the Serving Women in July. Juno Sospita was Juno the Savior. Juno Moneta (possibly meaning remembrancer) had a temple on the Capitoline Hill, dedicated in 344 BC; there were festivals of Juno Moneta on 1 June and 10 October. Juno Populonia blessed the people when they were under arms, and Juno Sispes was a protector of the state. Juno Sospita Mater Regina (Juno Savior, Mother, Queen) was a goddess mainly of fertility and protection, celebrated in a festival on 1 February. Juno Sororia was the goddess of protection of girls at puberty, and had a festival on 1 October. Juno Curitis (protector of spearmen) had a festival on 7 October. The Iunones, a triple version of Juno, was the name of a triad of mother goddesses worshipped in the territory of the Treveri; they were a local version of the Celtic triple mother goddesses. See also MATRES.

JUPITER: Identified with the Greek god Zeus. Like Zeus, he was regarded as the chief of the gods, and as such he was sometimes identified with the Egyptian god Amon. Jupiter had many epithets and was also known as Diespiter, the archaic nominative Latin form of Jupiter. As Jupiter Optimus Maximus (Jupiter Best and Greatest) he occupied the temple of Jupiter Capitolinus with the goddesses Juno and Minerva (the three making up the Capitoline Triad) on the Capitol (fig. 3.1), which made this the most sacred part of Rome. The Ludi Romani, games in honor of Jupiter Optimus Maximus, took place in September with a festival on 13 September. A temple of Jupiter Feretrius also stood on the Capitol, associated with an oak tree; the name Feretrius is obscure, but may mean one who blesses weapons or maker of agreements.

Originally Jupiter appears to have been a sky god controlling the weather, particularly rain and lightning. A place struck by lightning (*bidental*) was considered sacred to Jupiter and belonged to him alone. A stone inscribed *Fulgur Divom* (Lightning of the Gods) at Halton Chesters may mark such a place. As Jupiter Lapis he was associated with the stones used in taking oaths. (Presumably the stones were believed to be thunderbolts.) Jupiter Dolichenus was originally a Syrian sky and weather god (a Baal) who seems to have been a fusion of Jupiter and the local weather god at Doliche. The cult of Jupiter Dolichenus spread through the empire. He was identified with Jupiter Optimus Maximus and had Juno Regina as his consort. The main sanctuary of the cult at Doliche was sacked by the Persians in the mid-3rd century, and the cult subsequently lost support.

Jupiter was also sometimes identified with a Celtic sky god, and an altar from Chester was dedicated to Jupiter Optimus Maximus Tanarus—Tanarus being a Celtic thunder god. It is apparently as an identification with the Celtic sky god that Jupiter is portrayed on monuments known as Jupiter Columns (or Jupiter-Giant columns). About 150 of these stone columns are known, mainly in northeast Gaul and Germany. They were often ornamented to symbolize a tree, on top of which a figured Corinthian capital supported a carved group of figures, commonly a horseman riding down a monster with snake limbs. Jupiter is not normally portrayed on horseback, and so it is probably the Celtic sky god that is portrayed, although the dedication is to Jupiter. Other types of column are rare, but a Mercury column is shown on a plate from Berthouville, France, and Diana is shown on a column in a mosaic at Lillebonne, France. Jupiter is also sometimes portrayed with a spoked wheel, which is a symbol of the Celtic sun god.

In Noricum, Jupiter was identified with a local high-mountain god and was known as Jupiter Uxellinus. Jupiter Beissirissa is known from southern Gaul, and Jupiter Brixianus is known from Brescia. In northwest Spain Jupiter was identified with a local mountain god and was worshipped as Jupiter Ladicus. In northeast Dalmatia and Upper Moesia, Jupiter was worshipped as Jupiter Parthinus. In the Alps around the Great St. Bernard Pass he was worshipped as Jupiter Poeninus. Jupiter Lucetius was the bringer of light. Jupiter Stator (fig. 7.4) had the aspect of "stayer of the rout" and had festivals on 27 June and 5 September. Jupiter Liber was a god of creativity, Jupiter Dapalis a god of boundaries, Jupiter Conservator Orbis preserver of the world and Jupiter Pistor the god of bakers.

At Rome, Jupiter Victor (Victorious Jupiter) and Jupiter Libertas both had festivals on 13 April. There were also festivals of Jupiter on 15 March, 15 May and 15 October, and he was worshipped in the festival of Vinalia Priora on 23 April. Jupiter Latiaris was worshipped in the Feriae Latinae festival on 27 March. Jupiter Invictus (Unconquered Jupiter) had a festival on 13 June. Jupiter the Thunderer had one on 1 September, and Jupiter Liber on 1 September. There was a festival of Jupiter Fulgur on 7 October. The Capitoline Games, in honor of Jupiter, took place on 15 October, and the Plebeian Games on 4 to 17 November, with a festival of Jupiter on 13 November.

JUTURNA: An Italian goddess of springs. She had a temple at Rome in the Campus Martius and a shrine and pool in the Forum, the water from which was used in official sacrifices. Her festival was on 11 January.

JUVENTAS: The Roman goddess of youth, identified with the Greek goddess Hebe. There may have been a festival of Juventas on 19 December.

LARA: In mythology Lara was a talkative nymph whose tongue was cut out by Jupiter. Also known as Mania, she was the mother of the *lares*.

LARENTINA: Also known as Acca Larentia. She was a Roman goddess worshipped at the Larentalia on 23 December. She may have been the wife of the herdsman Faustulus, mother of the original *fratres arvales*, and nurse of Romulus and Remus.

LATIS: A Celtic goddess known from Cumbria, Britain. She was a local goddess of watery places, bogs and pools.

LATOBIUS: A Celtic god of mountain and sky worshipped in Noricum. He was equated with Mars and with Jupiter.

LATONA: The Latin name for the Greek goddess Leto, mother of Apollo and Artemis.

LAVERNA: The Roman goddess of thieves and impostors.

LIBER: An Italian fertility god. As Liber Pater he was often identified with Dionysus, even though Liber does not appear to have been associated with wine. He had an important cult on the Aventine Hill at Rome, along with Ceres and his female equivalent Libera. Liber was sometimes identified with the African god Shadrapa. Liber had a festival on 17 March, apparently shared with Libera.

LIBERA: The female equivalent of Liber. She was identified with the Greek goddess Persephone and apparently shared the festival of Liber on 17 March.

LIBERTAS: This goddess was the personification of liberty.

LIBITINA: An Italian goddess of funerals. She had a temple at Rome, in which registers of the dead were kept.

LIMENTIUS/LIMENTINUS: A god of the threshold.

LUA: (or Lua Mater) An Italian goddess, possibly of diseases and connected with Saturn.

LUCINA: The goddess of bringing things to light, often identified with Diana and Juno.

LUNA: The goddess of the moon. She had festivals on 31 March and 24 and 28 August.

LUPERCUS: This god seems to have been invented in the Augustan period to account for the festival of Lupercalia.

LUXOVIUS: A Celtic god and patron deity of Luxeuil, France. He is known only from this site, where he was worshipped as the male partner of Bricta. This divine couple were deities of the thermal spring, where other deities were also worshipped.

MAIA: An Italian goddess associated with Vulcan. She appears to be connected with the growth of living things, and the month of May is probably named after her. She became confused with a much better known Greek goddess of the same name, who was the mother of Hermes, and consequently she became associated with Mercury (the Roman equivalent of Hermes). As a fertility goddess, she was also associated with Fauna. Maia had a festival on 15 May.

MALAKBEL: A Syrian deity associated at Palmyra with Baal Shamin and Aglibol.

MAPONUS: A Celtic god worshipped in northern Britain and at Chamalières in Gaul. Maponus means divine youth or divine son. He was sometimes conflated with Apollo and appears to have been associated with music, poetry and hunting.

MARS: An Italian god of agriculture and guardian of fields and boundaries. He was identified with the Greek god Ares and so assumed the major role of a war god (fig. 7.5), and was regarded as the son of Juno. As Mars Pater (Mars the Father) his connection with agriculture was maintained, and the month of March is named after him. Mars had an altar in the Campus Martius at Rome and was served by the *flamen martialis*. There was a temple of Mars on the Appian Way outside Rome, and a temple of Mars Ultor (Mars the Avenger) was ordered by Augustus to be built in the Forum in 20 BC. The wolf and the woodpecker were his sacred animals. Mars had a succession of festivals in February, March and October. There was a festival on 1 June, and a festival of Mars Invictus (Unconquered Mars) on 14 May. Roman troops celebrated the birthday of Mars Pater on 1 March with the sacrifice of a bull. The Armilustrium, the festival of purification of arms in honor of Mars, was on 19 October.

Among the Celts, Mars was regarded not only as a war god but as peaceful protector, healer and tribal

Fig. 7.5 Reverse of a follis *of Constantine I showing Mars Conservator with spear and shield.*Courtesy of Somerset County Museums Service.

god. He was equated with many Celtic gods, such as Mars Cocidius, Mars Belatucadrus and Mars Braciaca. Mars Alator is known from a dedication at Barkway, Hertfordshire. Curse tablets from Uley, Gloucestershire are addressed to Mars Silvanus and Mars Mercury. In Noricum Mars was identified with a local god and was known as Mars Latobius. Mars Albiorix was worshipped as protector of the Albici tribe in southern Gaul as well as being regarded as a mountain god. Mars Camulos was a war god venerated in Britain and Gaul, and Mars Caturix (Mars king of combat) was worshipped in Gaul, possibly as the tribal god of the Caturiges. Mars Corotiacus is known from Martlesham, Suffolk, where he is portrayed as a horseman. Mars Lenus was an important god of healing of the Treveri tribe who had sanctuaries at medicinal springs at Trier and Pommern. At Trier, Lenus was also coupled with the Celtic goddess Ancamna and was sometime given the name Iovantucarus, indicating that he was a protector of the young. There is evidence that Lenus had been established as an important local god for some time before being equated with Mars. In Britain dedications to Mars Lenus are known from Chedworth and also from Caerwent, where he is identified with Ocelus Vellaunus. Also from Caerwent is a dedication to Mars Ocelus, which probably refers to the same deity (fig. 7.6).

Mars Loucetius is known from a dedication at Bath, where a divine couple of Mars Loucetius and Nemetona were worshipped; he may have been regarded as a god of healing since the dedication was on an altar in the temple of Sulis Minerva at the medicinal springs. Worship of Mars Mullo was popular in northern and northwestern Gaul. Mullo means mule, and so this god may have been connected with horses or mules. He was also known as a healer of eye ailments. Mars Nabelcus was a local mountain god worshipped in the Vaucluse Mountains of Provence; Nabelcus was also worshipped in other mountain areas of southern France. Mars Rigisamus (Mars King of Kings) is known from West Coker, Somerset, and Bourges in Gaul. The title implies a very high status for this god, more important than the usual roles for Mars. Mars Rigonemetis (Mars King of the Sacred Grove) is known from Nettlesham, Lincolnshire. Mars Vorocius was a god of healing worshipped as a healer of eye afflictions at the medicinal springs at Vichy. Mars Thincsus (a Germanic god) is known from a dedication at Housesteads, Hadrian's Wall,

Fig. 7.6 A small altar from Caerwent, Wales, dedicated to the god Mars Ocelus by Aelius Augustinus, an optio *[in the army], who willingly and deservedly fulfilled his vow* (VSLM).

where he is linked with two goddesses called the Alaisiagae; these goddesses are also linked with Mars on another dedication from Housesteads. Mars Segomo (Mars Victorious) was worshipped by the Sequani tribe in Gaul. Mars was also equated with many other Celtic gods.

MATRES: Also called Deae Matres or Matronae. They were mother goddesses, normally worshipped in a triad. They were often portrayed in art, particularly sculpture, usually as three seated women accompanied by various symbolic objects. They were worshipped largely in northwestern Europe under a variety of names and with differing attributes. The Matres Domesticae are known in Britain from Chichester, Stanwix and Burgh-by-Sands. They may be connected with the Matres Aufaniae who were worshipped by the Celto-Germanic tribes of the Rhineland. At Bonn they were called Aufaniae Domesticae. The Matres Comedovae were worshipped at Aix-les-Bains, where they were associated with healing and the medicinal properties of the hot springs. The Matres Griselicae were worshipped at Gréoulx in southern Gaul, again associated with medicinal springs. The Matres Vacallinehae were worshipped in the Rhineland and had a temple complex at Pesch. Apparently connected with the Matres are goddesses that have been called Deae Nutrices.

MATUTA: A goddess of dawn, who also had some connection with young growth and developed into a goddess of childbirth. She was later identified with the Greek goddess Ino (also called Leucothea). Matuta was worshipped at the festival of Matralia in June.

MEDITRINA: This goddess seems to have been a late Roman invention to account for the festival of Meditrinalia on 11 October.

MENS/MENS BONA: This goddess was the personification of "mind" or "right thinking" and had a festival on 8 June.

MERCURY: Regarded as the son of Maia and Jupiter, and identified with the Greek god Hermes. He was a messenger and a god of trade, particularly the corn trade, and a god of abundance and commercial success, especially in Gaul. He had a temple on the Aventine Hill, founded in 495 BC. He was often depicted bearing a *caduceus* (a herald's staff with two entwined snakes) and wearing a winged hat and winged shoes. He was also often accompanied by a cockerel (herald of each new day), a ram or goat (a fertility symbol) and a tortoise (a reference to Mercury's invention of the lyre from a tortoise shell). At Rome Mercury was not assigned a *flamen*, indicating that he was not worshipped there from earliest times, but there was a festival of Mercury on 15 May.

Caesar states that Mercury was the most popular god in Britain and Gaul and was regarded as the inventor of all the arts. In Celtic areas he was sometimes portrayed with three heads or faces. At Tongeren, Belgium, a statuette of Mercury with three phalli (an extra one on his head and one replacing his nose) is probably a good luck and fertility charm, enhanced by using the magical number three. In Celtic areas Mercury was often equated with native deities and was frequently accompanied by Rosmerta. Mercury Artaios was worshipped near Isère, France, and was probably connected with bears and hunting. Mercury Arvernus was worshipped in the Rhineland and was probably a god of that locality. The worship of Mercury Cissonius was more widespread, known from Cologne to Saintes. Cissonius was a Celtic god venerated mainly in Germany, and a goddess Cissonia is also known. Mercury Gebrinius was a god worshipped at Bonn. Mercury Moccus was probably associated with hunting and is known from Langres, France; the name Moccus (pig) suggests a connection with boar hunting.

MESSOR: A deity associated with reaping.

MINERVA: An Italian goddess of crafts and trade guilds. She was originally the Etruscan goddess Menrva and was identified with the Greek goddess Athena. She appears to have assumed the martial aspect of Athena Promachos (champion) and was regarded as a goddess of handicrafts and of war. In Noricum and Dalmatia she was identified with a local goddess Flanona and was known as Minerva Flanatica. Minerva had a shrine on Mons Caelius and a temple on the Aventine Hill. She had festivals on 19 March, 19 June and 13 September.

MOGONS: Also known as Mogtus, Mogunus, and Mountus, Mogons (great one) was a Celtic god worshipped mainly in northern Britain, particularly around Hadrian's Wall. On the continent dedications to Mogons Vitiris and Apollo Grannus Mogounus are also known.

NEHALENNIA: A Celtic goddess of seafarers, fertility and abundance. She is known at two coastal shrines at Domburg and Colijnsplaat in the Netherlands. She is frequently portrayed with symbols of sea travel, such as a steering oar, as well as symbols of abundance. Another frequent accompanying symbol is a dog, usually portrayed in a benign protective pose. The variety of symbolism suggests that the goddess presided over wide issues such as healing, death and rebirth, and not just travel at sea.

NEMAUSUS: An ancient local Celto-Ligurian god of Nîmes (Nemausus). Nemausus was probably originally the spirit of the healing springs at Nîmes, where local goddesses of healing and fertility (called Nemausicae or Matres Nemausicae) were also worshipped.

NEMESIS: The goddess of vengeance. An underworld goddess, she was always ready to punish impiety and reward virtue. She was sometimes regarded as one of the Furies.

NEMETONA: A Celtic goddess of the sacred grove (*nemeton* means sacred grove). She was worshipped mainly in the territory of the Nemetes in Germany. She is usually paired with a Celtic version of Mars, such as Mars Rigonometis or Mars Loucetius.

NEPTUNE: An ancient Italian god of water. He was later identified with the Greek god Poseidon and was therefore regarded as a sea god (fig. 7.7). Because of Poseidon's association with horses, Neptune also became identified with the Roman god Consus, who was associated with horses. Neptune had a festival, the

Fig. 7.7 Reverse of an as *of Caligula showing the god Neptune. Courtesy of Somerset County Museums Service.*

Neptunalia, on 23 July, and there was another festival on 1 December.

NERTHUS: A Germanic earth goddess mentioned by Tacitus in the *Germania* as riding in procession on a wagon.

NODENS: A Celtic god of healing found only in Britain. He was also called Nodons and had a major temple at Lydney, where he was equated with Mars and Silvanus. There is no known portrayal of Nodens in human form, but representations of a dog occur that may portray the god or an associated attribute.

NODUTUS: A god of the joints and knots on the stems of grain plants.

NOREIA: The patron goddess of Noricum. She had a shrine at Hohenstein and was sometimes identified with Isis.

NORTIA/NURTIA: An Etruscan goddess of fortune, worshipped at Bolsena.

OBARATOR: A deity associated with top dressing (such as manuring) the fields.

OCCATOR: A god of hoeing.

OCEANUS: The god of the ocean (which was regarded as the great river that surrounded the earth).

OCELUS: A Celtic god, known from three inscriptions in Britain where he was associated with Mars; one inscription was a dedication to Mars Ocelus.

OGMIOS: A Celtic god mentioned by Lucian, who encountered the cult of Ogmios in Gallia Narbonensis, apparently equated with Hercules. The god is also known from two curse tablets from Bregenz, Austria.

OLLOUDIUS: A Celtic god worshipped in Britain and Gaul. He was a god of fertility and abundance, healing and peaceful protection, and was sometimes equated with Mars. An image of Mars Olloudius is known from Custom Scrubs, Gloucestershire, where he is accompanied by a patera and a double cornucopia, symbolizing abundance.

OPS: A Roman goddess of abundance. She was usually associated with Saturn, and because Saturn was identified with the Greek god Cronus, Ops was identified with Cronus' consort Rhea. Ops had festivals on 25 August (Opsiconsivia) and 19 December (Opalia).

PALES: A Roman deity of shepherds and sheep. This deity was regarded as male by some authorities and female by others. There were festivals of Pales on 21 April and 7 July.

PATELANA: A goddess of the husks of corn when they are open to allow the ears to emerge.

PAX: The Roman goddess of peace, identified with the Greek goddess Irene. She is represented on coins as a young woman with a cornucopia in her left hand and an olive branch or staff of Mercury in her right hand.

PICUMNUS: The brother of Pilumnus. Both may have been ancient Roman agricultural gods. They were known as beneficent gods of matrimony and childbirth.

PICUS: An Italian god of agriculture who possessed prophetic powers. He usually took the form of Mars' sacred bird (the woodpecker) and was sometimes regarded as the son of Saturn.

POMONA: The Roman goddess of fruit, wife of Vertumnus.

PORTUNUS: Originally a Roman god protecting doors, who also became the protector of harbors. He was usually depicted holding a key. His festival, the Portunalia, was on 17 August. He was served by the *flamen portunalis.*

PRIAPUS: A god of flocks of sheep and herds of goats.

PROMITOR: A deity of the distribution of the harvest.

PROSERPINA: A goddess of germinating seeds and of the underworld, identified with the Greek goddess Persephone. In 249 and 207 BC the Senate ordered special festivals to appease Dis and Proserpina as deities of the underworld.

QUIRINUS: Originally a god (perhaps a war god) of the Sabines on the Quirinal Hill before Rome was founded. He was subsequently absorbed into the state religion. He had a wife called Hora. His festival was on 17 February. He was served by the *flamen quirinalis.*

REPARATOR/REDARATOR: The deity associated with the second plowing.

REDICULUS: This god was worshiped at Rome as the deity who caused Hannibal to retreat from the city gates.

RIDER-HUNTER GOD: The main god of Thrace. He appears not to have had a name and is referred to in inscriptions as "the hero." He has no connection with the Danubian Rider Gods.

ROBIGUS/ROBIGO: Sometimes called Robigo (the female equivalent of Robigus). He was a god of mildew or grain rust and had a festival on 25 April.

ROMA: The divine spirit of Rome.

ROSMERTA: A Celtic goddess whose name means the great provider. She was usually associated with Mercury as the female partner of a divine couple worshipped over much of Europe, particularly in central and eastern Gaul. In this couple Rosmerta was a goddess of prosperity and abundance, and was often depicted with a cornucopia and patera. She was occasionally worshipped on her own as a goddess of plenty, and at Gissey-la-Vieil, France, she was associated with a sacred spring.

RUDIANUS: A Celtic war god worshipped in southern Gaul. Rudianus means red.

RUMINA: A goddess protecting mothers suckling their children. She had a sanctuary at the foot of the Palatine Hill.

RUSINA: A goddess of fields or farmland.

SABAZIOS: A Phrygian god whose worship was widespread in Italy during the empire, and which seems to have been connected to that of the Magna Mater. He was sometimes identified with Jupiter and Dionysus. His chief attribute was the snake, and a characteristic of his cult consisted of votive offerings of representations of hands covered with magical symbols.

SALUS: An Italian goddess of health, equated with the Greek goddess Hygeia. During the empire she was called Salus Publica Populi Romani (Public Health of the Roman People). Her festival was on 5 August.

SARRITOR: A god of hoeing.

SATURN: An ancient Italian god, possibly of blight and/or of seed sowing. He is known mainly as a god of sowing and had a festival (Saturnalia) at the winter solstice. This festival was originally on 17 December, but from the late republic, it started on 17 December and continued for several days. Saturn was regarded as the husband of Ops and father of Picus and was identified with the Greek god Cronus. He had a temple at the foot of the Capitoline Hill, which served as the treasury (*aerarium Saturni*).

SEGETIA: A goddess of grain crops ripening aboveground.

SEIA: A goddess of sown seed.

SENTONA: A goddess worshipped at Tarsatica.

SEQUANA: A Celtic goddess of water and healing and a personification of the Seine River at its source northwest of Dijon.

SILVANUS: A god of uncultivated land, pastures and woods. He was sometimes identified with the Greek god Silenus or with satyrs, but was more often identified with the Greek god Pan. Silvanus was sometimes identified with Mars, and in Gallia Narbonensis he was equated with the Celtic hammer god. In Britain he was identified with various local deities, such as Cocidius in the Hadrian's Wall area, where he was probably a hunting god. He was linked with Nodens at Lydney, and at Colchester he was worshipped as Silvanus Callirius; Callirius was a local forest god whose name means King of the Woodland or God of the Hazel Wood.

SIRONA: A Celtic goddess of healing, fertility and regeneration, often associated with medicinal springs.

She was frequently worshipped as the consort of Apollo (usually Apollo Grannus), and this divine couple was particularly venerated in the territory of the Treveri. Sirona was worshipped over a much wider area, from western France to Hungary.

SMERTRIUS: A Celtic god of abundance. The name Smertrius appears to mean the provider. He was sometimes linked with Mars and worshipped as a partner in the divine couple Mars Smertrius and Ancamna.

SOL INVICTUS: The unconquered sun. He was a Syrian god, established as a supreme deity by Aurelian in the late 3rd century. It has been suggested that the cult of the sun influenced the east-west orientation of burials, so that the dead arose to face the rising sun on the day of resurrection. It is more certain that the sun's birthday (25 December: the midwinter solstice in the Julian calendar) could not be suppressed by Christianity, and so the festival was made out to be the birthday of Christ instead. There were festivals of Sol on 28 August and of Sol Indiges (possibly meaning native sun) on 9 August.

SORANUS: A Sabine sun god often identified with Apollo.

SPES: This deity was the personification of hope, with a festival on 1 August.

SPINIENSIS: The deity who presided over the digging out of thorn bushes.

STERCULINUS: A god of manure-spreading.

STRENIA: A goddess of health and vigor. At Rome she had a grove from which twigs were brought and exchanged as presents at New Year. These twigs, called *strenae*, were thought to bring good luck.

SUBRUNCINATOR: A deity of weeding.

SUCELLUS: A Celtic hammer god. Sucellus (the good striker) is usually portrayed as a mature bearded male with the identifying symbol of a long-handled hammer. He often occurs with a consort called Nantosuelta (winding river), who often carries a model of a house on a long pole. They are often accompanied by other symbols, such as barrels, pots, dogs and ravens, from which it is assumed that Sucellus and his consort were associated with beneficence, domesticity and prosperity. The hammer may denote a connection with thunder, rain and fertility.

SULEVIAE: A triad of Celtic mother goddesses worshiped in Gaul, Britain, Hungary and Rome. They were sometimes called Matres Suleviae or Suleviae Iunones. The Suleviae were concerned with fertility, healing and regeneration as well as maternity, and their cult was widespread. The Sulae Nantugiacae are known from Condado, Spain.

SULIS: The Celtic goddess of the medicinal thermal springs at Bath. Sulis was a healing goddess and was equated with Minerva, being worshipped as Sulis Minerva. The Suleviae were also worshipped at these springs.

SUMMANUS: A god closely associated with Jupiter, and possibly originally an aspect of that god and not a separate deity. Summanus appears to have been the god who wielded thunderbolts by night, as Jupiter wielded them by day. There was a festival of Summanus on 20 June.

TALASSIUS: God of marriage. He appears to have been invented to explain the ritual cry of *talassio* when the bride was escorted to the groom's house, the original meaning of which had been lost.

TANIT: A Phoenician goddess, also known as Astarte. She was a mother and fertility goddess, identified with Juno Caelestis.

TARANIS: Also called Tanarus and Taranus. He was a Celtic thunder god, mentioned by the poet Lucan. Altars to Taranis are known from Britain, Germany, France and former Yugoslavia. He was sometimes conflated with Jupiter and has therefore sometimes been identified with the Celtic sun-wheel god (who may also be conflated with Jupiter). However, there is no direct evidence that Taranis was regarded as a sun god, and it is likely that Jupiter, as omnipotent sky god, covered both functions of thunder and sun gods.

TARVOSTRIGARANUS: The bull with three cranes. The name is found inscribed on a sculptured panel from Paris depicting a bull and three cranes; a similar sculpture is known from Trier. In both cases other gods are represented and the stones form part of a religious dedication, but the significance of the Tarvostrigaranus is unclear.

TELLUS: An earth goddess associated with agricultural festivals such as the Paganalia in January and the Fordicidia in April. She was also known as Tellus Mater. There was a festival of Tellus on 13 December.

TELO: A Celtic goddess and personification of Toulon, being the goddess of the sacred spring around which the town developed. Dedications to Telo are also known from Périgueux, where on three occasions she is associated with a goddess called Stanna.

TEMPESTATES: Weather goddesses with a temple at Rome.

TERMINUS: The state god of boundary stones whose own boundary stone was in the temple of Jupiter Optimus Maximus on the Capitol. Each rural boundary stone had its own individual god, and these Termini were worshipped in an annual ritual (the Terminalia) on 23 February.

TETHYS: A goddess of the ocean and consort of Oceanus.

TEUTATES: A Celtic god mentioned by the poet Lucan. A number of dedications to Teutates are known from Britain and Gaul. He was normally equated with Mars and appears to have been a god of war and of the tribe. He is also sometimes linked with Apollo, and there is a dedication to Apollo Toutiorix at Wiesbaden. He was also called Toutatis.

TIBERINUS: The god of the Tiber River. There was a festival of Tiberinus on 8 December. See also GAIA.

TUTILINA: A goddess of harvested and stored grain.

UCUETIS: A Celtic god and consort of Bergusia. This divine couple was worshipped at Alesia, probably as deities of prosperity and deities of craftsmen.

VACUNA: An ancient Sabine goddess, whose function had already been forgotten by the time of Horace.

VAGDAVERCUSTIS: A goddess who is known from an inscription at Cologne. She was probably a Celto-Germanic mother goddess.

VALLONIA: A goddess of valleys.

VEDIOVIS: Also known as Vedius, Veiovis or Vendius. This god was closely connected with Jupiter but regarded by the Romans as "the opposite of Jupiter" (that is, harmful). He had festivals on 1 January, 7 March and 21 May. He is little known outside Rome.

VELLAUNUS: A Celtic god known from only two inscriptions. One at Caerwent, to Ocelus Vellaunus, was equated with Mars Lenus. One in southern Gaul identifies him with Mercury.

Fig. 7.9 *Reverse of a* denarius *of Plautilla showing the god Venus Victrix.* Courtesy of Somerset County Museums Service.

VENUS: Originally an Italian goddess, possibly presiding over the fertility of vegetable gardens, fruit and flowers. She was identified with the Greek goddess Aphrodite at an early date and acquired Aphrodite's mythology. She was the consort of Mars. In Roman legend Aeneas, one of the leaders in the Trojan war, was the son of Anchises (a Trojan prince) and of Venus (fig. 6.5). Venus Erycina had a temple on the Capitol at Rome, which was dedicated in 217 BC; the title Erycina is derived from the sanctuary on Mount Eryx in Sicily. Venus had another temple outside the Colline Gate at Rome. Venus Genetrix (the universal mother) had a festival on 26 September; Julius Caesar dedicated a temple to her in this aspect in the Forum Iulium in 46 BC (fig. 7.8). Venus Verticordia (the changer of hearts) had a festival called Veneralia on 1 April. Venus Cloacina was Venus the Purifier. There were festivals of Venus Victrix (Victorious Venus) (fig. 7.9) on 12 August and 9 October. Venus was also associated with the festival of Vinalia Priora in April.

VERMINUS: The god of protection of cattle against worms.

VERNOSTONUS: A Celtic god and personification of the alder tree, known from an inscription near Hadrian's Wall and linked with the war god Cocidius.

Fig. 7.8 *Temple of Venus Genetrix at Rome, dedicated by Julius Caesar in 46* BC.

VERTUMNUS: Sometimes called Vortumnus. He was the Roman god of orchards and fruit and also presided over the changes in the seasons. He was the husband of Pomona and had a festival on 13 August.

VERVACTOR: A deity associated with the first plowing of the fallow land.

VESTA: The goddess of the hearth fire. She was identified with Hestia, the Greek goddess of the hearth. In early Rome the family in each household would gather at the hearth once a day to perform a sacrifice to Vesta. There was a small circular temple of Vesta in the Forum at Rome, where the fire on her altar was kept constantly burning by the Vestal Virgins. This eternal flame represented the goddess, who was not portrayed by statues. Vesta had a festival on 9 June. On 14 May *argei* (bundles of rushes resembling men bound hand and foot) were carried from the 27 shrines of the *argei* in Rome, and after a procession of pontiffs, Vestal Virgins, magistrates and the priestess of Jupiter, the *argei* were thrown into the Tiber from the Bridge of Sublicius by the Vestal Virgins. The meaning of the ritual is unclear; it may have been to pacify the river god, or was possibly a substitute for human sacrifice said to have been carried out in times of acute famine.

VICA POTA An ancient Roman goddess identified with Victoria and later overshadowed by her. Vica Pota had a shrine at Rome, the anniversary of which was celebrated on 5 January.

VICTORIA: Goddess of victory. She had festivals on 17 July and 1 August and was worshipped during the games *(ludi Victoriae Caesaris)* in July and the games *(ludi Victoriae Sullanae)* in October.

VIRBIUS: A forest god, later identified with the Greek god Hippolytus. He was worshipped in association with Diana and Egeria in a grove at Aricia.

VIRTUS: The god of "virtue" in the sense of physical and moral excellence. There was a festival of Virtus on 17 July.

VISUCIUS: A Celtic god worshipped mainly in the frontier area of Gaul and Germany. He was usually equated with Mercury, but a divine couple of Mars Visucius and a goddess Visucia is known from Gaul.

VITIRIS: Also called Hvitiris, Vetus and Vitris. He was a Celtic god worshipped in northern Britain. His cult appears to have been exclusively male and was particularly popular among the lower ranks of the army in the 3rd century. Little is known about the character or function of the god. In an inscription at Netherby, he was invoked with another local god, Mogons, but he never seems to have been linked with classical deities.

VOLUTINA A goddess of the husks of corn when they are folded over the ears.

VOLTURNUS: The origin of this god is obscure. He may have been a water god or possibly a wind god. His cult seems to have dwindled by the late republic. His festival, the Volturnalia, was on 27 August.

VOSEGUS: The Celtic god of the Vosges Mountains. He was probably also a god of hunting and protector of the inhabitants of the Vosges forest.

VULCAN: Also known as Volcanus. He was an early Roman god of fire and perhaps also of the smithy. He was later identified with the Greek god Haephaestus. Vulcan was the father of Cacus, who in Roman myth was a fire-breathing monster that lived on a hill at Rome and was killed by Hercules. Cacus appears to have originated in Etruscan myth as a seer on the Palatine Hill. Vulcan had an important cult in Ostia, where he was the patron god. Vulcan Mulciber was the name of Vulcan with the aspect of "smelter of metals." Vulcan had festivals on 23 May and 23 August.

ZALMOXIS: An underworld deity worshipped in Romania and Bulgaria.

Spirits

The majority of Roman gods and *numina* were spirits of the local environment. Every place, object and process (even individual trees and rivers) could have its own spirit. Consequently there were almost limitless numbers of spirits, and most were nameless. In practice, a Roman would not worship all these deities, but only those closely associated with his or her own home and occupation. For example, propitiation of a local river spirit would be necessary to ensure a good water supply and guard against flooding or drowning.

GENII

A *genius* (pl. *genii*), meaning literally "begetter" was a man's guardian spirit that enabled him to beget children. The household worshiped the genius of the house on the birthday of the *paterfamilias*, in whom it was thought to reside. Its symbol was the house snake, and it was often identified with the *lar*. The idea was extended, so that groups of people and even places had their own *genius*, such as that of the Roman people and of the city of Rome. In women, the corresponding guardian spirit was called Iuno (Juno).

GENIUS LOCI

A *genius loci* was the spirit of the place. This was a formula used in dedications when the suppliant was uncertain of the name of the god for whom the sacrifice was meant.

LARES

Lares (sing. *lar*) were spirits whose original character is unclear. Each household had its own protective spirit. It was the role of the *paterfamilias* to ensure the continued protection of the *lar* and to maintain a *lararium* (shrine to the household gods), usually in a corner of the atrium. It is possible that the *lares* were originally farmland gods, later introduced into households as *lares familiares*. By the late republic they were guardian spirits of the house and household and were worshiped at the household hearth on the Kalends, Nones and Ides of each month. As in the domestic situation, the Romans came to recognize the *lares compitales* who protected a neighborhood and the *lares publici* or *lares praestites* who protected the whole city. At Rome the *lares praestites* had a temple at the head of the Via Sacra. The *lares compitales* were worshiped at the Compitalia, which was an agricultural festival. There was also a festival of the *lares* on 22 December.

DI PENATES

The *di penates (penates)* were regarded as protectors of the household, along with the *lares*. They were the spirits of the pantry, and their images were to be found in the atrium of houses. A portion of every family meal was set aside and thrown on the flames of the hearth fire for the *penates* and *lares*, and there was always a salt cellar and a small offering of first fruits for them on the table. Any notable event of family life usually involved a prayer to the *penates* and *lares*. There was a festival of the *penates* on 14 October. The state counterparts of the family *penates* were the *penates publici*, whose cult was attached to the temple of Vesta.

MANES

The Manes were the spirits of the dead, worshiped collectively as *di manes* (the divine dead) at the festivals of Feralia, Parentalia and Lemuria. They were later identified with the *di parentes* (the dead of the family), and the concept grew that each dead person had an individual spirit called a *manes* (a plural noun used as a singular noun). Similarly, graves were once dedicated to the dead collectively (*dis manibus sacrum*, sacred to the divine dead), but later on in the empire it became customary to name individuals in such dedications, meaning sacred to the divine spirit of (the named individual). Memories of the individual personalities of the dead were kept alive in the busts (*imagines*) of ancestors in houses. For the Romans, the seat of life was in the head rather than the heart, so ancestral busts had more than just decorative significance. With better-quality statues and busts, it is difficult to know if they were purely works of art or had a religious significance.

LEMURES

The *lemures*, also known as *larvae*, were spirits of dead household members believed to haunt the household on 9, 11 and 13 May, the festival days of the Lemuria. They were regarded as ghosts or hostile spirits in contrast to the spirits of dead members of the immediate family worshiped in the Parentalia.

THE FATES

The Fates (in Latin, *fata* or *parcae*) were assimilated from Greek myths and represented rather abstract powers of destiny. The Parcae were called Nona, Decima and Morta, meaning nine-month birth (premature by the Roman method of calculation), ten-month birth (normal by the Roman method of calculation), and stillbirth. The Parcae may originally have been birth-goddesses who became equated with the attributes of the Greek Fates. The triplism of these deities sometimes appears to have encouraged their fusion with the triads of Celtic mother goddesses, who are sometimes portrayed with spindle, distaff and scroll—symbols usually associated with the Fates. At Carlisle a triad of mother goddesses is actually called Parcae.

THE FURIES

The Furies (*furiae* or *dirae*) were the Roman equivalent of the Greek Erinyes or Eumenides. These were female spirits appointed to carry out the vengeance of the gods upon men and women, punishing the guilty on earth as well as in the underworld. According to most ancient authorities there were three furies, Tisiphone, Megara and Alecto, although Adrasta and Nemesis were sometimes regarded as furies.

NYMPHS

Nymphs were female personifications of natural objects such as springs, rivers, trees and mountains. These spirits were derived from Greek myth, where they were regarded as rather vague beings that were young and beautiful, fond of music and dancing and long-lived rather than immortal. The cult of nymphs was widespread through the Hellenistic world, and under the empire it extended to all the provinces, but the distinction between a nymph and a goddess is often vague. Coventina, for example, was sometimes portrayed as a nymph, as were other goddesses associated with water.

Myths

Many myths and legends about the gods had origins in Greek mythology. Myths are traditional stories that were often based on historical or supposedly historical events and people, and provided the Greeks with their entire early history. Many were a mixture of fact and fiction, and most featured stories about the Greek gods. The myths used by Roman poets were largely borrowed from Greek sources. Most early Roman gods were not anthropomorphic in nature until they became identified with Greek gods, so there is unlikely to have been much scope to invent myths

around Roman gods. There is very little surviving evidence for Roman and Italian myths before the Romans adopted many of the Greek myths.

RELIGIOUS OBSERVANCE

The Romans communicated with their gods largely through prayers, vows, sacrifice and divination.

Cultus and Pietas

Roman religion was one of *cultus* rather than *pietas*. The gods were "cultivated" by their worshippers in that rituals were strictly observed to make the gods favorably disposed, irrespective of the ethics and morals of the worshippers. It was thought that the gods required acknowledgment and propitiation of their power because they were largely spirits of natural forces, not because they were deliberately spiteful or particularly sympathetic. The worship of these gods was therefore designed to keep the natural forces benevolent, and rituals were performed to maintain peace and harmony with the gods (*pax deorum*).

A cult was the worship of a god, goddess or hero with rites and ceremonies. Some heroes, such as Hercules, were worshipped as gods by the Romans and were often identified with other gods in the Roman pantheon. Religious belief for the Romans was largely a matter of observing a cult or cults by performing rites and ceremonies correctly, rather than by committed belief, moral behavior or spirituality. Usually the most important part of cult ceremonies was an offering to the god by sacrifice, libation or dedication, accompanied by prayers on the theme "as I give to you, so you give to me." Over time, such rituals became static and formalized, to the point where the slightest error would invalidate a ritual, which would then have to be started again.

The idea of *pietas* was a sense of duty concerned with moral issues and the maintenance of good relations with family, friends, ancestors, institutions and fellow citizens as well as with the gods. This is a much wider meaning than in the modern derivative word piety. The concept of *pietas*, like other abstract concepts, was personalized and deified, and there was a festival of Pietas on 1 December.

Prayers

Prayers took the form of "I am doing this for you (or I am giving this to you), please do this for me." An example of such a prayer is recorded by Cato in *De Agri Cultura*.

> Whether you are god or goddess to whom this grove is dedicated, as it is your right to receive a sacrifice of a pig for the thinning of this sacred grove, and to this intent, I or one at my bidding do it, may it be rightly done. To this end, in offering this pig to you I humbly beg that you will be gracious and merciful to me, to my house and household, and to my children. Will you deign to receive this pig which I offer you to this end?

The basis of this prayer is the propitiation of the deity of the wood before the farmer cuts down some of the trees. The legal tone, which exemplifies the Roman attitude to the gods, can be summarized as: "With the sacrifice of this pig I am buying the god's permission to cut down some trees." As with other elements of ritual, the wording of prayers tried to cover all eventualities.

Vows

Vows took the form of "If you will do this for me, I will then do this for you (or give this to you.)" In a prayer, the god received a gift whether or not the prayer was answered, but with a vow, the god received a gift only if the suppliant's wish was granted. Public vows on behalf of the state were also made, promising the gods special sacrifices in return for some favor—often protection from some imminent disaster. These vows were recorded in writing, and the records were kept by the pontiffs. Similar private vows could be recorded on votive tablets deposited in temples. Curses were at times a form of vow. Fulfillment of a vow usually took the form of a votive offering, which might be the setting up of an altar or the deposition of a gift at a shrine or temple.

Sacrifice

A sacrifice was a gift to the gods, heroes and the dead. Both public and private sacrifice was practiced, and sacrifices were offered in different ways. For example, a food offering might be shared between gods and people in a sacrificial feast, or the food might be given entirely to the gods by burning it all. There were various types of offering, such as cakes, wine, incense, oil and honey as well as blood sacrifices, which involved the slaughter of various animals. There is very little evidence for human sacrifice, but it appears that after the battle of Cannae in 216 BC, two Greeks and two Gauls were buried alive in the Forum Boarium at Rome.

Sacrificial offerings can be divided into six broad categories, according to the motives for the offering, although there is some overlap between the categories. These are offerings made in fulfillment of a vow, thank offerings, offerings made in the expectation of favors, sacrifices made at the instigation of the gods, sacrifices as a result of divination and anniversary dedications. The evidence for these categories is derived largely from inscriptions on altars, which were themselves set up as sacrifices.

The most common form of sacrifice was the fulfillment of a vow, where a person had promised a sacrifice if a god undertook a particular action. Once the god performed his part of the transaction, the person was bound by the vow. The initial vow was called the *nuncupatio* (pl. *nuncupationes*), and its fulfillment was the *solutio*. The vow to the god was often the erecting of an altar, and inscriptions are often found on altars with the formulae *ex voto* (in accordance with a vow) and *votum solvit laetus libens merito* (paid his vow joyfully, freely and deservedly), usually abbreviated to VSLLM. Inscriptions on many altars show that they were set up in thanks to a god for favors granted freely rather than in response to a suppliant's vow, while other altars were set up in anticipation of a favor. Many of the latter were *pro salute* (for the health of) a named person.

Some sacrifices were made at the instigation of the gods, who may have suggested the sacrifice in a dream or by some other sign. Other sacrifices were as a result of consulting oracles. Sacrifices were also made on anniversaries, such as the anniversary of the founding of Rome—traditionally 21 April.

The slaughter and consumption of an animal was the most popular form of sacrifice. The animal had to be appropriate to the particular god—male for gods, female for goddesses, without blemish and often of an appropriate color (such as black for gods of the underworld). The person requiring the sacrifice usually made arrangements with the custodian (*aedituus*) of the relevant temple and hired the services of *popae* and *victimarii* (the people who actually cut the throats of the sacrificial animals and dissected them afterward),

and often of a flute player (*tibicen*) as well. Sacrifices were accompanied by music (on a flute or lyre) to prevent any sounds of ill omen being heard, which would mean starting the sacrifice again. The priest kept his head covered with his toga at all times to guard against sights and sounds of ill omen (fig. 7.10).

The precise way an animal was killed for sacrifice was probably important. The head of the animal was usually sprinkled with wine and sacred cake (*mola salsa*) before it was killed. It was stunned with a pole-ax and then stabbed with a sacrificial knife. Its blood was caught in a bowl and poured over the altar, and the animal was skinned and cut up. The entrails were roasted on the altar fire, and the important participants ate them first. The bones and fat were burned on the altar fire for the gods with other offerings, such

Fig. 7.10   A sacrificial scene depicted on an altar in the temple of Vespasian, Pompeii. A priest with head covered performs libations on a tripod. Behind are two lictors and a flute player. In front of the bull is the victimarius *with a two-edged axe, and an assistant leads the bull to sacrifice.*

Fig. 7.11 A scene on Trajan's Column, Rome. A boar, ram and bull are being led round the camp in a ritual procession by the victimarii, *prior to the animals being sacrificed to Mars (the* suovetaurilia) *inside the camp to purify the army starting on campaign. They are accompanied by horn and trumpet players.*

as wine and cakes. The rest of the animal was cooked for a feast for those taking part. Blood sacrifices where all the sacrifice was given to the gods were usually performed at times of crisis (such as before a battle) as well as at purification ceremonies and at the burial of the dead. Blood sacrifices were also given to gods of the underworld and to heroes. A holocaust was a sacrifice that was completely burned. Some sacrifices were of animals considered by some as unfit for human consumption, such as the dogs sacrificed to Hecate. The combined sacrifice of a pig, sheep and ox, the principal agricultural animals, was made at certain agricultural festivals and on other occasions, such as at the conclusion of a military campaign or a census. It was known as the Suovetaurilia (fig. 7.11).

LIBATIONS

Libations were sacrifices of liquids offered to the gods by pouring them on the ground. The most common was undiluted wine, but other liquids were used such as milk, honey and even water. Libations were also offered to the dead during burials and at subsequent ceremonies at the tomb.

Devotio

Devotio, an attempt to gain the favor of the gods by means of the suppliant offering his own life as a sacrifice, was usually undertaken by desperate generals facing the loss of a battle. The general used a complex ritual to dedicate himself to "Tellus and the Manes" (gods of the underworld), on the understanding that his death in battle was the sacrifice and the gods must also take the enemy army. *Devotio* was also the name given to a form of magical curse or charm.

VER SACRUM

In times of great crisis the *ver sacrum* (sacred spring) was performed by dedicating everything born in the spring to a god, usually Jupiter. The animals were sacrificed, but the children were expelled from the country to found a new community when they reached the age of 20. This ceremony was revived at Rome in 217 BC, during the Second Punic War, but without the expulsion of children.

Lustratio

Lustratio (lustration) was a purification ceremony to provide protection from evil influences and bring good luck. It consisted of a solemn procession of a beneficial object, such as an animal for sacrifice, around whatever was to be purified, with prayers and sacrifices being offered at various points on the route.

Mundus

A *mundus* was a pit dug to provide access to the spirits of the underworld. The one in Rome seems to have been called the *mundus cereris*, linking the pit with the goddess Ceres. It was closed by a stone except on 24 August, 5 October and 8 November, which were considered days of ill omen.

Divination

It was thought that the gods revealed their will to people in the form of signs or omens. Some might be fairly obvious, such as thunder, lightning, unusual natural phenomena or a casual word or phrase overheard in passing but most signs were less obvious, and in any case needed proper interpretation. Divination was the art of reading such signs to predict the future. The Romans had many methods of divination, known today mainly from Cicero's writings. Divination was of two kinds, artificial or natural. Early Christians saw divination as the work of the devil, and the edict of Theodosius in 391, which banned pagan worship, formally ended this practice.

ARTIFICIAL DIVINATION

Artificial divination was based on external observations of animals, plants, objects or phenomena and the observation of the entrails of sacrificed animals. Div-

ination by dice or drawing lots was common, and random consultation of works of famous poets was used. (See Virgil, chapter 6.) Unusual weather conditions were always considered significant, and from the 4th century BC astrology became increasingly popular. Necromancy (calling up the spirits of the dead) was practiced but was not considered respectable.

Augury (*auspicium*) was the interpretation of divine messages by augurs in the flight or feeding patterns of birds (see *augures*), and so auguries were taken before any major event, such as a voyage or battle. *Extispicium* was the interpretation of signs in the entrails of sacrificial animals (particularly the liver), and this procedure was carried out by an *haruspex*.

NATURAL DIVINATION

The interpretation of dreams is an example of natural divination, a dream being interpreted by the dreamer or a professional interpreter. This interpretation was the basis of "incubation" whereby a sick person slept in a temple of a healing god (usually Aesculapius) so that the god could appear in a dream and suggest a cure. A patient first had to observe three days of ritual purity followed by various sacrifices, a gift of money and an offering of three cakes to "Success," "Recollection" and "Right Order." The patient usually slept in a chamber in the temple precinct, wearing a laurel wreath, and hoped for a vision of the god. A god was also sometimes approached in this way for other purposes, such as to help locate lost property. Another natural form of divination was prophecy from the speech of someone possessed and used as a mouthpiece by a divine power, the basis of oracles such as that at Delphi.

Oracles

Oracles were a form of divination. In the Greek world the most famous oracle was the oracular shrine of Apollo at Delphi, where a priestess (the Pythia) prophesied in a similar manner to the Sibyls. The Delphic Oracle continued to be consulted during the Roman period, but declined in the 1st century BC. Despite a brief revival in the 2nd century during Hadrian's reign it was virtually abandoned by the mid-4th century.

There were no oracular shrines in Italy to compare with those of Greece, and during the republic the Sibylline books appear to have been the only oracle consulted by the state. At Palestrina, oracles were given at the temple of Fortuna. They were inscribed on tablets called *sortes* (lots), which were shuffled by a child who chose one and gave it to whoever was consulting the oracle. As well as Apollo, several other gods were regarded as providing prophesies, including Faunus and Carmentis. Incubation was practiced at the temple of Faunus at Tivoli, where a sheep was killed and the person consulting the oracle slept in its skin.

The Sibylline books were a collection of oracles that were consulted when a crisis threatened Rome. The original collection was believed to have been bought from a prophetess called the Sibyl who came from the east and settled in a cave at Cumae. The books were kept in a chest in a stone vault under the temple of Capitoline Jupiter, but after the temple was destroyed by fire in 83 BC, a new collection of oracles was made from different copies which existed in many places. These new Sibylline books were transferred by Augustus to the temple of Apollo on the Palatine Hill. Fourteen miscellaneous books of oracles still survive, which are of Judaeo-Hellenic and Christian origin. Because of the Christian interpolations in the Sibylline oracles, the Sibyls were later considered equal to Old Testament prophets and appear in Christian art and literature.

Sibyl (*Sibylla*) was the name given to various prophetesses, who often had individual names as well. The Sibyl at Cumae was the most famous, but other Sibyls lived in different places at different times. They prophesied in an ecstatic state and were thought to be possessed by Apollo. Albunea was the Sibyl who had a cult at Tivoli, and her oracular verses were kept with the Sibylline books at Rome. Under the empire, with increased worship of Greek and Oriental gods, there was increased interest in oracles. Many books of oracles circulated, and Augustus seized and burned 2,000 books of prophecies in an attempt to calm a panic.

Astrology

Astrology spread from Babylon and Egypt to Italy in the 2nd century BC, and gained a strong hold. It was regarded as compatible with religion because if the stars foretold the future, the gods must have willed it. Astrology became very fashionable in the early empire, although it was singled out as a target by skeptics, unlike other forms of divination. Astrological signs were often incorporated into charms and amulets. From the 1st century virtually everyone (including Christians and Jews) accepted the predictability of fate and the influence of the planets. Rome was particularly sensitive to the political implications, and at times of national crisis professional astrologers often were banished. However, such bans were only temporary, and the emperors had frequent recourse to astrology. It was not until Augustine's denunciation of astrology in the 4th century, and the rule of Christian emperors, that astrology was officially prohibited, although its practice continued nevertheless.

FESTIVALS

Feriae (or *dies ferialis*) were holidays or festivals for visiting temples and making sacrifices to gods. The same term was used for public festivals and for private occasions, such as celebrating a birthday. Festivals were days when the Romans renewed their relationships with particular gods, usually involving additional rituals to what was normally practiced. Failure either to celebrate a festival or to celebrate it absolutely correctly would cause the gods to cease being benevolent. There were, therefore, important public ceremonies conducted by state officials as well as private prayers and sacrifices. The public rites took place in the temple of the god being honored by the festival. Prayers, rituals and sacrifices were conducted by the priests outside the temple. Citizens might attend the ceremonies, but only as observers and not as participants.

There were many festivals during the year, but not all were public festivals recognized by the state and celebrated by state priests. On public holidays work and business (legal and political) were stopped to avoid polluting the sacred day. Some work was permitted (decided by the pontiff), but it is likely that much work went on regardless, and only the pious visited temples, while others took a holiday. Roman citizens were legally required to observe the rules about working but were not obliged to perform acts of worship. The large number of festivals obviously reduced the number of working days in the year, but only the Jews (who did not observe the festivals) had a regular "rest day" by observing the sabbath; others did not have a "weekend" so the number of working days lost through observance of festivals was not great.

Although festivals always had a religious aspect, no rigid distinction was made between religious and secular activities, and festivals were often occasions of merrymaking. Public festivals were originally literally "feast days" when the local aristocracy paid for a meal for their poorer fellow citizens. The public festivals (*feriae publicae*) fell into three groups: *feriae stativae* were annual festivals on fixed dates, *feriae conceptivae* were festivals whose dates were set annually by magistrates or priests and *feriae imperativae* were irregular holidays proclaimed by consuls, praetors or dictators for such purposes as celebrating a victory.

The games (*ludi*) had a religious element, having originated as votive games in honor of Jupiter Optimus Maximus, which before c. 220 BC were the only annual games. Other annual games were established later. The games were not strictly *feriae* but were regarded as festivals.

It is not clear how many festivals were celebrated outside Italy or outside Rome itself. With some gods, such as Vediovis, there is very little evidence for their worship outside Rome, and none outside Italy, so that celebration of their festivals was probably geographically limited. It is likely, though, that major festivals, such as the Saturnalia, were celebrated in many parts of the empire. With the rise of Christianity, many festivals were converted to the Christian calendar. For example, Caristia (22 February) was converted to the Feast of St. Peter and Lupercalia (15 February) was converted to the Feast of the Purification of the Virgin Mary. Perhaps the most significant of such conversions was that of the birthday of the sun god Sol (25 December) to the birthday of Christ.

List of Festivals

In Rome at least, some gods and goddesses had several festival days during the year. The main festivals are described below, with the most important marked by an asterisk (*). Games (*ludi*) formed part of some of the festivals. Bacchanalia was the festival of the largely Greek rites (*orgia*) of the god Dionysus (also known as Bacchus): little is known about these rites, but it seems likely that the festival was celebrated at different times in different places, and possibly with differing rites, until it was banned in 186 BC.

JANUARY

1 January: Dedicated to Janus. This marked the beginning of the new year, and small gifts were exchanged, especially lamps to light the way through the forthcoming year. Also the festivals of Aesculapius and of Vediovis.

3–5 January: The Compitalia* was a movable festival held between 17 December and 5 January (usually around 3 to 5 January). It was celebrated at Rome on a day announced by the city praetor. It was the festival of the *lares* of the crossroads, held to mark the end of the agricultural year. Shrines were erected at crossroads where three or four farms met. The shrine would be open in all four directions to allow passage for the *lar* of each farm. A plow was hung up at the shrine, a wooden doll for every free person in the household and a woolen ball for every slave.

5 January: The birthday of the shrine of Vica Pota at Rome.

9 January: The Agonalia* was held on 9 January, 17 March, 21 May and 11 December. On each occasion the *rex sacrorum* sacrificed a ram, probably an offering to Janus.

11 and 15 January: The Carmentalia* was celebrated to honor Carmentis. Juturnalia, festival of Juturna, was on 11 January.

24–26 January: The Sementivae* (or Paganalia) was a movable festival that was probably held around this time. It is not clear whether this was one or two festivals, particularly as it was held on two days with an interval of seven days. It appears to have been a festival of spring sowing or for protection of seed sown the previous autumn, or both. Offerings were made to Tellus on the first day and to Ceres on the second day.

27 January: Festival of Castor and Pollux.

FEBRUARY

Amburbium was a movable festival that appears to have been held sometime in February to purify the city of Rome. It seems to have involved a procession around the city, accompanied by prayers and sacrifices.

1 February: Festival of Juno Sospita.

5–17 February: Festival of Concordia. The Fornacalia* must have started around 5 February. It was a festival held at Rome on a day appointed by the leaders of the wards (*curiae*) and ended on 17 February. It appears to have been celebrated to benefit the *fornaces* (ovens used for parching grain).

13 February: Festival of Faunus held in Rome. A more popular festival was held in the countryside on 5 December. Parentalia* was the festival of the dead at Rome, from 13 to 21 February. The last day was for public ceremony, but the preceding days were for private commemoration of the dead. During this festival temples were closed, marriages forbidden and magistrates did not wear their insignia of office.

15 February: Lupercalia* involved purification and fertility rites. It was originally a shepherd festival in honor of Lupercus, a pastoral god, to ensure fertility of fields and flocks. The festival was ancient, and the Romans themselves were uncertain which god was being worshipped. Lupercus seems to have been invented in the Augustan period to account for the rituals. Ancient authors cited Inuus or Faunus (both identified with Pan) as the god of Lupercalia. Worshippers gathered at a cave called the Lupercal on the Palatine Hill, where Romulus and Remus were supposed to have been suckled by a wolf. At this cave priests called *luperci* sacrificed goats and a dog. Two youths of noble family were smeared with sacrificial blood, and the *luperci* clothed themselves with parts of the skin of the sacrificed goats. With strips of skin from the goats, they ran with some of the magistrates through Rome's streets, striking everyone they met with the strips to make them fertile. The festival involved much revelry and was very popular. Consequently the early Christian church could not abolish

it, and so in 494 Pope Gelasius I made 15 February the Festival of the Purification of the Virgin Mary.

17 February: Quirinalia,* the festival of Quirinus.

21 February: The Feralia* was the public festival of the dead, held on the last day of the Parentalia, when food was carried to tombs for use by the dead.

22 February: The festival of Caristia* or Cara Cognatio (Dear Relation). It was a day to renew family ties and patch up quarrels. There was a family meal and offerings to the family *lares*.

23 February: Terminalia* was an annual ritual to worship Terminus (god of boundary stones). Rituals (including a sacrifice and feast) were held at selected boundary stones by the owners of converging fields.

24 February: Regifugium* was regarded in the late republic as something of an independence day, celebrated as an anniversary of the expulsion of the last king and the beginning of the republic. The origin of this festival is likely to have been quite different, becoming confused with the expulsion of the king at a later date.

27 February: Equirria* was a festival of horse-racing in honor of Mars. It was held in the Campus Martius at Rome or, if that was flooded, on the Caelian Hill. A similar festival was held on 14 March.

MARCH

1 March: A festival of Mars* continuing to at least 24 March and possibly to the end of the month. The festival appears to have celebrated Mars both as a war god and an agricultural god. The celebrations included processions with ritual dances by the *salii*, who carried the sacred shields of Mars in procession. The Matronalia (festival of Juno Lucina) was held on 1 March (the old New Year's Day). Prayers were offered to Juno and her son Mars, husbands gave their wives presents and female slaves were feasted by their mistresses.

7 March: Festival of Vediovis.

9 March: The sacred shields of Mars were again carried in procession by the *salii*. (See 1 March.)

14 March: Equirria,* a horse-racing festival, was held at Rome in honor of Mars. (*See also* 27 February.) A festival of Mamuralia is also recorded for 14 March, but it is unclear if this was a separate festival for Mamurius Veturius, legendary maker of the sacred shields, or another name for the Equirria.

15 March: Festival of Anna Perenna. This goddess seems to have been a personification of the year, and both public and private sacrifices were made to her at what was effectively a New Year's Day festival. Also the festival of Jupiter.

16–17 March: Procession of the *argei*. (*See also* 14 May.)

17 March: The Liberalia,* the festival of Liber Pater and his consort Libera. It was celebrated with sacrifices, crude songs and masks hung on trees. Also the Agonalia.* (See 9 January.)

19 March: This day was called *Quinquatrus* because it was the fifth day after the Ides of March. It came to be regarded as the start of a five-day festival and holiday (the Greater Quinquatrus*) in honor of Mars. (*See also* 13 June.) Also the festival of Minerva.

23 March: Tubilustrium* was the last day of the Greater Quinquatrus (festival of Mars) when the *tubae* (sacred trumpets — originally war trumpets, but later used for ceremonial occasions) were purified. (See also 23 May.)

31 March: Festival of Luna.

APRIL

Feriae Latinae was a movable festival to honor Jupiter Latiaris in his role as god of the Latin League. This was a joint festival of Romans and Latins on the Alban Mount, usually held at the end of April on days set by the magistrates. The festival dates from the time when Alba Longa, not Rome, was the chief city of Latium, but the festival survived into the 3rd century. A white heifer was sacrificed and eaten in a communal meal by representatives from all the cities in the Latin League.

1 April: Veneralia, the festival of Venus Verticordia. The goddess Fortuna Virilis apparently was also worshipped as part of this festival.

4–10 April: The Megalesia* (Megalensia or Megalesiaca) was a festival with games at Rome in honor of Cybele. The games included theatrical performances and spectacles in the Circus Maximus (*ludi Megalenses*).

5 April: Festival of Fortuna Publica.

12–19 April: The Cerialia,* the festival in honor of Ceres, with games in the Circus Maximus on the final day (*ludi Cereales*). One of the cult rituals was to let foxes loose in the Circus Maximus with burning brands tied to their tails.

13 April: Festivals of Jupiter Victor and Jupiter Libertas.

15 April: Fordicidia* was a festival at Rome, at which a pregnant cow was sacrificed to Tellus in each of the 30 wards of the city to promote fertility of cattle and the fields. The unborn calves were burned and the ashes were used in a purification rite in the festival of Parilia.

21 April: Parilia* (or Palilia), the festival of Pales. This seems to have been a ritual for the purification of sheep and shepherds and was connected with Rome's foundation. Sheep pens were cleaned and decorated with greenery, and the sheep were purified in smoke from a bonfire on which sulfur was burned. Milk and cakes were offered to Pales, and shepherds washed themselves in dew, drank milk and leaped through the bonfire. At this festival at Rome ashes from calves burned at the Fordicidia were sprinkled on the bonfire.

23 April: Vinalia Priora* was the first of two festivals held in Rome connected with wine production. (*See also* 19 August.) Wine casks filled in the previous autumn were opened, and the first draft was offered as a libation (called *calpar*) to Jupiter. Originally in honor of Jupiter, this festival was later also connected with Venus.

25 April: At the Robigalia,* a rust-colored dog was sacrificed to appease Robigus, the deity of mildew or grain rust.

28 April–3 May: Floralia, a festival of Flora, was a flower festival and a spring festival; if the crops blossomed well, the harvest would be good. Under the empire games continued for six days (*ludi Florales*).

MAY

1 May: Festival of the *lares praestites*.

9 May: The Lemuria* was held on 9, 11 and 13 May to appease the spirits of the household dead at a time when they were supposed to haunt the house. (The most terrifying of these spirits were those who had died young, since they were thought to bear a grudge.) Each householder rose at midnight and made the *mano fico* sign (the thumb between the middle of the closed fingers — a fertility charm) and walked barefoot through the house. As he went he spat out nine black beans or else, having first washed his hands, cast black beans over his shoulder. These were for the ghosts to eat as ransom for the living members of the household whom the ghosts would otherwise carry off. This was accompanied and followed by other rites designed to drive away the ghosts.

11 May: Possibly as part of Lemuria, sacrifices were made to Mania (mother of the *lares*). Mania seems to have been regarded as a goddess of death, and so a sacrifice to her during Lemuria was likely.

14 May: Festival of Mars Invictus. Also on 14 May Vestal Virgins, pontiffs, praetors and others threw 30 *argei* into the Tiber River. The meaning of these ancient ceremonies has been lost. (See also 16–17 March.)

15 May: Festivals of Jupiter and Mercury. A festival of Maia was also on 15 May, because she was confused with the Greek goddess Maia, mother of Hermes. He was equated with the Roman god Mercury, who was worshipped on 15 May.

21 May: The Agonalia.* (*See* 9 January.) Also the festival of Vediovis.

23 May: A Tubilustrium* festival, a repetition of the ceremony held on 23 March. Also the festival of Vulcan.

25 May: Festival of Fortuna.

29 May: The Ambarvalia* was a movable festival celebrated at the end of May (probably around 29 May). It was both a public and private festival involving rituals to purify the crops. It therefore involved worship of gods of agriculture, such as Ceres and Bacchus. Sacrificial animals (pigs, sheep and oxen) were led in procession around the old boundaries of Rome, and sacrifices were offered at particular locations.

JUNE

1 June: Festivals of Juno Moneta and Mars.

3 June: Festival of Bellona.

4 June: Festival of Hercules the Great Custodian.

5 June: Festival of Dius Fidius.

8 June: Festival of Mens.

9 June: Vestalia,* the festival of Vesta.

11 June: The Matralia* (festival of mothers) was held at Rome in honor of the goddess Mater Matuta. Also the festival of Fortuna Virgo.

13 June: Festival of Jupiter Invictus. The Lesser Quinquatrus also took place 13 to 15 June, and was a festival of the guild of flute-players, who played an important part in religious ceremonies. See also Greater Quinquatrus (19 March).

19 June: Festival of Minerva.

20 June: Festival of Summanus. The cult of this god seems to have dwindled by the late republic.

24 June: Festival of Fors Fortuna.

25 June: The Taurian Games* were held every five years in honor of the gods of the underworld (*di inferi*).

27 June: Festivals of *lares* and of Jupiter Stator.

JULY

1 July: Festival of Juno.

5 July: The Poplifugia* (Flight of the People) was an ancient festival whose meaning seems to have been lost at an early date.

6–13 July: Games in honor of Apollo* (*ludi Apollinares*). Originally they took place on 13 July, but they proved so popular that they were gradually extended backward until, by the late republic, they began on 6 July. Following the games, six days were set aside for markets or fairs.

7 July: Festival of the Pales. This day was also the Nonae Caprotinae (*nones* of the wild fig) on which the feast of the serving women was held. Juno Caprotina was worshipped at this festival, which commemorated an incident in which serving women were instrumental in removing a Latin army's threat to Rome.

13 July: See 6 July.

17 July: Festivals of Honos and Virtus and of Victoria.

19 July: Lucaria* was held on 19 and 21 July. This festival was celebrated in a large grove between the Via Salaria and the Tiber, but its meaning has been lost.

20 July: The *ludi Victoriae Caesaris** (Caesar's Victory Games) lasted from 20 to 30 July. The games were in honor of Julius Caesar and of Victoria, a goddess closely connected with Caesar.

22 July: Festival of Concordia.

23 July: Neptunalia,* festival of Neptune.

25 July: Furrinalia,* festival of the goddess Furrina.

30 July: Festival of Fortuna Huiusque.

AUGUST

1 August: Festivals of Spes and Victoria.

5 August: Festival of Salus.

9 August: Festival of Sol Indiges.

12 August: Festivals of Hercules Invictus and Venus Victrix.

13 August: Festivals of Diana, Vertumnus, Fortuna Equestris, Hercules Invictus, Castor and Pollux, the Camenae and Flora.

17 August: Portunalia,* the festival of Portunus. Also the festival of Janus.

19 August: Vinalia Rustica* was a festival to celebrate the start of the grape harvest, in which the first grapes were broken off the vine by the *flamen dialis*. See also Vinalia Priora on 23 April.

21 August: Consualia,* the festival of Consus. Another Consualia was on 15 December.

23 August: Volcanalia,* the festival of Vulcan. Celebrations in honor of Maia and Hora, both at times regarded as consorts of Vulcan, also took place on this day. Ops and the nymphs were also worshipped, but their connection with Vulcan is unclear.

24 August: Festival of Luna. Also on this day the cover was removed from the *mundus* (ritual pit). This allowed the spirits of the underworld to roam abroad, and so the day was holy and public business was forbidden. The cover was also removed on 5 October and 8 November.

25 August: Opiconsivia,* festival of Ops. Her other festival was on 19 December. See also 23 August.

27 August: Volturnalia,* the festival of Volturnus. Observance of his cult appears to have declined by the late republic.

28 August: Festival of Sol and Luna.

SEPTEMBER

1 September: Festivals of Jupiter the Thunderer, Jupiter Liber and Juno Regina.

5 September: Festival of Jupiter Stator.

5–19 September: Ludi Romani* (or *ludi magni*) were games held in honor of Jupiter Optimus Maximus.

Originally taking place only on 13 September, they gradually expanded to cover half the month.

13 September: Festivals of Jupiter Optimus Maximus, Juno and Minerva.

23 September: Festival of Apollo.

26 September: Festival of Venus Genetrix.

OCTOBER

1 October: Festivals of Fides and Juno Sororia.

4 October: A fast in honor of Ceres. Fast days were very rare; most religious celebrations were feasts. Originally this fast day had been ordered by the Senate to take place every five years as prescribed by the Sibylline books, but by the Augustan period it was an annual event.

5 October: The cover was removed from the *mundus*. (See 24 August.)

7 October: Festivals of Jupiter Fulgur and Juno Curitis.

9 October: Festivals of the Genius Publicus, Fausta Felicitas and Venus Victrix.

10 October: Festival of Juno Moneta.

11 October: Festival of Meditrinalia.* It was concerned in some way with the new wine vintage and had some connection with Jupiter.

13 October: Fontinalia,* festival of the god Fons. In honor of this god of springs, garlands were thrown into springs and placed around the tops of wells.

14 October: Festival of the Penates.

15 October: Festival of Jupiter. The Capitoline Games in honor of Jupiter also took place on this day.

19 October: Armilustrium,* the festival of purification of arms, was held in honor of Mars. The *salii* danced in procession, and then the armor and the

sacred shields were purified and put away until the next year.

26 October–1 November: The *ludi Victoriae Sullanae** (Sulla's Victory Games) in honor of the goddess Victoria.

NOVEMBER

1 November: See above.

*4–17 November: Ludi plebeii** (Plebeian Games) in honor of Jupiter.

8 November: The cover was removed from the *mundus*. (See 24 August.)

13 November: Festival of Jupiter. A feast of Jupiter on this day provided a central point in the Plebeian Games. Also festivals of Feronia and Fortuna Primigenia.

DECEMBER

1 December: Festivals of Neptune and Pietas.

3 December: Festival of Bona Dea,* a celebration that fell between the categories of public and private worship. It was attended by the Vestal Virgins but was not celebrated in the temple of Bona Dea, but in the house of a consul or praetor with only women present.

5 December: Festival of Faunus, an ancient festival held in the countryside rather than the city.

8 December: Festival of Tiberinus. A deity called Gaia appears to have been worshipped in connection with Tiberinus at this festival.

11 December: The Agonalia.* (See 9 January.) Also Septimontia, apparently a festival conducted by the people of the seven hills of Rome in honor of the hills.

12 December: Festival of Consus.

13 December: Festival of Tellus.

15 December: Consualia,* the second major festival of Consus. See also 21 August.

17–23 December: Saturnalia* was originally celebrated on 17 December, but by the late republic the festival extended from 17 to 23 December. It was a winter solstice festival to honor Saturn as the god of seed sowing. This festival was replaced by Christmas, and many of the festivities and customs of the Saturnalia (such as it being a time of enjoyment, cheerfulness and goodwill, lighting of candles and the giving of gifts) were absorbed into the Christian festival. The festival began with a sacrifice at the temple of Saturn, followed by a public feast open to everyone. All business ceased, there was a general holiday and on this one occasion in the year people were allowed to play gambling games in public. Everyone wore holiday clothes and the soft cap (*pilleus*), slaves were let off their duties and might even be served by their masters, and each household chose a mock king to preside over the festivities.

18 December: Festival of Epona.

19 December: Opalia,* the second major festival of Ops. (See 25 August.) There may have been a festival of Juventas on this day.

21 December: Divalia Angeronae,* a festival in honor of Diva Angerona.

22 December: Festival of the *lares*.

23 December: Larentalia,* the festival of Acca Larentia. This consisted of funeral rites at the supposed tomb of Acca Larentia.

25 December: This day took on significance only after the rise of the cult of Sol Invictus in the 3rd century, since in the Julian calendar 25 December was the midwinter solstice. This "birthday of the sun" was later converted to a Christian festival.

DRUIDISM

Relatively little is known about the Druidic religion because the basic doctrines were kept secret. Much of what is known comes from the observations of ancient Roman authors such as Julius Caesar. Celtic society was controlled by an elite class that had three sections: Druids, Vates and Bards. According to Caesar, Druidic power originated in Britain, which remained the center of Druidism. The cult appears to have been centered around a belief that after death the soul passed to another body, human or animal. Not only did this lead to the Celts being fearless in battle, but it also sanctioned the human sacrifices that seem to have been part of some Druidic rituals. Criminals, captives in battle and innocent people were at times sacrificed for various purposes, such as propitiation of the gods after disasters or thanksgiving for victories, but mainly for purposes of divination.

Druids were more than priests, since they controlled the warriors and, through them, the rest of the people. They did not have a monopoly of religious power—the Vates and the Bards also had religious functions. The Druids appear to have dominated the ruling class and to have been a unifying element between tribes, presiding over religious assemblies involving more than one tribe. The Druids were educated and knowledgeable in astronomy and astrology, and divination was undoubtedly part of their duties. They were also thought to have powers over the elements and the ability to cast spells. Both Augustus and Tiberius published edicts against them, and Claudius proscribed Druidism in Gaul in 54. In 60 there was a concerted effort to break the power of the priesthood in Britain. The Druids were persecuted allegedly because the Romans objected to human sacrifice. However, as a unifying force between independent tribes for Celtic resistance, the Druids were also a political threat. It is difficult to assess what effect the suppression of the Druids and of human sacrifice had on Celtic religion. The ample evidence for worship of Celtic gods after the suppression implies that it was the priesthood rather than the religion that the Romans wished to eradicate. However, in the 4th century Ausonius alludes to Druids in Aquitaine, so it is doubtful whether their suppression was ever complete.

ORIENTAL RELIGIONS

By the late republic religious cults from the east had gained a popular following in Rome and Italy, mainly because they made a direct appeal to the individual, in contrast to other cults. Many were considered Mystery Religions, so called because their teachings were supposed to illuminate the mystery of achieving immortality—teachings that were themselves kept as a mystery and to which the faithful were initiated. As the empire grew, Oriental cults also grew in strength, but most Romans did not renounce state religion when initiated into such a religion and saw no conflict in this behavior. The insistence by Christians and Jews that converts must renounce all other religions was mainly responsible for conflict with the state in the later Roman period. Because Christians and Jews would not sacrifice to the cult of the emperor, they were accused of disloyalty.

Eleusinian Mysteries

The Eleusinian mysteries, as this cult is generally known, originated in pre-Roman Greece. It claimed to guarantee initiates a happy afterlife. The cult was celebrated each year at Athens in September and October at the time of sowing, when every participant bathed in the sea for purification and sacrificed a piglet. There was an initiation ceremony in the Eleusinion, a temple below the Acropolis at Athens. In the *telesterion* (initiation hall) a priest showed the sacred objects to the initiated. Then the sacred and secret objects, which had been brought from Eleusis to Athens a few days previously, were taken from the Eleusinion back to Eleusis accompanied by a great procession of initiates. The ritual was supposed to represent the myth of Demeter and Persephone and the symbolic death and rebirth of agricultural seed corn. On the following day the initiates fasted (as Demeter fasted when mourning the loss of Persephone). They broke their fast with a special drink of barley water flavored with pennyroyal (called *kykeon*). At a certain place on the procession route, obscenities were shouted as a reenactment of the abusive joking of a woman in Greek myth called Iambe who was supposed to have made Demeter smile. The shout of *Iakch' o Iakche* was raised regularly during the procession, and was usually regarded as referring to Iacchus, who was sometimes identified with Dionysus. The cult appears to have existed for more than 1,000 years until it was suppressed by Theodosius in 393.

Bacchic Mysteries

The Bacchic mysteries (*orgia*) were the rites of worship of Bacchus (the Greek god Dionysus). These rites do not appear to have been associated with specific cult sites, but were performed wherever there was a group of worshippers. Adherents to this cult were mainly women and were called Bacchants (also Bacchantes, Bacchanals or Maenads). Surrender to Bacchic frenzy in order to achieve a sense of freedom and well-being appears to have been at the heart of these mysteries (fig. 7.12), although there were also promises about an afterlife. Livy describes wild excesses and criminal acts performed by devotees of the cult. The Bacchants were supposed to roam mountains with music and dancing, performing supernatural feats of strength such as uprooting trees and catching and tearing apart wild animals, sometimes eating the flesh raw. They were often depicted wearing the skins of fawns or panthers with wreaths of ivy, oak or fir and carrying a *thyrsus* (wand wreathed in ivy and vine leaves and topped with a pinecone). This aspect of the religion symbolized the triumph of unfettered nature over man-made order.

The Senate banned the Bacchanalia from Rome and Italy with a decree in 186 BC. However, the cult revived despite being strictly controlled, and in the 2nd century there was a group of worshippers at Frascati nearly 500 strong; presumably other such groups existed as well. On sarcophagi dating to the 2nd and 3rd centuries are representations of scenes from Bacchic myth, portraying Bacchus as lord of life and thus demonstrating the hope of resurrection.

Cybele

Cybele was also known as Agdistis, Magna Mater (great mother), Kybele or Kybebe. The center of her cult was on Mount Dindymus at Pessinus in Phrygia, where she was known as Agdistis. She was considered to be the mother of all living things—an earth mother goddess and a goddess of fertility and of wild nature, the latter being symbolized by her attendant lions. She was also said to cause and to cure disease. Her cult was deliberately brought to Rome in 204 BC after a prophecy in the Sibylline books and advice from Delphi. However, the Romans regarded some of her rites as excessive, so the cult was restricted and Roman

Fig. 7.12   A Bacchanalian scene depicted on a coffin, with dancing and music.

citizens were forbidden to serve as priests. Restrictions were lifted by Claudius, and worship of Cybele and her consort Attis (or Atys) became part of the state religion and an important mystery religion. Phrygian myth states that Attis was the son of Nana, daughter of the river god Sangarius (a river in Asia Minor). Nana conceived him after gathering the blossom of an almond tree that had risen from the severed male organs of Agdistis (Cybele), who was born both male and female and had been castrated by the gods. Cybele loved Attis, and when he wished to marry, she was jealous and drove him mad, so that he castrated himself and died beneath a pine tree.

The rites of Cybele and Attis included the *taurobolium*, self-flagellation and castration of the priests, and ecstatic dances. In the *taurobolium* the worshipper stood in a pit, while a bull was sacrificed on a slatted floor overhead, bathing him in its blood. A similar ceremony was the *criobolium* where a ram was used instead of a bull. The *galli* were the eunuch priests of Cybele, thought to take their name from the Gallus River in Galatia near the original temple of Cybele. They were thought to castrate themselves in imitation of Attis. This was done on 24 March (*dies sanguinis*), apparently with the most primitive of instruments, such as of flint. Castration clamps for staunching the

flow of blood are known to have been used in gelding animals, and an example from the Thames River at London, decorated with busts of Cybele, may have had a ritual use. The Corybantes were priests associated mainly with the cult of Cybele, although they were also associated with other gods who had orgiastic cults. They followed Cybele with wild dances and music, and are often confused with the Curetes, who were attendants of the goddess Rhea. Guilds of *dendrophori* (tree bearers) were associated with the worship of Attis and also acted as burial societies, possibly because in myth Attis was buried and resurrected. The main festival of Cybele, the Megalesia, was on 4 to 10 April. As part of the Cybele cult, a festival of mourning was followed by a joyous ceremony (*hilaria*) to celebrate the rebirth of Attis and the start of the new year. Shrines for the worship of Cybele were called *metroons*.

Orphism

From about the 6th century BC, there are indications of mystery cults associated with Orpheus, but it is doubtful whether there was ever a unified cult that could be called Orphism. According to legend, Orpheus was a pre-Homeric Greek poet and a marvelous lyre player who tried and failed to recover Eurydice from the underworld and was later torn to pieces. There are several versions and variations of the legend, which was often used as a theme by poets and Roman mosaicists. The Derveni papyrus, an ancient book of the late 4th century BC found in Greece, gives a commentary on an Orphic religious poem. It indicates that good and evil in human nature were explained by the myth of Dionysus Zagreus (which involved death and resurrection and punishment of the wicked). Men were regarded as bearing the guilt of the death of Dionysus Zagreus and had to pay a penalty to Persephone after death before rising to a higher existence. This Greek myth was different in having as its central doctrine the punishment of individuals after death. The Orphic cult also recognized reincarnation. After three virtuous lives, as defined by Orphic doctrine, individuals were supposed to dwell in the Isles of the Blest forever. The high ethical tone and ascetic practices of some adherents of Orpheus in Greece became debased and ridiculed. The cult appears to have waned, but there was a revival of belief during the empire.

Mithraism

Mithras was an ancient Indo-Iranian god of truth and light. His cult reached Rome in the second half of the 1st century BC and was regarded as a mystery religion. It was confined exclusively to men and appealed particularly to merchants and soldiers. Mithraism was an offshoot of Zoroastrianism, which recognized Ahura Mazda as god and sole creator of the universe. The mythology of Mithraism is very complex, but essentially Mithras supported Ahura Mazda in a struggle against the evil Ahriman—the same struggle of good and light against evil and darkness that was central to Zoroastrianism. Mithras was sent to earth by Ahura Mazda to hunt and kill a divine bull, and from the bull's blood all living things sprang. This bull-slaying (tauroctony) was a central part of Mithraism and was depicted on stone reliefs in Mithraic temples (*mithraea*, sing. *mithraeum*). The cult had seven grades of initiation for worshippers and included a form of baptism and a ritual meal as well as bull-slaying. Mithras was often depicted with a bull, which he was

supposed to have captured and sacrificed in a cave, and the interior of his temples resembled caves. Mithras also appears to have been identified with the sun, and altars to *Sol Invictus* (unconquered sun), as well as to other gods, have been found in *mithraea*. Also found in *mithraea* are representations of a pair of figures in Persian dress—one (Cautes) holding an upright torch, and the other (Cautopates) with an inverted torch, representing light and darkness.

Isis

Isis was an Egyptian mother goddess, whose son Horus (called Harpocrates in the Roman world) is a heroic figure who avenged the death of his father Osiris (known to the Romans as Serapis or Sarapis—a conflation of Osiris and Apis). Osiris was killed and dismembered by the evil god Seth but was restored to life by Isis. Herodotus identified Isis with Demeter, but in the early Hellenistic period she was identified with Aphrodite. The worship of Isis reached Rome in the early 1st century BC and by the early 1st century AD was flourishing throughout the empire.

The triad of Isis, Harpocrates and Serapis represented the power of creation. Serapis was regarded as a god of the underworld, the sky and healing. Isis herself was a goddess of fertility and marriage, represented as loving and compassionate to individual suppliants. She was often portrayed as a loving mother, nursing her baby son Horus, an image that is often very similar to portrayals of the Virgin Mary. She is also commonly portrayed with a bucket for holy water (*situla*) and a rattle (*sistrum*, pl. *sistra*), which were objects used in her worship. The cult of Isis involved initiation, baptism and service, and promised eventual salvation. A shrine or temple to Isis was called an *iseum* (pl. *isea*).

JUDAISM

Judaism was an Oriental mystery religion. Of all the religions in the ancient world before Christianity,

Judaism was exclusive in allowing belief in and worship of only one god and only one acceptable way of worshipping that god. Worship of other gods was forbidden. To the Romans, it was this aspect of Jewish religion that made it appear at best intolerant and at worst impious and dangerous. This was not a serious problem for the Romans, since Judaea was a very small part of the empire, and Jews elsewhere generally maintained a low profile. Jews were legally entitled to follow their national religion because they were an ancient people and had been allies of Rome since the 2nd century BC. Pagan Roman tolerance of Jews (including Christians) persisted into the 1st century, despite growing nationalism on the part of the Jews, and hostility between Jews and Christians.

Jews regarded their god as the one and only creator of all things and the giver of natural and moral law. They also regarded the Jewish nation as the people especially chosen by god to receive his revelation and to play the central role in human salvation. Judaism was not exclusive to the Jewish nation, since non-Jews could convert to the religion, but there was no active missionary work to encourage such conversions. However, the dispersal of the Jews (Diaspora) throughout the empire, particularly after the second destruction of the temple in Jerusalem in 70, laid the foundations for the rise of Christianity: it was from small groups of Jews throughout the empire that Christianity initially spread, making use of the communications network that linked these groups.

CHRISTIANITY

Development

Romans first became aware of Christianity as a troublesome Jewish sect. Christianity initially spread rapidly to the scattered communities of Jews outside Palestine. It might have remained a religion of a Jewish splinter group had not Paul and subsequent missionaries deliberately spread the religion to non-Jews. In its early days, the end of the world was thought to be at hand and so little thought was given to organization or planning for the future. As the apocalypse did not arrive, attempts were made to organize and rationalize the religion. Early Christian groups were controlled by a single leader or by a council of elders, but this gave way to rule by an *episcopus* (bishop). The early church and its organization was at first financed by offerings (*oblationes*), but in time gifts, patronage by wealthy Christians and tax concessions made the church rich. The posts of bishops, who controlled this wealth, were greatly sought after and sometimes fought over. In 64 Nero found the Christians a convenient scapegoat for the fire in Rome, but the official attitude of tolerance toward Jews and Christians remained unchanged for two more centuries. By the end of the 2nd century, though, Christianity began to be regarded as a threat to the stability of the state.

In the second half of the 2nd century, a coherent Christian creed was being formulated, so that pagans could more easily understand it. In the 3rd century there is evidence that some pagans attempted to absorb the Christian god into their pantheon. Severus Alexander is supposed to have had statues of Orpheus, Abraham, Christ and Apollonius of Tyana in his private chapel, but the end of his reign marked the end of official tolerance of Christianity. Decius was the first emperor to try systematic extermination of the Christians, and several subsequent emperors attempted suppression. At this time, though, Christianity was becoming accepted in many communities, and by the late 3rd century public churches were beginning to take the place of house churches. Persecution of Christians ended in the west with the abdication of Diocletian in 305 and in the east in 311 when Galerius granted them religious tolerance. In 313 Constantine issued the Edict of Milan, which granted certain favors to Christians, and in 325 Christianity effectively became the religion of the Roman Empire after the Council of Nicaea. Julian attempted to restore paganism, but in 391 Theodosius I completed the process of making Christianity the state religion by banning all pagan cults (but not pagan beliefs) and removing their state subsidies.

Arianism

The Arian heresy (Arianism) was a heretical 4th-century Christian doctrine, named after its originator,

Arius, who denied the divinity of Christ. A compromise with orthodoxy was achieved in 359, after which Arianism declined sharply in popularity (except among the Goths), and orthodoxy was then reestablished at the Council of Constantinople in 391.

Donatism

Donatists were a schismatic party in the African Christian church. The split was caused by their refusal to accept as bishop of Carthage a man who had been consecrated by a Christian who had surrendered the scriptures when their possession became illegal during Diocletian's persecutions of 303 to 305. They elected their own bishop of Carthage, whose name was Donatus. The split persisted until the African church was destroyed by the Arabs in the 7th and 8th centuries.

Gnosticism

Gnosticism was a complex religious movement based on a myth of redemption. Possibly pre-Christian in origin, it came to prominence in the 2nd century in both Christian and pagan forms. It distinguished between a remote and unknowable divinity and a Demiurge—an inferior deity descended from this divinity. The Demiurge was the imperfect creator and ruler of the world (which was imperfect, having been made by an imperfect deity). However, some individuals were believed to possess a spark of the substance of the divinity and might hope to return to the divinity after death. A redeemer was sent by the divinity (perhaps Christ, or a redeemer still to come) who temporarily inhabited a human body and brought *gnosis* (knowledge).

Monasticism

By the late 4th century the organized church was very rich, and leading Christian thinkers such as Jerome and Martin of Tours began to question its values. This gave impetus to the monastic movement, which had been set in motion earlier in the 4th century. In Egypt,

Syria and Palestine, men began withdrawing into the desert, away from cities, often setting up small settlements that allowed both for solitude and communal life. Bishops were not slow to draw on the energies and talent within the monastic movement, and some monastic communities came to be set up within cities. In time the great monastic houses became the training ground for future bishops and eventually for the offspring of the aristocracy as well.

Miracles

In parallel with material power, the church needed to be able to demonstrate its spiritual authority. Nowhere was this better demonstrated than in the performing of miracles. Miracles were proof of sanctity, and the saints who performed them had the role of intercession between god and the people. This role was more effective if the saint was physically present, so that relics of saints became an important focus for local Christians. In the search for relics, many forgeries were accepted. Likewise in the search for saints, many pagan deities were absorbed into the church and "sanitized" as saints (such as St. Brigit, originally a deity of the Brigantes), in much the same way that pagan sites were often converted to Christian use.

Christian Objects

A few objects appear to have Christian associations, largely because they bear Christian symbols. The Christian symbol most commonly found is the chi-rho, which is the monogram of Christ made from the Greek letters chi and rho. A number of lead tanks with this symbol appear to be unique to Britain and may have been used as baptismal tanks. The symbol has also been found on more portable objects, such as silver spoons and bronze finger rings. The fish was also used as a symbol of Christianity. Finger rings of various metals are known with inscriptions that have a phrase such as "May you live in god." It is assumed that in most cases this is evidence of Christianity, and sometimes this is confirmed where such inscriptions are accompanied by the chi-rho or a fish symbol. Pewter and silver vessels with the chi-rho or fish symbol are known, and various other objects, such as stones, brick and tile fragments and a lead seal, have been found with the chi-rho on them. Of particular note are the fragmentary silver votive plaques with the chi-rho that were found with other Christian objects in a hoard from Water Newton, England. These votive plaques imply the use of pagan ritual in a Christian context.

Magic squares or word squares of letters and numbers were also used. The most well-known one is:

R	O	T	A	S
O	P	E	R	A
T	E	N	E	T
A	R	E	P	O
S	A	T	O	R

This has often been claimed as a Christian cryptogram, but there are very early examples of it. Two at Pompeii can be no later than AD 79, which implies that it predates Christianity, even if it was adopted by Christians later.

ATHEISM

Atheism was either a refusal to believe in any gods or the refusal to believe in the traditional pantheon of gods. Christians who refused to offer incense to the emperor were therefore accused of atheism. Generally atheism did not incur penalties unless it was so publicly proclaimed (as in the case of Christians and Jews) that it aroused fear. At times of crisis people became alarmed at signs of atheism that might offend the gods, with disastrous consequences, so that anyone branded an atheist was liable to be made a scapegoat.

MAGIC AND SUPERSTITION

Superstition is the irrational fear of the unknown allied to a false idea of the causes of events. Magic is the attempt to control such events by direct actions and rituals. Superstition and magic spring from the same origin as religion, in a belief in supernatural forces that control the lives of people. The dividing line between a religious ritual (asking for something to happen) and a magic ritual (directly attempting to make that thing happen) is often very fine, and the entire Roman religion was based on superstition and had a strong element of magic.

Superstitions and associated charms and rituals are often very ancient and extremely long lived, since many superstitions current today are attested in Roman literature, such as saying "good health" (nowadays "bless you" is more common) when someone sneezes. Magic was officially disapproved of, but it appears to have been widely used by private individuals, and there are descriptions of witches in Roman literature.

Necromancy, the summoning of the spirits of the dead for various purposes, was also practiced. Harmful magic was practiced privately and came to be repressed by Roman law, whereas nonharmful magic was often absorbed into or became indistinguishable from religious ritual. The practice of harmful magic was illegal and was suppressed not because of disbelief, but rather through fear of its possible consequences. Similarly, early leaders of the Christian church condemned magic as impious rather than as a delusion.

RELIGIOUS BUILDINGS

Temples

The Latin word *templum* originally denoted an area of sky designated by an augur as that in which he was taking auspices. It also meant a space on which to erect the shrine of a god or a space in which to conduct business. A building was only a *templum* if it had been consecrated by both pontiffs and augurs, because the augurs knew the will of the gods. Those buildings consecrated only by pontiffs were *sacrum* or *aedes*, because the consecration was only "by the will of

Fig. 7.13 Reverse of a denarius of Antoninus Pius celebrating the restoration of the classical temple of the deified Augustus and Livia. Courtesy of Somerset County Museums Service.

men" and not by the will of the gods. In most cases buildings that were recognized as temples of the state religion were referred to as *aedes*, but they were sited within a consecrated area called a *templum*. Only later was the name for the consecrated area extended to the building as well. This practice of erecting a sacred building in a consecrated area was later paralleled by the building of Christian churches within a consecrated area (the churchyard).

CLASSICAL TEMPLES (figs. 7.1, 7.2, 7.13, 7.14, 7.15, 7.16)

The earliest Roman temples were probably built of timber with a skin of decorative plaques and sculpture in terracotta. More substantial stone temples were constructed from the early republic. Early Roman temples were based on Etruscan examples (themselves based on Greek temples). They had a room (*cella*) containing a statue of the god and possibly a small altar for incense, fronted by columns and raised on a high platform (*podium*) with steps only at the front. On the facade above the columns there was normally an inscription naming the deity of the temple and

perhaps the name of the person who paid for its construction. These inscriptions were frequently made with bronze letters. There was an altar for sacrifice outside the temple, usually placed directly in front of the steps.

Temples were designed to house a statue of the deity and store offerings and did not provide accommodation for a congregation of worshippers.

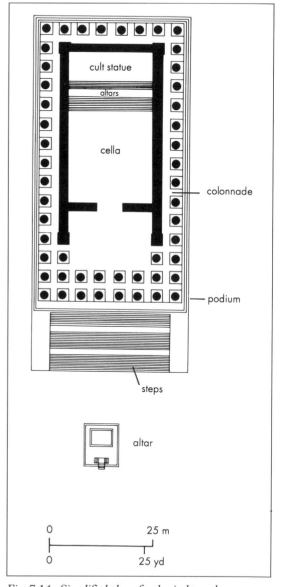

Fig. 7.14 Simplified plan of a classical temple.

Fig. 7.15   *The Pantheon at Rome, built by Hadrian around AD 125. The main inscription records Agrippa as the builder, because the temple replaced one originally built by him in 27 BC.*

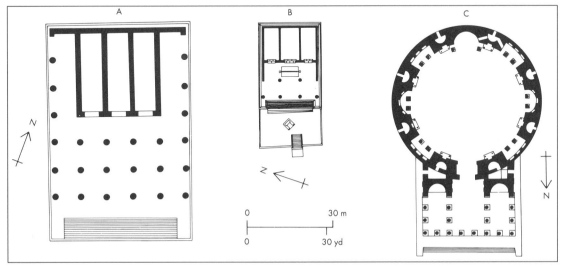

Fig. 7.16   *Plans of temples with varying orientations. A. Capitolium at Rome (5th century BC); B. Capitolium at Cosa (2nd century BC); C. Pantheon at Rome (2nd century AD).*

Later Roman temples (in the last two centuries of the republic) imitated late Greek temples, but mainly used the Corinthian order of architecture. Using arches, vaults and domes, they also developed styles of their own, such as the circular temple of Vesta. The Pantheon at Rome was a magnificent temple built by Hadrian to replace the one in the Campus Martius built by M. Agrippa. It was consecrated to all the gods and was built as a rotunda with a pedimented portico in the Corinthian style (fig. 7.15, 7.16). The interior was richly decorated in marble, with niches for statues of the gods. It was dedicated as a Christian church in 609, and the walls and bronze doors still survive.

Many of the major temples in Rome were paid for by the spoils of war, built by successful generals to mark their achievements. Others were paid for out of public funds, on authority of the Senate during the republic or later by order of the emperor. Augustus, probably the most prolific temple-building emperor, is recorded in the *Res Gestae* as having restored 82 temples in 28 BC and built 12 temples (including rebuilding some existing temples). In towns outside Rome temples appear to have been paid for out of public funds or by leading citizens. There appear to have been no fixed rules for the orientation of Roman temples, whose axes often seem to have been determined by the constraints of town planning (fig. 7.16). Although varying a great deal in plan and details of design, temples recognizable as of classical type are known throughout the empire.

ROMANO-CELTIC TEMPLES (figs. 7.17, 7.18)

Other groups of distinctive forms of temple had a more limited distribution. The Romano-Celtic temple was widespread in Gaul, Germany and Britain, although other examples have been found as far east as Budapest. This type of temple had a square, rectangular, polygonal or circular plan (rectangular was most common), with a small central chamber (cella) surrounded by a passage or gallery (ambulatory). Sometimes annexes were attached to one side of the ambulatory. Of polygonal temples, the eight-sided plan was by far the most common, and in some cases a circular cella was surrounded by a polygonal ambulatory. As in other Roman temples, the cella contained a statue and/or cult objects of the god. Except where a temple conformed to a town plan by facing onto a street, these temples faced east or southeast, and many were raised above ground level and were approached by a flight of steps. Since in most cases the only evidence for Romano-Celtic temples comes from their surviving foundations, it is often uncertain what form the building originally took. It appears that ambulatories with solid walls, with pillars supported on stub walls or with only columns supporting the roof were all variations of the same basic type of building. Generally the central cella was roofed, although in a few cases there is evidence that it may have been open to the sky.

In some cases Romano-Celtic temples were preceded by Iron Age timber-built temples or shrines of

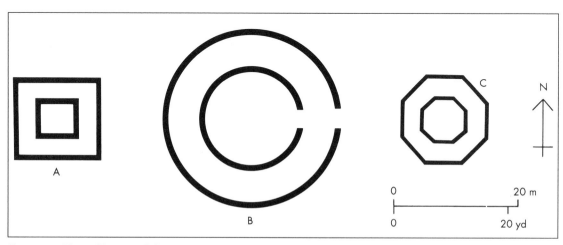

Fig. 7.17 *Plans of Romano-Celtic temples. A. square; B. circular; C. polygonal.*

Fig. 7.18 *Reconstruction of a square Romano-Celtic temple at Schwarzenacker, Germany.*

circular or rectangular plan, and in some instances such buildings continued in use into the Roman period.

NORTH AFRICAN TEMPLES

There is also evidence for rectangular, circular and polygonal temples or shrines, built of both timber and masonry, that do not conform to the Romano-Celtic plan. One type is found in north Africa and has a limited distribution. Its distinguishing feature is a row of three small chambers occupying most, or all, of one side of an enclosure or courtyard. Although often built in classical Roman style, they lack the high podium and impressive facade. They are probably a combination of Roman and Punic traditions of temple architecture, and good examples of this type occur at Thugga.

MITHRAEA (fig. 7.19)

The temples of Mithras (*mithraea*) were small, designed in imitation of caves. Some were partially or

wholly built underground. *Mithraea* were different from most other temples in that the worshippers of Mithras conducted their worship mainly inside rather than outside the temple. The focus of the temple interior was a marble relief or sometimes a painting, portraying as its main theme Mithras slaying the bull. This might be flanked by other sculptured scenes or

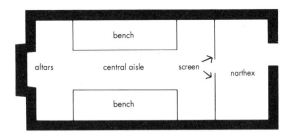

Fig. 7.19 *Stylized plan of a* mithraeum.

statues and by altars. There is evidence that at least some of these sculptures were pierced so that illumination from behind could shine through. In the main body of the temple the central aisle was flanked by raised benches on which the initiates reclined at ritual meals. At the end opposite the reliefs and altars was a narthex or porch, and there was sometimes a pit used for initiation ceremonies.

SYNAGOGUES

For dispersed Jewish communities that were far from the temple at Jerusalem, assembly houses for prayer and worship developed into synagogues. Such houses of prayer date back to at least the 3rd century BC in Egypt, and it appears that a deliberate attempt was made to avoid copying the temples of pagan deities. The fundamental difference between pagan temples and early synagogues was that the temples were regarded as the home of gods, with worshippers remaining outside, whereas synagogues were for prayer, worship, study, education and debate. With this difference in function, synagogues were modeled on Greek and Roman assembly halls, with smaller halls for other functions such as legal business. As a result, no distinctive architecture or layout distinguishes early synagogues. Many, if not most, dispersed Jewish communities had a synagogue by the 1st century AD, and the number of synagogues increased as Jewish communities became more widespread through the empire. Thirteen synagogues are known to have existed in Rome, and even before the destruction of the second temple in 70, there were many synagogues in Jerusalem itself.

Churches

During the early centuries of Christianity there seems to have been no move toward constructing special buildings (churches) for worship. Groups of Christians met for communal worship at convenient places, such as in houses, outdoors or in hiding during times of persecution. Even with the development of organized Christianity in the 4th century, there is little evidence for intentionally built churches, probably because of lack of funds to commission such buildings. The first churches probably used existing buildings, such as houses, partly or wholly converted for use by worshippers. As Christianity became more influential and wealthier, churches were constructed. Inevitably their design was rooted in the traditions of Roman architecture, and the basilica with aisles flanking a nave and an apse at one end greatly influenced the architecture of early churches.

Shrines

As well as temples, there were probably a great many shrines dedicated to local deities, particularly in rural areas. These were often simple and relatively insubstantial places of worship, probably consisting of little more than an altar. Therefore relatively few have survived in recognizable form. Some sites, such as some of the smaller Romano-Celtic temples, may have been shrines rather than temples. The term shrine is sometimes used to distinguish those places of worship without a building, although it has also been used as a general term covering a broader range of cult sites.

RELIGIOUS AND RITUAL ARTIFACTS

There are several groups of artifacts connected with ritual and religious use, including implements and vessels used in rituals, votive gifts to the gods, materials used for curses and charms and amulets. Some overlap exists between these groups. For instance, an altar may be a votive gift as well as being used in rituals. In the absence of definite proof, many artifacts are conveniently assumed to have a religious or ritual connection through lack of a better interpretation.

Cult Images

Cult images were representations of gods and goddesses and formed the center of a cult site such as a temple (where the cult image occupied the cella). The images were either statues or reliefs, usually of stone or bronze. Usually it is impossible to be certain that a surviving statue or fragment was originally a cult image, particularly as many were deliberately destroyed in the early Christian period.

Object Used in Rituals

ALTARS

Altars (*arae*, sing. *ara*) were used as sacrificial tables and were indispensable in the cult of most gods. (The exception was underworld gods, to whom offerings were made in pits.) Since nearly every religious act was accompanied by a sacrifice, altars were a focus of worship that predated the use of temples. When temples were built, the altar usually stood outside, opposite the main door (figs. 7.2, 7.14). Altars were of various shapes and sizes and were commonly a rectangular stone block bearing the name of the god to whom the altar was dedicated and the name of the person responsible for setting it up (figs. 2.3, 7.6). Sometimes altars were set on platforms approached by steps, and more sophisticated forms were elaborately carved, often with a hollow (*focus*) in the upper surface where a small fire could be lit to consume small sacrificial offerings. Private houses often had small altars, or else the hearth served as an altar. Small public altars served for bloodless sacrifices and for the burning of incense. Altars also served as a refuge for supplicants, who then came under the protection of that particular god.

The *Ara Maxima* (Greatest Altar) is the name of the altar of Hercules that stood in the Forum Boarium at Rome. Tithes of booty and commercial profit were offered at this altar, the site of which was connected with the legend of Hercules and Cacus. The *Ara Pacis* (Altar of Peace) was situated in the Campus Martius at Rome (fig. 3.2), and was built by order of the Senate in honor of Augustus' safe return from Gaul in 13 BC. It is of marble and measures 10.5 m by 11.6 m by 7 m (34 ft 5 in. by 38 ft by 23 ft), with numerous carvings on both interior and exterior walls.

RITUAL VESSELS

Flagons and shallow bowls called *paterae* (sing. *patera*) were commonly used in sacrifices, for liquids for ritual washing and for pouring libations. These vessels were made in a range of materials, including silver and pewter as well as bronze and pottery. Occasionally they bore inscriptions dedicating them to a particular god.

Silver and bronze strainers were also associated with religious use, mainly for removing impurities from wine, although some strainers could have been used to infuse wine with herbs or drugs. Knives, spoons and platters would have been used in ceremonial feasting and have been found on temple sites, sometimes with dedicatory inscriptions to particular gods.

VOWS AND VOTIVE OFFERINGS

Vows could be made on votive tablets and placed at temples; many have been found, such as at the temple of Mercury at Uley, England, where they were mostly inscribed on metal, mainly lead, and were largely of the type known as curse tablets. Votive tablets on tin, bronze and pewter are also known.

Votive offerings were often made after the fulfillment of a vow. Gifts to the gods could range in size from temples and monumental arches to small coins and could also range widely in value. They could be made of almost any material; many of the more perishable items will not have survived. For example, few wooden statuettes are known, but it is likely that these were relatively common offerings. Often votive offerings were deliberately broken or damaged, metal objects bent and coins bent or defaced; it is thought that this was an attempt to "kill" the object as a sacrifice, just as animals sacrificed to the gods were killed. Votive offerings were sold in shops at the more important temples and shrines, and in some cases such objects were not made locally. For example, pottery figurines were exported from Gaul and the Rhineland to Britain. Items commonly for sale included stone reliefs, bronze figurines, votive plaques, votive leaves or feathers, bronze letters and model implements.

Stone reliefs depicting gods and goddesses sometimes had a space prepared for the addition of an inscription. Small bronze figurines of gods and goddesses were also used as votive gifts and as cult figures in domestic shrines. Votive plaques were made of silver and bronze, with repoussé representations of gods and dedicatory inscriptions. Plaques with triangular handles (*ansae*) on each side had dedicatory inscriptions that appear to have been produced to order using a punch. Votive leaves or feathers were triangular sheets of bronze, silver or gold, decorated with a herringbone pattern of repoussé work. They often had a small hole at the base by which they could be nailed down or suspended by a thread. Some also have representations of gods and/or inscriptions, and a few have been found with the Christian chi-rho symbols flanked by the Greek letters alpha and omega. Bronze letters with nail holes are thought to have been used to make up inscriptions, possibly on wooden plaques. Some gilded letters have been found.

Miniature models of tools and weapons were also used as votive offerings. Miniature axes are commonly found on temple sites and may represent implements of sacrifice. Also frequently found are small enameled stands designed to stack one on top of another, the purpose of which is unclear. Model *caducei* (sing. *caduceus*) in bronze, iron and silver are known to have been offered to Mercury, and miniature weapons such as spears were used as votive offerings. A model ballista was found at the temple of Sulis Minerva, Bath.

Many votive offerings were made of pottery, including miniature pots, lamps and lamp covers, figurines and incense burners. Rings and brooches of bronze, silver and gold were commonly used as votive offerings, as were gifts of coins and precious metal. There are also records of valuable antiques being given to shrines and temples. In all these cases, the symbolic act of giving an offering to the gods was enhanced by the fact that the worshipper was giving up a real part of his wealth.

A particular class of votive offerings was medicinal in nature and consisted of models of parts of the human body. Someone with an ailment would deposit a model of the afflicted anatomical part in a shrine or temple of a god of healing. The person hoped to be healed by dedicating the afflicted part to the god. This was a common medical practice in the Roman world, and models of every part of the anatomy are known.

Ceremonial Equipment

Often priests wore the toga when officiating at ceremonies, but there is evidence for a variety of regalia, which was presumably worn on special occasions, such as festivals and processions. The variety of regalia probably reflects the requirements of different gods as well as local traditions. Crowns and diadems in various styles are known, often richly ornamented with real or glass paste gems and with decorative silver plaques. Another form of headdress consisted of medallions linked by chains.

Musical Instruments (fig. 7.11)

Music played a part in most religious ceremonies, often to drown out sounds of ill omen. Double pipes (*tibiae*) were used at most sacrifices. Tambourines and cymbals seem to have been used mainly in orgiastic cults, such as those of Cybele and Bacchus (fig. 7.12). Rattles were probably widely used, and a special kind of rattle (*sistrum*) was used in the cult of Isis. Singing of hymns may also have been widely practiced.

Processional Objects

Various items, such as standards and scepters, were usually carried in religious processions. Elaborate standards portraying gods accompanied by animals and other attributes are known, but more simple maces or scepters were more common. These were often surmounted with the bust or head of a god, or in some cases an emperor, and were made of wood, iron and bronze. Other sacred objects, such as the sacrificial implements, ceremonial plate used for lustrations, and incense burners, were also carried. Garlands and bouquets of flowers and the burning of incense were used to present the god with sweet smells and pleasing sights. In religious ceremonies carried out by the army, legionary standards and banners were also carried in processions.

Charms, Amulets and Curses

Various charms and amulets were used as protection against evil and to bring good luck, and the division

Fig. 7.20   Phallic symbol on the exterior wall of a house at Pompeii.

between superstition and religion in the Romans' attitude to charms and amulets is often unclear. Many such objects may have been on sale at shrines and temples. Rings and pendants were common forms of amulet, with inscriptions or magical symbols cut on them or occasionally cut on the semiprecious stones set into the ring. Phallic charms were also common, usually in the form of a pendant, although they occur on rings. There are examples of phalli being carved on buildings (fig. 7.20), paving stones and even stones in well linings in order to provide protection for that particular structure. The *fascinum*, a representation of the phallus, was used to protect children against witchcraft. The image of the Gorgon's head (the face that turned all who looked on it to stone) was regarded as having the power of attracting and holding evil

powers and thus diverting them from other targets. Consequently, the face or mask of the Gorgon was used as amulets and on buildings, tombstones and coffins. Representations of the club of Hercules were also used as amulets. The dividing line between images of gods used for religious or for superstitious reasons is very thin, and many gems with representations of deities may well have been amulets. Gems with representations of combined heads (several human, or human and animal heads fused together) also seem to have been used as amulets. Other amulets have a fusion of two or more protective symbols, such as a combination of a phallus and a human head, or a phallus and a hand making the *mano fico* gesture.

The division between vows and curses is similarly difficult to distinguish. Strictly speaking, curses involve magic powers that are summoned by a sorcerer, but the term is often used to cover requests to the gods to punish enemies and wrongdoers. *Devotio* was the name given to a form of magical curse or charm. The wax image of a person whose death or love was desired was treated in a way thought to bring about the desired outcome. For example, the image was melted to make the person melt with love, or pierced with nails to make the victim feel pain or even die. *Devotio* was also the name used for a form of sacrifice.

Curses were normally inscribed on curse tablets (*defixiones;* sing. *defixio*—nailing down). These were normally thin sheets of lead that could be inscribed with the person's name and even the desired course of action. Since the gods of the underworld were usually called on to undertake the desired course of action, the lead sheets were often rolled up and hidden, usually by burying them, placing them in tombs or at shrines or throwing them down wells. They often had nail holes for affixing to a tree or post. Similar tablets were used to attempt, for example, to recover lost or stolen property, affect the outcome of chariot races or bring back departed lovers. When a tablet was used to call on a god to perform such an action, the dividing line between magic and a religious vow becomes almost imperceptible. The phrasing on some curse tablets strongly suggests that they were written by professional scribes, and it is possible that such scribes may have offered their services at temples and shrines, writing curses, vows and dedications as required. Phrasing on other tablets suggests they were copied from other texts, with meaningful phrases being combined in a clumsy, semiliterate way.

READING

Several books deal with many aspects of Roman religion, including Henig 1984, Howatson (ed.) 1989 and Shelton 1988.

State Religion
Ferguson 1987: emperor worship; Howatson (ed.) 1989: priesthoods; Ogilvie 1969; Scullard 1981: contains a section on priests; Shelton 1988: priesthoods; Warde Fowler 1922: priesthoods.

Gods and Goddesses
Ferguson 1970; Grant 1971: mythology; Green 1976 and 1986: Celtic gods and goddesses; Green 1987; Green 1992: Celtic gods and goddesses, with an extensive bibliography; Hammond and Scullard (eds.) 1970 passim; Henig 1984: gods and goddesses, particularly in Roman Britain; Henig and King (eds.) 1986; Scullard 1981: contains a section on Roman cults; Shelton 1988: gods and goddesses, importation of foreign gods; Warde Fowler 1922: spirits.

Religious Observance
Howatson (ed.) 1989: divination; Jackson 1988: religion and medicine; Ogilvie 1969: prayer, sacrifice and divination; Scullard 1981: contains a section on priests; Shelton 1988; divination; Woodward 1992: sacrifice, particularly in Britain.

Festivals
Ogilvie 1969; Salzman 1990: includes festivals in relation to the calendar; Scullard 1981; Shelton 1988; York 1986.

Druidism
Piggott 1968; Ross and Robins 1989.

Oriental Religions
Henig 1984: Oriental cults, particularly in Britain; Howatson (ed.) 1989; Hutchinson 1991: review article of cult of Bacchus; Vermaserem 1963: Mithraism.

Judaism
Grant 1973; Wigoder 1986.

Christianity
Harries 1987; Lane Fox 1986: transition from paganism to Christianity; Thomas 1981: Christianity in Britain with continental parallels; Watts 1991: Christianity in Britain; Woodward 1992: includes Christianity in Roman Britain.

Atheism
Howatson (ed.) 1989.

Magic and Superstition
Ferguson 1970: includes magic and astrology; Henig 1984: mainly Britain; Howatson (ed.) 1989; Merrifield 1987; Shelton 1988; Warde Fowler 1922: magic.

Religious Buildings
Barton 1989: temples; Drury 1980: nonclassical shrines and temples; Henig and King (eds.) 1986: temples; Sear 1982: temples; Wilson 1980: Romano-Celtic temples; Wigoder 1986: synagogues; Woodward 1992: shrines and temples in Britain.

Religious and Ritual Artifacts
Green 1976: religious objects; Howatson (ed.) 1989: altars; Merrifield 1987.

8

ECONOMY AND INDUSTRY

COINAGE

Names

Many coins are known by names that are of modern origin (albeit Latinized), as their original names are unknown. Names up to the end of the 2nd century are generally those used by the Romans, but not later ones. Many ancient sources continued to use traditional names, such as *denarii* and *sestertii*, but they cannot be related to actual coins.

Origin of Coins

Coins were first produced in the Greek cities of Asia Minor in the later 7th century BC and were made of electrum (a mixture of gold and silver) with punched designs. Coin production spread to other Greek cities in the Aegean and to Greek colonies in southern Italy by 500 BC. These coins came to be made of pure silver formed between obverse and reverse dies. Bronze coins were first minted in the Greek areas of southern Italy.

In much of Italy currency originally consisted of irregular lumps of bronze (*aes rude*), valued according to weight. From the late 4th century BC large cast rectangular bars of greater uniformity were made. From the beginning of the 3rd century BC they were roughly standard in weight, with simple decoration such as an elephant or cattle (*aes signatum*), and some with the name of Rome.

Republican Coins

Around 289 BC at Rome the *tresviri monetales* were appointed. About this time heavy bronze pieces (*aes grave*) up to 100 mm (4 in.) in diameter were produced, cast in two-part stone molds. They gradually superseded the bronze bars. Each one was known as an *as* or *aes* (pl. *asses*) and weighed one Roman pound (335.9 g, 0.74 lb). They were subdivided into lesser denominations and had a distinctive mark on each side and a value sign. Subdivisions were the *semis*

(half-*as*), *triens* (third), *quadrans* (quarter), *sextans* (sixth) and *uncia* (ounce or twelfth).

From the early 3rd century BC struck silver coins appeared, based on Greek coins but bearing the legend ROMANO. They were probably made initially by Greek craftsmen in southern Italy, then from 269 BC in Rome, according to Pliny. The first silver *denarii* were probably issued just before 211 BC, and silver rather than bronze became standard. The *denarius* remained the principal silver coin to the 3rd century AD.

From the late 3rd century BC the *as* was reduced in weight and size, probably due to financial pressures in the Punic Wars, and after c. 155 BC it was only 1/12 of its original value (the uncial-*as*). When the *as* was worth one-sixth of a Roman pound, one *denarius* was equivalent to ten *asses*. There was also a half-*denarius* (*quinarius*) equivalent to five bronze *asses* and a quarter-*denarius* (*sestertius*) equivalent to 2½ *asses*. Even large sums of money were commonly expressed in *sestertii* (sesterces).

Around 100 BC the relationship between silver and bronze coinage was adjusted, so that one *denarius* was equivalent to 16 rather than 10 bronze *asses*, with the *as* being worth one-twelfth of its original weight. The value on the *denarius* changed from X, then to XVI, then X. The *as* went out of use in the early 1st century BC and was revived only by Augustus.

Gold coins (staters) were issued from the time of the Second Punic War, in three denominations, and Sulla, Pompey and Julius Caesar struck *aurei* of various weights. Silver *denarii* from the 2nd and 1st centuries BC continued in circulation into the 1st century AD. Silver *denarii* of Mark Antony struck in the east were so debased that they were not hoarded, and some continued in use to the 3rd century AD. These late republican gold and silver coins contained the features recognizable in imperial coinage and were struck in the provinces on behalf of the generals to pay their armies.

Early Imperial Coinage

The coinage system established by Augustus in 24 BC was based on four metals—gold, silver, brass (*orichalcum*—a new alloy containing about 80 percent copper and 20 percent zinc) and bronze or copper (*aes*), designed for all levels of use. Gold and silver were for official use (such as salaries), and base metals were small change for everyday use. Until the late 3rd century a variety of local currency was used as small change throughout the empire, especially in the east.

Table 8.1   Coins In Use From the 1st to the 3rd Centuries

Coin name	Metal	Number = 1 aureus
aureus	gold	1
denarius	silver	25
sestertius	brass	100
dupondius	brass	200
as	bronze	400
semis	brass	800
quadrans	bronze	1600

Gold and silver coins were minted in relation to their bullion weight. Under Augustus the *aureus* (or *denarius aureus*) was fixed at 40 to the Roman pound. It remained the standard gold coin of the early and middle empire, although from the mid-2nd century it became fairly scarce. Under Nero (54–68) its weight was reduced to 45 to the Roman pound. This remained its nominal weight until Caracalla (211–217), who reduced it to 50 to the Roman pound.

Under Augustus the silver *denarius* (or *denarius argenteus*) was fixed at 84 to the Roman pound (fig. 1.1). Nero retained the standard of 25 *denarii* to the *aureus*, but its weight was reduced to 96 to the Roman pound with additions of at least 10 percent copper alloy. This debasement continued under subsequent emperors. There were also occasional issues of the half-*aureus* or *aureus quinarius* (in gold) and the half-*denarius* or *denarius quinarius* (in silver).

The *sestertius* and *dupondius* were brass coins and the *as* and *quadrans* were of bronze. The brass *semis* and *quadrans* were rarely issued after the 60s. The coinage system remained unchanged for over 200 years, although some of the small bronze coins dropped out of use.

From the middle of Claudius' reign (41–54) through the first ten years of Nero's reign (54–68), there was a shortage of coinage in Britain and Gaul, which led to copies of the coins (known as Claudian copies) being minted, some very good and some very poor in quality. The resumption of official coinage by Nero in 64 alleviated the shortage.

Fig. 8.1 Obverse of a sestertius *of Trajan (dating to 103), bearing a realistic laureate portrait. The legend is longer than others up to this time.* Courtesy of Somerset County Museums Service.

In the 2nd century the *sestertius* dominated the coinage (fig. 8.1), although *asses* (figs. 1.9, 1.10, 7.3) and *dupondii* continued to play a large part in everyday transactions. By the middle of Marcus Aurelius' reign (161–180) the volume of bronze coinage fell very sharply. Even the *sestertius* became scarce in some provinces in the later 2nd and 3rd centuries, and in the later 3rd century it ceased altogether throughout the empire. In the mid-3rd century *dupondii* are difficult to distinguish from *asses*, except by the radiate crown of the *dupondii*.

Increased military expenditure led to continued debasement of the silver *denarius* (in weight and fineness), and at the same time it began to assume a dominant role in the coinage. By the time of Severus (193–211), the *denarius* contained only 40 to 50 percent silver, and it became virtually a bronze coin with only a small amount of silver. Some were silver-plated from this time and may have been forgeries. Bronze coins were in turn reduced in weight to match the metallic decline in the *denarius*.

Antoninianus

In 215 a new coin was introduced by Caracalla known now as the *antoninianus* ([coin of] Antoninus, i.e.,

Caracalla). It was larger than the *denarius* and differed from it by the treatment of the imperial image (radiate not laureate). Like the *denarius* it was also of debased silver. Although probably a double *denarius*, it contained 25 percent less silver than two *denarii*. It was not issued between 222 and 238 but was afterward struck in large numbers.

The 3rd century was generally a period of confusion for coinage. By 244 the *denarius* ceased to be issued regularly. The *antoninianus* was the only silver coin in circulation, although it too suffered rapid debasement affecting its weight and silver content. By 270 it had been reduced to a weight of about 2.5 to 3 g (0.088 to 0.1 oz) and contained less than 5 percent silver. *Antoniniani* changed to being copper coins with a silver coating, and the imperial silver currency collapsed.

Billon Coinage

Around 272 Aurelian attempted a currency reform. In place of the defunct *sestertius*, he issued a XXI billon (very debased silver) coinage as small change (a reformed *antoninianus*). Many of the new coins bore on the reverse a value mark of XXI (or in the east the Greek equivalent KA), possibly denoting that one radiate piece comprised 20 *sestertii*, although the interpretation of XXI is disputed. The coins were about the size of the *antoniniani* and had a radiate crown. They were made of copper washed in silver and contained about 5 percent silver.

Greek Imperial Coins

Some imperial coins were minted in the east, especially at Alexandria, and are known as Greek imperial issues, as they have Greek legends and designs. They tended to have simpler denominations. The *tetradrachm* (equivalent to a *denarius*) was a silver coin that became so debased that it resembled a copper coin by the time of its demise in Diocletian's currency reforms (294–295). Copper coins consisted of the *drachm* (equivalent to the *sestertius* in size and style), but they became rare by the mid-3rd century. Smaller denominations died out by the end of the 2nd century.

Gallic Empire

In the late 3rd century there were two main groups of coins—those struck by emperors whose power was centered on Rome and those struck by emperors whose power lay in Britain or Gaul (the Gallic Empire, 260–274). The latter emperors struck their own coins but followed Roman styles. Postumus tried to revive the old imperial system of the *sestertius* and its fractions, and large numbers of old *sestertii* were restruck as radiate double *sestertii*, but this measure failed.

Between c. 273 and c. 285 copies of earlier coins of the Gallic Empire were minted, particularly copies of *antoniniani* of Tetricus I and II. These radiate copies (barbarous radiates) were often of poor quality with a poor radiate crown (fig. 8.2), and their circulation probably ceased in 286 with the accession of Carausius. Some copies were tiny and bore little similarity to their prototype.

Argenteus and Follis

Around 294 to 295 Diocletian completed a thorough revision of the currency system so that there was a uniform system of coinage across the empire. The gold *aureus* was fixed at 60 to a Roman pound. A high-quality silver coinage, sometimes known as the

Fig. 8.2   Part of a hoard of barbarous radiates found near Glastonbury, Somerset, showing obverses and reverses. Courtesy of Somerset County Museums Service.

argenteus was reintroduced at 96 to the Roman pound (fig. 1.17) and based on the old *denarius*. Diocletian also reformed the bronze billon coinage—Aurelian's XXI radiate was phased out and was replaced by a new laureate issue weighing 10 g (0.35 oz), with about 3 percent silver content. This large coin, worth 20 *denarii*, is generally called a *follis* (figs. 7.5, 8.5). From 295 to c. 364 smaller copper coins existed with 1 to 2 percent silver.

After Diocletian's and Maximian's abdication in 305, the *follis* fell rapidly in weight and size to 3.5 g (0.123 oz) by 318. Smaller coinage ceased, and *argentei* were discontinued after 308. The value of gold rose, and the relationship among gold, silver and copper coins fluctuated daily. Political fragmentation led to the establishment of a number of conflicting coinage standards within the empire.

Solidus

In about 310 Constantine reduced the weight of the gold coinage from 60 to 72 to the Roman pound. This new gold coin, the *solidus*, became the standard high denomination of the Roman world and continued until the 11th century. The eastern mints continued to produce the heavier *aureus* until 324. There was also a half-*solidus* or *semis*. From 370 a third-*solidus*, *triens* or *tremis* (1/216th of a Roman pound) became important and formed the basis of the post-Roman coinage of 5th- and 6th-century Europe.

Centenionalis

Constantine's billon coinage initially followed the Diocletianic system, but c. 318 it diverged from the *follis* with the issue of even baser coins. This new coin weighed 3.0 g (0.1 oz), with the reverse type VICTORIAE LAETAE PRINC PERP (the joyful victories of our everlasting ruler). It appears to have been tariffed as a 12½ *denarius* piece and may have been called a *centenionalis* (since the base silver coin from which it had been developed had originally been tariffed at the rate of 100 to the *solidus*).

From 318 to 348, the *centenionalis* declined from 3.0 g to 1.7 g (0.1 oz to 0.06 oz), and so around 325 two new high-quality silver coins were introduced,

one at 96 to the Roman pound (known now as the *siliqua*), a continuation of the *argenteus*, and one at 72 to the Roman pound, known now as the *miliarense*, although these were subject to series of changes.

Fel Temp Reparatio Coinage

With the establishment of a high-quality gold coinage and a regularly produced silver coinage, although at erratic standards, the needs of the 4th and 5th centuries were met. Taxes could be collected in cash rather than payments in kind as in the 3rd century. In 348, to coincide with the 11th centenary of Rome's foundation, a comprehensive revision of the billon coinage was undertaken. All denominations bore a single reverse legend FEL(IX) TEMP(ORUM) REPARATIO (happy restoration of the Times). From 353 the reverse was a Roman soldier spearing a fallen horseman.

Three denominations were issued — the largest, weighing 5.2 g (0.18 oz), contained 3½ percent silver and was probably known as the *maiorina* (the big one). The middle coin weighed 4.2 g (0.148 oz) and contained 1½ percent silver and the third coin weighed 2.6 g (0.09 oz) and contained no silver. The *Fel Temp Reparatio* coinage suffered very rapid depreciation. In Gaul in the mid-4th century the usurper Magnentius (350–353) abandoned the issue of billion coinage, which he had struck at the same standard as the *Fel Temp Reparatio* issues, but with different types. After 353 the addition of silver appears to have ceased. By 361 only the largest coin survived, and Constantius II (353–361) abandoned the billon series.

Julian (361–363) attempted to reintroduce a billon coin, at 8.3 g (0.29 oz) containing 3 percent silver, with a bull on the reverse, but this did not survive his death. Attempts to introduce silver into the small-change system were now abandoned. Although of base metal, the subsidiary coinage underwent further changes before the end of the 4th century. In 378 a small and large copper coin were introduced. Except for Rome, in the west small bronze coins ceased to be minted in 402.

In the east completely different coins were struck that are found only rarely in the west, and larger denominations survived longer. Bronze coins were spasmodically minted in the east until the comprehensive reform by Anastasius in 498.

Minting

Coins are often classified into gold (AV), silver (AR) and first, second or third brass (AE 1, 2, 3). The two sides of the coin are called an obverse and a reverse. The early *as* was cast in a two-part mold as it was too heavy to be struck between dies. Later coins were made as blanks that were originally cast in open molds, although they may have been cast on flat surfaces. The blanks or flans were then stamped with a pair of dies — the lower die for the obverse and upper die for the reverse. Dies were made mainly of a high-tin bronze, but iron examples may have existed. The face of the die had a design engraved in intaglio, so that it appeared in relief on the coins. A blank was taken with tongs from the furnace and positioned on the lower die (pile), which was usually placed on an anvil. The upper die (trussel) was held over the blank and struck with a hammer. There is little evidence for striking coins when cold.

If the newly struck blank adhered to the upper die, the next blank received on its reverse an incuse impression from the obverse of the previous blank, known as a brockage. Misstrikes of blanks also occurred. Dies were capable of striking 10,000 coins before being discarded.

REPUBLIC

In the republic coinage was issued by authority of the Senate, the mint being controlled by a committee of three magistrates, *tresviri aere argento auro flando feriundo* (*III viri AAAFF*), also called *tresviri monetales*. Most coins were minted at Rome (in the temple of Juno Moneta) and at Capua, but other centers began to be used, especially during civil war. Later republican generals and early Augustan legates commanding troops in the provinces also began striking coins at mints within their provincial sphere of command.

EMPIRE

Under the empire the minting of gold and silver coins was the monopoly of the emperor, but bronze coins were technically struck by the Senate at Rome, while nearly all eastern cities struck their own copper or bronze coins to the mid-3rd century. From the time of Aurelian (270–275) all coinage was issued by the emperor.

MINTS

Until the late 2nd century Rome was the main source of currency, with a mint at Lyon from 10 BC to AD 82. The civil wars of the late 2nd century led to a revival of provincial mints in cities, but not all on a permanent basis. Mint marks proper to indicate the source began to appear in the reign of Gallienus and were a control device that had previously been used only intermittently. From the time of Diocletian (284–305) mint marks were systematically placed on coins and became more explicit. In the west only Rome survived as a mint in the 5th century, while all mints in the east (except for Heraclea) survived to the 7th century.

Table 8.2   Most Common Marks of the Main Coin Mints

Mint	Examples of abbreviations on coins (some were in Greek)
Alexandria	ALE
Antioch	A, ANT
Aquileia	AQ, AQP, AQS
Arles	AR, ARL, CON, CONST (Constantia was the 4th-century name)
Constantinople	CON
Cyzicus	KV, KA, SMK
Heraclea	HA, HTA
London	L, LN, LON, AVG (Augusta was the 4th- century name), PLN, PLON
Lyon	L, LG, LVG, LVGD
Nicomedia	SMN, SMNA
Rome	R, RM, ROM, ROMA
Serdica	SD, SM
Siscia	S, SIS, SISC, SISA, ASIS
Thessalonika	TES
Ticinum	T
Trier	TR, TRR, ATR, PTR

Early mint marks, especially those of Rome, often consisted of the *officina* (workshop) number only. In the late republic coins were freely marked with symbols, which sometimes identified a particular die or coinage batch and the *officina*. Later coins had an abbreviation of the location of the mint (such as TR for Trier) and the number of the *officina* within the mint (figs. 7.5, 8.3). This was stated in numerals, such as I, II, III or as OF I, OF II and so on. It could also be written in full — PRIMA, SECVNDA, TERTIA, or abbreviated P, S, T. Occasionally these numerals were in Greek.

Fig. 8.3 *Reverse of a bronze coin of Constantine I (306–337) with the mint mark STR (Trier). VOTIS XX on the altar refers to the vows of the emperor of the last 15 years and their renewal to the 20th anniversary.* Courtesy of Somerset County Museums Service.

The mint mark could also have an abbreviated prefix — P (*pecunia*), M (*moneta*), or S M (*sacra moneta*). There were sometimes marks of value, most commonly XXI. There were also marks indicating the quality of the metal, such as OB (*obryziacum*).

Obverse and Reverse

Legends (lettering) could appear on the obverse or reverse. Those on republican coins (such as the names of the moneyers or minters) were located at any convenient point as vertical or horizontal lines and could even continue from obverse to reverse or vice-versa. They ignored the circular outline of the coin. By the end of the 1st century all coins had legends that followed the circumference of the flan, starting from bottom left and running clockwise round the coin. The lettering could be normal (fig. 1.10) or retrograde (figs. 1.8, 8.4), and was usually abbreviated, with some ligatured letters.

OBVERSE

The obverse of republican coins varied but tended to be portraits of deities. Portraits of people began only

in late republican coins, starting with the recently murdered Pompey (issued by his supporters in 46 BC) and followed by portraits of Julius Caesar and other generals. Augustus (27 BC – AD 14) continued this tradition into the imperial period (fig. 1.1). The names of the moneyers could appear on the obverse or reverse.

The obverse of imperial coins usually bore the portrait of the reigning emperor (most facing right) or occasionally relatives or revered predecessors (fig. 1.4), surrounded by a legend. The portrait of the emperor could be laureate (wearing a laurel wreath) (figs. 1.8, 8.1, 8.5), radiate (wearing a crown of the sun's rays like spikes) or diademed (wearing a diadem or low crown of jewels). From Nero's reign the *dupondius* was distinguished from the *as* by a radiate crown instead of the traditional laurel wreath, a device used on *dupondii* until their demise in the 3rd century. The radiate crown (fig. 8.2) actually represented the sun's rays that surrounded the head of Apollo, a deity especially dear to Nero. Caracalla's new coin, the *antoninianus*, also differed from the *denarius* by the use of a radiate crown.

There was a wide variation in coin portraiture right across the empire, particularly in those from eastern mints, so that portraits of the same emperor could vary significantly. From the late 3rd century portraits became more stylized, and those from the

Fig. 8.4 *Retrograde abbreviated lettering on the obverse of a* denarius *of Titus (79–81):* IMP/TITVS/CAES/VESPAS-IAN/AVG/PM. Courtesy of Somerset County Museums Service.

Fig. 8.5 Obverse of a follis *of Maximian (286–305). The legend is sparse (MAXIMIANVS/NOB/CAES) and his portrait (a laureate bust) is very stylized.* Courtesy of Somerset County Museums Service.

4th century tended to present the portrait as an ideal in a Greek style rather than as an individual (fig. 8.5). Portraits of different emperors were therefore remarkably uniform (fig. 1.17), broken only briefly by Constantine I, and it is difficult to distinguish one emperor from another except by their names.

The obverse legend of imperial coins could be votive—commemorating the *vota* (vows) that the emperor took on accession and renewed every five years (fig. 8.3)—or else constitutional—dealing with the emperor's ranks and appointments and the reckoning of his years in various offices. Common imperial titles and constitutional terms (with abbreviations) that appear on obverse legends are AVGVSTVS, AVG (senior emperor), CAESAR, CAES, C (junior emperor), CONSVL, COS (consul), DN (Dominus Noster—Our lord), IMPERATOR, IMP (leader of the military), PATER PATRIAE, PP (father of the country), PIVS FELIX, PF (reverent or dutiful, and fortunate), PONTIFEX MAXIMVS, PON MAX, PM (chief priest), SENATVS CONSULTO, SC (by decree of the Senate), TRIBVNICIA POTESTAS, TRIB POT, TR P (holder of the tribunician power), and VOTA, VOTAE (vows undertaken by the emperor every five years). Obverse legends after 350 were stereotyped and contained little information (fig. 1.17).

REVERSE

The reverse of a coin bears the design (called a type). Republican coins tended to show personifications of deities and mythical scenes, and many have a prow of a ship. After 213 BC all bronze coins bore the prow of a ship on the reverse. The word ROMA was often at the base of the reverse of coins from 260 BC to the 2nd century BC. The legend on bronze coins was restricted to the names of the moneyers, either on the obverse or reverse, initially as symbols and then full names. Signed bronze coins date mainly to the 2nd century BC. Names of moneyers also appeared on silver coins.

The earliest imperial bronze coins bore the letters SC (*senatus consulto*) with no other design. From the mid-1st century the designs of reverses are much better and more intricately cut. Designs of imperial coins included representations of deities (figs. 1.22, 7.4, 7.5, 7.7, 7.9), personifications of a virtue (such as peace or justice) or propaganda (such as a military victory or a building program). The reverse can be divided into two parts, with the field containing the type set on a groundline and the exergue below it containing a mint mark (fig. 8.3). The legends were often related to the design (fig. 8.6).

From the time of Diocletian's coinage reform in 294, designs were mass produced throughout the

field
normal legend
groundline   exergue

Fig. 8.6 Reverse of a denarius *of Maximinus I (235–238) portraying the health of the emperor (SALVS AVGVSTI) personified. Courtesy of Somerset County Museums Service.*

empire, with little attention paid to reverses. Silver coins of the tetrarchs simply bore the numerals XCVI (96 to the Roman pound), gold coins bore simple religious themes such as *Sol Invictus* or an image of Jupiter, and bronze coins often had a military design, such as two soldiers, with a military legend such as GLORIA EXERCITVS. Pagan gods disappeared in the west in 318 and in the east in 324, and instead old-style personifications (such as Victory) appeared on coins with simple legends.

Reverses of Greek imperial coins vary considerably, and some have a portrait of heads of joint rulers or other members of the ruling family, so that the coins appear to have two obverses.

Dating

A coin can be dated by the portrait of the emperor and by his titles and offices held. The design (such as a military victory) may also assist with dating. The date when a coin was lost or hidden (and subsequently recovered in archeological deposits) is more difficult to establish, since many coins had a lengthy circulation.

Banking

In early Greece temples lent money to the local population and served as safe repositories for valuables and money. Bankers were originally moneychangers who operated at festivals, changing the money of travelers into the local coin. In the city-states of the Hellenistic period, banking was undertaken by important temples, private firms and the cities themselves, and written orders to bankers requesting payment to third parties are known. In Ptolemaic Egypt a complex public banking system collected the king's revenues and made payments, using a variety of paper transactions.

During the republic moneychangers (*argentarii*) were needed to exchange the coinage of communities in Italy and farther afield that reached Rome in the course of trade. In the 2nd and 1st centuries BC banks at Rome were fairly small and were run mainly by wealthy *equites*, not by the state. Valuables and money could be deposited with bankers, who could make loans to third parties at profitable rates of interest. The rate of interest in the late republic and early empire at Rome was normally 6 to 10 percent, but it was much higher in outlying provinces where investments were less secure. Using primitive exchange bills, bankers evolved a means of clearing payments in and outside Rome, allowing payments to be made without the actual transfer of coinage. The banking system spread across the empire, and Augustus reorganized the Ptolemaic banking system in Egypt.

During the empire moneychangers continued to be important in converting from one form of currency to another, particularly in small-scale local transactions such as payment of taxes. Money lending also continued to be profitable, and in the provinces money was often borrowed to pay taxes, so that enormous debts accrued. Much of the banking procedure was codified by Justinian in the 6th century and preserved by Europeans and Arabs throughout the Middle Ages.

Prices and Inflation

In the early empire inflation was apparently fairly low, but it increased rapidly from the 260s, mirrored by the debasement of silver currency. There was widespread hoarding, and the government refused to accept coinage for many taxes, insisting instead on payment in kind. Prices of many commodities are known in the republic and empire, but it is difficult to draw comparisons as they were dependent on many variables, such as poor harvests. Two reasonable indicators of inflation are army pay (see chapter 2) and wheat prices.

In conjunction with his revision of taxation and coinage, Diocletian undertook a measure unprecedented in Roman history, by decreeing fixed ceilings on wages and prices throughout the empire. Diocletian's Price Edict (*Edictum de pretiis*) was published in 301 and consisted of a preamble followed by an extensive list of maximum prices of goods of all kinds and a list of maximum wages for all types of work. Death or exile were the punishments for contravening the regulations. The Price Edict actually failed as many goods were driven from the market, and it was finally revoked.

WEIGHTS AND MEASURES

2½ *pedes*	= 1 *gradus*
2 *gradus*	= 1 *passus*
2 *passus*	= 1 *decempeda*
12 *decempeda*	= 1 *actus*
2 *actus*	= 1 *iugerum*

Measures of Length

Measures of length were based mainly on parts of the human body. The normal Roman foot (*pes*, pl. *pedes*) was around 296 mm (11.65 in.) and is usually called the *pes monetalis*, from the standard measure kept in the temple of Juno Moneta at Rome. There was an early foot of over 297 mm (11.7 in.), and the *pes Drusianus* of around 332 or 333 mm (13.1 in.) was used in at least Gaul and Germany in the early empire. From the 3rd century there was a shorter foot of 294 mm (11.5 in.). The foot was sometimes divided into 16 fingers (*digiti*), possibly Greek in origin, but was more usually divided into 12 Roman inches (*unciae*, sing. *uncia*).

as	= 12 *unciae* (inches)
deunx	= 11 *unciae*
dextans	= 10 *unciae*
dodrans	= 9 *unciae*
bes	= 8 *unciae*
septunx	= 7 *unciae*
semis	= 6 *unciae*
quincunx	= 5 *unciae*
triens	= 4 *unciae*
quadrans	= 3 *unciae*
sextans	= 2 *unciae*
semuncia	= 0.5 inch
sicilicus	= 0.25 inch
sesuncia	= 1.5 inches
dupondius	= 2 feet

For measuring road distances, the pace and mile were used, 5 *pedes* = 1 *passus* (pace — actually a double pace equivalent to 1.48 m [4 ft 10 in]). 1,000 paces (5,000 Roman feet) = *mille passus* or *milia passuum* (mile), equivalent to 1,480 m (4,856 ft). Leagues were also used: see chapter 5. For measuring distances by sea, the *stadium* was used: 125 paces = 1 *stadium*.

Land surveyors mainly used the *actus* (a driving) of 120 Roman feet (35.48 m [116 ft 6 in]) (see chapter 4), an agricultural term indicating the distance that oxen pulling a plow would be driven before turning. The Oscans and Umbrians used a *versus* (turning) of 100 Roman feet.

Measures of Area

1 square *actus* (known as an *actus quadratus* or *acnua*) = 14,400 square Roman feet (c. 0. 126 hectares [0.312 acres]).

2 square *actus* = 1 *iugerum* = 28,800 square Roman feet (c. 0. 252 hectares [0.623 acres]). A *iugerum* (yoke area, from *iugum*, yoke) was a common measurement of area in land survey and was the amount that could be plowed in one day. One-twelfth of a *iugerum* was an *uncia* (2,400 square Roman feet). A *triens* was one-third of a *iugerum*.

2 *iugera* = 1 *heredium* = c. 0. 504 hectares (c. 1. 246 acres). A *heredium* (inherited area) was an area of land sufficient for one person, but the term went out of use.

100 *heredia* = 1 *centuria* = c. 50.4 hectares (c. 124.6 acres). This was the normal size of a century (20 by 20 *actus*: 2,400 square Roman feet). Nonstandard centuries were also used, from 50 to 400 or more *iugera*.

Measures of Capacity

There were wet and dry measures of capacity, originally used for wine and oil (wet) and grain (dry). The smaller subdivisions of wet and dry measures were:

4 *cochlearia*	= 1 *cyathus* (borrowed from the Greek)
6 *cochlearia*	= 1 *acetabulum*
2 *acetabula*	= 1 *quartarius*
2 *quartarii*	= 1 *hemina*
2 *heminae*	= 1 *sextarius*

A *cochlear* or *cochlea* (snail shell) or *ligula* (spoonful) was the smallest unit, equivalent to 1.14 centiliters (0.34 fluid ounce).

Larger liquid measures were:

12 *heminae*	= 1 *congius*
8 *congii*	= 1 *amphora* or *cadus*
20 *amphorae*	= 1 *culleus* (about 144 U.S. gallons)

The *amphora* was a cubic Roman foot (25.79 liters, about 7 U.S. gallons). It was the chief unit of liquid measurement, and related to the pottery vessels whose cubic capacity actually varied. (See chapter 8.)

Larger dry measures were:

8 *sextarii*	= 1 *semodius*
16 *sextarii*	= 1 *modius* (the chief grain unit)

A *sextarius* was 0.546 liters (1.14 U.S. pint). A *modius* was nearly 2.4 U.S. gallons.

Weights

The weight system was based on natural units, the smallest for measuring barleycorn (equivalent to the troy grain). The word for weight was *pondus*, from *pendere* (to hang). Roman weight was based on the pound (*libra*, literally "balance") (335.9 g, 11.849 ounces avoirdupois). Originally the chief use of balance scales was to weigh bars of copper (*asses*), and so the term *as* is also used for a Roman pound. These bars were 1 Roman foot long and divided into 12 inches (*unciae*), and so the pound was divided into 12 ounces (*unciae*). The names of the subdivisions of the Roman pound are:

as or *libra*	= 1 pound
deunx	= 11 oz
dextans	= 10 oz
dodrans	= 9 oz
bes	= 8 oz
septunx	= 7 oz
semis	= 6 oz
quincunx	= 5 oz
triens	= 4 oz
quadrans	= 3 oz
sextans	= 2 oz
sesuncia	= 1½ oz
uncia	= 1 oz
semuncia	= ½ oz
sicilicus	= ¼ oz
sextula	= ⅙ oz
semisextula	= 1/12 oz
scriptulum	= 1/24 oz
siliqua	= 1/144 oz

1 *siliqua* = 3 *grana hordei* (barleycorns or troy grains). 1 *as* or *libra* = 5,184 barleycorns or troy grains (5,050 before 268 BC).

Weighing Instruments

A balance (*libra*) was used for weighing and consisted of a balance arm of bronze, iron or occasionally bone, from which two scale pans of bronze were suspended at equal distance from the point of suspension. The goods to be weighed were placed on one scale pan and weights of lead, stone, bronze, iron or bronze-covered lead were placed on the other pan until the two pans balanced.

A steelyard (*statera*) consisted of a balance arm, and the goods to be weighed were suspended from the short end. A steelyard weight was moved along the long arm until it balanced, and the weight of the object was measured from marks along the arm. The arm often could be suspended from different hooks, so as to cover a range of different weights; the weights were marked on one or two faces of the balance arm and corresponded to the hook used.

Grain (such as barley and wheat) was measured with a bucket-shaped vessel of bronze (*modius*). For instruments for measuring linear measurement, see chapter 4.

INDUSTRY

Most Roman industries were like well-organized crafts, and there was no distinction between a craft and an industry. They were labor-intensive, often very skilled and localized, although some goods were traded extensively. (See chapter 5.) Industries varied in their organization, from large-scale production for trade to very small-scale production to meet local needs on what would now be termed a craft industry.

Very little is known of the working population. Most miners were slaves or criminals condemned *ad metallum* (to work in the mines). Slaves undertook a variety of work, including that of skilled craftsmen. In Italy, and more so in the provinces, slaves probably constituted only a minority of the population. The majority of the work force probably consisted of free citizens and freedmen. Across the empire craftsmen were organized into guilds (*collegia*) that operated as dinner and funeral clubs.

Throughout the Roman period there was extremely little technical innovation, and labor-saving devices were rarely introduced. Despite the potential, there was no industrial revolution, and industrial capacity expanded only in response to increased markets. The failure of industry to put itself on a more efficient basis was probably due to a combination of factors. The prime reason may have been that the wealthy regarded investment in industry as socially unacceptable. While many profited from industry, agriculture was invariably the most prestigious form of investment. The widespread use of slaves in the late republic and early empire has also been considered as a further reason that industry and technology failed to develop.

POTTERY

Pottery was made throughout the Roman world, but only limited studies have been undertaken in some areas. While pottery manufacture was one of the most common trades and pottery is the most common artifact found in excavations, very little is known from ancient writers about the industry. Pottery vessels were used as tableware, in the kitchen and for storage and transport of goods. Most coarse pottery was made locally, while specialized wares were transported over long distances, including quality wares such as terra sigillata and those vessels made for the transport and storage of goods, such as amphorae. As well as pottery vessels, there was also a range of other ceramic goods, such as figurines, candlesticks and lamps.

Manufacture

As with brick and tile manufacture, the clay was dug from selected deposits and allowed to weather. The clay may have been refined by levigating—mixing it with water so that coarse particles sank and organic debris floated and could be skimmed off. It was then puddled (mixed and blended with temper and water).

Some coarse pottery was handmade, but most pottery was wheel-made. Some pots, particularly terra sigillata, were made in molds. Little information about potters' wheels exists. Potters may have worked at a broad flat wheel set on the ground, which acted as a combined flywheel and working surface. They may have also used small potters' wheels set at waist height and connected to a flywheel below. A few stone components, possibly from potters' wheels, are known, but most were probably of wood.

After drying, the pots were fired. Coarse wares were sometimes fired in simple bonfire kilns—the pots were stacked and baked in a pit under a bonfire. For most wares the single-flue updraft kiln was commonly used. The pots were stacked inverted in an oval or circular chamber over the fire on clay fire bars supported on a column of tiles or clay. There was a stokehole or stokepit on one side, and the hot gases rose up from the fire, around the pots and out of the top of the kiln. The type of kiln superstructure is uncertain—some kilns may have had a temporary covering and others a permanent dome with a central opening. The fuel was probably mainly wood.

Similar parallel-flue kilns were used to fire building materials such as tiles and large pots. They were stacked above tile arches that formed parallel flues. More sophisticated kilns seem to have been used for specialist wares such as terra sigillata.

Coarse Wares

Locally made pottery (native wares) tended to follow pre-Roman styles, so that there is a divergence of styles across the empire. They are usually termed coarse wares or kitchen wares, although some had fine fabrics. Most coarse wares consisted of relatively plain unglazed earthenware vessels, varying in color according to the source of the clay and the methods of firing. Some of the local industries were on a large scale, but their distribution tended to be limited. Many of the coarse ware forms were functional and therefore changed little over the centuries. Much local pottery supplied the military forces.

Terra Sigillata (or Samian) (fig. 8.7)

HISTORY

The terra sigillata industry was organized on a huge scale, and immense quantities were exported to various parts of the Roman world. In Britain terra sigillata is known as Samian and the earlier wares as Arretine. As a Latin term, *terra sigillata* (clay adorned with figures) should apply only to decorated vessels, but it is also used for plain vessels. Terra sigillata is also known as red-gloss pottery and red-coated pottery. Comparable wares made in Britain are known as color-coated wares and those in north Africa as red-slipped wares.

Terra sigillata was usually red, made from a fine red clay with a glossy surface (not a glaze) formed by a slip of fine clay. The red color was obtained by firing in the kiln in an oxidizing (oxygen-rich) atmosphere. Some marbled samian is known and also black samian, which was fired in a reducing (oxygen-starved) atmosphere.

Terra sigillata derives from much earlier Greek glossy black and red figure vases. Everyday Greek pottery with a similar surface treatment was "black glazed" tableware. This was imitated in various parts of Italy from the 4th century BC and was known as Campanian ware. In the mid-1st century BC tastes and different firing techniques led to the production of Arretine ware. They were red-coated vessels, made first in Arezzo and then elsewhere in Italy, with a branch workshop at Lyon, and included molded cups, jugs and tableware. Many were plain or with restrained decoration, and there were also some high-quality decorated vessels with figured and floral designs. Arretine ware superseded Campanian ware c. 50 BC. It was exported throughout the Mediterranean and as far as India and Britain.

In the early 1st century the terra sigillata industry spread to southern Gaul (mainly La Graufesenque). The vessels from these potteries were originally plain or simply decorated, but intricate designs with human and animal figures developed. Production moved to central Gaul (in the Allier valley, mainly at Les Martres-de-Veyre and Lezoux) in the 1st century, and by the end of the 1st century the quality of the south Gaulish wares had declined. Central Gaulish wares became predominant from the late 1st century and continued to c. 200. Highly decorated vessels were made, especially with human and animal figures. The south and central Gaulish wares were exported to the western provinces, including Italy.

East Gaulish potteries were established in the early 1st century and became predominant in the late 2nd century. There were several small potteries along the Moselle, Rhine and Danube rivers, in particular at Trier, Blickweiler and Rheinzabern. The east Gaulish potteries exported only to the northwestern provinces. Standards declined and production ceased c. 250. Other provinces, including Spain, Africa and Britain, produced similar pottery. African red-slipped wares became predominant in the Mediterranean by the end of the 2nd century, and production continued to the 7th century.

METHODS OF MANUFACTURE

Plain open vessels such as bowls and plates were wheel-thrown, probably using a wooden template, and then a footring was added. Simple decoration could be applied by barbotine and rouletting, but vessels with more complex decoration were made in molds manufactured from fine clay that had been impressed with decorative scenes and motifs. The clay was pressed inside the mold, and, when dry, it shrank and could be removed. The rim and footring were then added by hand. Before firing, plain and decorated vessels were dipped into a liquid clay slip that produced the glossy finish when fired.

STAMPS AND FORMS

Terra sigillata is useful for dating because of the potters' stamps and changing style of decoration, form and fabrics, which varied from center to center. Most of the vessels bear potters' name-stamps—the basal interior of the vessel was usually stamped with a die cut in reverse, so that the lettering was the right way round on the pot. The mold maker's name was sometimes present, usually incised with a stylus as a signature in the mold, so that a mirror image appeared on the vessel. On decorated vessels, stamps advertising the workshop (*officina*) were often used.

The vessels were made in a range of standardized forms classified by various authorities whose names have been used for the classification, in particular: Dragendorff (Dr. or Drag.), Déchelette, Knorr, Walters, Curle, Ludovici and Ritterling (fig. 8.7). Plain and decorated vessels were made, including dishes, plates, cups, bowls, jars, mortaria, candlesticks, inkwells and jugs.

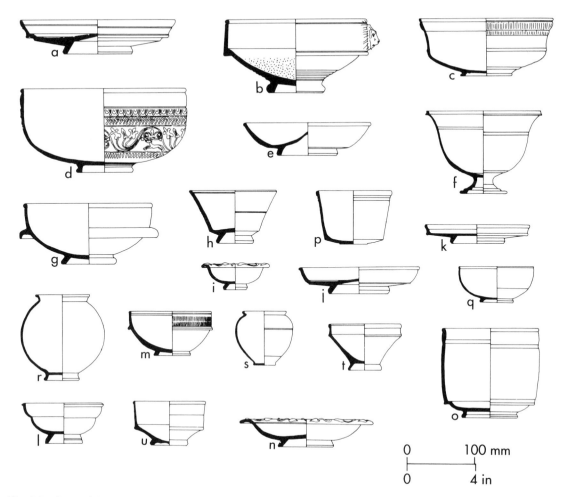

Fig. 8.7   Some of the major terra sigillata forms: Dragendorff forms: a. 15/17; b. 45 (mortarium); c. 29; d. 37; e. 31; f. 11; g. 38; h. 33; i. 35; j. 18; k. 17; l. 27; m. 24/25; n. 36; o. 30. Other forms: p. Knorr 78; q. Hofheim 8; r. Déchelette 72; s. Déchelette 67; t. Haltern 8; u. Hofheim 9. In addition to Dr. 37, the following forms were decorated: Dr. 11, Dr. 29 and Dr. 30.

Fine Wares

Apart from terra sigillata, other fine (thin-walled) vessels were manufactured, in particular drinking beakers and cups (fig. 8.13), some at the same centers of production. The industry lasted from the 2nd century BC to the late 2nd century AD, predominantly in Italy and then, from the early 1st century, in Gaul and Germany. Special finishes were created by colored slips (color-coated pottery), glazes (not common) and decoration. Several local potteries produced red-slipped tablewares as terra sigillata copies.

Mortaria

Mortaria (sing. *mortarium*) were mortars used for food preparation in the kitchen. They were large strong bowls with a flange for easy gripping and a spout. Grit (trituration) was incorporated in the interior surface to roughen and strengthen it. In the 1st and 2nd centuries *mortaria* were often stamped with the name of the potter or factory, enabling their origins to be traced. They were made in many areas and were traded over long distances. They are relatively rare in the eastern Mediterranean region.

Amphorae

In the Mediterranean region, liquids such as wine, oil and fish sauce were often transported in amphorae—pottery vessels that were usually wide at the girth, with a neck and mouth narrow enough to be corked and two opposed vertical handles near the mouth. The heights, girths and wall thicknesses of amphorae varied, but they usually stood over 1 m (3 ft 3 in) high. Many have a knob or spike at the base that could be used as a third handle when lifting or pouring. They could be carried upright or sideways. The Greek term *amphiphoreus* ([jar] that was carried on both sides) came to be shortened to *amphoreus*, which was borrowed by Latin as *amphora*.

CLASSIFICATIONS (fig. 8.8)

There are many classifications of amphorae by shape. Over 40 types were recognized by Heinrich Dressel in the 19th century, with subsequent additional classifications by others. Styles of amphorae were less susceptible to change than other goods and so are not very useful for dating purposes (except some with inscriptions). Many types of amphorae have a wide distribution, from one end of the empire to the other, even in the late Roman period. Analysis of the clay fabric has enabled the sources of manufacture to be identified, although very few kilns are known.

The main types of amphorae are described below in date order with alternative names in brackets.

Greco-Italic (Republicaine 1, Lamboglia 4): Originated in Magna Graecia, forerunners of Roman amphorae; one form was probably made in Sicily and the Aegean and another near Pompeii and Cosa. Date: late 4th century BC to c. 130 BC. Contents: possibly wine.

Dressel 1A: Made throughout Italy. Date: c. 130–50 BC. Contents: probably mainly wine.

Dressel 1B: Made throughout Italy, replacing Dressel 1A. Date: 1st century BC. Contents: probably mainly wine.

Dressel 1—Pascual 1: Made along Spain's northeast coast and possibly in southern France. They copied Dressel 1B. Date: mainly Augustan. Contents: possibly wine.

Lamboglia 2: From Apulia. Date: 2nd to mid-1st century BC. Contents: possibly olive oil or wine.

Dressel 6: Probably from Istria, in the former Yugoslavia. They had widespread distribution, especially in Dalmatia, the Aegean and northeast Italy. They were typologically similar to Lamboglia 2. Form: bag-shaped body with pointed or stub base. Date: 1st century. Contents: possibly mainly olive oil.

"Rhodian Type" (Ostia LXV, Camulodunum 184, Callender 7): Probably mainly from Rhodes. Form: simple rounded rim, cylindrical neck, long rod handles rising to a high peak, body often slightly corrugated, tapering to a solid spike. Date: late 1st century BC to early 2nd century AD. Contents: probably wine.

Dressel 2–4 ("Koan type," "Greco-Roman amphora"): made from the late 1st century BC, replacing Dressel 1B. They were mostly from the west Mediterranean and were the most important wine amphora of this area from the late 1st century BC to mid-2nd century AD. They were thin-walled and could therefore carry more wine. Contents: probably mainly wine.

During the latter 2nd century BC to the first decade of the 1st century AD, Dressel 1 and 2–4 amphorae were the most common forms, dominating the western Mediterranean and north European markets and also reaching many other places, including the Red Sea and eastern India. During this time amphorae such as the Rhodian type were still made in Greece, but not on a large scale.

"Carrot amphora" (Camulodunum 189, Schöne-Mau XV): Uncertain origin, commonly found on early military sites in Britain and Germany. Form: plain or rounded rim, usually no neck, small thick loop handles, small tapered body normally covered with horizontal rilling. Date: mainly 1st century. Contents: possibly dates.

Haltern 70 (Camulodunum 185A, Callender 9): from Baetica, Date: mid-1st century BC to mid-1st century AD. Contents: possibly mainly *defrutum*.

Dressel 7–11 (Beltrán I): Probably from Spain. Date: late 1st century BC to 1st century AD. Contents: mainly fish sauces.

Beltrán II (Camulodunum 186A, Schöne-Mau VII): From southern Spain. Date: late 1st century BC to early 2nd century AD. Contents: fish sauces.

Dressel 38 (Beltrán IIA, Ostia LXIII, Camulodunum 186C, Pélichet 46, Callender 6): From southern Spain. Form: broad neck, hooked rim, long flattened handles, a body that widened toward the base, terminating in a long hollow spike. Date: probably Flavian to early 2nd century. Contents: fish products.

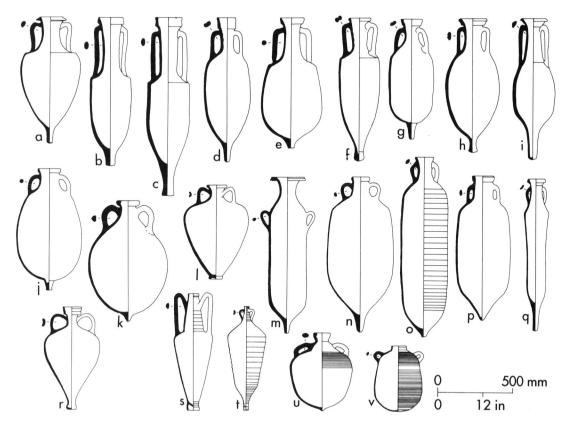

Fig. 8.8 Major amphora forms: a. Greco-Italic; b. Dressel 1A; c. Dressel 1B; d. Dressel 1—Pascual 1; e. Lamboglia 2; f. Dressel 2–4; g. Haltern 70; h. Dressel 7–11; i. Beltrán II; j. Oberaden 83; k. Dressel 20; l. Pélichet 47; m. "Neo-Punic"; n. Africana II; o. Late Roman North African; p. Tripolitanian I; q. "Spatheion"; r. Dressel 30; s. "Hollow Foot"; t. British Biv; u. British Bi; v. "Palestinian."

Oberaden 83 (Haltern 71, Dressel 25):   Probably from the Guadalquivir region; commonly found on forts of the German *limes.* Date: end of 1st century BC to 1st century AD. Contents: probably olive oil.

Dressel 20("Globular amphora," Beltrán V, Ostia I, Callender 2):   Developed from Oberaden 83 and were from the Guadalquivir area. They are one of the most common and widely distributed of amphorae, particularly in the west. Date: Tiberian period to late 3rd, possibly 4th century. Contents: olive oil.

Pélichet 47 (Gauloise 4, Ostia LX, Callender 10):   Mainly from southern France. Date: mid 1st–3rd centuries. Contents: wine.

Dressel 28:   Made in Spain and France. Form: "pulley-wheel" rim, short rounded handles with one, sometimes two, shallow furrows, well-rounded body ending in a thick footring base. Date: late Augustan to first half of 2nd century. Contents: possibly wine or fish products.

"Neo-Punic":   Made in Morocco and Tunisia. Date: mainly 2nd and 1st centuries BC, probably continuing to 1st century AD. Contents: unknown.

Africana I "Piccolo" (Beltrán 57, Ostia IV):   From north Africa, especially the Sahel region of Tunisia and the Carthage area. Form: thickened everted rim, short straight neck, small sharply bent handles, long cylindrical body, short hollow spike. Date: 3rd, possibly 4th century, some 2nd century. Contents: fish products, possibly olive oil.

Africana II "Grande" (Beltrán 56, Ostia III):   From the Sahel region of Tunisia. Date: late 2nd to at least 4th century. Contents: olive oil, possibly fish products.

Late Roman North African amphorae: Mainly from Tunisia. They developed into over 93 cylindrical forms differentiated mainly by the rim and spike. They became common from the late 4th century continuing to the 6th century.

Tripolitanian I (Ostia LXIV): Made in Tripolitania; widely distributed in the eastern Mediterranean. Date: 1st–4th centuries. Contents: probably olive oil.

Dressel 30 (Ostia V): Probably from Algeria. Date: 3rd–4th centuries. Contents: possibly olive oil.

British Bi (Kuzmanov XIX, Scorpan 7A, Carthage LR amphora 2, Benghazi LR amphora 2): Probably from the Aegean and Black Sea areas. Date: 4th to late 6th/early 7th centuries. Contents: unknown.

British Bii (Ballana 6, Kuzmanov XIII, Scorpan 8B, Carthage LR amphora 1, Benghazi LR amphora 1): From the eastern Mediterranean where they were a very common form, possibly from Syria or Cyprus. Form: relatively thin walls, thick slumping handles, thickened rim, widely spaced ridging in the center of the body narrowing at the shoulder and base. Date: early 5th–mid-7th century (especially frequent in the later 5th and early 6th centuries). Contents: possibly oil.

British Biv (Ballana 13a, Kuzmanov VII, Scorpan 5, Zeest 95, Carthage LR amphora 3, Benghazi LR amphora 10): From the eastern Mediterranean, possibly Asia Minor, with a widespread distribution. Date: one-handled forms—late 1st–5th centuries; two handled—very late 4th–late 6th centuries. Contents: unknown.

In the late 4th century, an increasing influx of bag-shaped amphorae from the eastern Mediterranean came to dominate the western Mediterranean in the later 5th century (for example, Palestinian type). The trade possibly persisted until the Arab conquests of the mid-7th century.

"Palestinian": Probably from Palestine, where they are common. There are usually corrugations over much of the body and white painted decoration. Date: 5th–6th centuries. Contents: possibly white wine.

"Hollow Foot" amphora (Ostia VI, Kapitän II, Kuzmanov VII, Niederbieber 77, Zeest 79, Benghazi MR amphora 7): Probably from the Aegean. Date: 3rd–4th centuries. Contents: possibly wine.

Zemer 53: Possibly from Gaza in Palestine; commonly found in the Levant, especially Palestine and Egypt. Form: small thickened rim, two ring handles on the shoulder, heavy bag-shaped body with a rounded base. Date: 3rd–4th centuries. Contents: possibly wine.

Almagro 54 (Kuzmanov XIV, Carthage LR amphora 4): Probably from Gaza in Palestine; common in the southeastern Mediterranean. Form: small everted rim, rough loop handles on the shoulders, narrow cylindrical body leading to a rounded or sometimes flat base, often heavy ridging on the shoulder and between the handles, accretions of clay on the shoulder and around the rim. Date: 4th–6th centuries. Contents: possibly wine, olive oil or sesame oil.

"Spatheion" (Benghazi LR amphora 8): Possibly from Spain and north Africa. The term spatheion refers to a group of amphorae with a long narrow body, long tapering spike, fairly high neck with an everted rim and two short handles on the neck. Date: the larger ones are late 4th–5th/6th centuries; the smaller ones are 6th–7th centuries. Contents: unknown.

SEALING

Amphorae were permeable but could be made leakproof in various ways, such as by rubbing the interior of olive oil amphorae with olive oil lees. Many amphorae have a black lining to make them impermeable. The lining is often described as bitumen, pitch, resin and rosin, but the terminology is confused. Bitumen is found associated with crude oil; wood tar (wood pitch) is residue from wood distillation; and resin is the sticky substance from certain trees. Rosin is the solid residue from pine tree resin distillation. Analysis of amphora linings has, in fact, shown them to be primarily rosin. Occasionally resin was carried as a commodity, but usually its residue represents a sealant. By studying the residues of amphorae that did not have a lining, it is possible to ascertain the original contents and therefore much about trade in foodstuffs.

Amphorae were sealed with a stopper or lid of cork or fired clay (*operculum*), held fast by a cement seal. The seals were occasionally stamped with a name, possibly that of the merchant rather than the producer.

SUPPLY OF AMPHORAE

Farms producing oil, fish products and wine bottled their commodities at the place of manufacture. Amphorae may have been made on the estate (possibly also supplying other estates) or by independent potters. Amphorae kilns have been found in north Africa, southern Gaul and Spain, some on estates, but little is known of amphora kilns in Italy. There were many major technical problems in producing such large vessels. They were probably mainly made on a wheel, removed with a wire, dried, and then the neck and rim were formed and the handles added. Some were probably made from coils of clay finished on a wheel. They were fired in large circular updraft kilns with diameters from 3.5 m (11 ft 6 in) to 5.5 m (18 ft). Kilns are usually found in pairs or groups.

INSCRIPTIONS

Many amphorae had inscriptions, which are very useful for ascertaining their date, origin and contents. Before firing, many were stamped on the handle, spike or body, but it is unclear what these mean: It seems most likely that they were the stamps of the estate owners rather than the potters.

Painted inscriptions (*tituli picti*) were added after firing. Probably present on most amphorae but seldom surviving, they were often written in red letters below the amphora neck. *Tituli picti* on Dressel 20 amphorae were the most complex and included the empty weight of the amphora, the weight of the contents, origin of the product and shipping and control details. The amphora was weighed when empty and when full, and the difference between the two weights was written on the amphora to denote the weight of the contents. Many amphorae could carry 24 to 30 liters (6 to 7.9 U.S. gallons), but there were variations, and Dressel 20 amphorae had a capacity of 40 to 80 liters (10.6 to 21.1 U.S. gallons). The inscriptions on other types of amphorae are less complex and therefore less informative.

Terracotta Figurines

Fired clay (terracotta or ceramic) figurines were very popular in Hellenistic times. This industry continued in workshops across the Roman world, with the figurines made in molds. Many followed Hellenistic patterns but were often of goddesses associated with local cults. From the early 2nd century figurine production became important in the Allier valley of central Gaul and then in the Rhineland; they were made in a white clay (pipeclay) and were widely exported, particularly Venus figurines and mother goddesses.

Figurines were largely for votive use in temples and household shrines. Also used as votive offerings were terracottas of various parts of the human body. (See chapter 7.) Other terracottas may have been ornaments, souvenirs or toys. The terracotta industry declined from the 4th century, possibly because of the increasing influence of Christianity

Lamps

Bronze and pottery lamps were used in the Mediterranean area from the 7th century BC. Most surviving Roman oil lamps are of pottery, but many were probably of bronze and other materials. They consisted of a chamber for the oil (usually olive oil), a filling hole, a nozzle for the wick and sometimes a handle. The wick was probably of linen. Some lamps had more than one nozzle. The upper surface of the lamp was often decorated, including scenes of everyday life and mythology, while other lamps were plain and functional. Many have the name of the maker on the base. A few lamps were wheel-made, but most were made in two-piece molds, probably of gypsum and plaster. When the lamp was removed from the mold, it was dipped in a slip of clay before firing, in order to make it more impermeable to oil. Lamps were fired in updraft kilns similar to those used for pottery.

Lamps of the 3rd and 2nd centuries BC in Italy were possibly imported from Athens. From the 1st century BC lamps were produced mainly in Italy. They were widely exported and were copied by local manufacturers. In Augustan times in Italy high-quality volute lamps were produced, with two curved ornaments flanking the nozzle and a wide upper surface for relief decoration. In the mid-1st century AD another type of lamp was commonly produced, with a circular body and short rounded nozzle. In northern provinces the *Firmalampe* became common, exported initially from Italy and then copied. This type of lamp was plain and functional, sometimes with simple decoration. From the mid-1st century AD lamps were made across the Roman world in various shapes and styles. The figure-of-eight shaped open tray with a loop handle is found in Britain, Gaul and Germany but rarely in the Mediterranean. It may have been used as a drip tray or as an actual lamp. In northwest

Europe lamp production ceased in the mid-3rd century, probably because of the disruption of the oil supply, and other means of lighting must have been used. In the Mediterranean, however, lamp production flourished throughout the Roman period.

BRICK AND TILE

The actual manufacturing process of bricks and tiles was protracted. First, suitable clay was dug and allowed to weather, usually over winter. The clay then underwent various treatments—stones and other impurities were removed and sand was added to produce the desired color. When the clay was the right consistency for working, it was shaped in wooden molds into bricks and tiles. These were taken to a drying area to harden before being fired in kilns, which were circular, square or rectangular in plan. Brickyards were run by the army, towns or private companies.

Bricks

Unbaked or mud bricks were very common in eastern areas and also appear to have been used in Italy and Rome itself. Baked bricks were a common building material long before the Roman period, being used in Babylon in the 4th millennium BC. They were occasionally used in buildings from the 2nd century BC but were not widespread until the mid-1st century AD. They were used mainly for facings of concrete walls, bonding courses in stone walls and in pillars supporting floors in hypocausts. (See chapter 4.)

A variety of shaped bricks was used for specific purposes, such as solid voussoir bricks for the construction of arches and semicircular bricks for the construction of pillars.

Tiles (fig. 8.9)

A great variety of tiles was made for roofing and for hypocaust flues, and drainage pipes were also manufactured. The main types of roofing tile were *tegulae* and *imbrices*. (See chapter 4.) Ridge tiles are relatively rare, as *imbrices* were often used for ridges. Baked clay antefixes decorated with relief patterns were set at the lower edges of roofs (at the ends of *imbrices*) along the eaves. Antefixes were also used as finials at the ends of roof ridges. Decorative baked clay revetments were used on some buildings in the republic from the 6th century BC. Other specialized roofing tiles were sometimes made, such as *tegulae* with holes or with molded hoods, which were probably used above heating flue vents. Roofing tiles were also sometimes used to build cistlike structures in place of coffins in tombs.

Tegulae mammatae were large flat tiles with a raised boss at each corner. The tiles were built against a wall, from which the bosses kept the tiles at a constant distance, forming a cavity for a heating flue in a hypocaust system. Half-box tiles (resembling box tiles cut in two lengthways) were used in a similar manner. An alternative method was to use flat tiles held away from the wall by cylindrical ceramic spacer bobbins, through which an iron pin or cramp was hammered to hold the tiles in place.

The hollow rectangular box tiles (*tubuli*) became most commonly used in heating flues. The term *tubuli* (or *tubi*) is also used for ceramic drainage pipes. In a hypocaust system the flues conducted hot air and gases from the underfloor cavity up the walls to roof vents. Hollow voussoir tiles were sometimes built into vaulted roofs to conduct the hot air and gases from these flues to a central vent, but for ridged roofs, vents were usually under the eaves. (*See also* "Heating," chapter 4.)

Markings

Tiles used for flues in walls were designed to be plastered over, and so their exterior surface was scored to provide a keying for plaster. This was done with a sharp instrument, often a comb so that the teeth created parallel score marks. In Britain a number of tiles from the south and east of the province have roller-printed patterns instead of scoring. Most of the patterns are purely abstract, but some include figures of animals and initials or names.

Many bricks and tiles were impressed with a stamp before firing, some with the name of the army unit that made them (fig. 8.10) and others with the name

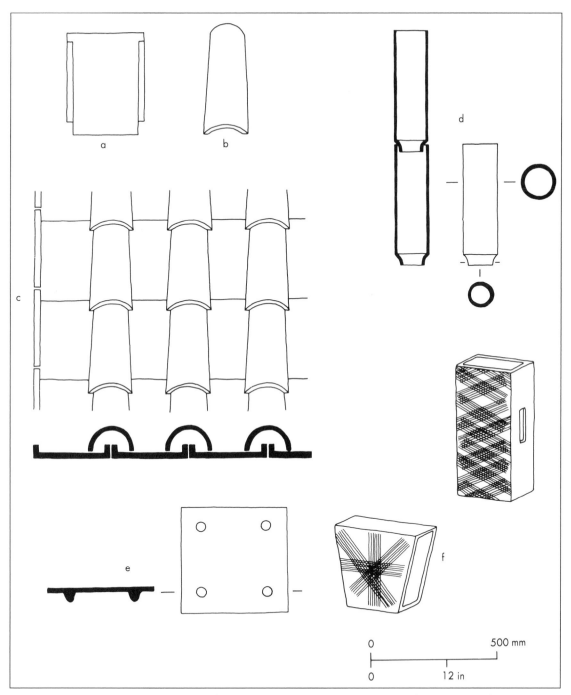

Fig. 8.9 Examples of tiles: a. tegula; *b.* imbrex; *c. reconstruction of part of roof of* imbrices *and* tegulae; *d. drainage pipes; e.* tegula mammata; *f. hollow voussoir tile; g. box tile.*

Fig. 8.10 A tile stamped LEGIIAVG— made by the II Augusta legion. The tile has also been marked with signatures.

of the person running the kiln or the controlling private company, imperial estate or municipal magistrates. Some stamps included the consular date. By the early 3rd century brick production at Rome had become an imperial monopoly. Very few bricks appear to have been stamped from the reign of Caracalla (211–217), although the practice was reinstated after the reorganization of the brick industry by Diocletian (284–305). Stamps were still being used as late as the reign of Theodoric (493–526).

Some bricks and tiles were deliberately marked by fingers to produce surface grooves (signatures) before firing (fig. 8.10). The purpose of this marking is unknown, but it may have denoted the person or brickyard that made the bricks or tiles or simply the end of a batch. Cuts on the edges of some bricks and tiles resemble Roman numerals and may have been tally marks.

GLASS (fig. 8.11)

Glass was made by heating a mixture of silica (usually sand), soda (from natural soda deposits or from ashes of certain sea plants) and lime (from limestone). Other ingredients were added to give the glass different colors.

Glass beads were produced from around the mid-3rd millennium BC, and glass vessels were made in Mesopotamia from before 1500 BC. By the 9th century BC the industry was established in Mesopotamia and north Syria. During the Hellenistic period, centers of production changed. Glass does not appear to have been made in Mesopotamia from the late 4th century BC for two or three hundred years, but it continued in Syria. Soon after Alexandria's foundation in 332 BC, the city became a glassmaking center, and it rapidly became the dominant center of production, its market including Rome. Glassmaking also spread to Italy and possibly to Cyprus and Rhodes. From these centers glass was exported widely through the Mediterranean area.

At this time, the Romans used four main methods of manufacturing glass vessels, none of which enabled the easy manufacture of large pieces. Closed vessels, such as bottles and vials, were formed from molten glass around cores (probably of mud), which were removed piecemeal when the glass had cooled. A second method was to assemble glass rods around a core, which were heated to fuse them together. Open vessels could be cut and ground from a block of glass. It is assumed that vessels showing signs of this method of manufacture were shaped from a piece of glass cast to approximately the right shape, rather than from a solid block. As techniques improved, vessels were cast in molds and finished off by grinding and fire-polishing (reheating at the furnace to give the vessel a shiny surface). All these methods were skilled and time-consuming, and so glass in the republic was an expensive luxury commodity and relatively unimportant.

In the 1st century BC glassblowing was invented, probably in Syria. This technique relied on the fact that glass will stick to hot iron. Iron tubes, long enough to protect the glassmaker (*vitriarius*) from being burned, were dipped into molten glass. The glassmaker blew down the tube to form a bubble of glass, which could be formed into the desired shape. This process was much faster and could also be used to make larger and more intricately shaped vessels, resulting in a virtual revolution in the glass industry. Glass became cheaper and much more widely available. By the early 1st century AD glass vessels were being used for everyday purposes such as storage, and bottles were made as packaging for items of trade.

Glassmaking spread across the Roman world, minimizing the distance that fragile glass vessels had to be transported to their markets. (See also chapter

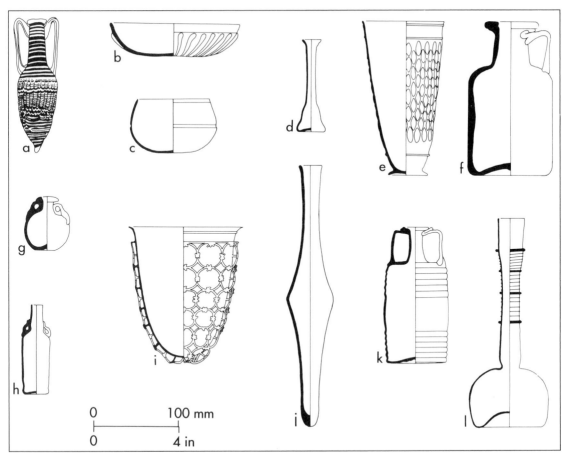

Fig. 8.11 Examples of glass vessel forms: a, amphoriskos, core-formed in brown-green glass (shown black), white and yellow opaque trails (shown white), with clear amber handles and base-knob, 2nd–1st century BC; b. pillar-molded bowl, made by casting, 1st century. Blown vessels: c. Hofheim cup, with wheel-cut lines, 1st century; d. unguent bottle, 1st century; e. faceted beaker, with cut facets, 1st century; f. square bottle, mold-blown, 1st century; g. aryballos, (oil flask), often used for taking oils to the baths, 2nd century; h. cylindrical bottle with dolphin handles, late 3rd century; i. cage cup, 4th century; j. unguent bottle, 4th century; k. mold-blown two-handled barrel-shaped bottle, sometimes with a name (such as "Frontinus") on the base, 4th century; l. flask with trail decoration, 6th century.

5.) Glass is known to have been made in Rome, Puteoli, Aquileia and Cologne, which became major centers for its production. Eventually most if not all provinces probably had several glassmaking centers, but relatively little has survived of furnaces and tools, and few glassmaking sites are known.

Some glassware continued as luxury goods, because of the craftsmanship involved. In the 1st century highly colored vessels were particularly popular, but they went out of fashion at the end of the century, giving way to clear colorless glass. Cutting and engraving by glass-cutters (diatretarii) as decoration continued throughout the Roman period, including the engraving of scenes with figures on clear glass vessels. Particularly fine examples of cutting were cameo vessels and cage cups, the latter with almost free-standing carved designs. Glass was also decorated by the addition of trails and blobs, by blowing glass vessels in decorated molds and by painting and gilding.

As well as vessels, many objects of glass were made, such as beads, bangles, decorative plaques and portrait busts. Window glass was a 1st-century Roman invention. It was probably made by simply casting it onto a flat surface, possibly a wooden mold. Probably in the

3rd century, window glass was made by the cylinder method, in which a cylinder was cut from an elongated bubble of glass. The cylinder was then cut lengthways and opened out to form a flat rectangular sheet.

The unrest during the 4th and 5th centuries resulted in declining markets for glass, particularly in the west, where glass again became an expensive luxury commodity, with a much narrower range of vessel forms. Decline was not so severe or rapid in the east, where high-quality glass continued to be made.

FOOD PROCESSING

Wine

Wine production was a major industry, giving rise to an export trade throughout the Roman world. (See chapter 5.) Most evidence for wine production comes from Italy but is probably representative of the methods used elsewhere. After picking, the grapes were sorted. Selected ones were taken to the press room, where the grapes were trodden on a raised paved floor. The juice was fed into an intermediate reservoir or straight into huge jars (*dolia*). A simple mechanical press then removed much more juice from the pulp. These presses consisted of a large wooden beam that was anchored at one end and acted as a lever. The grape pulp was placed on a hard surface beneath the lever toward its fixed end, and the other end of the lever was forced downward by using ropes and levers or else a screw mechanism. The residue (must) from treading and pressing was often mixed with water to make a drink.

The grape juice was left to ferment in *dolia*, which were usually sunk into the ground in a yard adjacent to the press room, or else it was fermented in barrels or vats. When fermentation was complete, the wine was transferred to amphorae and left to mature.

Olive Oil

Olive oil was traded extensively. It was a major source of food and lighting fuel, and was also used in other commodities, such as soaps, perfumes, medicaments, skin oils and cosmetics. After picking, the olives were pressed to extract the oil. They may have been stored for a few days before pressing, but ancient authors are contradictory about the storage period, with some advocating immediate pressing. The olives were crushed in a special mill that enabled the distance between the upper and lower stones to be adjusted to avoid crushing the bitter-tasting kernels. The juice was collected in a reservoir and the oil was ladled off the top into pottery vessels, leaving behind the bitter-tasting water from the olives. The paste from the crushed olives (excluding the kernels) was pressed in a beam press similar to that used for wine, and the resulting liquid was fed into a sedimentation tank from which further oil was recovered.

Fish Sauce

Fish sauce was an expensive luxury delicacy that was traded widely. It was exported in large quantities from

Fig. 8.12   A large mill in a bakery at Pompeii. On the left is an oven.

Baetica to Italy and elsewhere from the late 1st century BC. Fish sauce (*garum*) was a by-product of fish processing, made by fermenting the intestines and other waste parts of fish. The recipe for fish sauce varied according to the type of fish (usually vertebrate) being used. Mackerel, anchovies, sprats, tunny and red mullet are known to have been used and sometimes shellfish as well. Whatever the recipe, the manufacture seems to have consisted of putting the ingredients in a vessel and allowing them to ferment for several months, although some recipes advise boiling the ingredients together first. When fermentation was complete, the liquid fish sauce was strained, leaving a residue (*hallec*), which was also sold. Less well-known fish sauces included *liquamen* and *muria*.

Mills and Baking

The milling of grain into flour was originally a household occupation. Saddle querns were used—grain was placed on a flat quernstone and was crushed by rubbing another stone backward and forward over the top. From the early 2nd century BC rotary querns and mills were developed. Rotary hand querns remained in common use and consisted of an upper concave stone and a lower convex one. Grain was fed through an aperture in the upper stone, which was simultaneously rotated. However, larger rotary mills (donkey mills) powered by donkeys and mules became increasingly common (fig. 8.12). They consisted of a bell-shaped lower stone and an hourglass upper stone.

Watermills were developed from the 1st century BC and were capable of milling far greater quantities of grain. There is some evidence that watermills may occasionally have been used for other industrial purposes. The largest known watermill is at Barbegal, Provence, which was supplied by its own aqueduct and had a complex of 16 millwheels in two parallel rows. This is probably the most impressive Roman industrial monument to have survived, but it is an exception. Most milling remained a small-scale local occupation, usually carried out by bakers.

Milling and baking were often done on the same premises. In rural areas baking was a household task, but in towns and probably in many villages bakers provided not only bread but pastries and confectionery.

TEXTILES

As might be expected, the main finished products of the textile industry were clothing, but cloth had various other uses, such as blankets, rugs, bags, sacks and tapestries (fig. 8 .13). The manufacture of cloth consisted of three basic processes—fiber preparation, spinning, and weaving.

Fiber Preparation

The preparation varied according to the fiber. Wool was usually sheared in early summer using iron shears

Fig. 8.13 The Igel monument, Germany, erected by wealthy merchants, the Secundinii, to commemorate their connection with the textile industry. Scenes on the monument show the preparation and finishing of cloth.

similar to ones still occasionally used today. Impurities in long staple wool were removed using a flat iron comb with long teeth, but impurities in short wool were probably removed by hand.

Flax was harvested in high summer by pulling up the complete flax plants by hand. The flax was retted by soaking it in stagnant or slow-flowing water for about three weeks, after which it was dried, pounded with a wooden mallet and scutched. In scutching, the flax was bent over a narrow object and beaten with a wooden sword to loosen and separate the fibers. The fibers were combed (hackled) to remove impurities. Hemp fibers were prepared in a similar way.

Cultivated silk and silk fabrics were imported from China and wild silk from India and Cos. Cultivated silk was a single fiber and did not need spinning; wild silk probably was in short lengths that would have been spun, but otherwise no preparation was needed.

Instances of cotton are known, and occasionally the Romans experimented with other fibers such as rabbit and goat hair, mallow and asbestos.

Spinning

Spinning was a labor-intensive cottage industry. The quality of the finished yarn could be almost equivalent to modern machine-spun yarn. Spinning was done with a spindle and distaff. In its simplest form the distaff was a forked stick, which supported a mass of fibers and was held in the left hand. The spindle was a wooden or bone rod up to 200 mm (8 in) long, thicker toward the lower end to hold a spindle whorl. Spindle whorls were of various materials, commonly stone, bone or pottery. They acted as flywheels to aid the rotation of the spindle.

To spin yarn, fibers were drawn out from the mass on the distaff and were twisted into a thread, which was tied to the top of the spindle. The spindle was set spinning, and fibers were drawn out by hand to add to the lengthening thread. When the spindle reached the floor, the thread was wound onto it and the process was repeated.

Weaving

The warp-weighted vertical loom was used throughout the Roman world. It consisted of two wooden uprights with a horizontal beam across the top and a shed rod farther down to separate even and odd numbered warp threads. This created the gap (shed) through which the horizontal weft thread was passed. A heddle rod brought the odd-numbered warp threads backward and forward to alternate the shed so that the weft thread could be passed through as a single movement. The vertical warp threads were weighted with stone or baked clay weights (loomweights).

Another loom that came into use during the Roman period was the two-beam loom. This was also an upright loom, but the warp threads were held in tension between an upper and a lower cloth beam. This loom was often used for tapestry weaving. The horizontal loom is known to have been used in the later Roman period but was probably confined to a few specialist workshops, such as those of silk weavers. Weaving tablets and band looms were used for weaving braid.

Dyeing and Fulling

It was more usual to dye unspun fiber than yarn or finished cloth. Vegetable dyes were common, but lichens and shellfish were also used. Purple dye, often used by the Romans, was obtained from various sources (such as lichens and shellfish), with the shellfish *murex* being especially well regarded. Many dyes would not remain fast without a mordant, and so alum or iron salts were often applied beforehand.

Cloth was finished by fulling, which involved treading it in a tub containing a solution of fuller's earth or decayed urine to remove grease and dirt. Woolen cloth was sometimes bleached with sulfur, and some cloth was finished by raising and cropping the nap.

LEATHER

Leather was an important material throughout the Roman world, used for a wide range of articles such as saddles, shoes, harness, tents, bags, buckets, jugs, shields and some clothing.

Tanning

Tanning is a series of processes whereby raw animal skins are converted into leather. The exact combination of processes depends on what kind of leather is required. The raw hides had to be treated to prevent bacterial decay before they reached the tanyard. This was usually done by salting, but sometimes hides were merely sun dried, or they might be salted after drying.

At the tanyard, the hides were washed and then limed. This made them more receptive to the tanning liquids and loosened wool and hair, which were removed by scraping off the top layer of the hide (epidermis). Similarly, fat was scraped from the inner surface of the skin to leave the corium or derma, which is made into leather. The hide was then tanned by soaking in a solution of wood and bark or a solution of alum and salt. After tanning, leather underwent various processes, known collectively as finishing, to produce leather of the desired color, texture and surface appearance.

Decoration

Leather articles were decorated in several ways. The leather could be cut into patterned shapes, such as on openwork sandals. Patterns could also be made with stamps and punches to produce pierced or relief designs, and decorative stitching was also used, sometimes combined with an appliqué pattern.

Bone, Antler and Ivory

Animal bone and antler were used for objects such as hairpins, bracelets, rings, gaming counters, styli, weaving tablets, spindle whorls, spoons and dice. They were also used for parts of other articles, such as knife handles, hinges for cupboards and boxes and decorative inlays for furniture. It is not known if specialist craftsmen made bone objects. It is more likely that a variety of craftsmen used bone so that, for example, jewelers made bone bracelets. There do not appear to have been any specialized tools used in the working of bone, which was generally cut, carved and shaped in a similar way to wood.

Ivory was occasionally used in the early empire for furniture inlay. Diptychs were carved in wood or ivory, usually commemorating a consulate or other important event (see also chapter 6) and were presented to notables, cities and the emperor. In 354 a law was passed restricting the use of gilt and ivory to consuls.

Woodworking

Wood

Wood was extensively used in the construction of buildings, boats, ships, carts, fortifications, tools, weapons, barrels, furniture and carvings. Woodworking skills were highly developed, and specific types of wood were deliberately selected for different purposes. A great deal of timber used by woodworkers was locally grown, but it could be traded over long distances.

Tools

The range of woodworking tools is much the same as hand tools available today, and a high standard of craftsmanship was attained. There were various kinds of frame saw, the simplest of which was the bow saw. This had a saw blade fixed to the ends of a piece of wood that had been bent into a semicircle, so that the stress in the wood kept the saw blade taut. More commonly an H-shaped wooden frame was used; the saw blade was fixed across the bottom of the H, while a cord was fixed across the top of the H and tightened in order to keep the saw blade taut.

Axes, adzes and draw-knives were used for shaping wood, and chisels and gouges were used for much the same purposes as in modern carpentry and joinery. Rasps and files for smoothing and shaping wood are also known.

Planes were used for trimming and smoothing wood. Some had the blade set in a wooden body, while others also had an iron sole that made the plane more accurate and hard-wearing. Iron planes are known, with both the blade and the body of the plane made from iron, and the paneling on a 3rd-century wooden door found in Egypt suggests that molding planes were used.

Lathes were employed for turning wood to produce objects such as bowls, furniture legs and even small round tabletops. Holes in wood were made by bow drills or augers, and joinery techniques included mortise-and-tenon and dovetail joints. Wooden pegs, glue, iron nails or a combination of these were used to join pieces of wood, but not screws. For fixing larger timbers, joiners' dogs and T-clamps were common.

EXTRACTIVE INDUSTRIES

Mining

With the exception of agriculture, mining was one of the largest industries in the Roman world, and was organized on an immense scale. Evidence for mining is found in many provinces, but particularly in Spain, extremely important for gold, silver, copper, tin, lead and iron. Because many sites continued to be mined long after the Romans, much evidence for Roman mining techniques has been obliterated, and dating mines can be very difficult. Most mines were in imperial control, often leased out to companies.

UNDERGROUND MINING

In hard-rock formations, the usual mining method was digging of vertical shafts with galleries to follow the mineral vein. Most Roman shafts were square or rectangular, but occasionally circular. Entry down the shafts was by foothold notches cut in the sides of the shaft walls or sometimes by wood hammered into the walls. Adits (horizontal or sloping shafts) could be extremely long, some cutting through a large body of barren rock before reaching the ore. Galleries leading off the shafts varied in shape and size. Adits and galleries could be square, rectangular, arched or trapezoidal.

It is possible that adits and galleries were driven into the rock with the assistance of fire setting, a process whereby a fire is lit against the rock face and the heat causes the rock to expand and crack. The heated rock can be quenched with water, which causes rapid contraction and disintegration. Shoring was little needed in adits and galleries because of their small height and width, but wooden props for supporting roofs have been found occasionally.

Numerous types of iron tools were used in mining, including picks, chisels and wedges, and rock faces were carefully worked. Lighting was probably provided by oil lamps, small niches for which have been found. Ventilation would have been a problem, and the use of fire setting could have produced noxious fumes. This may explain the common occurrence of shafts in pairs. Lighting a fire at the bottom of one shaft would increase the draft down the other shaft and so provide fresh air.

The other problem when mining at depth is water. The Romans used three main methods to overcome this difficulty. The most simple was bailing with a chain of buckets. Another method, not commonly used, was to cut cross adits and drainage channels down which water could flow to a sump from where it was bailed. The most effective method of drainage was the use of machinery, and there is evidence for the screw pump and the water wheel to raise water from mines, powered by human labor. Screw pumps were mounted in a series and raised water from one sump to another by being rotated. Water wheels were more effective and more commonly used, often in pairs.

The ore could be removed from the mines by human chains with buckets. Buckets for bailing and removal of ore were probably made from various materials. In Spain ones of copper alloy and of esparto grass are known, the latter made waterproof by a lining of tar or pitch. Ore haulage baskets strengthened by wood were also used.

SURFACE MINING

For soft-rock deposits (such as the gold-bearing rocks in northwest Spain) and in some hard-rock deposits, opencast (surface) mining was used. This method required vast quantities of water, and so extensive aqueduct and tank systems had to be constructed. The tanks varied in shape and size, but most were rectangular. Two techniques were used—hushing and ground sluicing. In hushing (or booming) water was collected in large tanks fed by aqueducts and was then released in a wave to pour down over the deposit. This removed the overburden, exposing the mineral deposits, and also removed mining debris. In ground sluicing a more controlled, continuous supply of water was used to wash out the ore and remove the overburden.

SECONDARY MINING TECHNIQUES

Once the ore-bearing material had been mined or washed out by hushing or ground sluicing, the ore had to be extracted. Most ores could be retrieved by crushing and by the use of flowing water, because ores will settle out while the lighter waste is washed away.

Quarrying

Because of the high cost of transport, stone was normally used locally. However, some stones such as marble were shipped over considerable distances (see chapter 5), as were some stone products such as quernstones. Nearly all the major quarries were near the sea or rivers. In the western provinces there was no pre-Roman tradition of building in mortared stone, and so under the Romans there was a particularly great expansion in the quarrying industry. Most quarries producing fine stone were under imperial control, but others were private enterprises. Various stones were quarried, and inscriptions have been found on some rock faces. Stone was generally quarried by splitting blocks from their bed by driving wedges. The blocks were then trimmed and dressed at the quarry face. Quarrying tools included picks, axes and adzes.

Clay was quarried for the ceramics industry, and sand and gravel were excavated for aggregate in mortar and concrete. Large quantities of chalk and limestone were also quarried and burned in kilns for lime for mortar. (See chapter 4.)

Salt

Salt was usually produced by the evaporation of seawater or water from inland salt springs. The water was evaporated in lagoons by the sun or in shallow clay pans supported on cylindrical fire bars over hearths.

Fragments of the pans and bars, known as briquetage, are often found. The industry may have been under imperial control. Salt was used mainly for preserving foodstuffs and in the leather industry.

METALWORKING

The conversion of ores into metal ready for use involved several processes, including smelting with charcoal in a fire or furnace. Smelting was usually undertaken as close as possible to the mines, although ores were occasionally transported when charcoal was unavailable nearby. Iron ore smelting required techniques more sophisticated than those for other ores, and bowl furnaces and shaft furnaces were used. Silver was obtained from lead by a further process known as cupellation.

The smelted metals were poured into molds to form ingots (see chapter 5), which were transported to manufacturing centers for the production of artifacts. Metals were used for the production of coinage at official mints, and much was used to produce arms and armor (see chapter 2), but many other metal goods were also produced.

Gold

Several goldsmiths' workshops are known. Jewelry was the main product, including chain necklaces, rings, bracelets, earrings and pendants. Most objects were made from sheet gold, which was formed by hammering a gold ingot on an anvil. Gold wire was used to manufacture objects such as chains and earrings, and very occasionally objects were cast.

Silver

Syria, Alexandria and Italy were particularly famous for the production of silver ware, but most major cities probably had a silver industry. Much was produced in small workshops, but there is evidence for larger factories producing silver plate. Most plate is found in western provinces, but any signatures are generally those of Greek artists, who may have moved around seeking patronage. The techniques of silver working are similar to those in use today. Silver could be hammered into shape, and all traces of hammering removed by polishing. Decoration was done by repoussé work, engraving, chasing and gilding, and niello inlay was often used.

Silver was used mainly for jewelry, such as rings and bracelets, but also for vessels, strainers and spoons, for religious or domestic use (fig. 8.14). Some of the silver ware was highly decorated, often with pagan themes or Christian motifs. Silver plate was rare at Rome until the Second Punic War, when rich sources of metals became available in Spain and much booty was captured from elsewhere. In the later 4th and early 5th centuries much plate of high quality was made. Silver dishes were often presented to emperors and other notables as customary gifts, while a great deal was apparently purchased for domestic use. Silver and gold were also given to troops as donatives.

Fig. 8.14 *Part of a funeral monument from Neumagen, Germany, depicting a table set for a meal. The table was probably of marble and has carved lion's heads on the legs. The metal vessels were probably of bronze and silver. The man holds a pottery beaker and appears to be ready to serve the family.*

Bronze

Copper was most commonly used as an alloy with tin to produce bronze, although brass could be produced by the addition of zinc to copper. Bronze was used for a diverse range of objects, including tableware, coins weapons and jewelry. It was sometimes worked cold but was usually cast, with lead added to increase its fluidity. Objects could be made by being cast in stone molds or by the lost-wax method—a beeswax model was covered in clay and fired, melting the wax. Molten bronze was poured into the hollow, and when solidified, the clay was removed.

Larger hollow objects were made by core casting (hollow casting) — one method was to make a rough shape in clay with a wax model around it. This was covered with clay, and bronze pins were inserted so that the clay core remained in place after the wax was melted in the firing. Molten bronze was poured into the gap left by the wax. The outer clay mold was removed, sometimes in pieces so that it could be reused as a piece mold. This enabled the mass production of objects such as deities or portraits of the emperor. The clay core was removed through a hole, which was sealed over with bronze.

Open vessels could be formed by casting in stone molds or by hammering and shaping sheet bronze around a mold as it was rotated on a lathe. Closed vessels such as jugs (fig. 8.14) were formed in two-piece molds using the core-casting technique. The inner core was removed through the base, which was subsequently added. Many bronze objects were highly decorated, such as by the addition of bronzework and other metals to the surface or by enameling.

Enameling

Enamel is a vitreous material fused to a metallic surface (mainly bronze) as a means of decoration in various bright colors. Areas of bronze were cut out or cast as hollows, filled with glass powder and heated so that the glass powder fused with the bronze to form enamel.

Lead, Pewter, Tin

Various objects were made of lead, such as weights, seals and spindle whorls. Sheet lead was widely used for objects such as water tanks, water pipes, bath linings, containers and coffins. Lead was also used in the production of pewter.

Pewter, an alloy of lead and tin, was used as a solder throughout the Roman world. It was also popular in Britain in the 3rd century as a substitute for silver, particularly for tableware. Pewter was always cast, and stone molds have been found.

Tin was used as an alloy with copper to make bronze and with lead to make pewter. It was also used for tinning brooches and military bronzes as well as the interior of bronze cooking vessels.

Iron

Iron was worked by blacksmiths in forges with a variety of tools. Anvils were roughly squared blocks of iron. Most of the shaping and finishing of objects was done with variously shaped hammers, and holes were made with punches. Smithing was a particularly common industry throughout the Roman world, and a vast range of objects was produced, especially tools, weapons and fittings.

STONEWORKING

Stone served a large number of purposes, particularly in buildings, but was also used for objects such as sculptures, tombstones, altars and tables (fig. 8.14). Masons required a wide range of tools. In marble sculpture points, punches and chisels were commonly employed, with the bow drill for finer details. Projecting parts (such as arms) were often added separately, rather than being carved from a single block. They were joined with stone or metal dowels strengthened by lead or mortar, or sometimes glue. Columns for buildings appear to have been turned on a lathe.

Shale was used in the northwestern provinces for objects such as tabletops, table legs, bracelets, plates, trays, spindle whorls, counters and carvings. Because shale is a soft rock, many objects could be made on a lathe using techniques similar to woodworking. Amber and jet (organic in origin, unlike other gem-stones) were also skillfully carved. Amber (a fossil resin) came from the Baltic, and was used for decorative inlay and for objects such as rings, pendants, boxes and figurines. Jet (a form of fossilized wood) came from Whitby, Britain, and was used for various objects, including pins, finger rings, bangles, beads, pendants, spindle whorls, dice, handles and counters. Jet seems to have been used in the 3rd and 4th centuries when amber supplies became scarce.

The intaglio carving of precious stones for jewelry and seals set in rings was done with a simple drill with changeable heads. Although glass magnifying lenses existed, their use in this industry is uncertain. The carving techniques developed from the middle republic, and by the 1st century BC a wide range of stones was available and particular artists can be recognized. From the time of Augustus (27 BC–AD 14), large cameos were cut in state workshops, a tradition maintained throughout the empire. Apart from cut stones, gemstones with relief decoration were also made of glass paste impressed in molds. They were intended for the popular market but had blurred impressions. Vessels, free-standing portraits and figurines were occasionally carved from precious stones.

READING

Oleson 1986: comprises annotated bibliography on many aspects of craft and technology.

Coinage
Burnett et al. 1992: late republican and early imperial coinage; Casey 1980: imperial coinage, with particular reference to Britain; Carson 1978: illustrated description of republican coins; Carson 1980: illustrated description of coins of the principate; Carson 1981: illustrated description of coins of the late empire; Carson 1990: description of all types of coins with plates and numerous references; Crawford 1985: republican coinage with many photographs and maps; Greene 1986, 45–66: coinage, banking and monetary economy, with numerous references; Hammond and Scullard (eds.) 1970, 160–1, 261–63, 698–99; Jones 1990: dictionary of coins; Kent 1987: imperial coins;

Lewis and Reinhold 1990: includes Diocletian's Price Edict; Oleson 1986; Reece 1970: types of coins, designs and legends; Reece 1983: artistic designs on coins in the republic and empire; Sellwood 1976: minting of coins.

Weights and measures
Hammond and Scullard (eds.) 1970, 659, 1138; Sandys (ed.) 1921, 436–41.

Industry
Bradley 1991, 103–24: child labor; including apprentices; Burford 1972: various aspects of craftsmanship, including patronage and *collegia*; Greene 1986; Manning 1987; Oleson 1986; Wacher 1987: includes an overview of industry in the empire.

Pottery
Bailey 1976: manufacture of lamps; Bailey 1983: lamps and figurines; Bailey 1991: lamps of metal and clay, listing the major publications from 1980; Brown 1976b: techniques of pottery manufacture; Greene 1979: fine wares of pre-Flavian date, with many illustrations and references; Greene 1986, 156–68: trade and manufacture of pottery, especially terra sigillata; Johns 1971: terra sigillata; King 1983: decorated pottery from the republic to the late empire; Oleson 1986; Peacock 1982: manufacture of various types of pottery, with extensive references; Peacock and Williams 1986: types, uses and trade of amphorae with a revised classification of forms; Swan 1984: illustrated analysis of kilns in Britain, methods of pottery manufacture and references.

Brick and Tile
Bailey 1983: terracotta revetments; Brodribb 1987; McWhirr (ed.) 1979; McWhirr 1982; Oleson 1986; Sear 1982.

Glass
Harden 1970; Harden et al. 1968; Harden et al. 1987; Isings 1957; Newby and Painter (eds.) 1991: articles on glass of 1st centuries BC and AD, extensive bibliography; Oleson 1986; Price 1976, 1983.

Food Processing
Bateman and Locker 1982: fish sauce; Hill 1984, 155–64: water power for milling; Mattingly 1988: olive oil; Oleson 1986; Peacock and Williams 1986, 31–39: wine, olive oil, fish sauce; Shelton 1988, 85–86:

a recipe for fish sauce; Tchernia 1986: wine; White 1984: wine, olive oil.

Textiles
McWhirr 1982; Manning 1985, 33–37: wools used in wool and cloth processing; Oleson 1986; Wild 1970, 1976, 1988.

Leather
McWhirr 1982; Manning 1985, 39–42: leatherworking tools; Oleson 1986; Waterer 1976.

Bone, Antler, Ivory
Henig 1983, 163–64; MacGregor 1985: describes technology and gives examples of artifacts; Strong 1976: includes ivory diptychs.

Woodworking
Liversidge 1976; Manning 1985, 15–29: woodworking tools; Meiggs 1982: supply of timber; Oleson 1986.

Extractive Industries
Dodge 1991: review article on the marble industry, with bibliography; Edmondson 1989: mining in the late empire; Healey 1978: mining; Hill 1984, 127–54: water-raising machines; Landels 1978, 58–83: water pumps; Oleson 1986; Woods 1987: mining, including drainage methods.

Metalworking
Brown 1976a: bronze and pewter working; Butcher 1976: enameling; Cameron 1992: late Roman silver plate; Cleere 1976: ironmaking; Healey 1978: processing of ores; Henig 1983: includes decorative metalwork; Higgins 1976: goldsmithing; Higgins (ed.) 1980: jewelry manufacturing techniques; Kent and Painter (eds.) 1977: gold and silver of the late empire; Manning 1976: blacksmithing; Manning 1985: metalworking tools and ironwork of various kinds; Oleson 1986; Sherlock 1976: silversmithing; Strong 1966: gold and silver plate up to the 5th century, including manufacturing methods; White 1984, 120–26: metallurgy.

Stoneworking
Henig 1983: includes engraved gems, amber and jet; Strong and Claridge 1976: marble sculpture; Manning 1985, 30–32: stoneworking tools; Oleson 1986.

9

EVERYDAY LIFE

TIME

Dates of Years

The Romans usually dated their years by the names of the consuls (in the empire, those who took office on 1 January) and sometimes by the regnal year of the emperor. Dating by consuls was used until 537 when Justinian introduced dating according to regnal years of emperors, although dating by consuls continued to 611 in Egypt. Lists of consuls (*fasti*) exist from 509 BC but are unreliable before 300 BC. Years were occasionally dated from the foundation of Rome (*ab urbe condita*). Many other dating systems were used across the empire, including eras that were used only locally. The method of dating the Christian era using BC and AD was introduced in the mid-6th century, starting with year 1 from the birth of Christ: there was no year 0.

Indictio (indiction) originally meant the announcement of the compulsory delivery of food and other goods to the government. From 287 the term was used for the annual assessment of taxation in kind, numbered serially in five-year cycles and from 312 in 15-year cycles. It was often used for dating financial years (which usually began on 1 September) and then as a general means of dating. The population usually knew the year of indiction better than the consular year.

Converting ancient dates to the modern calendar can be difficult. Exact dates before Caesar's calendar reform in 45 BC are questionable, giving rise to discrepancies in converted dates, and numerous other factors can affect conversions.

Calendar

The lunar month (the period between one new moon and the next) measures 29½ days, but the yearly cycle of the earth around the sun is about 365¼ days (about 11 days longer than 12 lunar months). All calendars were originally lunar.

MONTHS

The word calendar and the names and order of the months are of Roman origin. Knowledge of Roman calendars derives from literary sources and from surviving fragments of inscribed calendars (*fasti*), including the *fasti consulares*. The original Roman calendar (year of Romulus) was an agricultural ten-month year. There were ten irregular months (totaling 304 days) from March to December (month ten). The names of the months originated in this first calendar, with an uncounted gap from December to March when no agricultural work was possible.

The change to a 12-month lunar calendar probably occurred in the 6th century BC. In 153 BC January was made the first month of the year. Until Caesar's calendar reform, the Roman year comprised 355 days divided into 12 months, four with 31 days (March, May, July, October), seven with 29 days (January, April, June, August, September, November, December) and February with 28 days. Their names were adjectives relating to *mensis* (month): *Ianuarius, Februarius, Martius, Aprilis, Maius, Iunius, Quin(c)tilis* (fifth month, renamed *Iulius* in 44 BC after Julius Caesar), *Sextilis* (sixth month, renamed *Augustus* in 8 BC after the emperor Augustus), *September* (seventh month), *October* (eight month), *November* (ninth month), *December* (tenth month). Many of the names were a legacy from the ten-month year.

Evidence for intercalation (addition of days to adjust to the solar year) is limited, but apparently 22 or 23 days (called *Mercedonius* or *Intercalaris*) were added every other year in February, so that on average there were 366¼ days per year (about one day too many). Intercalation became a function of the pontiffs but was not properly undertaken, so that by Julius Caesar's time, the civic year was about three months ahead of the solar year. Caesar therefore extended 46 BC to 445 days to remove this discrepancy. From 1 January 45 BC he made the year consist of 365 days, with the months containing their present numbers of days. Caesar also introduced the leap year by inserting an extra day between 23 and 24 February. It was originally every three years, then corrected to four years from 8 BC. The resulting Julian calendar (named after Julius Caesar) was about 11 minutes longer than the solar year.

The modern Gregorian calendar is essentially the same as the Julian calendar. The only substantial changes took place under Pope Gregory XIII, who in 1582 omitted ten days from that year alone to adjust the discrepancy between the Julian calendar and the solar year, and ordered that three days be omitted in leap years every four hundred years.

DAYS

The days of the month were not numbered serially but in relation to three named days, from which the dates were counted retrospectively. The Kalends (*Kalendae*) was the first of the month. The Nones (*Nonae*) was the ninth day before the Ides (according to the Roman method of inclusive counting). This was equivalent to the 5th (or 7th in a month of 31 days), and was originally the first quarter of the moon. The Ides (*Idus*) was the 13th (or 15th in a month of 31 days), originally corresponding with the full moon of the lunar month. The number of the day was calculated by so many days (*ante diem*) before the Kalends, Nones, or Ides, although the day before a named day was *pridie*. All these names were usually abbreviated.

Table 9.1   Roman Julian Calendar for November

Modern Date	Roman Date
1 Nov	*Kalendis Novembribus* (*Kalendae*)
2	*a(nte) d(iem) IV Nonas Novembres*
3	*a.d. III Non. Nov.*
4	*pridie Nonas Novembres*
5	*Nonis Novembribus* (*Nonae*)
6	*a.d. VIII Id. Nov.*
7	*a.d. VII Id. Nov.*
8	*a.d. VI Id. Nov.*
9	*a.d. V Id. Nov.*
10	*a.d. IV Id. Nov.*
11	*a.d. III Id. Nov.*
12	*pridie Idus Novembres*
13	*Idibus Novembribus* (*Idus*)
14	*a(nte) d(iem) XVIII K(alendas) Dec(embres)*
15	*a.d. XVII Kal. Dec.*
16	*a.d. XVI Kal. Dec.*
17	*a.d. XV Kal. Dec.*
18	*a.d. XIV Kal. Dec.*
19	*a.d. XIII Kal. Dec.*
20	*a.d. XII Kal. Dec.*
21	*a.d. XI Kal. Dec.*
22	*a.d. X Kal. Dec.*
23	*a.d. IX Kal. Dec.*
24	*a.d. VIII Kal. Dec.*
25	*a.d. VII Kal. Dec.*
26	*a.d. VI Kal. Dec.*
27	*a.d. V Kal. Dec.*
28	*a.d. IV Kal. Dec.*
29	*a.d. III Kal. Dec.*
30	*pridie Kal. Dec.*
1 Dec	*Kalendis Decembribus*

The official calendar was drawn up by the pontiffs and contained the dates of religious festivals. Days on the calendar were marked with various letters, including C (*comitialis*—days when *comitia* might be held), F (*fasti*) or N (*nefasti*). (See chapter 7)

WEEKS

From earliest times, a market day (*nundinae*) occurred every eight days—every ninth day, according to the Roman method of inclusive reckoning. It was a day of rest from agricultural labor and a time to take produce to market. The intervening period was a *nundinum*. The seven-day period was used in the east, particularly by astrologers in Hellenistic times, with some days receiving the names of the planets. The earliest reference to a seven-day period at Rome is in the time of Augustus (27 BC–AD 14), and it was gradually adopted during the empire.

Clocks

The day was divided into 12 hours of night and 12 hours of day, so that a daylight hour was not the same length as a night hour (except at an equinox) and varied from month to month. A daylight hour in midwinter was about 45 minutes, and in midsummer one and a half hours. The length also varied with latitude. Midnight was always the sixth hour of night, and midday the sixth hour of day. The time of day was referred to in terms such as "first hour" (the hour after sunrise), "twelfth hour" (the hour before sunset) and "midday" (*meridies*). *Ante meridiem* (AM) was before midday (morning), and *post meridiem* (PM) was after midday (afternoon).

Clocks (*horologia*) were used—the shadow clock or sundial and the water clock. Shadow clocks in the form of sundials (*solaria*) were introduced to Rome in the 3rd century BC. They had the disadvantage of relying on sunshine, needed different scales according to the latitude, needed seasonal correction and could not be used at night. In its most simple form, the sundial consisted of a *gnomon* or staff. The Horologium or Solar Clock of Augustus (fig. 3.2) was erected in the Campus Martius at Rome in 9 BC, with an Egyptian obelisk for its *gnomon*.

Water clocks (*clepsydrae*) also needed seasonal adjustment, but could be used at night—for example, in military camps to measure the four watches into which the night was divided. The outflow *clepsydra* consisted of a vessel, with orifices, that was filled with water and measured time as it emptied. More elaborate examples had a constant supply of water and consisted of a mechanism for a 24-hour clock operated by water. An elaborate example is the Horologion of Andronicus (or Tower of the Winds) at Athens, erected in the second half of the 1st century BC.

The Family

As in many aspects of Roman life, much more is known of families of the upper classes than of others. The household (*familia*) consisted of the "nuclear" family—the conjugal pair, their children and slaves. There is no evidence for extended families of grandparents and so on. The *paterfamilias* was the legal head of the family and had absolute control (*patria potestas*—power of a father) over all his children, whether or not they were married. His power extended to life and death (*ius vitae necisque*)—he had the right to expose newborn infants or to kill, disown or sell a child into slavery. Only at his death did children become independent (*sui iuris*), although a son could be emancipated by his father.

Women

In practice, women were excluded from public life, except occasionally as priestesses. They could not, for example, become magistrates or vote in elections. Political power was generally exercised by women only if they were the wives or close relatives of someone in power. From the late republic women gained much greater freedom in managing their own business and financial affairs. Unless married *in manu* (in her husband's control), they could own, inherit and dispose of property. Many women were involved in the running of the household and the care of children. Women had no legal rights over children.

A woman who married *sine manu* (without her husband's control) nevertheless retained a guardian (*tutela*) throughout her life, although from the time of Augustus she became independent if she had three children (four children for freedwomen). From the 2nd century the guardianship of adult women became a formality.

Female slaves and free women of the lower classes must have undertaken various types of work, but comparatively little is known about their lives.

Marriage

Roman marriage was monogamous. A full Roman marriage could occur only if both parties were Roman citizens or had been granted *conubium*. The minimum legal age of marriage was 12 for females and 14 for males, but in practice age at marriage tended to be higher. In early times a formal betrothal (*sponsalia*) usually occurred before marriage. Some children were betrothed at a young age by their fathers. Until 445 BC patricians could not marry plebeians, and a free person could not marry a freedman or freedwoman until legislation under Augustus made it permissible (except for senators).

Roman marriage was a private act resting on the initial consent of the partners. What was necessary in marriage was the living together of a man and woman with the intention of forming a lasting union. There was no prescribed formula of words or written contract (except for dowries). There were marriage ceremonies, but these carried no legal status although they did indicate that the relationship was a marriage. The law was primarily interested in the legitimacy of children and so needed to know if there was a valid marriage. A dowry (*dos*) was also an indication that the relationship was marriage. Dowries were moral but not legal requirements.

In early times, a woman passed into her husband's control (*manus*) on marriage and was *in manu* (*in manu mariti*). By the end of the republic, the woman tended to remain in the power of her father (*sine manu*—without control) as long as he lived, and was not integrated into her husband's family. Under the empire, marriage became unpopular and the birth rate fell, and so Augustus granted privileges to parents of three or more children—*ius trium liberorum* (right of three children).

Confarreatio was the oldest and most solemn form of marriage, from which it was virtually impossible to become divorced. It was apparently confined to certain priesthoods. The *flamen dialis* and *pontifex maximus* were present at the ceremony, and a cake made of *far* (grain) had some significance. Other marriage ceremonies commonly took place in June, and included various rituals such as a sacrifice and a wedding feast.

DIVORCE

More is known about Roman divorce than marriage. There was no religious ban on divorce, and no social stigma was attached to a divorced spouse. From early times a husband could divorce his wife for adultery, but not vice versa—it was taken for granted that men would make use of mistresses, slaves and prostitutes. Later on it became acceptable for a husband to divorce his wife for reasons such as infertility. By the late republic both men and women could inititiate divorce, and no cause had to be given.

Divorce was apparently common, at least among upper classes. It is estimated that about one in six upper-class marriages ended in divorce in the first ten years, and another one in six ended through the death of one spouse. On divorce, a woman usually had the right for her dowry to be returned.

REMARRIAGE

Remarriage was fairly frequent. Many men remarried without difficulty after divorce, although it was more difficult for a divorced woman to remarry. For widows, remarriage was fairly normal and was required by Augustan legislation. Among the upper classes, marriages, divorces and remarriages were often politically expedient.

Children

There was some knowledge of contraception, and abortion was practiced for unwanted pregnancies. Only occasionally was it regarded as criminal, if the father was being defrauded of an heir. The birth of a child was apparently a relatively public occasion, which took place at home with a midwife (generally not a doctor) and several female relatives in atten-

dance, but the husband or other males were not present. The mother gave birth in a special chair in an upright position. After nine days a ceremony (the *lustratio*) was held, and the child was given its name. Infants were swaddled, and wet nurses (*nutrices*) were commonly employed in all social classes.

The father was able to deny the right of the newborn child to be reared. This was one way of limiting family numbers—all children inherited equally (the daughters' share usually given as a dowry), and so too many children fragmented the family property. Many other reasons existed for not wanting to rear a child, such as poverty. A posthumous child, though, could not be denied the right to be reared, as the child belonged to the deceased father. Newborn children could be killed, sold or exposed. Usually sons rather than daughters were required by the family, and so girls may have been exposed more commonly than boys, but there is little definite evidence for this. Exposure took place outside the house or in a public place, and deformed children were exposed or drowned. Exposure was made criminal in 374, although it still continued to be practiced.

There was no assumption that children should always be with their mothers, either during the day or if death or divorce ended the marriage. In law, the child of a marriage belonged to the father, and after divorce children remained by law in the household of the father. An orphan was a child who had lost its father, not both parents, and sometimes went to live with a tutor rather than with the mother. Illegitimate children took their mother's name and had no rights.

Children played with a wide range of toys, including dolls made of wood or bone, although it is not known if they were given to girls and boys. There is some evidence in art for the activities of children, but before the imperial period children had virtually no place in public or private art.

ADOPTION

Adoptio was not the humanitarian adoption of orphans or abandoned children, although this occasionally occurred in response to a couple's sterility. It was normally the transferring of a son from the power of one *paterfamilias* to another, with the son losing all rights within his old family. Adoption often occurred for political expediency, particularly where there was an absence of male descendants. Most commonly adopted were close relations. Females were rarely adopted, and women could not adopt by law. A person who was *sui iuris* (himself a *paterfamilias*) could also place himself under the power (*potestas*) of another of his own accord, known as *adrogatio*. In the late republic several young patricians had themselves adopted by plebeians in order to be eligible for the tribunate of the plebs.

POPULATION

Despite evidence for censuses (see chapter 1), very little information about population has survived. Most useful are the figures for totals of citizens registered under Augustus and Claudius. These suggest that around AD 14 there were about 5 million free inhabitants of Italy, to which some demographic analysts conjecture that a population of 2 to 3 million slaves should be added. Rome had a population of between 500,000 and 1 million, and other large cities had populations of 100,000 to 200,000. Egypt seems to have had a total population of around 7 million. At the beginning of the 1st century, there is likely to have been a minimum of 50 million to 60 million people within the frontiers of the empire, possibly 100 million. However, the scarcity of figures means that these population totals can be taken only as approximations. There are few indicators to suggest whether the population was rising or falling.

Life expectancy was shorter than today, although there is evidence for people surviving to an old age, especially within the upper classes. Infant and child mortality was high, as was the incidence of mortality due to childbirth. Many people died in their 20s and 30s. Most of the evidence for mortality comes from epitaphs.

SLAVES

The civilization of the Roman world was enjoyed by the few at the expense of the majority. Wealth and resources were distributed unequally and there was relatively little social mobility. There was a large labor force of slaves and of poorly paid free labor, to some extent indistinguishable from slaves. Other types of unfree workers, such as debt bondsmen and peasants who were tied to the land, did not fit into the category of slaves. Slaves and their children were the property of their owners, to be traded like any other commodity. They were sold or rented out by slave dealers, or they could be bought and sold between individuals.

Slaves were used at Rome from earliest times, but there was a huge increase from the 2nd century BC. Most were foreigners, not Italians or Greeks. Slave dealers obtained them as prisoners-of-war (fig. 9.1), from pirates (see chapter 5) and through trade outside Roman territory. Parents also sold their children, particularly to pay debts. From the 1st century the external sources of supply possibly dwindled, but many slaves were probably bred. Home-bred slaves may therefore have eventually outnumbered those

Fig. 9.1 Pillar base from Mainz, Germany, showing two prisoners-of-war, who were likely to be sold as slaves. Later 1st century AD. Photo: Ralph Jackson.

enslaved. Slaves became very expensive and unprofitable to use in unskilled labor, and by the 4th century free labor tended to replace them in the mines and in private industries. The ownership of slaves by the upper and middle classes was widespread, but the extent of their use outside Italy is uncertain.

Slaves were employed in every form of skilled and unskilled labor. No tasks were performed solely by slaves, but they formed the overwhelming majority of workers in mining, factories and private households. They were also owned by towns and cities to undertake public works, such as road construction or maintenance of aqueducts, but slave ownership by the state was limited by the practice of contracting out many public enterprises. The agricultural labor force was more complex, though, with large farming estates worked entirely by slaves existing alongside smaller farms worked by peasants or leased to tenants.

The treatment of slaves varied enormously, depending on their employment and their owner. Harsh treatment was often restrained by the fact that the slave was an investment, and impairment of the slave's performance might involve financial loss. Treatment tended to be more harsh in factories, agriculture and mining, where slaves might work seven days a week with no holidays. There is evidence that slaves on agricultural estates were chained, working in gangs in the fields in the daytime and locked in prisons at night, particularly in southern Italy and Sicily. They could also be branded or wear inscribed metal collars, so that they had little chance of successful escape. Treatment was worse in the mines and life expectancy was short. In contrast, many slaves were educated, practicing as doctors, architects and teachers, and some amassed large fortunes.

Slaves became freedmen (*liberti*, *libertini*) or freedwomen (*libertae*) by being granted manumission (freedom) by their owner, or they could buy freedom if they were able to raise sufficient money. Formal manumission (before a magistrate) granted both freedom and Roman citizenship, when the master let the slave go (*manumisit*). Clients were free men who owed legally binding services to a patron, and freedmen automatically became clients of their former owners (now their patrons). They owed them obligations and sometimes even continued working for them. Although they gained citizenship, freedmen were not eligible for political office. Any children subsequently born to them became free citizens and were eligible for political office.

Informal manumission (before friends) did not grant citizenship; these freedmen were known as Junian Latins (*Latini Iuniani*), and at their death their property reverted to their former owners. Manumissions were fairly frequent, and the prospect of freedom was probably one of the main incentives to efficient labor. Slave revolts occurred, but mainly during the republic. Three great revolts took place in the late republic—two in Sicily (135–132 BC, 104–101 BC) and one led by Spartacus (73–71 BC) in Italy. In the imperial period slaves did not apparently organize many revolts or commit many violent acts against their owners.

FOOD AND DRINK

Food

Diet and dining customs depended on the standard of living and geographical region. The diet of most people was frugal, based on corn (grain), oil and wine, but exotic foods and recipes were available for the dinner parties of the wealthy. Cereals, mainly wheat, provided the staple food. Originally husked wheat (*far*) was prepared as porridge (*puls*), but later on naked species of wheat (eventually known as *frumentum*) were cultivated and made into bread. Bread was sometimes flavored with other foods such as honey or cheese. It was eaten at most meals, accompanied by products such as sausage, domestic fowl, game, eggs, cheese, fish and shellfish. Fish and oysters were particularly popular. Meat, especially pork, was also available. Delicacies such as snails and dormice were specially bred, and game and small wild birds were also eaten. There was a great variety of cakes, pastries and tarts, sweetened with honey.

Vegetables formed an important part of the diet and included cabbage, parsnips, lettuce, asparagus, onions, garlic, marrows, radishes, lentils, beans and beets. For many people meat was a luxury, and their diet consisted largely of bread and vegetables. Various fruits and nuts were also available. Strongly flavored sauces such as *garum* were very popular (see chapter

8) as well as spices and herbs. Much Roman food was highly spiced, disguising its natural flavors.

Evidence for food comes mainly from ancient authors, archaeological deposits (such as seeds and animal bones) and still-life wall paintings of food. There were various writings on cooking by ancient authors, but the only one to survive in any length is the cookbook attributed to Apicius. See also farming, chapter 4.

Cooking

Bread, cakes and pastries were produced commercially and at home. Circular domed ovens were used mainly for baking bread and pastries—a fire was lit inside the oven and was raked out before the food was put in. Most food was cooked over a brazier or open hearth, with cauldrons suspended from a chain or cooking vessels set on gridirons or trivets. Cooking was done in the kitchen, and smoke from fires escaped through the roof or a vent in the wall. Cooking was also done outside. Many people, particularly tenement dwellers, probably had no cooking facilities, although communal ovens may have been available.

Food was often cooked with fruit, honey and vinegar, to give a sweet-and-sour flavor. Meat was more often boiled than roasted, with spicy sauces. Honey was very important for sweetening. The preservation of food would have been difficult. Fish and shellfish were probably transported live in barrels to their destination. Various foods could be preserved by pickling, and meat and fish by drying, smoking and salting. Nevertheless, contaminated food must have been eaten, and food poisoning was probably not uncommon.

There were regional variations throughout the empire in the food eaten and the cooking methods used, caused by the influence of local traditions and the availability of foodstuffs.

Drink

Wine was drunk most commonly, generally watered down, as well as spiced and heated. Drinking undiluted wine was considered barbaric. Wine concentrate (must) diluted with water was also drunk. *Posca*

was a particularly common drink among the poorer classes, made by watering down *acetum*, a low-quality wine very similar to vinegar. Beer and mead were drunk mainly in the northern provinces. Milk, usually from sheep or goats, was regarded as an uncivilized drink and was reserved for making cheese and for medicinal purposes.

Meals

The Romans generally ate one main meal a day. Breakfast (*ientaculum*) was not always taken, but was in any case a very light meal, often just a piece of bread. Breakfast originally appears to have been followed by a main meal of dinner (*cena*) at midday and by supper (*vesperna*) in the evening. However, dinner came to be taken later in the day, eventually becoming the evening meal. Supper was then omitted and a light lunch (*prandium*) was introduced between breakfast and dinner, so that the Romans came to eat two light meals in the day and a main meal (*cena*) around sunset.

For the poor, most meals consisted of cereal in the form of porridge or bread, supplemented by meat and vegetables if available. For the reasonably wealthy, the main meal consisted of three courses, *ab ovo usque ad mala* (from the egg to the apples). The first (*gustatio* or *promulsis*) was an appetizer, usually eggs, raw vegetables, fish or shellfish, prepared in a simple manner. The main course (*prima mensa*) consisted of cooked vegetables and meats—the type and quantity of such dishes depended on what the family could afford. This was followed by a sweet course (*secunda mensa*) of fruit or sweet pastries.

The Romans often sat upright to eat their meals, but the wealthy reclined on couches, particularly at dinner parties, and often dined outdoors in their private gardens when the weather was fine. A variety of cooking vessels was used, largely in coarse pottery and bronze. For the poorer classes, tableware probably consisted of coarse pottery, but there was also available a range of vessels in fine pottery, glass, bronze, silver, gold and pewter. (See chapter 8.) Food was eaten with the fingers, cut up by knives with iron blades and handles of bone, antler, wood or bronze. Bronze, silver and bone spoons are also known, for eating liquids and eggs, and their pointed handles were used for extricating shellfish or snails from their shells.

PERSONAL APPEARANCE

Clothing

Men's and women's clothes were similar and changed little in fashion over the centuries, although clothes varied in style in different parts of the empire. Children tended to wear smaller versions of adult clothing. For many types of clothing, there is evidence for the use of gaudy colors for both men and women.

Fig. 9.2 Part of a funeral monument from Neumagen, Germany, portraying a husband dressed in a toga with umbo and sinus. His wife wears a close-fitting bonnet and a stola, and their son wears a long-sleeved tunic and cloak. They wear leather shoes of various kinds.

TOGAS

The toga was the formal outer garment of the Roman male citizen and also his shroud. Originally only a toga was worn, but later it was worn as an outdoor garment over a tunic. The toga was an expensive, heavy garment of fine natural white wool, and required frequent cleaning by the fuller. It was roughly semicircular in shape, about 5.5 m (18 ft) wide and 2.1 m (7 ft) deep. It had to be draped in a complicated manner around the body, and several emperors had to issue decrees to enforce its use on public occasions.

The oldest representations date to the late republic and depict the *toga exigua*, a short, simple toga. Toward the end of the republic, it became more complex with a *sinus* and *umbo* (fig. 9.2). The *sinus* consisted of the drapes that fell from the left shoulder to the right thigh as a pocket and could be brought up over the right shoulder, forming a sling. The *umbo* was a projecting mass of folds in front of the body that could be pulled up to form a hood. A Roman shown with the toga drawn over his head is represented as a priest (fig. 9.3).

The toga showed differences in the social order. The *toga praetexta* (bordered toga) had a purple stripe and was worn by curule magistrates. It was also worn by boys until the age of about 15 or 16, when they

Fig. 9.3 Reverse of a denarius *depicting Caracalla (211–217) sacrificing over a tripod. The toga is drawn over his head, indicating his role as a priest.* Courtesy of Somerset County Museums Service.

assumed the plain *toga virilis* (man's toga). The togas for senators had a broad purple stripe (*latus clavus*); for equestrians a narrow purple stripe (*clavus angustus*); emperors' togas were entirely purple.

A *toga candida* (white toga) was worn by candidates for office, the togas made whiter by being rubbed with chalk. A *toga pulla* was of natural black wool and was worn at funerals.

TUNICS

The basic garment was the short-sleeved tunic (*tunica*), tied round the waist with a belt. It was commonly worn by slaves and children and was the usual indoor garment. Wearing a long tunic with sleeves was considered effeminate. In cold weather extra tunics were worn. Senators wore tunics with a broad purple stripe, and equestrians with a narrow purple stripe, running from the shoulder to the hem, front and back. Tunics worn by charioteers were dyed the color of their faction. A dalmatic (*dalmatica*) was originally a short-sleeved or sleeveless tunic, but by the late empire it had long sleeves. It was made of various materials, such as wool, linen and silk, and was worn by people in high position. It was adopted as an ecclesiastical garment.

TROUSERS

Short leather trousers were worn by soldiers, in particular cavalrymen, but long woolen trousers (*braca*) were mainly worn by barbarians outside the boundaries of the empire.

CAPES/CLOAKS

Capes and cloaks of various styles and sizes are also known (figs. 1.5, 1.16, 1.21), of wool or leather, some with hoods. They included the *palla* (*pallium*), *lacerna*, *paenula*, *caracallus*, *cucullus*, *sagum* and *byrrus*.

WOMEN'S CLOTHES

Women of early Rome also wore togas, but later only prostitutes and other women considered of ill repute wore them. Women then wore tunics. Married women (matrons) wore a tunic covered by a *stola*, a long, full dress gathered up by a high girdle (fig. 9.2), with a colored border around the neck. It became a symbol of the Roman matron. Women also wore cloaks. The clothes of the wealthy were in rich colors and fine materials, such as muslins and silks. In some areas women also wore close-fitting bonnets and hairnets (fig. 9.2).

UNDERCLOTHES

Evidence for underclothes is limited, but a loincloth was worn in Rome and Italy, and women sometimes wore a breast band or bikini-type underclothes, occasionally of soft leather. There is some evidence for socks and stockings.

SHOES

Various types of leather shoes and boots were worn (figs. 1.16, 9.2), varying from heavy hobnailed examples to light sandals and slippers. A *carbatina* was a sandal made from one piece of leather, with a soft sole and an openwork upper fastened by a lace. A *soccus* had a sole without hobnails and a separate leather upper. A *calceus* was a hobnailed shoe secured by laces. A *solea* was a simple sandal with a thong between the toes and a sole with hobnails. A *caliga*, worn by soldiers, was a heavy sandal with a hobnailed sole and a separate leather upper, fastened by thongs. Shoes could also be of wood.

Toiletries

In the empire the Romans spent much time in bathing and massaging. Toilet instruments are common finds, singly or in sets, and were usually made of bronze. They include nail cleaners, tweezers, toothpicks and earpicks. Razors were of bronze or iron, and combs were of bone or wood. Strigils made of bronze and sometimes iron were used to scrape oil, sweat and dead skin from the body after bathing. *Ligulae* (sing. *ligula*) were used for extracting cosmetics or medicines from narrow unguent bottles. Mirrors were of polished bronze and silver, and occasionally of silvered glass. Toilet boxes for storing toilet instruments, perfumes and cosmetics have also been found.

Fig. 9.4 A hairdressing scene in which four women attend their mistress. They wear plain long-sleeved tunics, and their hair is pinned up in buns. One woman holds a mirror. Their mistress is wearing a stola *and is seated in a basketwork chair. Copy of a monument from Neumagen, Germany.*

HAIRSTYLES

Details of hairstyles are well known from sculptured portraits and altered considerably over the years. In the late 1st and early 2nd centuries elaborate female hairstyles became popular, with a mass of curls or plaits piled high on a wire framework. By the mid-2nd century less elaborate styles with waves and plaits had been adopted. Women's hairdressing was undertaken at home (fig. 9.4), usually by slaves. Men and women used various dyes on their hair, and blond hair was fashionable. Wigs made from the blond hair of Germans captured in battle were very popular, and black hair was sometimes imported from India.

In early Rome most men wore beards and long hair, but from the 3rd century BC they began to shave their beards. Beards were again more common from the time of Hadrian (117–138), who grew a beard to hide a facial blemish. There were many barbers' shops.

COSMETICS

Various perfumes and facial cosmetics were used. Cosmetics were of various materials such as charcoal and saffron. Chalk and white lead were used to whiten the face.

JEWELRY

Many types of jewelry were worn. Particularly common were brooches (*fibulae*), used for fastening clothes such as the toga. As well as brooches, men wore finger rings, and women wore necklaces, earrings, bracelets, armlets, anklets, finger rings and hairpins.

ENTERTAINMENT

Public entertainment in particular played an important part of life in Rome and to a large extent in the provinces as well. Juvenal remarked that the city mob in Rome was only interested in *panem et circenses* (bread and circuses). Although this was a satirical exaggeration, it demonstrates the important place of entertainment in their everyday lives.

Public Entertainment

PUBLIC GAMES

Originally public games (*ludi*) were held at some religious festivals, but gradually the entertainment aspect became more important and the number of annual games increased. By 100 BC the games in the city of Rome included the *ludi Megalenses* (4–10 April), *ludi Cereales* (12–19 April), *ludi Florales* (28 April–3 May), *ludi Apollinares* (6–13 July), *ludi Romani* (5–19 September) and *ludi plebeii* (4–17 November). See also "Festivals," chapter 7.

In the 1st century BC military leaders also celebrated victories with private games which became so lavish that they rivaled the public ones. Magistrates also used the games to gain favor and support for election and to keep the populace under control. Emperors found it expedient to continue this tradition. With each emperor seeking to surpass his predecessor, enormous sums of public and private money came to be spent on the games. Admission to the games was free.

By the end of the 2nd century, the number of official celebrations at Rome reached 135, and by the 4th century it was 176. There were also special celebrations, such as the games that lasted for over 100 days in AD 107 to celebrate Trajan's victory over the Dacians. Publicly financed *ludi* also spread to provinces throughout the empire.

Restrictions were imposed on the games during the 4th century. Gladiatorial combats ceased in the east at the end of the 4th century and in the 5th century in the west, but combats with wild animals appear to have continued until the 6th century throughout the empire. Chariot racing died out in the west in the late empire, although it continued in the east throughout the Byzantine Empire.

There were three main types of performances— circuses, shows in the amphitheater and theater performances.

CIRCUSES (See also chapter 4)

Chariot racing was the oldest and most popular entertainment in the Roman world, dating back to at least the monarchy and in legend to the founding of Rome itself. Greek chariot races were held in hippodromes, and this continued in the east during the Roman period, but in the west races were held in circuses. Other events came to form part of the circus games (*ludi circenses*), such as Greek athletics and wrestling, but chariot racing was the most popular event.

Chariot racing was very expensive and was run for profit as a highly organized business. There were four racing factions in Rome, the blues, greens, whites and reds, which were the colors worn by the charioteers. Successful charioteers became rich and famous, and portrayals of them in sculpture, mosaic and molded glassware have survived, sometimes with their names. There was great rivalry among the factions, sometimes leading to violence among their supporters, but the greens and blues were usually the favorites.

AMPHITHEATERS (See also chapter 4)

Several different kinds of show were staged in amphitheaters, all taking place in the *arena* (*harena*), meaning literally "sand," which was placed in the arena to soak up the blood from the spectacles (figs. 4.7, 9.5). One of the most popular spectacles was gladiatorial combats—fights for life between two gladiators. This type of performance appears to have developed from Etruscan funeral rites called *munera* (duties). The earliest recorded gladiatorial combat in Rome took place at a funeral in 264 BC, but by the late 1st century BC these contests had lost their ritual significance.

Gladiatorial training schools were established to supply an increasing demand for gladiators. In the 1st century the schools came under state control to prevent them becoming private armies. The gladiators were condemned criminals (*damnati*), slaves bought for the purpose, prisoners-of-war or volunteers who had signed on for a fee and were bound by oath. There were four main types of gladiator: the *murmillo*

Fig. 9.5   An amphitheater at Trier, Germany, with the arena and raised banks for seating for the spectators.

(*mirmillo*) had a helmet (with fish crest), oblong shield and sword, and usually fought a *retiarius*, who was lightly armed with a net and trident or dagger. The Samnite had a sword, visored helmet and oblong shield, and the Thracian was armed with a curved scimitar and round shield. Combats between gladiators armed in various other ways also took place (fig. 9.6), and women and dwarves were also used.

Performances involving wild animals (*venationes*, huntings) were introduced to Rome as entertainment in the early 2nd century BC and became very popular. They were often based on the hunt, with men fighting wild animals on foot or occasionally from horseback, but fights between wild animals were also staged. These fights often took place in spectacular stage sets, and huge numbers of animals were slaughtered. Greater numbers of increasingly exotic animals were sought, leading to an extensive trade in wild animals, mainly from frontier provinces. The men who fought wild animals were *bestiarii* and were condemned criminals, prisoners of war or paid trained fighters.

Fig. 9.6   Combat between two gladiators depicted on a mosaic at Nennig villa, Germany.

Originally fights with wild animals took place on the morning of the games, public executions at midday and gladiatorial contests in the afternoon, but gradually these divisions became blurred. Numerous gladiatorial combats often took place simultaneously, giving the appearance of a battle in the arena. Sometimes mock naval battles (*naumachiae*) were staged, but not as once thought in amphitheaters, but elsewhere, such as in artificial lakes. There were also shows of performing animals, often accompanied by music, and musicians performed during the intervals (fig. 9.7).

THEATERS (See also chapters 4 and 6)

Theatrical performances (*ludi scaenici*) became popular from the 3rd century BC, with their origins in Greek theater. No women were allowed on stage, and so male actors probably wore masks to distinguish clearly their male or female role. The actors were

Fig. 9.7 A musical interlude at the games in the amphitheater, depicted on a mosaic at Nennig villa, Germany. One musician plays a cornu, *and the other musician plays a* hydraulis, *a water organ—there would have been an attendant to pump the air.*

Fig. 9.8 Reconstructed view of the tepidarium *(warm room) in the Forum Baths, Pompeii, with bronze benches and a bronze brazier (far end).* From W. Gell (1832) *Pompeiana.*

trained slaves or freedmen, under the direction of a manager.

From the 1st century BC pantomimes and mimes became popular. Actors in pantomimes mimed their roles to the accompaniment of singing, dancing, music and elaborate visual effects to produce a performance similar to an extravagant ballet, whereas in a mime the actors had speaking roles. Women were allowed to take part in mimes and pantomimes, which became much more popular than plays, but which degenerated into vulgar and tasteless spectacles. Musical performances and literary recitals were performed in *odea*.

Private Entertainment

BATHS (See also chapter 4)

Bathing became a recreational activity. As such, it was both a private and a public entertainment — most people used the public baths (fig. 9.8), but the wealthy often possessed private baths. As well as the baths, there were often associated facilities for various exercises, ball games, swimming and massage as well as gardens, meeting rooms and food shops. In their developed form, the public baths were similar to modern fitness clubs or community centers.

OTHER LEISURE ACTIVITIES

Those who could afford it enjoyed entertaining at home, with meals that ranged from modest dinner parties to lavish banquets, often in the open air. Apart from conversation, there might be music, dancing and singing by professional musicians. In some social circles, after-dinner entertainment consisted of recitation of literary works—often poetry, but also speeches and essays. For the plebeians, associations (*collegia*) sometimes presented opportunities for dinner parties. Eating and drinking as a recreational activity for the poor usually meant frequenting taverns, of which there was probably a large number in most towns. Their quality varied, some functioning as brothels and others as gaming houses. Gambling was popular with people of every class, and dice, knucklebones

and gaming counters are common finds. Board games were probably played by both adults and children, and many traditional children's games, such as hide-and-seek and leap-frog, are portrayed in Roman art. Children's toys are known, although in some cases it is difficult to distinguish between toys and votive offerings. In rural areas hunting and fishing were leisure pursuits of the wealthy, but for the poorer classes such activities were more often a necessity than an entertainment (fig. 4.22).

ART

Public art, such as images of deities and statues of illustrious citizens erected in public places, is known in Rome from at least the late monarchy. By the end of the republic such works of art were often the ostentatious gifts of the upper classes, carrying an element of propaganda. Patronage of art for private enjoyment does not seem to have developed until the late 1st century BC, when the houses and possessions of the wealthy became as ostentatious as their public benefactions. This was probably a direct result of the importation of artists and looted art treasures into Rome after the conquest of Greece. Despite the number of works of art, Roman artists, unlike Greek artists, remain largely unknown. (See also "Architectural styles," chapter 4.)

Sculpture

The earliest sculpture in Rome, during the monarchy and early republic, seems to have been Etruscan, which was itself greatly influenced by Greek sculpture from the 6th century BC. Greek sculpture was imported to Rome from the 4th century BC. The importation of Greek sculpture and sculptors reached a peak in the 2nd and 1st centuries BC. Many sculptures were copies of Greek originals, but a Roman style of sculpture subsequently developed, reaching a peak of excellence in the 1st and 2nd centuries.

Sculptures were produced in the round in marble and bronze, from small figurines to full-size statues, with a range of subjects including deities, emperors (fig. 1.12) and animals. Roman sculpture was at its best in expressing character, particularly in portrait busts. Also produced were reliefs on public buildings, often commemorating historical events, such as on triumphal arches and Trajan's Column (fig. 1.2). Funerary sculpture included tombstones, funerary busts and sarcophagi. Like Greek sculpture, Roman sculpture was painted in lifelike and often garish colors. (See also "Stoneworking," chapter 8.)

Portraiture

From the 3rd century BC portraiture became a highly developed aspect of Roman art in sculpture, full-size statues and busts. The unflatteringly accurate depiction of facial features was probably closely connected with the custom of preserving *imagines* of ancestors. Realistic portraits of people were also portrayed in scenes, such as the life–size carvings of the family of

Augustus, walking in funeral procession, on the reliefs of the Altar of Peace (Ara Pacis). Portraiture began to decline from the 3rd century, becoming much more stylized in sculptures and on coins (figs. 1.16, 8.5). Portraits were also painted on walls, and examples from Egypt painted on wood and sometimes linen have been found with burials.

Painting

Roman painting was derived from Greek traditions and was mostly done on walls and ceilings or on wood. The paintings were generally strong, bright and colorful, and sometimes depict brightly colored furnishings such as inlaid furniture, curtains and cushions. Such furnishings, and the paintings themselves, must have created highly decorated and colorful interiors.

Little Roman painting has survived in comparison with other art forms, and virtually no evidence survives from earlier than the 1st century BC. By the

Fig. 9.9 Reconstructed view of a small garden and portico in a house at Pompeii, with wall paintings in Style III. From W. Gell (1832) *Pompeiana.*

mid-1st century BC painting was being used widely for interior decoration. Some painting was purely decorative, such as that imitating marble on walls, while others depicted landscapes, architectural settings, scenes of everyday life and figures and scenes from Greek mythology. Some scenes were deliberately painted to give an illusion of three-dimensional space.

Many surviving paintings come from Pompeii. Pompeian paintings have been divided into four overlapping styles, which are sometimes used to categorize other Roman paintings. Style I (also called First Style) probably dates from the early 2nd century BC, derived from Greek traditions. The decoration is very simple, mainly imitating blocks of colored marble, sometimes with molded stucco forming architectural features. Style II (Second Style) dates from around 90 BC and is a development of Style I. The decoration is still often painted to imitate marble panels, but three-dimensional architectural features, such as columns, are realistically painted on the flat wall, rather than molded in stucco, to give an illusion of a three-dimensional surface. A later development depicts figure or landscape scenes instead of architectural features, with walls resembling windows beyond which other scenes could be seen.

Style III (Third Style) began in the reign of Augustus (27 BC–AD 14). The elaborate realism of Style II is replaced by a restrained decorative treatment of the flat wall surface. This often consisted of insubstantial architectural details and abstract designs against a monochrome background with small central vignettes (fig. 9.9). Style IV (Fourth Style) dates from the mid-1st century. It is a combination of styles II and III, mixing unrealistic elements of pattern with realistically portrayed architectural elements and figure scenes.

Pompeii was destroyed in AD 79, and so there are no Pompeian styles beyond this date. Relatively little painting survives from the 2nd century onward. By the end of the 3rd century technical standards were apparently falling, but no radical change of style occurred until the Byzantine, which was becoming established in the east before 700. The upheavals in the west effectively destroyed the Roman tradition of painting. (See also chapter 4.)

Mosaics

Roman mosaics developed from Greek mosaics in the 2nd century BC. Some were in black and white, with geometric patterns (fig. 9.10) or figured scenes in silhouette on a white background. They were very popular in Italy in the 1st to 3rd centuries. In addition, there were polychrome mosaics with figured and landscape scenes, some combined with geometric patterns (fig. 9.11).

Thousands of Roman mosaics are known, but few have been closely dated by means other than the style of the design, so it is not possible to trace an accurate chronological development of mosaic styles. The situation is complicated further by the copying of paintings in mosaics, the copying of polychrome mosaics in monochrome and the development, from the mid-2nd century, of distinct regional schools of mosaicists in various provinces. (See also chapter 4.)

Portable Art

Numerous types of portable objects were decorated, and in some cases the decoration became more important than the object itself. For example, some of the glass cage cups are likely to have been works of art rather than functional drinking vessels. Other objects, such as jewelry, had a purely decorative function. Functional tableware, such as terra sigillata, or gold or silver plate, was often decorated with high-quality patterns or figured scenes. (See also chapter 8.)

Fig. 9.10 Part of a black and white geometric mosaic from the House of the Gem, Herculaneum.

Fig. 9.11 Personification of spring with flowers in her hair and a bird on her shoulder, depicted in the polychrome Four Seasons mosaic found at Cirencester, England. From Prof. Buckman and C.H. Newmarch (1850) *Illutrations of the Remains of Roman Art, in Cirencester, the Site of Antient Corinium.*

PUNISHMENT

The Roman penal system distinguished between public and private penalties, reflecting the division between public and private law. Private law developed as a substitute for retaliation and vengeance, and the penalty came to be a compulsory payment of money as compensation by the offender to the injured party. Public penalties were more concerned with vengeance and deterring others than correcting the offender or compensating the injured party. The division between public and private law is not always as might be expected. For example, treason against the state and some forms of murder were public offenses, normally carrying the death sentence, while theft or assault against a person were usually civil offenses dealt with by private law. There were also differences in punishment for different classes of people. (See also "Laws," chapter 1.)

Capital punishment was carried out in a number of ways according to the severity of the crime and the status of the condemned person. The methods included decapitation with a sword (for military personnel), crucifixion, burning alive, drowning in a sack and exposure to wild animals.

Punishment for crimes against the public also included beatings, fines, condemnation to mines and quarries, banishment to gladiator training schools and partial or total confiscation of property. Slaves could be punished in any way by their owners. They were commonly beaten, as well as punished by branding and other mutilation. In the case of murder by a slave, all the owner's slaves could be executed (often by crucifixion), largely to suppress possible revolts and to encourage slaves to report plots.

Torture

During the republic torture was commonly used to extract information from slaves during criminal proceedings. A slave required to give evidence in court was tortured first, on the grounds that a slave would not otherwise tell the truth. From the 1st century the emperors tried to restrict the use of torture to the most serious criminal cases, although from the reign of Tiberius torture was used on free people as well. Torture gradually became more widespread, eventually being employed in civil as well as criminal proceedings.

Prisons

Under Roman criminal law imprisonment was not recognized as a form of punishment. The public prison was regarded as a coercive measure applied to those disobeying magistrates' orders, and periods of imprisonment were short. Prisons were also used to detain accused persons during a criminal trial or to detain condemned criminals awaiting execution. In some larger households there were private domestic prisons for holding slaves.

Exile

The rules governing imprisonment were lax, and sometimes magistrates delayed arrest to provide time for a person accused of a capital crime to go into voluntary exile (*exsilium*) before sentence was pronounced. This allowed the escape of the accused who nevertheless lost their citizenship and suffered confiscation of property. From the 1st century BC magistrates were obliged to allow a condemned person time to go into exile before carrying out the death sentence. *Exsilium* therefore became an alternative to the death penalty.

Exsilium also came to be used loosely for all other types of expulsion or banishment, so that it is not always clear what is meant. *Relegatio* was temporary banishment to a place or exclusion from living in certain places. *Deportatio* was perpetual banishment to a place with loss of citizenship and confiscation of property.

Exile was a punishment used largely for the upper classes. For similar offenses, the lower classes were punished with forced labor on public works or in the mines, banishment to the gladiator training schools or the death penalty.

MEDICINE

Roman medicine absorbed much from Greek medicine, and many doctors in the Roman world were Greek. The fusion of Greek and Roman medicine was in part scientific (mainly from the Greeks) and in part magical and religious (mainly from the Romans), resulting in a sometimes bizarre collection of treatments and practices.

Most, if not all, Roman deities were attributed some healing powers, but some deities were thought to be particularly beneficial. Their healing powers were sought by prayer, votive offerings and incubation. (See chapter 7.) Amulets and magical incantations were widely used to ward off or attempt to cure disease. Herbs and drugs also appear to have been widely used, for their supposed magical properties as much as for their proven effectiveness.

Alongside this religious and magical view of medicine was a more rational approach, mainly derived from Greek medicine, which rejected the idea of divine intervention and looked for more practical explanations and remedies. Treatment of wounds and injuries often consisted of cleaning and bandaging. The use of wine, vinegar, pitch and turpentine as mild antiseptics was known, but infection and gangrene often necessitated amputation. Artificial limbs are known, but probably only the wealthy could afford them.

Diagnosing and curing diseases were more difficult, and relied on observation and recording of symptoms to compare with experience of similar cases to predict the course of the disease and find a suitable treatment. Medicine was a subject dealt with by many authors, of whom the most important was probably Galen.

Some medical treatment, particularly surgery, was fairly advanced. For those who could afford it, dental treatment could be very elaborate, and capped teeth and bridgework are known. Gold was generally used for repairing teeth, and it was forbidden by law to bury gold with a body except where it had been used to repair teeth. The causes of tooth decay were not understood, but due to diet the incidence of dental caries was much lower than nowadays.

Other surgery, such as removal of small tumors, trephination and various eye operations was carried out relatively routinely, and in Italy at least some doctors practiced as *medici ocularii* (eye specialists). Opium and henbane for sedation and pain relief were known, but surgeons were hampered by the lack of an effective anaesthetic, so that a successful surgeon had to be strong, dexterous, accurate and, above all, fast.

Army surgeons were very important in improving medical practice, particularly in treating wounds and injuries and also in spreading medical knowledge throughout the empire as surgeons moved with the legions. Army surgeons also benefited from coming into contact with new ideas and particularly new herbs and drugs. The army was therefore probably the single most important force for the improvement and spread of Roman medicine.

There were no set qualifications for doctors and no standardized form of training. Doctors never enjoyed very high status, and many were Greek slaves or freedmen or the descendants of freedmen. Their standing gradually improved, and in 46 BC foreign doctors working in Rome were granted citizenship by Julius Caesar. As well as private practitioners and army surgeons, doctors were attached to wealthy families and the emperor's retinue, and some were employed by town councils to provide treatment for anyone needing it.

Medicine was one of the few professions open to women, and a number of female doctors (*medicae*) are known, often of Greek origin as well. More common were midwives (*obstetrices*) who specialized in childbirth and women's diseases and disorders. They often worked under the guidance of doctors, but were capable of carrying out treatments on their own and appear to have been highly skilled and literate.

Military hospitals were relatively common, but no civilian hospital has yet been certainly identified. Wealthy patrons were treated in their own homes by resident or visiting doctors, while others were treated in rooms rented by the doctor or in his own house. Other doctors worked out of *tabernae medicae*, which were small shops of the type used by traders and craftsmen.

Many surgical instruments for various tasks have been found, made of bronze or brass and occasionally iron. They included probes, hooks, forceps, needles and scalpels. Collyrium stamps (oculists' stamps) are small inscribed stone tablets that were used for marking eye ointment (which was made in a fairly solid form). The stamps are found particularly in Gaul, Germany and Britain.

PHILOSOPHY

The Romans were initially suspicious of Greek philosophers, banning them from Rome in 173 BC and 161 BC. By the end of the 2nd century BC philosophy was beginning to gain favor at Rome, particularly Epicureanism and Stoicism, which became the leading schools of philosophy there. In general, the Romans were more interested in the ethical and religious aspects of philosophy than in theory and speculation.

Epicurus, an Athenian living around 300 BC, was responsible for the Epicurean philosophy, much of which is known from Lucretius' writings. Epicurus believed that the gods existed in mortal bliss but did not interfere with mortals to reward or punish. He believed that the soul was mortal and good could be attained and evil endured, and that there was nothing to fear from the gods and nothing to feel in death.

Stoicism was developed by Greek philosophers in the late 3rd and early 2nd centuries BC after it had been founded by Zeno c. 300 BC. Official Roman policy generally favored the Stoics; its most famous proponent was Seneca the Younger. The Stoics were pantheists and determinists. They believed that a person's part in the divine plan was determined, so that he or she only had freedom in the way that part was played, not a choice of what part to play. Consequently the Stoics advocated acceptance of whatever life had to offer, good or bad.

In the Greek world, the philosophy of Plato remained a powerful influence. However, Roman adherents disregarded many of the metaphysical and mystical aspects of Plato's philosophy, adopting an intellectual skepticism that replaced certainty of truth with probabilities. Plato's philosophy was based on two main ideas — that human beings could be improved and that the intellect was supreme.

Neoplatonism was founded in the 3rd century and was a revival of Platonism, incorporating elements from Pythagoras, Aristotle and the Stoics. It was the dominant pagan philosophy from around the mid-3rd century until philosophy schools were closed by Justinian in 529. Neoplatonism was an attempt at a comprehensive philosophy that also showed how the individual soul might reach God. As such it offered a path to salvation comparable with Christianity and the mystery religions and came to have a great influence on Christian thinking.

DEATH AND AFTER-LIFE

Afterlife

There was a range of views about whether there was an afterlife, and, if so, what it was like. These views are reflected in the range of burial rites. Around the mid-3rd century there was a marked change in burial rites, with inhumation becoming more popular than cremation, the reason for which is unclear. It may reflect a general increase in the hope and expectation of an afterlife as a result of the influence of the

Oriental cults and Neoplatonism (but not Christianity, which had not yet risen to predominance). Alternatively, it may be the result of a growing fashion that favored the more ostentatious rites and monuments associated with inhumation.

No generally accepted view on an afterlife existed, but there was a long-lasting and widely held view that the dead lived on in their tombs and could influence the fortunes of the living in a vague, undefined way, and so offerings were regularly made to them. Gifts were brought to the tomb, libations were poured for the dead and in some instances graves were provided with pipes so that wine could be poured into the burial itself. Although only a few instances of such pipe burials are known (both cremation and inhumation), it is possible that they were quite common. Holding celebrations at the tombs was also thought to appease the spirits of the dead.

Belief in an afterlife sometimes gave rise to superstitious practices. Cases are known of burials being weighted down to stop the dead from rising and haunting the living, while some corpses appear to have been decapitated for the same reason. The souls were thought to go to the underworld after death (not heaven or hell), but those souls that the gods of the underworld would not admit were destined to wander for eternity. The mystery religions, including Christianity, offered the promise of a happy afterlife (albeit defined in different ways in different religions) and helped to foster a more widespread belief that the soul (an entity defined by Plato and later philosophers) survived death.

Funerals

Funerals were organized by professional undertakers who provided mourning women, musicians and sometimes dancers and mimers. Most funerals were fairly simple, but upper-class funerals were often elaborate, particularly if the deceased was in any way illustrious. For such a person, the body might lie in state until the funeral, which started with a procession out of the city, taking a route along the main streets. The procession might pause in the forum for a ceremony of *laudatio*, during which the deceased, carried on a bier, was displayed, usually in an upright position, and a funeral oration (*laudatio funebris*) was read out.

During the republic and early empire part of the procession consisted of members of the deceased's family dressed as his ancestors and wearing masks of the ancestors (*imagines*). The masks were of wax until the 1st century BC, when other materials were used. These representatives of the ancestors rode in chariots and were a prominent part of the funeral procession. The right to display ancestral images publicly was restricted to families who had held curule magistracies. From the forum, the procession moved outside the city to the place of burial or cremation.

In contrast, lower-class funerals took place soon after death, and the corpse was taken from the city by the shortest route with a less elaborate procession of mourners. The poor could belong to funeral clubs (*collegia funeraticia*), so that the club paid the funeral expenses.

At the grave or cremation site, various rites took place, including a feast for the mourners and offerings of food and drink to the deceased. At the end of full mourning, nine days later, there was another feast (*cena novendialis*), and the dead continued to be remembered, particularly during the festivals of Parentalia and Lemuria. Nine was often of importance being three times three, a number used much in ritual. The exact funeral and burial rites varied widely according to the beliefs of the deceased's family and local customs. All people concerned with a funeral were considered polluted and had to be purified through ritual acts before they mixed with other people.

Burial

The Romans either buried their dead (inhumations) or burned them (cremations). Cremation replaced inhumation by the late republic and remained the dominant rite until the mid-3rd century, when inhumation became most common. At all times, however, both cremation and inhumation were practiced. To avoid religious pollution, most burials were in cemeteries outside towns, often beside roads. Some cemeteries must have contained thousands of burials.

CREMATIONS

In cremations, the Romans burned the dead on pyres. Cremations could take place in part of the cemetery set aside for that purpose (*ustrinum*). They could also take place where the ashes were to be buried, normally over a ready-dug grave called a *bustum*. Gifts and personal belongings of the dead were sometimes burned as well. The resulting ashes and bones were buried in a container, of which various types were used, including cloth bags, pottery, glass or metal vessels, gold caskets and marble chests. Jews and Christians objected to cremation, and the practice died out by the 5th century.

INHUMATIONS

In inhumations, the body was usually protected in some way. For poor burials probably only a sack or shroud was used. Wooden coffins were common, but there were also lead coffins and stone coffins (sarcophagi). Graves could also be lined with stones or wood, or the body protected by roof tiles or even broken amphorae. Young infants were usually buried rather than cremated, often near houses — presum-

ably they were not thought to cause pollution. In some regions embalming was carried out, including the encasing of bodies in gypsum plaster inside coffins. Christian burials tended to be oriented east-west.

TOMBS AND TOMBSTONES

Many graves (inhumations and cremations) were marked with tombstones. These varied enormously, but many were sculpted with some representation of the dead and had a dedicatory inscription (figs. 6.8, 6.9). Many more graves were probably marked with wooden grave markers that have not survived.

Tombs of various shapes and sizes (fig. 9.12) also were built to accommodate one or more burials in coffins or cremation vessels. Many tombs stood within carefully defined plots of ground, marked at the very least by boundary posts at the corners or surrounded by a low wall. To the Romans, a mausoleum was the same as a tomb, but it has come to mean a monumental tomb, sometimes enclosed within a

Fig. 9.12   Tombs in one of the main cemeteries at Pompeii, parallel to the town wall outside the Nuceria gate. The tombs were rectangular or circular in plan, and their interiors were decorated by paintings.

building. One of the largest was Hadrian's mausoleum at Rome (fig. 3.2). The burials of the upper classes were often marked by impressive and sometimes eccentric monuments, such as the pyramid-shaped tomb of Gaius Cestius at Rome.

In some cases, the dead person seems to have had the status of a hero and was treated almost like a god. Such people occupied temple tombs or temple mausolea, where the living could gain access to their presence. This seems to be a forerunner of the Christian belief in the power and sanctity of the tombs of martyrs. However, many of the temple mausolea may have only been elaborate tombs. Large mounds (barrows) built over the burial were also impressive monuments, examples of which have been found in northern provinces.

Rock-cut tombs were used for burial as well as catacombs in the late Roman period, the latter mainly by Christians. Catacombs were networks of underground passages carved out of soft rock, and burials were placed in chambers cut into the sides of the passages. There were catacombs at Rome and a few other Italian towns and also in Sicily, Malta and north Africa.

In Rome, funeral clubs and large households often deposited vessels of cremated remains in a collective tomb called a *columbarium* (dovecote), with each vessel in its own *nidus* (pigeonhole).

GRAVE GOODS

Many burials, both inhumations and cremations, were furnished with grave goods, presumably for use by the deceased in an afterlife, although Christian burials lack grave goods. The range of grave goods probably reflects the beliefs and wealth of the deceased's family. A rich burial would be likely to contain a variety of vessels full of food and drink, a flagon and patera (dish) for ritual libations, perhaps a gold ring as a symbol of high status, and almost anything else that the dead might be thought to require in the afterlife, including perfumes such as myrrh and frankincense. Poorer burials had only a few grave goods, often one or two vessels, food and drink and a few personal items.

Some inhumations have a coin in the mouth as the traditional fee for Charon, the mythical ferryman of the dead, and other inhumations and cremations had a pair of boots or shoes and sometimes lamps as grave goods, possibly for the deceased's journey through the underworld.

READING

The Falco novels by Lindsey Davis (Davis 1989, 1990, 1991, 1992) give an entertaining and well-researched look into life in the Roman world in the early empire.

Time
Bickerman 1980: various aspects of ancient chronology, including calendars, lists of consuls and problems of dating; Gordon 1983, 226–33; Hill 1984, 223–42; Oleson 1986: includes bibliography on time-keeping; Salzman 1990: discusses the calendar, in particular an illustrated one for AD 354 and its contents; Scullard 1981, 41–49.

The Family
Allason-Jones 1989: women in Britain; Balsdon 1962: women; Balsdon 1969: includes children; Bradley 1991; Clark 1989: various aspects relating to women, with numerous references; Dupont 1989, 103–21; Grant 1992, 27–37: women; Jackson 1988, 86–111: women's diseases, contraception, birth; Rawson (ed.) 1991: marriage, divorce, children, families; Treggiari 1991: marriage; Veyne 1987, 9–49: children, women, marriage, adoption.

Population
Brunt 1987; Duncan-Jones 1982: population size; Hammond and Scullard (eds.) 1970, 863–64.

Slaves
Bradley 1984: various aspects of slavery, including manumission; Bradley 1989: slave rebellions; Dupont 1989, 56–69; Grant 1992, 100–22: slaves, freedmen and freedwomen; Phillips 1985, 16–39; Shelton 1988, 168–205; Veyne 1987, 51–93: slaves and freedmen; Yavetz 1988: compilation of slave revolts.

Food and Drink
Dupont 1989, 269–75: meals; Hammond and Scullard (eds.) 1970, 443–44; Jackson 1988, 32–55: diet and hygiene; Oleson 1986: includes bibliography on food; Shelton 1988, 81–88.

Personal Appearance
Boon 1991: razors; Houston 1947: illustrated account of Roman and Byzantine costume and hairstyles;

Wild 1968: clothing in the northwest provinces; Wilson 1924: togas.

Entertainment
Balsdon 1969: various types of entertainment; Cameron 1976: circus factions; Dupont 1989, 275–86: dinner parties; Humphrey 1986: circuses; Shelton 1988; Olivová 1984; Veyne 1987; Welch 1991: review article of amphitheaters and *naumachiae*.

Art
Bandinelli 1969 and 1970: sculpture, paintings, mosaics, portable art; Barbet (ed.) 1983: paintings; Beckwith 1979: early Christian and Byzantine art; Bonanno 1976: portraiture; Brilliant 1974; Blagg 1987; Dorigo 1966: paintings and mosaics; Henig (ed.) 1983: includes articles on numerous aspects of art; Liversidge (ed.) 1982: paintings; Ramage and Ramage 1991; Ridgeway 1991: useful list of references on Etruscan art; Wilson 1986: various types of art, with numerous references.

Prisons and Punishment
Hammond and Scullard (eds.) 1970, 426, 911–12; Saller 1991.

Medicine
Jackson 1988 and 1990a; Jackson 1990b: collyrium stamps; Hammond and Scullard (eds.) 1970; Scarborough 1969; Shelton 1988.

Philosophy
Howatson (ed.) 1989, 434–35; Meredith 1986: includes numerous references; Shelton 1988, 426–37.

Death and Afterlife
Henig 1984: death, burial and afterlife; Howatson (ed.) 1989: death, burial and afterlife; Jones 1987: burial; Reece (ed.) 1977: burial; Shelton 1988: death, burial and afterlife: Toynbee 1971: burials and tombs.

BIBLIOGRAPHY

Adam, J.-P. 1984. *La Construction romaine. Materiaux et techniques.* Paris: Grands Manuels Picard.

Alföldy, G. 1974. *Noricum.* London and Boston: Routledge & Kegan Paul.

Allason-Jones, L. 1989. *Women in Roman Britain.* London: British Museum Publications.

Anderson, A.S. 1987, "The Imperial Army." In J. Wacher, ed., *The Roman World*, vol. 1, pp. 89–106. London and New York: Routledge & Kegan Paul.

Anderson, J.K. 1985. *Hunting in the Ancient World.* Berkeley, Los Angeles and London: University of California Press.

Andreae, B. 1973 *The Art of Rome* (translated and published in English in 1978). London: Macmillan.

Applebaum, S. 1987. "Animal Husbandry." In J. Wacher, ed., *The Roman World*, vol. 2, pp. 504–26. London and New York: Routledge & Kegan Paul.

Baatz, D. and Herrmann, F.-R., eds. 1982. *Die Römer in Hessen.* Stuttgart: Theiss.

Bailey, D. 1983. "Terracotta Revetments, Figurines and Lamps." In M. Henig, ed., *A Handbook of Roman Art: A Survey of the Visual Arts of the Roman World*, pp. 191–204. Oxford: Phaidon.

Bailey, D.M. 1991. "Lamps Metal, Lamps Clay: A Decade of Publication." *Journal of Roman Archaeology* 4, 51–62.

Balsdon, J.P.V.D. 1962. *Roman Women: Their History and Habits.* London: Bodley Head.

———. 1969. *Life and Leisure in Ancient Rome.* London: Bodley Head.

———. 1970. *Rome: The Story of an Empire.* London: Weidenfeld and Nicolson.

Bandinelli, R.B. 1969. *Rome. The Centre of Power, Roman Art to AD 200* (translated and published in 1970). London: Thames and Hudson; New York: George Braziller.

———. 1970. *Rome. The Late Empire. Roman Art AD 200–400* (translated and published in 1971). London: Thames and Hudson; New York: George Braziller.

Barbet, A., ed. 1983. *La peinture murale romaine dans les provinces de l'Empire: Journées d' étude de Paris 23–25 Septembre 1982.* Oxford: British Archaeological Reports International Series 165.

Barnwell, P.S. 1992. *Emperors, Prefects & Kings. The Roman West, 395–565.* London: Duckworth.

Barton, I.M. 1989. "Religious Buildings." In I.M. Barton, ed., *Roman Public Buildings*, pp. 67–96. Exeter: University of Exeter.

Barton, I.M., ed. 1989. *Roman Public Buildings.* Exeter: University of Exeter.

Bass, G.F., ed. 1972. *A History of Seafaring Based on Underwater Archaeology.* London: Thames and Hudson.

Bateman, N. 1985. "Warehousing in Roman London." In G. Milne, *The Port of Roman London*, pp. 68–78. London: Batsford.

Bateman, N., and Locker, A. 1982. "The Sauce of the Thames." *London Archaeologist* 4, 204–7.

Beckwith, J. 1979. *Early Christian and Byzantine Art*, 2nd ed. Harmondsworth: Penguin.

Bennett, J. 1980. *Towns in Roman Britain.* Princes Risborough: Shire Publications.

Bickerman, E.J. 1980. *Chronology of the Ancient World.* 2nd ed. London: Thames and Hudson; Ithaca, NY: Cornell University Press.

Bidwell, P., Miket, R., and Ford, B. 1988. *Portae cum turribus. Studies of Roman Fort Gates.* Oxford: British Archaeological Reports 206.

Birley, E. 1988. *The Roman Army. Papers 1929–1986.* Amsterdam: J.C. Gieben.

Bishop, M.C. 1985. "The Military *Fabrica* and the Production of Arms in the Early Principate." In M.C. Bishop, ed., *The Production and Distribution of Roman Military Equipment*, pp. 1–42. Oxford: British Archaeological Reports International Series 275.

Bishop, M.C., ed. 1985. *The Production and Distribution of Roman Military Equipment.* Oxford: British Archaeological Reports International Series 275.

Bishop, M.C., and Coulston, J.C. 1989. *Roman Military Equipment.* Princes Risborough: Shire Publications.

Black, E.W. 1987. *The Roman Villas of South-East England.* Oxford: British Archaeological Reports 171.

Blackman, D.J., ed. 1973. *Marine Archaeology.* Colston Papers no. 23. London: Butterworths.

Blagg, T. 1983. "Architecture.". In M. Henig, ed., *A Handbook of Roman Art*, pp. 26–65. Oxford: Phaidon.

Blagg, T.F.C. 1987. "Society and the Artist." In J. Wacher, ed., *The Roman World*, vol. 2, pp. 717–42. London and New York: Routledge & Kegan Paul.

Boardman, J., Griffin, J., and Murray, O. 1986. *The Roman World.* Oxford: Oxford University Press.

Boethius, A. 1970. *Etruscan and Early Roman Architecture.* Harmondsworth. Penguin Books. 2nd integrated ed. published 1978.

Bonanno, A. 1976. *Portraits and Other Heads on Roman Historical Relief up to the Age of Septimius Severus.* Oxford: British Archaeological Reports Supplementary Series 6.

Bonner, S.F. 1977. *Education in Ancient Rome From the Elder Cato to the Younger Pliny.* London: Methuen.

Boon, G.C. 1991. "*Tonsor Humanus:* Razor and Toilet-knife in Antiquity." *Britannia* 22, 21–32.

Bowder, D., ed. 1980. *Who Was Who in the Roman World 753 BC–AD 476.* Oxford: Phaidon.

Bowman, A.K. 1986. *Egypt after the Pharaohs 332 BC–AD 642 from Alexander to the Arab Conquest.* London: British Museum Publications.

Bowman, A.K., and Thomas, J.D. 1983. *Vindolanda: The Latin Writing Tablets.* London: Britannia Monograph Series 4.

Bradley, K.R. 1984. *Slaves and Masters in the Roman Empire. A Study in Social Control.* Brussels: Latomus.

———. 1989. *Slavery and Rebellion in the Roman World 140 B.C.–70 B.C.* Bloomington: Indiana University Press. London: Batsford.

———. 1991. *Discovering the Roman Family. Studies in Roman Social History.* Oxford: Oxford University Press.

Bradley, P. 1990. *Ancient Rome. Using Evidence.* Victoria: Edward Arnold.

Braund, D.C., ed. 1988. *The Administration of the Roman Empire (241 BC–AD 193).* Exeter: University of Exeter.

Breeze, D.J. 1982. *The Northern Frontiers of Roman Britain.* London: Batsford.

———. 1987. "The Frontiers: Britain." In J. Wacher, ed., *The Roman World*, vol. 1, pp. 198–222. London and New York: Routledge & Kegan Paul.

Bridger, C.J. 1984. "The *Pes Monetalis* and the *Pes Drusianus* in Xanten." *Britannia* 15, 85–98.

Brilliant, R. 1974. *Roman Art from the Republic to Constantine.* London: Phaidon Press.

Brodribb, G. 1987. *Roman Brick and Tile.* Gloucester: Alan Sutton.

Brothers, A.J. 1989. "Buildings for Entertainment." In I.M. Barton, ed., *Roman Public Buildings*, pp. 97–125. Exeter: University of Exeter.

Brown, D. 1976a. "Bronze and Pewter." In D. Strong and D. Brown, eds., *Roman Crafts*, pp. 24–41. London: Duckworth.

———. 1976b. "Pottery." In D. Strong and D. Brown, eds., *Roman Crafts*, pp. 74–91. London: Duckworth.

Brunt, P.A. 1987. "Labour." In J. Wacher, ed., *The Roman World*, vol. 2, pp. 701–16. London and New York: Routledge & Kegan Paul.

Buck, D.J., and Mattingly, D.J., eds. 1985. *Town and Country in Roman Tripolitania: Papers in Honour of Olwen Hackett.* Oxford: British Archaeological Reports International Series 274.

Burford, A. 1972. *Craftsmen in Greek and Roman Society.* London: Thames and Hudson.

Burnett, A., Amandry, M., and Ripollès, P.P. 1992. *Roman Provincial Coinage. Volume I from the Death of Caesar to the Death of Vitellius (44 BC–AD 69). Part I: Introduction and Catalogue. Part II: Indexes and Plates.* London: British Museum Press; Paris: Bibliothèque Nationale.

Burnham, B.C., and Wacher, J. 1990. *The "Small Towns" of Roman Britain.* London: Batsford.

Burton, G. 1987. "Government and the Provinces." In J. Wacher, ed., *The Roman World*, vol. 2; pp. 423–39. London and New York: Routledge & Kegan Paul.

Butcher, S.A. 1976. "Enamelling." In D. Strong and D. Brown, eds., *Roman Crafts*, pp. 42–51. London: Duckworth.

Cameron, A. 1976. *Circus Factions Blues and Greens at Rome and Byzantium.* Oxford: Clarendon Press.

———. 1992. "Observations on the Distribution and Ownership of Late Roman Silver Plate." *Journal of Roman Archaeology* 5, 178–85.

Carson, R.A.G. 1978. *Principal Coins of the Romans. Volume I. The Republic c. 290–31 BC.* London: British Museum Publications.

———. 1980. *Principal Coins of the Romans. Volume II. The Principate 31 BC–AD 296.* London: British Museum Publications.

———. 1981. *Principal Coins of the Romans. Volume III. The Dominate AD 294–498.* London: British Museum Publications.

———. 1990. *Coins of the Roman Empire.* London and New York: Routledge.

Carter, J. 1989. "Civic and Other Buildings." In I.M. Barton, ed., *Roman Public Buildings*, pp. 31–65. Exeter: University of Exeter.

Casey, P.J. 1980. *Roman Coinage in Britain.* Princes Risborough: Shire Publications.

Casson, L. 1991. *The Ancient Mariners, Seafarers and Sea Fighters of the Mediterranean in Ancient Times* 2nd ed. Princeton: Princeton University Press.

Chapman, H. 1978. "Writing Tablets." In *Southwark Excavations 1972–1974*, pp. 397–401. London and Middlesex Archaeological Society/ Surrey Archaeological Society joint publication 1.

Chevallier, R. 1976. *Roman Roads.* London: Batsford.

———. 1988. *Voyages et Déplacements dans l'empire romain.* Paris: Armand Colin.

Clark, G. 1989. *Women in the Ancient World.* Oxford: Classical Association, Oxford University Press.

Clarke, J.R. 1991. *Houses of Roman Italy 100 B.C.–A.D. 250.* Los Angeles: University of California Press.

Clayton, P.A. 1988. "The Pharos at Alexandria." In P.A. Clayton and M.J. Price, *The Seven Wonders of the Ancient World*, pp. 138–57. London and New York: Routledge.

Clayton, P.A., and Price, M.J. 1988. *The Seven Wonders of the Ancient World.* London and New York: Routledge.

Cleere, H. 1976. "Ironmaking." In D. Strong and D. Brown, eds., *Roman Crafts*, pp. 126–41. London: Duckworth.

Collingwood, R.G. and Wright, R.P. 1965. *The Roman Inscriptions of Britain. I. Inscriptions on Stone.* Oxford: Oxford University Press.

Connolly, P. 1981. *Greece and Rome at War.* London: Macdonald & Co.

———. 1987. "The Roman Saddle." In M. Dawson, ed., *The Roman Military Equipment*, pp. 7–27. Oxford: British Archaeological Reports International Series 336.

Cornell, T., and Matthews, J. 1982. *Atlas of the Roman World.* Oxford: Phaidon.

Coulston, J.C. 1985. "Roman Archery Equipment." In M.C. Bishop, ed., *The Production and Distribution of Roman Military Equipment. The Accoutrements of War*, pp. 220–336. Oxford: British Archaeological Reports International Series 275.

Crawford, M.H. 1985. *Coinage and Money under the Roman Republic. Italy and the Mediterranean Economy.* London: Methuen.

Crummy, N. 1981. *The Roman Small Finds from Excavations in Colchester 1971–9.* Colchester Archaeological Report 2.

Cüppers, H., ed. 1990. *Die Römer in Rheinland-Pfalz.* Stuttgart: Theiss.

Curchin, L.A. 1991. *Roman Spain. Conquest and Assimilation.* London: Routledge.

Daniels, C. 1987. "The Frontiers: Africa." In J. Wacher, ed., *The Roman World*, vol. 1, pp. 223–65. London and New York: Routledge & Kegan Paul.

Davies, R.W. 1985. *Service in the Roman Army*, eds. D. Breeze and V.A. Maxfield. Edinburgh: Edinburgh University Press with University of Durham.

Davis, L. 1989. *The Silver Pigs.* London: Sidgwick & Jackson.

———. 1990. *Shadows in Bronze.* London: Sidgwick & Jackson.

———. 1991. *Venus in Copper.* London: Hutchinson.

———. 1992. *The Iron Hand of Mars.* London: Hutchinson.

Davison, D.P. 1989. *The Barracks of the Roman Army from the 1st to 3rd centuries A.D. A Comparative Study of the Barracks from Fortresses, Forts and Fortlets with an Analysis of Building Types and Con-*

struction, *Stabling and Garrisons.* Oxford: British Archaeological Reports International Series 472.

Dawson, M., ed. 1987. *The Roman Military Equipment. The Accoutrements of War.* Oxford: British Archaeological Reports International Series 336.

De Alarcão, J. 1988. *Roman Portugal: Introduction and Gazetteer.* Warminster: Aris & Phillips.

DeLaine, J. 1988. "Recent Research on Roman Baths." *Journal of Roman Archaeology* 1, 11–32.

De Ruyt, C. 1983. *Macellum. Marché Alimentaire des Romains.* Louvain-la-Neuve: Publications d'Histoire de l'Art et d'Archéologie de l'Université Catholique de Louvain 35.

Dilke, O.A.W. 1971. *The Roman Land Surveyors: An Introduction to the Agrimensores.* Newton Abbot: David & Charles.

———. 1985. *Greek and Roman Maps.* London: Thames and Hudson.

Dixon, K.R. and Southern, P. 1992. *The Roman Cavalry from the First to the Third Century AD.* London: Batsford.

Dobson, B. 1981. "Army Organization." In P. Connolly, *Greece and Rome at War*, pp. 213–27. London: Macdonald & Co.

Dodge, H. 1990. "The Architectural Impact of Rome in the East." pp. 108–20. In M. Henig, ed., *Architecture and Architectural Sculpture in the Roman Empire.* Oxford University Committee for Archaeology Monograph 29.

———. 1991. "Ancient Marble Studies: Recent Research." *Journal of Roman Archaeology* 4, 28–50.

Dorigo, W. 1966. *Late Roman Painting. A Study of Pictorial Records 30 BC–AD 500*, trans. and pub. in 1971. London: Dent.

Drack, W., and Fellmann, R. 1988. *Die Römer in der Schweiz.* Stuttgart: Theiss.

Drinkwater, J.F. 1987. "Urbanization in Italy and the Western Empire." In J. Wacher, ed., *The Roman World*, vol. 1, pp. 345–87. London and New York: Routledge & Kegan Paul.

Drury, P.J. 1980. "Non-Classical Religious Buildings in Iron Age and Roman Britain: A Review." In W. Rodwell, ed., *Temples, Churches and Religion*, pp. 45–78. Oxford: British Archaeological Report 77.

Duncan-Jones, R. 1982. *The Economy of the Roman Empire Quantitative Studies*, 2nd ed. Cambridge: Cambridge University Press.

du Plat, J. Taylor, and Cleere, H., eds. 1978. *Roman Shipping and Trade: Britain and the Rhine Provinces.* London: Council for British Archaeology Research Report 24.

Dupont, F. 1989. *Daily Life in Ancient Rome*, trans. and pub. in 1992. Oxford, UK. and Cambridge, Mass.: Blackwell.

Edmondson, J.C. 1989. "Mining in the Later Roman Empire and Beyond: Continuity or Disruption?" *Journal of Roman Studies* 79, 84–102.

Fabre, G., Fiches, J.-L., and Paillet, J.-L. 1991. "Interdisciplinary Research on the Aqueduct of Nîmes and the Pont du Gard." *Journal of Roman Archaeology* 4, 63–88.

Ferguson, J. 1970. *The Religions of the Roman Empire.* London: Thames and Hudson.

———. 1987. "Ruler-worship." In J. Wacher, ed., *The Roman World*, vol. 2, pp. 766–79. London and New York: Routledge & Kegan Paul.

Filtzinger, D., Planck, D., and Cämmerer, B. eds. 1986. *Die Römer in Baden Württtenberg.* Stuttgart: Theiss.

Flemming, N.C. 1980. "Structures under water." In K. Muckelroy, ed., *Archaeology under Water*, pp. 162–77. New York and London: McGraw-Hill.

Frere, S. 1967. *Britannia. A History of Roman Britain.* London: Routledge & Kegan Paul.

Frere, S.S., Roxan, M., and Tomlin, R.S.O., eds. 1990. *The Roman Inscriptions of Britain. Volume II. Instrumentum Domesticum. Fascicule 1.* Gloucester: Alan Sutton.

Golvin, J.-C. 1988. *L'amphithéâtre romain. Essai sur la théorisation de sa forme et de ses fonctions.* Paris: Publications du centre pierre.

Gordon, A.E. 1983. *Illustrated Introduction to Latin Epigraphy.* Berkeley, Los Angeles and London: University of California Press.

Grant, M. 1971. *Roman Myths.* London: Weidenfeld & Nicolson.

———. 1973. *The Jews in the Roman World.* London: Weidenfeld & Nicolson.

———. 1974. *The Army of the Caesars.* London: Weidenfeld & Nicolson.

———. 1980. *Greek and Latin Authors 800 B.C.–A.D. 1000.* New York: H.W. Wilson Company.

———. 1990. *The Visible Past. Greek and Roman History from Archaeology 1960–1990.* London: Weidenfeld & Nicolson.

———. 1992. *Greeks and Romans. A Social History.* London: Weidenfeld & Nicolson.

Green, E. 1987. "Laws and the Legal System in the Principate." In J. Wacher, ed., *The Roman World*, vol. 2, pp. 440–54. London and New York: Routledge & Kegan Paul.

Green, M.J. 1976. *A Corpus of Religious Material from the Civilian Areas of Roman Britain*. Oxford: British Archaeological Report 24.

———. 1986. *The Gods of the Celts*. Gloucester: Alan Sutton; Totowa, N. J.: Barnes and Noble.

———. 1987. "Provincial Cults." In J. Wacher, ed., *The Roman World*, vol. 2, pp. 785–92. London and New York: Routledge & Kegan Paul.

———1992. *Dictionary of Celtic Myth and Legend*. London: Thames and Hudson.

Greene, K. 1979. *Report on the Excavations at Usk 1965–1976: The Pre-Flavian Fine Wares*. Cardiff: University of Wales Press.

———. 1986. *The Archaeology of the Roman Economy*. London: Batsford.

Greenhill, B. 1976. *Archaeology of the Boat. A New Introductory Study*. London: Adam and Charles Black.

Grew, F., Pritchard, F., and Richardson, B. 1985. "Traffic and Trade." In G. Milne, *The Port of London*, pp. 103–26. London: Batsford.

Grimal, P. 1983. *Roman Cities*, trans., ed. and a descriptive catalogue of Roman cities by G.M. Woloch. Madison: University of Wisconsin Press.

Gwinup, T., and Dickinson, F. 1982. *Greek and Roman Authors: A Checklist of Criticism*, 2nd ed. Metuchen, N.J.: Scarecrow Press.

Hague, D.B. 1973. "Lighthouses." In D.J. Blackman, ed., *Marine Archaeology*, pp. 293–314. Colston Papers no. 23. London: Butterworths.

Hammond, N.G.L., and Scullard, H.H., eds. 1970. *The Oxford Classical Dictionary*, 2nd ed. Oxford: Clarendon Press.

Hanley, R. 1987. *Villages in Roman Britain*. Princes Risborough: Shire Publications.

Harden, D.B. 1970. "Ancient Glass. II: Roman," *Archaeological Journal* 126, 44–77.

Harden, D.B., Hellenkemper, H., Painter, K., and Whitehouse, D. 1987. *Glass of the Caesars*. Milan: Olivetti.

Harden, D.B., Painter, K.S., Pinder-Wilson, R.H., and Tait, H. 1968. *Masterpieces of Glass*. London: British Museum.

Harries, J. 1987. "The Rise of Christianity." In J. Wacher, ed., *The Roman World*, vol. 2, pp. 796–811. London and New York: Routledge & Kegan Paul.

Healey, J.F. 1978. *Mining and Metallurgy in the Greek and Roman World*. London: Thames and Hudson.

Heinen, H. 1985. *Trier und das Treverland in römischer Zeit*. Trier: Spee-Verlag.

Heinz, W. 1983. *Römische Thermen*. Munich: Hirmer Verlag.

Henig, M. 1983. "The Luxury Arts: Decorative Metalwork, Engraved Gems and Jewellery." In M. Henig, ed., *A Handbook of Roman Art*, pp. 139–65. Oxford: Phaidon.

———. 1984. *Religion in Roman Britain*. London: Batsford.

Henig, M., ed. 1983. *A Handbook of Roman Art: A Survey of the Visual Arts of the Roman World*. Oxford: Phaidon.

———. 1990. *Architecture and Architectural Sculpture in the Roman Empire*. Oxford: Oxford University Committee for Archaeology, Monograph 29.

Henig, M., and King, A., eds. 1986. *Pagan Gods and Shrines of the Roman Empire*. Oxford: Oxford University Committee for Archaeology, Monograph 8.

Higgins, R. 1976. "Jewellery." In D. Strong and D. Brown, eds., *Roman Crafts*, pp. 52–61. London: Duckworth.

———. 1980. *Greek and Roman Jewellery*, 2nd ed. London: Methuen.

Hill, D. 1984. *A History of Engineering in Classical and Medieval Times*. London: Croom Helm.

Hodge, A.T. 1989. "Aqueducts." In I.M. Barton, ed. *Roman Public Buildings*, pp. 127–49. Exeter: University of Exeter.

———. 1992 *Roman Aqueducts & Water Supply*. London: Duckworth.

Holder, P.A. 1982. *The Roman Army in Britain*. London: Batsford.

Horn, H.G., ed. 1987. *Die Römer in Nordrhein-Westfalen*. Stuttgart: Theiss.

Houston, M.G. 1947. *Ancient Greek, Roman and Byzantine Costume & Decoration*, 2nd ed. London: Adam & Charles Black.

Howatson, M.C., ed. 1989. *The Oxford Companion to Classical Literature*, 2nd ed. Oxford: Oxford University Press.

Humphrey, J.H. 1986. *Roman Circuses. Arenas for Chariot Racing*. London: Batsford.

Hutchinson, V.J. 1991. "The Cult of Dionysos/Bacchus in the Graeco-Roman World: New Light from Archaeological Studies." *Journal of Roman Archaeology* 4, 222–30.

Hyland, A. 1990. *Equus: The Horse in the Roman World.* London: Batsford.

Ireland, R. 1983 "Epigraphy." In M. Henig, ed., *A Handbook of Roman Art*, pp. 220–33. Oxford: Phaidon.

Isaac, B. 1988. "The Meaning of the Terms *Limes* and *Limitanei.*" *Journal of Roman Studies* 78, 125–27.

———. 1992. *The Limits of Empire: The Roman Army in the East*, 2nd ed. Oxford: Clarendon Press.

Isings, C. 1957. *Roman Glass from Dated Finds.* Groningen/Djakarta: J.B. Wolters.

Jackson, R. 1988. *Doctors and Diseases in the Roman Empire.* London: British Museum Publications.

———. 1990a. "Roman Doctors and Their Instruments: Recent Research into Ancient Practice." *Journal of Roman Archaeology* 3, 5–27.

———. 1990b. "A New Collyrium Stamp from Cambridge and a Corrected Reading of the Stamp from Caistor-by-Norwich." *Britannia* 21, 275–83.

Johns, C. 1971. *Arretine and Samian Pottery.* London: British Museum.

Johnson, A. 1983. *Roman Forts of the 1st and 2nd centuries AD in Britain and the German Provinces.* London: A & C Black.

Johnson, S. 1983. *Late Roman Fortifications.* London: Batsford.

———. 1989. *English Heritage Book of Hadrian's Wall.* London: Batsford/English Heritage.

Johnston, D.E. 1979. *An Illustrated History of Roman Roads in Britain.* Bourne End: Spurbooks.

Johnston, D.E., ed. 1977. *The Saxon Shore.* London: Council for British Archaeology Research Report 18.

Johnstone, P. 1988. *The Sea-craft of Prehistory*, 2nd ed. London: Routledge.

Jones, B., and Mattingly, D. 1990. *An Atlas of Roman Britain.* Oxford: Basil Blackwell.

Jones, J.M. 1990. *A Dictionary of Ancient Roman Coins.* London: Seaby.

Jones, R. 1987. "Burial Customs of Rome and the Provinces." In J. Wacher, ed., *The Roman World*, vol. 2, pp. 812–37. London and New York: Routledge & Kegan Paul.

Kapitän, G. 1973. "Greco-Roman Anchors and the Evidence for the One-armed Wooden Anchor in Antiquity." In D.J. Blackman, ed., *Marine Archaeology*, pp. 383–94. Colston Papers no. 23. London: Butterworths.

Keay, S.J. 1988. *Roman Spain.* London: British Museum Publications.

Kennedy, D. 1987. "The Frontiers: The East." In J. Wacher, ed., *The Roman World*, vol. 1, pp. 266–308. London and New York: Routledge & Kegan Paul.

———. 1992. "The Roman Frontier in Arabia (Jordanian sector)." *Journal of Roman Archaeology* 5, 473–89.

Kennedy, D., and Riley, D. 1990. *Rome's Desert Frontier from the Air.* London: Batsford.

Kent, J. 1987. "The Monetary System." In J. Wacher, ed., *The Roman World*, vol. 2, pp. 568–85. London and New York: Routledge & Kegan Paul.

Kent, J.P.C., and Painter, K.S. 1977. *Wealth of the Roman World. Gold and Silver AD 300–700.* London: British Museum Publications.

Keppie, L. 1984. *The Making of the Roman Army: From Republic to Empire.* London: Batsford.

———. 1991. *Understanding Roman Inscriptions.* London: Batsford.

King, A. 1983 "Pottery." In M. Henig, ed., *A Handbook of Roman Art*, pp. 179–90. Oxford: Phaidon.

———. 1990. *Roman Gaul and Germany.* London: British Museum Publications.

Kleiner, F.S. 1989. "The Study of Roman Triumphal and Honorary Arches 50 Years After Kähler." *Journal of Roman Archaeology* 2, 195–206.

Landels, J.G. 1978. *Engineering in the Ancient World.* London: Chatto & Windus.

Lander, J. 1984. *Roman Stone Fortifications. Variation and Change from the First Century A.D. to the Fourth.* Oxford: British Archaeological Reports International Series 206.

Lane Fox, R. 1986. *Pagans and Christians.* Harmondsworth: Viking Penguin.

Lengyel, A., and Radan, G.T.B., eds. 1980. *The Archaeology of Roman Pannonia.* Lexington: University Press of Kentucky; Budapest: Akademia Kiadó.

Levick, B. 1987. "Urbanization in the Eastern Empire." In J. Wacher, ed., *The Roman World*, vol. 1, pp. 329–44. London and New York: Routledge & Kegan Paul.

Lewis, N., and Reinhold, M., eds. 1990. *Roman Civilization. Selected Readings. Volume II: The Empire*, 3rd ed. New York: Columbia University Press.

Liebeschuetz, J.H.W.G. 1987. "Government and Administration in the Late Empire (to AD 476)." In J. Wacher, ed., *The Roman World*, vol. 2, pp. 455–69. London and New York: Routledge & Kegan Paul.

Ling, R. 1976. "Stuccowork." In D. Strong and D. Brown, eds., *Roman Crafts*, pp. 209–21. London: Duckworth.

Lintott, A. 1990. "Electoral Bribery in the Roman Republic." *Journal of Roman Studies* 80, 1–16.

Liversidge, J. 1976. "Woodwork." In D. Strong and D. Brown, eds., *Roman Crafts*, pp. 154–66. London: Duckworth.

Liversidge, J., ed. 1982. *Roman Provincial Wall Painting of the Western Empire*. Oxford: British Archaeological Report International Series 140.

———. 1983. "Wall Painting and Stucco." In M. Henig, ed., *A Handbook of Roman Art*, pp. 97–115. Oxford: Phaidon.

London Association of Classical Teachers. 1971. *Some Inscriptions from Roman Britain*, 2nd ed. Original Records no. 4.

MacDonald, W.I. 1982. *The Architecture of the Roman Empire. I. An Introductory Study*, rev. ed. New Haven and London: Yale University Press.

———. 1986. *The Architecture of the Roman Empire. II. An Urban Appraisal*. New Haven and London: Yale University Press.

MacGregor, A. 1985. *Bone, Antler, Ivory & Horn. The Technology of Skeletal Materials Since the Roman Period*. London and Sydney: Croom Helm; Totowa, N.J.: Barnes & Noble.

McKay, A.G. 1975. *Houses, Villas and Palaces in the Roman World*. London: Thames and Hudson.

Macready, S. & Thompson, F.H., eds. 1987. *Roman Architecture in the Greek World*. London: Society of Antiquaries.

McWhirr, A. 1982. *Roman Crafts and Industries*. Princes Risborough: Shire Publications.

———. 1987. "Transport by Land and Water." In J. Wacher, ed., *The Roman World*, vol. 2, pp. 658–70. London and New York: Routledge & Kegan Paul.

McWhirr, A. ed. 1979. *Roman Brick and Tile: Studies in Manufacture, Distribution and Use in the Western Empire*. Oxford: British Archaeological Reports International Series 68.

Magie, D. 1950. *Roman Rule in Asia Minor to the End of the Third Century After Christ*. New York: Arno Press, orig. pub. 1950. Princeton: Princetown University Press, reprint.

Mann, J.C. 1977 "*Duces* and *Comites* in the 4th Century." In D.E. Johnston, ed., *The Saxon Shore*, pp. 11–15. London: Council for British Archaeology Research Report 18.

———. 1983. *Legionary Recruitment and Veteran Settlement During the Principate*, University of London Institute of Archaeology Occasional Publication 7.

Manning, W.H. 1976. "Blacksmithing." In D. Strong and D. Brown, eds., *Roman Crafts*, pp. 142–53. London: Duckworth.

———. 1985. *Catalogue of the Romano-British Iron Tools, Fittings and Weapons in the British Museum*. London: British Museum Publications.

———. 1987. "Industrial Growth." In J. Wacher, ed., *The Roman World*, vol. 2, pp. 586–610. London and New York: Routledge & Kegan Paul.

Marsden, E.W. 1969. *Greek and Roman Artillery. Historical Development*. Oxford: Clarendon Press.

Marsden, P. 1972. "Ships of the Roman Period and After in Britain." In G.F. Bass, ed., *A History of Seafaring*, pp. 113–32. London: Thames and Hudson.

Mattingly, D.J. 1988. "Oil for Export? A Comparison of Libyan, Spanish and Tunisian Oil Production in the Roman Empire." *Journal of Roman Archaeology* 1, 33–56.

Mattingly, D.J., and Hayes, J.W. 1992. "Nador and Fortified Farms in North Africa." *Journal of Roman Archaeology* 5, 408–18.

Maxfield, V.A. 1981. *The Military Decorations of the Roman Army*. London: Batsford.

———. 1987. "The Frontiers: Mainland Europe." In J. Wacher, ed., *The Roman World*, vol. 1, pp. 139–97. London and New York: Routledge & Kegan Paul.

Maxfield, V.A., ed. 1989. *The Saxon Shore. A Handbook*. Exeter: University of Exeter.

Maxfield, V.A., and Dobson, M.J., eds. 1991. *Proceedings of the XVth International Congress of Roman Frontier Studies*. Exeter: University of Exeter.

Meiggs, R. 1982. *Trees and Timber in the Ancient Mediterranean World*. Oxford: Oxford University Press.

Meijer, F. 1986. *A History of Seafaring in the Classical World*. London and Sydney: Croom Helm.

Meredith, A. 1986. "Later Philosophy." In J. Boardman, J. Griffin, and O. Murray, *The Roman World*, pp. 288–307. Oxford: Oxford University Press.

Merrifield, R. 1987. *The Archaeology of Ritual and Magic*. London: Batsford.

Miller, J. 1969. *The Spice Trade of the Roman Empire 29 B.C. to A.D. 641*. Oxford: Clarendon Press.

Miller, L., Schofield, J., and Rhodes, M. 1986. *The Roman Quay at St Magnus House. London. Excavations at New Fresh Wharf. Lower Thames Street. London 1974–78*. London: London & Middlesex Archaeological Society.

Milne, G. 1985. *The Port of Roman London*. London: Batsford.

Mócsy, A. 1974. *Pannonia and Upper Moesia. A History of the Middle Danube Provinces of the Roman Empire*. London and Boston: Routledge & Kegan Paul.

Morris, P. 1979. *Agricultural Buildings in Roman Britain*. Oxford: British Archaeological Reports 70.

Morrison, J.S. 1976. "The Classical Traditions." In B. Greenhill, *Archaeology of the Boat*, pp. 155–73. London: Adam and Charles Black.

Muckelroy, K., ed. 1980. *Archaeology Under Water. An Atlas of the World's Submerged Sites*. New York and London: McGraw-Hill.

Newby, M., and Painter, K. (eds.) 1991. *Roman Glass. Two Centuries of Art and Invention*. London: Society of Antiquaries of London.

Nicol, D.M. 1991. *A Biographical Dictionary of the Byzantine Empire*. London: Seaby.

Ogilvie, R.M. 1969. *The Romans and Their Gods*. London: Chatto & Windus.

Oleson, J.P. 1986. *Bronze Age. Greek and Roman Technology. A Select Annotated Bibliography*. New York and London: Garland Publishing.

Olivová, V. 1984. *Sports and Games in the Ancient World*. London: Orbis Publishing.

Owens, E.J. 1989. "Roman Town Planning." In I.M. Barton, ed., *Roman Public Buildings*, pp. 7–30. Exeter: University of Exeter.

———. 1991. *The City in the Greek and Roman World*. London: Routledge.

Paddock, J. 1985. "Some Changes in the Manufacture and Supply of Roman Bronze Helmets Under the Late Republic and Early Empire." In M.C. Bishop, ed., *The Production and Distribution of Roman Military Equipment*, pp. 142–59. Oxford: British Archaeological Reports International Series 275.

Parker, A. 1980. "Mediterranean Wreck Sites and Classical Seafaring." In K. Muckelroy, ed., *Archaeology Under Water. An Atlas of the World's Submerged Sites*, pp. 50–61. New York and London: McGraw-Hill.

Peacock, D.P.S. 1982. *Pottery in the Roman world: An Ethnoarchaeological Approach*. London and New York: Longman.

Peacock, D.P.S. and Williams, D.F. 1986. *Amphorae and the Roman Economy: An Introductory Guide*. London and New York: Longman.

Percival, J. 1976. *The Roman Villa*. London: Batsford.

———. 1987. "The Villa in Italy and the Provinces." In J. Wacher, ed., *The Roman World*, vol. 2, pp. 527–47. London and New York: Routledge & Kegan Paul.

Phillips, W.D. 1985. *Slavery from Roman Times to the Early Transatlantic Trade*. Manchester: Manchester University Press.

Piggott, S. 1968. *The Druids*. London: Thames and Hudson.

———. 1983. *The Earliest Wheeled Transport. From the Atlantic Coast to the Caspian Sea*. Ithaca, N.Y.: Cornell University Press.

Potter, T.W. 1987. *Roman Italy*. London: British Museum Publications.

Poulter, A. 1987. "Townships and Villages." In J. Wacher, ed., *The Roman World*, vol. 1, pp. 388–411. London and New York: Routledge & Kegan Paul.

Pratt, P. 1976. "Wall Painting." In D. Strong and D. Brown, eds., *Roman Crafts*, pp. 223–9. London: Duckworth.

Price, J. 1976. "Glass." In D. Strong and D. Brown, eds., *Roman Crafts*, pp. 110–25. London: Duckworth.

———. 1983. "Glass." In M. Henig, ed., *Handbook of Roman Art*, pp. 205–19. Oxford: Phaidon.

Ramage, N.H., and Ramage, A. 1991. *The Cambridge Illustrated History of Roman Art*. Cambridge and New York: Cambridge University Press.

Rawson, B., ed. 1991. *Marriage, Divorce and Children in Ancient Rome*. Oxford: Oxford University Press.

Reddé, M. 1986 *Mare Nostrum. Les Infrastructures, le dispositif et l'histoire de la marine militaire sous l'empire romain*. Rome: Ecole française de Rome.

Reece, R. 1970. *Roman Coins*. London: Ernest Benn.

———. 1977. "Coinage and Currency." *Institute of Archaeology Bulletin* 14, 167–78.

———. 1983 "Coins and Medals." In M. Henig, ed., *Handbook of Roman Art*, pp. 166–78. Oxford: Phaidon.

Reece, R., ed. 1977. *Burial in the Roman World*. London: Council for British Archaeology.

Rees, S.E. 1979. *Agricultural Implements in Prehistoric and Roman Britain*. Oxford: British Archaeological Reports 69.

———. 1981. *Ancient Agricultural Implements*. Princes Risborough: Shire Publications.

———. 1987. "Agriculture and Horticulture." In J. Wacher, ed., *The Roman World*, vol. 2, pp. 481–503. London and New York: Routledge & Kegan Paul.

Rickman, G. 1971. *Roman Granaries and Stone Buildings*. Cambridge: Cambridge University Press.

Rickman, G. E. 1980. *The Corn Supply of Ancient Rome*. Oxford: Clarendon Press.

Ridgway, F.R.S. 1991. "Etruscan Art and Culture: A Bibliography 1978–1990." *Journal of Roman Archaeology* 4, 5–27.

Rival, M. 1991 *La Charpenterie Navale Romaine, Matériaux, méthodes, moyens*. Paris: Editions du centre national de la recherche scientifique.

Rivet, A.L.F. 1988. *Gallia Narbonensis. Southern Gaul in Roman Times*. London: Batsford.

Rivet, A.L.F., and Smith, C. 1979. *The Place-Names of Roman Britain*. London: Batsford.

Robertson, D.S. 1945. *Greek and Roman Architecture*, 2nd ed. Cambridge: Cambridge University Press.

Rodwell, W., ed. 1980. *Temples, Churches and Religion: Recent Research in Roman Britain with a Gazetteer of Romano-Celtic Temples in Continental Europe*. Oxford: British Archaeological Reports 77.

Ross, A., and Robins, D. 1989. *The Life and Death of a Druid Prince*. London: Rider.

Rossiter, J.J. 1978. *Roman Farm Buildings in Italy*. Oxford: British Archaeological Reports International Series 52.

———. 1989. "Roman Villas of the Greek East and the Villa in Gregory of Nyssa *EP*. 20," *Journal of Roman Archaeology* 2, 101–10.

Saller, R. 1991. "Corporal Punishment, Authority, and Obedience in the Roman Household." In B. Rawson, ed., *Marriage, Divorce and Children in Ancient Rome*, pp. 144–65. Oxford: Oxford University Press.

Salmon, E.T. 1969. *Roman Colonization under the Republic*. London: Thames and Hudson.

Salway, P. 1981. *Roman Britain*. Oxford: Oxford University Press.

Salzman, M.R. 1990. *On Roman Time: The Codex-Calendar of 354 and the Rhythms of Urban Life in Late Antiquity*. Berkeley, Los Angeles, and Oxford: University of California Press.

Sanders, I.F. 1982. *Roman Crete. An Archaeological Survey and Gazetteer of Late Hellenistic, Roman and Early Byzantine Crete*. Warminster: Aris & Phillips.

Sandys, J.E. 1927. *Latin Epigraphy. An Introduction to the Study of Latin Inscriptions*, 2nd ed. revised by S.G. Campbell. Cambridge: Cambridge University Press.

Sandys, J.E. ed. 1921. *A Companion to Latin Studies*, 3rd ed. Cambridge: Cambridge University Press.

Scarborough, J. 1969. *Roman Medicine*. London: Thames and Hudson.

Scott, I.R. 1985. "First Century Military Daggers and the Manufacture and Supply of Weapons for the Roman Army." In M.C. Bishop, ed., *The Production and Distribution of Roman Military Equipment*, pp. 160–219. Oxford: British Archaeological Reports International Series 275.

Scullard, H.H. 1980 *A History of the Roman World 753–146 BC*, 4th ed. London and New York: Routledge.

———. 1981. *Festivals and Ceremonies of the Roman Republic*. London: Thames and Hudson.

———. 1982. *From the Gracchi to Nero. A History of Rome 133 BC to AD 68*. 5th ed. London and New York: Routledge.

Sear, D.R. 1981. *The Emperors of Rome and Byzantium. Chronological and Genealogical Tables for History Students and Coin Collectors*, 2nd ed. London: Seaby.

Sear, F. 1976. "Wall and Vault Mosaics." In D. Strong and D. Brown, eds., *Roman Crafts*, pp. 231–52. London: Duckworth.

———. 1982. *Roman Architecture*. London: Batsford.

———. 1992. "Introducing Roman Public Buildings." *Journal of Roman Archaeology* 5, 291–93.

Sellwood, D. 1976. "Minting." In D. Strong and D. Brown, eds., *Roman Crafts*, pp. 62–73. London: Duckworth.

Shaw, J.W. 1972. "Greek and Roman Harbourworks." In G.F. Bass, ed., *A History of Seafaring*, pp. 87–112. London: Thames and Hudson.

Shelton, J.-A. 1988. *As the Romans Did: A Source Book in Roman Social History*. New York: Oxford University Press.

Sherlock, D. 1976. "Silver and Silversmithing." In D. Strong and D. Brown, eds., *Roman Crafts*, pp. 10–23. London: Duckworth.

Smith, D.J. 1983. "Mosaics." In M. Henig, ed., *A Handbook of Roman Art*, pp. 116–38. Oxford: Phaidon.

Speidel, M. 1984. *Roman Army Studies Volume 1*. Amsterdam: J.C. Gieben.

Starr, C.G. 1960. *The Roman Imperial Navy 31 B.C.–A.D. 324*, 2nd ed. Cambridge: Heffe.

Strong, D.E. 1966. *Greek and Roman Gold and Silver Plate*. London: Methuen.

———. 1976. *Roman Art*. Harmondsworth and New York: Penguin, reprint in an integrated, 1980.

Strong, D., and Brown, D., eds. 1976. *Roman Crafts*. London: Duckworth.

Strong, D., and Claridge, A. 1976. "Marble Sculpture." In D. Strong and D. Brown, eds., *Roman Crafts*, pp. 194–207. London: Duckworth.

Swan, V.G. 1984. *The Pottery Kilns of Roman Britain*. London: Royal Commission on Historical Monuments, HMSO.

Talbert, R.J.A. 1992. "Mapping the Classical World: Major Atlases and Map Series 1872–1990." *Journal of Roman Archaeology* 5, 5–38.

Talbert, R.J.A., ed. 1985. *Atlas of Classical History*. London: Routledge, reprint.

Tchernia, A. 1986. *Le Vin de l'Italie Romaine. Essai d'Histoire économique d'après les amphores*. Rome: Ecole française de Rome.

Thébert, Y. 1987. "Private Life and Domestic Architecture in Roman Africa." In P. Veyne, ed., *A History of Private Life. 1. From Pagan Rome to Byzantium*, trans. A. Goldhammer, pp. 313–409. Cambridge, Mass.: Harvard University Press, Belknap Press.

Thiel, J. H. 1946. *Studies on the History of Roman Sea-Power in Republican Times*. Amsterdam: North-Holland Publishing Company.

Thomas, C. 1981. *Christianity in Roman Britain to AD 500*. London: Batsford.

Thompson, D.J. 1987. "Imperial Estates." In J. Wacher, ed., *The Roman World*, vol. 2, pp. 555–67. London and New York: Routledge & Kegan Paul.

Todd, M. 1978. *The Walls of Rome*. London: Paul Elek.

Todd, M., ed. 1978. *Studies in the Romano-British Villa*. Leicester: Leicester University Press.

Tomlin, R. 1981a. "The Mobile Army." In P. Connolly, *Greece and Rome at War*, pp. 249–59. London: Macdonald & Co.

———. 1981b. "Fortifications, AD 284–378." In P. Connolly, *Greece and Rome at War*, pp. 300–2. London: Macdonald & Co.

———. 1981c. "Siege Warfare, 4th century." In P. Connolly, *Greece and Rome at War*, pp. 302–3. London: Macdonald & Co.

Tomlin, R.S.O. 1987. "The Army of the Late Empire." In J. Wacher, ed., *The Roman World*, vol. 1, pp. 107–20. London and New York: Routledge & Kegan Paul.

Toynbee, J.M.C. 1971. *Death and Burial in the Roman World*. London: Thames and Hudson.

Throckmorton, P. 1972. "Romans on the Sea." In G.F. Bass, ed., *A History of Seafaring*, pp. 65–86. London: Thames and Hudson.

Treggiari, S. 1991. *Roman Marriage Iusti Coniuges from the Time of Cicero to the Time of Ulpian*. Oxford: Clarendon Press.

Tusa, V. 1973 "Ancore antiche nel Museo di Palermo." In D.J. Blackman, ed., *Marine Archaeology*, pp. 411–37. Colston Papers no. 23. London: Butterworths.

van Doorninck, F. 1972. "Byzantium, Mistress of the Sea: 330–641." In G.F. Bass, ed., *A History of Seafaring*, pp. 133–58. London: Thames and Hudson.

Vermaserem, M.J. 1963. *Mithras the Secret God*. London: Chatto and Windus.

Veyne, P. 1987. "The Roman Empire." In P. Veyne, ed., *A History of Private Life*, pp. 5–233. Cambridge, Mass. and London: Harvard University Press, Belknap Press.

Veyne, P., ed. 1987. *A History of Private Life 1. From Pagan Rome to Byzantium*, trans. A. Goldhammer. Cambridge, Mass. and London: Harvard University Press, Belknap Press.

Wacher, J. 1974. *The Towns of Roman Britain*. London: Batsford.

———. 1987. *The Roman Empire*. London: J.M. Dent.

Wacher, J., ed. 1987. *The Roman World*, vols. 1, 2. London and New York: Routledge & Kegan Paul.

Warde Fowler, W. 1922. *The Religious Experience of the Roman People from the Earliest Times to the Age of Augustus*. London: Macmillan.

Ward-Perkins, J.B. 1970. *Roman Imperial Architecture*. Harmondsworth: Penguin Books, 2nd integrated ed. pub. 1981.

Warmington, B.H. 1954. *The North African Provinces from Diocletian to the Vandal Conquest*. Cambridge: Cambridge University Press.

Waterer, J.W. 1976. "Leatherwork." In D. Strong and D. Brown, eds., *Roman Crafts*, pp. 178–93. London: Duckworth.

Watson, G.R. 1969. *The Roman Soldier*. London: Thames and Hudson.

———. 1987. "The Army of the Republic." In J. Wacher, ed., *The Roman World*, vol. 1, pp. 75–88. London and New York: Routledge & Kegan Paul.

Watts, D. 1991. *Christians and Pagans in Roman Britain*. London and New York: Routledge.

Webster, G. 1985. *The Roman Imperial Army of the First and Second Centuries A.D.*, 3rd ed. London: A & C Black.

Welch, K. 1991. "Roman Amphitheatres Revived." *Journal of Roman Archaeology* 4, 273–81.

Welsby, D.A. 1982. *The Roman Military Defence of the British Provinces in its Later Phases*. Oxford: British Archaeological Reports 101.

White, K.D. 1967. *Agricultural Implements of the Roman World*. Cambridge: Cambridge University Press.

———. 1970. *Roman Farming*. London: Thames and Hudson.

———. 1975. *Farm Equipment of the Roman World*. Cambridge: Cambridge University Press.

———. 1978. *Country Life in Classical Times*. London: Elek.

———. 1984. *Greek and Roman Technology*. London: Thames and Hudson.

Wightman, E.M. 1985. *Gallia Belgica*. London: Batsford.

Wigoder, G. 1986. *The Story of the Synagogue*. London: Weidenfeld & Nicolson.

Wild, J.P. 1968. "Clothing in the North-West Provinces of the Roman Empire." *Bonner Jahrbuch* 168, 166–240.

———. 1970. *Textile Manufacture in the Northern Roman Provinces*. Cambridge: Cambridge University Press.

———. 1976. "Textiles." In D. Strong and D. Brown, eds., *Roman Crafts*, pp. 166–77. London: Duckworth.

———. 1988. *Textiles in Archaeology*. Princes Risborough: Shire Publications.

Wilkes, J.J. 1969. *Dalmatia*. London and New York: Routledge & Kegan Paul.

———. 1989. "The Frontier of Noricum." *Journal of Roman Archaeology* 2, 347–52.

Wilson, D.R. 1980. "Romano-Celtic Temple Architecture: How Much Do We Actually Know?" In W. Rodwell, ed., *Temples, Churches and Religion*, pp. 5–28. Oxford: British Archaeological Reports 77.

Wilson, L.M. 1924. *The Roman Toga*. Baltimore: John Hopkins Press.

Wilson, R.J.A. 1986. "Roman Art and Architecture." In J. Boardman, J. Griffin, and O. Murray, *The Roman World*, pp. 361–400. Oxford: Oxford University Press.

———. 1990. *Sicily Under the Roman Empire. The Archaeology of a Roman Province, 36 BC–AD 535*. Warminster: Aris & Phillips.

———. 1992. "Terracotta Vaulting Tubes (*Tubi Fittili*): On Their Origin and Distribution." *Journal of Roman Archaeology* 5, 97–129.

Wiseman, T.P., ed. *Roman Political Life 90 BC–AD 69*. Exeter: University of Exeter.

Woods, A. 1987. "Mining." In J. Wacher, ed., *The Roman World*, vol. 2, pp. 611–34. London and New York: Routledge & Kegan Paul.

Woodward, A. 1992. *English Heritage Book of Shrines and Sacrifices*. London: Batsford/English Heritage.

Yavetz, Z. 1988. *Slaves and Slavery in Ancient Rome*. New Brunswick, N.J. and Oxford: Transaction Books.

York, M. 1986. *The Roman Festival Calendar of Numa Pompilius*. American University Studies Series 17, Classical Languages and Literature vol. 2. New York: Peter Lang.

INDEX

Main entries are in **boldface**. Pages in *italics* denote a figure (f), map (m) or table (t).

witchcraft 301
witches 293
wives 78
wolves 169, 256, 265, 282
women 286, **339**, 341, *346f see also*
  mother goddesses; Vestal Virgins
    actors 212, 349–350
    clothes *344f*, 344–345, *346f*
    deity of 260
    diseases 355
    in divorce 340
    doctors (*medicae*) 355
    epitaphs 236
    exclusive worship of Bona Dea
      258
    gladiators 348
    guardian spirit (Iuno) 274
    hairstyles 346, *346f*
    mourning 356
    names of 244
    pregnant 260
    punishment 275
    worshippers of Bacchus 288
wood
  coffins 357
  diptychs 329

dolls 281
fuel 194, 315
plaques 299–300
portrait paintings 351
sheets used in writing 209
shoes 345
statuettes 299
swords 78, 328
woodland, deities of 259–260, 270,
  276
woodpeckers 265, 269
woodworking 329–330, 333
wool 163, 327–329, 344–345
woolen balls 281
word squares 293
workshops
  along streets (in towns) 144
  cameos 333
  coins 309, *309t*
  goldsmiths' 331
  military 65, 82, 94
  pottery 316, 321
world guides (*periegeses*) 171
world maps 169–170
wreaths 279, 288, 310
wrecks *see* shipwrecks

wrestling 347
writers *see* authors; literature
writing 205, *206–207t*, 206–208, 234–
  235 *see also* alphabet
    cursive *206–207t*, **206–208**, 235,
      237
    inscriptions 237
    materials *208f*, 208–210
    on papyrus 208
    punctuation 208
    sacred 251
    tablets 207, *208f*, **209**, 235
Wroxeter   *see*   Viroconium
  Cornoviorum

X

Xanten (Colonia Ulpia Traiana), Germany 72, *99m*, *124t see also* Vetera
Xanthus (Kinik), Turkey *121m*, 128

Y

year of Romulus 337
years (dates) 337
yokes 184–185, 313

York (Eburacum), Britain 25, 31–32,
  124t, 132, 175 *see also* Eburacum

Z

Zaitha, Syria 26
Zalmoxis (deity) **273**
Zama, battle of 4, 18
Zama Regia (Zama), Tunisia *119m*,
  127t
Zaragoza *see* Caesaraugusta
Zela (Zile), Turkey *121m*, *127t*
  battle of 6, 14, 56, 58
Zeno 10, *12t*, **37**
Zeno (Stoic) 355
Zenobia, Septimia 8, *11t*, 28, **29**, 224
Zeugma, Turkey *122m*, *127t*
Zeus 256, 260, 263
zinc 305, 332
Zmyrna (Cinna) 219
Zollfeld (Virunum), Austria *121m*,
  127t
Zoroastrianism 290
Zosimus **234**